Commercial Law in East Asia

The Library of Essays on Law in East Asia
edited by Roman Tomasic

Titles in the Series:

Law and Society in East Asia
Christoph Antons and Roman Tomasic

Public Law in East Asia
Albert H.Y. Chen and Tom Ginsburg

International Law in East Asia
Zou Keyuan and Jianfu Chen

Commercial Law in East Asia
Roman Tomasic and Leon Wolff

Commercial Law in East Asia

Edited by

Roman Tomasic
University of South Australia, Australia

Leon Wolff
Bond University, Australia

ASHGATE

© Roman Tomasic and Leon Wolff 2014. For copyright of individual articles please refer to the Acknowledgements.

All rights reserved. No part of this publication may be reproduced, stored in a retrieval system or transmitted in any form or by any means, electronic, mechanical, photocopying, recording or otherwise without the prior permission of the publisher.

Wherever possible, these reprints are made from a copy of the original printing, but these can themselves be of very variable quality. Whilst the publisher has made every effort to ensure the quality of the reprint, some variability may inevitably remain.

Published by
Ashgate Publishing Limited
Wey Court East
Union Road
Farnham
Surrey GU9 7PT
England

Ashgate Publishing Company
Suite 3-1
110 Cherry Street
Burlington
VT 05401-3818
USA

www.ashgate.com

British Library Cataloguing in Publication Data
A catalogue record for this book is available from the British Library.

The Library of Congress has cataloged the printed edition as follows: 2013942290

ISBN 9780754628682

Printed in the United Kingdom by Henry Ling Limited,
at the Dorset Press, Dorchester, DT1 1HD

Contents

Acknowledgements vii
Series Preface ix
Introduction: Mapping the Contours of East Asian Commercial Law for the Asian Century xi

PART I GENERAL ISSUES

Rationale: What is the Importance of East Asian Commercial Law both Now and into the Future?
1 Richard P. Appelbaum (1998), 'The Future of Law in a Global Economy', *Social and Legal Studies*, 7, pp. 171–92. 3

Rule of Law: Does the Rule of Law Matter in East Asian Commercial Law?
2 Douglas W. Arner, Charles D. Booth, Paul Lejot and Berry F.C. Hsu (2007), 'Property Rights, Collateral, Creditor Rights, and Insolvency in East Asia', *Texas International Law Journal*, **42**, pp. 515–59. 25
3 Donald C. Clarke (2003), 'Economic Development and the Rights Hypothesis: The China Problem', *The American Journal of Comparative Law*, **51**, pp. 89–111. 71
4 John Gillespie (2009), 'Testing the Limits to the "Rule of Law": Commercial Regulation in Vietnam', *The Journal of Comparative Asian Development*, **8**, pp. 245–72. 95

Global and Local Influences: To What Extent is Asian Commercial Law a Mix of the Global and the Local?
5 Mohammad Rizal Salim (2006), 'Legal Transplantation and Local Knowledge: Corporate Governance in Malaysia', *Australian Journal of Corporate Law*, **20**, pp. 55–83. 123
6 Hwa-Jin Kim (1999), 'Living With the IMF: A New Approach to Corporate Governance and Regulation of Financial Institutions in Korea', *Berkeley Journal of International Law*, **17**, pp. 61–94. 153
7 Li-Wen Lin (2009), 'Legal Transplants through Private Contracting: Codes of Vendor Conduct in Global Supply Chains as an Example', *The American Journal of Comparative Law*, **57**, pp. 711–44. 187

PART II CASE STUDIES

Negotiations
8 John A. Pearce II and Richard B. Robinson Jr (2000), 'Cultivating *Guanxi* as a Foreign Investor Strategy', *Business Horizons*, **43**, pp. 31–8. 223

9   James K. Sebenius (2002), 'Caveats for Cross-Border Negotiators', *Negotiation Journal*, **18**, pp. 121–33. 231

Commercial Transactions

10 Quan H. Nguyen (2007), 'The Norms and Incentive Structures of Relational Contracting in Vietnam – Two Surveys', *Australian Journal of Asian Law*, **9**, pp. 44–65. 245
11 Yoshiro Miwa and J. Mark Ramseyer (2000), 'Rethinking Relationship-Specific Investments: Subcontracting in the Japanese Automobile Industry', *Michigan Law Review*, **98**, pp. 2636–67. 267

Commercial Dispute Resolution

12 Saadia M. Pekkanen (2001), 'Aggressive Legalism: The Rules of the WTO and Japan's Emerging Trade Strategy', *The World Economy*, **24**, pp. 707–37. 299
13 Junji Nakagawa (2007), 'No More Negotiated Deals?: Settlement of Trade and Investment Disputes in East Asia', *Journal of International Economic Law*, **10**, pp. 837–67. 331

Corporate Law and Corporate Governance

14 Chen Su (2009), 'The Establishment and Development of the Chinese Economic Legal System in the Past Sixty Years', *Columbia Journal of Asian Law*, **23**, pp. 109–36. 363
15 Philip Lawton (1996), 'Berle and Means, Corporate Governance and the Chinese Family Firm', *Australian Journal of Corporate Law*, **6**, pp. 348–79. 391
16 Roman Tomasic (1995), 'Company Law and the Limits of the Rule of Law in China', *Australian Journal of Corporate Law*, **4**, pp. 470–87. 423
17 Curtis J. Milhaupt (2001), 'Creative Norm Destruction: The Evolution of Non-legal Rules in Japanese Corporate Governance', *University of Pennsylvania Law Review*, **149**, pp. 2083–129. 441
18 Dan W. Puchniak (2009), 'Delusions of Hostility: The Marginal Role of Hostile Takeovers in Japanese Corporate Governance Remains Unchanged', *Journal of Japanese Law*, **28**, pp. 89–120. 489

Name Index 521

Acknowledgements

Ashgate would like to thank the researchers and the contributing authors who provided copies, along with the following for their permission to reprint copyright material.

American Journal of Comparative Law for the essays: Donald C. Clarke (2003), 'Economic Development and the Rights Hypothesis: The China Problem', *The American Journal of Comparative Law*, **51**, pp. 89–111; Li-Wen Lin (2009), 'Legal Transplants through Private Contracting: Codes of Vendor Conduct in Global Supply Chains as an Example', *The American Journal of Comparative Law*, **57**, pp. 711–44.

Australian Journal of Asian Law for the essay: Quan H. Nguyen (2007), 'The Norms and Incentive Structures of Relational Contracting in Vietnam – Two Surveys', *Australian Journal of Asian Law*, **9**, pp. 44–65. Copyright © 2007 *Australian Journal of Asian Law*.

Berkeley Law, University of California for the essay: Hwa-Jin Kim (1999), 'Living With the IMF: A New Approach to Corporate Governance and Regulation of Financial Institutions in Korea', *Berkeley Journal of International Law*, **17**, pp. 61–94. Copyright © 1999 by the Regents of the University of California.

Chen Su for the essay: Chen Su (2009), 'The Establishment and Development of the Chinese Economic Legal System in the Past Sixty Years', *Columbia Journal of Asian Law*, **23**, pp. 109–36.

Elsevier for the essay: John A. Pearce II and Richard B. Robinson Jr (2000), 'Cultivating *Guanxi* as a Foreign Investor Strategy', *Business Horizons*, **43**, pp. 31–8.

Journal of Japanese Law for the essay: Dan W. Puchniak (2009), 'Delusions of Hostility: The Marginal Role of Hostile Takeovers in Japanese Corporate Governance Remains Unchanged', *Journal of Japanese Law*, **28**, pp. 89–120.

LexisNexis for the essays: Mohammad Rizal Salim (2006), 'Legal Transplantation and Local Knowledge: Corporate Governance in Malaysia', *Australian Journal of Corporate Law*, **20**, pp. 55–83. Copyright © 2006 Mohammad Rizal Salim and LexisNexis; Philip Lawton (1996), 'Berle and Means, Corporate Governance and the Chinese Family Firm', *Australian Journal of Corporate Law*, **6**, pp. 348–79; Copyright © 1996 Philip Lawton and LexisNexis; Roman Tomasic (1995), 'Company Law and the Limits of the Rule of Law in China', *Australian Journal of Corporate Law*, **4**, pp. 470–87. Copyright © 1995 Roman Tomasic and LexisNexis.

The Michigan Law Review Association for the essay: Yoshiro Miwa and J. Mark Ramseyer (2000), 'Rethinking Relationship-Specific Investments: Subcontracting in the Japanese Automobile Industry', *Michigan Law Review*, **98**, pp. 2636–67. Copyright © The Michigan Law Review Association.

Oxford University Press for the essay: Junji Nakagawa (2007), 'No More Negotiated Deals?: Settlement of Trade and Investment Disputes in East Asia', *Journal of International Economic Law*, **10**, pp. 837–67. Copyright © 2007 Oxford University Press.

Sage Publications for the essay: Richard P. Appelbaum (1998), 'The Future of Law in a Global Economy', *Social and Legal Studies*, **7**, pp. 171–92. Copyright © 1998 Sage Publications, London, Thousand Oaks, CA, and New Delhi.

Taylor and Francis for the essay: John Gillespie (2009), 'Testing the Limits to the "Rule of Law": Commercial Regulation in Vietnam', *The Journal of Comparative Asian Development*, **8**, pp. 245–72. Copyright © 2009 National Communication Association, reprinted by permission of Taylor & Francis Ltd, www.tandfonline.com on behalf of the National Communication Association.

University of Pennsylvania Law Review for the essay: Curtis J. Milhaupt (2001), 'Creative Norm Destruction: The Evolution of Non-legal Rules in Japanese Corporate Governance', *University of Pennsylvania Law Review*, **149**, pp. 2083–129.

University of Texas for the essay: Douglas W. Arner, Charles D. Booth, Paul Lejot and Berry F.C. Hsu (2007), 'Property Rights, Collateral, Creditor Rights, and Insolvency in East Asia', *Texas International Law Journal*, **42**, pp. 515–59.

John Wiley and Sons for the essays: James K. Sebenius (2002), 'Caveats for Cross-Border Negotiators', *Negotiation Journal*, **18**, pp. 121–33; Saadia M. Pekkanen (2001), 'Aggressive Legalism: The Rules of the WTO and Japan's Emerging Trade Strategy', *The World Economy*, **24**, pp. 707–37. Copyright © 2001 Blackwell Publishers Ltd.

Every effort has been made to trace all the copyright holders, but if any have been inadvertently overlooked the publishers will be pleased to make the necessary arrangement at the first opportunity.

Publisher's Note

The material in this volume has been reproduced using the facsimile method. This means we can retain the original pagination to facilitate easy and correct citation of the original essays. It also explains the variety of typefaces, page layouts and numbering.

Series Preface

This new *Library of Essays on Law in East Asia* brings together important examples of legal scholarship that has sought to analyse law and legal change in East Asia in recent times. Rapid political change and economic development of East Asian economies has sparked a growing interest in the laws and the legal systems of these countries. We have seen the passage of extensive bodies of new laws and the revision of some older laws, in many areas, especially in commercial law.

At the same time we have seen the growth in the size and complexity of legal institutions such as courts, the legal profession, law schools and regulatory bodies in East Asian countries. To some extent, East Asian law reformers have looked to Western legal models, but there has also been a strong emphasis on creating laws and legal institutions that reflect local culture and political structures. Law reform models and influences have also come from within East Asia itself and not simply from particular Western countries.

This is likely to become an increasingly important source of legal ideas in the region as the experiences of neighbouring countries are often seen as more applicable to local circumstances. Thus we have seen Japanese and Taiwanese legal models being influential in China, China's legal reforms inspiring interest in Vietnam, and Singapore and Malaysia being influential in South East Asia. Values drawn from Islamic and Confucian traditions have also had increasing impact on law making and legal institutions in East Asia.

Where laws have been externally imposed, such as after the Asian financial crisis and during earlier colonial periods, they have often not been as effective as laws that have emerged organically through domestic law making processes. The pervasive and sometimes subtle effect of Americanization and American legal education has however been widely felt in many areas, although this has sometimes been diffused through the efforts of multilateral bodies such as the World Bank and the International Monetary Fund. The effects of globalization have also been evident in patterns of East Asian legal changes.

This wide-spread pattern of energetic legal institution building and legal change has sparked considerable public policy debate and research into the distinctive features of laws and legal institutions in increasingly robust East Asian legal systems. Theories of path dependency and convergence have sometimes been drawn upon to explain the trajectories of different law reforms and legal institutional arrangements in East Asia; and political, historical and economic theories have also been brought to bear in explaining patterns of legal change in the region. This has seen the reappraisal of Western derived models of the role of law.

The adoption of a variety of approaches to the rule of law in East Asia has added to the diversity of market based legal systems and provided contrasts with once dominant European and North American models. To some extent, comparative research has also allowed us to better understand the nature and limits of Western laws and legal institutions. An increasing body of new legal research is being undertaken by East Asian legal scholars, and their international impact is likely to increase over the next decade or so as many return from undertaking graduate studies in other countries. This is bound to invigorate the tradition of legal scholarship in the wider region and has both provided exciting new insights and enlivened scholarly and wider debates about the role of law and legal institutions in society and their relationship to politics, economic development and the protection of individual rights.

These legal developments have also provoked important theoretical debates and new empirical research into the role of law and legal institutions in East Asian countries, as well as into the problems of implementing these changes in the face of the powerful influence of traditional ideas and political structure in East Asian societies. This research has ranged from studies of the operation of particular laws and legal institutions to comparative law studies, which have highlighted the distinctive features as well as similarities with the laws and legal institutions of Western legal systems.

Finally, with regard to the scope and coverage of the volumes in this series, although there is a diverse body of legal scholarship written in different languages, we have drawn primarily upon English language writing with a view to making this material as widely accessible as possible. It might also be noted that there has not been an even spread of English language legal scholarship across the region with some larger countries, such as China and Japan, inevitably generating more such research by virtue of their size.

ROMAN TOMASIC
Series Editor
University of South Australia and Durham University

Introduction: Mapping the Contours of East Asian Commercial Law for the Asian Century

The centre of economic gravity in the new century is shifting to the East. Since 2001, according to the International Monetary Fund (IMF), Asia's contribution to world economic growth has matched that of the United States and Europe combined, and, since 2006, has even exceeded it (IMF, 2011; Neumann and Arora, 2011). This surge is easy to explain: China has emerged as a global super-power; Japan remains the third-largest world economy, despite only recently emerging from over twenty years of economic stagnation (The Age, 2013); South Korea and the 'tiger' economies of Taiwan, Hong Kong and Singapore have achieved high-level economic development through capital investment and technological innovation; and Indonesia, Thailand, the Philippines and Malaysia have supplied riches in labour and resources to the regional economy (MacIntyre and Naughton, 2005, p. 78). A growing middle class is lifting consumption. 'Billions of Asians,' writes Mahbubani (2008, p. 3), 'are marching to modernity.'

This book examines scholarly interpretations for the role commercial law has played in East Asia's economic rise. At first blush, this might seem a daunting task. After all, as some theorists have argued, the East Asian experience is largely neglected in writings on law generally and commercial law more broadly (Wolff, 2012). This is because law, as a discipline, was largely forged in the prior European and American centuries; these 'Anglo-American moorings' ill-serve legal analysis in the new Asian Century (Cossman, 1997, p. 539).

Consider comparative law, for example. As Fauvarque-Cosson argues, the major goal of comparative law is to 'eradicate pluralism and diversity by unifying or at least harmoni[s]ing major fields of the law' (Fauvarque-Cosson, 2001, p. 427). This project resonates in the West because Europe and the United States share a common political, economic and cultural heritage. Its application is more troublesome in Asia given greater intraregional diversity politically, economically, philosophically and even culturally. Upham (1997) provides empirical support for this thesis. The first 46 issues of the *American Journal of Comparative Law* – a journal representative of mainstream comparative law scholarship – carried barely 2.41 per cent of its articles on China, 2.37 per cent on Japan and 8.67 per cent on Asia as a region.

International law and global law, two other legal scholarly traditions, have similar criticisms levelled against them (Wolff, 2012). Gaubatz and MacArthur (2001), for example, provocatively question the extent to which international law is truly international. Despite the rhetoric that international law embodies universal norms, the authors conclude that, in truth, its values are largely the bastion of a small number of powerful Western states.

Darian-Smith (2000) identifies the same Western normative bias in global law. The core tension in global law, she submits, revolves around the role of the nation-state in global governance: some believe global law is about transnational market regulation; others think that global law is about geopolitical integrity and state sovereignty. For Darian-Smith, however, this is a sterile debate. Either way, she argues, global law is fundamentally Eurocentric because it represents 'modernist understandings of sovereignty, constitutionalism, nationalism, and

Western superiority' (Darian-Smith, 2000, p. 815). De Sousa Santos (1987) agrees. He argues that the modern conception of law involves a misreading of the legal landscape or maps of the world; it is for this reason that globalization should also be understood from below, from the perspective of the global South (de Sousa Santos and Rodriguez-Garavito, 2005; de Sousa Santos, 2002, p. 254–7).

These criticisms might have been fair at the turn of the twenty-first century (when most of them were made). But they are losing some of their force today. If anything, the literature on East Asian commercial law is burgeoning. This might be because comparative law is reinventing itself: embracing interregional diversity in Asia (Glenn, 2000); seeking new interdisciplinary connections with international law (Kennedy, 1997; Obiora, 1998); and escaping its Anglo-American biases by drawing on broader jurisprudential (Valcke, 2004) or social scientific (Whitman, 2007) analytical techniques. Or it might be because an emerging breed of Asia-literate legal specialists is building an entirely new discipline of 'Asian law' (Antons, 1995; Taylor, 1997; Jayasuriya, 1999a and 2000).

Either way, the literature on East Asian commercial law does not lack in volume. It does, however, lack in settled shape. On nearly every issue canvassed in the literature – from the rationale for engaging with East Asian commercial law to the relevance of law in the East Asian economic experience; from the distinctiveness of East Asian commercial law in a global economy to the variables that explain law's economic function in the region – scholars are divided. In this book, we neither shy away from nor explain away the cleavages, conflicts and controversies in this literature. Instead, we highlight them.

We do so because we want to foster Asia-literacy in commercial law analysis. 'Asia literacy', as defined in the Australian Government's White Paper on *Australia in the Asian Century* (2012, p. 167), is the decision-making, cultural and representational skills to make informed decisions in an increasingly complex environment. It draws on cultural literacy in communication theory – the idea of navigating different system of meanings (Schirato and Yell, 1996, pp. 1–2, 11, 15–19, 21, 22; Birch et al., 2001, pp. x–xi). To the extent that a legal system is also a 'culture' – that is, a system of legal ideas and meanings as opposed to simply a collection of legal texts (statutes and case reports) – 'literacy' in the law is more than just knowing the black-letter of the law, but also negotiating (making sense of) legal meanings. Asia-literacy in law, therefore, is the way both domestic and foreign legal practices produce and 'normalize' certain cultural values and preferences in the legal systems of Asia (Ruskola, 2000). The purpose of this volume is to introduce readers to the range of meanings that, at least according to the scholarly literature, underscore East Asian regulation of the economy.

This rationale has informed our selection of essays for this volume. We have chosen journal articles representative of the different schools of thought on key issues in East Asian commercial law. As such, we have generally avoided descriptive, technical analyses of the law in favour of more theoretically-focussed writing. Further, we have eschewed formal citation analyses in choosing pieces, instead selecting those that contribute the widest range of views on the specific issues. As far as possible, we have sought a balance between articles that deal with East Asia as a whole and those that focus on particular countries. This is to demonstrate how scholarly diversity underpins the entire corpus of scholarly literature on East Asian commercial law, regardless of content coverage or scope. Our effort to balance treatment of individual legal regimes, however, was less easy to achieve: given the size of China and

Japan, it is not surprising that they have received more attention in the literature than other jurisdictions. Our selection of articles, especially the case studies, reflects this reality.

We have structured this volume into two parts. Part I deals with general issues, while Part II explores more specific commercial law case studies.

General Issues

The articles in Part I debate the rationale for engaging with East Asian commercial law; the extent to which, if any, the rule of law matters in East Asian economies; and whether East Asian commercial law represents a distinctive approach to economic regulation or is converging on global standards.

Rationale: What is the Importance of East Asian Commercial Law both Now and into the Future?

'In terms of time, centuries happen. In terms of history, centuries are made' (Fidler, 2005, p. 25). If the eighteenth and nineteenth centuries were the European and American centuries, due to the economic, cultural and military might of the West over the past 200 years, the twenty-first century is said to belong to Asia (Weiss, 1989; Lingle, 1997; Black III, 1990; Abbott and Bowman, 1994; Sanders, 1997). Some are unshakeable in this belief. Mahbubani (2008) is typical. 'The rise of the West,' he writes, 'transformed the world. The rise of Asia will bring an equally significant transformation' (Mahbubani, 2008, p. 1). Others are more cautious. Fidler (2005, p. 25), for example, senses the coming of 'a historical moment for the region dawning ..., a "tipping point" of history'.

Political leaders are recognizing the global economic implications of the Asian Century. Australian Prime Minister, Julia Gillard, for example, commissioned a White Paper on *Australia in the Asian Century* (2012), specifically addressing the trade, investment and training implications of Asia's rise. US President Barak Obama, in an address to the Australian House of Representatives on 17 November 2011, declared the 'future' lay in the Asia-Pacific:

> As the world's fastest growing region and home to more than half of the global economy, the Asia-Pacific is critical.... With most of the world's nuclear power and some half of humanity, Asia will largely define whether the century ahead will be marked by conflict or cooperation, needless suffering or human progress. As President, I have therefore made a deliberate and strategic decision: as a Pacific nation, the United States will play a larger and long-term role in shaping this region and its future ... (Obama, 2011, p. 12848).

What are the implications of the Asian Century for law and legal practice? In a globalized world, lawyers now work beyond the jurisdictional confines of the local and the national (Trubek et al, 1994, pp. 407–10). There is a shift from a 'purely local conception of law' to one where the 'world [is] an archipelago of jurisdictions' (Chesterman, 2008, p. 60). Firms are branded globally; standards regulation is transnational; issues require international normative solutions (Chesterman, 2008, p. 63). Problems – legal, political, economic, social – are now 'without passports' (Annan, 2002). Asia, therefore, is becoming an increasingly important site for commercial legal practice. In 'The Future of Law in a Global Economy' (Chapter

1), Richard Appelbaum goes even further. He argues that the ascendance of Asian power will transform global legal practice. The US template premised on precise rules, adversarial dispute resolution and formal business structures will give way to a more Asian (or, more accurately, Chinese) model of informal relationships, cooperative dispute resolution and flexible organization.

Appelbaum's thesis is certainly bullish. Others are more sceptical. For Baruma, for example, the idea of an Asian Century borders on the 'absurd': '"Asia" is too big, too vague and too diverse to serve as a useful concept' (Baruma, 1999, A25). For Fidler (2005, p. 26), there are several reasons why East Asia is unlikely to dominate in the same way as the European states did in the nineteenth century and the United States has in the twentieth. First, US hegemony will not completely disappear. Second, EU power will not dissipate to render it vulnerable to Chinese and Indian power. Third, Asian powers are not unified politically or economically to allow them to project their power outwards. Finally, East Asia lacks a common ideological position that can seriously threaten the current liberal orthodoxy.

Indeed, an emerging line of comparative law scholarship makes the opposite case to Appelbaum's – that the 'Americanization' of law is, if anything, marginalizing the significance of East Asian commercial law. This is particularly evident in some comparative law work on Japan. According to this scholarship, Japanese law is inching inexorably towards American standards of legal regulation. Keleman and Sibbitt (2002), for example, submit that Japan is witnessing a more pronounced American flavour to its corporate and commercial laws due to accelerating economic liberalization and political fragmentation. Milhaupt (2002), too, sees evidence of Japanese corporate governance assuming a more American shape, despite the 'stickiness' of its traditional corporate governance norms. Other legal scholars pursue similar reasoning but boldly extend the thesis beyond Japanese law. Hansmann and Kraakman (2001), law professors from Yale and Harvard respectively, prophesy the 'end of history for corporate law', predicting the inevitable convergence by other legal systems on Anglo-American principles of shareholder-oriented corporate governance. Chesterman (2008) posits the Americanization of legal education and research. 'Globalization,' Yves Dezalay submits, 'is for the most part an Americanization' (1990, p. 281).

But some American scholars, such as Lawrence Friedman, have long criticized the imprecision of 'Americanization' to describe a more globalized approach to law and legal institutions. Friedman (2002, pp. 23–7) argues that 'Americanization' has in fact been very selective. A better approach is to see globalization as essentially a cultural movement across borders. As he argues, 'Everything follows from global culture'. Like a number of critics of globalization, Friedman (2002, pp. 28–30) warns that, insofar as law is concerned, 'We should not exaggerate the scope of the globalized legal sphere. Most lawyers remain firmly rooted in their own legal habits and traditions, even those who work for transnational corporations ...' However, he concedes, the legal culture of lawyers in different parts of the world may well be seen as looking increasingly like the culture of American lawyers. This is certainly applicable to styles of lawyering in East Asian law firms.

Rule of Law: Does the Rule of Law Matter in East Asian Commercial Law?

Is the economic rise of East Asia *because of* – or *despite* – its commercial laws? A strand in the literature on East Asian legal systems compares levels of 'legalization' in the East and

West. The conclusion, invariably, is that Europe and North America set the benchmark for high legalization; Asia, by contrast, displays an 'allergy' to legalization (Alvarez, 2007, p. 16). Asians, it is said, simply 'do not like law' (Noda, 1976, p. 160; Alvarez, 2007, p. 16).

This is the thrust of 'Property Rights, Collateral, Creditor Rights, and Insolvency in East Asia' by Douglas Arner, Charles Booth, Paul Lejot and Berry Hsu (Chapter 2). In their wide-ranging multi-jurisdictional analysis of property, creditor and investor rights, they find East Asian financial and transactional legal standards range from acceptable to inadequate. They defend these judgments on the theoretical premise that commercial law, legal institutions and economic policy are essential to a fully-functioning market economy.

This link between law and capitalism has a long intellectual pedigree. Weber, Marx and Durkheim have all contributed greatly to understandings of the place of law in the development process.[1] The thrust of this early scholarship is that a well-developed rational legal system is a pre-requisite for economic development. But what type of legal system? For Weber, economic development was more likely in codified legal systems (such as in Germany) rather than where law is established more pragmatically through court decisions (as in the United Kingdom). However, Britain's emergence as the first major industrial power undermined Weber's assumption that codified rationality was a pre-condition for the rise of capitalism (see also Ginsburg, 2000, p. 832).

The 'legal origins' thesis – a relatively recent scholarly turn in the law and finance literature to which Arner and his colleagues offer cautious endorsement – makes the opposite case. Contrary to Weber, its adherents claim that common law systems are generally more effective in protecting the rights of investors than civil law systems (La Porta et al., 1998 and 2008). The theory, however, has attracted its share of critics (see generally Deakin and Pistor, 2012). Milhaupt and Pistor (2008), for example, question the general proposition that legal systems derived from common law have had more economic success than those derived from civil law. They point to the experience of the so-called East Asian 'miracle' economies, such as China, Japan, South Korea and Indonesia – all with civil law-inspired traditions (see further, Stiglitz, 1996; Page, 1994).

Legal origin theory has also failed to examine institutional functional equivalents to Western legal rules on such topics as investor protection, which can be found in civil law- influenced countries such as those in East Asia (Pistor, 2000). Further, the theory relies upon an idealized view of unrestrained markets and their capacity to foster economic development when compared to systems dominated by state-led activity. This neo-liberal conception of markets has itself now been more widely questioned in the West following the global economic crisis of 2007–2008. It has also been seriously questioned by the success of heavily state-influenced East Asian economies. As Deakin and Pistor sum up:

> Legal origin theory has some considerable way to go in providing a theory of law and development that can fit what we know about the relationship between institutions and sustainable economic growth. Despite the range of empirical studies demonstrating a link between legal origin, market-oriented legal rules, and particular aspects of financial and labor market development, it has not been

---

[1] For a review of this scholarship see further: Tamanaha (1995, pp. 470–86). See also Trubek and Galanter (1974); Trubek (1972); Trubek and Santos (2006); Trebilcock and Daniels (1999); McAlinn and Pejovic (2012).

possible to demonstrate, using the same statistical techniques, a correlation between common law origins and higher level of GDP growth. (Deakin and Pistor, 2012, p. xvi)

Arner and his colleagues, however, build their analysis more on the so-called 'rights hypothesis'. This is the insight of economic historian Douglas North who shifted the focus away from issues of rationality in legal rules, and instead explained economic development by the degree to which the law enforced property rights and contract and thereby limited the degree to which governments interfered in the free market (see further D. Chen, 2013).[2] In 'Economic Development and the Rights Hypothesis: The China Problem' (Chapter 3), Donald Clarke expresses reservations with this hypothesis. The difficulty, Clarke argues, is that it does not explain China's massive economic growth (see also Clarke et al., 2008, pp. 375, 376). Clarke notes that (functionally equivalent) mechanisms other than law may well have produced a business environment in China conducive to economic growth, 'such as stable growth-oriented governmental administration, social relationships, a culture of trustworthiness, and so on' (Clarke et al., 2008, p. 376). Added to this, local government has also played an important role in regard to the protection of property rights in China.

Other factors which promoted the development of general rules for China included decentralization (which saw powers devolved to local government), the growth in the size of the market and the emergence of the private sector which was outside traditional bureaucratic controls (Clarke et al., 2008, p. 378; Garnaut, 2001; Garnaut and Song, 2004). In some ways, administrative directives were replaced by legal rules as China simply grew out of the old five-year economic plans which had been developed by the state (Naughton, 1995). Clarke et al. sum up:

> the experience of the reform era in China seems to refute the proposition that a necessary condition for growth is that the legal system provide secure property and contract rights. Given the centrality of security of property and contract in current thinking on the determinants of economic growth, the obvious next question to ask is where such security could come from, if not from the legal system ... We argue that the political structure itself has served as an alternative to the formal legal system in providing a reasonable degree of security to certain non-state investors at the local level. (Clarke et al., 2008, p. 400)

This conclusion directly challenges the direct link between law and economic development: regardless of whether it finds expression in Weber's formal rationality, the legal origins thesis or the rights hypothesis. Instead, as Ginsburg observes, in explaining the causes of economic development in East Asia, '[s]cholars have placed more emphasis on particular policies, institutions, and cultural underpinnings rather than on law *per se*' (Ginsburg, 2000, p. 830). An example is 'Testing the Limits to the 'Rule of Law': Commercial Regulation in Vietnam' (Chapter 4) by John Gillespie. In his analysis of Vietnam's transplanted corporate law, Gillespie found that the fragmented corporate legal landscape in Vietnam was due to its socio-political structure. Norms – legal ideology, legal culture and special interest groups

---

[2] This shift in perspectives also parallels the move from law and development debates of the 1970s and the second wave of such debates in the 1990s. As these models were based on European experiences (particularly in Britain and Germany) there is a need for a new model of capitalist development that is built upon Asian experiences where the state has played a much more significant role in markets and where the shape of markets was often seen as an expression of state power (Ginsburg, 2000, p. 834)

– were instrumental in the layered and uneven reception of corporate regulation. Informal rules have long governed commercial relations for centuries – both in the East and the West. Even Douglas North recognized that they could be effective substitutes for formal institutions. Consider, for example, the traditional importance of *guanxi* in China and trust in modern banking relations in the West (see generally, Stout, 2011; Ginsburg, 2000, pp. 850–52; Tomasic and Akinbami, 2011). Indeed, since the Middle Ages, the *Lex Mercatoria* or the Law Merchant, operated to some degree amongst business actors without the need for formal state legislation (see further, Gessner, 2007, pp. 41–2; and Teubner, 1997).[3]

Global and Local Influences: To What Extent is Asian Commercial Law a Mix of the Global and the Local?

Linked to the scholarly debate over the causal link (if any) between law and capitalism in East Asia is the question over the proper identity of East Asian commercial law. Ever since the rise of Japan during the Meiji period, East Asia has transformed its economies by reforming its legal infrastructure and passing a body of commercial laws committed to achieving the rule of law. But to what extent did East Asia itself – through its own branded laws, policies, institutions and norms – engineer the Asian Century? Or was its economic success a gift of Western (or, at least, Western-inspired) commercial laws and market-oriented ideologies? Who, in short, authored East Asian commercial law?

The Western imprint is undeniable. In some jurisdictions, Western-style commercial laws were originally introduced by colonial powers, as in Indonesia, Malaysia, the Philippines and Vietnam. Others were copied from European models of law, as in Japan which was heavily influenced by European Civil Code precedents; these were, in time, influential in other parts of East Asia, such as in Taiwan and South Korea. China has also been influenced by Japanese commercial law models, sometimes via Taiwan, and has relied upon European and American models in the drafting of new laws since the commencement of the opening up of China in the mid-1970s.

The literature identifies three channels through which the East has received Western commercial law, policy and ideology: (1) wholesale colonial transplants of commercial laws and codes; (2) the involvement of global institutions in domestic law reform in East Asia; and (3) transnational private contractual and regulatory networks that have influenced domestic legal and commercial practice. In 'Legal Transplantation and Local Knowledge: Corporate Governance in Malaysia' (Chapter 5), Mohammad Rizal Salim provides an example of the first type: Malaysia's corporate law statute, a transplant from its English colonizer. In 'Living with the IMF: A New Approach to Corporate Governance and Regulation of Financial Institutions in Korea' (Chapter 6), Hwa-Jin Kim illustrates the second: the role of international lending agencies, such as the International Monetary Fund (IMF) and the World Trade Organisation (WTO), in reforming South Korea's system of corporate governance. And in 'Legal Transplants through Private Contracting: Codes of Vendor Conduct in Global

---

[3] It should be noted that some argue that there is little evidence to support the existence of a *lex mercatoria* during the Middle Ages; see further, Sachs, (2006), Volckart and Mangels (1999), and Dasser (2001).

Supply Chains' (Chapter 7), Li-Wen Lin demonstrates the third: how multinational firms have 'smuggled' social and environmental regulatory standards into China by incorporating codes of vendor conduct into contracts with local suppliers.

This is not to suggest that East Asia lacked any commercial legal tradition pre-dating this Western intrusion. Prior to their colonization, Malaysia and Indonesia, for example, had adat law, usually less formal or customary in nature, especially in more settled communities. As Geertz (1993, pp. 209–19) has pointed out, Malay adat law reflected an outlook, rather than the culture, and that this law could be seen as a reflection of 'local knowledge' rather than 'placeless principle' (Geertz, 1993, p. 218). China had its own indigenous legal tradition, with great imperial codes which could be traced back centuries to successive dynasties. However, these were generally concerned with public order issues, such as criminal law and administrative law. As Menski notes, '[s]ubjects like contract and topics of commercial law were conspicuously absent from the imperial codes [in China]' (Menski, 2006, p. 536). Japan, like China, had a stronger legal tradition in public rather than private law. This was because Japan was concerned with maintaining national unity among competing warlords, especially during its forced isolation from foreign powers during the two centuries of the Tokugawa period. However, Japan did develop a customary law on secured transactions and commercial loans and there was evidence of contract consciousness among Tokugawa merchants (Henderson, 1975).

This indigenous legal tradition matters. As Salim notes, even where whole law has been transplanted, its operation takes shape from the cultural, institutional and political setting of the receiving country. In Malaysia, for example, British colonial policy was to transplant commercial law across the Empire, and Malaysia's company law statute was modelled on the English template. However, it did not operate in the same way as its colonial parent. This is due to the distinction between 'hard' and 'soft' law. In Malaysia – and, indeed, in most of East Asia – soft law conceptions tend to dominate. As Heller (2003, p. 382) points out, 'governance through law is normally only one element in a wider portfolio of substitutable mechanisms for the various functions development requires'. He adds that:

> Those who design, fund, and implement rule of law activity should understand that law services are a scarce resource that should be used where other public and private substitutes are relatively less effective. That understanding may lead programs to become less judicial centric and prone to place inflated demands on courts and the law that result in only formal, ineffective, and delegitimating change. (Heller, 2003, p. 383)

The same observation applies to China and Japan. Neither country was colonized; both, however, received foreign law. In the dying days of the Tokugawa Period, Japan was subject to unequal treaties with Western nations and was forced to accept that consular rather than Japanese courts would apply to foreign nationals (Zweigert and Kotz, 1998, p. 297). However, Japanese governments were more quickly able to gain the upper hand over foreigners by adopting Western bodies of law and Westernizing their educational and military systems. A new German inspired Civil Code came into force in 1898 and a Commercial Code in 1899. After Japan's defeat in the Second World War, American-inspired common law ideas were introduced into Japan; noteworthy amongst these was the introduction of a strong anti-monopoly law and a new company law. However, especially recently, Japanese legal scholarship has 'increasingly emancipated itself from foreign models and become increasingly conscious of its autonomy' (Zweigert and Kotz, 1998, p. 299). The German-inspired Japanese Commercial Code and US-modelled corporate laws evolved over time as a result of local modifications and enforcement practices (Kanda, 2008, pp. 60–61).

The State and Commercial Law Reform in East Asia: Many commentators have reminded us that it is misleading to leave politics out of the relationship between law and development in East Asia (see further, Ginsburg, 2000, pp. 841–3; Jayasuriya, 1999). The state has therefore continued to play an important part in the development of commercial laws in many parts of Asia. This is illustrated by Antons (1993, pp. 216–17) who argues that the Asian Economic Crisis exposed weaknesses in the regulatory framework in East Asian states; this led to a strengthening of the role of the state. Despite a considerable degree of state control over the economy in these countries, economic liberalization took place after the 1997 Asian financial crisis in areas such as banking. Antons (2003, pp. 236–7) points out that: 'As a result of liberalization measures [in Japan] during the 1980s and 1990s, the stock market has become more attractive' leading to a revision being made to relevant laws in regard to this area. He adds, in regard to legal developments in Indonesia and Singapore, that, during this period, 'state enterprises have continued to play an important role, in spite of liberalization measures in other sectors of the economy …' (2003, p. 237).

In contrast to China, state ownership of enterprises was less prevalent in other Asian countries, despite the existence of broad schemes of state control and supervision. China's state-owned enterprises have, if anything, become stronger after economically weaker enterprises were sold to private interests. In Singapore, for example, government-linked companies account for only 10 per cent of economic output and 25 per cent of stock market capitalization (Antons, 2003, p. 237); but the state in Singapore retained control over strategic industries. In Indonesia, although a new Anti-Monopoly and Unfair Competition Law was passed in 1999, the President of the Republic retains considerable influence over the impact of this law as the law fails to specify the conduct that will be regarded as 'unfair' or 'detrimental' to society under this law (Antons, 2003, p. 238).

Antons (2003) also notes that the classic public-private distinction has been blurred in East Asian countries due to the continued influence of the State which has continued to issue administrative decrees in relation to commercial regulation. Privatization efforts by multilateral aid bodies such as the World Bank and the IMF during the Asian Financial Crisis were resisted in varying degrees; this was especially so in China where the state was in a stronger position to devise alternative strategies (see further, Peerenboom, 2007). Key features of commercial law reform in Indonesia, Japan and Singapore have been described as follows:

> All three countries to a certain extent instrumentalized their imported commercial laws for developmental purposes. In Japan, Western law was introduced to revise the unequal treaties and litigation for individual goals was never encouraged. Singapore impresses with its formal legal system, but some essential parts of the developmental strategy have been removed from judicial scrutiny. In Indonesia, the court system has been largely unreliable and Western derived business laws served to appease foreign investors and to justify developmental policies of the government. (Antons, 2003, p. 239).

So Asian governments have continued to play a central role in East Asian countries despite the extent to which there may have been an adoption of Western neo-liberal market models which assumed that markets were self-balancing; during the Asian financial crisis, for example, Asian governments played major roles, such as the actions of the Hong Kong government to prevent a collapse of the local stock market by buying shares of listed companies (Draper and Fung, 2002), or by the imposition of capital controls in Malaysia (Johnson et al., 2006). But, in other parts of East Asia, and Japan in particular, the degree of state intervention has been more limited, with political instability being notorious; this has meant that commercial law reform has often been slow to develop (see generally Bayoumi and Collyns, 2002). However, the collapse of Japan's bubble economy in the early 1990s did provoke some major commercial law reforms.[4]

Despite these economic problems, Japan as a patriarchal society has remained an important model for other countries in East Asia; this is evident if we look at the way that Chinese law reformers have been influenced by Japanese models of law in areas such as company law. The British sociologist Anthony Woodiwiss (1998, p. 56) argued that 'it is Japanese-style rather than American-style capitalism that has become archetypal within the region'. Woodiwiss also described what he saw as 'Pacific capitalism' in East Asia; he argued that this had acquired 'a distinctive institutional silhouette' which was characterized by a centralized and sometimes authoritarian state; with a small number of very large companies dominating commodity chains and society being subject to a patriarchalist ideology (Woodiwiss, 1998, pp. 56–7).

More recently, others such as Ginsburg (2007), have pointed to the emergence of a 'Northeast Asian Legal Complex' which is characterized by the patriarchal style adopted by legal institutions sustaining strong state governance in economies such as Japan, South Korea and Taiwan.[5] This model reflects the manner in which Japan adopted Western models during the Meiji era; it subsequently exported these ideas to its nearby colonies. Similarly, Gillespie and Peerenboom (2009, p. 1) note that 'Japan is now a major supporter of legal reforms from The Philippines to central Asia. It also exerts a strong influence over law reforms sponsored by the Asian Development Bank (ADB).'

China as a Rising Hegemonic Power in Asia: Given its increasing power and influence in East Asia, China's rise has generated considerable interest from legal researchers. For this reason, we devote particular attention in this Introduction to the comprehensive commercial law reform process that has been occurring in China. China's legal history has some similarities to that of Japan. As in Japan, foreign traders in China were reluctant to be subject to Chinese laws and insisted upon foreign laws being extraterritorially applicable to their dealings in China, leading to the Opium War in 1839–42. By the end of the nineteenth century, in response to

---

[4] This saw the introduction of a new corporate rescue law in 1999, a new company law in 2005 and a new securities law in 2006 (see further, Oda, 2009; Upham, 1987).

[5] Ginsburg (2007, p. 45) points to the Northeast Asian complex as being characterized by 'a professional, somewhat autonomous and competent court system; a small, cartelised private legal profession without much political influence; and administrative law regimes that insulate bureaucratic discretion exercised by developmental regimes.' Each of these elements of the complex were seen by Ginsburg (2007, p. 49) to interact 'to produce a set of stable and reinforcing institutions'.

the intrusions of foreign powers, China took a broader interest in commercial law-making. This accelerated after the collapse of the Qing Dynasty in 1911 with Republican governments having mixed success in transplanting Western laws into China. However, this process only began in earnest in 1926 after the Nationalists had gained power over the War Lords. Drawing upon European models, six comprehensive Codes were promulgated by the Nationalists, such as the Civil Code on private and commercial law in 1929–31.

These new laws did not have much impact and traditional ideas tended to persist and were often dominant (Menski, 2006, p. 365). So when the Communists took power in 1949, they abolished all pre-existing Nationalist laws. But it was harder to abolish legal customs and attitudes that can be traced back to China's Confucian traditions; these traditions were drawn upon in more recent times under President Hu Jintao as governments sought to create greater social harmony. In the meantime, Soviet legal models were copied in China and Soviet legal experts gave advice on fashioning a new economic system. But it was not until after the death of Mao Tse-tung and the rise of Deng Xiao Ping that a new commitment to the rule of law and commercial law-making emerged in China (see further, Potter, 2003).

After the disaster of the Cultural Revolution, China dramatically turned to greater reliance upon the use of law from the late 1970s. The fact that China began this journey of commercial law reform and modernization at this time is significant as it took place against the backdrop of the end of the Cold War and hostility to all things foreign; during the Cultural Revolution, Western influences were much criticized and eliminated. After the turmoil of the Cultural Revolution, China became increasingly committed to adopting an approach to governance that was more oriented to the rule of law; by 1992 this was couched in terms of establishing a 'socialist market economy' and thereby fostering an instrumental view of the rule of law (J. Chen, 1999, pp. 73–4). This has seen both 'thick' and 'thin' versions of the rule of law develop in China, although mainly the latter form.

China's Paramount Leader, Deng Xiao Ping, brushed aside the conflict between the old attitude to foreign laws and the new interest in transplanting modified Western legal models into China with his somewhat folksy expressions – such as 'It doesn't matter if a cat is black or white, so long as it catches mice'. Thus it was now possible for China to adopt Western legal forms without threatening socialist ideological purity. But this was not to be a concession to capitalist or neo-liberal models as it was evident that there were a number of different market-based models of capitalist ordering that were available (Hall and Soskice, 2001). Commitments to preserving state control over the economy and the dominance of the Party were affirmed recently by former President Hu Jintao in his address to the historic 18th National Congress of the Chinese Communist Party in November 2012 (see further Evans-Pritchard, 2012; Guardian, 2012).

The rapid growth of new commercial laws in China was an illustration of this new commitment to modernization. These laws were often themselves revised a few years later, responding to the pace of economic and social change taking place as the market developed. This showed an on-going process of commercial law reform aimed at ensuring that commercial laws remained in touch with the changing demands of the market. Thus, 1979 saw the passage of the PRC Law on Chinese-Foreign Equity Joint ventures (updated on a number of occasions over the following years). It has been said that this law was a way of officially welcoming foreign investment into China (Clarke et al., 2008, p. 381). In contrast to attitudes in Western countries, in China, the rule of law was not seen as an end in itself, but as an instrument of Party policy (J. Chen, 1999, p. 71; also see J. Chen, 2003).[6]

As Jianfu Chen has observed, these laws 'were distinctively Western in style, form, structure and language' even though China remained committed to being a socialist country (J. Chen, 1999, p. 79). The passage of the comprehensive new Contract Law in 1999 was another important milestone in the development of the market economy in China. To a large degree these legislative reforms were the result of internal efforts, drawing liberally on foreign ideas which had been carefully reshaped to suit Chinese circumstances; this might be described as law making with Chinese characteristics. However, there were clearly limits to the globalization of commercial laws, such as those relating to bankruptcy (see generally, Halliday and Carruthers, 2007 and 2009). This has seen slowness in the implementation at the provincial level of new business rescue laws in China (Tomasic and Zhang, 2012a and 2012b).

Nevertheless, in modernizing its laws, China's law reformers felt free to draw liberally upon Western precedents to internationalize Chinese law. As Chen has noted, '[w]hat has now been emphasised is the urgency of assimilating or harmonizing Chinese law with international practice. Law has been seen as a tool; this instrumental approach has helped to defuse ideological objections to change' (J. Chen, 1999, pp. 80, 82). Despite the parallels with Western laws, the legal system of China's socialist market economy has been built upon preserving three guiding principles or philosophies: instrumentalism, utilitarianism and authoritarianism (J. Chen, 1999, p. 85).

In addition to this extensive body of new legislation, China has also seen the issue of Supreme Court Opinions on the meaning of laws, as well as administrative regulations and opinions issued by agencies, such as the State Council and local government, regarding the emerging market economy. China has also adopted new 'soft laws', such as its Code of Corporate Governance for Listed Companies in China (2001) developed by the China Securities Regulatory Commission.[7] To some extent, external factors, such as the requirements

---

[6] In 1980 China passed a Law approving the regulation of Special Economic Zones in Guangdong province, whilst 1981 saw the passage of the Economic Contract law (revised in 1993); 1982 saw the passage of a new Trademark Law in China (revised in 1993) and 1984 saw the passage of a new Patent Law (revised in 1992 and 2000), whilst a new Copyright Law was passed in 1990 (and revised in 2010). Other notable new commercially oriented laws passed in the early years after the opening up of China included the Accounting Law in 1985 (revised in 1993 and 1999) and the Enterprise Bankruptcy Law of 1986 (replaced in 2006). In 1986, the passage of the General Principles of Civil Law saw the creation of basic legal principles of the kind that would be necessary to support a market economy. By 1993 the pace of economic law reform had quickened with the passage of a new Company Law (revised in 1999 and replaced in 2005), an Unfair Competition Law and a law regarding the Protection of Consumer Rights and Interests. The following years saw the passage of many new commercial laws such as the new Foreign Trade Law (1994 and 2004), the Law on Commercial Banks (revised in 1995 and 2003), the Guaranty Law (in 1995), the Negotiable Instruments Law (in 2004), the Insurance Law (1995 and revised in 2002), the Partnership Law (in 1997) the Securities Law (in 1998 and revised in 2005) and the Trust Law (2001).

[7] This Code was to a large degree modelled upon the OECD's 1999 Principles of Corporate Governance (revised in 2004). The adoption by banks of the voluntary Equator Principles, issued by the International Financial Corporation (IFC), aims to foster green environmental principles and relates to

for China's admission to the WTO in 2001, had an effect upon the pace of commercial law reform, although major events, such as the Asian Financial Crisis in 1997–98, had little real effect upon shaping China's commercial laws, in contrast to the position of countries such as Indonesia, Thailand and South Korea where foreign multilateral bodies such as the IMF and the World Bank had more influence during this economic crisis. Since China's entry into the WTO, and especially from the mid-2000s, the pace of law reform may have slowed in China and implementation problems at the local level have become more intense (see generally, Biddulph et al., 2012).

This is hardly surprising as the process of embedding such a vast body of new commercial laws and practices across China was bound to be problematic, even in an authoritarian political system. In the circumstances, it has, however, been remarkably successful given the dimensions of China's 'Great Economic Transformation' (Brandt and Rawski, 2008). As Stephen Green has noted in regard to the reform of China's commercial banking system from the mid-1990s: 'The ongoing transformation of China's banking system is a particularly impressive achievement, given both the scale and depth of the challenges over the last 30 years, as the country made the rapid transition from a planned economy to a market-oriented one' (Green, 2009, p. 92). Similarly, Chen (2011, p. 110) has noted that the massive amount of law-making in China represents 'fundamental changes in Chinese law'; he suggests that this law is a product of China's 'politico-economic system' and that 'Chinese law is unambiguously becoming Western law in its form, terminologies and, to a lesser extent, its structure.' It is likely that China's state-led model of commercial law reform (the so-called 'Beijing consensus') will be mirrored in other parts of East Asia (such as in Vietnam) as well as in other parts of the world.

Economic Law Reform Elsewhere in East Asia: In other parts of East Asia the pace of economic law reform has been less brisk and has not been subject to the same internal pressures for change as existed in China. As Clarke et al. (2008, p. 380) point out: 'Although the main motor of change in the Chinese legal system has been domestic developments, the policy of opening up to foreign trade and investment has had an unmistakeable impact on both substance and procedure.' On the other hand, in many other countries, such as Indonesia, Malaysia and Hong Kong, somewhat dated bodies of commercial law which can be traced back to their respective colonial eras were retained for much longer than they should have been. Pressure for change accelerated after the Asian Financial Crisis, although the forces of globalization (such as private actors, financial institutions and professional communities) also encouraged a modernization of commercial and financial laws.

This of course raises the parallel question of the degree to which the forces of globalization have led to a convergence in the nature of commercial laws in different parts of the region (see generally, Pistor and Wellons, 1999). To some extent, a degree of harmonization has been occurring in areas such as corporate governance, securities regulation and bankruptcy

---

the social and environmental impact of project financing of US$10 million, or more. In this regard, the Shanghai branch of the China Banking Regulatory Commission now requires banks in China to report on the corporate social responsibility initiatives (Green, 2009, p. 104).

law, but this convergence has often only been a convergence in form rather than in substance; significant implementation problems remain.

However, Asian cultural values and structural features of Asian economies created important differences from patterns in the West. For example, the State continued to play an important role in most East Asian economies and in law reform priorities; also, individualism was tempered by a strong commitment to collective or communitarian factors in shaping and enforcing new commercial laws. Even where economies have become globalized through their participation in global markets, as in Taiwan, the 'corporate law system and financial markets remain parochial' as the local political economy has had a critical role in shaping the system of corporate law (Liu, 2003, pp. 400–401).

This has seen a negative reaction to globalization with different patterns of business regulation emerging in East Asian jurisdictions as a result of the interactions of state and non-state actors in their respective regulatory spaces (Gillespie and Peerenboom, 2009, pp. 2–6). This illustrates the interrelationship that exists between global and local forces in shaping the regulatory environment to create what has been described as a 'localized globalism' (de Sousa Santos, 2002, p. 179). In reaction to perceived deficiencies in globalized norms that have usually been created in Western states, business regulation has been localized in different ways in East Asia, with the State playing a greater role in non-democratic countries such as China and Vietnam. This 'pushback' or resistance has been explained by Gillespie and Peerenboom as follows:

> At the most general level, some countries have resisted the trend toward liberal democracy and a liberal interpretation of human rights, most notably Vietnam and China...Northeast Asian states have also rejected aspects of the dominant development models promoted by Western states and the major international donor agencies such as the IMF and the World Bank. In particular, they have rejected certain aspects of the Washington Consensus. While they generally accepted the basic macroeconomic principles for their domestic economy, they have rejected or modified the neoliberal emphasis on a small state, deregulation, and privatization. They also rejected or modified the prescribed relationship between the domestic and international economies by advocating that the domestic economy be only gradually exposed to foreign competition. (Gillespie and Peerenboom, 2009, p. 8)

Case Studies

The articles in Part II discuss the implications of East Asian law for commercial negotiations; the Asian identity of East Asian contracts; the East Asian approach to commercial dispute resolution; and the institutional features of East Asian corporate governance.

The identity of East Asian commercial law has practical implications for transnational lawyers. Whether the law is Western or Eastern, global or local, or – as Salim, Kim, Lin and most other commentators conclude – a complex confluence of influences, legal practitioners need to know the ramifications for negotiating business deals, drafting transactions, resolving disputes, arranging finance and structuring investment opportunities in and across the region. The lesson from comparative law – that the 'law in the books' is not the same as 'law in action' – is well understood. But the question remains: what is the key variable that determines how commercial law in East Asia operates in practice?

This is no easy task. East Asia is a diverse region lacking an overarching identity. The region speaks multiple languages from different linguistic families; practises a pastiche of religions – Islamic, Buddhist, Confucian, Shinto, Christian; and comprises people from different ethnic backgrounds with little intra-regional immigration. Economically, the region is less integrated than Western Europe, the Gulf States and North America; politically, governance systems vary from constitutional democracies (Japan) to illiberal authoritarian regimes (Singapore) to one-party Communist states (China); and, historically, colonization has affected some, but not all, states and, even then, the outcomes have diverged.

Some have argued that such intra-regional diversity and divisions render an East Asian approach to commercial law a theoretical and practical impossibility (see, for example, Taylor, 1997). Others, however, have sought to find 'unifying concepts' (Antons, 1995) or geopolitical commonalities (Jayasuriya, 1999a) to facilitate comparative analysis of both capitalism and commercial law in East Asia. Multilateral bodies (such as UNCITRAL, the OECD and the Asian Development Bank) have nevertheless sought to fashion templates of principles that could be (and have been) adopted to varying degrees in different parts of Asia; also 'soft law' principles developed by banks and financial institutions (such as the Equator principles regarding environmentally responsible investment practices) have also been adopted (Conley and Williams, 2011). Even so, scholars are divided over the best way to characterize law and the economy in East Asia. Does East Asian capitalism – and the commercial laws that underpin it – function according to neo-classical, rational market economics? Or does East Asian culture provide a more convincing explanation? Perhaps the region is defined by its own unique set of economic institutions, in which cases its structural or institutional properties determine its capitalist design? Or perhaps it is a hybrid of more than one of these explanatory models?

Negotiations

One of the more popular explanations of East Asian commercial law emphasizes cultural norms of behaviour. This is especially evident in the literature on negotiations. An illustrative piece is 'Cultivating *Guanxi* as a Foreign Investor Strategy' by John Pearce II and Richard Robinson (Chapter 8). The authors argue that personal connections (*guanxi*) matter more than business considerations (such as price and product quality) in Chinese business deals. Therefore, successful business deals with Chinese partners must accord with Chinese cultural preferences for relationship-building and non-legal, informal means for entering into business relationships and resolving disputes. Hutchings and Murray (2003, pp. 27–30), in their exploration of the broader literature on the cultural attributes that underpin the cultural dynamics of doing business in China, similarly note that Chinese business culture is built on close, family relationships, personal connections, face, reciprocity, trust and favours. The same cultural analysis informs much of the literature on negotiations with the Japanese (Zhang and Kuroda, 1989; Walters, 1991).

This cultural model of negotiations is not without its critics. James Sebenius, in 'Caveats for Cross-Border Negotiators' (Chapter 9), for example, argues that cultural explanations of negotiating strategy – from surface etiquette and protocol to deeper cultural characteristics and decision-making processes – are prone to four fallacies: (1) stereotyping, (2) over-attribution, (3) skewed perception and information-processing, and (4) uncritical oversimplification. In the case of China, specifically, some scholars argue that *guanxi* is less important than most assume and that negotiators must pay closer attention to the institutional environment and more rational 'market' imperatives such as price and product quality. Yi and Ellis (2000), for instance, question the cultural underpinnings of *guanxi*. The authors instead suggest that *guanxi* is a response to institutional weakness in the legal system insofar as interpersonal trust is needed when institutionalized law is inadequate for underpinning transactions.

Guthrie (1998) builds on this idea to suggest that the use of *guanxi* in business deals is on the decline as China moves towards a market economy and the rule of law. China is in the process of constructing a rational-legal system at the state level and formal rational bureaucracies at the firm level. Further, as the state places more and more economic responsibilities directly on the shoulders of firms, there is increasing pressure from market constraints: in the face of self-responsibility policies and tightening fiscal constraints, organizations can no longer afford to favour personal relationships and ignore the imperatives of price and quality. For Guthrie, market questions of price, quality, service and reliability must underline any negotiating strategy with urban Chinese business partners. Hutchings and Murray (2003), although accepting that Chinese business may have distinctly national cultural attributes such as family, face and favour, question the continuing significance of these historical cultural concepts. They query whether a system of networks consolidated during 50 years of state-owned enterprises can still have application on the considerably larger scale of multinational corporate business of today's China. Based on interviews with expatriate Australians, the authors conclude that *guanxi* is of declining significance in large-scale, global areas of business but of enduring relevance in regional, start-up or small-scale businesses.

Similar counter-explanations exist for negotiations in Japan. Janosik (1987) does not deny the relevance of Japanese culture on the negotiating process, but questions whether Japanese culture can be packaged as homogenous, static and deterministic. Buckley and Parkin (1985) are more critical of cultural explanations of Japanese negotiating style, especially those accounts which hold out the Japanese to be inscrutable, mysterious and even treacherous. They prefer the view that the Japanese, like all good business-people, are rational in their approach to bargaining.

Commercial Transactions

A similar debate over the relevance of norms plays out in the literature on East Asian contracts. A strong view that emerges in the scholarship is an East Asian cultural preference for relational contracting. Quan Nguyen, in 'The Norms and Incentive Structures of Relational Contracting in Vietnam – Two Surveys' (Chapter 10), makes this claim in the context of Vietnamese commercial transactions. Among Vietnamese local merchants, relationships of personal trust and harmony matter more than a formally-documented deal. 'A contract does not have the meaning of a 'sharp in, sharp out' deal. Instead, it is embedded within social relationships built between family members, friends, or social networks' (Ngyuyen, 2007, p. 53).

This view is reminiscent of the debate about Japanese contract consciousness sparked by Kawashima's (1974) classic essay on Japanese contracting. Drawing on his observations of contracting practices in the pre-war and immediate post-war periods, Kawashima concluded that, for cultural reasons, the Japanese prefer not to arrange their affairs by means of formal contracts. Where contracts are entered into, they are typically vague and open-ended, and evidence the priority given to personal relationships over formal terms and conditions. As Japan modernizes, Kawashima predicts, the Japanese will increase their reliance on formal contracting.

Informality in contract norms is also said to be evident in China. According to Boettcher (1999), for example, Chinese contract law – both the new fundamental law and the former collection of subject-matter-specific contract laws – is premised on specific Chinese ideas about 'fairness', 'equality', 'good faith' and 'mutual benefit'. It is misleading to assume that Western and Chinese contract law regimes share a 'common denominator'. Pattison and Herron (2003) agree; they contend that there is not yet sanctity of contract in China, because, despite the appearance of a modern law, centuries of cultural practices will resist the new law. Therefore, they recommend some 'stop-gap' measures for foreign businesses wishing to engage contractually with Chinese business partners.

Critics counter that relational contracting in East Asia is not a cultural preference. In the scholarship on Japanese law contracts, for example, Taylor (1993) is dismissive of the Kawashima thesis. Taylor questions the extent to which relational contracting is unique to Japan, is intrinsically harmonious, removes the need to document the relationship between the parties, and reflects a disdain for formal law. Indeed, for Taylor, the law seems to *facilitate* relational contracting. Kobayashi (2005) offers a sophisticated institutional analysis to explain the prevalence of relational contracting. Exogenous factors – in particular, the lack of professional drafting experience in Japanese history – explains why discrete contracts never dominated Japanese business practice. Kuzuhara (1996) adds that Japanese contract law allows for 'extrinsic' evidence in the interpretation of bargains, thereby facilitating shorter and organic deals, whereas the *parol* evidence rule in the Anglo-American tradition mandates precise and detailed contractual terms. Yoshiro Miwa and Mark Ramseyer, in 'Rethinking Relationship-Specific Investments: Subcontracting in the Japanese Automobile Industry' (Chapter 11), go even further. The empirical evidence does not reveal a trend of relationship-specific investment in Japanese industry, they claim; rather, Japanese firms enter into arm's length contracts due to 'standard competitive market' principles.

Commercial Dispute Resolution

At first blush, the scholarship on dispute resolution in East Asia produces a similar range of views. As with relationship-building in precontractual negotiations and relationship-specific investments in documented deals, the East Asian approach to dispute resolution is distinctive: litigation is a last resort; informal dispute resolution is the preference. Take Japan, for example; in the mid-1990s, Japan had only 9.3 cases per 1,000 people compared to 123.2 cases in Germany, 74.5 in the United States, 64.4 in the United Kingdom and 40.3 in France (Sato, 2002, p. 5). Some commentators claim that litigation rates are steadily increasing, especially since the beginning of the twenty-first century (Ginsburg and Hoetker, 2006). However, others explain that most of the increase is attributable to the surge in expedited debt-recovery cases following the bursting of the economic bubble; ordinary contested cases – a better barometer of litigiousness – still remain at relatively low levels. (Tanase, 2010, p. 158). China, too, is said to prefer mediation over formal litigation (Colatrella, 2000; Wong, 2000).

Why is litigation so much lower in East Asia compared to other modern democratic economies? One of the more popular explanations is the cultural model of civil justice.

Japanese national traits of harmony and groupism, for example, explain low levels of litigation in Japan (Port, 1994, pp. 659–70); Chinese philosophical and religious traditions underpin the Chinese preference for mediation (Wong, 2000; Colatrella, 2000). However, comparative law researchers have strongly criticized the cultural model and offered alternative explanations. One such counter-explanation stresses institutional factors over cultural attributes. Specifically, this model points to a number of institutional disincentives in the legal system which deters litigation (Port, 1994, p. 659).

For example, Haley (1978), while acknowledging that Japanese citizens file proportionately fewer civil suits compared to citizens in other industrialized countries, points to evidence that the Japanese are not reticent about asserting their legal rights. Rather, institutional incapacity – few lawyers and judges, discontinuous nature of trials, and an inadequate range of remedies and enforcement powers – sets up a barrier to bringing suits in Japan. Other institutional barriers include a lack of pre-trial discovery procedures, high contingency fees, prohibitive court costs and the absence of a jury system (Yamanouchi and Cohen, 1991). Likewise, the Chinese settle their disputes through informal mediation mainly because of the difficulties in accessing justice provided by law (Fu, 2002, p. 179). Indeed, according to Lo (2001), mediation is actually instituted and controlled by the Chinese government to entrench its political agenda.

The twist in this line of scholarship, however, is that there is little evidence of aversion to formal dispute resolution in international trade disputes. Rather, Saadia Pekkanen in 'Aggressive Legalism: The Rules of the WTO and Japan's Emerging Trade Strategy' (Chapter 12), describes Japan's international dispute resolution strategy as both legalistic and aggressive. In 'No More Negotiated Deals?: Settlement of Trade and Investment Disputes in East Asia' (Chapter 13), Junji Nakagawa explores the scholarship that makes similar claims for other jurisdictions in the East Asian region. Nakagawa, however, notes that East Asian economies vary in their strategy towards international trade disputes: some, such as China, are relatively reticent to file international trade complaints; others, such as Japan, are more willing to do so but prefer to join with other complainants; and yet others, such as South Korea, are even more aggressive. East Asian assertiveness in international commercial dispute resolution, Nakagawa predicts, might very well grow, especially as the region intensifies regional integration through free trade agreements, economic partnership agreements and bilateral investment treaties. Even so, he cautions, it still significantly lags behind the more aggressive stance towards trade disputes adopted by the United States and the European Union.

Corporate Law and Corporate Governance

Corporate law and corporate governance in East Asia, too, are also taking on more sophisticated shape. As already observed, some even predict that East Asian corporate law will march inexorably towards shareholder primacy that is the orthodoxy in the West (Hansmann and Kraakman, 2001; see also Keleman and Sibbit, 2002). In 'The Establishment and Development of the Chinese Legal System in the Past Sixty Years' (Chapter 14), Chen Su charts the positive, but uneven, development of Chinese corporate and other economic laws throughout modern Chinese legal history. Although Chen does not go so far as to argue that Chinese corporate and commercial laws are inevitably converging on the global template, he does suggest that China is erecting a legal infrastructure that respects such universal values as respect for the market economy and the principle of the rule of law.

Others are more cautious. In 'Berle and Means, Corporate Governance and the Chinese Family Firm' (Chapter 15), Philip Lawton argues that the Chinese firm in Hong Kong still has a Chinese heart beating within its modern legal body. The tradition of the family firm, for example, will lead to unpredictable results when corporate law reforms seek to impose culturally alien concepts, such as independent non-executive directors. Likewise, Roman Tomasic, in 'Company Law and Limits of the Rule of Law in China' (Chapter 16), contrasts the schizophrenic commitment to the rule of law: although formally embodied within the legal language of the PRC company law statute, it remains elusive in the broader institutional make-up of the legal system. Drawing on a case study demonstrating the lack of judicial independence from official manipulation, Tomasic concludes that, until rule of law values permeate China's legal system, corporate law, despite its modern appearance, will be unlikely to inspire the confidence of foreign investors.

Japanese corporate law and governance, too, are said to be undergoing a 'gradual transformation' towards market-driven governance (Nottage et al., 2008). Corporate and securities laws have been comprehensively re-written to ensure a more flexible regime of regulation. Banking laws have been reformed to increase competition among providers of financial services. Employment law reforms have allowed for greater flexibility in hiring practices. Restrictions on M&A activity have been eased. For Curtis Milhaupt, in 'Creative Norm Destruction: The Evolution of Non-legal Rules in Japanese Corporate Governance' (Chapter 17), all this suggests that the traditional norms which have evolved to support a peculiarly Japanese-style corporate governance are beginning to weaken. These norms have underpinned main-bank monitoring, lifelong employment, distaste for hostile takeovers and a large board of largely inside directors. But as they break down, Milhaupt suggests, Japanese corporate governance will look increasingly likely to converge (although not precisely) with Western-style management practices. Dan Puchniak, however, in 'Delusions of Hostility: The Marginal Role of Hostile Takeovers in Japanese Corporate Governance Remains Unchanged' (Chapter 18), expresses caution. Despite confident predictions that corporate Japan is increasingly embracing American-style corporate law practices in its adoption of more overtly market-driven reforms to kick-start its flagging economy, the evidence is still overwhelming that the Japanese prefer friendly, over hostile, takeovers. Puchniak, in short, is an advocate of path-dependence in Japan's corporate law reforms.

Conclusions

This volume has sought to cover a vast area of legal scholarship and a broad range of themes relating to the field of commercial law in East Asia. Inevitably, we have had to generalize if we are to obtain any capacity to identify broader trends over time; inevitably, in such a process, there will be exceptions to some of the broader points being made, as well as changes over time. What is clear, however, is that there is now a multi-layered body of commercial law scholarship which has sought to engage with broader patters of change over this region and this body of scholarship is increasing in both its depth and its theoretical sophistication.

We have increasingly seen a movement from narrow jurisdictional and technical legal scholarship to more widely based studies. This movement is essential if we are to make the best use of comparative law, especially as East Asia becomes a more important area of commercial law practice. Up until recent times, the shape of East Asian commercial law has been heavily influenced by Anglo-American and European models, but this has been rapidly changing; at the same time, Americanization has increasingly had an effect on the shape of institutions, such as large law firms and major corporations in East Asia. This Americanization may have the effect of marginalizing East Asian commercial law, especially where global soft law norms are used as a basis for agreements and dispute handling.

Over the last 40 years or so we have seen an increasing commitment to using law as a means of shaping relationships and dealing with conflicts; but this has tended to be a 'thin' version of the rule of law and has also tended to involve a more instrumental approach to the use of law. This has arisen from the widespread dominance of the state in East Asian legal systems; at the same time, politics remains an important means of protecting interests in some areas. This is in contrast to the model of liberal legalism that characterizes many Western legal systems. This dominance of the state has helped to stabilize markets in times of crisis as we saw in the Asian Financial Crisis and more recently in the Global Financial Crisis that came to a peak in 2008.

Consequently, economic development in East Asia has occurred as a result of an interplay of forces; and commercial law reform often has followed rather than caused such development. This has been possible because of the strength of other social systems in supporting investor confidence and commercial transactions in these markets; some of these are political, some are cultural and others are historical. All this means that progressive convergence of East Asian and Western bodies of commercial law cannot be taken for granted, even where Western-style laws have been adopted in East Asian countries. Problems of implementation of these laws remain.

But, these problems may be counterbalanced by other mechanisms supporting commercial activity. We look forward to the emergence of a more extensive body of East Asian commercial law scholarship which further highlights the limits of law and the increasing similarities and differences that exist both within East Asia and between East Asian states and Western legal systems. This is important because, for too long, our conceptions of commercial law have been filtered through the limited lens of the Anglo-American experience.

ROMAN TOMASIC and LEON WOLFF

Bibliography

Abbott, K.W. and G.W. Bowman (1994), 'Economic Integration for the Asian Century: An Early Look at New Approaches', *Transnational Law and Contemporary Problems*, **4**, pp. 187–226.

Age, The (2013), 'Japan Returns to Growth in Boost to Abe', 8 March 2013: available at http://www.theage.com.au/business/world-business/japan-returns-to-growth-in-boost-to-abe-20130308-2fq46.html.

Alvarez, J.E. (2007), 'Institutionalised Legalisation and the Asia-Pacific "Region"', *New Zealand Journal of Public International Law*, **5**, pp. 9–28.

Annan, K.A. (2002), 'Problems without Passports', *Foreign Policy*, 132: 30–31.

Antons, C. (1993), 'Japan as a Model? Comparing Law and Development in Japan, Singapore and Indonesia', in C Antons (ed.), *Law and Development in East and Southeast Asia*, London: Routledge Curzon, pp. 216–48.

Antons C. (1995), 'Analysing Asian Law: The Need for a General Concept', *Law in Context*, **13**, pp. 106–23.

Antons, C. (2003), *Law and Development in East and South East Asia*, London and New York: Taylor & Francis.

Australian Government (2012), *Australia in the Asian Century* (White Paper), October 2012: available at http://asiancentury.dpmc.gov.au.

Baruma, I. (1999), 'What Happened to the Asian Century?' *New York Times*, 29 December 1999, A25.

Bayoumi, T. and Collyns, C. (eds) (2000), *Post-Bubble Blues: How Japan Responded to Asset Price Collapse, International Monetary Fund*: available at http://www.imf.org/external/pubs/nft/2000/bubble/index.htm .

Biddulph, S., S. Cooney and Y. Zhu (2012), 'Rule of Law with Chinese Characteristics: The Role of Campaigns in Lawmaking', *Law & Policy*, **34**, pp. 373–401.

Birch, D., T. Schirato and S. Srivastava (2001), *Asia: Cultural Politics in the Global Age*, Sydney: Allen & Unwin.

Black III, W.L.R. (1990), 'Maritime Arbitration in the Asian Century', *Tulane Maritime Law Journal*, **14**, pp. 261–2.

Boettcher, J.G. (1999), 'Attempting a New Commercial Code: China's New Commercial Sale Maize', *Business Forum*, **24**, pp. 39–44.

Brandt, L. and T.G. Rawski (eds) (2008), *China's Great Economic Transformation*, Cambridge: Cambridge University Press.

Buckley, S. and J. Parkin (1985), 'Negotiation: Understand Ethnic, but Build on Commonsense with Japan Inc.', *Rydges*, **58**, pp. 84–6.

Chen, D. (2013), *Corporate Governance, Enforcement and Financial Development*, Cheltenham Edward Elgar Publishers.

Chen, J. (1999), 'Market Economy and the Internationalisation of Civil and Commercial Law in the People's Republic of China', in K. Jayasuriya (ed.), *Law, Capitalism and Power in Asia*, London: Routledge, pp. 69–94.

Chen, J. (2003), 'Policy as Law and Law as Policy: The Role of Law in China's Development Strategy', in C. Antons (ed.), *Law and Development in East and Southeast Asia*, London: Routledge Curzon, pp. 251–70.

Chen, J. (2011), 'China's Civil and Commercial Law Reforms: Context and Transformation', in J. Garrick (ed.), *Law, Wealth and Power in China: Commercial Law Reforms in Context*, London: Routledge, pp. 109–29.

Chesterman, S. (2008), 'The Globalisation of Legal Education', *Singapore Journal of Legal Studies*, July: pp. 58–67.

Clarke, D., P. Murrell and S. Whiting (2008), 'The Role of Law in China's Economic Development', in L. Brandt and T.G. Rawski (eds), *China's Great Economic Transformation*, Cambridge: Cambridge University Press, pp. 375–428.

Colatrella, M.T. (2000), '"Court-performed" Mediation in the People's Republic of China: A Proposed Model to Improve the United States Federal District Courts' Mediation Programs', *Ohio State Journal on Dispute Resolution*, **15**, pp. 391–424.

Conley, J.M. and C.A. Williams (2011), 'Global Banks as Global Sustainability Regulators?: The Equator Principles', *Law & Policy*, **33**, pp. 542–76.

Cossman, B. (1997), 'Turning the Gaze Back on Itself: Comparative Law, Feminist Legal Studies and the Postcolonial Project', *Utah Law Review*, **2**, pp. 525–44.

Darian-Smith, E. (2000), 'Structural Inequalities in the Global Legal System', *Law and Society Review*, **34**, pp. 809–28.

Dasser, F. (2001), 'Lex Mercatoria – Critical Comments on a Tricky Topic', in R.P. Appelbaum, W.L.F. Felstiner and V. Gessner (eds), *Rules and Networks: The Legal Culture of Global Business Transactions*, Oxford: Hart Publishing, pp. 189–200.

De Ly, F. (2001), '(New Law Merchant): Globalisation and International Self-Regulation', in W.L.F. Felstiner and V. Gessner (eds), *Rules and Networks: The Legal Culture of Global Business Transactions*, Oxford: Hart Publishing, pp. 159–88.

Deakin, S. and K. Pistor (eds) (2012), *Legal Origin Theory*, Cheltenham: Edward Elgar Publishing.

De Sousa Santos, B. (1987), 'Law: A Map of Misreading. Toward a Postmodern Conception of Law', *Journal of Law and Society*, **14**, pp. 279–302.

De Sousa Santos, B. (2002), *Towards a New Common Sense: Law, Globalization, And Emancipation*, 2nd edn, London: Butterworths LexisNexis.

De Sousa Santos, B. and C.A. Rodriguez-Garavito (eds) (2005), *Law and Globalization from Below: Towards a Cosmopolitan Legality*, Cambridge: Cambridge University Press.

Dezalay, Y. (1990), 'The Big Bang and the Law …', *Theory, Culture and Society*, **7**, pp. 279–83.

Draper, P. and J.K.W. Fung (2002), 'Discretionary Government Intervention, and the Mispricing of Index Futures', Paper Number 02/07: available at http://business-school.exeter.ac.uk/documents/papers/accounting/2002/0207.pdf.

Evans-Pritchard, A. (2012), 'China's Hu Jintao clings to socialist economy in Mao nostalgia speech', *The Telegraph*, 8 November 2012: available at http://www.telegraph.co.uk/finance/china-business/9665384/Chinas-Hu-Jintao-clings-to-socialist-economy-in-Mao-nostalgia-speech.html.

Fauvarque-Cosson, B. (2001), 'Comparative Law and Conflict of Laws: Allies or Enemies? New Perspectives on an Old Couple', *American Journal of Comparative Law*, **49**, pp. 407–28.

Fidler, D.P. (2005), 'The Asian Century: Implications for International Law' *Singapore Yearbook for International Law*, **9**, pp. 19–35.

Freidman, L.M. (2002), 'One World: Notes on the Emerging Legal Order', in M. Likposky (ed.), *Transnational Legal Processes: Globalisation and Power Disparities*, London: Butterworths LexisNexis, pp. 23–40.

Fu, H. (2002), 'Shifting Landscape of Dispute Resolution in Rural China', in J. Chen, L. Yuwen and J.M. Otto (eds), *Implementation of Law in the People's Republic of China*, The Hague, Boston and London: Kluwer Law International, pp. 179–96.

Garnaut, R. (2001), *Private Enterprise in China*, Canberra: ANU Asia Pacific Press.

Garnaut, R. and L. Song (eds) (2004), *China's Third Economic Transformation: The Rise of the Private Economy*, New York: Routledge.

Gaubatz, K.T. and M.C. MacArthur (2001), 'How International is International Law?', *Michigan Journal of International Law*, **22**, pp. 239–82.

Geertz, C. (1993), *Local Knowledge: Further Essays in Interpretive Anthropology*, London: Fontana Press.

Gessner, V. (2007), 'Legislation and the Varieties of Capitalism', in C. Antons and V. Gessner (eds), *Globalisation and Resistance: Law Reform in Asia since the Crisis*, Oxford: Hart Publishing, pp. 27–51.

Gillespie, J. and R. Peerenboom (eds) (2009), *Regulation in Asia: Pushing Back on Globalization*, London: Routledge.

Ginsburg, T. (2000), 'Does Law Matter for Economic Development? Evidence from East Asia', *Law & Society Review*, **34**, pp. 829–56.

Ginsburg, T. (2007), 'Law and the Liberal Transformation of the Northeast Asian Legal Complex', in T. Halliday, L. Karpik and M. Feeley (eds), *Fighting for Freedom*, Oxford: Hart Publishing, pp. 43–63.

Ginsburg, T. and G. Hoetker (2006), 'The Unreluctant Litigant? An Empirical Analysis of Japan's Turn to Litigation', *Journal of Legal Studies*, **35**, pp. 31–59.

Glenn H.P. (2000), *Legal Traditions of the World: Sustainable Diversity in Law*, Oxford: Oxford University Press.

Green, S.K. (2009), 'China's Financial Transformation and New Challenges', in Zhu Min, Cai Jinqing and M. Avery (eds) *China's Emerging Financial Markets: Challenges and Global Impact*, Singapore: John Wiley & Sons (Asia) Pte Ltd, pp. 91–122.

Guardian, The (2012), 'China's Hu Jintao's last hurrah', *The Guardian*, 9 November 2012; available at http://www.guardian.co.uk/commentisfree/2012/nov/09/china-hu-jintao-last-hurrah-editorial.

Guthrie, D. (1998), 'The Declining Significance of Guanxi in China's Economic Transition', *China Quarterly*, **154**, pp. 254–82.

Haley, J.O. (1978), 'The Myth of the Reluctant Litigant', *Journal of Japanese Studies*, **4**, pp. 359–90.

Halliday, T.D. and B.G. Carruthers (2007), 'Fooling the Financial Hegemons: Limits to the Globalisation of Corporate Insolvency Regimes in Indonesia, Korea and China', in C. Antons and V. Gessner (eds), *Globalisation and Resistance: Law Reform in Asia since the Crisis*, Oxford: Hart Publishing, pp. 255–301.

Hall, P.A. and D. Soskice (2001), *Varieties of Capitalism: The Institutional Foundations of Comparative Advantage*, Oxford: Oxford University Press.

Halliday, T.D. and B.G. Carruthers (2009), *Bankrupt – Global Lawmaking and Systemic Financial Crisis*, Stanford: Stanford University Press.

Hansmann H. and R. Kraakman (2001), 'The End of History for Corporate Law', *Georgetown Law Journal*, **89**, pp. 439–68.

Heller, T.C. (2003), 'An Immodest Postscript', in E.G. Jensen and T.C. Heller (eds), *Beyond Common Knowledge: Empirical Approaches to the Rule of Law*, Stanford: Stanford University Press, pp. 382–417.

Henderson, D.F. (1975), *Village 'Contracts' in Tokugawa Japan: Fifty Specimens With English Translations and Comments*, Seattle: University of Washington Press.

Hutchings, K. and G. Murray (2003), 'Family, Face, and Favours: Do Australians Adjust to Accepted Business Conventions in China?', *Singapore Management Review*, **25**, pp. 25–49.

International Monetary Fund (2011), *Regional Economic Outlook: Asia and the Pacific* (April 2011), Washington D.C.: International Monetary Fund.

Janosik, R.J. (1987), 'Rethinking the Culture-Negotiation Link', *Negotiation Journal*, **3**, pp. 385–95.

Jayasuriya, K. (1999a), 'Introduction: A Framework for the Analysis of Legal Institutions in East Asia', in K. Jayasuriya (ed.), *Law, Capitalism and Power in Asia: The Rule of Law and Legal Institutions*, New York: Routledge, pp. 1–27.

Jayasuriya, K. (ed.) (1999b), *Law, Capitalism and Power in Asia: The Rule of Law and Legal Institutions*, New York: Routledge.

Jayasuriya, K. (2000), *The Rule of Law and Regimes of Exception in East Asia*, Asia Research Centre Working Paper 96, Murdoch University, Perth.

Johnson, S., K. Kochhar, T. Mitton and N. Tamirisa (2006), 'Malaysian Capital Controls: Macroeconomics and Institutions', IMF Working Paper, WP/06/51, available at http://www.imf.org/external/pubs/ft/wp/2006/wp0651.pdf.

Kanda, H. (2008), 'What Shapes Corporate Law in Japan', in H. Kanda, K.S. Kim and C.J. Milhaupt (eds), *Transforming Corporate Governance in East Asia*, London: Routledge, pp. 60–67.

Kawashima, T. (1974), 'The Legal Consciousness of Contract in Japan', *Law in Japan*, **7**, pp. 1–21.

Keleman R.D. and E.C. Sibbitt (2002), 'The Americanization of Japanese Law', *University of Pennsylvania Journal of International Economic Law*, **23**, pp. 269–323.

Kennedy, D. (1997), 'New Approaches to Comparative Law: Comparativism and International Governance', *Utah Law Review*, **2**, pp. 545–638.

Kobayashi, I. (2005), 'The Interaction between Japanese Corporate Governance and Relational Contract Practice', *NYU Journal of Law & Business*, **2**, pp. 269–322.

Komesar, N. (1994), *Imperfect Alternatives: Choosing Institutions in Law, Economics and Public Policy*, Chicago: Chicago University Press.

Komesar, N. (2001), *Law's Limits: The Rule of Law and Demand of Rights*, Cambridge: Cambridge University Press.

Kuzuhara, K. (1996), 'Contracting between a Japanese Enterprise and an American Enterprise: The Differences in the Importance of Written Documents as the Final Agreement in the United States and Japan', *ILSA Journal of International & Comparative Law*, **3**, pp. 57–92.

La Porta, R., F. Lopez-de-Silanes, A. Shleifer and R.W. Vishny (1998), 'Law and Finance', *Journal of Political Economy*, **106**, pp. 1113–55.

La Porta, R., F. Lopez-de-Silanes and A. Shleifer (2008), 'The Economic Consequences of Legal Origins', *Journal of Economic Literature*, **46**, pp. 285–332.

Lingle, C. (1997), *The Rise and Decline of the Asian Century: False Starts on the Path to the Global Millennium*, Hong Kong: Asia 2000 Ltd.

Liu, L.S. (2003), 'Global Markets and Parochial Institutions', in C.J. Milhaupt (ed.), *Global Markets, Domestic Institutions*, New York, Columbia University Press, pp. 400–434.

Lo, V.I. (2001), 'Resolution of Civil Disputes in China', *UCLA Pacific Basin Law Journal*, **18**, pp. 117–56.

Macintyre, A. and B. Naughton (2005), 'The Decline of the Japan-Led Model of the East Asian Economy', in T.J. Pempel (ed.), *Remapping East Asia: The Construction of a Region*, Ithaca: Cornell University Press, pp. 77–100.

Mahbubani, K. (2008), *The New Asian Hemisphere: The Irresistible Shift of Global Power to the East*, New York: Public Affairs.

McAlinn, G.P. and C. Pejovic (eds) (2012), *Law and Development in Asia*, New York: Routledge.

Menski, W. (2006), *Comparative Law in Global Context: The Legal Systems of Asia and Africa*, 2nd edn, Cambridge: Cambridge University Press.

Milhaupt, C.J. (2002), 'On the (Fleeting) Existence of the Main Bank System and Other Japanese Economic Institutions', *Law & Social Inquiry*, **27**, pp. 425–36.

Milhaupt, C. and K. Pistor (2008), *Law and Capitalism: What Corporate Crises Reveal about Legal Systems and Economic Development around the World*, Chicago: University of Chicago Press.

Naughton, B. (1995), *Growing out of the Plan*, Cambridge: Cambridge University Press.

Neumann, F. and T. Arora (2011), 'Can Asia Save the World?', *Macro Asian Economics*, 26 August 2011: available at www.research.hsbc.com.

Noda, Y. (1976), *Introduction to Japanese Law*, Tokyo: University of Tokyo Press.

Nottage, L., L. Wolff and K. Anderson (eds) (2008), *Corporate Governance in the 21st Century: Japan's Gradual Transformation*, Cheltenham and Northampton: Edward Elgar.

Obama, Barak (2011), 'Address by the President of the United States of America', *House of Representatives Official Hansard*, **17**, pp. 12843–52.

Obiora, L. Amede (1998), 'Toward an Auspicious Reconciliation of International and Comparative Analyses', *American Journal of Comparative Law*, **46**, pp. 669–82.

Oda, H. (2009), *Japanese Law*, Oxford: Oxford University Press.

Page, J. (1994), 'The East Asian Miracle: Four Lessons for Development Policy', *NBER Macroeconomics Annual 1994, Volume 9*, Cambridge, MA: MIT Press, pp. 219–82: available at http://www.nber.org/books/fisc94-1.

Pattison, P. and D. Herron (2003), 'The Mountains are High and the Emperor is Far Away: Sanctity of Contract in China', *American Business Law Journal*, **40**, pp. 459–510.

Peerenboom, R. (2007), *China Modernizes: Threat to the West or Model for the Rest?*, Oxford: Oxford University Press.

Pistor, K. (2000), 'Patterns of Legal Change: Shareholder and Creditor Rights in Transition Economies', *European Business Organisation Law Review*, **1**, pp. 589–110.

Pistor, K. and P.A. Wellons (1999), *The Role of Law and Legal Institutions in Asian Economic Development, 1960–1995*, New York: Oxford University Press.

Port, K.L. (1994), 'The Case for Teaching Japanese Law at American Law Schools', *Depaul Law Review*, **43**, pp. 643–71.

Potter, P.B. (2003), *From Leninist Disciplne to Socialist Legalism: Peng Zhen on Law and Political Authority in the PRC*, Stanford: Stanford University Press.

Ruskola, T. (2000), 'Conceptualizing Corporations and Kinship: Comparative Law and Development Theory in a Chinese Perspective', *Stanford Law Review*, **52**, pp. 1599–730.

Sachs, S.E. (2006), 'From St Ives to Cyberspace: The Modern Distortion of the Medieval Law Merchant', *American University International Law Review*, **21**, pp. 685–812.

Sanders, S. (ed.) (1997), *The US Role in the Asian Century*, Lanham, MD: University Press of America.

Sato, I. (2002), 'Judicial Reform in Japan in the 1990s: Increase of the Legal Profession, Reinforcement of Judicial Functions and Expansion of the Rule of Law', *Social Science Japan Journal*, **5**, pp. 71–83.

Schirato, T. and S. Yell (1996), *Communication and Cultural Literacy: An Introduction*, Sydney: Allen & Unwin.

Steele, S. (2000), 'Evaluating the New Japanese Civil Rehabilitation Law', *Australian Journal of Asian Law*, **2**, pp. 1–35.

Stout, L. (2011), *Cultivating Conscience: How Good Laws Make Good People*, Princeton: Princeton University Press.

Stiglitz, J.E. (1996), 'Some Lessons from the East Asian Miracle', *World Bank Research Observer*, **11**, pp. 151–77.

Tamanaha, B.Z. (1995), 'The Lessons of Law and Development Studies', *American Journal of International Law*, **89**, pp. 470–86.

Tanase, T. (2010), *Community and the Law: A Critical Reassessment of American Liberalism and Japanese Modernity*, trans. L. Nottage and L. Wolff, Cheltenham and Northampton: Edward Elgar.

Taylor, V.L. (1993), 'Continuing Transactions and Persistent Myths: Contracts in Contemporary Japan', *Melbourne University Law Review*, **19**, pp. 352–8.

Taylor, V. (1997), 'Beyond Legal Orientalism', in V. Taylor (ed.), *Asian Laws through Australian Eyes*, Sydney: Law Book Company, pp. 47–62.

Teubner, G. (ed.) (1997), *Global Law without a State*, Aldershot: Ashgate.

Tomasic, R. and F. Akinbami (2011), 'The Role of Trust in Maintaining the Resilience of Financial Markets', *Journal of Corporate Law Studies*, **11**, pp. 369–94.

Tomasic, R. and Z. Zhang (2012a), 'China's Enterprise Bankruptcy Law: Implementation of the Corporate Reorganization Provisions', in J. Garrick (ed.), *Law and Policy for China's Market Socialism*, New York: Routledge, pp. 55–69.

Tomasic, R. and Z. Zhang (2012b), 'From Global Convergence in China's Enterprise Bankruptcy Law 2006 to Divergent Implementation: Corporate Reorganisation in China', *Journal of Corporate Law Studies*, **12**, pp. 295–332.

Trebilcock, M.J. and R.J. Daniels (1999), *Rule of Law Reform and Development: Charting the Fragile Path of Progress*, Cheltenham: Edward Elgar.

Trubek, D. (1972), 'Max Weber on Law and the Rise of Capitalism', *Wisconsin Law Review*, **3**, pp. 720–53.

Trubek, D. and M. Galanter (1974), 'Scholars in Self-Estrangement: Some Reflections on the Crisis in Law and Development Studies in the United States', *Wisconsin Law Review*, **4**, pp. 1062–1101.

Trubek, D. and A. Santos (2006), *The New Law and Economic Development: A Critical Approach*, Cambridge: Cambridge University Press.

Trubek, D.M., Y. Dezalay, R. Buchanan and J.R. Davis (1994), 'Global Restructuring and the Law: Studies of the Internationalization of Legal Fields and the Creation of Transnational Arenas', *Case Western Reserve Law*, **44**, pp. 407–98.
Upham, F. (1987), *Law and Social Change in Post-war Japan*, Cambridge, MA: Harvard University Press.
Upham F. (1997), 'The Place of Japanese Legal Studies in American Comparative Law', *Utah Law Review*, **2**, pp. 639–56.
Valcke, C. (2004), 'Comparative Law as Comparative Jurisprudence – The Comparability of Legal Systems', *American Journal of Comparative Law*, **52**, pp. 713–40.
Van der Sprenkel, S. ([1962] 1976), *Legal Institutions in Manchu China: A Sociological Analysis*, London: Athlone Press.
Volckart, O. and A. Mangels (1999), 'Are the Roots of the Modern Lex Mercatoria Really Medieval?', *Southern Economic Journal*, **65**, pp. 427–50.
Walters, R.J. (1991), 'Now That I Ate the Sushi, Do We Have a Deal?' – The Lawyer as Negotiator in Japanese–U.S. Business Transactions', *Journal of International Law and Business*, **12**, pp. 335–63.
Weiss, J. (1989), *The Asian Century: The Economic Ascent of the Pacific Rim and What It Means for the West*, New York: Facts on File.
Whitman, J.Q. (2007), 'Consumerism Versus Producerism: A Study in Comparative Law', *Yale Law Journal*, **117**, pp. 340–407.
Wolff, L. (2012), 'Should Law Look East?' *Journal of Civil & Legal Sciences*, **1**, pp. 1–4.
Wong, B.K.Y. (2000), 'Traditional Chinese Philosophy and Dispute Resolution', *Hong Kong Law Journal*, **30**, pp. 304–19.
Woodiwiss, A. (1998), *Globalisation, Human Rights and Labour Law in Pacific Asia*, Cambridge: Cambridge University Press.
Yamanouchi, N. and S.J. Cohen (1991), 'Understanding the Incidence of Litigation in Japan: A Structural Analysis', *International Lawyer*, **25**, pp. 443–54.
Yi, L.M. and P. Ellis (2000), 'Insider-Outsider Perspectives of Guanxi', *Business Horizons*, **43**, pp. 25–30.
Zhang, D. and K. Kuroda (1989), 'Beware of Japanese Negotiation Style: How to Negotiate with Japanese Companies', *Journal of International Law and Business*, **10**, pp. 195–212.
Zweigert, K. and H. Kotz, (1998), *An Introduction to Comparative Law*, 3rd edn, Oxford: Oxford University Press.

Part I
General Issues

[1]
THE FUTURE OF LAW IN A GLOBAL ECONOMY

RICHARD P. APPELBAUM
University of California at Santa Barbara

ABSTRACT

In this paper I challenge the notion that an emerging global legal culture modeled on US legal practices will necessarily come to dominate global legal practices in the economic sphere. Rather, I argue that the ascendance of Asian economic power will have significant implications for the sorts of legal as well as business institutions that are likely to dominate in the next century. Specifically, I argue that Chinese business culture, with its emphasis on informal relationships and flexible organization, has a strong affinity for the new forms of flexible production that characterize an important and growing portion of the world economy. Drawing on world-systems theory, research on Chinese business organization and culture, and my own fieldwork, I argue that the 'legal convergence' hypothesis may well be premature: that the rise of the East Asian economies, linked together through the Chinese business diaspora, may well herald not only the decline of North American and European global economic dominance, but along with it the hegemony of their associated legal forms

INTRODUCTION

On one of Beijing's busiest shopping streets, an eye-catching display for a small Chinese beer and soda company hangs in a glass case. The highlight of the display is a photograph of President Clinton and the first lady, smiling at a White House Christmas party as they pose with the Chinese company's chairman and two other men. Beneath the photo sit an oversized beer bottle and two mugs. The California entrepreneur who arranged the photo, and who appears in it, Johnny Chien Chuen Chung, has donated $391,000 to the Democratic Party since mid-1994, and he has visited the White House at least 50 times, often with foreign visitors like Chen in tow. (Drew, 1997)

Clinton calls for a 'vigorous' and 'thorough' investigation into reports that representatives of the People's Republic of China tried to direct financial contributions from foreign sources to the DNC. Rep. Gerald Solomon tells reporters,

'The potential finding is that our foreign policy has been sold for a price, national security has been sold for a price'. (Associated Press news item, 13 February 1997)

AMONG THE many scandals that have plagued Clinton's second term, none has raised as much partisan attack as the allegation that foreign businesses and governments have channeled funds to the Democratic Party. Millions of dollars reportedly raised from within the Asian-American community are now claimed to have originated in Asian companies, including the Indonesian-based (but Chinese-owned) Lippo Bank, whose US operations were once headed by former Deputy Assistant Commerce Secretary and Democratic Party vice-chair Johnny Huang. Potentially even more scandalous have been the claims that the government of the People's Republic of China funneled money into the Democratic Party in the hope of countering the influence of the Taiwan lobby on sensitive pending trade negotiations. In the USA, it is illegal for political parties or candidates to accept money from foreign companies and governments.

Chinese contributors are at the centre of the storm, providing grist for a new wave of anti-Chinese fear and recrimination in the USA. A century ago, Sino-phobia grew out of the fear that cheap Chinese immigrant labour would take jobs away from hard-working American citizens. Today, reflecting the shifting fortunes of global capitalism, the worry is that all-powerful Chinese businesses will somehow come to control American politics. Such fears easily play into long-standing anti-Asian prejudices – the belief that a secret, behind-the-scenes, peculiarly Chinese way of doing business will subvert the rule of law that presumptively governs American business and political transactions. This concern is fueled by the growing importance of global trade in the world economy, a trade that is increasingly centred on East Asia.

In this paper I will examine what might be called the 'East Asian challenge' to US and European business hegemony, and particularly its implication for the emerging frameworks of international law that regulate and govern global trade. I specifically question the argument that the creation of a global capitalist system heralds the inevitable triumph of western (and specifically North American) business and legal institutions, by focusing on the principal challenge to North American and European economic hegemony: East Asia, especially Greater China and the Chinese diaspora (China, Hong Kong and Taiwan, as well as Vietnam, Singapore, Malaysia, Indonesia – countries in which the overseas Chinese constitute a dominant industrial and merchant class). I shall argue that a Chinese business culture exists which is distinct from those characteristic of the USA and Europe; I shall also claim that Chinese business culture has a strong affinity for the highly informal relationships that characterize the most rapidly growing part of the global economy. Any shift in the economic centre of gravity to Asia has strong implications for the emergence of a regime of international business law.

I first review the argument that the current phase of capitalist expansion into Hong Kong and China entails the wholesale importation of North American legal institutions as well. In particular, I challenge the notion that western legal universalism will necessarily triumph over the particularism of Chinese social relations, which – against the legal universalistic position – I believe to be rooted in long-standing cultural and institutional practices characteristic of Chinese business and trade. This is significant in light of the argument I make in the next section of the paper: that global capitalism does not necessarily mean North American/European economic hegemony. Drawing on world-systems theory I will argue that the world capitalist system is entering a new, polycentric phase in which economic power (although not necessarily political power) is shifting across the Pacific. If this is the case, there is no reason to assume that western businessmen (and their lawyers) will set the tone for global business (and legal) practices; at the very least, this should be a highly contested field. Next, I turn to an analytic framework that seeks to explain the functioning of business in a global capitalist system: global commodity chains. This framework, by emphasizing global business networks as a key feature of the world economy, provides insights concerning the circumstances under which common global business practices are likely to emerge – and which practices are likely to predominate. I then build on this insight to argue that a preference for informal, extra-legal forms of business organization characterizes East Asian business culture, and that this preference is compatible with the flexible forms of production that are increasingly important in global commodity chains. Finally, I draw on my own research to conclude with some examples of the importance of relying on personal networks when doing business in East Asia.

LEGAL CONVERGENCE OR PLURALISM?

The notion that modernity brings with it a global homogenization of cultures and institutions has an impeccable western pedigree. The emergence of European social theory in the 19th century was inextricably tied up with the Enlightenment belief that science, technology and secularization herald an inexorable global march from mind-numbing tradition to a golden age of reason. Theorists might disagree on the particulars, for example, whether the move was evolutionary (Tönnies, Durkheim), revolutionary (Marx) or both (Weber), but that the end-point was a society organized according to rational principles was never questioned. The most detailed classical exposition of this view – Weber's meticulous historical writings on the long-term western secular trend towards legal–rational forms of social, economic and political organization – remains paradigmatic for thinking throughout the social sciences. These classical views became incorporated into a wide range of social thinking in the 20th century: multilinear evolutionary theory in anthropology (Sahlins and Service, 1960; Service, 1976); Parsonian modernization theory in sociology (Parsons, 1966; Levy, 1972); rational choice theory in economics (Becker, 1976, 1996). The rapid acceleration in globalization

(Robertson, 1992; but see also Harvey, 1995; Hirst and Thompson, 1996) during the past quarter of a century has, not surprisingly, brought with it a resurgence of this perspective: global economics portends global homogeneity, whether the result of market processes (neo-liberalism), political economy (world-systems theory) or the more neo-Weberian processes of institutional isomorphism (Meyer et al., 1987; Thomas et al., 1987).

Obvious parallels exist within the study of legal institutions. Legal pluralism, which challenges liberal political theory's privileging of the nation-state as the sole source of political and legal initiative, emphasizes the importance of 'powerful supra-state processes (general intensification of transnational practices, and above all transnational capital, interstate regional agreements ... [including] globalization of legal phenomena [such as] the transnational *lex mercatoria* ...' (de Sousa Santos, 1992: 133). The 'new wave' of legal pluralism is characterized by 'the coexistence within the nation-state of international or transnational legal orders articulated in different ways with the nation-state legality' (de Sousa Santos, 1992: 133) in which the nation-state no longer enjoys a legal monopoly; it remains an open question the extent to which there is an 'isomorphism between state-produced law and non-state produced law' (de Sousa Santos, 1992: 137). Significantly, 'the transnationalization of the legal field is underway' (de Sousa Santos, 1992: 135).

DOING BUSINESS IN HONG KONG AND CHINA: ARE LAWYERS REALLY NECESSARY?

A strong argument for this 'transnationalization of the legal field' on the basis of American legal practices and professional norms is associated with the work of Yves Dezalay and Bryant Garth (see, for example, Dezalay, 1990; Dezalay and Garth, 1996). The Dezalay–Garth project seeks to show that a combination of global business hegemony and educational imperialism on the part of American law schools and corporate law firms is responsible for the global triumph of the North American legal model, particularly in the realm of international business law.

In his earlier work on European legal practice, Dezalay argued that legal convergence is driven by the growing need for global commerce to generate and abide by a common normative–legal framework, with American corporate law firms providing the model. Lawyers, Dezalay notes, 'for centuries have tied their fate to that of the nation-states'. Now that the global marketplace seems to be superseding the nation-state, lawyers are hardly likely to surrender their 'royal prerogatives' (Dezalay, 1990: 279). Instead, lawyers have reoriented their sights: 'The ideal of social law has been killed off, replaced by the *lex mercatoria*, the transnational law of market relations' (Dezalay, 1990: 280), creating a vastly increased role for lawyers in the field of international finance and trade. 'It is no coincidence that, throughout Europe, the *legal big bang* followed straight after the *financial big bang* ... The financial predators who are restructuring the economic terrain do not have to look far before they are surrounded by all the legal talent that they need' (Dezalay, 1990: 280–1). Legal advances relevant to international trade include codes of conduct for international enterprises, the harmonization of accounting practices, and the growth of international commercial arbitrage. The largest multinationals may be able to make up their own rules, profiting from national differences in law; for most businesses, however, 'a general set of rules for the economic field is what is required' (Dezalay, 1990: 283). A host of management professionals has arisen to fill this international breach – 'international lawyers, corporate tax accountants, financial advisors, and management consultants', comprising a 'new international market in consultancy'. Their proliferation 'constitutes a motive force, and is the best indicator of the importance of the process of homogenization of global economic space' (Dezalay, 1990: 283–4):

> The opening and expansion of the market in legal services has unleashed a process of homogenization and interconnection between national legal systems which until now have strongly preserved their own identities. The breaking down of barriers favours the strongest performers – in this case, the great North American firms – and forces the others to align themselves on their model if they wish to survive. (Dezalay, 1990: 285)

American legal hegemony is not only the result of American economic hegemony; it is also because for over a century 'American lawyers had become legal entrepreneurs, creating "law factories" so as to provide a better service for their clients' (Dezalay, 1990: 286). Today's Wall Street 'mega-firms' have accelerated this process. The 'new generation' of lawyers thrive on the basis of merit rather than good manners: 'social connections lost their importance in favour of technical competence' (Dezalay, 1990: 287). This has meant the spread of 'American-style litigiousness' to Europe, breaking up the 'local networks of business leaders' who had long preferred to settle their differences in private so as not to endanger their long-term relationships (Dezalay, 1990: 287). 'It appears today that the restructuration of the legal field around the axis of commercial justice is irreversible' (Dezalay, 1990: 288).

In a recent work, Dezalay and Garth extend this analysis to China and Hong Kong (Dezalay and Garth, 1996: 250–80). These East Asian economies constitute a hard test of their legal isomorphism thesis, since Chinese business practices are widely believed to rest on values that denigrate formal law in favour of the informal personal relations of mutual obligation termed *guanxi*.[1] Dezalay and Garth argue that while *guanxi* unquestionably survives, formal law is playing an increasingly important role in both Hong Kong and China. (Dezalay and Garth do acknowledge that *guanxi* still predominates in intra-Chinese dealings, for example, in Hong Kong trade relations with China.) This is because the explosion in trade has created a space for commercial law, particularly in dealings with non-Chinese people. The legal profession has also grown in prestige, fueled by the 'missionary efforts' of American corporate law firms, which have actively sought to promote their image (Dezalay and Garth, 1996: 259). Commercial arbitration has also grown, at least in some areas.

According to Dezalay and Garth, neither Confucianism (with its hostility to lawyers and conflict) nor communism (with its emphasis on Party rule) afford real cultural barriers to the adoption of western legal practices in China and Hong Kong. Rather, the barriers are mainly due to the lack of an historical legal tradition, itself explicable in terms of the particular role of commercial capital in the British (and subsequently Chinese) development of China trade – a role framed more by personal relations than by formal legal considerations. During the 19th century, the great British trading houses played the pivotal role, with disputes settled informally at the Jockey Club rather than in courts of law. The reasons for this were found not only in the gentleman's tradition of the British trading houses, but also in the nature of the trade itself – much of it centred on opium, bordering on extra-legal piracy. Legal institutions were poorly developed; legal practice was marginal and low status. When Chinese merchants began to get economic power comparable to the British colonialists at the end of the century, 'it was no surprise that they maintained the same kind of relational, familial capitalism', drawing on their family connections and informal networks to build a power base (as the British had done before them) (Dezalay and Garth, 1996: 253). Hong Kong's 'imported state' was, after all, 'mainly a gloss on the personal and familial relations in a merchant-dominated society' (Dezalay and Garth, 1996: 255). The obstacles to the growth of an autonomous politico-legal system in Hong Kong are thus less cultural than institutional, for example, the lack of any substantial historical tradition, uncertainties posed by the Chinese takeover of Hong Kong and the absence of an indigenous legal scholarship (Dezalay and Garth, 1996: 268–9).

But times change, and in the view of Dezalay and Garth the Chinese can be expected to adopt formal legal practices to the extent that these will serve their interests in the global economy. In Hong Kong, the 'key engines of legal transformation' have been American law firms, which came in two waves, first in the late 1970s, and then subsequent to the Tiananmen Square uprising in 1989. There are some 4000 solicitors and 500 barristers in Hong Kong today (Dezalay and Garth, 1996: 257). It is true that lawyers remain marginal in intra-Chinese business transactions, being brought in mainly after the deal is done, to make certain it is legal. Even this is changing, however, especially among the larger enterprises, whose Chinese leaders are frequently graduates of American MBA programmes and are comfortable with using lawyers (Dezalay and Garth, 1996: 261).

When it comes to doing business with American multinationals, however, the law plays an increasingly central role, although even the growth of 'hugely more sophisticated' contracts is tempered by pressure for 'Sinocized contracts with shorter sentences and fewer words' (Dezalay and Garth, 1996: 262). In China, the explosion in global trade has been followed by a substantial increase in the role of commercial law: there are today an estimated 60,000 to 75,000 lawyers, of which perhaps 2000 have experience in international matters (Dezalay and Garth, 1996: 264). The older ideology ('chain the lawyers to the tree outside the courthouse') is being replaced with a more lawyer-friendly one ('don't lock lawyers out') (Dezalay and Garth, 1996: 265). All this is not to argue that formal law is replacing *guanxi* in Hong Kong and China; even large-firm lawyers emphasize problem-solving rather than legal formalism, and business relationships involve a mix of the personal and the legal. 'Nevertheless, we would expect some movement towards more formal law and in particular the US variant' (Dezalay and Garth, 1996: 273).

Dezalay and Garth (1996: 273–80) also trace the growth of commercial arbitration in Hong Kong and China, noting that the Hong Kong Commercial Arbitration Center handled some 139 commercial cases in 1993, with commercial arbitration well established in shipping and construction and that in China, the Chinese International Trade and Arbitration Commission (CIETAC) has a growing caseload growing from 37 in 1985 to 513 in 1993. They argue that these efforts at building an arbitration capacity 'will serve mainly to reinforce the power of US, English, and other large international law firms and the ICC world of arbitration' (Dezalay and Garth, 1996: 280).

CHINESE BUSINESS CULTURE AND THE RULE OF LAW

What ethnic Chinese from Hong Kong, Macau, and Taiwan did was to demonstrate to a skeptical world [that] *guanxi* connections through the same language and culture can make up for a lack in the rule of law and transparency in rules and regulations. (Statement by Lee Kuan Yew, former President of Singapore, at the World Chinese Entrepreneur's Convention, Hong Kong, 1993 (cited in Ong, 1997: 181))

From Asia, the accusations of influence-peddling at the White House look a bit different. The immediate reaction is often not outrage but surprise — at the low American prices. Corruption and gift-giving to curry favor are widespread in most Asian countries. And a few highly publicized scandals, including cases that involved former presidents of South Korea, have highlighted what is widely accepted here: the practice is entwined with building relationships and doing business here, and the amounts are usually far greater than the sums that have sparked uproar in Washington. (WuDunn, 1997: 4)

How convincing is the Dezalay/Garth argument that *guanxi* is being superseded by American legal practices in Hong Kong and China, at least in the exploding area of international commerce? Their argument partly rests on the assumption that American and European transnational corporations (and their associated legal practices) will continue to dominate global trade, an assumption I will question in the next section of this paper. It also rests on their assertion that *guanxi* is the result of relatively recent historical accident, rather than more historically rooted cultural beliefs and practices. While it is beyond the scope of this article to examine the historical and cultural roots of *guanxi*, I do want to argue that a wide range of social relationships in China – and in particular business relationships – are deeply embedded in cultural practices and economic institutions that long predate the arrival of European colonialists. We will discuss the cultural practice of *guanxi* in this section, and the centuries-old Chinese trading system in the next.[2]

Mayfair Mei-hui Yang's (1994) book *Gifts, Favors, and Banquets: The Art of Social Relationships in China*, provides a detailed examination of the historical roots and multiple meanings of the practice of *guanxi*, a concept whose roots she traces to several historical sources, including Confucian philosophy. *Guanxi* carries the sense of social connections based on mutual interest and benefit: 'Once *guanxi* is established between two people, each can ask a favor of the other with the expectation that the debt incurred will be repaid sometime in the future' (Yang, 1994: 1–2). 'Indeed, it can be said that implicit in the very act of accepting [a gift, banquet, or favor] is an agreement in trust to repay in another form at a later date' (Yang, 1994: 142). The art of *guanxi*:

> ... typically involves the exchange of gifts, favors, and banquets; the cultivation of personal relationships and networks of mutual dependence; and the manufacturing of obligation and indebtedness. What informs these practices and their native descriptions is the conception of the primacy and binding power of personal relationships and their importance in meeting the needs and desires of everyday life. (Yang, 1994: 6)

Yang's informants indicated that along with its positive meanings (in terms of relationships), the term *guanxi* frequently has negative connotations as well (using one's personal connections instrumentally, by 'pulling strings' or 'going through the back door'). The related term *renqing* (personal ties based on affect and obligation) implies mutual obligation through feeling and sentiment, rather than purely instrumental calculations (Yang, 1994: 67). Her (1994: 112–15) informants, and the folk-sayings they provided for her, enabled her to identify four principal bases of *guanxi*, at least in urban China: family and kinship ('cousins are close, close through generations; smash their bones, but they are still attached by tendons'), neighbours and home-place ties ('an official seal is not as good as a fellow from the same hometown'), non-kin relations of roughly equal status (for example, classmates, coworkers, and friends), and non-kin superior–subordinate relations (for example, teacher–student, master–apprentice). China, in Yang's view, is a 'society of gatekeepers', in which *guanxi* is necessary to open the gates. This is evidenced by the following ditty, related by two economists who had learned it while working in a factory:

> First class people get gifts delivered to the door;
> second class people go through the back door;
> third class people rely on others;
> fourth class people can only fume. (Yang, 1994: 86)

One measure of the persistence of *guanxi* in Chinese culture is the strength with which it has survived all attempts by the communist state to purge it – not only from practice, but from discourse itself. According to Yang's research, *guanxi* is once again being acknowledged in China, after years of being officially suppressed as a feudal remnant rooted in the kinship-based morality (*lunli daode*) of the Chinese clan system (*zongfa zhidu*). The terms *guanxixue* (the art of *guanxi*) and *guangxiwang* (*guanxi* networks) first appeared in China's official newspapers and journals around 1978 (Yang, 1994: 156), where such practices were roundly condemned as 'a backward ethical system whose particularistic ethics of interpersonal relations hamper the development of universalistic loyalty to the country and the "socialist system"' (Yang, 1994: 59). More recently it has been attributed to the corrupting influence of bourgeois individualism, imported along with foreign businesses. Whatever its origins, *guanxi* is once again a central feature of Chinese social, political and economic relationships – a half century after the communist revolution first sought to obliterate it as a feudal legacy, and a quarter of a century after the Cultural Revolution (1966–76) punished any hint of familiar or personal loyalty as counter-revolutionary (Yang, 1994: 156).[3]

There is by now a large social science literature which documents the importance of *guanxi* relationships as a distinguishing characteristic of Chinese businesses, comprised of firms that are formally independent of one another but closely affiliated and tied by informal networks, equity ties and family relationships (Wong, 1985; Hamilton and Kao, 1990; Orrú et al., 1991; Granovetter, 1993). I will discuss this argument in detail below, in the section 'Towards a Global Business Culture?'.

GLOBAL SHIFT: THE RISE OF EAST ASIA

> Today, there are some twenty-five million ethnic Chinese outside of China, the bulk of whom are concentrated around the fast-growing Pacific Rim. Individually and collectively, they are well-placed to play a key role in realizing the potential and promise of globalization, particularly in making the Pacific Century come true. (Statement by the Singapore Chinese Chamber of Commerce and Industry at the World Chinese Entrepreneur's Convention, Singapore, 1991 (cited in Nonini and Ong, 1997: 4))

There are various ways to track the economic changes that are occurring in the world economy today, including a large and growing popular literature on the seeming 'Pacific Shift' (Thompson, 1985) or even 'destiny' (Elegant, 1990).[4] In this section I draw on a specific body of political economy, the world-systems theory associated with the work of Immanuel Wallerstein (1974, 1979a, b). Specifically I will claim, following Giovanni Arrighi (1994), that the 'long twentieth century' associated with American economic hegemony is coming to an end – to be followed by a more multipolar world with a strong East Asian presence.

World-systems theory argues that capitalism first emerged as a global system with the extension of markets and trade in Europe in the 15th and 16th centuries.[5] Among the powerful core countries competing with one another, at any given time, one is likely to be hegemonic, possessing the greatest economic and military power, with the latter helping to guarantee the former (Chase-Dunn, 1989). According to Arrighi, the world capitalist system is currently completing its fourth expansionary phase,[6] the American-dominated 'long twentieth century' (which actually began in the latter part of the 19th century). Arrighi argues that this phase has lasted about 100 years, and is now breaking down as the world system emerges into a new, uncharted period of capitalist expansion. Each succession has been briefer than the previous one, and more expansive.

In a recent work, Arrighi (1994), drawing partly on the writings of Japanese historians Takeshi Hamashita (1994) and Heita Kawakatsu (1986), argues that for at least 1000 years East Asia was integrated through a 'tribute-trade system' unified by an extensive China-centred trading network – one in which it was legitimate to view tribute exchange as a commercial transaction (Hamashita, 1994). Contrary to the previously discussed arguments of Dezalay and Garth, the existence of a Chinese trading system operating outside the law predates English colonialism by centuries; the English colonial merchants hardly 'set the tone' for the marginality of law in Hong Kong (Dezalay and Garth, 1996: 252).

This system eventually resulted in the growth of an overseas Chinese business diaspora which linked the regional economies to one another, in growing conflict with the state-centred tribute system that originally spawned it:

> The Chinese merchants and migrants were operating outside the control of their own government and had already established their relations with other authorities. They had their own social and economic institutions and they had their own agendas... Chinese merchants and laborers were not simply pioneers of the economy; they were also pioneers of state expansion. (Trocki, 1997: 64, 70)

The principal organizational vehicle for Chinese businesses was the *kongsi*, a share-holding partnership based in real or fictive family ties, and which was highly compatible with family business patterns (Trocki, 1997: 69). *Kongsi* were interlinked through marriage or common share-holding, with the largest *kongsi* (tied to the opium trade) assuming considerable social and political power (Trocki, 1997: 69). The economic success of the *kongsi* organizational form has been attributed to:

> ... its flexibility, its looseness, and its more or less segmented structure ... [which extended] into a wide range of ventures all over the world ... held together with little more than handshakes and relationships between brothers-in-law.... (Trocki, 1997: 81)

Eventually, the tribute system withered away, weakened both by regional nationalisms and, by the end of the 19th century, economic encroachment by the expanding Europe-centred world economy. But the overseas Chinese business communities remained a powerful source of regional economic integration, providing an infrastructure for today's East Asian economic expansion – and one that predates western capitalism by many centuries:

> More important, structures and business practices that characterized Chinese businesses during these formative years have proven quite durable. Although there were compromises with western-style corporate forms, the old *kongsi* structure continued to underlie many Chinese business ventures, particularly the informal ones. This has continued to buttress the family–business relationship. (Trocki, 1997: 82)

The cross-border business structure of today's East Asian Newly Industrializing Economies (NIEs), unified through the Chinese business diaspora, is a direct organizational legacy of the *kongsi*. Such networks are 'emerging as a leading agency of processes of capital accumulation in East Asia' (Arrighi, 1994: 9–10, drawing on Hui, 1995). The growing economic power of the Chinese diaspora has greatly accelerated with the incorporation of China into the world economy, with some four-fifths of foreign investment in the People's Republic of China today originating in the overseas Chinese business community (Arrighi, 1994: 15). This provides a significant advantage to East Asia in the global economy:

> If the problem with nation-states is that they are either 'too large' or 'too small' to operate effectively, gifts of history and geography seem to have provided East Asia with a solution to the problem by endowing it with a variety of territorial and non-territorial organizations that are either something less, or something more, or something different than nation-states. (Arrighi, 1994: 16)

During the 'long twentieth century' of American hegemony, 'the nation-state form of political organization became universal. But as the form of national sovereignty expanded, its substance contracted like never before' (Arrighi, 1994: 22). In fact, for the USA the strong nation-state has proved to be a mixed economic blessing: 'the main tendency of the last twenty-five years has been for all nation-states, including the US, to become the servant rather than the master of extraterritorial high finance' (Arrighi, 1994: 24–5).

American hegemony has been challenged most directly by the explosion of transnational corporations, and particularly those centered in East Asia:

> By the 1980s, it was the turn of East Asian capital to outcompete both US and Western European capital through the formation of a new kind of transnational business organization – an organization that was deeply rooted in the region's gifts of history and geography, and that combined the advantages of vertical integration with the flexibility of informal business networks. (Arrighi, 1994: 25)

In Arrighi's view, these 'gifts of history and geography' have favoured the growing global economic importance of East Asia, insofar as:

> the leading agencies of the formation and expansion of the capitalist world system appear to [be] organizations that are either something less (city-states

and quasi-states) or something more (quasi-empires) or something different (business diasporas and other transterritorial capitalist organizations) than nation-states. (Arrighi, 1994: 26)

It is to these 'business diasporas and other transterritorial capitalist organizations' that provide East Asia with its putative advantage that we now turn, in order to better understand Asian business culture and its ramifications for the global diffusion of American legal forms.

Towards a Global Business Culture? Doing Business across Global Space

Does economic globalization mean that a single global business culture is likely to emerge, one that requires a common legal structure? In this section I draw on the concept of global commodity chains to provide a framework for understanding how governance of business transactions takes place across a global space. The concept originated with Terrance Hopkins and Immanuel Wallerstein, who initially defined a commodity chain as 'a network of labor and production processes whose end result is a finished commodity' (Hopkins and Wallerstein, 1986: 159). As subsequently elaborated by Gary Gereffi and others (including the present author), commodity chains are conceptualized in terms of 'nodes' or operations that comprise pivotal points in the production process: raw materials supply, production, export and marketing, taking us 'across the entire spectrum of activities in the world-economy' (Gereffi, 1992: 94).

It is useful to distinguish two ideal types of commodity chains that have emerged since the 1970s: producer-driven and buyer-driven (Gereffi, 1994). Producer-driven commodity chains are found in those industries 'in which large integrated industrial enterprises play the central role in controlling the production system (including its forward and backward linkages)' (Appelbaum and Gereffi, 1994: 44). They are most characteristic of capital- and technology-intensive industries dominated by large transnational corporations (TNCs), such as the automobile, computer, aircraft and electrical machinery industries. Control, which lies with the TNC that coordinates production, is vertical: 'these vertical networks are producer-driven in the sense that the main manufacturing firms in the commodity chains are crucial in coordinating the entire chain' (Gereffi and Hamilton, 1996: 31). The principal profits to be realized in producer-driven commodity chains are typically associated with the core manufacturing stages, deriving from economies of scale and scope, production volume and advanced technology. These include such things as research and development, product conception and product design. In other words, the highest value activities are typically associated with production rather than consumption.

Buyer-driven commodity chains, on the other hand, are found in those industries in which 'large retailers, brand-named marketers, and trading companies play the pivotal role in setting up decentralized production networks in a wide range of [low-wage] exporting countries' (Appelbaum and Gereffi, 1994: 44). This pattern of trade-led industrialization is common in labour-intensive, consumer goods industries such as the garment, footwear, toy and consumer electronics industries. Commercial capital, rather than industrial capital, holds the greatest power. Buyer-driven commodity chains tend to be horizontally (rather than vertically) organized; 'hollow' manufacturers source out their production through formal and informal networks that are frequently intermediated by buying offices. In buyer-driven commodity chains, profits derive 'from unique combinations of high-value research, design, sales, after-sales services, marketing, and financial services' (Gereffi, 1994: 99). In other words, the highest value-added activities are often more closely associated with consumption than production.

Buyer-driven commodity chains have become increasingly important in shaping global export relations, as mega-mergers and retail consolidations have greatly strengthened the hand of large retail buyers. In fact, there is 'a movement from producer-driven to buyer-driven commodity in many less capital intensive industries', largely because 'technologies of mass marketing ... allow ... retailers ... to create significant barriers of entry into successful merchandising' (Gereffi, 1996a: 16). This movement has 'allowed commercial capital to gain the upper hand vis-a-vis industrial capital' (Gereffi and Hamilton, 1996: 14).[7]

Buyer-driven commodity chains lend themselves to extensive subcontracting, and in fact today there is a China-centred hierarchy for buyer-driven commodity chains (Gereffi, 1996a). This is arguably at least partly due to the similarity between the organizational form of buyer-driven commodity chains and that of Chinese enterprises where trust – rather than formal legal contracts – govern business transactions (Nonini and Ong, 1997: 19–20). Personal networks among Chinese transnationals, cemented in *guanxi* relations, have a powerful affinity for forms of global business organization that emphasize flexibility, subcontracting and trust.

CHINESE BUSINESS CULTURE

Richard Whitely has sought to show that different cultures produce different types of business systems, which he defines as 'particular forms of economic organization that have become established and reproduced in certain institutional contexts – local, regional, national, or international' (Whitely, 1996: 412). Most generally, Whitely notes that Chinese, Japanese and Korean business systems differ in important ways from their western counterparts, reflecting the relative ethnic and cultural homogeneity of their (differing) pre-industrial societies and their isolation from the West. In all of these countries formal law played a very reduced economic role in pre-industrial times. Conversely, the family played a very large role. Compared to western business systems, therefore, East Asian business systems reflect a much lower commitment to legal rational authority principles, as well as a lower emphasis on individual identities, rights and duties (Whitely, 1992: 237).

In Whitely's (1996: 411) view, culturally distinct business systems 'are unlikely to converge to a single efficient type through some universalizing competitive process'. While this point is debatable,[8] Whitely does identify a number of distinguishing features of Chinese family businesses that are useful for the present discussion, noting in particular their differences from Japanese and Korean businesses on the one hand, and European and North American businesses on the other. In Whitely's (1992) characterization, Chinese businesses are characterized by a high degree of control on the part of the owner (who is typically the family patriarch), with managers playing a strictly subordinate role to the owner–leader. Reliance on informal personal networks and connections tends to be high. Chinese businesses tend not to cultivate long-term obligations with their suppliers, with whom they develop little by way of mutual dependence (unless they are related through family connections, community ties, or other forms of *guanxi*). As a consequence, risk is more likely to be transferred to subcontractors and partners, rather than shared. Inter- and intra-firm loyalties tend to be low, again unless personal commitments are made or family connections are involved. Integration therefore tends to be horizontal and informal, rather than vertical and contractual, with horizontal coordination based on short-term needs rather than long-term obligations.

It should be evident that in Chinese business culture the ability to have a business relationship based on personal knowledge and trust is extremely important (Hakansson, 1982; Willis and Hutson, 1990). When relationships between firms and individuals are embedded in pre-existing social relationships, there is greater confidence in the reliability of transactions. Such 'networks of trust' – handshake arrangements – are typically mediated by intense familistic ties. This is no less true of international transactions, where risks of misunderstanding business practices and regulations, controlling quality, and assuring timely delivery are much greater than in local transactions (see, for example, Smart and Smart, 1991). One of the most important organizational features of the East Asian NIEs is that they are organized through business groups (Hamilton and Kao, 1990; Gerlach, 1992). Informal alliances between firms in these large business groups allow the network as a whole, rather than individual firms, to organize and manage a large portion of the commodity chain. Rather than using vertical integration to solve problems of opportunism and information flow, these problems are managed through inter-firm trust and communication (Gerlach, 1992; Granovetter, 1993). Firms can therefore remain small and more responsive to quickly changing market conditions, while at the same time gaining access to the large capital, resource and information pools of the business group (Hamilton and Kao, 1990).

LAW IN A GLOBAL ECONOMY 185

Doing Business in China: The Importance of Personal Connections

In my own research on the global apparel industry, apparel executives in Hong Kong and Los Angeles consistently assert that Chinese entrepreneurs (whether in Los Angeles, Hong Kong, Taiwan or elsewhere in the Chinese diaspora) are in a better position to source production in Asia than anyone else, largely because of their ability to draw on *guanxi* networks. The ability of European and North American firms to operate successfully in East Asia depends on their ability to work through such Chinese networks (Chan, 1993; Cheng, 1993; Walton, 1993). In one survey of Los Angeles' 184 largest apparel manufacturers, for example, it was found that three-quarters of Chinese-owned firms produced in Asia – compared with only a quarter of all firms owned by Koreans, and almost no firms owned by Latinos (who tended to contract for sewing in Los Angeles) (Appelbaum and Bonacich, 1993).

My research has repeatedly documented the central role placed by such personal connections, in an industry in which orders take place on a handshake. As Jim Cunningham, The Gap's Vice President for Offshore Sourcing explained it, with the exception of Korea and Japan:

> Every country's apparel industry is dominated by ethnic Chinese, the merchants of past centuries, who live in Chinatowns the world over – branches of families from the same province. In this business, things take place on trust. (Cunningham, 1991)

Even when the world's largest apparel manufacturers (The Limited, The Gap, Benneton) want to do business in China, they must work through the trading companies owned by Hong Kong's powerful China-connected families (Walton, 1993). Personal connections are especially important if a manufacturer wants to produce in China. Having a personal relationship means having the ability to get what one wants when one wants it:

> Having a relationship doesn't mean you can demand lower prices, it means you can get things done. Price is irrelevant in China. The problem is getting what you want when you want it. You need relationships for this. Westerners can work in China and be very successful. It just takes being there constantly. Few people are willing to make that effort. (Birnbaum, 1993)

Many visits are required to earn a reputation, establish relationships and ascertain which governmental officials are the important ones to cultivate (Ng, 1991). The person with the most connections is the person with whom one must establish contact, not necessarily the highest ranking official (Wong, 1993). County-level government officials are especially important, since they have the official right to issue the licenses and rubber stamp all decisions, as well as assign land and local government resources like construction materials and workers (Tsang, 1993). Cultivating relationships with important officials in smaller towns close to Hong Kong is reportedly easier than in larger cities (Chan, 1993; Walton, 1993). Even the largest European or North American retailers and manufacturers cannot ordinarily directly access Chinese factories: typically they must work through Hong Kong or Taiwanese intermediaries (Walton, 1993). Partly this has to do with Chinese restrictions on profit repatriation or joint venture foreign ownership (Sung, 1993), although requirements can occasionally be circumvented (Walton, 1993). If a person has a family history in a particular locale, they are treated as kin, as sharing a 'common language'. While such connections do not guarantee a business relationship, they do provide a 'starting point for conversation' (Cheng, 1991). This does not imply that non-Chinese people cannot do business with Chinese factories (Birnbaum, 1993); but few Europeans or North Americans have the patience to sit down, drink some tea and cultivate the necessary relationships. Steve Walton (1993), Managing Director of Innova,[9] suggests the following:

> I would advise anyone doing business in China to take at least two trips to visit officials or whomever you are doing business with, and don't mention anything about business. Bring pictures of your family. You don't have to have a Hong Kong firm to go through. In fact, there is often tension between Hong Kong and Mainland Chinese. Hong Kong Chinese are seen as greedy traitors. They do not have those kinds of bad feelings for Westerners. If you are dealing with a state-owned factory, you need to know the people in the local government. You need to know people in the town council, the planning and development committee, the Import Export Textile Corporation, etc.

David G. Birnbaum (1993), owner of the apparel investment company Third Horizon Ltd, adds:

> In a state factory, there are usually five people on the management committee. These are key people. Invite them to Hong Kong for a business meeting, but don't talk business. Just put them up in a nice hotel, and give them some spending money for their trip. You also need to have relationships with local governments. You also need to build relationships with textile mills. One of the biggest problems in working in China is getting access to raw materials. You need to build relationships with factories that have quota. You also need connections with transport.

Conversely, Ringo Ng (1993), Vice President and General Manager of Manhattan Industries, describes why he prefers not to source in China:

> You have to have connections with every official from the top to the bottom. If there is a break in the chain – if there is one official with which you have no *guanxi* – you get killed. If you are a large and famous company, relationships can be built fairly quickly. You can make a few trips to China, have some large fancy banquet for all the officials, and give them gifts. A couple of these banquets and you can begin to work. If you are a small firm, however, it is more difficult. You have to have personal connections. You may know someone who can introduce you to a particular official. You can then begin to build a relationship with him. Then he can see what he can do to use his connections to try to get quota or access to capacity. This takes a lot of time and effort.

With the growth of the East Asian manufacturing and service economies, companies that once specialized in sourcing production for core country capital have diversified into a range of economic activities, including manufacturing and design. Such diversification greatly amplifies the reach of personal networks, increasing their significance. To take one example, the Cheng family conglomerate *Wing-Tai* was founded in 1955 by Cheng Yik Hung, who had fled China and started the company in Hong Kong to make jeans for the British market (Kingman, 1992). *Wing-Tai* opened a Singapore office in 1962 when quota was imposed on Hong Kong, and a Malaysia office in 1985. The 1960s–1970s saw an enormous growth in the demand for apparel, exceeding Hong Kong's capacity to produce. *Wing-Tai* saw its next step as getting into wholesaling and distribution as well as manufacturing. By 1993 *Wing-Tai* had acquired controlling ownership of a number of apparel manufacturing companies, including Polly Peck in London, Baxter International in New York City, and Styl-land in Orange County, California.

With its holdings encompassing apparel manufacturing, design and wholesaling, sourcing and even real estate development, *Wing-Tai* in 1991 aptly described itself as 'a diversified multi-national corporation with the confidence, ability, and determination to broaden the scope of its operations still further'. In the Southeast Asian garment industry alone it had over 8000 employees and produced 'over 13 million pieces of quality fashion garment every year' (*Wing-Tai*, 1991). *Wing-Tai* factories made clothing for such retailers as Macy's and The Gap, as well as its own offshoot manufacturers such as Styl-land/PCH (Kingman, 1991). *Wing-Tai* employed some 17,000 people worldwide (Cheng, 1991).

Today, *Wing-Tai* is owned and run by the three sons of the founder, all of whom hold American MBA degrees (from Columbia, Wisconsin and Chicago) (Cheng, 1991). Yet our interviews with Chinese and European managers who work for *Wing-Tai* or its affiliated businesses suggest that it continues to operate in much the traditional manner. Despite numerous and complex dealings with European, North American and Japanese companies, *Wing-Tai* remains very much a family business, with power residing in the Cheng brothers, and global operations maintained through a tightly coordinated network of personal contacts.

Conclusions

In this paper I have sought to counter the notion that 'western' business and legal practices are becoming universal, as a consequence either of the globalization of capital or the diffusion of professional training and norms. Rather, I have argued that the changing nature of global capitalism, both geographically and organizationally, may favour business practices that avoid formal organizational forms as well as codification into universal systems of law. In particular, the rise of the East Asian economies, especially Chinese, may herald not only the decline of North American and European global economic dominance, but along with it the hegemony of their associated legal forms. New regimes of flexible accumulation, seen especially in buyer-driven commodity chains, would seem to have an affinity for the informalism and personal networks long associated with Chinese businesses.

Economic decentering has not yet brought with it sufficient discursive decentering, at least not in our understanding of the intersection of business and law. Perhaps it is time we stopped viewing emerging global economic institutions and practices from the exclusive standpoint of Europe and North America, and became more open to the possibility that new, hybrid ones will emerge – along with new associated legal forms.

Notes

This paper was prepared for a Workshop on Changing Legal Cultures II, Oñati International Institute for the Sociology of Law, Oñati, Gipuzkoa – Euskadi, Spain, 24–25 April 1997.

1. *Guanxi* 'means literally "a relationship" between objects, forces, or persons'; it can most broadly be defined as 'relationship, personal connections' (Yang, 1994: 1, 326). *Guanxi* relationships entail reciprocal obligations, cemented through various forms of gift-giving. For a detailed analysis of both the nature of *guanxi* and its changing role in Chinese society, see Yang (1994). I shall return to a more detailed discussion of the notion of *guanxi* below.
2. This is not to argue that a unique, timeless, unchanging, intrinsically 'Chinese culture' exists that is unthinkingly embraced by a quarter of the world's population: beliefs, values and practices throughout China and the Chinese diaspora (as well as everywhere) reflect differences of national and regional identifications, social class, gender and other aspects of social location through which people engage the world and construct their cultural understandings. I will argue, however, that in business practices *guanxi* has long played a central role. The book by Nonini and Ong (1997) challenges the reification of Chinese culture by academics (and business people) eager to explain China's economic ascendance in terms of ageless cultural values. 'In contrast, in this book we fruitfully view "Chinese culture", Chinese family values, *guanxi*, "Confucian capitalism", and so on as discursive tropes, each with a genealogy, each having been constantly cast in cultural terms both by Chinese and by Westerners, including academics . . . Such discourses and their connections to power in large part *constitute* Chinese identities and transnational practices, and are therefore in need of deconstruction and study' (Nonini and Ong, 1997: 9).
3. Interestingly, some of Yang's informants saw the resurgence of *guanxixue* in the late 1970s as a reaction to the excesses of the Cultural Revolution; personal connections provided humane relief following a decade in which children denounced their teachers and even their parents. Yang's larger argument is that in China today, *guanxi* constitutes a set of oppositional practices 'working *against* state power'; in her view, the 'gift economy' subverts and diffuses the state apparatus, forming a basis for the emerging civil society. See part II of her book.
4. For a telling critique of such 'triumphalist discourse', see Nonini and Ong (1997).
5. World-systems theory has been criticized for over-emphasizing the role of

European expansion in the world system. Relevant to the present discussion, Andre Gunder Frank – a key figure in world systems theory – has recently sought to demonstrate that an Asian world system predated the European one by thousands of years. Frank argues that Europe's role in Asia remained one of trade (financed by silver extracted from the Americas beginning in the 16th century) until inter-Asian struggles weakened Ottoman, Moghul and Qing rule (Frank, 1994).

6. Prior to American dominance, British capitalism held sway for some 130 years; before the British were the Dutch, for about 180 years; and before the Dutch, the Italians (Venice and especially Genoa) for 220 years.

7. In fact there is reason to believe that the 'retail revolution' may even overtake producer-driven commodity chains; even the automobile industry seems to be moving towards more flexible forms of production – achieved partly through increased subcontracting – in order to achieve mass customization and sales through large retail outlets (Kassler and Appelbaum, 1998).

8. See, for example, Gereffi's (1996b) response to Whitely. Gereffi claims that 'there is a global economic structure to which all countries need to adapt in order to be successful. There is a considerable scope for national variations, but the scope is not unlimited' (p. 435).

9. Innova is an investment company loosely affiliated with *Wing-Tai*, a Hong Kong-based conglomerate that will be discussed below. Innova is headed by Chris Cheng, who is also the head of *Wing-Tai*; it is a vehicle for investments that Cheng wishes to make independently of *Wing-Tai* and its various holdings.

REFERENCES

Appelbaum, Richard and Edna Bonacich (1993) *A Tale of Two Cities: The Garment Industry in Los Angeles*. Los Angeles, CA: Report to The Haynes Foundation.

Appelbaum, Richard and Gary Gereffi (1994) 'Power and Profits in the Apparel Commodity Chain', in Edna Bonacich, Lucie Cheng, Norma Chinchilla, Norma Hamilton and Paul Ong (eds) *Global Production: The Apparel Industry in the Pacific Rim*. Philadelphia, PA: Temple University Press.

Arrighi, Giovanni (1994) *The Long Twentieth Century*. London: Verso.

Becker, Gary Stanley (1976) *The Economic Approach to Human Behavior*. Chicago: University of Chicago Press.

Becker, Gary Stanley (1996) *The Economic Way of Looking at Behavior: The Nobel Lecture*. Stanford, CA: Stanford University, The Hoover Institution, Essays in Public Policy No. 69.

Birnbaum, David G. (1993) President, Third Horizon Ltd, Hong Kong, Brad Christerson interview, 1 July 1993.

Chan, Jan (1993) Managing Director, David and David Fashion Wholesale and Retail Ltd, Hong Kong, Brad Christerson interview, 29 July 1993.

Chan, Joseph (1993) General Manager, Innova Ltd, Hong Kong, Richard Appelbaum interviews, 22 April and 2 May 1993.

Chase-Dunn, Christopher (1989) *Global Formation: Structures of the World-Economy*. Cambridge, MA: Basil Blackwell.

Cheng, Francis Man-Piu (1991) Assistant Managing Director, Wing-Tai Exporters, Ltd, Hong Kong, Richard Appelbaum interview, 25 November 1991.

Cheng, Francis Man-Piu Cheng (1993) Assistant Managing Director, Wing-Tai Exporters, Ltd, Hong Kong, Brad Christerson interview, 19 July 1993.

Cunningham, James P. (1991) Vice President, Offshore Sourcing, The Gap (Far East) Ltd, Hong Kong, Richard Appelbaum interview, 28 November 1991.
de Sousa Santos, Boaventura (1992) 'State, Law, and Community in the World System: An Introduction', *Social and Legal Studies* 1: 131–42.
Dezalay, Yves (1990) 'The *Big Bang* and the Law: The Internationalization and Restructuration of the Legal Field', *Culture and Society* 7: 279–93.
Dezalay, Yves and Bryant Garth (1996) *Dealing in Virtue: International Commercial Arbitration and the Construction of a Transnational Legal Order.* Chicago: University of Chicago Press.
Drew, Christopher (1997) 'Asian Links of a Donor Put Gifts to Democrats in Doubt', *The New York Times* 22 February.
Elegant, Robert S. (1990) *Pacific Destiny: Inside Asia Today.* New York: Crown.
Frank, Andre Gunder (1994) 'The World Economic System in Asia Before European Hegemony', *The Historian* 56(2): 259–76.
Gereffi, Gary (1992) 'New Realities of Industrial Development in East Asia and Latin America: Global, Regional, and National Trends', in Richard P. Appelbaum and Jeffrey Henderson (eds) *States and Development in the East Asian Pacific Rim.* Newbury Park, CA: Sage.
Gereffi, Gary (1994) 'The Organization of Buyer-Driven Global Commodity Chains: How US Retailers Shape Overseas Production Networks', in Gary Gereffi and Miguel Korzeniewicz (eds) *Commodity Chains and Global Capitalism.* Westport, CT: Greenwood Press.
Gereffi, Gary (1996a) 'Commodity Chains and Global Capitalism in East Asia', *Journal of Asian Business* 12(1): 75–112.
Gereffi, Gary (1996b) 'Global Commodity Chains: New Forms of Coordination and Control Among Nations and Firms in International Industries', *Competition and Change: The Journal of Global Business and Political Economy* I(4) (fall): 427–39.
Gereffi, Gary and Gary Hamilton (1996) 'Commodity Chains and Embedded Networks: The Economic Organization of Global Capitalism', paper presented at the Annual Meeting of the American Sociological Association, New York, 16–20 August.
Gerlach, Michael L. (1992) *Alliance Capitalism: The Social Organization of Japanese Business.* Berkeley: University of California Press.
Granovetter, Mark (1993) 'Business Groups', in Neil Smelser and Richard Swedberg (eds) *Handbook of Economic Sociology.* New York: Russell Sage Foundation.
Hakansson, H. (ed.) (1982) *International Marketing and Purchasing of Industrial Goods*, 2nd edition. Chichester: John Wiley & Sons.
Hamashita, Takeshi (1994) 'The Tribute Trade System and Modern Asia', pp. 91–107 in A. J. H. Latham and H. Kawakatsu (eds) *Japanese Industrialization and the Asian Economy.* London and New York: Routledge.
Hamilton, Gary G. and Cheng-shu Kao (1990) 'The Institutional Foundations of Chinese Business: The Family Firm in Taiwan', *Comparative Social Research* 12: 95–112.
Harvey, David (1995) 'Globalization in Question', *Rethinking Marxism* 8(4) (winter): 1–17.
Hirst, Paul Q. and Grahame Thompson (1996) *Globalization in Question: The International Economy and the Possibilities of Governance.* Cambridge, MA: Blackwell Publishers.
Hopkins, Terence K. and Immanuel Wallerstein (1986) 'Commodity Chains in the World-Economy Prior to 1800', *Review* 10(1): 157–70.
Hui, Po-keung (1995) 'Overseas Chinese Business Networks: East Asian Economic Development in Historical Perspective', PhD dissertation, Department of Sociology, SUNY Binghamton.

Kawakatsu, Heita (1986) 'International Competitiveness in Cotton Goods in the Late Nineteenth Century: Britain versus India and East Asia', pp. 619–43 in W. Fischer, R. M. McInnis and J. Schneider (eds) *The Emergence of a World Economy, 1500–1914*. Weisbaden: Franz Steiner Verlag.

Kessler, Judi and Richard P. Appelbaum (1998) 'The Growing Power of Retailers in Producer-Driven Commodity Chains: A "Retail Revolution" in the US Automobile Industry?'. Santa Barbara, CA: ISBER-CGS, Working Papers, no. 11 (March).

Kingman, Matt (1991) Senior Vice President of Styl-land, PCH-Innova, Richard Appelbaum interview, 25 November 1991.

Kingman, Matt (1992) Senior Vice President of Styl-land, PCH-Innova, Hong Kong, Brad Christerson interview, 26 August 1992.

Levy, Marion J. (1972) *Modernization: Latecomers and Survivors*. New York: Basic Books.

Meyer, John W., John Boli and George M. Thomas (1987) 'Ontology and Rationalization in Western Cultural Account', in George M. Thomas, John W. Meyer, Francisco O. Ramirez and John Boli (eds) *Institutional Structure: Constituting State, Society, and the Individual*. Newbury Park, CA: Sage.

Ng, Ringo (1991) Vice President and General Manager, Manhattan Industries (Far East) Ltd, a division of Salant Corporation, Hong Kong, Richard Appelbaum interview, 3 December 1991.

Ng, Ringo (1993) Vice President and General Manager, Manhattan Industries (Far East) Ltd, a division of Salant Corporation, Hong Kong, Brad Christerson interview, 9 July 1993.

Nonini, Donald M. and Aihwa Ong (1997) 'Chinese Transnationalism as an Alternative Modernity', pp. 3–33 in Aihwa Ong and Donald M. Nonini (eds) *Ungrounded Empires: The Cultural Politics of Modern Chinese Transnationalism*. New York: Routledge.

Ong, Aihwa (1997) 'Chinese Modernities: Narratives of Nation and of Capitalism', pp. 171–202 in Aihwa Ong and Donald M. Nonini (eds) *Ungrounded Empires: The Cultural Politics of Modern Chinese Transnationalism*. New York: Routledge.

Orrú, Marco, Nicole Woolsey Biggart and Gary G. Hamilton (1991) 'Organizational Isomorphism in East Asia', in Walter Powell and Paul DiMaggio (eds) *The New Institutionalism in Organizational Analysis*. Chicago: University of Chicago Press.

Parsons, Talcott (1966) *Societies: Evolutionary and Comparative Perspectives*. Englewood Cliffs, NJ: Prentice-Hall.

Robertson, Roland (1992) *Globalization: Social Theory and Global Culture*. Newbury Park, CA: Sage.

Sahlins, Marshall D. and Elman R. Service (1960) *Evolution and Culture*. Ann Arbor: University of Michigan Press.

Service, Elman (1976) *Origins of the State and Civilization: The Process of Cultural Evolution*. New York: Norton.

Smart, J. and A. Smart (1991) 'Personal Relations and Divergent Economies: A Case Study of Hong Kong Investment in South China', *International Journal of Urban and Regional Research* 15(2): 216–33.

Sung Yun-wing (1993) Senior Lecturer in Economics, The Chinese University of Hong Kong, Richard Appelbaum interview, 4 November 1993.

Thomas, George M., John W. Meyer, Francisco O. Ramirez and John Boli (eds) (1987) *Institutional Structure: Constituting State, Society, and the Individual*. Newbury Park, CA: Sage.

Thompson, William Irwin (1985) *Pacific Shift*. San Francisco: Sierra Club Books.

Trocki, Carl A. (1997) 'Boundaries and Transgressions: Chinese Enterprise in Eighteenth- and Nineteenth-Century Southeast Asia', pp. 61–85 in Aihwa Ong and Donald M. Nonini (eds) *Ungrounded Empires: The Cultural Politics of Modern Chinese Transnationalism*. New York: Routledge.

Tsang, Paul C. M. (1993) General Manager, Unimix Limited, Hong Kong, Brad Christerson interview, 17 July 1993.

Wallerstein, Immanuel M. (1974) *The Modern World-System*. New York: Academic Press.

Wallerstein, Immanuel M. (1979a) *The Capitalist World Economy*. Cambridge: Cambridge University Press.

Wallerstein, Immanuel M. (1979b) *The Modern World-System II*. New York: Academic Press.

Walton, Steven R. (1993) Managing Director, Innova Ltd, Hong Kong, Richard Appelbaum interview, 2 May 1993.

Whitely, Richard (1992) *Business Systems in East Asia: Firms, Markets, and Societies*. Newbury Park, CA: Sage.

Whitely, Richard (1996) 'Business Systems and Global Commodity Chains: Competing or Complementary Forms of Economic Organization', *Competition and Change: The Journal of Global Business and Political Economy* I(4) (fall): 411–25.

Willis, T. H. and C. R. Hutson (1990) 'Vendor Requirements and Evaluation in a Just-In-Time Environment', *International Journal of Purchasing Management* 10(4): 41–50.

Wing-Tai (1991) *Brochure and Report*.

Wong, Siu-lun (1985) 'The Chinese Family Firm: A Model', *British Journal of Sociology* 36: 58–72.

Wong, Victor Witt H. (1993) Assistant Production Manager, Production Planning Department, Wing Tai Garment International, Ltd, Hong Kong, Brad Christerson interview, 4 July 1993.

WuDunn, Sheryl (1997) 'In Asia Some Ask, Why a Fuss Over Cash to Clinton?', *The New York Times* 6 April: A-1.

Yang, Mayfair Mei-hui (1994) *Gifts, Favors, and Banquets: The Art of Social Relationships in China*. Ithaca, NY: Cornell University Press.

[2]

Property Rights, Collateral, Creditor Rights, and Insolvency in East Asia[1]

DOUGLAS W. ARNER,[*] CHARLES D. BOOTH,[**] PAUL LEJOT,[***] & BERRY F. C. HSU[****]

SUMMARY

I.	INTRODUCTION	516
II.	GOVERNANCE, ECONOMIC AND LEGAL SYSTEMS	518
III.	THE SIGNIFICANCE OF PROPERTY RIGHTS	524
IV.	COLLATERAL AND SECURED TRANSACTIONS	525
	A. Real Property	530
	B. International Standards for Movables	531
	C. Collateral in East Asia	532
	1. Overview	534
	2. Real Property	535
	3. Movables and Unsecured Property	537
	D. Securitization	540
V.	CREDITOR RIGHTS AND INSOLVENCY	542
	A. Insolvency	543
	B. Interaction between Creditor Rights and Insolvency	545

---

[1]. This is an expanded and updated version of a study that was published as Douglas W. Arner, Charles D. Booth, Berry F. C. Hsu, Paul Lejot, Qiao Liu & Frederik Pretorius, *Property Rights, Collateral and Creditor Rights in East Asia*, in EAST ASIAN FINANCE: SELECTED ISSUES (Ismail Dalla ed., World Bank 2006). The authors thank Dean Polizzotto of the Asian Institute of International Financial Law of the Faculty of Law of the University of Hong Kong for research assistance, and the Hong Kong Research Grants Council Competitive Earmarked Research Grant program and the University of Hong Kong Strategic Research Areas initiative for financial support.

[*] Associate Professor; Director, Asian Institute of International Financial Law (AIIFL); & Director, LLM (Corporate & Financial Law) Program, Faculty of Law, University of Hong Kong.

[**] Professor & Director, Institute of Asian-Pacific Business Law, William S. Richardson School of Law, University of Hawaiʻi at Manoa.

[***] Visiting Fellow, AIIFL, Faculty of Law, University of Hong Kong; & Visiting Research Fellow, ICMA Centre, University of Reading.

[****] Associate Professor, Faculty of Architecture, & Deputy Director, AIIFL, Faculty of Law, University of Hong Kong.

  C. *Creditor Rights and Insolvency in East Asia* 546
    1. Insolvency: Pre-1997 Overview 547
    2. Insolvency: Post-Financial Crisis Legal Reforms 550
    3. Insolvency: Post-Financial Crisis Out-of-Court Reforms 553
    4. Interaction between Creditor Rights and Insolvency 555
    5. Summary 556

VI. CONTRACT ENFORCEMENT AND DISPUTE RESOLUTION 558

I. INTRODUCTION

  A number of common preconditions must prevail if a market-orientated financial system or national economy is to develop and function effectively.[2] Those relating to financial sector development rest on three principles: the first, institutional and legal; the second, largely legal; and the third, related mainly to policy.

  First, a market economy and a market-based financial system cannot exist if certain institutional and legal supports are not in place, namely, a governance mechanism that establishes property rights and provides for the consistent enforcement of contracts and resolution of commercial disputes. It is also important that the setting provides for the development of human capital.[3]

  With these institutional foundations in place, a number of legal underpinnings must then be available for a market-based financial system to function effectively. These include the availability of collateral to support secured transactions, a system of law for the establishment and dissolution of corporate bodies, and a transparent system of government funding, including taxation. To maintain such effectiveness, national and sub-national governance should also provide more widely for the rule of law, which is taken to be transparent and non-discriminatory, in addition to establishing specific property rights, enforcing contracts and supporting commercial dispute resolution.

  Third, a financial sector functions most effectively in the context of appropriate macroeconomic policies. These policies, while largely outside legal and institutional concerns, operate best in the context of an appropriately designed and transparent institutional framework.

  No sophisticated market economy or market-based financial system can exist without these prerequisites, regardless of indigenous or acquired national characteristics or the form manifested by that system. In this context, this article examines the relationships within East Asia between economic development, governance, property rights, provisions for the deployment of collateral and the creation of secured financial transactions, and creditor rights and their relationship with insolvency.

---

  2. The framework of analysis underlying this study is based upon DOUGLAS W. ARNER, FINANCIAL STABILITY, ECONOMIC GROWTH AND THE ROLE OF LAW (2007).
  3. Human capital development is not examined here. It became an acknowledged feature of growth studies with Lucas's 1985 Marshall lectures. *See* Robert E. Lucas, Jr., *On the Mechanics of Economic Development*, 22 J. MONETARY ECON. 1, 17 (1988).

The eleven subject jurisdictions appear in two groups, shown in Table 1. First is a core group of nine, which have undergone, or intend to enact, reforms in the subject areas. Second are two common law jurisdictions that are perceived as being among the most sophisticated in the region in terms of the issues examined, and which may represent benchmarks for reform elsewhere. It is not suggested that either jurisdiction represents an institutional or practical optimum.[4]

TABLE 1: JURISDICTION CLASSIFICATIONS

Study Core Jurisdictions		Regional Benchmarks
Cambodia	South Korea	Hong Kong
China	Taiwan	Singapore
Indonesia	Thailand	
Malaysia	Vietnam	
Philippines		

Neither law nor practice is advanced in relevant areas in most of the remaining jurisdictions within the region, but the issues addressed in this article have begun to receive attention from policymakers and commercial interests. The issues of policy and principle raised in this article have been regularly debated in official and legal circles since the economic and social shocks associated with the 1997-98 Asian financial crisis. In no national case can the legal, regulatory, or policy background be described as either complete or fully integrated, even in the two examples of benchmarks, or elsewhere in countries where specific reforms have been recently instigated or completed, for example, China or the Philippines.

Later sections include tables that give appraisals of the legal framework for creditor rights, especially in relation to secured claims; the effectiveness of national insolvency systems; specific or general provisions for private securitized transactions; and the mutual compatibility of systems for enforcement. Thus in Tables 2, 5, 7 and 8, a scale rising from 1 to 5 is used to indicate the quality or effectiveness of specific factors that are self-explanatory, with "NA" used to signify where the law makes no provision in a specified matter, based primarily upon qualitative analysis. Unless stated, these tables use terms such as "security" and "interest" in a generic sense without attachment to any legal system or jurisdiction. In each case, the appraisals acknowledge not only pure aspects of law and regulation (often clear where the law includes recent legislation), but also qualifications to reflect enforcement issues, integration with related law, and the stability of the regulatory setting. Commercial participants throughout the region have often found that while the law appears clear, it suffers from uncertain application. The results appear in complex private financial transactions that seek to mitigate such risks.

It is now generally accepted that the form and practice of law influences economic behavior. In particular, institutional quality is an important determinant of

---

4. Certain reforms in Japan's civil code and statutes have guided changes elsewhere among civil law jurisdictions in the study group. *See infra* note 80.

credit creation and flows of capital, both among the main sectors of an economy and in cross-border savings and investment. Factors such as legal origin, the nature of the acquisition or founding of law, and details of its application and enforcement are seen in features of governance, economic systems and structure, commercial culture, corporate behavior, and financing patterns. These conditions also affect broader variables such as national output or personal income. The appraisals in this article and the research upon which they are based thus adopt the view of users, that is, principals and agents, that become subject to the law rather than those involved in its creation or administration.

At the same time, the efficiency and consistency of the law's operation will always form part of its institutional costs, so that no assessment can ignore the organization and management of legal systems. This is especially valid in the context of creditor claims and corporate distress. In general, the main objective of the reform of laws governing security and creditor rights will be to influence behavior through changes in costs. The following two parts of this article discuss respectively, its theoretical background and the role of property rights in transaction formation and credit creation. Parts IV and V then examine collateral and secured transactions, and creditor rights and insolvency, respectively. Part VI concludes with an outline of provisions in Asia for contract enforcement and commercial dispute resolution.

II. GOVERNANCE, ECONOMIC AND LEGAL SYSTEMS

State governance and the appropriateness of political and economic structure have been of interest for over ten thousand years, prompted by specialized human activity encouraging the first agricultural settlements. This in turn allowed the development of writing systems appropriate and necessary to sustain the administrative structures of such settlements. Building the "perfect society" and creating governance systems to encourage its development has been a focus of many thinkers, including Confucius, Plato, Aquinas, Locke, and Marx. All political and economic systems function in close parallel, even though the interplay may not always be acknowledged by political theorists. Certainly, the relationship between politics (or governance) and economics has been a central interest of Smith, Marx, and more recently Keynes, Hayek, and Friedman. Although politics and economics became increasingly distinct disciplines in the twentieth century, the end of the millennium saw a reviving interaction between governance and economics, partly encouraged by the experience of market orientation undertaken by many centrally planned economies, and from the conspicuous failure of earlier economic development models in neglecting institutional issues of governance.

The role and development of financial intermediaries have become a focus of attention only recently in law, financial policy, and economics, although each discipline is directly concerned with both the problem and its several explanations. Similarly, conditions influencing how financial structure develops have begun to interest scholars in the developed and developing world, and those helping to create supportive policy. Until the 1970s few economic or finance theorists gave attention to the nature of financial systems or how they may affect economic development. Similarly, the importance and influence of the characteristics of financial markets and intermediaries has been accepted only since the late-1980s, with the inception and success of the law and finance and institutional economics schools. Financial intermediation is now recognized as vital to many aspects of economic development, and what determines the nature of financial intermediaries and financial system infrastructure is susceptible to both quantitative analysis and the tools of legal and economic theory.

By the beginning of the 1990s, two traditionally polar alternatives—central planning under state ownership and laissez-faire—had been subsumed into an apparent consensus as to the general superiority of a market economy, but one functioning under the framework of an appropriate and transparent regulatory system, with the state taking a benign but active role in addressing the interests of any society through the provision of largely agreed public goods, systems to limit or ameliorate market failure, and sanctions to penalize market abuse, whether arising from monopoly or the occurrence of asymmetric information available to privileged participants. Nonetheless, as Shleifer and others have recognized, many differences remain among today's economic and governance models.[5] The question then arises as to what may represent the best choices among available options, and to what extent those choices lead to the disadvantage of certain interests.

For institutional economists such as North, and writers in the law and economics school, governance systems must provide for two fundamental features to support a market economy, regardless of its ideological identity and consequent form. First, the system must provide for clear and usable property rights. Second, it must facilitate practical and fair contract enforcement. Both literatures agree that these conditions are essential in the context of imperfect markets where there exist discernable transaction costs. While there appears to be agreement as to the need to satisfy these basic points, the governance structure that best supports a market economy is less apparent, and may change in relation to the relative development of the host economy.

Many scholars have argued further that democratic models of governance are optimal in protecting property rights and enforcing contracts, albeit this was the result they sought most often to prove. However, Olson has presented a convincing argument that a variety of governance structures can provide each of these necessary features.[6] Specifically, he suggested that an autocrat with a long-term time horizon will have a strong incentive to support both property rights and contract enforcement in order chiefly to maximize revenue from taxation.[7] Conversely, Olson argues that any democracy, while potentially providing for property rights and the enforcement of contracts, may nevertheless become subject to inefficient outcomes due to its responsiveness to representative but factional interests.[8] Thus neither autocracy nor democracy is necessarily a superior political system in providing the most beneficial support for a market economy. Instead, what is necessary is a "market-augmenting government."[9] There is contemporary anecdotal evidence that

---

5. *See* Simeon Djankov et al., *The New Comparative Economics*, 31 J. COMP. ECON. 595 (2003).

6. MANCUR OLSON, POWER AND PROSPERITY: OUTGROWING COMMUNIST AND CAPITALIST DICTATORSHIPS (2000).

7. *Id.*

8. *Id.*

9. Charles Cadwell, *Foreword* to MANCUR OLSON, OUTGROWING COMMUNIST AND CAPITALIST DICTATORSHIPS, at x (2000).

certainly supports Olson's theory,[10] and recent empirical research has begun to test these ideas and appears to be supportive.[11]

North sums up the interaction between the political system and property rights thus:

> Broadly speaking, political rules in place lead to economic rules, though the causality runs both ways. That is, property rights and hence individual contracts are specified and enforced by political decision-making, but the structure of economic interests will also influence the political structure. In equilibrium, a given structure of property rights (and their enforcement) will be consistent with a particular set of political rules (and their enforcement). Changes in one will induce changes in the other.[12]

The result is that a national governance structure is important and must provide for property rights and the enforcement of contracts, as well as human capital development. However, while some governance structures are clearly not conducive to liberty (any state run by the myopic autocrat-bandit), there is at present no clearly preferable model. Both autocratic and democratic governance systems can support a market economy. Similarly, each can provide for institutional choices that fail to result in efficient, wealth-maximizing outcomes in a given economy.

Two further underlying issues are present throughout this study: those relating to the mechanisms that transmit influences on economic growth, and those involving the means by which finance affects economic development, including the relationship between legal systems and financial structure. Neoclassical economic theory, post-1940s growth theories and traditional finance theory all ignore or assume away the nature of financial systems.[13] While finance and corporate finance theory examine commercial organizations in terms of contract or cost, a similar approach has been applied only recently to financial intermediaries, and rarely to examine financial systems. Thus, early modern studies of the determinants of economic growth identified a strong correlation between the "rule of law" and per capita growth.[14] These analyses were weak in terms of identifying with any practical precision the ways in which legal reform might be invoked to promote growth, given

---

10. *Cf.* China, Singapore.

11. *See* Djankov et al., *supra* note 5 (indicating that policies are more important than democratic institutions, and specifically, that human capital is a more basic source of growth than democratic institutions; that poorer states can alleviate poverty through sound policies, even when pursued by dictators; democratic institutions are developed after economic "take-off").

12. DOUGLASS C. NORTH, INSTITUTIONS, INSTITUTIONAL CHANGE, AND ECONOMIC PERFORMANCE 48 (1990).

13. This growth school pattern probably began with WALTER ROSTOW, THE PROCESS OF ECONOMIC GROWTH (1952); Lucas, *supra* note 3, perhaps the most willful financial agnostic, based indifference upon the thesis that at firm level, financial performance is unrelated to the composition of funding. Certain Marxian analysis asserts a causal relationship running from economic activity to financial structure to accord with the primacy of capitalist production. It is often unspecific in its treatment of both law and financial activity in this area, perhaps reflecting Marx's disdain for "merchant" or "commercial" capital; an exception is J. J. McManus *The Emergence and Non-emergence of Law*, 5 BRIT. J. LAW & SOC'Y 185, 190 (1978) (describing the origin of English consumer credit legislation).

14. Notably, Robert J. Barro, *Economic Growth in a Cross Section of Countries*, 106 Q. J. ECON. 26-28 (1971); ROBERT J. BARRO, DETERMINANTS OF ECONOMIC GROWTH: A CROSS-COUNTRY EMPIRICAL STUDY 26-28 (1997).

that the measures used to specify rule of law explanatory variables were primitive and included subjective components such as commercial indexes of sovereign risk.

The law and finance school asserts that there exist significant causal links between the origins of law or the means by which a national system of law is acquired, and the nature of financial system development.[15] Certain scholars further suggest a causal relationship that flows from financial development to economic performance, although most accept that such links are unlikely to be unicausal.[16] Questions investigated or prompted by the law and finance school include: first, the relationship of institutional development to general economic welfare; second, the relationship between legal origin and the effectiveness and even-handedness of legal systems; third, whether the effectiveness of a national legal system is significantly determined by its origin or the form of its acquisition; and finally, whether common law is inherently more effective than other systems in encouraging financial development, stimulating credit growth or protecting property rights.[17]

While the general premise of law and finance protagonists has become accepted, especially in suggesting more specific legal research agendas, the school has been criticized for two main methodological reasons. The first is its choice and specification of explanatory variables,[18] which may either be incomplete or endogenously related to the objective questions that the analysis seeks to answer;[19] which may not signify close substitutes or take account of compensatory mechanisms in different legal systems;[20] or may reflect customary choice appropriate mainly to

---

15. Djankov et al., *supra* note 5; Robert G. King & Ross Levine, *Finance & Growth: Schumpeter Might Be Right*, 108 Q. J. ECON. 717 (1993), Ross Levine, *Finance & Growth: Theory & Evidence* (Nat'l Bureau of Econ. Res. Working Paper No. 10766, 2004); Ross Levine, *Financial Development and Economic Growth: Views and Agenda*, 35 J. ECON. LIT. 688 (1997); Raghuram G. Rajan & Luigi Zingales, *Financial Systems, Industrial Structure, and Growth*, 17 OXFORD REV. ECON. POL. 467 (2001).

16. Notably Thorsten Beck et al., *Law and Finance: Why Does Legal Origin Matter?* (World Bank Pol'y Res. Working Paper 2904, 2002); Thorsten Beck & Ross Levine, *Legal Institutions and Financial Development* (Nat'l Bureau of Econ. Res. Working Paper No. 10126, 2003); Rafael La Porta et al., *Law and Finance*, 106 J. POL. ECON. 1113 (1998); *Legal Determinants of External Finance*, 52 J. FIN. 1131 (1997); Paul G. Mahoney, *The Common Law and Economic Analysis: Hayek Might be Right*, 30 J. LEGAL STUD. 503 (2001); Peter L. Rousseau & Richard Sylla, *Financial Systems, Economic Growth and Globalization* (Nat'l Bureau of Econ. Res. Working Paper No. 8323, 2001).

17. Given that the quality of creditor and shareholder protection measures the effectiveness of a national legal system. This is not synonymous with financial development but is often so taken, with the protection of claims used as a proxy for financial sophistication.

18. Philip Arestis & Panicos Demetriadis, *Financial Development & Economic Growth: Assessing the Evidence*, 107 ECON. J. 783 (1997); Daniel Berkowitz et al., *The Transplant Effect*, 51 AM. J. COMP. L. 163 (2003); David Blum et al., *The Financial-Real Sector Nexus: Theory & Empirical Evidence* (Res. Inst. for European Affairs Working Paper No. 43, 2002); Charles Kenny & David Williams, *What do we know about Economic Growth? Or, Why don't we know very much?*, 29 WORLD DEV. 1 (2001); Michael Thiel, *Finance & Economic Growth: A Review of Theory & the Available Evidence* (Eur. Comm. Econ. Pap. No. 158, 2001); Paul Wachtel, *How much do we really know about Growth & Finance?*, 88 FED. RES. BANK ATLANTA ECON. REV. 1 (2003).

19. *See* Rajan, *supra* note 15.

20. MARK J. ROE, STRONG MANAGERS, WEAK OWNERS: THE POLITICAL ROOTS OF AMERICAN CORPORATE FINANCE (1994); KATHARINA PISTOR & PHILIP WELLONS, THE ROLE OF LAW AND LEGAL INSTITUTIONS IN ASIAN ECONOMIC DEVELOPMENT 1960-1995 (1999); Katharina Pistor et al., *Law and Finance in Transition Economies*, (European Bank for Reconstruction & Dev. Working Paper No. 48, 2000); Sofie Cools, *The Real Difference in Corporate Law Between the United States and Continental Europe: Distribution or Powers*, 30 DEL. J. CORP. L. 697 (2005); Mathias Siems, *Legal Origins: Reconciling Law & Finance And Comparative Law*, *available at* SSRN: http://ssrn.com/abstract=920690.

developed, homogenous markets.[21] The second attack concerns the usefulness of the school's conclusions in indicating legal or regulatory reform, given that legal related explanatory variables have of necessity been general and unspecific.[22]

As examples, the scale of finance evident in an economy has often been used as an explanatory variable, but it may not measure financial sophistication, contrary to the intentions of La Porta, López-de-Silanes, Shleifer & Vishny (LLSV) or Rousseau & Sylla;[23] no distinction is made between types of claims against a debtor or firm. Rather, all debt is generally taken as secured. The chain of causation identified by the law and finance school (especially LLSV) runs from legal origin to enforcement, to financial development and finally to growth. This is unreliable for policy development if legality impacts growth but legal origin does not impact legality. A more fully informed identification of explanatory variables will assist with these problems. It may also overcome problems caused by the static nature of the law and finance school's analysis, for example, ignoring the convergence of civil and common commercial law with political regionalization and financial harmonization, more extensive financial and trade treaty networks, and the activity of international self-regulatory bodies.

Theoretical interest in the structure and operation of financial systems was largely absent from legal and financial studies before the 1970s, and in schools of economics was confined to political economy.[24] That such indifference has vanished results largely from the influence of two trains of scholars. First, Goldsmith sought ways to test whether financial structure could be related to levels of economic development.[25] This work was to become a foundation of the law and finance school. Second, North and others synthesized hitherto separate concepts from law, finance and economics in what has become modern institutional economics, which stresses the nature and effect of core rights, duties and incentives. While the first is primarily concerned with whole markets or national economies and the latter is initially microeconomic in its emphasis, the two disciplines share certain interests, and meet in the analysis of the effects of legal systems and property rights, for example, on economic conditions and development.

The approach of the traditional financial development school was to examine the role of banking and bank credit creation. More recent law and finance analysis has taken account of environmental and cultural factors, and indeed all measurable financial variables. None has yet examined in detail the quality of law enforcement in a commercial context, for example, in the willingness of national courts to enforce foreign judgments and accept non-exclusive jurisdiction transaction provisions. Instead, where quality of law and regulation is included in analysis, its tendency to date has been on subjective index measures of the "rule of law." In addition, while law and finance scholars have sought to quantify the effects on financial

---

21. Naomi R. Lamoreaux & Jean-Lamoreaux Rosenthal, *Legal Regime and Business Organizational Choice: A Comparison of France and the United States* (Nat'l Bureau of Econ. Res. Working Paper No. 10288, 2004).

22. Frank B. Cross, *Law and Economic Growth*, 80 TEX. L. REV. 1736 (2002); Kevin E. Davis, *What Can the Rule of Law Variable Tell Us About Rule of Law Reforms?* (N.Y.U. L. & Econ. Res. Paper Series Working Paper No. 04-026, 2004); Kevin E. Davis & Michael J. Trebilcock, *Legal Reforms and Development*, 22 THIRD WORLD Q. 210 (2001); Roe, *supra* note 20.

23. *See supra* note 16.

24. Due largely to Marx, Schumpeter, and Weber and their later acolytes, but in no instance with the dedication to detail of the modern law and finance school.

25. RAYMOND GOLDSMITH, FINANCIAL STRUCTURE AND DEVELOPMENT (1969).

development of national legal systems or their origins,[26] no systematic attempt has yet appeared in this context that together considers legal origins, their form of acquisition and the distinct nature of jurisdictions, especially when their roots are mixed.[27] Nor has analysis yet recognized that the nature of commercial legal disputes may itself be endogenous to the legal system.

Related work includes a considerable body of empirical studies in the style pioneered by Goldsmith and following the methods adopted by King & Levine and LLSV in seeking evidence of causal relationships between financial market or institutional sophistication or structure (including legal origins and conditions), and economic development, commonly measured by growth in national output. While not unanimous, these generally suggest that finance often has a positive effect on growth, although contrary to popular belief there is no theoretical school that asserts the contrary: that the primary causal flow is from economic growth to financial development.[28]

The remainder of this article contains summaries of appraisals of the effectiveness of current law and practice as to collateral and creditor rights in eleven prominent East Asian jurisdictions. In particular, it examines discrete aspects of the creation and treatment of secured creditor interests, processes for insolvency, securitization, and the functional relationship between these related aspects of law. The effects of globalization on both market practice and harmonization of financial regulation mean that the private law governing international financial transactions differs less by virtue of the location of parties or the place of transaction execution than by issues of judicial enforcement, including the willingness of courts to provide equitable and predictable judgments to domestic and foreign creditors.[29] The quality of legal and practical provisions for insolvency is also central to the willingness of lenders and investors to provide funds for capital investment. By contrast, legal frameworks for the taking or enforcement of collateral may be influenced by informal or traditional national or local commercial custom, although remaining subject also to the prevailing form of law and the roots of national law.

---

26. *See* La Porta et al., *supra* note 16 (classifying forty-nine national legal systems by their origins in English common law or French, German or "Scandinavian" civil law); Berkowitz et al., *supra* note 18 (dividing the same sample among ten original systems); PHILIP WOOD, COMPARATIVE FINANCIAL LAW (1995) (perceiving seven categories, not including states that lack a clear legal system or for which it may be "emerging"). Earlier comparatists found different solutions, the most contemporary being David, who identifies eight "families" of law, see RENÉ DAVID & JOHN E. C. BRIERLEY, MAJOR LEGAL SYSTEMS IN THE WORLD TODAY: AN INTRODUCTION TO THE COMPARATIVE STUDY OF LAW (John E. C. Brierley trans., 2d ed. 1978), not all of which subsist in the form described.

27. Philip Wood, Global Law Maps: Key Map of Jurisdictions (mimeo, 2001) identified up to 307 distinct national and state jurisdictions. The number is certain to change.

28. That a body of scholarship contends that financial development largely responds to economic growth was first suggested against the theme of his study by Richard C. Porter, *The Promotion of the "Banking Habit" and Economic Development*, 2 J. DEV. STUD. 346, 363 (1966) (asserting in a footnote that "the few economists who have proposed a clear direction of causation between real and financial growth usually suggest [that real growth precedes financial sector development]"). The remark is often repeated without substantiation.

29. This appears in contemporary comparative analyses of commercial law. *See* WOOD, *supra* note 26.

III. THE SIGNIFICANCE OF PROPERTY RIGHTS

Property rights were an important concern for Smith, Marx and Weber but received little attention from economists for generations until becoming subject to intensive research in the late 1970s. Until recently the nature of finance and thus the preconditions for its provision were ignored or assumed away by generations of economists and finance specialists; only "maverick" opinion appears to have considered otherwise.

The importance of property rights began to receive significant contemporary attention when the disintegration of the Soviet bloc introduced the challenge of transforming command economies to market-based systems. Development specialist de Soto deserves considerable credit for increasing awareness of the importance of property rights in this respect, especially in relation to the potential impact of formally endowing individuals with such rights.

Classically, property is seen as a "bundle of rights." More specifically, "property" includes some or all of a variety of different "rights," including the rights to hold, use, modify, transfer, or destroy a real or intangible asset. Questions of degree and time relate to all such varied rights, and the extent to which a property owner may exploit such rights may be constrained by the competing rights of others within a legal system or as part of public policy. In addition, property can be real or personal, tangible, or intangible. The more complex a system of property rights, the more effective is their potential use in the context of finance and capital-raising.

According to North:

> Property rights are the rights individuals appropriate over their own labor and the goods and services they possess. Appropriation is a function of legal rules, organizational forms, enforcement, and norms of behavior — that is, the institutional framework.[30]

De Soto argues that capital is the engine of a market economy, with property rights the mechanism that allows it to be effectively deployed.[31] Further, relatively poor countries often fail to produce capital sufficient for economic development due to five main failings in property systems. First, such societies may have substantial masses of capital,[32] yet it represents "dead" resources in that it is constituted by assets, interests or claims that cannot be used or mobilized as capital. Second, capital is intrinsically difficult to define or recognize. Third, many states have neglected the importance of the preceding two factors, an attitude that has begun only slowly to change.[33] Fourth, while de Soto's process of mobilizing property rights

---

30. DOUGLASS NORTH, INSTITUTIONS, INSTITUTIONAL CHANGE AND ECONOMIC PERFORMANCE 33 (1990).

31. HERNANDO DE SOTO, THE MYSTERY OF CAPITAL: WHY CAPITALISM TRIUMPHS IN THE WEST AND FAILS EVERYWHERE ELSE (2000).

32. *Id.* at 35. By his calculation, "the total value of the real estate held but not legally owned by the poor of the Third World and former communist nations is at least [US]$ 9.3 trillion." *Id.*

33. De Soto states this best:

> The substantial increase of capital in the West over the past two centuries is the consequence of gradually improving property systems, which allowed economic agents to discover and realize the potential in their assets, and thus to be in a position to produce the non-inflationary money with which to finance and generate additional production.

needed in emerging or transition economies had occurred earlier elsewhere, it was often poorly understood or documented, even in relatively sophisticated states. Finally, laws need to reflect national or local circumstances in order to allow the effective transformation of property rights into capital.

For de Soto:

> A well-integrated legal property system in essence does two things: First, it tremendously reduces the costs of knowing the economic qualities of assets by representing them in a way that our senses can pick up quickly; and second, it facilitates the capacity to agree on how to use assets to create further production and increase the division of labor.[34]

De Soto concludes that formal property systems are required to produce six effects so as to allow individuals to generate usable capital. These are: first, making certain the economic potential of existing assets; second, integrating dispersed information into a single dependable system; third, making individuals accountable for their economic actions; fourth, increasing the fungibility of assets; fifth, marshalling individuals into valuable social networks; and sixth, protecting the integrity of legitimate transactions.[35]

Established and accepted property rights and their identification and protection, including rights over intellectual property are, therefore, essential in any market economy.[36] Unfortunately, de Soto notes that such rights have evolved in advanced economies over protracted periods, making it difficult even for the legal historian to discern how they function or become established. Without complete templates of this kind it may never be simple for emerging, transition or developing economies to introduce those experiences or systems, even when respecting the integrity of local or state culture. Furthermore, the recognition of property rights is not self-justifying; the need is for such rights to be available for use other than in instantly completed transactions. This is an underlying theme of the remainder of this article.

IV. COLLATERAL AND SECURED TRANSACTIONS

Collateral exists to meet commercial customs, national practices, and socio-economic constraints that differ strongly between jurisdictions, even in an era when commercial practice and financial regulation are often well-integrated and the international harmonization of financial markets is well-advanced. Several World Bank studies have surveyed law, institutions, and secured transactions,[37] but the reasons for security differ everywhere by intention, nature, and degree. This affects whether the granting of collateral is an efficient choice for commercial or individual

---

Id. at 65.

34. *Id.* at 63.
35. *Id.* at 49-62.
36. Leora Klapper et al., *Business Environment and Firm Entry: Evidence from International Data* 27-28 (World Bank Policy Research, Working Paper No. 3232, 2004).
37. *See* World Bank, *1989 World Bank Dev. Rep.* (1989); *2002 World Bank Dev. Rep.* (2002); Yoram Keinan, *The Evolution of Secured Transaction's Background Study for World Development Report 2002* (2001).

borrowers, or for creditors at large. Recent analysis of European transition economies suggests that the provision of collateral is important in inducing early-stage development.[38]

Schumpeter's 1939 description of the working of capitalism[39] draws on his earlier theoretical approach to interest and credit creation that came to be disputed by contemporary traditional classicists (Cannan), radicals (Keynes and Joan Robinson), and for some remains controversial. It includes a generic description of the role of credit creation in banking not attempted by his contemporary critics. Schumpeter's approach includes a customary means by which a creditor bank may seek to overcome transaction obstacles and thus lessen the costs resulting from asymmetric information, which otherwise would often force the adoption of incomplete lending contracts. Modern structured finance techniques such as non-recourse project finance or securitization are intended to limit to the greatest possible extent the incompleteness of financing contracts. In each case, contractual structuring results in the debtor having no surplus value, so as to become theoretically constrained from engaging in activity outside the financed enterprise.

By contrast, lending conducted under typical incomplete contracts involves credit risks subject to unquantifiable Knightian uncertainty, since lenders can only be partially informed as to the scope of activities of companies to which they lend. Even though lenders may hope to mitigate the effects of incomplete contracts by incorporating covenants and assignments of actual or potential revenue into contracts, the result will inevitably be subject to general practice and comparative strengths in negotiation. Even if a lender has full knowledge of a debtor enterprise, the volition of the debtor may lead to default, which on occasion may be economically rational.[40] Other mechanisms to encourage contract compliance (given that few non-fraudulent debtors in advanced economies now face the threat of prison) include socioeconomic forces of the kind traditionally associated with distinct lending markets, for example, in the financing of the trade in diamonds or ship purchase. By this view, the taking of collateral is thus not related to information discontinuities but represents a sanction to encourage contract compliance by the debtor. In terms of institutional analysis it will typically constitute a distortion,

---

38. Rainer Haselmann, Katharina Pistor & Vikrant Vig, *How Law Affects Lending* (Colum. L. Econ. Working Paper No. 285, 2005). By contrast, this may not have been the case in the British industrial revolution, when the existence of reliable non-possessory land mortgages failed to induce banks to lend in a major way to industrial capitalists, allowing historians to discount the importance of finance in development; *see* MAURICE DOBB, STUDIES IN THE DEVELOPMENT OF CAPITALISM (1947); MICHAEL FLINN, ORIGINS OF THE INDUSTRIAL REVOLUTION (1966) 52-53. A similar pattern of bank passivity is observed in the United States at the turn of the twentieth century; *see* Naomi R, Lamoreaux, Margaret Levenstein & Kenneth L. Sokoloff, *Financing Invention during the Second Industrial Revolution: Cleveland Ohio 1870-1920*, 27-30 (Nat'l Bureau of Econ. Res. Working Paper No. 10923, 2004). Yet only after 1850 did a reliable form of non-possessory chattel mortgage emerge in Britain, and it was arguably not fully trusted by lenders until the early twentieth century. ROY GOODE, COMMERCIAL LAW 586 (3d ed. 2004). Neal observes that England's preceding seventeenth to eighteenth century "financial revolution" has long been underestimated in its effect on later commercial development, *see* Larry Neal, *The Finance of Business during the Industrial Revolution*, *in* 1 THE ECONOMIC HISTORY OF BRITAIN SINCE 1700, 151 (Roderick Floud & Deirdre McCloskey eds.(1994). Hartwell similarly acknowledges a lack of attention to private finance in growth studies, describing the service sector as the "neglected variable"; *see* RONALD MAX HARTWELL, THE INDUSTRIAL REVOLUTION AND ECONOMIC GROWTH (1971).

39. JOSEPH SCHUMPETER, BUSINESS CYCLES: A THEORETICAL, HISTORICAL, AND STATISTICAL ANALYSIS OF THE CAPITALIST PROCESS (1939).

40. For example, in the case of home mortgage loans where the value of collateral falls below the amounts outstanding, given certain limits to creditor rights in bankruptcy.

enabling credit substitution to become the means by which a bank lender avoids the moral hazard associated with asymmetric information.

At the same time, contrary to the findings of certain studies of domestic U.S. practice—except in cases where recourse to the principal debtor is non-existent or limited—taking security is not generally a device to signal credit quality but the converse,[41] as with conventional non-recourse project finance. Rather, it serves three main purposes for the principals involved or prospectively engaged in financial bargaining, shown in Figure 1.

FIGURE 1: PRINCIPAL FUNCTIONS OF COLLATERAL

Transformative

(A) Mitigation or substitution in credit risk for a potential financier.

(B) Change in capital asset use to make financing available.

Informative

(C) Signal credit risk strengths or borrower status.

(D) Signal risk or bargaining weaknesses.

(E) Facilitate credit substitution.

Providing incentives

(F) Effect on costs and information for credit creation.

(G) Provide financiers with known credit risks.

(H) Encourage contractual compliance by collateral providers.

Adequate institutional infrastructure enable banks to extend the duration of their loans and reduce regulatory capital costs by providing greater confidence as to the credit risk associated with likelihood of repayment. In this regard, two aspects of lending infrastructure are especially important for risk management: an effective system for taking security, and sufficient sources of information through accounting standards, audit practice, credit rating methodology and oversight, and acceptable credit information systems. In addition, banks need systems to manage risks appropriately, these typically being required by capital adequacy and other prudential regulatory requirements.

---

41. This and other motivations for borrowers to grant security have been questioned notably by Schwartz, who (assuming with Modigliani and Miller that the value of an enterprise is unrelated to the composition of its capital) asks whether security represents an efficient practice, given its effect on other potential creditors and the interplay of priority of claims with U.S. precepts of bankruptcy. *See* Alan Schwartz, *Security Interests and Bankruptcy Priorities: A Review of Current Theories*, 10 J. LEGAL STUD. 1, 1 (1981) [hereinafter Schwartz, *Security Interests*]; Alan Schwartz, *The Continuing Puzzle of Secured Debt*, 37 VAND. L.R. 5, 1051 (1984) [hereinafter Schwartz, *Puzzle of Secured Debt*]; Franco Modigliani & Merton Miller, *The Cost of Capital, Corporation Finance and the Theory of Investment*, 48 AM. ECON. REV. 261 (1958). A more recent study suggests that collateral provides incentives for lenders to monitor loan performance and is correlated with generally poor business conditions or the debtor's financial distress. *See* Raghuram Rajan & Andrew Winton, *Covenants and Collateral as Incentives to Monitor*, 50 J. FIN. 1113 (1995).

As an institution of risk management, an effective system to create security allows lenders to obtain collateral to reduce unwanted credit risk and have confidence that such collateral may be realized where necessary to permit the full or partial repayment of a loan. Effective security creation and registration thus provides two advantages for lenders. First, it allows the limiting of monitoring costs by means of partial or complete credit risk substitution, providing that no failure to monitor collateral results in the erosion of security protection. Second, it increases simplicity in lending decision-making, thereby increasing the probability that such decisions will be made.[42]

If property rights are to create capital, they must be applied to procure funding so that the taking of security is the lender's simplest form of risk mitigation. Loans are disbursed provided the lender is given a contingent claim to property of a proportionately equivalent or greater value. If the debt is not satisfied, the lender retains the property and need take little or no account of the credit risk of the borrower. In this simple case, the availability of collateral induces marginal lending. However, to prompt this simple transaction, the lender must be confident of retaining rights to the property given contractual non-payment by the debtor. Thus, the borrower must have valid initial title to the property, and the law must provide for certain and effective transfer of ownership in the event of the security being enforced. Finally, the lender will need a means to appraise supporting collateral. This has often been a problematic feature of all economies, whether developed, emerging, transition, or developing, and usually in the context of loans secured by real property.

Complex collateral-based lending involves sophisticated distinctions between property rights and the certainty of contractual enforcement, derived from the prevailing legal and institutional framework. For example, in the simple transaction of the preceding paragraph, a borrower provided physical, recognizable collateral to secure its indebtedness, as in the common South Asian example of personal loans secured by quantities of gold or silver. This is collateral deployed in its most simple form. For reasons presented in the preceding paragraphs, the use of collateral in secured transactions can become more complex only to the extent that it is supported by an adequate legal and institutional framework. If a borrower must deliver physical collateral to a lender then poorly capitalized enterprises will lack access to most secured lending, and excessive transaction costs render the exercise sub-optimal.

With institutional support for more advanced practices, a borrower may be allowed physical possession of collateral pre-dating the creation of a new loan, thus keeping day-to-day control of the use and enterprise value of existing assets, whether land, buildings, plant, or machinery. At a still more sophisticated legal level, a loan might be used to purchase real property or productive assets, secured by those newly-acquired assets, with the borrower retaining their full use in ways that may be expected to assist in the servicing of the loan. While the mechanics of such transactions are simple to describe, this type of purchase money security is not universally supported by security or bankruptcy law. Whether national law allows or

---

42. The contrary argument is that over-reliance on collateral in lending to commercial enterprises represents an inefficient solution and raises a moral hazard, in each case by disassociating the creditor from a true interest in the borrower's commercial prospects. Even if this is not the case, in certain common law jurisdictions where banks may be encouraged to seek security interests in order to gain a degree of contractual influence over the debtor.

limits such arrangements reflects an underlying view of the economic welfare associated with security and collateral. This is seen in the competing views of a commercial enterprise as being either revenue generating or a custodian of assets, and may result in the legal treatment of the purchase of money security as unfairly benefiting individual creditors at the expense of others.[43]

In each case, transaction complexity requires greater legal sophistication, and deploying moveable property as collateral typically requires a more complex legal framework than real property. Furthermore, while real or movable physical collateral is associated with the largest share of secured lending in most emerging and developed economies, intangible property may also represent potential collateral, including intellectual property or trade receivables. The rights of a secured creditor could thus extend to defined classes of assets such as inventory or receivables, to a company's entire asset base if it becomes subject to whole business securitization, or where debts are secured by floating charges as found in English law and certain other common law jurisdictions. They might also extend to the right to receive revenues rather than actual receipt of revenues, providing in each case that the institutional system is sufficiently supportive.

Simple financial markets are greatly enhanced when the availability of collateral increases, even though there may be diminishing returns in the welfare created by collateral-based lending. As a minimum, functional markets require that real property used as security be left in the possession of the borrower, and that security over movable assets does not hinder their normal commercial use.[44] Developed financial markets typically operate with a wide range of feasible collateral assets, and sophisticated financial markets similarly require commensurate techniques for taking security, for example, in using future receipts and providing for securitization. Nonetheless, questions and anomalies exist even in advanced financial markets. De Soto asserts that property must be allowed in use as collateral in order to encourage economic development, but then fails to distinguish between the legal and institutional issues concerning property, which he addresses in a "capitalization process," and in the use of property as collateral, except in relation to the recording or registration of property rights. In reality, capital is created or released only given both aspects of the framework supporting the use of property and property rights as collateral for secured transactions. To refine de Soto's analysis, property rights must exist and property must also be usable in support of funding for a financial system to develop comprehensively beyond a basic level.[45]

Despite the importance of collateral and secured transactions, this is an area of law involving highly varied legal systems, which in developed jurisdictions is also highly technical. Perhaps as a result, secured transactions tend to receive analytical attention at relatively advanced levels and involve those emerging economies that are already well-progressed in systems supporting basic secured transactions. Once

---

43. An alternative approach distinguishes between the common law view of the firm as a nexus of contractual bargains, following Ronald H. Coase, *The Nature of the Firm*, 4 ECONOMICA 386 (1937), and the more civilian view of the firm as a commercial hub of rights and obligations.

44. Which might be the case, for example, under the traditional English common law mortgage or civil law possessory pledge.

45. Note that in certain jurisdictions in the study core group, sophisticated financial transactions and state funding mechanisms exist alongside relatively primitive consumer banking or low-scale credit creation.

such transactions are supported by a legal and institutional system, there is considerable development potential in enhancing similar support for more advanced secured transactions. Furthermore, sophisticated transactions may provide an interim financing solution for states with incomplete or emerging legal systems.

A. Real Property

Recent research supports the view that systems of finance based upon property are highly relevant to financial and economic development.[46] Byamugisha's 1999 World Bank study develops a theoretical framework to guide the empirical analysis of the effects of property finance on an entire economy,[47] arguing that the conceptual framework linking real estate finance to financial development and economic growth has five main features. First, land tenure security and investment incentives; second, land title, collateral, and credit; third, land liquidity, deposit mobilization, and investment; fourth, land markets, transactions, and efficiency; and last, labor mobility and efficiency. All must be effective to facilitate real estate-based finance, and each demands the existence of appropriate legal infrastructure.

Given the significance of real estate finance for economic development, an ensuing question focuses on markets in which the secondary refinancing of mortgage lending is prominent. For example, a 1997 World Bank study analyzed factors hindering the development of home loan markets in the transition economies of Central and Eastern Europe and proposed a strategy to expedite their development.[48] The analysis shows that banks in transition economies may be reluctant to make mortgage loans for house purchase because of the scale of risks they perceive in such lending; that is, the extent of credit, interest rate basis, and liquidity risks. It suggests that a secondary mortgage market is likely to assist in solving these problems by allowing banks to manage their loan books to meet preferences over risk concentration and duration, assuming that the initial primary provision of loans meets certain institutional standards.

A third World Bank study argues that successful land and real estate reforms must be "comprehensive in design, even if implementation is phased in over time."[49] It contends that such reforms include three elements: first, institutional reforms that better define property rights, reduce information asymmetries and improve contract performance (termed Property Rights, Information, Contracting and Enforcement);

---

46. In addition to de Soto's suggestion, *supra* note 31, that legal reform in developing economies can energize idle capital, North & Thomas, *supra* note 12, argue that efficient economic organization is the key to growth; Nathan Rosenberg & L. E. Birdzell, Jr., HOW THE WEST GREW RICH: THE ECONOMIC TRANSFORMATION OF THE WESTERN WORLD (1986), argue that Western economic development hinged on factors promoting experimentation; Goldsmith, *supra* note 25, provides empirical evidence that the growth of democratic freedoms and property rights in poor countries may lead to increased local prosperity; Johan Torstensson, *Property Rights and Economic Growth: An Empirical Study*, 47 KYKLOS 231 (1994), applies empirical analyses of property rights and economic growth to substantiate the findings of both Rosenberg & Birdzell and North & Thomas.

47. Frank Byamugisha, *The Effects of Land Registration on Financial Development and Economic Growth: A Theoretical and Conceptual Framework* (World Bank Pol'y Res. Working Paper No. 2240, 1999).

48. Dwight M. Jaffe & Bertrand Renaud, *Strategies to Develop Mortgage Markets in Transition Economies* (World Bank Pol'y Res. Working Paper No. 1697, 1996).

49. Ahmed Galal & Omar Razzaz, *Reforming Land and Real Estate Markets* 31 (World Bank Policy Research Working Paper No. 2616, 2001).

second, capital market reforms making mortgage finance available at reasonable costs, especially for the poor (Finance and Risk Management); and third, market reforms that reduce or eliminate distortions in the price of goods and services, the production of which is enabled by land and real estate assets (Market Regulation and Fiscal Policy). Their conclusions tie effective mortgage markets to the broader concept of using real estate finance to encourage all aspects of financial and economic development.

Jaffee and Renaud suggest that secondary mortgage markets confer two main benefits: allowing lenders to shed risks associated with holding mortgages, and creating common standards for credit evaluation and collateral procedures that lead to greater efficiency in new mortgage lending. They suggest that governments adopt catalytic policies in developing secondary mortgage market systems and institutions. This follows the experience of the U.S. and certain other developed countries, and has been adopted by several of the jurisdictions considered in this article.

B. International Standards for Movables

Wide disparities exist in secured transactions law in developed economies, and are often central in distinctions between common and civil law traditions.[50] As a result of those disparities, there exist no internationally agreed standards or principles governing secured transactions.[51] Creating effective provisions for secured transactions demands a mastery of many aspects of an entire legal system, including laws of property, obligations, insolvency, and civil procedure, and of administrative practices and procedures such as registration and enforcement. Nonetheless, research shows that the sound development of legal infrastructure underlies functioning collateral-based credit provision and that inadequacies in such infrastructures hinder financial and economic development.[52]

Recent guidance from the Bank for International Settlements (BIS) describes the features of a generic collateral and credit law,[53] which include two main elements. First are credit laws to govern creditor-debtor relationships in commercial transactions. These may be established by common law, contract law, civil codes or specific legislation, for example, in usury laws, banking statutes or creditor-debtor statutes. Second, are pledges and collateral laws helping to create and enforce rights in collateral security, preferably through legislation of specific or general application, rather than through contract or common law. Such laws establish priority rankings among secured and unsecured claims in situations of default or insolvency, requiring legislation of a specific or general application.

---

50. For an excellent discussion, see Frédérique Dahan, *Secured Transactions Law in Western Advanced Economies: Exposing Myths, in* EUROPEAN BANK FOR RECONSTRUCTION AND DEVELOPMENT, LAW IN TRANSITION 37 (2000), and sources cited therein.

51. *See* Arjun Goswami & Hamid Sharif, *Preface* in Nuria de la Pena, Heywood Fleisig & Philip Wellons, *Secured Transactions Law Reform in Asia: Unleashing the Potential of Collateral, in* LAW AND POLICY REFORM AT THE ASIAN DEVELOPMENT BANK 2 (2000).

52. *See generally* de la Pena et al., *supra* note 51.

53. BANK FOR INT'L SETTLEMENTS COMMITTEE ON PAYMENT AND SETTLEMENT SYSTEMS, GENERAL GUIDANCE FOR NATIONAL PAYMENT SYSTEM DEVELOPMENT 65-5 (2006).

Example of such laws and regulations include the U.S. Uniform Commercial Code (UCC) Article 9; the European Union Directive 2002/47/EC on financial collateral arrangements; the 1997 OHADA Uniform Law on Security Rights; the 1994 European Bank for Reconstruction and Development (EBRD) Model Law on Secured Transactions; the UNCITRAL Legislative Guide on Secured Transactions; the Cape Town Convention on International Interests in Mobile Equipment; and the West African Economic and Monetary Union Regulation 15/2002/CM/UEMOA Regarding Payment Systems in the Member States.

Among multilateral agencies, the EBRD's Model Law is one of the few international standards for secured transactions that has been applied successfully as part of an established process to collateral law reform, drawing also upon the Bank's core principles and glossary.[54] The Asian Development Bank (ADB) has assisted in creating specific new secured transaction frameworks and the World Bank has addressed some of these issues in relation to insolvency. More directly, the United Nations Commission on International Trade Law (UNCITRAL) is completing a Legislative Guide on Secured Transactions.[55] Other significant international efforts have been made by the International Institute for the Unification of Private Law (UNIDROIT),[56] while regional efforts are under way in North America,[57] Asia,[58] and Europe. In addition, important harmonization efforts were made in respect of U.S. UCC Article 9 and Canada's Personal Property Security Acts, with both frameworks often serving as models in East Asia and elsewhere.

C. Collateral in East Asia

A sound framework for secured lending can encourage the provision of credit and assist in the development of domestic financial markets. At the same time, any system that involves the widespread use of collateral assets to support corporate lending may risk fostering a monopolistic banking sector. The use of secured lending as a proxy for informed risk appraisal can become inefficient to the economy as a whole, both by encouraging wasteful credit risk substitution and acting as a force oppressive to non-financial trade creditors.[59] In East Asia, an over-reliance by lenders on the use of private and corporate real estate as collateral for corporate credit may have contributed to the scale and rapidity of the 1997-98 financial crisis. Following the widespread collapse of asset values, this over-reliance provoked a severe subsequent credit squeeze affecting otherwise "healthy" borrowers, even in national markets that were the least affected by the general loss in confidence. Collateral must be available as security to release the flow of capital but not so unreasonably as to protect the oppressive and inefficient.

---

54. *See* John Simpson & Joachim Menze, *Ten Years of Secured Transactions Reform*, *in* EUROPEAN BANK FOR RECONSTRUCTION AND DEVELOPMENT, LAW IN TRANSITION 20 (2000).
55. *See* UNCITRAL, http://www.uncitral.org (last visited Nov. 24, 2006).
56. *See* UNIDROIT, Convention on International Factoring, May 28, 1988, *available at* http://www.unidroit.org/english/conventions/1988factoring/main.htm (last visited Nov. 24, 2006); UNIDROIT Convention on International Interests in Mobile Equipment (2001), *available at* http://www.unidroit.org/english/conventions/mobile-equipment/main.htm (last visited Nov. 24, 2006).
57. *See* American Law Institute, International Secured Transactions Project (1997), *available at* http://www.ali.org (last visited Nov. 24, 2006).
58. *See* de la Pena, Fleisig & Wellons, *supra* note 51.
59. *See also supra* notes 41 and 42.

These concerns prompt a series of questions applicable to any jurisdiction. First, to what extent is commercial secured lending or title finance possible? Second, what legal provisions exist for home mortgages? Third, what provisions are made for the transfer of secured claims? Fourth, what are the principal effects of related legal reforms, for example, in civil jurisdictions that choose to enact wholesale securitization legislation? Fifth, what is the position of secured claims vis-à-vis statutory priority, for example, in government or employee creditor claims? Last, is there simplicity of execution, perfection, notification, registration, and enforcement? Table 2 synthesizes an analysis of these issues in the economies addressed by this study, using a rising 1-5 scale. Scores such as 2/3 represent an intermediate appraisal between two given levels. As with Tables 5, 7, and 8, these "split" scores are intended to reflect degrees of uncertainty as to commercial outcomes.

TABLE 2: LEGAL FRAMEWORK FOR CREDITOR RIGHTS

	Enforcement of Unsecured Rights	Security Interest Legislation	Registration and Disclosure of Secured Rights	Enforcement of Secured Rights
Cambodia	1	1[60]	1[61]	1
China	2	2	2	2
Indonesia	1	2	1/2	1
Malaysia	5	4	4	5
Philippines	2	2/3	2/3	2
South Korea	3	1/2	1/2	2/3
Taiwan	3	4	3	3/4
Thailand	2	1/2	2	2
Vietnam	1	1	1	1
Hong Kong	5	4	4	5
Singapore	5	4	4	5

Here, granting and making security effective is treated as a form of property right, regardless of the nature of the legal systems under review. Any appraisal will therefore question how the law links the granting of security to the rights of general creditors in both normal and distressed circumstances. Table 2 thus shows how the system now supports, undermines, or confuses all aspects of secured transactions. No account is taken of informal systems, even if commercially entrenched.[62] Ideally, the law will allow simple cost-effective creation of security without affecting rights of

---

60. When enacted, a forthcoming secured transactions law is expected to allow a score of "4" in this category.

61. When implemented, new provisions are expected to allow a score of "4" in this category.

62. But account is taken of legal provisions peculiar to certain jurisdictions, such as Taiwan's right of *dien* which is recognized in the Civil Code Art. 911 as a form of leasehold interest in immovable property, or the contractual antichresis permitted under the Philippines Civil Code Art. 2132, but which is increasingly disused as a form of pledge.

conventional day-to-day collateral usage. It will be public, transparent, function without discrimination, and be enforceable in ways compatible with declared public policy, especially in relation to insolvency, receivership, and rearrangements following corporate distress.

The effectiveness of a national legal and administrative framework permitting the creation of collateral for secured transactions is revealed in several elements, not all of which are consistently present in the review countries. Among the matters to be considered are the ease and cost of creating reliable security interests, the systems for such interests to be disclosed, the costs and risks associated with the enforcement of charges, the relationship of security and collateral with insolvency and receivership practice, and the operation of creditor protection and stays to enforcement. These are contained in Table 2.

Civil and common law traditionally have different approaches to security interests, and the introduction of reform always needs to be sensitive to the existing contractual and legal setting. While the EBRD Model Law on Secured Transactions was intended to be adopted by jurisdictions of all types, it is likely that the presence of relatively well-developed legal systems in the core review group make a single benchmark impractical. Such a device might have value, however, in other developing Asian jurisdictions.[63] Elsewhere, recent legislative reforms appear to be effective in supporting transaction creation, but have yet to be tested in cases involving economic stress, in particular a downward phase in the credit risk cycle or weakening. This applies to Indonesia, South Korea, and Thailand, for example, as well as to Cambodia's pending Secured Transactions Law and the registry that will support its implementation. In each case, a further concern for the integrity of new laws in relation to existing and succeeding legislation may arise, given that measures are often introduced in discrete steps despite leading to a complex commercial whole. In China, for example, legislation introduced since 2003 has necessitated the reconsideration of statutes that were created in recent but earlier days of reform. Likewise, implementation of China's 2007 Property Law is likely to have significant impact, though the exact scope is as yet unclear.

In a related area of law, securitization legislation or decrees have been adopted in recent years and remain largely untested in Indonesia and the Philippines.[64] Those introduced in South Korea, Taiwan, and Thailand appear to be transactionally sound but have not yet been made subject to credit or valuation stress of the kind indicated in the preceding paragraph.

1. Overview

Asia's legal provisions for secured credit transactions regimes at the onset of the 1997-98 financial crisis were at least as outdated and inefficient as its insolvency laws. Yet less effort has since been made to reform those laws. Immediately after the crisis, most attention was directed to reforming corporate reorganization procedures and other features of insolvency law, even though such laws cannot work

---

63. Vietnam, for example, introduced a general bankruptcy law in 1993 (and a new bankruptcy law in 2004) and commercial and property laws in 1991.

64. A recent unreported decision of the Indonesian Supreme Court may affect the use of a special purpose vehicle to facilitate foreign currency borrowing by Indonesian entities. *See* Kate Linebaugh, *How Indonesia's Bond Market Stayed Hot Despite Court Ruling*, WALL ST. J. ASIA (Nov. 10, 2006) at A22.

efficiently when secured creditors find it difficult or impossible to enforce their rights in bankruptcy. Such delays were common in Asia prior to the financial crisis.[65] Similarly, credit creation is adversely affected when either valid collateral must be held in possession by a secured creditor or limits exist to the permissible categories of assets that may be used as collateral. As will be seen in the country-specific discussion below, these problems were also endemic prior to the crisis,[66] but its impact finally drew attention to the need for coordinated legal reform as well as the creation of modern provisions for secured transactions. Thailand is an example of how this acceptance has been made, as legislation was under preparation immediately prior to the suspension of the legislature in September 2006.

2. Real Property

In each jurisdiction within this study, the legal system provides for real property to be offered and taken as collateral. However, there is considerable divergence as how best to resolve a variety of issues, including the following: the ease and efficiency with which mortgages, charges or liens may be created; the requirements for registration and its usefulness to third parties; whether a mortgagor retains title to collateral while the extension of credit that the charge purports to secure remains outstanding; and how secured creditors may enforce their collateral rights. Differences also exist in some cases in the treatment of collateral arising from varying statutory provisions for real property ownership by domestic and foreign interests.

Table 3 does not address the distribution of property rights, which is a focus of de Soto's work that merits further attention in the context of the relationship between state governance and property rights, and economic outcomes.

TABLE 3: TREATMENT OF REAL PROPERTY

Cambodia	Real property may be mortgaged, but enforcement can be extremely problematic. Registration is efficient and effective. A foreign creditor may take a mortgage over land but not become the owner of land.
China[67]	Land may not be mortgaged, but mortgages over land-use rights are permitted. Registration is necessary to protect secured creditor rights. The enforcement of a mortgage can require litigation in cases in which the mortgagee and mortgagor cannot reach agreement as to how the mortgagee claim may be satisfied. Transactions involving mortgages to be held by foreign entities are subject to prior approval and registration with the State Administration of Foreign Exchange (SAFE).

---

65. *See* ADB Office of the General Counsel, *Insolvency Law Reforms in the Asian and Pacific Region*, Report of the Office of the General Counsel on TA 5795-Reg: Insolvency Law Reforms, Law and Policy Reform at the ADB 10-11, 70-75 (2000) [hereinafter Report on Insolvency Law Reforms].

66. *See* Lampros Vassiliou, *The Restructuring Revolution in the Asia-Pacific Region, in* THE ASIA-PACIFIC RESTRUCTURING AND INSOLVENCY GUIDE 2006 18, 21 (2006).

67. After extensive discussions and the withdrawal of an earlier draft law in 2006, a new property rights law was approved by the 10th National People's Congress in March 2007, to take effect on October 1, 2007. *See* Property Rights Law of the People's Republic of China 2007. This covers both real property

Indonesia	Security interests may be taken in land, but it often proves difficult for creditors to enforce a security interest. The process is inefficient; enforcement can take many years. Auction fees and taxes are high and, in practice, recourse to the courts is almost always necessary.[68] Official registers are maintained manually, which causes difficulties for potential lenders wishing to search for title or prior claims.[69] Security rights may be impaired by the creation of a parent company guaranty in respect of like debt.
Philippines	Real property may be mortgaged (under provisions of the Civil Code). While both registration and notarization are necessary for creditor protection, the requirements are set out in a mix of statute and presidential decree. Ownership is retained by the mortgagor while a charge is outstanding. Delays in foreclosure can occur because the secured party must use the courts in the absence of any contractual agreement for extrajudicial foreclosure.[70] Contractual antichresis was a common form of commercial pledge, but it is becoming increasingly less used. Unless stated by agreement, mortgages over land will embrace subsequent buildings or improvements to the land, and may gain inadvertent priority over other subsequent charges. Foreign creditors may become mortgagees of land but not buildings, and may subsequently not take possession of land.
South Korea	Most real estate rights must be registered. However, there are important exceptions from this rule (e.g., property acquired through inheritance or pursuant to a judgment auction).
Taiwan	The Civil Code allows mortgages to be created over defined classes of real property,[71] and for possessory security or attachments. In addition, the right of "dien" is allowed as a form of possessory pledge similar to a leasehold interest, and may be created effectively over assets not specified in law. Registration in all cases is mandatory and efficient, without which the charge will be void. There is some uncertainty as to whether notice or consent is required of a secured creditor for the creation of a subsequent mortgage. Foreign creditors are restricted as to the types of real property over which they may hold security interests.

---

and movable assets, and for the first time establishes rights in respect of both state and non-state interests. The law makes most real property ownership rights contingent upon registration. *See id.* Art. 9-22. Art. 170-240 establish conditions for the granting of security interests by a property owner, including the right to mortgage real property and specified movable assets, and the right to pledge other assets, including certain defined intangibles. The creation of registry facilities throughout China will be a considerable administrative burden.

68. EMIR NURMANSYAH, THEODOOR BAKKER, CLIFFORD REES & DAVID ADAMS, INDONESIA: THE ASIA PACIFIC RESTRUCTURING AND INSOLVENCY GUIDE 80 (2006).

69. *Id.*

70. RICARDO ONGKIKO, CARINA LAFORTEZA, CARLOS FRANCISO & COSETTE CANILAO, PHILIPPINES: THE ASIA PACIFIC RESTRUCTURING AND INSOLVENCY GUIDE 135 (2006), noting that mortgage contracts now usually provide for extra-judicial foreclosure to address this problem.

71. It was until recently customary for lenders to require registration of a "comprehensive mortgage" over an undefined amount prior to approving a loan (compared to the widespread practice elsewhere making disbursal subject to security conditions) but the practice was held invalid by the courts as being contrary to the specificity required of charges by the Civil Code. Reform has not yet been completed.

Thailand	Real property may be mortgaged and registration is necessary to protect the secured creditor's rights, but foreclosure cannot occur unless loan interest or charges have been outstanding for five years, contributing to an inefficient enforcement process that can extend over many years. Separate charges are necessary in respect of plant or equipment contained in a mortgaged property, and may be subject to official inspection.
Vietnam	The 1992 constitution adopted the general recognition of private property rights but land ownership continues to be vested solely in the state. Nonetheless, rights of land use are clear and may be mortgaged under the Land Law of 1993.
Hong Kong, Malaysia, Singapore	All allow for a charge to be taken over land, which must be registered.[72] Hong Kong and Singapore also provide for mortgages to be taken over land, but in Hong Kong (since 1984) the mortgage may be created only by a legal charge. The Malaysian courts will generally recognize a charge that is executed but not yet registered. All three jurisdictions allow for the appointment of a receiver to protect the creditor's interest and in all three jurisdictions there is a high level of predictability and efficiency as to the creditor's ability to enforce its rights. Hong Kong land ownership is (with a single exception) held by the territory's government but this does not materially affect rights of use or the creation of security.

3. Movables and Unsecured Property

The treatment of secured rights over movable property is still more varied throughout the study group. Although none of the jurisdictions within this study has adopted a U.S. Article 9-style regime, the English origin systems of Hong Kong, Malaysia and Singapore work relatively well. However, Table 4 shows that delays and inefficiencies in the enforcement of secured rights are common. Similarly, limits to the movable assets that may be used as collateral is problematic or constraining in most jurisdictions. These include bars to taking security interests in chattel paper or accounts receivable, and more broadly a lack of provisions for charges over future property or the use of security to collateralize future loans.

---

72. Laws governing land registration differ between Peninsular and East Malaysia, the latter excluding Labuan, which became a federal territory in 1990 upon being designated an offshore financial center. The taking of land and movable assets owned by Labuan companies as collateral is governed largely by the Offshore Companies Act 1990.

TABLE 4: TREATMENT OF MOVABLES

Cambodia	A new Secured Transactions Law is expected to be enacted in the foreseeable future, providing a modern legal framework for security, including support through an electronic registration system. However, enforcement is likely to remain problematic, and the commercial effectiveness of the law may be colored by other current omissions in law.
China[73]	Mortgages may be taken over existing tangible movable property, but not over future property. Secured creditors must register their claims to protect all such non-possessory rights. They may also protect themselves through possession in the form of a pledge. As with real property, foreign entities seeking security over movable property must comply with SAFE approval and registration procedures. The treatment of security interests in intangible assets such as bank accounts or receivables is less straightforward. Regulations have been issued allowing mortgages over such assets, but the effectiveness of these new forms of collateral is largely untested. Enforcement of unsecured claims can sometimes run into resistance at a local level; there have been reported instances in which banks and their clients have colluded to hide assets from the court.
Indonesia	Under the Fiduciary Security Law, a debtor may transfer title in goods to a creditor and retain possession of the goods in the absence of any default. Pledges are also permitted. A fiduciary assignment may be taken for security purposes over intangible property and receivables.[74] As with real property, enforcement over movable property requires recourse to the courts, and both auction fees and taxes are punitive.[75] In essence, secured creditors foreclosing on collateral are forced to resort to substantially the same court proceedings as unsecured creditors.[76]
Philippines	Chattel mortgages and pledges are permitted over movable property. Chattel mortgages must be recorded. Philippine law does not recognize chattel mortgages over future property; but the courts have created exceptions for interests in inventories of raw materials, goods in process, and finished goods. Future obligations cannot be secured by chattel mortgages.
South Korea	Rights in personal property may only be protected by possession. South Korean law does not recognize purchase money security interests or floating liens.

---

73. The treatment of movables will be clarified by the introduction of the new Property Rights Law of the People's Republic of China 2007, to come into force in October 2007. *See supra* note 67, providing at Arts. 179-202 for the creation of mortgages over specified movable assets. Such mortgages will take effect only upon registration.
74. NURMANSYAH ET AL., *supra* note 68, at 80.
75. *Id.*
76. *Id.*

Taiwan	Non-possessory charges are possible under the Chattel Secured Transaction Act and by separate laws regarding ships and aircraft. Registration is mandatory in each case in order to protect priority. Enforcement is generally procedural and not subject to judicial uncertainty.
Thailand	Only certain forms of movable property may be mortgaged, including large ships, boats, floating houses, beasts of burden, and classes of machinery. Creditors holding rights of retention are also recognized as secured creditors. Other types of property may be pledged. Enforcement of secured rights requires either a court judgment or a public auction. Enforcement is slow and costly. Fixed and floating charges are not permitted at present, but would be allowed under draft secured transactions law. The enforcement of unsecured debts in Thailand can extend for many years.
Vietnam	Private property rights are constitutionally recognized and charges over movables permitted by the civil code. Improvements were made to Vietnam's secured transaction framework in 2005 amendments to the civil code, which took effect in January 2006. Further decrees are expected to assist with the implementation of these changes. A National Registration Agency for Secured Transactions has been established with offices in Hanoi, Ho Chi Minh City, and Danang. However, enforcement of security interests remains difficult. Unless bankruptcy proceedings have been commenced, a court order is not necessary for the enforcement of a secured transaction.
Hong Kong Malaysia Singapore	The laws in all three jurisdictions provide a variety of security over movable property (both tangible and intangible), including charges, liens, and pledges. Retention of title is also permitted. Security may be taken over future property. Fixed charges may be taken over tangible assets and floating charges may be taken over classes of variable assets such as inventory or book debts. The taking of fixed charges over book debts by secured creditors is much more difficult..[77] These English-origin systems require the registration of many types of charges, including charges over book debts and floating charges over the general undertaking of a company, but statutory rules are less clear and comprehensive than U.S. UCC Article 9. Usual practice in these three jurisdictions is for a debenture to provide a secured financial creditor with contractual remedies upon default, allowing appointment of a receiver or special manager. All have efficient debt collection procedures for unsecured creditors.

---

77. In these three jurisdictions the decision by the U.K. House of Lords limiting the validity of fixed charges over book debts to cases in which the secured creditor exercises sufficient control over the collateral (e.g., through including a provision in the debenture requiring the deposit of proceeds of book debts into a blocked account *and* in fact operating the account as a blocked account) would be persuasive authority. *See* Re Spectrum Plus Ltd; National Westminster Bank plc v. Spectrum Plus Ltd. and others [2005] 2 BCLC 269.

D. Securitization

Securitized transactions require a permissive framework of existing or dedicated law, acceptance of certain accounting principles, acceptable regulatory assent, and a non-discriminatory taxation background.[78] They also require accepted commercial precepts that are not matters of legal policy; for example, a lack of contractual restrictions to the transfer of financial claims. Such restrictions are common in all review markets, except in Hong Kong and Singapore.

The details of typical transactions will vary among jurisdictions, but are assumed to entail the irrevocable transfer of assets to an insubstantive special purpose vehicle (SPV) to which the asset seller has no ties of ownership or control. Funding for the asset purchase is provided by the sale of public or private securities to third party investors. The transaction must withstand any legal claim in bankruptcy against the asset seller; its economics must withstand taxes and duties on transfer; in most cases, securities issued by the SPV must provide for the dependable subordination of claims.

In general, the elements of law typically associated with securitized transactions in advanced markets are present in the three common law review jurisdictions, especially those affecting existing or future claims originated by financial intermediaries. However, certain future claims that cannot be specified in ways required by current law may be seen as hazardous source material by investors or third party monoline insurers, such as credit card receivables.

A summary of the provisions for securitized transactions and their effectiveness is given in Table 5. Its assessments of the effectiveness of enabling legal provisions (column 2), the enforcement of foreclosure or repossession of source assets (column 5), and ongoing threats to the integrity of transfer of assets to a SPV (column 6) are in each case based on transactional evidence and appraisals of governing laws. However, it must be noted that in most jurisdictions, transactional integrity has yet to be fully tested through a complete credit cycle. This would apply in relation to new rules such as the creation of real estate investment trusts in common law jurisdictions such as Hong Kong and Singapore. Nevertheless, in each case the probability is small that a completed transaction will be successfully challenged.

While aspects of law may now be clear in some cases, it may be little used, such as law regarding private contracts in the Philippines or Thailand, and is thus yet untested. Further, no significant number of completed securitized transactions has yet to undergo periods of economic stress or be attacked by creditors of the originator. In contrast, since 1998, South Korean reforms seem to be demonstrably successful.

Malaysian common law supports securitization. Rules setting out general parameters for securitization were first published only in 2001, but sales of whole or partial interests in pools of home mortgages began in the mid-1980s. Shariah-compliant transactions have been few to date and involve intricate structuring at all stages, but are now considered to be generally feasible, at least as single deals.

---

78. *See* Douglas Arner, *Emerging Market Economies and Government Promotion of Securitization*, 12 DUKE J. COMP. & INT'L L. 505 (2002).

TABLE 5: PROVISIONS FOR SECURITIZATION

	Sale, assignment, or other conveyance of assets by originators to securitization vehicles				Creation, maintenance, and operation of SPV		Other
	Legal framework for creating, transferring, and perfecting ownership interests	Restrictions on types or terms of financial assets that can be transferred	Taxation and capital gain recognition issues by the SPV	Default, foreclosure, or repossession at the level of source individual assets	Legal and regulatory impediments (e.g. bankruptcy remoteness)	Taxation or licensing requirements	Restrictions on securitization vehicles issuing multiple tranches with varying characteristics
Cambodia	NA	NA	NA	NA	NA	NA	NA
China	1/2	1	1	1	1	1	1
Indonesia	2	2	2	2	1	2	2
Malaysia	5	4	4	3/4	4	4	5
Philippines	2/3	2/3	1/2	2/3	2/3	1/2	2/3
South Korea	5	4	3/4	4	5	5	5
Taiwan	4/5	4	3/4	4	4	2/3	4
Thailand	3/4	3	3/4	3/4	2/3	4/5	2/3
Vietnam	NA	NA	NA	NA	NA	NA	NA
Hong Kong	5	5	4	5	5	5	5
Singapore	5	5	5	4	5	5	5

Since 1998, four of the eight civil law review jurisdictions have introduced, or are planning to introduce, enabling laws that permit the creation of securitized transactions recognizable by international standards. The most notable provisions are shown in Table 6. In particular, these allow for the creation of SPVs, which would not otherwise be permitted by the general provisions of national civil codes.[79]

Indonesia permits certain transactions under authority granted to the principal securities regulator, Bapepam. Several Indonesian securitized transactions were completed before 1997 but post-crisis deals are virtually non-existent because counterparties may have been more willing to enter deals in a time of moderate

---

79. A recent unreported decision of the Indonesian Supreme Court has created transaction uncertainty in the context of foreign borrowing by affirming the contiguous treatment of a company guarantor and its subsidiary SPV and voiding a financing contract to which the two entities purported to be separate parties. This may increase the legal risks of securitized transactions. *See also supra* note 64.

confidence than thereafter. Since 2000, there has been some doubt that regulatory decrees, upon which any new transaction will depend, may subsist during its lifetime. Finally, certain jurisdictions are affected by related issues of law, tax, or market rules, rather than pure securitization provisions. This increases contractual uncertainty, and applies, for example, in the Philippines and for domestic transactions in Taiwan.

TABLE 6: STATUS OF ENABLING LEGISLATION FOR SECURITIZATION[80]

	Years of Enactment or Proclamation
Cambodia	None
China	Major bank and possibly other sector securitization legislation forthcoming 2007-08
	Trial deals permitted by banking and securities regulators in 2006-07
Indonesia	Pre-1997 Securitization Decrees
	2002-03 Securities Regulator Guidelines
Philippines	2003 Special Purpose Vehicle Act
	2004 Securitization Act (largely untested)
	Implementing Rules and Regulations (2005) over credit rating requirements and the use of SPVs.
South Korea	1998 Asset-backed Securities Law
	1999 Mortgage-backed Securities Law
	2003 Korea Housing Finance Corporation law
Taiwan	2002 Financial Asset Securitization Act
	2003 Real Estate Securitization Act
Thailand	1997 Securitization Decree
	2003 Asset-backed Securitization Act
	2004 Special Purpose Vehicle Act
Vietnam	None

V. CREDITOR RIGHTS AND INSOLVENCY

At the formative stage of economic development, the risk and incidence of defaults by debtors often prevent the efficient deployment of funds for investment. A proper framework of law that provides both for company incorporation and the orderly resolution of proceedings for recovery and insolvency is therefore a crucial foundation of development.

---

80. A model for other Asian civil law jurisdictions may have been legislation enabling securitization in Japan, including notably its 1998 Perfection Law, 1998/2000 Asset Liquidation Law, and 2004 Trust Business Law (Amendment).

A. Insolvency

A functioning legal framework for insolvency management is essential in the operation of any modern market-based economy. No commercial sector can function effectively without mechanisms to recognize and govern the exit of insolvent participants. Furthermore, the financial sector will limit credit creation for many companies and individuals if lenders are uncertain that their status as secured creditors will prevail upon the liquidation of their debtors, or that a reliable means will be available for the enforcement of properly-constituted security. The general objectives of a system of corporate insolvency have been described as the reduction of uncertainty, promotion of efficiency, and fair and equitable treatment for all participants.[81] A functioning insolvency regime can thus help reduce and simplify the risks associated with lending and the potential cost of debt service; if this is the case, long-run credit availability and capital investment will increase.[82]

Functioning insolvency procedures are thus central to the legal and institutional environment for sound finance in any market-based economy, regardless of whether public policy requires the law to favor debtors or creditors. A well-administered insolvency system may be valuable in promoting market discipline. Effective insolvency laws provide the means for the identification of non-competitive participants and, in some cases, for their controlled exit. It thus provides an effective penalty for the least competitive as well as a potential solution to the ensuing reallocation of resources. While this view stresses the retroactive character of insolvency law, it also has a considerable preventive element by creating incentives for the uncompetitive to improve performance and to avoid the sanction of administration by a third party on its creditor's behalf.

A number of international organizations and associations have assisted the development of standards for modern insolvency law and related systems. Many of these activities have focused in particular on norms and standards for cross-border insolvency cases, such as the UNCITRAL Model Law on Cross-Border Insolvency and the EU Insolvency Regulation of 2000.[83] A working group chaired by the legal department of the IMF presented a document containing detailed principles for the development of workable, modern insolvency legislation.[84] While there is no internationally agreed key standard in the area of insolvency, the World Bank is coordinating efforts to develop such a benchmark and is working with UNCITRAL to develop a suitable framework for its implementation.

The World Bank first issued its Principles and Guidelines for Effective Insolvency and Creditor Rights Systems in April 2001[85] and a revised version under

---

81. *See* Report of the G-10, Report of the Contact Group on the Legal and Institutional Underpinnings of the International Financial System (Sep. 2002), *available at* http://www.bis.org/dcms/fd.jsp?p=1&uri=/publ/gten06.htm (last visited Nov. 24, 2006).

82. IMF Legal Department, Orderly & Effective Insolvency Procedures: Key Issues (1999), *available at* http://www.imf.org/external/pubs/ft/fandd/2000/03/hagan.htm (last visited Nov. 24, 2006). Note that this argument is silent as to the quality of investments so financed.

83. UNCITRAL MODEL LAW ON CROSS BORDER INSOLVENCY WITH GUIDE TO ENACTMENT (1997); Council Regulation 1346/2000 O.J. (L 160).

84. IMF Legal Department, *supra* note 82.

85. World Bank, Principles and Guidelines for Effective Insolvency & Creditor Rights Systems (Apr. 2001), *available at*

development will take into account feedback from insolvency assessments conducted under the IMF-World Bank Reports on Observance of Standards and Codes (ROSC) initiative.[86] The Bank is also preparing a technical report containing detailed implementation guidelines to support the principles. UNCITRAL released a Legislative Guide on Insolvency Law in 2005, a combination of model provisions, recommendations, and explanatory notes that builds upon the work of other international organizations, including the World Bank, IMF, and ADB.[87]

The World Bank identifies nine objectives for effective corporate insolvency:[88]

1) Integrate with broader national legal and commercial systems.

2) Maximize the value of a firm's assets by providing an option to reorganize.

3) Strike a careful balance between liquidation and reorganization.

4) Provide for equitable treatment of similarly situated creditors, including foreign and domestic creditors.

5) Provide for timely, efficient, and impartial resolution of insolvencies.

6) Prevent the premature dismemberment of a debtor's assets by individual creditors seeking quick judgments.

7) Provide a transparent procedure that contains incentives for gathering and dispensing information.

8) Recognize existing creditor rights and respect the priority of claims with a predictable and established process.

9) Establish a framework for cross-border insolvencies, with recognition of foreign proceedings.

In supporting these objectives, the thirty-five World Bank insolvency principles cover five main areas: first, a legal framework for creditor rights (principles 1-5);[89]

---

http://web.worldbank.org/WBSITE/EXTERNAL/TOPICS/LAWANDJUSTICE/GILD/0,,CONTENTMD K:20086184~menuPK:146153~pagePK:64065425~piPK:162156~thesitePK:215006,00.html. The Principles (ICRPs) were prepared in collaboration with the AfDB, ADB, EBRD, IADB, IFC, IMF, OECD, UNCITRAL, INSOL International, and International Bar Association.

86. The latest draft dates from 2005. *See* http://www.worldbank.org/ifa/rose_icr.html (last visited Nov. 24, 2006).

87. *See* Legislative Guide on Insolvency Law, UNCITRAL, *available at* http://www.uncitral.org/pdf/english/texts/insolven/05-80722_Ebook.pdf (last visited Nov. 24, 2006).

88. World Bank ICRP 6, 24, (Apr. 2001) (stating that these elements were identified by the G-22). *Id.* at 24, n.10 (citing G-22 16, 44-45 (1998)).

second, a legal framework for corporate insolvency (principles 6-16); third, corporate rehabilitation (principles 17-24); four, informal workouts and restructuring (principles 25-26); and five, institutional and regulatory frameworks for implementation of the insolvency system (principles 27-35).

The most recent version of the UNCITRAL Guide has two parts.[90] The first deals with the design of the key objectives and structure of an insolvency law, while Part II includes core insolvency law provisions. Regretfully, until the revised World Bank principles and final UNCITRAL Guide are integrated, approved, and released, it is impossible to identify an international consensus in this area.

B. Interaction between Creditor Rights and Insolvency

Debtor-creditor laws include systems for collecting debts and insolvency systems for terminating the collection of unpaid debts. Collection systems include: secured transactions, using movable property as collateral; mortgages, using fixed property as collateral; and unsecured lending, a system that employs no property or other rights as collateral.[91] One view of the interaction between secured lending and insolvency law sees each as addressing distinct problems, with separate solutions. A secured lending system determines how lenders are repaid, whereas an insolvency system establishes the appropriate treatment for defaulting borrowers.

At the same time, there are important points of intersection between secured transactions and insolvency, and the two systems must be integrated. Neither system can substitute for the other. Thus, reforms of debtor-creditor laws must embrace both secured lending and insolvency law, as well as other closely related areas of law. The need for such drafting integration may be more widely realized in East Asia now, as governments contemplate reform, than would have been the case prior to the 1997-98 financial crisis.

Secured transactions have often been seen as important in improving general welfare by helping create and encourage certain benefits for society as a whole. Regardless of the nature of preferred insolvency laws, East Asian national economies are likely to advance by improving their respective laws on secured lending. This relies on the premise that general access to credit, and the specific terms on which it becomes available, will improve in the borrower's favor as the quality of collateral-taking improves.[92] Effective secured transactions systems that allow for movable property to be used as collateral may allow distressed firms to gain access to credit and so avoid the final resort of insolvency. In such conditions, creditors may anticipate repayment without necessarily initiating the insolvency process.

---

89. This Section, while at first glance appearing to address collateral and secured transactions, addresses these only in the context of insolvency.

90. UNCITRAL, Draft Legislative Guide on Insolvency Law, A/CN.9/WG.V/WP.70 (Parts I and II) (2003).

91. Banking practice in civil law jurisdictions often treats guarantees as providing security, which is not usual in common law systems, regardless of the effect on credit risk.

92. This is not universally accepted. For an example, see Schwartz, *Security Interests*, *supra* note 41, and Schwartz, *Puzzle of Secured Debt*, *supra* note 41 (questioning the economic efficiency of secured lending).

All security interests must be properly publicized. An effective method of publication puts both existing and potential creditors on notice that a debtor company has fewer unencumbered assets available in which potential lenders might obtain meaningful interests. It also provides notice as to the order of priority for the distribution of assets if a company becomes insolvent. Filing or registration systems are comparatively more effective than inefficient systems that rely on possession as a form of security. The efficient enforcement of security interests is central to an effective secured transactions system. It also promotes both informal and judicially supervised workouts. An efficient system will minimize the need for judicial assistance wherever possible and expedite the enforcement process.

In the interaction between secured transactions and insolvency, the essential need is for insolvency law to respect the pre-existing priority rights of secured creditors. If the law poses unreasonable threats to secured lending, banks might increase transaction charges or restrict access to credit. In addition, when a company contemplating insolvency charges or mortgages assets to a creditor in exchange for identifiable value to the company, then as a general rule such charges or mortgages should not be voided by subsequent insolvency proceedings. Secured creditors should also be permitted to convert unsecured debts into secured debts, providing such transactions are completed substantially before the commencement of any insolvency proceedings. The law should provide that fraudulent or commercially unfair transactions that have a security component may be avoided. As a general rule, pre-petition interests should continue in post-petition proceeds, while post-petition grants of security should be permitted. Last, as a general rule, priorities in insolvency should be abolished.

Overall, East Asian economies would benefit from enacting insolvency laws that respect the pre-existing rights of secured creditors. However, in deciding to what extent exceptions may be permitted and how best to balance the needs of secured transactions and insolvency, law-makers in East Asia must first determine which approach they believe most appropriate.

C. Creditor Rights and Insolvency in East Asia

The appraisals given in Table 7 acknowledge extra-legal regulatory guidance for collaborative multi-creditor practice, for example in Hong Kong, Indonesia, Malaysia and Thailand. Regulators in these jurisdictions have attempted to instill informal out-of-court corporate workout practices similar to the well-established "London Rules," or "London Approach," promoted in the 1970s by the Bank of England as an alternative to formal court-based corporate insolvency proceedings involving multiple financial creditors.[93] After the onset of the Asian financial crisis, such out-of-court workout procedures were applied more frequently than court-based formal reorganizations, although the results were not consistent in all jurisdictions.[94] Most jurisdictions also set up public administrative agencies to assist

---

93. Their precept is that financial creditors act in concert rather than any single creditor competitively advancing its position in ways that might provoke premature liquidation.

94. *See supra* note 65 and accompanying text. Informal practice has tended to be successful where the courts have stood ready to support a consensus reached among creditors and debtors, and where debtors or their controlling owners have been unable to challenge the enforcement of foreign judgments.

with the restructuring of domestic financial intermediaries and the disposal of non-performing loans (NPLs).

In both Hong Kong and Singapore, systems and practice are well-established and generally sophisticated, but legislative reform has tended to lag both market practice and the willingness of the courts to intervene creatively in cases of corporate distress.

TABLE 7: DEVELOPMENT OF EFFECTIVE INSOLVENCY SYSTEMS

	Legal framework for corporate insolvency	Corporate insolvency implementation	Judicial decision-making and enforcement	Effective insolvency practitioners
Cambodia	NA	NA	1	1
China[95]	2/3	1	1	1/2
Indonesia	2/3	1	1	1/2
Malaysia	4	4	4	4
Philippines	2/3	2/3	2	2/3
South Korea	4	3/4	3	3/4
Taiwan	3	3	3	3
Thailand	3	2/3	2/3	2/3
Vietnam	1/2	1/2	1	1
Hong Kong	4	5	5	5
Singapore	4/5	5	5	5

1. Insolvency: Pre-1997 Overview

Among the jurisdictions in this study, only Singapore had an insolvency regime adequate to deal with a high number of corporate failures at the opening of the Asian financial crisis. All other jurisdictions were hampered by antiquated or inadequate laws and procedures, many of which dated from colonial times. None maintained an effective formal corporate rescue procedure. Hong Kong and Malaysian corporate insolvency procedures were modeled on mid-20th century English law. Thai law dating from 1940 was influenced by English personal bankruptcy laws, while Indonesian law was mainly Dutch in origin and dated from the late 19th century. South Korea's insolvency regime drew on Japanese law, which derived from German, Austrian, and U.S. principles and statutes. Taiwan's laws were also derived from Japan's laws and later, to a lesser extent from U.S. law, with the last pre-1997 amendments dating from the early 1980s. China's insolvency laws were written more recently, with bankruptcy provisions for state-owned enterprises (SOEs) enacted in 1986, and provisions for non-SOE enterprises with legal person status, in 1991. Vietnam's laws dated from 1994. These regimes used liquidation-

---

95. In regards to the recently enacted bankruptcy law that came into operation on June 1, 2007.

based procedures, with the exception of Singapore. Cambodia still lacks an insolvency framework. For the most part, these insolvency laws were under-utilized.

Insolvency law in Hong Kong, Malaysia, and Singapore share the same basic structure of detailed liquidation or winding-up procedures and an abbreviated scheme of arrangement procedure for use in corporate rescue. The liquidation procedures in these jurisdictions are still the region's most efficient, although in need of modernization, but the scheme of arrangement procedure is cumbersome and expensive. Hong Kong and Malaysian procedures do not provide for an automatic stay on creditor claims in the absence of a winding-up order; Singapore operates a stay only on unsecured creditors. In none of these three jurisdictions are there mechanisms to force uncooperative secured creditors to the bargaining table. The result is that prior the Asian financial crisis, the procedure was rarely employed, although it saw more use in Singapore than in Hong Kong and Malaysia.. Singapore also introduced judicial management procedures in 1987. These procedures may be initiated either by a debtor company or its creditors, and the procedure provides for an automatic stay while a judicial manager assumes the responsibility for running the company and proposing a plan of reorganization for creditor approval.[96]

The evolution of South Korea's insolvency regime has been more complicated. Until recently, the law had three parts, all dating from 1962, which concerned bankruptcy, composition, and reorganization. Rather than develop an insolvency solution, South Korea translated and enacted Japanese laws, so that the Bankruptcy Act was based on the Japanese Bankruptcy Act 1922, itself derived from German law. The Composition Act was based on a Japanese composition law taken from Austrian law; the Reorganization Act copied the Japanese Reorganization Act 1952, derived in turn from the U.S. Bankruptcy Act 1898. The composition law was triggered by a debtor's filing and only provided for temporary relief until creditors voted on a composition plan. The more complicated reorganization process was better suited for larger, public companies..

The Philippines civil law system has long-standing common law aspects, found also in some contemporary European jurisdictions, in that its supreme court decisions are binding as precedents. The pre-1997 Philippines insolvency law dated from 1909 and included a rarely used liquidation procedure and a corporate rescue suspension of payments process taken from Spanish law that was available only to solvent companies experiencing temporary cash flow problems. Any proposal for debt rearrangement required the full payment of debts, and so was rarely used. A rehabilitation procedure was introduced as an alternative to the inflexible suspension of payment process under a 1976 presidential decree, later amended in 1981. Rather than giving jurisdiction for rehabilitation and suspension of payments to the judiciary, however, the amendment granted jurisdiction to the Securities and Exchange Commission (SEC). The rehabilitation procedure provided few rules and contained curiosities, such as providing that creditors were not obliged to approve a rehabilitation plan, and at times treating secured and unsecured creditors alike.

Indonesian and Thai insolvency law also provided for liquidation and suspension of payments procedures, which were also rarely used. Indonesian debtors are able to present a plan of composition even within the liquidation process. The suspension of payments process provides the debtor with additional time to

---

96. Lee Suet Lin Joyce, *Is Singapore's Insolvency Regime Excessively Pro-Creditor?*, 12 INT'L INSOLVENCY REV. 37 (2003) (discussing Singaporean corporate insolvency law).

finalize a repayment plan. Under Thai bankruptcy law, composition is possible either pre-petition or post-petition. An unusual aspect of the Thai Bankruptcy Act 1940 is that its presumption of insolvency appears to have been influenced by the acts of bankruptcy in 19th century English law.

Taiwanese bankruptcy law dates from 1935 and provides for both liquidation and composition. The reorganization law under the Company Law, applicable to public companies, was similar to that in Korea. The reorganization law had not been amended in many years and was over-reliant on the court. The effectiveness of the old law has been criticized for its inconsistency "due in part to a lack of commercial viability on the part of the companies undergoing reorganization."[97] The lengthy reorganization process also enabled some companies to avoid bankruptcy by abusing the reorganization procedures.[98]

China was spared the most severe economic problems of the Asian financial crisis, and as of 1997 was the only jurisdiction in the study group whose bankruptcy laws had recently been promulgated. Nevertheless, at the time of the financial crisis, China was affected by domestic concerns resulting from the poor financial condition of its SOEs and state-owned banks. The insolvency framework in China at that time was an overlapping patchwork that included: a forty-three provision 1986 Bankruptcy Law for SOEs; eight provisions in Chapter XIX of the 1991 PRC Civil Procedure Law applicable to non-SOE enterprises with legal person status; judicial interpretations of these short laws, notably the 2002 interpretation by the Supreme People's Court; and most importantly, several policy decrees issued by the central government which are crucial in understanding the government's approach to insolvency issues. Although the number of insolvencies in China has been increasing, it is generally considered to be far lower than the number of insolvencies that would correspond to the true condition of most SOEs and banks, gauged by generally accepted accounting standards. A new bankruptcy law, under discussion for more than a decade, was finally enacted in August 2006 and is discussed below.

Vietnam enacted a bankruptcy law in 1993 that came into operation in the following year. Unlike China's bifurcated approach—with separate laws for SOEs and non-SOE legal person enterprises,—Vietnam had a unified law. The Vietnamese law was also more expansive than the former Chinese act in that it also applied to enterprises lacking legal personality (e.g. partnerships and sole proprietorships). . In practice, however,, the law was cumbersome in application and rarely used. Its requirement that a debtor exhaust "all financial measures" before being eligible for bankruptcy effectively led to a two-year delay before a bankruptcy could be commenced. A new Vietnamese bankruptcy law came into operation in 2004.[99] Cambodia is currently considering enactment of its first insolvency law.

The profound impact of the 1997 crisis led to an immediate call to reform or replace archaic liquidation regimes and supplement them with modern corporate rescue procedures, including both formal court-based regimes and out-of-court and administrative procedures. Since the crisis, two waves of reform have crossed the

---

97. Eric Tsai & Hui-Erh Yuan, *Taipei, China, in* THE ASIA-PACIFIC RESTRUCTURING AND INSOLVENCY GUIDE 2006 154, 156 (2006).

98. *Id.*

99. *See* Charles Booth, *Drafting Bankruptcy Laws in Socialist Market Economies: Recent Developments in China and Vietnam*, 18 COLUM. J. ASIAN L. 93 (2004).

region. The first included insolvency reforms in Indonesia, Malaysia, the Philippines, South Korea, Taiwan and Thailand. The second includes the new bankruptcy laws enacted in Vietnam in 2004 and China in 2006 and ongoing law reform efforts in Cambodia, Hong Kong, and Singapore, although the reform process in both China and Hong Kong began prior to mid-1997.

2. Insolvency: Post-Financial Crisis Legal Reforms

Thailand was among the states most severely affected by the 1997-98 financial crisis. A new chapter on business reorganization was added to the Bankruptcy Act in 1998 to facilitate corporate rescues. One reform provided for the appointment of a bankruptcy planner to manage the affairs of the debtor company and prepare a plan of reorganization. The new procedure was intended for large corporate debtors owing at least Bt10 million (US$273,000) to their creditors and further provisions would be appropriate to create an efficient procedure for smaller debtors. Further amendments were made to the bankruptcy law in 2000.

An important part of the Thai reforms was the establishment of a bankruptcy court with exclusive jurisdiction for such cases pursuant to the 1999 Act for the Establishment of and Procedure for Bankruptcy Court. The act was amended in 2004, while perceptions of the introduction of the bankruptcy courts have been varied. Initial views were positive, but concerns have increased as to the overall efficacy of these changes. There have been claims of inconsistency among individual courts; a fear that much of the expertise gained through the formation of the courts is lost when judges are rotated into other courts; an increasing backlog of cases; and there are concerns that corruption and fraud may be affecting the courts' work.[100] At present, these concerns appear to have eased somewhat and there is a re-emerging sense that the judicial reforms were for the best.

Indonesia was more severely impacted by the 1997 crisis. In 1998, the Bankruptcy Ordinance was amended by a Government Regulation in Lieu of Law. Indonesia established a Commercial Court after the crisis to hear bankruptcy cases, but according to one commentator the court "has been beset by concerns of corruption and inconsistent application of the Bankruptcy Act"[101] and "[t]he Indonesian Corruption Watch reports of corruption in the legal system is staggering."[102] Many abuses have been publicized, with cases involving Canadian insurer Manulife and the Indonesian-controlled group APP (Asia Pulp & Paper) the most well-known, having been the subject of much controversy and media coverage. However, the IMF and ADB funded a group of local lawyers and judges known as "Team 7" to address such problems and evaluate the Commercial Court's decisions.[103] Further amendments to Indonesian law were enacted in 2004.

South Korea has made the most significant changes to the formal insolvency laws of all the jurisdictions in this study. Its corporate sector, especially the closely-controlled chaebol conglomerates, was traditionally highly-leveraged, which proved an immediate burden in the light of a post-crisis withdrawal of available credit. South

---

100. Vassiliou, *supra* note 66, at 21.
101. Lampros Vassiliou, *The Asian Recovery: Progress and Pitfalls,* Presented at the Global Forum on Insolvency Risk Management, Washington, DC (Jan. 28-29, 2003) at 6.
102. *Id.* at 7.
103. *Id.* at 35.

Korea agreed to enact substantial changes in law at the instigation of the IMF and World Bank in the form of amendments to its tripartite insolvency legislation covering liquidation, composition and reorganization. U.S. bankruptcy law influenced many of these changes. Among notable reforms was the inclusion of creditor committees in composition proceedings and management committees in reorganizations, while the time limit for reorganizations was halved from twenty to ten years. Many changes were intended to expedite reorganization procedures. Further amendments were made in 2000 and 2001, the latter including formalizing an out-of-court Workout Accord in the reorganization legislation to enable creditors to file proceedings to bind foreign creditors. A more recent major change to insolvency law was a Debtors' Rehabilitation and Bankruptcy Act (DRBA), which came into effect on April 1, 2006, and for the first time consolidated the three parallel insolvency acts. The new act further expedites corporate rescue processes, expands the reorganization system and abolishes the Composition Act. The task for South Korea may now be to ensure that its new legal framework is properly implemented, for which further practitioner training is likely to be necessary.

Amendments to Philippines law were made in July 2000. Among the most significant changes was the transfer of jurisdiction for rehabilitation and suspension of payment cases from a state regulatory agency to the courts.[104] Interim Rules of Procedure for Corporate Rehabilitation were promulgated in December 2000, in far more detailed form than the procedures under a prior Presidential Decree. Suspension of payment cases and corporate rehabilitation have become more common since the financial crisis, but delays remain a problem under the new regime obtaining post-petition financing has remained difficult. Other reforms are currently under discussion, notably a Corporate Recovery and Liquidation Act and a Corporate Recovery Act. It is hoped that the former includes a provision for fast-track rehabilitation but congressional passage of these bills has been slow. The goal for the Philippines is also to increase the institutional capacity of the judiciary and of insolvency practitioners. Transferring jurisdiction for insolvency cases from the SEC to the courts is understandable, but it ensures that the Philippines is the sole jurisdiction in the study core where administrative and judicial enforcement capacity have decreased since the financial crisis. Another goal for the Philippines will be to better protect the rights of secured creditors.

A reform of the Taiwanese Company Law in 2001 streamlined the reorganization procedures. These were the first major reforms to the procedures in roughly thirty years. Among the changes to the law were reducing the length of the reorganization process and requiring that companies using the procedures "be capable of being revived through reorganisation."[105] It has been noted that several successful reorganizations have recently been carried out and that the changes have enhanced the viability of the new law as a restructuring tool and reduced the incentives for debtors to abuse the reorganization process.[106] Further changes to the insolvency laws are also being considered, including a proposal to unify the bankruptcy and reorganization laws into a single code.

---

104. *See supra* Part V(C)1.
105. Tsai & Yuan, *supra* note 97, at 156.
106. *Id.*

In August 2006, China enacted a new insolvency law that came into operation in June 2007. This new law is the result of an insolvency law reform process that dates back to 1994. This law applies to all legal person enterprises and unifies the existing patchwork of bankruptcy laws, decrees, and judicial interpretations. This new law radically improves both the liquidation and corporate rescue processes. At the heart of these reforms is the introduction of an office of the professional administrator to replace the current inefficient liquidation team model. The new law includes a detailed corporate rescue process that draws heavily on Chapter 11 of the U.S. Bankruptcy Act (for example, providing for post-petition financing and a limited cramdown). These procedures will allow for reorganizations led either by the administrator or a debtor-in-possession (under the supervision of the administrator).

The main substantive issue delaying the enactment of the new law was a conflict as to how to resolve the interests of secured creditors and employees in cases where company funds prove insufficient to meet wages in full. A compromise was reached providing that secured creditors will have priority over all workers' claims arising after August 27, 2006, but that certain wage, medical, and insurance claims of workers arising before that date will have priority over the claims of secured creditors. Another controversial issue during the drafting process was whether SOEs should be made subject to the new law. The new law provides that special matters regarding the bankruptcy of SOEs shall no longer continue to be handled under State Council regulations. Time will tell whether that will be the case.

In reforming its insolvency law, Vietnam was interested in China's approach to similar issues. When both Vietnam and China issued new draftlaws in 2002, the former was at an earlier stage of development. However, Vietnam avoided the contentious delays that occurred in China and enacted its law in 2004. This abolished the former requirements that a debtor must first exhaust "all financial measures" to become eligible for bankruptcy relief, and represents a significant reform. However, in comparison to China, Vietnam's reform approach was gradualist, lacks a "driver" of the new legal process (i.e., does not have an official equivalent to the Chinese administrator), and has fewer checks and balances.

Attempts at Hong Kong insolvency law reform pre-date the 1997 financial crisis. In 1996 the Hong Kong Law Reform Commission set out the framework for a new regime, by which a qualified specialist called a "provisional supervisor" would after commencement of the process take control of the company and be responsible for drafting a proposal for creditor agreement. The first draft bill was gazetted in 2000, and offered many advantages over current law, but a primary flaw has been a proposal that employees' salaries be paid in full or sufficient funds placed in trust for the purpose.[107] Fortunately, in a line of cases beginning in 2002, the judiciary was receptive to the use of provisional liquidation as a mechanism to facilitate corporate rescue. However, the use of provisional liquidation to assist with corporate rescue was narrowly re-interpreted in the recent case of *Re Legend International Resorts Ltd.*, which required that a company's assets first be in jeopardy for a provisional liquidator to be appointed.[108] The enactment of a provisional supervision regime in the foreseeable future is quite unlikely.[109]

---

107. *See* Philip Smart & Charles Booth, *Reforming Corporate Rescue Procedures in Hong Kong*, 1 J. OF CORP. L. STUD. 485 (2001); Booth, *supra* note 99.
108. [2006] HKCA 67; CACV000207/2005, Mar. 1, 2006.
109. *See* Charles Booth, *The Race of Two Tortoises: Insolvency Law Reform in Hong Kong and*

Singapore's insolvency regime is currently the most comprehensive of the study group. For more than five years, schemes of arrangements have proven more popular than judicial management cases. Among the reasons are that a stay on unsecured creditor action in the scheme of arrangement procedure gives the debtor company sufficient time to proceed to propose such a scheme; it can remain in possession of assets and equipment; and less adverse publicity and commercial stigma appears to arise in relation to a scheme of arrangement than from many judicial management cases. As with Hong Kong and Malaysian law, a weakness of Singapore's model is the bifurcation of corporate insolvency procedures in company law, and the personal insolvency procedures in bankruptcy law. Singapore is considering the enactment of unified legislation to address this problem, but this will not take place in the short term.

3. Insolvency: Post-Financial Crisis Out-of-Court Reforms

Although legal insolvency reforms received much attention due to the needs created by the Asian financial crisis, the time taken to enact and implement any such legislation is inevitably protracted. While legislative reforms were first considered, other efforts began to save companies whose businesses could create value for creditors and other stakeholders. These efforts led to two types of reforms, the first being the promulgation of out-of-court workout procedures based on the London Approach.[110] These included the Bangkok Approach, Malaysia's Corporate Debt Restructuring Committee (CDRC), the Hong Kong Approach, the Jakarta Initiative, and the Workout Accord in South Korea. In contrast to the general experience in Europe, this semi-formal approach has been successful in cases where the parties involved are overwhelmingly of a single domicile. Still, they have been only modestly helpful in Asia's many post-1998 cross-border multi-creditor restructurings, despite a large number of such cases being managed by banks operating in Hong Kong.[111]

More radically, where national banking sectors were severely affected by delinquent loans, the second alternative provided for establishment of administrative asset management agencies to assist with the restructuring and disposal of NPLs, including the Indonesian Bank Restructuring Agency (IBRA), Malaysia's Pengurusan Danaharta Nasional Bhd (Danaharta), and the Thai Asset Management Company (TAMC). For the most part, these entities were created as part of emergency measures and several are in the process of being shut down.[112]

Hong Kong established its Hong Kong Approach to Corporate Difficulties in 1999, modeled on the London Approach, with the backing of the self-regulated

---

China, CHINA L. REP., Nov. 2006, at 3.

110. *See supra* note 93 and accompanying text, but note that the "the effectiveness of such semi-voluntary arrangements has been eroded by the growing use of loan sales and other forms of credit risk transfer"; *see* BERRY HSU ET AL., FINANCIAL MARKETS IN HONG KONG: LAW & PRACTICE 154 (2006). Outside Asia, the practice has influenced the recent development of protocols for the settlement of credit default swaps.

111. *Id.*

112. The forerunner model of these entities was the U.S. Resolution Trust Corporation, which from 1989-95 acted as a federal asset disposal conduit for failed savings and loan and other housing finance organizations.

Hong Kong Association of Banks and the government's Hong Kong Monetary Authority.

South Korea established an out-of-court workout process in June 1998, in the form of a Workout Accord among financial intermediaries. The process was imperfect, though, as it excluded foreign creditors and provided no priority for post-commencement financing. In 2001 the Workout Accord procedure was promulgated as part of the reorganization law to address these two problems and formally expired on December 31, 2005. The Korean Asset Management Company (KAMCO) assisted in resolving the commercial banking sector's sizeable accumulation of NPLs. Unlike similar Asian asset management companies (AMCs), KAMCO was not a temporary entity established to deal with the 1997 crisis, and had been formed in 1962. Indonesia established the Jakarta Initiative to assist with out-of-court restructuring and set up IBRA to deal with the impaired assets of Indonesian financial intermediaries. IBRA became very substantial, and was the largest national landowner before its dissolution in 2004.[113] Its results were less effective than those of state-sponsored AMCs elsewhere, notably KAMCO or Danaharta, in particular due to a policy of acquiring distressed assets at inflated balance sheet prices rather than establish a realistic market value—even though the payments made to the transferor banks were not necessarily of the same order.

Malaysia established CDRC to assist with informal out-of-court rescues and an asset management entity (Danaharta) to assist with problems encountered by the financial sector. Danaharta had strong powers of enforcement and its results are still viewed as important in addressing post-crisis problems in Malaysia.

In 1998, the Bank of Thailand established an informal out-of-court restructuring procedure for financial creditors known as the Bangkok Approach, headed by the Corporate Debt Restructuring Advisory Committee. TAMC was created pursuant to emergency legislation in June 2001 to assist in the disposal of financial sector NPLs.

China established four AMCs to address accumulated NPLs at each of the largest state-owned commercial banks. The first, China Xinda Asset Management Company (Cinda) for Construction Bank of China and China Development Bank, was formed in April 1999. It was followed by China Huarong Asset Management Corporation for Industrial and Commercial Bank of China, Dongfang Asset Management Company (Oriental) for Bank of China, and China Great Wall Asset Management Company for Agricultural Bank of China. Regional AMCs were also established, including the important Guangdong Guangye Asset Management Company.

Like China, Vietnam established AMCs connected to the commercial banks to dispose of NPLs. In addition, Vietnam established a national Debts and Assets Trading Company managed by the Ministry of Finance.

Taiwan also has established AMCs to assist with the disposal of NPLs through the promulgation of the Financial Institutions Merger Act of 2000.

---

113. Vassiliou, *supra* note 101, at 35.

4. Interaction between Creditor Rights and Insolvency

A theme of this study is that effective insolvency regimes go hand-in-hand with effective secured transaction regimes. This parallel development of secured transaction laws is absent from most of the jurisdictions considered. The overall implementation of insolvency regimes throughout the region would benefit from the improvement or introduction of effective secured transactions systems, for it is within insolvency cases that the integrity of secured transactions and the rights of secured creditors are fully tested.

The English system of company law adapted in Hong Kong, Malaysia, and Singapore puts secured creditors in a relatively strong position in insolvency matters, and there is thus a high level of predictability as to the rights of secured creditors in these three jurisdictions. Secured creditors act outside a liquidation and are not subject to a general stay against creditors. Unless agreed otherwise, they also act outside any scheme-of-arrangement process. It is only in judicial management cases in Singapore that secured creditors are made subject to the general stay.

TABLE 8: COMPATIBILITY OF CREDITOR RIGHTS AND INSOLVENCY SYSTEMS

	Principal source and system of current law[114]	Form of legal transplant	Compatibility of systems relating to creditor rights and those permitting secured transactions
Cambodia	French civil	Imposition	NA
China[115]	Mixed (German civil; Socialist)	Adoption	1/2
Indonesia	Dutch civil	Imposition	1/2
Malaysia	English common	Imposition	3/4
Philippines	Mixed (Spanish civil; U.S.)	Imposition	1/2
South Korea	German civil	Mixed	3/4
Taiwan	German, Japanese civil	Imposition / adoption	3/4
Thailand	French civil	Adoption	1/2
Vietnam	Mixed (French civil; Socialist)	Imposition / adoption	1
Hong Kong	English common	Imposition	4/5
Singapore	English common	Imposition	4/5

114. For guidance only: questions of legal inheritance or transplant are beyond the direct scope of this article. The indications given in Table 8 take no real account of mixed jurisdictions, or of what has been termed "chthonic law," whether ancient or contemporary. See H. PATRICK GLENN, LEGAL TRADITIONS OF THE WORLD: SUSTAINABLE DIVERSITY IN LAW 58-114 (2004).

115. In regard to the recently enacted bankruptcy law that came into operation in June 2007.

In China, the rights of a secured creditor historically have depended upon whether a bankruptcy case is entered pursuant to government policy decrees or bankruptcy laws, though the new bankruptcy law claims to bring this distinction to an end. Under the old regime, there was a traditional priority scheme in the bankruptcy laws whereby employee claims ranked after those of secured creditors. In contrast, in policy bankruptcies, secured creditors could lose priority in land-use rights and other secured assets to employees, so as to assist the latter with resettlement and other entitlements. However, as noted above, under the recently agreed compromise, the new Chinese bankruptcy law provides that secured creditors will have priority over all workers' claims arising after August 27, 2006, but that certain wage, medical, and insurance claims of workers arising before that date will have priority over the claims of secured creditors. Although secured creditors are subject to a stay in liquidations and reorganizations, they retain priority in payment to the extent of their collateral.

In summary, China, Indonesia, the Philippines, and Vietnam adopt the U.S. approach by which secured creditors are subject to an automatic stay in both liquidations and reorganizations. In contrast, in South Korea, Singapore, and Thailand, secured creditors are subject to a moratorium in reorganizations, but not in liquidations or compositions. Last, secured creditors of companies in Hong Kong, Malaysia, and Taiwan may act unilaterally outside both bankruptcy and reorganization. In jurisdictions where secured creditors are subject to an automatic stay, the courts have rarely applied principles of adequate protection when those creditors seek to be exempt.[116] In the Philippines, less account is taken than elsewhere of the views of secured creditors in the preparation and sanction of reorganization plans. In some instances, secured creditors have been required to share *pari passu* with unsecured creditors.

Two main areas of law in the interaction of secured creditors and insolvency needing improvement in most jurisdictions are first, protection for secured creditors seeking exemption from the automatic stay; and second, limiting employee priority in claims over properly established secured interests.

5. Summary

In an immediate post-crisis review of regional insolvency law reforms, the ADB found that the number of insolvency cases remained low in Indonesia, Malaysia, the Philippines, South Korea, and Thailand, despite rising from pre-crisis levels. Indonesia, the Philippines, and Thailand were identified as having "extraordinarily low" liquidations, and Indonesia and Thailand were identified as jurisdictions in which the use of new formal reorganization laws was surprisingly low. Liquidations were most numerous in South Korea and Malaysia, with Malaysia having more. South Korea had by far the greatest number of reorganizations, but lower than might have been predicted based on national output losses in 1997-98.

The review also found that out-of-court processes were used far more often than formal insolvency laws except in South Korea, where their overall use was also "surprisingly low."[117] Data for the study were obtained from observations up to mid-

---

116. Vasiliou, *supra* note 101, at 8.
117. *See* Report on Insolvency Law Reforms, *supra* note 65, at 10-11, 70-75.

1999, but subsequent anecdotal observations support these findings. It remains difficult to obtain accurate insolvency case data from most jurisdictions in Asia, and harder still to locate accurate assessments of out-of-court workouts. However, case data may not be the sole benchmark of success. One benefit of enacting formal corporate rescue laws is that by setting outvoting minimums and implementation requirements for reorganization plans, a framework for extra-judicial negotiations is created that addresses problems of the type caused by intransigent holdout creditors, both before and since the region's financial crisis. If recalcitrant creditors currently use such tactics, a debtor or creditor may threaten formal insolvency proceedings so as to cause the holdout creditor to be outvoted.

The ADB study demonstrates that the promulgation of new insolvency laws is only part of achieving an effective insolvency system. Although a new law may be modern in design and enacted to facilitate corporate rescue, its impact will take time to discern. In contrast, the benefits from enabling out-of-court rescue processes have typically been more immediate.

Of the core jurisdictions discussed in this article, implementation of an effective corporate insolvency regime is best achieved in Singapore and Hong Kong, which are also the jurisdictions that have made the least changes to their laws since the 1997-98 crisis. Hong Kong is unusual in that while it lacks an effective formal corporate rescue law, it scores highly, largely due to the adaptation of the provisional liquidation procedure and the creativity of judiciary and insolvency practitioners in crafting out-of-court corporate rescues. The main goals for both Hong Kong and Malaysia remain the need to enact modern corporate rescue systems and to update aspects of liquidation procedures. The latter is also relevant for Singapore and most other countries examined here. It is expected that Cambodia will soon enact a modern insolvency law.

The demand following the enactment of formal insolvency laws is to stimulate human resources through greater judicial competence as well as training effective insolvency practitioners. Specialized courts or benches are valuable but experiences in Indonesia and Thailand demonstrate that the creation of such courts is not a panacea. It is important for the judiciary to strive for consistency, and to eliminate corruption and the trading of influence. Professional and judicial training are crucial in this process. Another important feature of strengthening the implementation of the law is the development of a government agency to regulate insolvency processes. The Official Receiver's Office in Hong Kong and the Official Assignee's offices in Malaysia and Singapore each perform this function effectively. It is also crucial for practitioners to discuss regularly contemporary insolvency developments among themselves and with national regulators. Hong Kong currently offers a good example of such interaction, which contributes to the overall effectiveness of the sector. Lawyers and accountants meet regularly for training sessions run by the Insolvency Interest Group, housed in the Hong Kong Institute of Certified Professional Accountants. The latter runs insolvency training courses including an advanced diploma course that is recognized by the Official Receiver's Office. Such arrangements could serve as a model for the region.

The activities of the World Bank and UNCITRAL show that there is no single set of provisions for an effective insolvency regime. Nonetheless, three issues have commonly caused difficulties in the implementation of new insolvency laws in the region. First, the granting of over-generous priority or preference to employees can lead to an unconstructive response by secured creditors and ultimately adversely affect bank lending and secured transactions. Second, it may be a serious disincentive for many officers and directors of distressed companies to be replaced immediately by an outside administrator, especially among smaller family-controlled companies that are seeking relief from creditors. Last, the commencement criteria should be as clear as possible, for example, avoiding balance sheet insolvency tests that may rely on imperfect accounting standards.

VI. CONTRACT ENFORCEMENT AND DISPUTE RESOLUTION

The most critical neglect throughout the region is in enforcement and implementation, with the partial exceptions of Hong Kong and Singapore. According to Haselman, Pistor, and Vig:

> The major function attributed to law is that it empowers creditors to enforce their contracts. Effective legal institutions reduce the risk of lending and therefore result in greater lending volume in an economy as a share of GDP. Implicit in this view of how law affects economic outcome is that all actors in the economy benefit from better law.[118]

This may suggest that the law matters less than its enforcement. Both theory and experience support this position. Coase was first to describe the importance of delineation and enforcement of commercial contracts, in analyses based upon observations of industrial practice.[119] In an environment of imperfect markets with real transaction costs, parties will seek efficient results through contracting. Unfortunately, transaction costs extend to the expense of enforcement, without which contracting cannot produce solutions to market imperfections nor lead to stable long-term outcomes. Rather, contracting will tend towards sub-optimal instantaneous transactions such as barter, which is in part a state from which the least developed members of the study core have recently emerged.

The enforcement of contracts requires a system of governance capable of producing, applying, and policing effective solutions. Part II of this article showed that a range of such systems may be theoretically capable of producing this result, and history has provided many disparate examples. Enforcement of contracts is not synonymous with the existence of the rule of law, but just one component of a system that can be so described. The rule of law is not a precondition for a market economy, despite generally being considered an important factor in economic development and highly conducive to financial market development. Yet a governance system that enforces contracts and resolves commercial disputes in a credible and predictable manner is essential to a basic market economy, as well as allowing financial markets to develop beyond the simplest single instantaneous transactions. This is important for institutional concerns such as the enforcement of financial contracts, efficient insolvency, and collateral systems, and dispute resolution procedures. In this context, mechanisms for contract enforcement and resolving commercial disputes may also be more important than specific laws.

---

118. Haselmann, Pistor & Vig, *supra* note 38.
119. *See* Coase, *supra* note 43; R. H. Coase, *The Problem of Social Cost*, 3 J. L. & ECON. 1 (1960).

There are four further concerns. First, broadening the availability of real property ownership and mechanisms to support its use, especially relating to enforcement and commercial dispute resolution mechanisms. Second, the need more simply to delineate the provisions for secured transactions, in particular to provide for security interests in intangible property. Third, the development of effective registration systems to cover a range of assets, including real property, security, and intangibles, and to simplify the use and availability of collateral and its enforcement, leading to reductions in transactions costs. Last, where judicial systems for enforcement and dispute resolution are ineffective, the support of appropriate mechanisms for creditor and debtor self-assistance deserve, provided that they are transparently fair and just. This includes encouraging greater use of commercial arbitration.

The foregoing Tables 2, 5, 7, and 8 show that most jurisdictions addressed in this Article have developed generally acceptable laws relating to creditor rights and insolvency but have failed fully to reform their collateral and secured transaction regimes. At the same time, where such insolvency or collateral laws have been enacted, few jurisdictions have been effective in their implementation and enforcement. This is the concern to which legislative and administrative attention needs to be devoted and which clearly demonstrates the linkage between effective governance, economic, and legal systems and property, collateral, and creditor rights in East Asia.

[3]

Economic Development and the Rights Hypothesis: The China Problem

DONALD C. CLARKE

1. Introduction

An important school of thought in institutional economics holds that economic growth requires a legal order offering stable and predictable rights of property and contract because the absence of such rights discourages investment and specialization. In general, the legal order described by this school is something along the lines of the legal systems of the developed countries of the West (excluding Japan, which is rarely discussed). I will call this proposition the "Rights Hypothesis." Without the security of expectations offered by such a legal order, according to the Rights Hypothesis, the risks of a great number of otherwise beneficial transactions far outweigh their expected return, and as a result such transactions simply do not occur. Society is mired in an economy of short-term deals between actors bound by non-legal ties such as family solidarity which by their nature cannot bind large numbers of strangers.[1]

The best known discussion of the relationship between legal institutions and the economy is, of course, Max Weber's.[2] A classic Weberian formulation of the role of legal institutions in the economy states: "The universal predominance of the market consociation requires . . . a legal system the functioning of which is *calculable* in accordance with rational rules."[3] (As will be shown later, this is not exactly the Rights Hypothesis in its most ambitious form.) The law and development movement in the 1960s produced a great deal of literature advancing the view that "through institutions such as contract and private property rights, modern law promotes the develop-

---

DONALD C. CLARKE is Professor of Law at the University of Washington School of Law.

1. See Knack & Keefer, "Institutions and Economic Performance: Cross-Country Tests Using Alternative Institutional Measures," 7 *Econ. & Pol.* 207, 210-11 (1995).

2. See generally, *Max Weber on Law in Economy and Society* (Max Rheinstein ed., 1954); Trubek, "Max Weber on Law and the Rise of Capitalism," 1972 *Wisc. L. Rev.* 720 (1972).

3. *Max Weber on Law in Economy and Society*, supra n. 2 (emphasis in original). See also Max Weber, *The Protestant Ethic and the Spirit of Capitalism* 25 (Talcott Parsons trans., 1958) ("[M]odern rational capitalism has need, not only of the technical means of production, but of a calculable legal system and of administration in terms of formal rules.").

ment of markets and hence economic growth."⁴ More recently, institutional economics has given new energy to the Rights Hypothesis. A typical formulation can be found in the work of Douglass C. North, who asserts that "impersonal exchange with third-party enforcement . . . [via an effective judicial system] has been the crucial underpinning of successful modern economies involved in the complex contracting necessary for modern economic growth"⁵ and that "the inability of societies to develop effective, low-cost enforcement of contracts is the most important source of both historical stagnation and contemporary underdevelopment in the Third World."⁶ North and others also emphasize the importance of secure property rights: "In response to expropriatory threats of one kind or another, entrepreneurs not only reduce investment, they also invest in less specialized capital (human and physical), which can be moved more easily from one activity to another".⁷ It is probably not unfair, therefore, to sum up the Rights Hypothesis in the words of a recent critic: "productive capitalism needs formal adjudication, judicially enforced contracts,⁸ and inviolable property rights".⁹

---

4. Trubek, "Toward a Social Theory of Law: An Essay on the Study of Law and Development," 82 *Yale L. J.* 1 (1982) (criticizing this conception). For a list of representative studies in this vein, see id. at 3, n.7. For a critique and subsequent defense of the law and development movement, see respectively Trubek & Galanter, "Scholars in Self-Estrangement: Some Reflections on the Crisis in Law and Development Studies in the United States," 1974 *Wisc. L. Rev.* 1062 (1974) and Burg, "Law and Development: A Review of the Literature and a Critique of 'Scholars in Self-Estrangement'," 25 *Am. J. Comp. L.* 492 (1977).

5. Douglass C. North, *Institutions, Institutional Change and Economic Performance* 35 (1990)

6. Id. at 54.

7. Knack & Keefer, supra n. 1, at 219.

8. In this article I generally try use the term "judicial enforcement of contracts" to refer to the enforcement of contract rights through a formal legal system of the kind envisaged in the Rights Hypothesis.

9. Upham, "Speculations on Legal Informality: On Winn's 'Relational Practices and the Marginalization of Law'," 28 *Law & Soc'y Rev.* 233, 237 (1994). As Sussman and Yafeh note, "The idea that the protection of property rights is of utmost importance for the economic and financial development of nations has become extremely influential in economics in recent years." Nathan Sussman & Yishay Yafeh, Constitutions, Commitment, and the Historical Evidence on the Relation between Institutions, Property Rights and Financial Development (January 7, 2003) (unpublished manuscript, on file with author), available at http://papers.ssrn.com/sol3/papers.cfm?abstract_id=347640.

The literature here is too vast to cite; influential works include North, supra n. 5; Weingast, "Constitutions as Governance Structures: The Political Foundations of Secure Markets," 1 *J. Inst'l & Theoretical Econ.* 286 (1993); North & Weingast, "Constitutions and Commitment: The Evolution of Institutions Governing Public Choice in Seventeenth-Century Britain," 49 *J. Econ. Hist.* 803, 803-32 (1989); La Porta, Lopez-de-Silanes, Shleifer & Vishny, "Legal Determinants of External Finance," 52 *J. Fin.* 1131 (1997); La Porta, Lopez-de-Silanes, Shleifer & Vishny, "Law and Finance," 106 *J. Pol. Econ.* 1113 (1998).

2. The Problem

The history of China's post-Mao economic reform has provided interesting material against which to test the Rights Hypothesis.[10] Two features of that history in particular stand out for the purposes of this article. First, the institutions by which rights are enforced, in particular courts, are perceived to be weak, and thus rights are perceived to be unenforceable.[11] (It is perception, which determines whether persons are willing to invest and make deals, that counts for purposes of the Rights Hypothesis.[12]) Second, China has indeed enjoyed substantial economic growth in recent years.[13]

There are several ways to interpret these observations together with the Rights Hypothesis. First, the hypothesis could be right and the observation that rights are not enforced wrong, or at least incomplete: rights are necessary for growth to occur, and growth is occurring: although courts don't effectively enforce rights, rights are enforced somewhere else in the system through some other mechanism. There are, of course, various mechanisms for the vindication of claims arising out of contractual relationships that do not involve the court system. For reasons beyond the scope of this article, I believe that it is often inappropriate to think of this as the enforcement of *rights* as such.[14] Nevertheless, it is important not to assume that a

---

10. For a recent qualitative attempt to assess the impact of legal institutions upon economic development in several East Asian countries, see Katharina Pistor & Philip A. Wellons, *The Role of Law and Legal Institutions in Asian Economic Development* (1999); see also Ohnesorge, "The Rule of Law, Economic Development, and the Developmental States of Northeast Asia," in *Law and Development in East and Southeast Asia* 91 (Christoph Antons ed., 2003).

11. For a detailed look at the enforcement powers of Chinese courts, see Clarke, "Power and Politics in the Chinese Court System: The Enforcement of Civil Judgments," 10 *Colum. J. Asian L.* 1 (1996) and Randall Peerenboom, *China's Long March Toward Rule of Law* 326-28 (2002).

12. See Johnson, McMillan & Woodruff, "Courts and Relational Contracts," 18 *J. L. Econ. & Org.* 221, 227 (2002) (in the theory of repeated games, "the relevant question is . . . what [the entrepreneur] believes would happen if there is a dispute in the future").

13. Both the proposition that China's legal system does not provide strong enforcement of rights and the proposition that China has enjoyed strong economic growth in the era of economic reform will, for reasons of space, be taken for granted in this article and not specifically supported by argument. Obviously, a great deal could be said about both these propositions.

14. For example, it is frequently suggested in the literature that criminal gangs could constitute a kind of informal mechanism for the enforcement of rights when the formal legal system is unable to do so. See, e.g., McMillan & Woodruff, "Private Order Under Dysfunctional Public Order," 98 *Mich. L. Rev.* 2421, 2457-58 (2000) (viewing mafia as an element of "private ordering" that arises when legal systems do not function costlessly); Leitzel, Gaddy & Alexeev, "Mafiosi and Matrioshki: Organized Crime and Russian Reform," 13 *Brookings Rev.* (Winter 1995), at 26, 28 ("[P]erhaps [the mafia's] main benefit is contract enforcement."); Hay, Shleifer & Vishny, "Toward a Theory of Legal Reform," 40 *Eur. Econ. Rev.* 559, 560 (1996) (viewing organized crime as one of several "mechanisms of enforcing agreements and resolving disputes"). This literature fails to consider a crucial distinction between "enforcement" by criminals and enforcement by other informal actors such as peer groups, chambers of commerce,

mechanism for the enforcement of rights *cannot* exist simply because it turns out that courts are not that mechanism.

Second, the hypothesis could be right and the observation of growth a misinterpretation of the data: although substantial growth is occurring now, it may be that much *more* growth would have occurred with a different set of legal institutions, or that the growth we see is a one-time transitional phenomenon that will soon stall out in the absence of legal reform along the lines suggested by the Rights Hypothesis. This interpretation is grounded in the fact that the beginning of the reform era saw numerous unsatisfied market segments, particularly in household goods and services, caused by the standard socialist restrictions on economic activity in these sectors. The relaxation of restrictions meant extraordinary profit opportunities for early entrants — so much so that there was substantial resentment among salaried workers and intellectuals at the hitherto unimaginable sums of money being earned by shoe repairers and hairdressers. Ultimately, however, one would expect additional entrants to compete profits down to normal levels, and indeed the statistics appear to bear out this prediction.[15] At some point all niches will be filled except those in which success requires security of property rights or effective judicial enforcement of contracts. At this point, if the Rights Hypothesis is correct, growth will taper off.

Third, the hypothesis could simply be wrong: rights aren't protected but significant growth occurs, and therefore there is not an important connection between the two. As David Trubek pointed out thirty years ago, to say, as did Weber, that a *market* requires a system of effectively enforced rights of property and contract is not the same as saying that *economic development* requires such a legal system unless we take the further step of positing that the only path to economic development is through the market.[16] But the history of the Soviet Union and of the People's Republic of China shows that development, at least up to a certain level, can in fact be achieved through planning and without a substantial role for the market.[17]

Moreover, it does seem that a market system can go a considerable distance in the absence of a functioning formal legal system that enforces rights of property and contract. McMillan and Woodruff, for example, document a thriving private sector in Vietnam, even though virtually none of the enterprise managers they interviewed believed

---

clan elders, and the like: criminals generally make no attempt to ascertain the rights and the wrongs of the dispute, and act on behalf of the party that pays them. Criminals enforce not rights but *demands*; they do not concern themselves with whether such demands are morally or legally justified.

15. See Barry Naughton, *Growing out of the Plan* 150-51 (1995).
16. See Trubek, supra n. 4, at 15.
17. See, e.g., Naughton, supra n. 15, at 53 ("[T]he Chinese economy appears to have strong growth potential regardless of system. Even before reforms, China's economy was growing at respectable rates.").

that courts were of any value in dispute resolution.[18] Certainly it would be difficult to assert that contract rights were *better* enforced in Vietnam today than in Vietnam under socialism, and it is by no means clear that contracts are better enforced in China today than in China in the Qing dynasty or as far back as the Han two millennia ago,[19] yet growth rates are surely very different. It may therefore be an overstatement to identify the absence of "effective, low-cost enforcement of contracts" as "*the* most important source of both historical stagnation and contemporary underdevelopment in the Third World."[20] Perhaps while having institutions for the low-cost enforcement of contracts is better, all other things being equal, than not having them, the contribution to growth made by such institutions is swamped by the contributions made by other factors.

Equally important and often overlooked is that Weber's formulation, whatever its accuracy, does not strictly speaking require that the legal system provide enforceable *rights* — that is, the actual ability, in certain special circumstances, to choose to invoke the coercive power of the state in support of one's personal interests. All that is needed is that the system operate in a predictable manner. Therefore, the Rights Hypothesis could be wrong in focusing so strongly on the particular institution of rights.[21]

As can be seen, each of the above interpretations has a certain plausibility. On the other hand, they cannot all be correct. In this article I will attempt to propose an understanding of Chinese legal institutions and their impact on economic transactions (and on investment in particular) that will allow us, if not to reconcile, at least to refine these different interpretations to make them less mutually inconsistent. More broadly, I will propose a reformulation of the Rights Hypothesis that retains the emphasis on security of property but substantially downgrades the importance of a formal legal system that provides effective enforcement of contract rights.

3. ANALYSIS

Perhaps the main problem with the Rights Hypothesis is that it is too sweeping and fuses concepts that ought to be kept separate. Its

---

18. See McMillan & Woodruff, "Dispute Prevention Without Courts in Vietnam," 15 *J. L. Econ. & Org.* 637, 639-41 (1999).
19. On enforcement of contracts in the Qing, see generally Philip C. Huang, *Civil Justice in China: Representation and Practice in the Qing* (1996) (arguing that the traditional Chinese legal system was more concerned with civil matters than previously believed); on enforcement of contracts in the Han, see Scogin, "Between Heaven and Man: Contract and the State in Han Dynasty China," 63 *S. Cal. L. Rev.* 1325 (1990) (making a similar argument); see also Scogin, "Civil 'Law' in Traditional China: History and Theory," in *Civil Law in Qing and Republican China* 35 (Kathryn Bernhardt & Philip C. Huang eds., 1994).
20. North, supra n. 5, at 54 (emphasis added).
21. See infra text accompanying nn. 64-67 for further discussion.

proponents too often forget the difference between a market system in particular and economic development in general, between rights in particular and predictability in general, and between contract rights and property rights.[22]

a. Contract Rights and Property Rights

Proponents of the Rights Hypothesis assert that the legal systems of developed capitalist economies do two important things: they enforce contractual rights against one's contractual partners, and they provide security for one's property. Thus, if a contract is breached, one gets damages or specific performance, and the government neither confiscates one's property unpredictably nor allows other private parties to do so.

These two things, however, are very different. It is quite possible in principle to imagine a system where there exists no effective machinery for the impartial third-party enforcement of contracts through a formal legal system, but where the government neither engages in unpredictable confiscation of property nor allows others to do so. In such a system, one will not, of course, see any economic activity that requires effective third-party enforcement of contracts through a formal legal system, but one will see activity that merely requires security of property from confiscation.

For what kind of activity is the enforcement of contract rights through a formal legal system the *sine qua non*? The substantial literature on informal and social sanctions, repeated games, and self-enforcement mechanisms[23] suggests that in the end there is perhaps only one kind of deal that can *never* be done without an effective formal legal system: a one-shot deal between strangers who have neither the desire nor the expectation of ever doing business again with the other or with anyone known by the other. In all other kinds of deals, it is possible in principle for another mechanism to provide

---

22. By "contract rights" I mean roughly the right to have a promisor of equal legal status held to her promise or required to pay damages; by "security of property rights" I mean roughly the probability that one's property will not be confiscated unpredictably by (a) government or (b) other parties that government is unwilling or unable to stop. Predictable confiscation is economically indistinguishable from a tax, and while excessive taxes can of course stifle economic activity, that is not an issue within the scope of this article.

23. See, e.g., Black & Kraakman, "A Self-Enforcing Model of Corporate Law," 109 *Harv. L. Rev.* 1911 (1996); Bull, "The Existence of Self-Enforcing Implicit Contracts," 102 *Q. J. Econ.* 147 (1987); Greif, "Contract Enforceability and Economic Institutions in Early Trade: The Maghribi Traders' Coalition," 83 *Am. Econ. Rev.* 525 (1993); Telser, "A Theory of Self-Enforcing Agreements," 53 *J. Bus.* 27 (1980); Winn, "Relational Practices and the Marginalization of Law: Informal Practices of Small Businesses in Taiwan," 28 *L. & Soc. Rev.* 193 (1994); and sources cited in North, supra n. 5.

the needed security and protection from bad faith.[24] (In the real world, of course, the cost of that other mechanism may be greater than the benefit of the transaction to the parties.[25])

In assessing the impact on the economy of the lack of such an effective system for enforcing contract rights, one must therefore ask just how important such one-shot deals (as well as any other deals for which there exists no reasonably effective informal method of sanctioning breaches) are in that economy or to its development. North and others seem to assume that they are common in advanced capitalist economies. This is a question calling for empirical research,[26] although defining and measuring such transactions is clearly difficult.

---

24. This might be viewed as an extreme position. I believe it is defensible if the qualifications — particularly the words "never" and "in principle" — are taken seriously.

25. The degree to which informal sanctions can replace formal legal institutions in supporting contractual commitments is much debated. It is generally agreed that where legal institutions are weak, bilateral relationships and other informal institutions can be at least a partial substitute. See Johnson et al., supra n. 12. See also Kathryn Hendley & Peter Murrell, Which Mechanisms Support the Fulfillment of Sales Agreements? Asking Decision-Makers in Firms (January 23, 2003) (unpublished manuscript, on file with author), available at http://papers.ssrn.com/sol3/papers.cfm?abstract_id=337042 (listing six types of mechanisms on a rough scale of formality, ranging from bilateral relations of personal trust to court action). Some scholars have argued that such relationships can go a very long way, perhaps being a complete substitute for legal institutions. See, e.g., Jones, "Capitalism, Globalization and the Rule of Law: An Alternative Trajectory of Legal Change in China," 3 *Soc. & L. Stud.* 195, 213 (June 1994) (discussing role of *guanxi* (relationships) in China). In a series of articles, however, John McMillan and his colleagues have argued that the scope of transactions beyond the capacity of relational contracts is substantial and important. See, e.g., McMillan & Woodruff, "The Central Role of Entrepreneurs in Transition Economies," 16 *J. Econ. Persp.* 153 (Summer 2002) (describing the types of transactions for which relational contracting is inadequate) [hereinafter McMillan & Woodruff, The Central Role of Entrepreneurs]; McMillan & Woodruff, supra n. 18, at 63) (same). Even weak courts can play an important role in facilitating economic activity; ease of entry, for example, has been critical to economic success in transition economies, see McMillan & Woodruff, The Central Role of Entrepreneurs, supra, and entrepreneurs in transition economies who believe that courts are effective offer more trade credit and are more willing to take on new trading partners, thus lowering barriers to entry, see Johnson et al., supra n. 12. Raja Kali has also written in a similar vein, arguing that while networks of relationships can arise in response to inadequate legal institutions and even do a good job in replacing them, their negative effects on non-members could outweigh their beneficial effects on members, and thus, from an economy-wide standpoint, reduce overall economic efficiency. See Kali, "Business Networks in Transition Economies: Norms, Contracts, and Legal Institutions," in *Assessing the Value of Law in Transition Economies* 211-28 (Peter Murrell ed., 2001).

None of this, of course, solves the problem of how governments with limited resources should spend their money in societies at a particular level of economic development. Strengthening courts in order to protect contract rights will apparently do something, but putting the same resources into building other kinds of institutions – or preventing certain kinds of behavior – might do more.

26. See, for example, Macauley, "Non-Contractual Relations in Business: A Preliminary Study," 28 *Am. Soc. Rev.* 55 (1963), in which one-shot relationships between strangers were conspicuously absent in the business community under study.

Turning now to property rights, for what kind of economic activity is freedom from fear of arbitrary confiscation by government (or by those whom government allows to act) the *sine qua non*? The answer is clear: just about any kind of investment other than investments with the very shortest of time horizons. In other words, the greater the fear of arbitrary confiscation, the shorter will be the time horizon of any investments. This means that a whole class of economically rational investments — those with a large payoff, but one which is delayed or stretched out over several years — will not get made.

In sum, my minimum claim is that the enforcement or lack thereof of contract rights and the security of property rights can involve very different consequences and ought to be conceptually distinguished. My stronger claim is that whether contract rights are judicially enforced is less important than whether property rights are secure: the lack of an effective formal judicial system that enforces contract rights puts definitely out of reach only a relatively small number of growth-enhancing transactions, whereas the fear of confiscation of one's property by government makes a very large number of growth-enhancing investments impossible.

b. The Idea of Rights vs. the Idea of Predictability

Suppose we grant the claim of the Rights Hypothesis that, all other things being equal, it is more conducive to economic development to have predictability than not to have it. Clearly, predictability has economic value; businesspeople often spend money, for example, to see if people are likely to buy a product before they invest in the factory needed to make it. More important to the Rights Hypothesis, however, is the claim that economic development is furthered by predictability in certain specific areas: the enforcement of contract rights and the security of property rights.

Where the Rights Hypothesis again goes too far, however, is in failing to distinguish between predictability and rights. Just as investment in agriculture depends on predictability about matters respecting which the farmer has no legal rights — for example, that spring will follow winter, or that seeds, if watered and fertilized, will grow — so we can imagine a legal system that contains no rights but that operates in a predictable manner. A system composed entirely of reglementation — defined by Weber as "those norms which only embody instructions to state officials as regards their duties, but, in contradistinction to what may be called 'claim norms,' do not establish any 'rights' of individuals"[27] — could in principle provide sufficient stability of expectations to support a reasonably well

---

27. *Max Weber on Law in Economy and Society*, supra n. 2, at 42.

functioning market.²⁸ Thus, it is a mistake to look solely at institutions that support rights — such as courts — to see if stability of expectations can exist. One must look at all the government agencies that adjust relations between parties and have the power to order the transfer of resources from one party to another.

c. Reformulating the Rights Hypothesis

The analysis above suggests that there are some serious internal problems to the Rights Hypothesis in its standard form, to say nothing of the problems created by evidence that appears to contradict it. This section of the article examines the arguments and evidence in favor of the proposition that a reasonable assurance to would-be investors that the fruits of their investment will not be confiscated unpredictably is far more important to economic development than a formal legal system that enforces contract rights.

Douglass C. North is one of the foremost proponents of the Rights Hypothesis in its full form: that is, the claim that enforcement of contract rights and security of property rights are both necessary to economic development.²⁹ If one looks closely, however, at North's illustrative examples of the institutions and practices that enabled England on the one hand to grow and prosper and caused Spain on the other to stagnate, one finds that he never, except in the most abstract way, cites the predictable enforcement of contract rights. Instead, he cites examples of greater or lesser security of property against government depredation. The bad old days of the Stuarts, for example, saw "repeated fiscal crises . . . that led them to engage in forced loans, to sell monopolies, and to engage in a variety of practices (including wealth confiscation) that rendered property rights less secure."³⁰ North sees the Glorious Revolution as an attempt, among other things, "to solve the problem of controlling the Crown's exercise of arbitrary and confiscatory power."³¹ The success of this attempt led, in North's view, to a rapid development of capital markets and access by the government to an unprecedented level of funds, because lenders had "a clear perception that the government would honor its agreements."³² North concludes that

> [t]he security of property rights and the development of the public and private capital market were instrumental factors

---

28. As Weber further remarked, "[P]rivate interests enjoy protection, not as guaranteed rights, but only as the obverse aspect of the effectiveness of these regulations." Id. at 44. In other words, if the regulations are effective, private interests can be protected in the absence of any system of rights.
29. See, for example, North, supra n. 5, and Douglass C. North & Robert P. Thomas, *The Rise of the Western World* (1973).
30. North, supra n. 5, at 139.
31. Id.
32. Id.

not only in England's subsequent rapid economic development, but in its political hegemony and ultimate dominance of the world.[33]

When he looks at Spain and the reasons for its decline in the 17th century from the mightiest empire in the West since Rome to the status of second-rate power, North tells a story of "the expulsion of Moors and Jews, rent ceilings on land and price ceilings on wheat, [and] confiscations of silver remittances to merchants in Seville" as disincentives to productive activity.[34] In *The Rise of the Western World*, North and his co-author also note the disincentives to agricultural investment in Spain occasioned by the Crown's grant to the sheepherders' guild of the right to run sheep over agricultural land owned by others.[35]

What all these examples have in common is that they essentially involve the government either keeping a promise to preserve the expected value of an asset or else not allowing others to deprive one of the expected value of an asset.[36] They simply do not show anything one way of the other about the need for enforcement of laws of property and contract against third parties with whom one deals.

A similar emphasis on freedom from arbitrary and unpredictable confiscation can be found in a study by Stephen Knack and Philip Keefer,[37] an often-cited effort to test the Rights Hypothesis empiri-

---

33. Id. Recent work by Sussman and Yafeh has questioned the empirical premises of the claim that Britain's supremacy stemmed from institutions that secured property rights and thereby lowered the cost of borrowing both to the government and to private investors. They show that after the institutional changes pointed to by North, supra n. 5, and North & Weingast, supra n. 9, interest rates remained high, and the volume of British government debt low, for nearly a century. See Sussman & Yafeh, supra n. 9. The same authors made similar findings with respect to Japan in the Meiji period. See Sussman & Yafeh, "Institutions, Reforms, and Country Risk: Lessons from Japanese Government Debt in the Meiji Period," 60 *J. Econ. Hist.* 442 (2000) (finding that institutional change, reforms, a constitution and other similar factors had little impact on the interest rate on bonds issued by the Japanese government between 1870 and 1914). See also Stasavage, "Credible Commitment in Early Modern Europe: North and Weingast Revisited," 18 *J. L. Econ. & Org.* 155 (2002) (also casting doubt on specific empirical premises).
34. See North, supra n. 5, at 115
35. See North & Thomas, supra n. 29, at 4.
36. In buying a house, writes North,
    the discount from the frictionless exchange envisaged in economic theory will be greater to the degree that the institutional structure allows third parties to influence the value of the attributes that are in the utility function of the buyer. These could include the behavior of neighbors, the likelihood of theft, and the possibility of changes by local authorities in zoning ordinances that may affect the value of the property. The greater the uncertainty of the buyer, the lower the value of the asset. It is worth emphasizing that the uncertainties described above with respect to the security of rights are a critical distinction between the relatively efficient markets of high income countries today and economies in the past as well as those in the Third World today.
North, supra n. 5, at 63.
37. See Knack & Keefer, supra n. 1.

cally. While the authors state or imply at several points in their study that what they are testing is the importance of rights of both property and contract to economic growth, an examination of their methodology shows that in fact contract enforceability, even if measurable and measured accurately, has little or no part in the indices with which they correlate economic growth and private investment.

Knack and Keefer use two indices, both based on indicators compiled by private international investment risk consultants, that they believe measure directly the dimensions of property rights emphasized by North and others. The first of these indices is derived from the International Country Risk Guide (ICRG)[38] and is the aggregate of five variables measuring expropriation risk, rule of law, repudiation of contracts by government, corruption in government, and quality of bureaucracy. The second index is derived from Business Environment Risk Intelligence (BERI)[39] and is the aggregate of four variables measuring contract enforceability, infrastructure quality, nationalization potential, and bureaucratic delays. They find that both the ICRG and the BERI indices outperform other indices of property and contract rights used in previous studies,[40] and that while the ICRG index explains growth best, the BERI index explains private investment best.

What the authors do not do is to attempt seriously to distinguish property rights from contract rights — i.e., the security of an expectation that one will not be subject to arbitrary and unpredictable confiscation as opposed to the security of an expectation that one will be able to enforce a promise made by another with whom one does business. They attempt to tie unreliability of government promises to unreliability of all third-party promises with the assertion that "[i]t is likely that if private actors cannot count on the government to respect the contracts it has with them, they will also not be able to count on the government enforcing contracts between two private parties,"[41] but this assertion rests on only a superficial symmetry and is not convincing. While the ICRG and BERI indices both present plausible measures of security against unpredictable expropriation, the ICRG contains no measures of contract enforceability and only

---

38. For further information on this source, including a description of the methodology, see PRS Group, International Country Risk Guide, at http://www.prsgroup.com/icrg/icrg.html.

39. For further information on this source, see Business Environment Risk Intelligence, at http://www.beri.com.

40. These other indices did not purport to measure property and contract rights directly, but instead used measures of political violence or political freedoms and civil liberties in the belief that these measures could be a suitable proxy for the absence or presence of secure property and contract rights. See, e.g., Barro, "Economic Growth in a Cross Section of Countries," 106 *Q. J. Econ.* 407 (1991) (using measures of political violence) and Gerald W. Scully, "The Institutional Framework and Economic Development," 96 *J. Pol. Econ.* 652 (1988) (using measures of civil liberties).

41. See Knack & Keefer, supra n. 1, at 210.

one of the four BERI variables attempts to do so. Consequently, while the Knack and Keefer study supports the Rights Hypothesis with respect to security of property rights, it simply does not address the importance of contract rights. Furthermore, security of property rights — at least as discussed by North and as measured by Knack and Keefer — has little to do with formal legal institutions. It is much more a question of political institutions.[42]

Other studies, whatever their conclusions, in fact share the emphasis on security of property. A recent study by Rodrik and his colleagues, for example, examines the respective contributions of geography, institutions, and openness to trade to wealth levels around the world, and concludes that the quality of institutions trumps everything else. The institutional environment, however, is measured by "observers' views as to the likelihood that investors will retain the fruits of their investments, the chances that the state will expropriate them, or that the legal system will protect their property rights."[43]

In short, while the Rights Hypothesis is generally stated in terms of a formal legal system that protects rights of property and contract, the qualitative and quantitative work that purports to support the hypothesis tends to focus almost exclusively on security from arbitrary expropriation, without being concerned about whether that security comes from a well functioning legal system or simply a wise government that prudently declines to exercise the power it has to expropriate in order to maximize its ultimate revenue from taxing the income stream. Contract rights are simply not addressed at all.

d. The China Problem

We can now return to the issue raised at the beginning of Section 2: what are the implications of the evidence from China for the Rights Hypothesis as reformulated to stress freedom from fear of confiscation?

Imagine two plots of land side by side in the Chinese countryside. On one sits a typical TVE[44] making buttons. On the other toils a

---

42. See Weingast, supra n. 9, at 286.

43. Rodrik, Subramanian & Trebbi, "Institutions Rule: The Primacy of Institutions Over Geography and Integration in Economic Development," (Nat'l Bureau of Econ. Research, Working Paper No. W9305, 2002), available at http://www.nber.org/papers/w9305. For another study in this vein, see Acemoglu, Johnson, & Robinson, "The Colonial Origins of Comparative Development: An Empirical Investigation," 91 Am. Econ. Rev. 1369 (2001) (using an index of protection against expropriation).

44. TVE is the general term used for township and village enterprises: businesses that are typically founded and run by local government. Technically they belong to the collective sector, as opposed to the private sector or the state sector, and are therefore said to be "owned" by the citizenry of a particular locality. This ownership is for all intents and purposes meaningless even as a formality; all the important indices of ownership rest with local government. Naughton, "Chinese Institutional Innovation

farmer. Both the factory and the farmer carry on their business under the same local government. If they have a contract dispute, the same court system will hear (or refuse to hear) their case. In short, from the standpoint of the ability of the formal legal system to protect their contract rights, they are similarly situated. Yet it is very likely that the TVE fits the general national pattern of solid growth in investment and output in its sector,[45] while the farmer fits the pattern of slow growth in agriculture relative to the remarkable growth of the early 1980s.[46] Why might this be so?

---

and Privatization from Below," 84 *Am. Econ. Rev.* 266, 267 (1994). Indeed, TVEs have been plausibly characterized as similar to subsidiaries of the township, viewed itself as a diversified corporation. See Oi, "Fiscal Reform and the Economic Foundations of Local State Corporatism in China," 45 *World Pol.* 99 (1992); Nee, "Organizational Dynamics of Market Transition: Hybrid Forms, Property Rights, and Mixed Economy in China," 37 *Admin. Sci. Q.* 1 (1992).

Although it is important in understanding TVEs to know that they are run by and for government bodies, not private investors, it is equally important to understand that these government bodies in many cases wish to maximize profits and operate in a competitive market environment. Most importantly, unlike state-owned enterprises, TVEs have no hope of central government support if they run into trouble, and their workers, unlike SOE workers, have no implicit guarantee or expectation of employment. Thus, they face a hard budget constraint. For a contrary but distinctly minority view, holding that "money-losing TVEs typically stay in business, despite their inability to repay debts," see Wang, "Capital Formation and Utilization," in *China's Rural Industry: Structure, Development, and Reform* 225 (William Byrd and Q. Lin eds., 1990). This is hard to reconcile with the finding of Weitzman and Xu that in 1989 alone, a full sixth of TVEs, some three million, went bankrupt or were taken over by other TVEs, although the term "taken over" may in fact conceal a bailout. See Weitzman & Xu, "Chinese Township-Village Enterprises as Vaguely Defined Cooperatives," 18 *J. Comp. Econ.* 121, 135-36 (1994) (citing Chinese statistical sources). A concise and insightful summary of relevant TVE characteristics can be found in Jin & Qian, "Public vs. Private Ownership of Firms: Evidence from Rural China," 113 *Q. J. Econ.* 773, 776-79 (1998).

45. Available statistics show a steady rise over the ten-year period from 1990 through 1999 in a number of relevant indices of TVE activity: fixed investment, circulating funds, profits, business revenues, and value added. Employment, however, has remained steady since 1993, and the total number of TVEs has decreased from a peak of about 25 million in 1994 to about 21 million in 1999. *Zhongguo Xiang-Zhen Qiye Nianjian* 2000 [China Township and Village Enterprise Yearbook 2000], 15-18 (2000). See also Wang & Kalirajan, "On Explaining China's Rural Sectors' Productivity Growth," 19 *Econ. Modelling* 261 (2002); Nongye Bu Xiangzhen Qiye Ju Xinxi Tongji Chu [Ministry of Agriculture, Township and Village Enterprise Bureau, Information and Statistics Office], "2001 Niandu Quanguo Xiangzhen Qiye Fazhan Tongji Gongbao" [Statistical Report on the Development of Township and Village Enterprises Nationwide in 2001], Zhongguo Xiang-Zhen Qiye Kuaji [Chinese Township and Village Enterprise Accounting], No. 6 (2002), at 4-7.

46. See generally Li, Rozelle & Brandt, "Tenure, Land Rights, and Farmer Investment Incentive in China," 19 *Ag. Econ.* 63 (1998). Between 1955 and 1980, when reforms began spreading in earnest, the annual per-person increase in grain production was 1.3 kilograms. From 1980 to 1984, that figure rose to 16.2 kilograms. Between 1984 and 1993, the figure fell to 2.9 kilograms even though agricultural policies had, if anything, become more liberal than before. See Prosterman, Hanstad & Li, "Can China Feed Itself?," *Sci. Am.* (November 1996), at 90. The explanation appears to be strongly connected with the move from collective farming to family farming. At the beginning of 1980, 1% of rural households had made this shift. By the end of 1984, 99% of rural households had. Lin, "Rural Reforms and Agricultural Growth in

It would be foolhardy, of course, to attempt a single-factor explanation of what is undoubtedly a complex phenomenon. First, the TVE and the farmer are not *identically* situated with respect to the ability of the formal legal system to enforce their contract rights. The TVE is a bigger actor and has more resources and clout in the community than a single farmer. Second, the TVE, again because it is bigger and has more resources and clout, is better situated than the farmer to take advantage of other mechanisms that might substitute for enforcement of contract rights through the formal legal system — mechanisms ranging from gathering information about the trustworthiness of prospective contractual partners to hiring thugs to collect on contract debts.[47] But these explanations do not really contradict, and in fact can be viewed as supporting, the reformulated Rights Hypothesis, which downgrades the importance of a formal legal system that can enforce contract rights between strangers.

From the standpoint of incentives for investment, it may simply be that all the large returns that can be obtained from investment in agriculture at China's current technological level have already been achieved, whereas light industry is still far from this point. But empirical research seems to suggest that there is in fact room for significant further returns from agricultural investment:

> Many agricultural scientists in China have concluded that farmers could obtain crops two to three times larger than what they currently harvest. The farmers we talked to also acknowledged that the land could afford much larger yields. Yet few of them had made any major alterations to their plots, even though they all knew that such changes would boost their output.[48]

Why are these investments not being made?

> The farmers' reluctance to sink money and labor into any extensive modifications can be directly attributed to their underlying fear that they may not be able to hold on to their property long enough to realize a return on their investment. (In contrast to the changes already made, the costs of which were recovered quickly, the next phase of improvements will take many years to pay for themselves.) Back in 1984 the central government ordered that land con-

---

China," 82 *Am. Econ. Rev.* 34, 38 (1992). Once the shift was complete, apparently, there were no more gains to be had from it.

47. For a good review of various theories of TVE advantages as well as an attempt to generate and test hypotheses from them, see Jin & Qian, supra n. 44. There has been some debate on whether TVEs are in fact efficient; for a review, see Whiting, "Contract Incentives and Market Discipline in China's Rural Industrial Sector," in *Reforming Asian Socialism: The Growth of Market Institutions* 65-67 (John McMillan & Barry Naughton eds., 1996).

48. Prosterman et al., supra n. 46, at 93.

tracts be extended for 15 years, but local officials have not implemented this policy to any significant degree. Indeed, very few farmers even possess written contracts granting them the right to tend a specific plot. And when they do obtain a contract, the expiration date is often left blank, or the term may change without warning, or the contract may be terminated far short of what was originally promised.[49]

This analysis is reinforced by a survey study conducted by Li, Rozelle, and Brandt,[50] which found a strong and robust connection between the right to use land for long (or indefinite) periods of time and the making of land-saving investments, although they did not conclude that the lack of such rights carried a high efficiency cost.[51]

---

49. Id. Note that the contract spoken of here is not an ordinary commercial contract with another party of equal legal status, but a contract with the local government for long-term land tenure. Thus, a violation of that contract by the local government in redistributing the land is more appropriately viewed as a problem of security of property against government confiscation than as one of enforcement of contract rights in business dealings.

50. Li et al., supra n. 46.

51. It should be noted that the diagnosis of Prosterman et al., supra n. 46, is not unchallenged. James Kung and Shouying Liu review the literature on the relationship between tenure security and agricultural productivity, and question this diagnosis on the basis of survey results showing that farmers did not have a strong preference for private ownership and that a majority reported that they preferred the existing system of periodic land redistribution to account for changes in family size. Kung & Liu, "Farmers' Preferences Regarding Ownership and Land Tenure in Post-Mao China: Unexpected Evidence from Eight Counties," 38 *China J*. 33 (1997). The key flaw in the authors' argument, however, is that a preference by farmers for a particular system is by no means equivalent to a refutation of the proposition that that system contains severe disincentives to agricultural investment. A detailed discussion of their findings is, however, beyond the scope of this article.

Other studies have explored the link between security of tenure and fertilizing practices specifically. Li et al., supra n. 46, do find a link, but only a small one. Kung and Cai state that "[w]hile the [popularly] postulated negative relationship between ill-defined property rights in land and suboptimal fertilizing practices is an intuitively plausible hypothesis, it is not adequately supported by empirical evidence." Kung & Cai, "Property Rights and Fertilizing Practices in Rural China: Evidence from Northern Jiangsu," 26 *Mod. China* 276 (2000). There are several difficulties, however, with the argument of Kung and Cai. First, the conventional wisdom they set out to refute is the claim that ill-defined property rights in land lead to sub-optimal fertilizing practices and other inefficient uses of land. But what they show is that non-private property rights do not necessarily give rise to tenure insecurity. This is not the same thing; non-private property rights need not be ill-defined, and tenure insecurity is of course a different thing from sub-optimal fertilizing practices. Second, they show that land tenure was not in fact as unpredictable in the villages they studied as has been assumed; reallocations of land within the villages they studied were frequently announced well ahead of time, so that farmers could adjust their input investments. Third, they found some anecdotal evidence of informal mechanisms (the exclusion from reallocation of families that had not taken proper care of their land) operating to ensure that all families made appropriate input investments. Thus, farmers had an incentive to take proper care of their land and some assurance that land they received upon reallocation would have been equally well cared for.

The differing conclusions of various studies may be the result in part of the wide variation across the country in land tenure regimes, despite the ostensible primacy of central government policy. See Brandt, Rozelle, Huang & Li, "Land Rights in China:

While agricultural growth has slowed considerably, growth in the TVE sector continues steadily. Apparently TVEs (or more precisely, the investors and managers of TVEs) do not have the same fear of confiscation of the fruits of their investment that farmers have. If indeed this is part of the explanation, it makes sense, for a key feature distinguishing TVEs from farmers is that TVEs are the creatures of local government, precisely the same body that farmers fear will confiscate or redistribute their land. While farmers, therefore, may face uncertainty as to the results of long-term investments such as well-digging or the terracing of fields, TVEs, whatever their other problems, face no real uncertainty in this area at all. Provided the economics are right, the only concern of the investor (local government) is the unlikely one that several years down the road the central government might confiscate all or part of its treasury.[52]

Whether TVEs do indeed enjoy a unique security of expectations in investment is controversial. A substantial body of literature exists asserting that the Rights Hypothesis, even when limited to property rights, is refuted by the success of TVEs in what is claimed to be an environment of vague and insecure property rights. As will be shown below, I believe that this literature places undue emphasis on formal instead of realistic categories of ownership and therefore does not succeed in its challenge to the property rights element of the Rights Hypothesis.

Weitzman and Xu, for example, noting correctly the hollowness of the formal ownership rights of "the community," go on to conclude that TVEs have "no owner in the spirit of traditional property rights theory."[53] They reject the local government as a candidate for the role of owner on the grounds that it lacks several elements of full control: it is restrained from firing workers who are community residents, for

---

Fact, Fiction, and Issues," 47 *China J.* 67 (2002) (finding that in a sample of 31 villages in northeast China, land resources were organized in almost 20 different ways). Another contributing factor may simply be inconsistent terminology. Rozelle and his colleagues, for example, cite approvingly a Chinese study that "found almost no evidence of expropriations of investments in the land in rural China during the last 10 years." Rozelle, Huang, & Zhang, "Emerging Markets, Evolving Institutions, and the New Opportunities for Growth in China's Rural Economy," 13 *China Econ. Rev.* 345, 350 (2002). Another article published in the same year, however, and sharing two coauthors with the first, states (a) that more than half of all cultivated land in a broad sample of villages surveyed in 1996 had been reallocated at least once, and (b) that households are typically not compensated for investments they have made in land when it is reallocated. See Brandt et al., supra. A taking without compensation *is* expropriation. The Chinese study cited may have been using a narrow legal definition of expropriation, and not an economic one.

52. Even this concern may not have a substantial effect on investment patterns, since all alternative investments will carry the same risk. The only way open to local government leaders for the certain avoidance of confiscation is to consume government funds now through the familiar rituals of banqueting and travel at public expense.

53. Weitzman & Xu, supra n. 44, at 132.

example, and "has to take into account . . . the preferences of residents" in its decision making respecting the establishment of TVEs.⁵⁴ This hardly disqualifies local government as owner. If a private entrepreneur faced statutory limits on her ability to discharge workers, we would not conclude that she was for that reason not a true owner. With respect to taking into account the views of residents, a decision to establish a TVE is hardly the same as the continuing series of decisions involved in running one, and in any case Weitzman and Xu fail to distinguish between what the local government *must* do and what it would be *wise* to do as a matter of policy. There is no question that the local government could, if it wished, set up a TVE without popular approval, in the same way that it can levy taxes and fees without popular approval.

Because they reject the notion that local government is an owner with clear rights of management, usufruct, and disposition over the assets of the TVE, they find TVE success a puzzle, and resort to a concept of cultural propensity to cooperate (*lamda*) in order to resolve it. They assert that conventional property rights theory assumes a low-*lamda* culture in which clearly defined property rights are needed to prevent shirking and opportunistic behavior. Perhaps China's TVEs are able to succeed, they hypothesize, because they exist in a high-*lamda* culture where formal rights and binding legal rules are less important.

The problem with *lamda* as an explanatory variable is that it turns out not to explain anything. Weitzman and Xu use it to account for different outcomes (*e.g.*, differential rates of success for firms with a TVE structure) when all other factors are held equal. The question, however, is what these "other factors" are. If they turn out to be everything that we can think of that might be relevant to TVE success, then *lamda* is by definition simply a residual category for things we cannot think of. In other words, *lamda* is just a label for things we cannot explain. But there is no particular reason to equate the unexplained with "culture." Given that *lamda* is a residual category, one would expect it to get smaller and less important the more we learn about identifiable factors contributing to TVE success.

The claim of unclear property rights is repeated by David Li in another frequently-cited article:

> [N]o one can claim that the Chinese non-state sector enjoys clearly defined property rights. Most of the non-state firms are collectives and other kinds of non-private firms. The owners of these collective firms are often loosely specified, e.g., all residents in a community.⁵⁵

---

54. Id. at 134.
55. Li, "A Theory of Ambiguous Property Rights in the Transition Economies: The Case of the Chinese Non-State Sector," 23 *J. Comp. Econ.* 1, 2 (1996).

Li then develops a theory to explain why ambiguity and vagueness could actually be advantageous. The analysis is flawed, however, by its origin in the notion that there is any vagueness about ownership of a TVE. While the category of "all residents in a community" is indeed vague, and while one can certainly find various pronouncements to the effect that the owners of a TVE are "all residents in a community," this ownership is no more meaningful than the "ownership" interest of French citizens in Air France and deserves equal attention — that is to say, none — in a legal or economic analysis. Thus, one can indeed claim that property rights in the non-state sector are, at least sometimes, clear:

> Local residents possess no "right of membership" in TVEs, nor do TVE workers possess any rights to participate in TVE management. In most cases that have been studied, township and village officials in their official capacity possess all the key components of property rights: control of residual income; the right to dispose of assets; and the right to appoint and dismiss managers and assume direct control if necessary.[56]

Other scholars whose analysis is distracted by the perceived need to take into account somehow the ownership rights of "the community" or "local citizens" (as opposed to the local government) include Chang and Wang,[57] Che and Qian,[58] and Hong.[59]

---

56. Naughton, supra n. 44, at 267.
57. See Chang & Wang, "The Nature of the Township-Village Enterprise," 19 *J. Comp. Econ.* 434, 447 (1994). The authors argue that TVEs are afflicted by a problem of separation of ownership from control that stems from ownership by citizens combined with management by the local government. But this is to get caught up in formalisms. *De facto* ownership is in the hands of local government. The separation of ownership from control occurs because the local government, as an abstract entity, can act only through human agents such as government officials. Yet another layer of agency is created when those officials in turn appoint others to manage the TVE. In any case, the principal-agent problem is no different from that faced by state-owned enterprises (SOEs) or large private enterprises in market economies:
> The problem is that the state as the owner was unable to manage each enterprise by its own, and needed to appoint managers to do it. Similar principal-agent conflict within large private enterprises also exists in market economies. In other words, the ownership and management of SOEs have always been separated. The managers of SOEs were appointed or recruited by the state.

Lin, Cai & Li, "Creating an Environment for Fair Competition Is the Core of Enterprise Reform," in *The Reformability of China's State Sector* 47, 55 (Guanzhong James Wen & Dianqing Xu eds., 1997).

58. See Che & Qian, "Institutional Environment, Community Government, and Corporate Governance: Understanding China's Township-Village Enterprises," 14 *J. L. Econ. & Org.* 1 (1998). The authors analogize the township to a multidivisional firm, with each TVE as a division within the firm, the local government as the board of directors, and local citizens as stockholders. While the analogy of the TVE to a division within a multidivisional firm is well taken, the notion of local citizens as equivalent to stockholders is difficult to accept. Among other things, they have no vote in "firm" management and they have no identifiable, protected, and transferable right

If, as I argue, ownership rights over TVEs and their cash flow are not significantly ambiguous or vague, then a critical distinction between a TVE run by local government and a privately-run enterprise is that the TVE does not need to fear arbitrary expropriation, either direct or indirect through oppressive taxes and fees.[60]

The threat of arbitrary expropriation in China today does not come from the central government; it comes from local government.[61] It is local government that is the most closely acquainted with a firm's financial health and that has the greatest incentive and ability to loot it. A firm owned by local government is obviously not subject to this uncertainty, since the local government internalizes the cost of whatever decision it makes about distribution of TVE profits. Local government investment in an enterprise, then, is (unlike local private investment) absolutely undeterred by the worry that the investor cannot fully capture the return on the investment. With respect to superior levels of government, it appears that the property rights of local levels of government are quite robust.[62] Superior levels of government do not in general take from inferior levels without compensation.

With this security against expropriation, local governments not only can invest more than private entrepreneurs, but they can invest more efficiently. As Knack and Keefer point out, an investor concerned about expropriation is likely to invest in less specialized capital (human and physical) that can be moved more easily from one activity to another.[63] Not only does this have static efficiency effects, but it also discourages dynamic gains from innovation, since such innovation in more likely to thrive where there is specialization.

The Chinese example also sheds some interesting light on the question of whether economic development actually requires rights or simply predictability. While China's legal system does not seem to protect the former very well, it may offer a reasonable degree of the latter.

A good deal of discussion of the Chinese legal system is in terms of what it lacks: there is a lack of enforcement, a lack of legal con-

---

to any of the wealth created by the "firm". Simply being in a position to benefit from local government expenditure if one still resides in the area when the expenditure is made is not enough to support this analogy in a meaningful way.

59. See Hong, "The Shareholding Cooperative System and Property Rights Reform of China's Collective Township-Village Enterprise," 23 *Asian Profile* 359 (1995).

60. For an attempt to assess the importance of various differences, see Jin & Qian, supra n. 44.

61. For this reason, I do not find convincing the claim of Chang and Wang that local citizens are designated as formal owners of TVEs in order to make credible a commitment by the central government not to expropriate. See Chang & Wang, supra n. 57, at 447.

62. See generally David Granick, *Chinese State Enterprises: A Regional Property Rights Analysis* (1990) and Naughton, supra n. 15, at 43.

63. See Knack & Keefer, supra n. 1, at 219.

sciousness, a lack of trained judges.[64] All this is true, and indeed in many cases these lacks are seen as deficiencies by Chinese legal scholars and others working in the system. In part because the institutions of the Chinese legal system come with labels that are customarily translated using familiar English words — "courts", "judges", "laws", etc. — without much thought about whether such words are really appropriate, pointing out the ways in which the Chinese system is *not* in fact like the system in which we use these terms is a necessary part of understanding that system. But it is far from sufficient. The Chinese legal system itself, like the society of which it is a part, does not function on the basis of what it lacks; it functions on the basis of what it has. Because the Rights Hypothesis is essentially oriented to the would-be investor's ability to predict what will happen to the investment, the question should be not whether China possesses or lacks courts that enforce rights, but simply whether investors and others engaged in business in China have adequate predictability for their needs.

To the extent the legal system has anything to contribute to this, China's — or any other country's — system is not any the less capable in principle of doing so simply because it consists largely of Weberian "reglementation" and not "claim norms".[65] Further inquiry, therefore, would be more usefully focused on the question of predictability than on the presence or absence of enforceable legal rights.[66]

The inquiry into predictability must also ask: predictability for whom? Proponents of the Rights Hypothesis typically assume that there must be predictability for private economic actors, because they assume that economic development requires a market and that a market requires private actors. Putting aside the question of whether or not economic development in fact requires a market, it does not appear to be true that a market requires private actors. What it does generally require in order to have meaningful bargaining over prices is actors that are trying to buy low and sell high. The Chinese case certainly demonstrates that governmental actors such as TVEs are

---

64. I confess to engaging in this kind of discussion myself. See Clarke, supra n. 11. I am grateful to Ellen Hertz for discussions regarding the problems with this approach.

65. This characterization of the Chinese legal system raises more issues than can be dealt with adequately in a mere footnote. I discuss these issues more fully in Clarke, "Justice and the Legal System," in *China in the 1990s* (Robert Benewick & Paul Wingrove eds., 1995). See also Thomas B. Stephens, *Order and Discipline in China* (1992).

66. As Albert Chen points out, modern critical social and legal theory, while by no means denying that Western societies have seen significant economic development, does deny that law in Western societies is autonomous, rational, and determinate, and therefore challenges the central causal claim of the Rights Hypothesis. See Chen, "Rational Law, Economic Development and the Case of China," 8 *Soc. & L. Stud.* 97 (1999). Critical theory does not, however, deny that there is predictability in societies; it just denies that it comes from an autonomous legal system and a regime of rights.

capable of fulfilling this role and that a market can flourish in the absence of significant true private actors.[67] Therefore, even if it could be shown that private actors do not enjoy the benefits of predictability in contract and property, that need not be fatal to economic growth. We might find at the same time that non-private actors *do* have predictability and can create flourishing markets and economic growth.

4. Conclusion

One of the reasons why proponents of the Rights Hypothesis have so often lumped security of property together with enforcement of contract rights may be that societies characterized by security of property from arbitrary government confiscation also tend to be characterized by the relatively effective enforcement of contract rights. Thus, they have mistaken effect for cause. China presents an invaluable case study for the hypothesis because although it seems that rights of any kind are not well protected through courts and the legal system, economic growth does take place, and it seems to take place in those sectors that are free of the fear of arbitrary government confiscation. Such sectors can exist in China in a way they cannot in other developing countries because of the near absence of a true private sector in industry and the dominant role played by governmental bodies — however much they may be forced to play by the rules of the market — as economic actors.

The reformulation of the Rights Hypothesis presented here may also offer a solution to Max Weber's "England problem."[68] Weber believed that "the degree of legal rationality [in England] is essentially lower than, and of a type different from, that of continental Europe."[69] Yet he could not avoid observing the strength in England of precisely the kind of capitalism for which he had posited the necessity of legal rationality. It may be, of course, that Weber simply defined too narrowly the type of legal rationality truly necessary. On the other hand, it is worth pointing out what England *did* have in common with the successful capitalist countries of Western Europe, a feature tirelessly pointed out by North: a government that made cred-

---

67. As numerous scholars have pointed out, the key difference between TVEs and state-owned enterprises is that TVEs face a much harder budget constraint. See, e.g., Che & Qian, supra n. 58, at 3; Jin & Qian, supra n. 44; Li, "The Institutional Foundation of Self-Enforcing Contracts: The Township Enterprise" (unpublished manuscript, on file with author) (1997). But see Edward Steinfeld, *Forging Reform in China: The Fate of State-Owned Industry* 239-40 (1998), who asserts that as TVEs become large and successful, they may be able to attract central bank loans, enjoy a softer budget constraint, and experience a decline in performance. See also Wang, supra n. 44, at 225.
68. See generally the discussion in Trubek, supra n. 2, at 746-48.
69. 1 *Max Weber, Economy and Society* 890 (Guenther Roth & Claus Wittich eds., 1968).

ible promises not to confiscate and that did not allow others to do what was in effect the same thing.

What about the contract rights half of the Rights Hypothesis? It makes intuitive sense to suppose that a large class of economically advantageous transactions will not take place if there is no legal system in place to enforce the promises parties make to each other. Why is it that this part of the Rights Hypothesis, if not outright wrong, at least has not nearly so much explanatory power as has been claimed for it by its adherents?

Part of the answer, as suggested earlier in this article, may lie in the fact (if it is a fact) that in most economic transactions, third-party enforcement through government coercion is not in fact the only effective enforcement mechanism available, because one-shot deals between people who are and intend to remain strangers are in practice not of great importance in modern capitalist economies. Obviously such a proposition requires empirical support. An excellent study of so-called "relational practices" in Taiwan shows just how very far you can go even in the absence of an effective formal legal system.[70]

The analysis presented here has policy implications in addition to academic ones. The World Bank, for example, now considers "governance" issues in the award of loans, with such issues defined as whether a country has "the rule of law": a system in which

> a) there is a set of rules which are known in advance, b) such rules are actually in force, c) mechanisms exist to ensure the proper application of the rules and to allow for departure from them as needed according to established procedures, d) conflicts in the application of the rules can be resolved through binding decisions of an independent judicial or arbitral body and e) there are known procedures for amending the rules when they no longer serve their purpose.[71]

However desirable it might be to have such a system for a number of reasons, it is far from clear that it is the *sine qua non* of economic development or, more prosaically, the effective use of World Bank loans.[72]

A further policy consequence follows from the relative unimportance of a formal system for the enforcement of contract rights. If a national government has limited resources to devote to growth-enhancing institutions, those resources would be better used in creating

---

70. Winn, supra n. 23, at 193.
71. Shihata, "The World Bank and 'Governance' Issues in Its Borrowing Members," in *The World Bank in a Changing World* 85 (F. Tschofen and A.R. Parra eds., 1991), cited in Upham, supra n. 9, at 233. Shihata was General Counsel of the World Bank when he made these remarks.
72. For a spirited critique of "rule of law" rhetoric in policymaking circles concerned with economic development, particularly in the World Bank, see Ohnesorge, supra n. 10.

an effective structure for the prevention of arbitrary confiscation (either outright or in the form of excessive fees, bribery demands, arbitrary taxes, etc.) instead of for the creation of courts that could fairly adjudicate contract disputes and enforce their decisions. While a fair and efficient court system for the adjudication of contract disputes is no doubt a desirable thing for any country to have, there is a great deal of evidence to suggest that non-governmental actors can set up substitute institutions that do the job reasonably well, even if they do not have the state's monopoly on the legitimate use of force. There is not, however, any such thing as a social remedy for confiscation of one's investment. Thus, businesses need state protection less from each other than from organs of the state. It may be that an advanced level of contractual protection is necessary in advanced economies, but even in advanced economies it appears that a great deal of business is done without resort to court enforcement of contract rights.[73]

At some point, however, we must perhaps admit that the *complete* absence of a formal legal system in a society is going to have a detrimental effect on economic development that cannot be fully or even substantially remedied by informal social or other sanctions. Yet it would be profoundly misleading to view the real barrier to economic development in such a society as the lack of an effective formal legal system. To say that a society needs enforcement of contract rights in order to get economic development begs the question of what would have to be true about that society for it to be able to have judicial enforcement of contract rights. Arguably, the society needs a commercial culture, an effective tax collection and fiscal disbursement system to pay for courts and judges, a tradition of honesty among public officials, control over crime, and a host of other factors — in short, a whole new society.[74] Suppose that new society were somehow in place and we observed an upsurge in economic growth: it would be missing the point to give all the causal credit to the judicial enforcement of contracts that came along with those social changes.

---

73. See, for example, the landmark study by Macauley, supra n. 26, at 55.
74. On the deeper determinants of economic success, see, inter alia, Hall & Jones, "Why Do Some Countries Produce So Much More Output per Worker than Others?" 114 *Q. J. Econ.* 83 (1999) (measuring "social infrastructure" favorable to production); Acemoglu et al., supra n. 43; Rodrik et al., supra n. 43 (finding that the quality of institutions trumps other factors such as geography and openness to trade); Rodrik, "Institutions for High-Quality Growth: What They Are and How to Acquire Them," 35 *Stud. Comp. Int'l Dev.* 3 (2000) (arguing that there is no single blueprint for the right institutions, but that democratic governance is the meta-institution that results generally in better institutions for growth).

[4]

Testing the Limits to the "Rule of Law": Commercial Regulation in Vietnam

John GILLESPIE[*]

Asia Pacific Business Regulation Group, Department of Business Law and Taxation, Monash University, Australia

Abstract

This article takes issue with conventional "rule of law" explanations for economic development that emphasize the regulatory role of the state. It draws on a detailed empirical study about entrepreneurs to show that commercial regulation in Vietnam is polycentric and that state, hybrid and non-state actors variously compete and collaborate with each other to order the regulatory space. What we conventionally recognize as the "rule of law" — state-based laws and legal institutions — does not so much control behaviour directly, as co-ordinate among a number of other, often non-state regulatory systems. The article concludes with the counter-intuitive proposition that the state can increase its regulatory reach over the market by recognizing and supporting socially beneficial self-regulatory practices. Rather than striving for particular regulatory settings, such as protecting property rights and contractual enforcement, the state needs to promote institutions that can flexibly respond to transitional conditions.

Keywords: Rule of law; Vietnam; regulatory theory; entrepreneur

---

[*] The author wishes to thank the anonymous referees of this article and the Australian Research Council for funding (Grant DP0665517) this research. (Correspondence concerning this article may be e-mailed to the author at: John.Gillespie@buseco.monash.edu.au)

Introduction

Given the long period of socialist governance in Vietnam, it is unsurprising that much analysis about the commercial regulation in this country is state-centred. The literature is state-centred not only because it locates the regulation of entrepreneurs in statutory rules and bureaucratic regulation, but also because it assumes the state has the regulatory solutions to commercial problems. Findings from the Survey of Vietnamese Entrepreneurs (SVE), which is discussed in this article, raise questions about the applicability of this conventional analytical framework to commercial regulation in Vietnam. In particular, the "rule of law" notion that only the government can bring order to commercial transactions is queried (Gillespie, 2006, pp. 261–286).

In this article, I posit a more complex, polycentric regulatory environment in which central laws play only a marginal regulatory role in many economic arenas. I suggest that central and local regulators variously compete and collaborate with each other, with the result that state and non-state regulation is often mutually constituted. What we conventionally recognize as the "rule of law" — state based laws and legal institutions — does not so much control behaviour directly, as co-ordinate among a number of other, often non-state regulatory systems. To understand this regulatory environment, new analytic approaches to commercial regulation that acknowledge the interaction and hybridization between state and non-state regulators are needed.

In this article, I extend regulatory theory to an analysis of commercial regulation in Vietnam to better understand the interaction between state and non-state regulation. Regulation is taken to mean a process involving a sustained attempt to alter behaviour for identified purposes (Parker et al., 2004). After first examining the competing conceptual understandings of commercial regulation, I use data from the SVE to show that four types of regulation complete with each other to control entrepreneurs. They are specified and examined in turn: facilitative regulation, state-bureaucratic regulation, flexible regulation, and non-state regulation.

The term "entrepreneur" refers to state-owned enterprises, private firms and hybrid entities. Hybrid actors take many forms: some resemble state agencies but pursue private (non-state) objectives, while others look like non-state agencies but aim to realize state policies. In some circumstances entrepreneurs orientate their behaviour according to "command and control" legislation passed by the state, but more typically, they form "self-regulatory networks" that negotiate regulatory outcomes with local officials. For example, I shall presently show how traders in Hanoi formed a self-regulatory network that sets the transactional conditions governing the wholesale distribution of copper wire in Northern Vietnam — an industry that is worth millions of dollars a year.

I conclude with the counterintuitive proposition that if the state wants to increase its regulatory reach it must recognize and support socially beneficial self-regulatory practices. This is not neo-liberal deregulation in disguise, but rather a recognition that there are limitations to the effectiveness of a state-based "rule of law" in Vietnam.

Conceptualizing State Control over Entrepreneurs

A careful reading of regulatory literature suggests that the prevailing assumptions about commercial regulation in Vietnam are problematic (Black, 2002; Parker et al., 2004). In what follows, I shall briefly examine current thinking about commercial regulation in Vietnam. Next, I shall review the alternative perspectives on regulation, highlighting evidence from East Asia and Vietnam that suggests non-state forms of self-regulation deserve more attention than they currently receive.

Commercial regulation in Vietnam: Prevailing modes of state-centred analysis

State mythology in Vietnam attributes private economic development to far-sighted action by the Communist Party during the Sixth Party Congress in 1986 (Do, 1994, pp. 69–70). According to this narrative, having recognized the shortcomings of the command economy, the party initiated *doi moi* (renovation) reforms that gradually relaxed controls over private enterprises and opened the economy to foreign investment and trade. As the story goes, centrally formulated policy and legal reforms, such as the Enterprise Law 1999, were instrumental in encouraging entrepreneurs to form business entities, invest capital and develop the economy.

Although most foreign-donor projects in Vietnam endorse the official narrative (Carlier & Son, 2005), they also pursue their own ideological agenda. Donors routinely invoke Hayek's (1944, p. 54) proposition that transparent, universal and predictable legal rules (a procedural rule of law) provide the optimal regulatory environment for entrepreneurs to maximize their self-interest. Both state and private entrepreneurs are supposed to seek out profit-making opportunities through spontaneous individual action, that is primarily (though not exclusively) guided by facilitative statutory rules implemented by state institutions that act as "neutral" umpires.[1] Most foreign donors conclude that only a procedural rule of law can bring order to the unbounded, inefficient and potentially anarchic self-regulatory networks.

Thus, for different reasons, both the Vietnamese government and foreign donors/investors see a state-centred legal system as the solution to private sector development. Where they differ is in the regulatory role reserved for state institutions. Foreign donors and investors support neo-liberal reforms that shift some regulatory power from the executive to enable courts to use statutory norms to resolve disputes — a facilitative legal system. Although moving in this general regulatory direction, the state is less enthusiastic about rights-based norms and places more trust in discretionary bureaucratic regulation.[2]

Alternative perceptions on commercial regulation: Decentring the analysis of regulation

Some commentators challenge state-centred explanations for private sector development (Fforde & de Vydler, 1996, pp. 3–4). Rather than leading reforms, they argue that policy-makers have struggled to control a vibrant entrepreneurial economy with state policies and laws. In this account, entrepreneurs survived decades of central planning and official suppression by co-opting, corrupting and evading state regulators (Beresford & Fforde, 1997; Gainsborough, 2003, pp. 98–109). Some state officials joined with entrepreneurs to use state-owned enterprises and assets for non-state purposes and personal gain.

This research implies that decades of legal reform have not fundamentally changed commercial behaviour and most entrepreneurs continue to rely on self-regulation and collaborative arrangements with state officials

---

[1] Hayek (1979, p. 146) recognized that humans have a collective side, but dismissed these impulses as a dangerous hangover from primitive times.
[2] "Resolution No. NQ/TW on the Judicial Reform Strategy to 2020", Politburo CPV, 2005.

rather than the facilitative legal system. As Fforde (2005, p. 242) put it: "formal law need not be important to economic life; markets can function efficiently enough, and accumulation processes can be robust enough, without identifiable and certain legal formality." If this analysis is correct and entrepreneurs do not readily identify with and support state regulatory objectives, what "rules of the game" do they follow?

Theorists for decades have recognized that both state and private order regulate entrepreneurs in Western (MacNeil, 1978, pp. 890–900) and East Asian settings (Winn, 1994). Many studies have shown that firms the world over use family and relational affiliations to either augment or substitute for facilitative property and contractual rights. There is a large *guanxi* literature about the regulatory influence of personal relationships in China (Gold, Guthrie & Wank, 2002). In a similar vein, McMillan and Woodruff (1999, pp. 1290) used relational theory to posit that "Vietnamese private firms do not yet have a formal legal system to fall back on" and instead rely on community norms, trade associations and market intermediaries; a claim that almost certainly underestimates the level of development of the Vietnamese legal system.

Using social capital theories, Dalton et al. (2002) and Norlund (2003) reached a similar conclusion about the importance of self-regulation. Dalton et al. (2002) found that business networks in Vietnam were generally less integrated with family structures than in China, the Philippines and Japan. While Norlund (2003) challenged the notion that state and private orders are mutually exclusive by showing that state relationships supplemented traditional trading linkages that had been undermined by commodity markets.

These theories offer a significant advance over state-centred analysis, because they take into account the rich and varied private order that profoundly shapes entrepreneurial behaviour. But they do not adequately explain why some modes of state regulation guide entrepreneurs more effectively than other modes. Nor do they show how the state can extend its regulatory power to correct shortcomings in self-regulatory systems.

In this article I have turned to regulatory theory for an analytical framework that does not assume that regulation is an activity exclusively performed by the state. It leaves open the possibility of mutually constituted state- and self-regulatory systems and does not assume any particular institutional or organizational arrangements or any particular techniques or normative standards. The framework is broad enough to encompass the four types of regulation discussed in this article: facilitative regulation, state bureaucratic regulation, flexible regulation and self-regulation.

The Survey of Vietnamese Entrepreneurs

Evidence presented in this article is based on qualitative interviews I conducted with 80 private companies between 2004 and 2008 — the Survey of Vietnamese Entrepreneurs (SVE).[3] Company managers and owners were interviewed at least twice, and in some cases many times, to construct a detailed picture of the regulatory framework governing their businesses. I found that ethnographic case studies furnished more reliable and insightful information than questionnaires and quantitative indicators, because they provided glimpses of the subtle processes and tacit understandings that bound the business networks. Moreover the sample size in each industry was insufficiently large to support the compilation of meaningful statistical data. The SVE covered firms in seven industry sectors (construction, wood-processing, clothing and textiles, computer manufacturing, together with trading in copper wire, electric batteries, and sunglasses). In this article I shall consider four case studies (construction, computer manufacturing and trading in copper wire and car batteries) in detail.

The Facilitative Regulatory System

Following *doi moi* reforms the state devoted considerable resources to develop the trappings of a law-based state (*nha nuoc phap quyen*) (Quinn, 2002; Gillespie, 2009, pp. 203–211). Although the reforms left the Leninist organizational structures such as party leadership over the state and society intact, at least in the commercial arena, they adopted the neo-liberal economic principle that statutory laws are supposed to facilitate rather than direct behaviour. The facilitative system is meant to protect property rights and promote contractual enforcement through the courts. These concerns lie at the heart of most legal writings about Vietnam.

This literature shows that legislative reforms have relaxed many market entry restrictions, enacted a plethora of rights-based commercial laws and improved market exit processes (Quinn, 2002). Amendments to the Civil Code and Commercial Law in 2005, for example, removed the last vestiges of the command legal system. Though much remains to be done to improve

---

3 Some of the 400 interviews were conducted with the assistance of Vietnamese lawyers (N. H. Quang and Associates and Investconsult), others were conducted with the assistance of research assistants.

the courts and judgment enforcement mechanism,[4] the reforms have established a legislative framework that covers most types of commercial transactions. Yet the SVE suggests that most domestic entrepreneurs are unmoved by the facilitative legal system and do not structure their transactions according to legal rights.

Contractual rights

In facilitative theory, self-regulatory systems function well enough in "dense social networks," but entrepreneurs are supposed to need third parties to enforce the transactions when they move outside their social network (North, 1990). Contractual rights, backed by courts, are meant to provide the transactional certainty that underpins efficient markets. Research from East Asia presents a more complex picture. It confirms the importance of state-based contractual enforcement mechanisms in reducing the risk associated with "arms-length" transactions (Haley, 1997, pp. 167–180), but it finds that family and relational networks are generally more important than public order in stabilizing long-term transactions that require ongoing co-operation (Schaede, 2000).

Analysis of data from the SVE reached similar conclusions. Vietnamese entrepreneurs only consummated long-term trading relationships involving trade credit after an extended period of trust building. During this time, which could last over two years for important business relationships, entrepreneurs attempted to generate feelings of trust, reciprocity and mutual obligation. They drank together in karaoke parlours to shed inhibitions and reveal their "true self." Entrepreneurs in the construction and computer parts industries preferred the elite world of sporting clubs and golf ranges to socialize and cement friendships. Excluded from this largely male orbit, female entrepreneurs relied more on social engagements such as weddings, birthdays and festivals to cultivate relationships.

In building trading relationships, entrepreneurs also made discreet inquiries about each other's creditworthiness and trading history. Some entrepreneurs looked for signs that their prospective business partners

---

4　A UNDP (2004) survey of attitudes towards the courts conducted in 2004 showed that only 9 per cent of respondents in high income groups had used the courts, while less than a third believed that the courts could deliver "just and fair" results. For a comprehensive review, see Nicholson (2007, pp. 247–273).

would use spiritual intervention to minimize bad luck. They felt more comfortable dealing with partners who believed in the spirit world and made offerings to spirit houses, visited pagodas and attended spiritual mediums (*len dong* or *thay cung*). They explained that in a rapidly changing business environment, good luck more than good planning and hard work underpinned success. Thus it makes sense to deal with partners who secure spiritual insurance to minimize bad luck.

Most of the entrepreneurs surveyed regularly used written agreements to document business transactions. At first glance, this development seems to support the facilitative theory that as Vietnamese firms grow in size and integrate internationally, they will augment relational transactions with the security of the "rule of law" (Clarke, 2003). Interviews with managers of two comparatively large (over 100 employees), vertically integrated wood-processing enterprises offered a different explanation. They thought the disputes between Vietnamese catfish exporters and US anti-dumping agencies in 2003 alerted many Vietnamese exporters to the dangers of poorly drafted international contracts (Intellasia, 2003). Local press reports depicted Vietnamese exporters as hapless victims of an international legal system and suggested that legal advice might have protected them from anti-dumping actions initiated by American competitors. The managers consulted foreign and Vietnamese law firms to renegotiate their export and shipping documents, not to secure more favourable commercial terms, but to clarify legal terms and conditions.

Follow-up interviews revealed that the managers had no intention of using the redrafted agreements as legally enforceable weapons to secure and protect their private interests. Instead, the contracts were viewed as "passports" to do something that would otherwise be unlawful. Though clearly wanting transactional security and certainty, they believed this objective was best secured through procedural conformity with international rules and bargaining with state regulators. They did not seriously contemplate the facilitative notion that contractual rights could check the behaviour of commercial partners and state officials.

With few exceptions, the entrepreneurs surveyed used written agreements to record transactional intentions, and not as legally binding covenants. They were uninterested in the normative standards and processes stipulated in the commercial legislation, because they did not consider the law a source of transactional guidance or security. Stable trading relationships based on family connections or friendships were overwhelmingly considered more important than rights-based laws.

Property rights

Theorists in the facilitative tradition, such as Hernando de Soto (2004), claim that statutory property rights are of fundamental importance to entrepreneurs, because they establish who can trade with what. They postulate a causal relationship between the emergence of property rights and economic development. In apparent contradiction to this theory, Vietnamese entrepreneurs for decades have flourished without resort to statutory property rights.[5] In fact, a distinguishing feature of Vietnam's land tenure system is the large number (75–80 per cent) of private land transactions that take place outside the state land title system (Dang & Palmkvist, 2001).

A survey conducted by the Ministry of Natural Resources and Environment in 2006 showed that formal land titles had been issued to less than half of the land-holdings in large urban centres such as Hanoi and Ho Chi Minh City.[6] It found that entrepreneurs sold, leased and mortgaged unregistered land through relational processes. For example, land sales were secured by a chain-of-title that was traced through a series of hand-written sale notes back to the original holder of French colonial land titles. Gold shops took physical possession of the chain-of-tile as collateral to secure loans.

More perplexingly, entrepreneurs holding registered land use right certificates (*quyen su dung dat*) routinely deal in land through relational transactions. It is commonplace to grant unregistered sub-leases or circumvent government registration charges by securing loans from gold shops by depositing title documents. Even land sales proceed without reference to state registration processes. Land is sold informally to avoid land transfer fees, but buyers can register their purchase by paying back fees and fines/bribes.

Despite recent attempts by the Land Law 2003 to systematize land tenure, it remains difficult to classify land use rights according to formal and informal categories (Tenev et al., 2003, p. 69). Studies point instead to a decentralized self-regulating land market that coexists with, and sometimes co-opts, state-issued land use rights (Kerkvliet, 2006). For example, *phuong* (ward) authorities certify and levy taxes on the sale of uncertified

---

5 Private sector industrial output rose from 7.9 per cent in 1996 to 20 per cent in 2004 (Government Statistics Office, 2006).

6 Comments about informal land use are based on information gathered by the author from government officials and private sector entrepreneurs as a consultant to the Foreign Investment Advisory Service Land Law Impact Assessment Project 2005–2007. Similar results have been observed in rural areas (ADB, 2005, pp. 17–26).

land and housing. They also validate vendors' claims to exclusive occupancy of uncertified land by affixing an official seal (*dau*) on informal house ownership papers (*chu quyen ti nhan*) issued by French colonial authorities and provisional revolutionary bodies. Officials treat formality and informality as a matter of regulatory style, where each shade of informality attracts different levels of toleration and legality.

Most entrepreneurs in the SVE expressed mixed feelings about the state-sponsored land regime. They wanted official land use rights certificates, but thought the benefits did not justify the cost of conversion, which included a transfer tax, surveying and other charges. An empirical study of the Ho Chi Minh City real estate market revealed a 3–7 per cent price differential between advertisements for land sold with land use rights certificates and informal land (Kim, 2004, pp. 294–302). In fact, many advertisements do not differentiate between the different types of title. Some vendors advertise property with legal papers (*giay to hop le*), others offer informal house ownership papers (*chu quyen ti nhan*), while surprisingly some advertisements claim to have both sets of rights.

To sum up, the facilitative property regime offers entrepreneurs commercial advantages such as state certification and mortgageable land use rights. Nevertheless, with the support of local officials, most entrepreneurs find that non- or quasi-state land tenure rights meet their core needs for transactional security and access to finance. They do not look to the facilitative property regime for transactional guidance or security.

Enforcing rights

Most of the entrepreneurs in the SVE thought that statutory rights were worthless without an effective system of legal enforcement. Even by regional standards, the commercial litigation rates in Vietnam are extremely low.[7] Making matters worse, the recovery rates for debts remains low by regional standards, 19.2 cents in the dollar in Vietnam compared with 91.3 cents in Singapore and 43.9 cents in Thailand (Nguyen, 2008, p. 13).

It is perhaps too early in the reform cycle to accurately assess whether domestic relational structures can complement or compete with the

---

7 In 2002 the annual inflow of cases filed in Vietnamese courts was approximately 200,000 or 0.00251 cases per person. During the same period there were approximately 7 million cases in China or 0.00583 cases per person, more than double the rate in Vietnam.

facilitative legal system. As the economy grows and domestic firms transact more frequently with foreigners (especially those requiring formal contracts and property rights), statutory norms may increasingly supplement familial and relational bonds in ordering commercial exchanges. However, this transformation is by no means inevitable. The SVE found that only the small number of enterprises directly dealing with foreign entities felt any compulsion to take the facilitative legal system seriously. The vast majority of entrepreneurs in the SVE wanted an orderly and predictable trading environment, but did not believe the facilitative legal system could secure this outcome. Instead they placed their trust in familial and relational transactions — self regulation.

The State Bureaucratic Regulatory Systems

State-backed regulatory systems not only protect rights, they also co-ordinate market activity. For instance, they set the terms for new market entrants, determine what constitutes fair market competition and establish the ground rules for markets. There is a growing body of opinion that where the protective (facilitative) function of law is underdeveloped, such as in Vietnam, entrepreneurs bargain outcomes with state regulators and the co-ordinating function of law dominates (Milhaupt & Pistor, 2008, pp. 4–8).

During the high socialist period (1954–86), the Leninist "state economic management" (*quan ly nha nuoc kinh te*) system was introduced to link central planning and economic production (Nguyen, 1976). It differed from Western forms of bureaucratic regulation in possessing a "party nature" (*tinh dang*) that gave party and state authorities broad extra-legal "prerogative" powers to fine-tune economic production (Hoang, 1973, pp. 8–12). Although two decades of neo-liberal-inspired deregulatory reforms have closed licensing gateways and streamlined administrative procedures, entrepreneurs in the SVE believed that contemporary officials still shared a similarity in regulatory style with socialist "state economic managers." They claimed that officials used three main modes of regulation to co-ordinate market relationships: subordinate legislation, discretionary licensing and official inspections.

The paramountcy of subordinate legislation

Most commercial laws passed by the National Assembly (NA) lack normative detail. Open-ended drafting techniques devolve responsibility for co-ordinating market activity to government agencies such as ministries (Office of Government, 2003). Ministries enact subordinate legislation that co-exists with, and not infrequently contradicts, superior laws in a complicated network of overlapping and contradictory rules (Truong, 1999). Compounding the problem, bureaucratic regulators rely more on subordinate rules issued by their leaders than on hierarchically superior laws passed by the NA. The confusion generated by thousands of subordinate rules gives government regulators considerable discretionary latitude to micro-manage entrepreneurs.

Discretionary licensing

The reforms introduced by the Enterprise Law 1999 (EL) abolished 159 business licences (*giay phep kinh doanh*), allowing entrepreneurs to enter many economic sectors without bureaucratic approval. Studies show that in some localities, the deregulatory reforms have induced a "strong commitment to simple, transparent and abridged transactions between public officials and businesses" (CIEM, 2003). Yet the Enterprise Enforcement Mission Group (*Nhom Nhiem Vu Cuong Che Doanh Nghiep*), formed by the prime minister to prevent re-regulation under the EL, found that "many local authorities still hold on to their powers to issue sub-licenses and continue to employ the 'ask-favour system' (*co che xin cho*) without regard for the consequences for the business community" (CIEM, 2003, p. 23). By 2007, the number of business licences had crept back to the pre-Enterprise Law levels (Nguyen, 2007).

Most entrepreneurs in the SVE reported few major difficulties in incorporating their businesses, but they encountered significant problems once their firms were incorporated. Discretionary controls had migrated from market entry to sub-licences and permits covering health and safety, environmental standards and fire and building controls. Regulators used licences to arrogate discretionary power to control business activities, such as the location of business premises, opening hours, and product standards — areas that were frequently unregulated by statutory law.

Official inspections

State inspections are a feature of every regulatory system. Most entrepreneurs in the SVE complained that inspections in Vietnam were not confined to monitoring compliance with legally-prescribed standards and practices, but rather act as a regulatory instrument. Inspectors take advantage of the previously mentioned overlap and contradiction between superior and subordinate legislations to extend their investigatory powers. Even where the text of legislation seems reasonably clear, its meaning is often determined by confidential policy directives. Take for example the computer trading sector: entrepreneurs interviewed in the SVE complained that the legislation governing trade promotion (*xuc tien thuong mai*) did not limit the use of advertising.[8] But the guidelines explaining "healthy advertising" contained in the internal "policy regimes" (*che do chinh sach*) instructed state agencies to limit expenditure on advertising for trade promotion. Entrepreneurs could face administrative and even criminal sanctions for violating the "policy regimes." Without knowing the nuances of the policy, they exercised caution in using advertising to increase their market share. Officials used regulatory uncertainty in this case to induce conservative marketing strategies.

The criminalization (*hinh su hoa*) of specific kinds of commercial activities is a potent regulatory instrument because it induces a psychology of compliance (Pham, 2000, pp. 3036). Politically-unconnected entrepreneurs are never certain when business activities will offend vague principles and policies. The mere threat of prosecution transforms calculable commercial risk into incalculable criminal risk and encourages entrepreneurs to form collusive arrangements with state officials (this will be discussed below).

Findings from the SVE intimate that bureaucratic regulation undermines the commercial rights championed by the facilitative system. Several factors contribute to this phenomenon. The porous boundaries between policy and law allow regulators to arrogate discretionary power. At the same time, the neo-liberal deregulatory ideas that animate facilitative legal reforms seldom percolate down to the local level. Most local regulators remain embedded in a tradition of "state economic management" and are themselves entrepreneurial in their search for opportunities to re-regulate entrepreneurs. Many entrepreneurs in the SVE were never entirely sure why they were being regulated. They felt that some officials treated "state economic management" as an objective in its own right.

---

8 Ordinance No. 39-2001-PL-UBTVQH10 on Advertising 2001; and Decree No. 24-2003-ND-CP on Providing Detailed Regulations for Implementing the Ordinance on Advertising 2003.

Entrepreneurial responses to bureaucratic regulation

The SVE indicates that bureaucratic regulation profoundly shapes private trading networks. With few exceptions, entrepreneurs worked hard to develop "relationship friendships" (*quan he*) with state officials through social events, goodwill payments and bribes. They used friendships to moderate bureaucratic inspections and gain preferential access to state regulatory policy.

Unsurprisingly, entrepreneurs responded strongly to bureaucratic regulation in the economic sectors that were heavily policed, such as the computer industry. Consider the self-regulatory networks developed by computer wholesalers. These medium-scale traders operate in a highly competitive industry in which large state and private firms use exclusive import licences and predatory pricing to squeeze smaller competitors out of the wholesale markets. In order to compete with the cartels, the medium-scale traders cut costs by avoiding import tax on brand-name computer parts.[9]

Traders have developed three strategies to "manage" their relationships with the economic police and market control inspectors. The first is to negotiate "relationship friendships." Long-term stable relationships are much preferred to short-term bribes (*dut lot*). Traders encourage feelings of reciprocity and mutual obligations by infusing relationships with sentiment (*tinh cam*). Networks based on family and friends are used to provide "good introductions" (*gioi thieu tot*) and cement relationships with state officials. Officials are then invited to karaoke parlours and plied with goodwill payments (*khoan thien chi*) and gifts on special occasions, such as weddings, birthdays and *Tet* (lunar new year). Officials generally respond by giving wholesalers advance warning about inspections and overlook irregularities in customs documentation.

Traders also negotiate standard tax payments with local officials. Payment formulas are loosely based on business turnover and aim to curb excessive claims by officials and prevent socially disruptive preferential deals. They also give traders leverage over new market entrants, who must agree to follow local trading rules in return for receiving the payment formula. Officials tacitly support this type of market network by only negotiating payments with traders familiar with the formula.

---

9 Traders estimate that approximately 70 to 80 per cent of imported computer parts avoid import taxes.

The second strategy is to avoid detection by selling smuggled goods with VAT invoices purchased on the black market. VAT invoices not only provide a cloak of legality, because only components that have been certified by customs authorities are issued with official VAT invoices, they are also needed when wholesalers sell to businesses that want to claim tax deductions for business expenses.

Given that the VAT invoices purchased on the black market are expensive, as a third strategy traders form distribution networks with small retail outlets that do not require the VAT invoices. Such networks are designed to distribute smuggled or counterfeit goods in ways that minimize payments to state inspectors. The wholesale distributors sacrifice their market share to remain close to ward (*phuong*) officials who evidently are more easily persuaded than higher-level officials to tolerate counterfeit or smuggled components priced for the domestic market.

Entrepreneurs in the SVE portrayed local regulation as *lam luat* (literally "make law"), a term that has the positive connotation of finding flexible solutions to rigid centrally imposed laws and the negative implication of inventing rules to extract rents. They negotiated with officials in a personal and highly contextual language that often (but not always) disregarded statutory rights. Officials were expected to intervene on behalf of family, friends and neighbours, and display a morality of good neighbourliness or sentiment among neighbours (*tinh cam lang gieng*) that balanced community interests against state or official interests. Correct official behaviour was assessed in terms of "being right and compassionate" (*co ly co tinh*).

To summarize, there are distinct differences between central and local modes of bureaucratic regulation. Central-level regulation is more rule-based and closely aligned to the facilitative and co-ordinating objectives of the legal system. In contrast, local regulation is best described as a series of negotiated relationships. Public and private actors negotiate policy outcomes creating a type of participatory regulation that blurs the legal distinctions between public and private realms implicit in law-based regulation.

It is important to emphasize that in some circumstances, bureaucratic regulation produces beneficial outcomes for entrepreneurs. Especially at a local level, officials often feel more responsible to the people in their locality than to higher-level authorities and central rules. They arrogate discretion to overcome rigidities in central laws, provide privileged information, enforce debts and selectively enforce administrative and criminal sanctions. They also protect private property rights and profits that have been accumulated in politically and socially responsible ways — a practice that establishes localized trading standards. In short they perform many of the functions the facilitative legal system fails to deliver.

Flexible Regulation

State regulation does not exclusively reside in statutory rules and legally prescribed bureaucratic powers. Sometimes the state enlists non-state regulatory processes to realize policy objectives. Flexible regulation involves a hybridization of state and non-state actors, where the state does not impose substantive objectives; rather it works with non-state actors to formulate regulatory policy for particular industries (Hira, 2006). In flexible regulatory arrangements, state regulators become one of the many interest groups, and are discouraged from exercising a determining judgement about what the public interest involves and how best to achieve it.

Pham Chi Lan, the former vice-president of the Vietnam Chamber of Commerce and Industry (VCCI) and an influential economic commentator, described the relationship between the state and private entrepreneurial associations in flexible regulatory terms as a "partnership," in which the state assists private firms to follow party and state socioeconomic policy.[10] In return for market information, training and access to the state tendering systems, VCCI members are expected to comply with the nuances of state socioeconomic policy (Nguyen & Stromseth, 2002).

Efforts to promote this form of flexible regulation are limited by the reluctance of private entrepreneurs to join business associations. Studies show that most entrepreneurs believe the VCCI and other state-directed associations are more interested in transmitting state policies than advocating their members' interests (Tran & Dau, 2006). Not only is membership low, but a survey conducted by the Mekong Project Development Facility in 2002 showed that entrepreneurs were much more likely to join business associations to network with other businesses (67 per cent), gain market information and access technical training (41 per cent) than rely on these bodies to promote the private sector (15 per cent) (Nguyen & Stromseth, 2002; Do, 2001). For the present, business associations play a marginal role in ordering private-sector behaviour.

10　Interview with Pham Chi Lan, Vice-President VCCI, Hanoi, March 2003.

Stronger evidence for flexible regulation can be found in the informal alliances formed between state regulators, state-owned enterprises and private enterprises in the construction industry. Tendering laws establish complex procedural and disclosure rules that co-ordinate government and foreign donor-funded (e.g., the World Bank) construction projects.[11] Government agencies form project management units to oversee the tendering process and ensure that construction projects proceed according to approved plans and building specifications. The legislative framework is closely modelled on templates supplied by the World Bank and other foreign financiers. The rules allow two types of contractors to participate in construction tenders: the first level comprises general or Equipment Procurement Construction (EPC) contractors. Sub-contractors make up the second level.

Evidence collected in the SVE shows that although the construction consortiums outwardly comply with the tendering rules, in practice the industry is regulated by a different set of normative values and strategic objectives. In direct violation of the tendering rules, the general and EPC contractors are led by SOEs that are owned, controlled or associated with the tendering authority. The lead contractors use confidential information about prices and construction standards conveyed by tendering authorities to gain a competitive advantage during public tenders.

The lead SOEs form construction "groups" (*thau con*), comprised of other SOEs and private companies that are bound together with interlocking ownership, management and profit-and-loss-sharing arrangements. Small private construction companies that lack the relational connections to join the "group" form a sub-stratum within the industry. As peripheral players, they survive on sub-contracts allocated on a project-by-project basis. Sub-contractors must pay illegal kick-back commissions, consisting of 10 to 15 per cent of the contract value, to secure work from the "group" members.

The construction "groups" qualify as trading networks, because they are bound together by family, friendships, sentiment and mutual obligation bonds. But they also serve a state regulatory function. Government authorities worry that the construction laws and regulations cannot adequately enforce the complex building codes, workplace health and safety rules and other standards needed to successfully complete construction projects. They cannot rely on

---

11 See Decree 58/2008/ND-CP guiding the implementation of the Law on Tendering and selection of constructional contractor in accordance with the Law on Construction dated May 5, 2008.

building inspectors, who lack technical skills and are easily corrupted, to enforce building codes. Poor-quality construction invites the unwelcome attention of the State Inspectorate and other investigation bodies.

To overcome shortcomings in statutory and bureaucratic regulation, government authorities cultivate construction "groups" with the skills and capital needed to implement complex tender standards and specifications. They also rely on the construction "groups" to moderate their demands for commissions, thus allowing sub-contractors to profit without cutting costs and compromising building quality.

From a central regulatory perspective, this type of flexible regulation constitutes bureaucratic corruption. Construction "groups" pay commissions in return for privileged access to information pertaining to state tenders. But this is only part of the regulatory story. For government regulators struggling to control a highly competitive and complex industry, construction "groups" provide an effective extra-legal mechanism to augment facilitative and state bureaucratic regulation. Flexible regulation allows the state to extend its regulatory reach by enlisting private order to project state policies and objectives into the construction industry. It also calls into question law-based distinctions between public and private order and intimates the importance of self-regulation in governing commercial activity.

Self-regulation

The extensive interaction and interdependence between state regulators and entrepreneurs in Vietnam suggests the need to decentre the analysis to include self-regulation. The term "self-regulation" is used to denote organizational structures and trading networks that primarily (though not exclusively) aim to secure private advantage. Self-regulation draws on norms, beliefs and personal relationships that straddle both public and private domains and includes hybrid state/private regulatory networks.

Trading networks

The SVE showed that trading relationships soon outgrew family connections and came to rely on broad relational networks for support. Entrepreneurs in each sector surveyed formed trading networks. In the computer, but more especially construction industries, trading networks were closely integrated with government bureaucracies. As the following case studies reveal, trading networks in the copper wire and battery industries are more detached from state regulators.

Copper wire trading case study

During the 1920s, shops selling copper wire began to open in Hang Bong Street in Hanoi to supply the building and electric motor industries. By the early 1960s, these businesses were collectivized into a *hop tac xa tieu thu cong ng hiep* (small industrial co-operative) to produce electric transformers. When the party decriminalized entrepreneurialism in 1988, the co-operative dissolved and private trading in copper wire resumed.

Currently the four key copper wire wholesale businesses operating in Hang Bong Street are either owned by relatives of the original copper wire shops or belong to former members of the co-operative. Business co-operation among wholesalers developed from friendships formed in the co-operative and it has been maintained and reinforced over the intervening years by social engagements, such as weddings, funerals and other special occasions. Co-operation is also predicated on the normative belief that businesses in local communities (*phuong*) should support each other (*buon co bau ban co phuong*). Although business meetings are now more frequent than social gatherings, the wholesalers do not differentiate the mutual assistance (*tuong tro lan nhau*) underpinning the trade network from the sentiment cementing personal relationships.

The wholesalers describe two spheres of co-operation. An inner group comprising the four main wholesale businesses co-operates closely, meeting regularly at early morning "tea clubs" to share market information about prices, quality and supply as well as to negotiate deals with each other. They work together to price competitors out of the northern market. Market stability is valued above short-term profits and competition. Members are expected to regularly attend "tea club" meetings, and will be excluded from the network for providing misleading or inaccurate information to other members.

Most of the business norms and tacit assumptions that guide business transactions in this industry are generated by the inner group. The complex rules governing wholesale transactions, which may exceed US$100,000 in value, are formulated during "tea club" meetings.

A set of explicit and tacit understandings are used to balance competition and co-operation. Members, for example, are expected not only to share commercially sensitive market information, but also to loan copper wire to each other to make up large orders. They co-operate with each other to collect debts by sharing information about the creditworthiness of retail purchasers and by withholding supply to repeat offenders. Members are also encouraged to promote the image of the copper wire traders and avoid sharp business practices, misleading advertising, poaching customers by paying high commissions (kick-backs) and selling counterfeit goods.

Attempts to promote product standards and fix market prices, delivery terms and credit conditions have been less successful. For example, suppliers are expected to compensate buyers for losses caused by late delivery and/or defects in products supplied. But members could not agree on whether compensation should take into account the full economic harm sustained, including loss of profits. Failing agreement, compensation is negotiated on a case-by-case basis, taking into account the commercial value of each customer.

Occasionally, members join together to combat state interference, such as excessive demands for bribes or delayed payments by SOEs — a common problem for all entrepreneurs. Typically a leading member of the group uses political connections and the collective voice of the group as social leverage in negotiations with officials. This strategy sends the message that officials cannot interfere with one member without dealing with all the members. Group mediation is most effective at the local level; central regulators apparently have less to gain from maintaining good relationships with traders.

The outer group comprises approximately 30 copper wire retailers located in Hang Bong Street and the thieves market (*choi du*) in Hanoi. Co-operation among this group is loose and rarely extends beyond sharing market information and advancing short-term credit. Attempts to build a more cohesive association have been frustrated by the limited means available to control opportunistic behaviour among group members. There are too many copper wire suppliers for the inner group to use supply constraints to prevent retailers from undercutting each other to gain market share.

Battery trading case study

Much higher levels of co-operation have been achieved by the Northern Areas Battery Shops Group (*Hiep Hoi Cac Cua Hang Ac Qui Khu Vuc Phia Bac*). In 1997, a respected battery shop owner contacted 25 other battery traders in the Hanoi area to establish a network to share information, control market territory and settle internal grievances. As one member put it, "in the market-oriented economy today, enterprises compete harshly, and ethical principles seem to be ignored. We have established this group to preserve people's sentimental and ethical principles. This group also aims to help all members to survive and develop in the face of competition" (Cuong, 2007). The group has been remarkably successful in maintaining market share. No new battery shops have opened in the northern region since 1997, even though the market for batteries has almost doubled in size. Competitors have been excluded from the market by a combination of predatory pricing and supply restrictions.

At first, members organized the group through informal social engagements, such as dinners, karaoke nights and weddings — social engagements that generated *tinh cam* (sentiment). The group is now more formalized with a written charter, fee structure and office bearers, including an elected head who performs a co-ordinating role. A member recalled that "our head was elected because of his age and experience. He is the person who collects members' opinions to reach agreement among the group, not the person who imposes his own view on others." Like the copper wire network, the group has remained unregistered to avoid strict state control over business associations.

Internal rules and processes formalized as the group developed. For example, the group's first charter covered matters such as membership and attendance at meetings. It also encouraged group members to co-operate to avoid market manipulation, hoarding and predatory pricing in the unregulated market, but stopped short of stipulating prescriptive rules.

In 2002, some members thought it was time to revise the charter and prescribed formal steps to stabilize the market. But other members rejected this development on the grounds that further formalization would undermine the sentimental bonds that held the group together. They argued that informal agreements that subdivided the market into separate territories were remarkably stable and that social pressure and threats to limit the supply of batteries provided effective controls over opportunistic behaviour.

The group has also successfully promoted business norms and practices among its members. Members are discouraged from using sharp trading practices that may damage the reputation of battery suppliers and traders. For example, members are expected to supply goods that comply with basic contractual warranties regarding quality, fitness for purpose and product service. In addition the group supplies a standard sales contract to its members. Although the agreements look like legally binding sales contracts, in practice they operate more like advertising brochures. They promote battery sales by listing the after-sales services provided by the group members.

Both the copper wire and battery groups function like self-regulatory communities. Members rarely order their behaviour according to statutory provisions, and their collaborative and monopolistic networks could hardly differ more from the market assumptions underpinning the rights-based facilitative law. Although group members emphasize the importance of *tinh cam* in promoting shared understandings about the correct approach to regulatory problems, other constituting factors are important. Members repeat particular stories that depict those outside the group as ruthless, irrational and fraudulent. They stress the need to form a trading network based on respect and market stability to protect them against unconscionable market competition.

With varying degrees of success, the self-regulatory groups have created their own regulatory universe by prescribing transactional standards and dispute resolution processes. These precepts and practices not only encode certain assumptions about proper business behaviour, they also distance and distinguish members from the *luat rung* (law of the jungle) in the market place.

Regulatory communities

The SVE suggests that entrepreneurs in northern urban centres inhabit three regulatory orbits — the state, family and trading networks. Of these, the facilitative legal system exerts the least influence over entrepreneurial behaviour. Had the survey included foreign investors, or even large export-oriented SOEs, the findings may well have revealed more interest in this type of "rule of law."

State bureaucratic regulation, on the other hand, touched virtually every business activity and was characterized by power differentials and rent-seeking. In some sectors, it blurred distinctions between public and private order, while in other sectors it left entrepreneurs space to develop self-regulatory networks. Though most entrepreneurs reluctantly accepted bribery and gift-giving as a cost of doing business in Vietnam, they turned to the regulatory networks for strategies to moderate predatory behaviour by state officials.

The central players in regulatory networks acted like nodes, collecting, moderating and transmitting information within the community. In addition to industry experience and social standing, the central players displayed political skills in dealing with state regulators. In the computer, and especially the construction industries, connections with state regulators were the single most important attribute.

Because network members lived significant parts of their lives together, they influenced each other to act for collective interests. Although sometimes pursuing their own economic objectives, in general they worked towards their common objectives. Members repeated particular stories that stressed the need to form a network to protect the group against unconscionable competition. Over time particular story-lines about the nature of business problems and the correct regulatory solution gathered authority. In this way the communities seemed to act as constitutive forums in which appropriate commercial behaviour was being constantly defined and redefined. Assumptions about the morally correct modes of business were used to differentiate members from non-members.

The degree of cohesion varied among the networks surveyed. The copper wire traders were rather heterogeneous in their use of language and ideas to construct regulatory meanings, while the battery traders formalize particular story-lines to create their own regulatory universe.

Decentring the Regulation of Entrepreneurs

The SVE findings send a clear message that the state cannot rely on facilitative legislation to order private commercial activity. To improve the public and private order, it is necessary to understand that the public and private regulation in Vietnam is closely intertwined. They influence each other. Poor public order in the form of inappropriate imported legislation and corrupt bureaucratic regulation induces poor private order.

There are four main reasons for decentring regulation in Vietnam. One, state power and market knowledge are fragmented in Vietnam. The blurred roles of the party and state, and especially the central and local governments, produce polycentric power structures that resist classification as state-centric regulation. A decentred perspective envisages a wide set of techniques such as flexible regulation that can accommodate the regulatory diversity.

Two, in a highly fragmented market, moreover, it cannot be assumed that any one actor, including the state, has sufficient knowledge to solve complex regulatory problems. State-centred regulation assumes that only states have the capacity to command and control entrepreneurs.

Three, entrepreneurs are autonomous and difficult to govern with centrally formulated "command-and-control" rules. Regardless of what the state does, entrepreneurs are likely to self-regulate to moderate bureaucratic controls and stabilize markets. Shared understandings within self-regulatory communities shape the way members perceive the world, define their self-interests and devise strategies to realize those interests.

Four, especially at the local level, the public and private order is mutually constituted. Local-level bureaucrats negotiate regulatory outcomes with entrepreneurs — a process that undermines the normative aims of facilitative law. Hybrid public/private organizations and networks blur the boundaries separating the public and private, legal and extra-legal and state-centred and decentred regulation.

All this suggests that rather than dictating from above, state authorities need to work together with entrepreneurs to steer commercial regulation toward socially desirable objectives. However there are several hurdles to implementing a more decentred and flexible regulatory approach in Vietnam. The first is conceptual. Governance is grounded on the twin notions of party leadership over the state and society and the Soviet doctrine of democratic centralism — both require inferior levels to obey superior levels (Gillespie, 2006, pp. 105–130). Together these approaches leave little conceptual space for the state to experiment with decentred regulation. Despite some movement towards a more participatory form of law-making, the state still struggles with the notion that successful regulation needs popular consent.

International donors and investors are also unlikely to accept a decentred understanding of law that recognizes and validates self-regulatory practices. Informed by the Hayekian proposition that productive capitalism needs a "rule of law," many international donor projects aim to establish a centralized legal system that promotes facilitative regulation. But efforts to promote the "rule of law" end up as "rule by law" and all sorts of entrepreneurial behaviour among state officials are intent on applying, expanding, and protecting their powers, legitimately or otherwise.

The second hurdle is finding practical ways to counter shortcomings with self-regulation, such as anticompetitive and discriminatory practices. Solutions to these problems are not to be found within self-regulatory practices or "traditional" commercial norms. Yet if remedies are borrowed from foreign laws, much more effort is required to broaden the dialogue between the law-makers and entrepreneurs, so that imported norms are naturalized to meet local needs. Genuine participation in law-making can foster public acceptance, if not agreement with laws. Currently the commercial laws reflect primarily the interests of SOEs and foreign investors who have political connections to influence law-making and enforcement.

The third hurdle is that state bureaucratic regulation induces pathologies in self-regulatory networks. To improve bureaucratic regulation, the state needs to develop more effective structures to prevent arbitrary property confiscation (either directly or through excessive fees, arbitrary taxes, demands for bribes, etc.). This transformation is the most complex of all, because it requires increased public accountability for state officials — a reform that the party and state have so far not seriously tackled (Gillespie, 2009).

Calls for decentred regulation are not neo-liberal deregulation in disguise. The state is part of the solution, because states regulate for the public good — a normative concern that is largely absent from most private order. States have higher obligations than maximizing wealth accumulation. They have the potential to transcend self-interest and promote a common good that can guide socially responsible self-regulation.

In contrast, self-regulatory networks focus primarily on the well-being of their members and rarely address broader societal concerns. They may generate efficiencies that are not possible in state regulatory systems, and yet the underlying assumptions of self-interest and wealth maximization are not fertile ground for developing the notions of common good required for unified markets. State-centred regulation requires entrepreneurs to trust in the state, however private order does not create the civic faith needed to generate broad-based systems of trust.

This does not mean that the public order should supplant self-regulation, since there are many areas such as the ordering of long-term trading relationships where private order is superior. But in order to promote socially beneficial self-regulation the state needs to find alternatives to a "rule of law" based on facilitative regulation, because this mode of regulation lacks social acceptance. Findings from the SVE suggest that flexible regulation that enlists non-state actors in state-sanctioned regulatory projects offers a promising way of extending the "rule of law" without relying on facilitative regulation.

References

ADB. (2005). The impact of land markets on the poor: Implementing de Soto's "Making Markets Work Better for the Poor." Discussion Paper 3. Hanoi: Asian Development Bank.

Beresford, M., & Fforde, A. (1997). A methodology for analyzing the process of economic reform in Vietnam: The case for domestic trade. *Journal of Communist Studies and Transitional Politics*, 13(4), 99–128.

Black, J. (2002). Regulatory conversations. *Journal of Law and Society*, 29(1), 163–196.

Carlier, A., & Son, Thanh Tran. (2005). *Promoting business to business commercial contracts in Vietnam*. Vietnam private sector development policy note. Hanoi: World Bank.

CIEM. (2003). Comparative provincial performance in private business development. VIE01/025, November. Hanoi: CIEM.

Clarke, D. (2003). Economic development and the rights hypothesis: The China problem. *American Journal of Comparative Law*, 51, 89–100.

Cuong, Phung Quang. (2007). Interview with Phung Quang Cuong, battery shop owner, Hanoi, March 2007.

Dalton, R., Hac, Minh Pham, Nghi, Thanh Pham, & Ong, Nhu-Ngoc. (2002). Social relationships and social capital in Vietnam: Findings from the 2001 World Values Survey. *Comparative Sociology*, 1(3–4), 369–386.

Dang, H., & Palmkvist, G. (2001). *Sweden–Vietnam cooperation on land administration reform in Vietnam*. Hanoi: SIDA.

De Soto, H. (2004). *The mystery of capitalism*. New York: Basic Books.

Do, Anh Tuan. (2001). *Business associations and promotion of small and medium eEnterprises in Vietnam*. Working Papers No. 7. Leipzig: Universitat Leipzig.

Do, Muoi (trans.). (1994, January 24). Political report to the mid-term National Party Conference, 20 January 1994. *FBIS East Asia Daily Report*, 94(15), 68–70.

Fforde, A. (2005). SOEs, law and a decade of market-orientated socialist development. In: J. Gillespie & P. Nicholson (Eds.), *Asian socialism and legal change: The dynamics of Vietnamese and Chinese reform* (pp. 239–266). Canberra: Asia-Pacific Press.

Fforde, A., & de Vydler, S. (1996). *From plan to market: The economic transition in Vietnam*. Boulder, CO: Westview.

Gainsborough, M. (2003). *Changing political economy of Vietnam*. London: Routledge Curzon.

Gillespie, J. (2006). *Transplanting commercial law reform: Developing a "rule of law" in Vietnam*. Aldershot, UK: Ashgate.

Gillespie, J. (2009). The juridification of administrative complaints and review in Vietnam. In: Tom Ginsburg & Albert Chen (Eds.), *Administrative law and judicialized governance in Asia: Comparative perspectives* (pp. 203–227). London: Routledge.

Gold, T., Guthrie, D., & Wank, D. (Eds.). (2002). *Social connections in China*. Cambridge: Cambridge University Press.

Government Statistics Office. (2006). Retrieved online on August 14, 2009 from: http://www.gso.gov.vn/Default.aspx?tabid=217

Haley, J. (1997). Relational contracting: Does community count? In: Harold Baum (Ed.), *Japan: Economic success and legal system* (pp. 167–180). Berlin: de Gruyter.

Hayek, F. (1944). *The road to serfdom*. Chicago, IL: University of Chicago Press.

Hayek, F. (1979). *Law, legislation and liberty*, Vol. 2. London: Routledge & Kegan Paul.

Hira, A. (2006). Governance crisis in Asia: Developing a responsive regulation. In: Michael Howlett & M. Ramesh (Eds.), *Deregulation and its discontents: Rewriting the rules in Asia* (pp. 13–28). Cheltenham: Edward Elgar.

Hoang, Quoc Viet. (1973). Tang Cuong Che Xa Hoi Chu Nghia Trong Cong Tac Quan Ly Xi Nghiep [Strengthening socialist legality in management enterprises]. Hanoi: Nhan Xuat Ban Su That (Truth Publishing).

Intellasia. (2003). Anti-dumping seminar, 12 Dec. 2003, Ministry of Finance. Retrieved online on June 12, 2008 from the Intellasia website: http://www.intellasia.net/news/articles/legal/111182047.shtml

Kerkvliet, B. (2006). Agricultural land in Vietnam: Markets tempered by family, community and socialist practices. *Journal of Agrarian Change*, 6(3), 285–305.

Kim, A. (2004). A market without the "right" property rights. *Economics of Transition*, 12(2), 275–305.

MacNeil, I. (1978). Contracts: Adjustment of long term economic relations under classical, neoclassical and relational contract law. *North Western University Law Review*, 72(1), 854–900.

McMillan, J., & Woodruff, C. (1999). Interfirm relationships and informal credit in Vietnam. *Quarterly Journal of Economics*, 114(4), 1285.

Milhaupt, C., & Pistor, K. (2008). *Law and capitalism*. Chicago, IL: University of Chicago Press.

Nguyen, Nien. (1976, September 30). Several legal problems in the leadership and management of industry under the conditions of the present improvement of economic management in our country (J.P.R.S. Trans.). *Luat Hoc*, 33(14), 34–36.

Nguyen, Sa. (2007, October 15). Licenses torment businessmen. Retrieved online on August 14, 2009 from *Vietnamnet*: http://english.vietnamnet.vn/news/2005/10/501069/

Nguyen, Thi Thom. (2008). Improving business environment. *Vietnam Economic Review*, 7, 3–13.

Nguyen, Phuong Quynh Trang, & Stromseth, J. (2002). *Business associations in Vietnam: Status, roles and performance*. Private sector discussions No. 13. Hanoi: MPDF

Nicholson, P. (2007). *Borrowing court systems: The experience of socialist Vietnam*. Leiden: Martinus Nijhoff.

Norlund, I. (2003). Social capital or social capitalism: Diversification of the Vietnamese rural scenery. Unpublished paper presented to the International Conference on "Modernization and Social Transformation in Vietnam: Social Capital Formation and Institution Building," organized by the Munich Institute for Social Sciences, Germany and Hanoi Institute of Socio-economic Development Studies, Vietnam.

North, D. (1990). *Institutions, institutional change and economic performance*. Cambridge: Cambridge University Press.

Office of Government. (2003). Study report to improve the quality of law and ordinances, drafted by the government to be submitted to the NA and NA Standing Committee. Unpublished report, Working Delegation No. 804. Hanoi: Office of Government.

Parker, C., Scott, C., Lacey, N., & Braithwaite, J. (2004). *Regulating law*. Oxford: Oxford University Press.

Pham, Duy Nghia. (2000). Hinh Su Hoa Cac Giao Dich Dan Su Kinh Te: Quan Niem Bieu Hien va Mot So Giai Phap Khac Phuc [The process of criminalization of civil and economic transactions: Ideas, manifestations and some solutions]. *Tap Chi Nghien Cuu Lap Phap*, 6, 30–36.

Quinn, B. (2002). Legal reform and its context in Vietnam. *Columbia Journal of Asian Law*, 15, 219–275.

Schaede, U. (2000). *Cooperative capitalism: Self-regulation, trade associations and the antimonopoly law in Japan*. Oxford: Oxford University Press.

Tenev, S., Carlier, A., Chaudry, O., & Nguyen, Quynh-Trang. (2003). *Informality and the playing field in Vietnam's business sector*. Washington: IFC, World Bank, & MPDF.

Tran, Huu Huynh, & Dau, Anh Tuan. (2006). *Draft report business associations*. Unpublished. Hanoi: VCCI.

Truong, Thanh Duc. (1999). Nhung Bat Cap Trong Viec Xay Dung va Ban Hanh Van Ban Quy Pham Phap Luat [Defects in building and promulgating legal instruments]. *Nha Nuoc va Phap Luat*, 2, 22–29.

UNDP. (2004). Access to justice: Survey from the people's perspective. Unpublished paper (pp. 12–13). Hanoi: UNDP.

Winn, J. (1994). Relational practices and the marginalization of law: A study of the informal financial practices of small businesses in Taiwan. *Law and Society Review*, 28, 193.

[5]

Legal transplantation and local knowledge: Corporate governance in Malaysia

*Mohammad Rizal Salim**

Malaysia's company law is based on the British template, brought about by British colonial policy of transplanting British commercial laws to the whole of the British Empire. This has long guided legal development in this area of law. This article argues that the British template is not wholly appropriate for many of Malaysia's governance problems. The shareholding structure in Malaysia gives rise to a specific agency problem, the powers of controlling shareholders, which was inadequately addressed by a corporate regime which focuses on the duties of directors. There are other issues which impact on the efficacy of corporate governance regulation in Malaysia. These include culture and value systems, the quality of legal institutions, issues relating to access to courts, and the influence of the state in businesses. The problems arising from these can neither be resolved merely by reforming the law-in-the-books nor by adopting foreign legal templates. Reforms should instead be more comprehensive and pay attention to the uniqueness in the local setting.

1 Malaysia — Background

Malaysia today comprises of Peninsular Malaysia (formerly known as Malaya) and the states of Sabah and Sarawak in the island of Borneo. 'Malaya' is a European invention.[1] It was a collection of isolated feudal kingdoms separated by untouched wilderness.[2] The feudal kingdom of Malacca was once the dominant power. This ended with Malacca's defeat at the hands of the Portuguese in the sixteenth century. The Dutch occupied Malacca in the seventeenth century, followed by the British in the eighteenth. The British initially established settlements on the island of Penang and later spread their influence in Malacca and Singapore.[3] The primary reason for the establishment of these settlements was to protect British trade — Penang was founded as a naval base for this purpose. Early British policy was thus one of non-interference in local affairs. This policy was reversed to better promote British commercial interests.[4]

The first colonial court was officially established in 1807, the date of the first Charter of Justice. This Charter paved the way for the establishment of a Court of Prince of Wales on the island of Penang and conferred upon the court

---

* Ph D Lecturer, Faculty of Law, Universiti Teknologi MARA, Malaysia. I thank Philip Lawton and the anonymous reviewer for their comments on earlier drafts. I take full responsibility for errors. Comments welcomed, please email to <riz.salim@gmail.com>.
1 R O Winstead, *The Malays: A Cultural History*, Graham Brash, Singapore, 1981 (revised and updated).
2 B Simandjuntak, *Malayan Federalism 1945–1963*, Oxford UP, Kuala Lumpur, 1969, p 1.
3 Singapore was a part of the Straits Settlement but made a crown colony in 1946, and later a self governing colony. In 1963, it merged with Malaya, and, together with Sabah and Sarawak, formed the Federation of Malaysia. It separated from the Federation by mutual consent two years later to become an independent republic.
4 Simandjuntak, above n 2, pp 6–7.

'the jurisdiction and powers of the Superior Court of England ... so far as local circumstances will admit' and as an Ecclesiastical Court 'so far as the several religions, manners and customs of the inhabitants will admit'. The Second and Third Charters of Justice in 1826 and 1855 respectively extended the jurisdiction of English law to Malacca and Singapore. The Charters required colonial courts to give recognition to the diverse races, customs and religions of the inhabitants as a matter of necessity to prevent 'injustice or oppression which would ensue if that law were applied to alien unmodified'.[5] In practice, only personal laws of the locals were recognised[6] while British commercial laws were applied uncontested. The successive Charters of Justice made it possible to import British statutes, common law and rules of equity, while British administration in these settlements and other Malay states made it possible to import British-style bureaucratic and legal institutions.[7]

Like other former British colonies, Malaysia adopted British-style political democracy and exercises the separation of powers with the judiciary independent from both the executive and the legislature. Also common to other former British colonies, Malaysia inherited the British common law system and borrowed the British Companies Act. The first local company law statute was the Straits Settlements Companies Ordinance 1889,[8] later replaced by successive Companies Ordinances of 1915, 1923 and 1940. For the Federated Malay states,[9] the applicable law was the Companies Enactment 1897 and later 1917. The Unfederated Malay states[10] had similar Company Enactments. The different statutes were necessitated by the different administrative structures. More importantly, these statutes reflected the company law as then existed in England.

A Malayan Union which unified the administrative structure in all of the Malay states was established after the Second World War. Following this, the Companies Ordinance 1946 was enacted which extended the application of the Straits Settlement Companies Ordinance 1940 to the other Malay states. This statute continued to be in force even after Malaya achieved independence in 1957. Following the formation of Malaysia in 1963,[11] the Companies Act 1965 was enacted to replace the 1946 Ordinance. It was based on the British Companies Act of 1929, but in some respects was closer to the Australian Uniform Companies Act 1961, a modernised version of the 1929 Act. As a result of these transplantations, the doctrines of separate legal personality and

---

5 *Khoo Hooi Leong v Khoo Chong Yeok* [1930] AC 346 at 355.
6 Barry Hooker said that the application of British precedents and statutes to personal laws gave rise to a 'hybrid' law, a 'pure invention of the nineteenth century English judicial mind': B M Hooker, 'English Law and the Invention of Chinese Personal Law in Singapore and Malaysia' in B M Hooker (Ed), *Law and the Chinese in Southeast Asia*, Institute of Southeast Asian Studies, Singapore, 2002, pp 95–6.
7 In the Malay states under the British resident system (ie, the Federated Malay States comprising Perak, Selangor, Negeri Sembilan and Pahang) the Resident-General usurped the powers of the Malay Sultan as the highest authority in the administration of justice. In the Unfederated Malay States (Johor, Terengganu, Kedah, Kelantan and Perlis), a British advisor was appointed.
8 Prior to this the Indian Companies Ordinance 1866 was applied in the Straits Settlements.
9 Above n 7.
10 Ibid.
11 See above n 3.

limited liability as applied in Britain were made part of the law of the land.[12] This and the landmark decision by the House of Lords in *Salomon v Salomon & Co Ltd*[13] had formed the basis of the company's existence in Malaysia as it has been in Britain.

In terms of corporate regulation, Malaysia was generally regarded as having one of the best legal regimes in Asia, rivalling her closest neighbour Singapore and also Hong Kong.[14] She has excellent accounting standards.[15] Auditing standards complied with international standards, which was said to exceed even US' standards.[16] Even to critical observers, Malaysia was seen to be committed in improving her corporate legal environment. As far back as 1994, the requirements for independent directors and independent audit committees had been put in place.[17] A new disclosure based regulatory regime was introduced in 1996.[18] The establishment of a Financial Reporting Foundation to oversee corporate reporting standards was established a year later.

Despite having all these rules and legal structure, Malaysia was not spared from the financial crisis which swept the region beginning 1997.[19] In fact, the crisis exposed some inherent problems in Malaysian corporate governance regime, in particular those related to the protection of minority shareholders. The government took the initiative to address this by establishing the High Level Finance Committee on Corporate Governance in 1998 with a mandate to enhance the standards of corporate governance in Malaysia. The committee came up with the *Report on Corporate Governance* in early 1999, in which it proposed a draft code on corporate governance, together with some proposals for further reforms to improve governance.[20] Since the publication of the Report, new governance measures have been taken, among them the publication of the *Code of Corporate Governance* in 2000: the requirement for beneficial owners of securities to declare their status,[21] quarterly reporting of financial information,[22] the requirement to include a director's report in the annual reports to shareholders, income statement, balance sheet, cash flow

---

12 Malaysian Companies Act 1965 ss 16(5), 18(3) and 214(1)(d). Section 16(5) of the Act provides that the company 'shall be a body corporate . . . capable forthwith of exercising all the function of an incorporated company'.
13 [1897] AC 22.
14 Economic Analytical Unit, Department of Foreign Affairs and Trade Australia, *Changing Corporate Asia: What Business Needs to Know*, Vol 2, Regional Economic Studies, Canberra, 2002.
15 The Malaysian Accounting Standards Board reviews international accounting standards and modifies them where necessary so that it suits local conditions.
16 Economic Analytical Unit, above n 14, p 144.
17 Bursa Malaysia, *Listing Requirements*, paras 15.10, 15.10(1)(a) and 15.11.
18 Securities Commission Act 1993. See M R Salim, 'The Prospectus Disclosure Regulatory Regime in Malaysia' (2001) 1 *UiTM L Rev* 24.
19 The crisis started in Thailand and affected the currencies and stock market of several Asian economies including Malaysia. The combination of the currency devaluation, depressed share and asset prices resulted in a severe recession in the affected countries.
20 Malaysian High Level Finance Committee on Corporate Governance, *Report on Corporate Governance*, 1999.
21 A 1998 amendment to the Securities Industry (Central Depository) Act 1991 now requires securities accounts to be opened in the name of beneficial owners or authorised nominees.
22 Bursa Malaysia, *Listing Requirements*, para 9.22 amended in 1999.

statement and detail equity changes,²³ and new laws imposing stringent disclosure standards for prospectuses and heavy sanctions for false or misleading statements or material omission.²⁴ All directors of listed companies are now required to attend an accreditation program to ensure competency and a limitation has been imposed on the number of their directorships so that they might give better attention to their responsibilities.²⁵ A shareholder watchdog group in the form of Minority Shareholder Watchdog Group has been established by some large institutional investors, led by a public institution, the Employees Provident Fund (EPF), to establish the foundation for the growth of shareholder activism. These new governance initiatives were further enhanced with the publication of the *Capital Market MasterPlan* by the Securities Commission in 2001 with promises for increased efficiency and creating a more conducive environment for investors.²⁶ The Companies Commission established a Corporate Law Reform Committee in 2003 which has published five Consultative Documents.²⁷

While reforms have resulted in improvement of corporate governance, this article argues that there are some weaknesses. Law reforms have not been grounded on local knowledge. Differences in shareholding structure, as well as economic, political and cultural differences, mean that the nature of the problems and the solutions to them vary across markets. In particular, a governance regime which has as its focus the shareholder-director agency conflict may not be wholly appropriate in a corporate environment where the excessive powers of controlling shareholders creates the biggest agency problem. Additionally, culture and value systems, the quality of legal institutions, issues related to access to courts, and the influence of politics in business, have so far undermined reform efforts.

2 Legal transplants

It was said that legal transplants was one of the most important sources of legal development.²⁸ Reception of laws occurred both voluntarily and involuntarily. The European legal harmonisation project and the adoption of corporate governance codes are examples of voluntary transplants. Forced transplant occurred primarily through the imposition of colonial laws.²⁹ In

---

23 Bursa Malaysia, *Listing Requirements*, para 9.25.
24 Securities Commission Act, Pt IV Div 3.
25 Bursa Malaysia, *Listing Requirements*, paras 15.09 and 15.06.
26 Securities Commission Malaysia, *Capital Market MasterPlan Malaysia*, 2001.
27 They are: *A Strategic Framework for the Corporate Law Reform Programme*, 2004; *On Capital Maintenance Rules and Share Capital, Simplifying and Streamlining Provisions Applicable to Share*, 2005; *On Engagement with Shareholders*, 2006; *On Company Liquidation — Reforms and Restatement of Law*, 2006; and *On Clarifying and Reformulating the Directors' Role and Duties*, 2006.
28 Alan Watson said that legal transplantation is 'extremely common' and forms 'the most fertile source of [legal] development': A Watson, *Legal Transplants: An Approach to Comparative Law*, 2nd ed, The University of Georgia Press, Athens, 1993, p 95.
29 A legal transplant from this perspective overlaps with legal colonialism, a field of study which examines the relationship between the coloniser and the colonised, in particular how the colonisers sought to exert control over the indigenous population. This was done in various ways, including the co-option of local elites, formalising and creating new customary laws: R Gordon, 'The White Man's Burden: Ersatz Customary Law and Internal

many colonised countries, there existed a multiplicity of legal systems in which the colonial system existed alongside the customary one, thus providing a link between legal colonialism and legal pluralism.[30]

Law was not only a core institution of colonial control, it was the cutting edge of colonialism.[31] The imposition of colonial laws has two main purposes. First, it served the needs of commerce and capitalism by allowing the appropriation of labour and land; and second the imposition of the rule of law was seen as an 'ideological cornerstone of the civilizing process'.[32] From another perspective, the imposition of colonial laws served as a double-edged sword — it was not only an oppressive instrument of power but also an avenue to limit the excesses of colonial control.[33] Regardless of the motivations, colonialism often involved large-scale transfer of laws and legal institutions from one society to another notwithstanding the differences of socio-cultural organisation and legal culture.[34]

Alan Watson controversially asserted that the autonomy of law means that it can be freely transplanted from one jurisdiction to another. Contemporary comparative law scholars however take the view that law is culture-specific and cannot be transferred from one society to another and have the exact same effect. The transplanted law will inevitably develop as it interacts with indigenous laws and other elements in the host country.[35] Questions remain,

---

Pacification in South Africa' (1989) 2 *Jnl of Historical Sociology* 41; F Snyder, 'Colonialism and Legal Form: The Creation of "Customary Law" in Senegal' (1981) 19 *Jnl of Legal Pluralism* 49; B M Hooker, *Legal Pluralism: An Introduction to Colonial and Neo-colonial Laws*, Clarendon, Oxford, 1975; Hooker, above n 6, pp 95–6. More recently researchers have turned their attention to the ways the indigenous population has attempted to resist the imposition of these laws: S E Merry, 'Law and Colonialism' (1991) 25 *Law and Society Review* 889; F Snyder and D Hay, 'Comparisons in the Social History of Law: Labour and Crime' in F Snyder and D Hay (Eds) *Labour, Law and Crime*, Tavistock, London, 1987.

30 S E Merry, 'Legal Pluralism' (1988) 22 *Law & Society Rev* 869 at 872–3.
31 M Chanock, *Law, Custom, and Social Order: The Colonial Experience in Malawi and Zambia*, Cambridge UP, Cambridge, 1985, p 4.
32 S E Merry, *Colonizing Hawai'i: The Cultural Power of Law*, Princeton UP, Princeton, 2000.
33 D Harris, *Fish, Law and Colonialism: The Legal Capture of Salmon in British Columbia* Toronto UP, Toronto, 2001, p 196.
34 Merry, above n 29, at 890.
35 A Watson, 'Comparative Law and Legal Change' (1978) 37 *Cambridge Law Jnl* 313. His critics include Otto Kahn-Freund who asserted that it cannot be assumed that all laws are transplantable. For Kahn-Freund, laws which are deeply embedded in a society will not be suitable for legal transplants. It will be necessary to first determine the relationship between the legal rule to be transplanted (whether mechanical or organic) and the socio-political structure of the origin jurisdiction. It will also be necessary to compare the socio-political environment of both the origin and the receiving jurisdiction. This two-pronged process is necessary to determine the viability of the transplantation: O Kahn-Freund, 'On Use and Misuse of Comparative Law' (1974) 37 *Modern L Rev* 1. Ann and Robert Seidman, drawing from their experience in China where they were involved in a law drafting project concluded that 'save accidentally, no country can copy another country's law and achieve similar outcomes': A Seidman and R B Seidman, 'Drafting Legislation for Development: Lessons from a Chinese Project' (1996) 44 *Am J Comp L* 1 at 34. See also A Seidman and R B Seidman, *State and Law in the Development Process: Problem Solving and Institutional Change in the Third World*, Macmillan, Hampshire/London, 1994. Gunther Teubner claimed that the essential question is how closely a particular area of law is 'coupled' to one or more 'social processes'. He says that received ideas act as an 'irritant', resulting in distortion of the ideas behind the law which is being transplanted: G Teubner, 'Legal Irritants: Good Faith in British Law or How Unifying Law Ends Up in New Divergences' (1998) 61 *Mod L Rev*

however, on whether transplanted laws can be as effective in their host country as in the country of origin. One view was that these laws, at least in the early stages of transplantation, would not be as effective as laws which have been developed locally. This is due to the absence of a lawmaking process which can be as important as the law itself, if not more. A series of studies by Katharina Pistor and others found evidence of shortcomings in transplanted laws in their new environment. They concluded that legal institutions in transplant countries were less effective compared to those in the origin countries,[36] transplant countries were less innovative than the origin countries,[37] and transplanted corporate laws were often retained despite substantial economic changes.[38]

These and other scholars also presented persuasive arguments that Western approaches to law have sometimes been ignored or were slow to gain acceptance[39] and that strong path dependence between economic development, legality and the transplant effect helps explain why legal technical assistance projects that focus primarily on improving the laws on the books frequently have little impact.[40] These views are consistent with another study which showed evidence that transplanted legal systems and rules of procedure lead to inefficiency due to high levels of procedural formalism.[41] The other cause for this lack of efficiency may be due to the transplanted law's struggle to assimilate with indigenous laws. This is especially the case when there are cultural differences between the origin and host countries, as it will complicate the assimilation process which is often the case where Western law is transplanted in non-Western countries. Japanese Law Professor Masaji Chiba argued that it was very common for received Western law to conflict with indigenous non-Western law. While foreign laws sometimes do

---

11. However, even Alan Watson acknowledged that transplanted laws will inevitably develop. He compared it to a human body: it will grow in its new body. The development of the law in the host country is a natural process which should not be seen as a rejection. However, Watson said that this development should not always be viewed as an improvement over the original transplanted laws. When the origin jurisdiction is much more advanced, materially and culturally, to the receiving country, transplantation is possible and easy, 'though changes leading to simplification, even barbarization, will be great': Watson, above n 28, pp 27 and 99. For example, the strong influence of Scots law on the modern day of Botswana, Lesotho and Swaziland because many of their lawyers, judges and legal bureaucrats were trained in Scotland: A Watson, 'Aspects of Reception of Law' (1996) 44 *Am J Comp L* 335 at 339–40.
36 K Pistor, Y Keinan, J Klenheisterkamp and M D West, 'Evolution of Corporate Law and the Transplant Effect: Lessons from Six Countries' (2003) 18 *The World Bank Research Observer* 89 (particularly at 90, 93).
37 K Pistor, Y Keinan, J Kleinheisterkamp and M D West, 'Innovation in Corporate Law' (2003) *Jnl of Comparative Economics* 676.
38 K Pistor, Y Keinan, J Kleinheisterkamp and M D West, 'The Evolution of Corporate Law: A Cross-Country Comparison' (2003) 23 *Jnl of International Economic Law* 791.
39 K Pistor and P Wellons, *The Role of Law and Legal Institutions in Asian Economic Development 1960-1995*, Asian Development Bank, Manila, 1998. See also H Kanda and C J Milhaupt, 'Re-examining Legal Transplants: The Director's Fiduciary Duty in Japanese Corporate Law' (2003) 51 *Am J Comp L* 887.
40 K Pistor, D Berkowitz and J F Richard, 'Economic Development, Legality and the Transplant Effect', research paper, SSRN, 1999.
41 S Djankov, R La Porta, F Lopez de-Silanes and A Shleifer, 'Courts: The Lex Mundi Project', research paper, Harvard Institute of Economic Research, 2002.

assimilate with indigenous laws, at other times they conflict with these laws which result in the indigenous laws either rejecting the received law outright, or adapting it to preserve the cultural identity. Thus, Chiba argues that the contemporary laws of Asian countries are found in 'an ongoing process of self-developing indigenous laws whether successful or not'.[42] He also said that the problem with the idea of law which was a product of long Western history and was biased towards Western culture, resulted in not only assimilation problems but also confining discussion to how Western law has been adopted and little on 'its conflict with or rejection by indigenous systems'. The main concern, he argued, should be the whole structure of the indigenous systems of the receiving people, which should focus 'upon assimilation of the received law while firmly maintaining their cultural identities'.[43]

The foregoing provides some justification for the argument that law should ideally be developed by the society and made 'part of the institutional fabric of society'.[44] As Clifford Geertz famously puts it, law is 'local knowledge'.[45] To be sure, this is not to say that transplanted laws have no real value and should be rejected outright. Given time it will evolve to accommodate the specific needs and peculiarities of the society in the host country. However, at the very least it cannot be assumed that laws across boundaries worked in the exact same way and produced the exact same results.[46]

3 Theories on corporate ownership structure

The foundation of corporate governance regulation in Malaysia can be traced to the work of two US academics, Adolf Berle and Gardiner Means in *The Modern Corporation and Private Property*.[47] Writing in 1932, Berle and Means gave an insight into the division of powers in a modern company. The evolution of dispersed shareholding, they explained, was an incident of capital needs. Companies have grown so large that their capital requirements can only be met by a large and dispersed group of shareholders. Such ownership structure left a control gap which was filled by corporate managers. Directors

---

42 M Chiba, 'Introduction' in M Chiba (Ed), *Asian Indigenous Law in Interaction with Received Law*, KPI, London/New York, 1986, pp v, 7.
43 Chiba, ibid, pp 4–5. Richard Nisbett forwarded convincing arguments of the fundamental differences between Eastern and Western cultures: *The Geography of Thought: How Asians and Westerners Think Differently and Why*, Nicholas Brealey, London, 2003.
44 Pistor et al, above n 36, at 90, 93.
45 He said that the law is 'local not just as to place, time, class, and variety of issue, but as to accent — vernacular characterizations of what happens connected to vernacular imaginings of what can': C Geertz, *Local Knowledge: Further Essays in Interpretative Anthropology*, 3rd ed, Basic Books, USA, 2000, p 215. In another passage he said (p 167): 'Like sailing, gardening, politics, and poetry, law and ethnography are crafts of place: they work by the light of local knowledge.'
46 Compare with R La Porta, F Lopez-de-Silanes, A Shleifer and R Vishny, 'Legal Determinants of External Finance' (1997) 52 *Jnl of Finance* 1131; 'Law and Finance' (1998) 106 *Jnl of Political Economy* 1113; R La Porta, F Lopez-de-Silanes and A Shleifer, 'Corporate Ownership Around the World' (1999) 54 *Jnl of Finance* 471.
47 A Berle and G Means, *The Modern Corporation and Private Property*, Harcourt, Brace & World Inc, NY, 1932; Transaction Publishers ed, New Brunswick/London, 1991. Even today, an exposition on power structures within a company may seem incomplete without a mention of this highly influential work.

therefore have almost complete discretion in management. Berle and Means were concerned that management may not have the same objectives as directors and managers and they may not be accountable to shareholders. The core purpose of corporate governance regulation is thus to align the interests of directors and managers with that of the owners.

An assumption that underlies this 'managerialism' theory was that shareholders as the providers of capital are the rightful owners of the company.[48] This therefore justifies the notion that the company should be managed primarily to further shareholders' economic interests. The concentration of powers in the hands of corporate managers however necessitates the control of such powers and the creation of incentive structures to align the interests of managers with those of shareholders. Managerialism quickly became the mainstream view in the United States. The Cohen Committee confirmed the acceptance of managerialism in Britain when it commented on the 'illusory nature of the control theoretically exercised by the shareholders over directors'.[49]

Managerialism remains an important influence on corporate governance regulation in both the United States and Britain. The role of boards of directors, in particular independent board members, became central to governance reform programmes.[50] This is complemented by takeovers and derivative actions as mechanisms to discipline corporate managers.[51] The theory on dispersed shareholding and the problems caused by it continue to wield great influence, despite contradicting studies which have found evidence of concentrated ownership even in the largest corporations in the United States.[52] It is now conceded that internationally concentrated corporate

---

48 See A Berle, 'Corporate Powers as Powers in Trust' (1931) 4 *Harv L Rev* 1049 (arguing that the agency problem be solved by regarding shareholders as beneficiaries, to whom the managers, as trustees, must serve). But see M E Dodd, 'For Whom Are Corporate Managers Trustees?' (1932) 45 *Harv L Rev* 1145; A Berle, 'For Whom Corporate Managers Are Trustees: A Note' (1932) 45 *Harv L Rev* 1365. However, the view of directors as trustees, at least in Britain, is flawed and has been rejected in part because directors' duties of care and skill permit directors to take reasonable risks in the exercise of their duties while trustees are required to be cautious and avoid risks: see *Re City Equitable Fire Insurance Co* [1925] Ch 407; *Daniels v Anderson* (1995) 37 NSWLR 438; 16 ACSR 607. For comments on Berle and Means, see M L Weidenbaum and M Jensen, 'Introduction to the Transaction Edition' in Berle and Means, ibid, pp ix–xviii; W W Bratton, 'Berle and Means Reconsidered at the Century's Turn' (2001) 26 *Iowa J Corp L* 737; M S Mizruchi, 'Berle and Means Revisited: The Corporate Governance and Power of Large US Corporations' (2004) 33 *Theory and Society* 579.
49 Cohen Committee, *Report of the Committee on Company Law Amendment*, Cmnd 6659, HMSO, London, 1945, para 7(e). This view was endorsed by the Jenkins Committee in 1962: *Report of the Company Law Committee*, Cmd 1749, HMSO, London, para 106.
50 See, eg, the American Law Institute, *Principles of Corporate Governance: Analysis and Recommendations*, 1992. For a discussion, see S M Bainbridge, 'Independent Directors and ALI Corporate Governance Project' (1993) 61 *Geo Wash L Rev* 1034.
51 For a comparison of the use of these two mechanisms in the United States and Britain, see G Miller, 'Political Structure and Corporate Governance: Some Points of Contrast between the United States and England' (1998) 51 *Colum Bus L Rev* 51.
52 H Demsetz, 'Corporate Control, Insider Trading, and Rates of Return' (1983) *American Economic Review* 313; A Shleifer and R Vishny, 'Large Shareholders and Corporate Control' (1986) 94 *Jnl of Political Economy* 461; R Morck, A Shleifer and R Vishny, 'Management Ownership and Market Valuation: An Empirical Analysis' (1988) 20 *Jnl of*

ownership structure is very much the norm rather than the exception.[53]

There were also challenges to the problems identified by Berle-Means. One area of study concentrated on social networks. This stream of research accepted Berle-Means finding on the evolution of dispersed shareholding but disputed that this resulted in the rise of the managerial class. The demise of the capitalist class, it was argued, was a myth. Maurice Zeitlin, a prominent advocate of this line of thought, found 'discrepant findings on the alleged separation of ownership and control' and lamented on 'the problems entailed in obtaining reliable and valid evidence on the actual ownership interests involved in a given corporation', prompting him to challenge the very foundation of the Berle-Means theory on managerialism as 'unsupported generalisations' and lacking empirically.[54]

Another area in which Berle-Means theory has been challenged was the evolution of the shareholding structure in the United States. It started with Mark Roe's thesis that it was the legal rules governing financial intermediaries, brought about by political and ideological factors, which contributed to dispersed shareholding in the United States.[55] Others have sought to examine the ownership structure of companies around the world. The quality of the law, the protection of property rights and the effectiveness of legal institutions are alternative theories why corporate structures in some countries are dispersed while others are concentrated.[56]

Financial Economics 293. See also P D Hall, 'A Historical Overview of Family Firms in the United States' (1988) 1 *Family Business Review* 51.

53 R La Porta et al, (1998), (1999), above n 46; S Claessens, S Djankov and L Lang, 'The Separation of Ownership and Control in East Asian Corporations' (2000) 58 *Jnl of Financial Economics* 81.

54 M Zeitlin, *The Large Corporation and Contemporary Classes*, Rutgers UP, NJ, 1989, pp 36–7. See also Pt II Ch 5, 'Who Owns America? The Same Old Gang', pp 142–61 and his work in 'Corporate Ownership and Control: The Large Corporation and the Capitalist Class' (1974) 79 *American Jnl of Sociology* 1073. For a summary of the sociological work based on Berle-Means work, see Mizruchi, above n 48. Continuing with this theme, British sociologist John Scott found that in both US and British companies, strategic control resides not with managers but through a 'constellation of interests', in which institutions, primarily financial intermediaries, play a major part. This constellation of interests is further strengthened through the extensive networks of inter-corporate business relations and business powers either formally in the form of business cooperations or informally in the form of interlocking shareholdings and interlocking directorates. Like Zeitlin in the United States, Scott maintained that propertied capitalist classes still existed in Britain. They are however 'no longer merely collections of individually powerful families', but have 'spread their shareholdings across a large number of companies, rather than holding controlling blocks in particular companies, and they form a pool from which the top corporate managers are recruited': J Scott, *Corporate Business and Capitalist Classes*, Oxford UP, Oxford, 1997, pp 19–20 and Ch 3. See also J Scott, 'Networks of Corporate Power: A Comparative Assessment' (1991) 17 *Annual Review of Sociology* 181 at 182.

55 M J Roe, 'Some Differences in Corporate Structure in Germany, Japan, and the United States' (1993) 102 *Yale LJ* 1927; *Strong Managers, Weak Owners: The Political Roots of American Corporate Finance*, Princeton UP, Princeton, 1994.

56 La Porta et al (1998), above n 46; (the law matters theory); C J Milhaupt, 'Property Rights in Firms' (1998) 84 *Va L Rev* 1145 (the property rights theory); and K Pistor, 'Patterns of Legal Change: Shareholder and Creditor Rights in Transition Economies', working paper, European Bank for Reconstruction and Development, 2000 and K Pistor, M Raiser and S Gelfer, 'Law and Finance in Transition Economies', working paper, European Bank for Reconstruction and Development, 2000 (the quality of institutions theory).

Despite findings of the dominance of concentrated share ownership (outside of the largest companies in the United States and Britain), managerialism and the problems caused by it continue to influence the shape of governance regimes in many, if not all, common law countries. One factor which has contributed to this was the spread of the British Companies Act. The legislation, together with court decisions and prevailing practices, contributed to the detachment of shareholders from the company. At the core of the power structure of the company are the shareholders in general meeting and the board of directors. The Act provides for the division of duties between shareholders and directors but does not specifically require that management should be left in the hands of the directors. Table A of successive British Companies Acts (the 1929 Act, 1948 Act and the current 1985 Act) however provide that the business of the company shall be managed by directors, although they were not explicit as to the division of powers.

In large companies where shareholders are dispersed and each owns a small portion of the shares, delegation is efficient (to borrow the term as employed by law and economics scholars). The shareholders may neither have sufficient financial interest nor expertise in managing the company — this is best left to better qualified managers. The practice, however, is to adopt this Table A provision, regardless of the size of the company, which means that corporate powers are generally left in the hands of directors. Recognising this practice, the courts have formulated various duties for directors, such as the duty to act in the best interests of the company and fiduciary duties. The counterbalance of this is reduced shareholders' powers. A number of court decisions have reinforced the separation of powers, first by preventing shareholders from interfering in the directors' exercise of powers,[57] and then by limiting the 'supervisory' powers of shareholders over directors.[58]

The financial interest of shareholders, together with the perceived 'ownership' rights of shareholders,[59] means that they retain one important weapon in their arsenal — that of appointing and removing directors. In private companies this is a very useful power as it provides a form of indirect control over the company. In companies with dispersed shareholding, typically large listed companies found in both the United States and Britain, these powers may mean little in practice. The shareholding structure creates a

---

57 *Automatic Self-Cleansing Filter Syndicate Co v Cunninghame* [1906] 2 Ch 34. This view was regarded controversial at the time of the case as the traditional view regarded shareholders in general meeting as the company and directors as their agents. See also *Breckland Group Holdings v London & Suffolk Properties* [1989] BCLC 100.

58 Directors are not obliged to carry out the views, opinions or even instructions of shareholders, even those voiced at the general meeting: *Shaw & Sons (Salford) Ltd v Shaw* [1935] 2 KB 113 (a resolution in general meeting disapproving the commencement of an action by the directors a nullity); *Scott v Scott* [1943] 1 All ER 582 (a resolution in general meeting giving instructions to pay interim dividend or to make a loan a nullity). The formal relationship between the shareholders and the board has been described in the following manner: 'the shareholders elect the directors, the directors report on their stewardship to the shareholders and the shareholders appoint the auditors to provide the external check on the directors' financial statements': Committee on the Financial Aspects of Corporate Governance, *Report on the Committee on the Financial Aspects of Corporate Governance*, London, 1992.

59 For a critique of this, see, eg, P Ireland, 'Company Law and the Myth of Shareholder Ownership' (1999) 62 *Mod Law Rev* 32.

collective action problem, compounded by management's control over agenda and proxy machineries, reinforced in some instances by the use of pyramids to further separate corporate assets from shareholders.[60] The concentration of powers in the hands of directors necessitates a legal regime which focuses on making directors accountable to shareholders and seeks to redress the agency problem caused by the director — shareholder conflict.[61]

4 Limits to the law-in-the-books

The companies' legislation, like other colonial commercial laws, was brought by British colonial government to its colonies to serve British business interests and, despite being unsuitable for local conditions, little effort was made to modify the laws to suit these businesses.[62] Corporate governance regulation in Malaysia provides good evidence for this assertion. The law which has as its focus the agency problem of director-shareholder conflict was not designed for the concentrated nature of Malaysia's companies. In Malaysia, the high degree of concentration occurs not only in the concentration of control in specific companies, but also the concentration of control over the financial assets and productive capacity of the corporate economy. The concentration of control over these large companies is consolidated by the use of interlocking share ownership and interlocking directorates.[63] The state also plays a significantly different role in Malaysia. Not only is the state the majority or controlling shareholder of many of the largest listed companies,[64] it also has direct influence on the management of

---

60 M Eisenberg, 'Megasubsidiaries: The Effect of Corporate Structure on Corporate Control' (1971) 84 *Harv L Rev* 1577.
61 In the 1980s there had been a move to corporate democracy by the insertion of a number of provisions which required directors to obtain the sanction of the general meeting for certain acts, eg, allotment of shares (s 80 of the UK Companies Act 1985); variation of class rights (s 125); special resolution to approve the giving of financial assistance by a private company (s 155); authorisation for the purchase of own shares (s 166). These provisions were however regarded as a failure in terms of increasing corporate democracy: see L A Bebchuck, J M Fried and D I Walker, 'Managerial Power and Rent Extraction in the Design of Executive Compensation' (2002) 69 *University of Chicago L Rev* 751; C T Bogus, 'Excessive Executive Compensation and the Failure of Corporate Democracy' (1993) 41 *Buffalo L Rev* 59; L J Barris, 'The Overcompensation Problem: A Collective Approach to Controlling Executive Pay' (1992) 68 *Indiana L Rev* 59.
62 It was British colonial policy to transplant the Companies Act to facilitate and promote British business in its colonies: R S Rungta, *The Rise of Business Corporations in India 1851–1900*, Cambridge UP, Cambridge, 1970; R McQueen, 'Company Law as Imperialism' (1995) 5 *Aust Jnl Corp Law* 187. L C B Gower said that there was a time when the English Companies Act was so widely copied that it was virtually a Commonwealth Act of Parliament: L C B Gower, 'Company Law Reform' (1962) 4 *Malaya L Rev* 36 at 36.
63 M H Lim, *Ownership and Control of the One Hundred Largest Corporations in Malaysia*, Oxford UP, Kuala Lumpur, 1981. See also The Economist Intelligence Unit, *Beyond the Bamboo Network: Successful Strategies for Change in Asia*, London/New York/Hong Kong, 2000, pp 8–10. Pyramidal holdings are common not only in East Asia but also in developed countries: La Porta et al (1999), above n 46. For empirical studies of the use of pyramids in East-Asian companies, see Claessens et al, above n 53.
64 Seven of the top 10 listed companies in Malaysia are majority owned by the state through its investment arms. Most of these are privatised infrastructure companies in which the state maintains the majority shareholding (eg, Tenaga Nasional Berhad, the national power company, and Telekom Malaysia Berhad, the national telecommunication company). Others

many companies.⁶⁵ To the extent that the state benefits as direct and indirect beneficiaries of businesses, it cannot be considered as merely an impartial intermediary seeking to benefit the whole populace by implementing appropriate development strategies and ensuring free competition and fair-play to all.⁶⁶

In view of the fact that real control of Malaysian companies is exercised by majority or controlling shareholders and not directors, the focus on the regulation of directors is misplaced.⁶⁷ Therefore the theory of the separation of ownership and control and the problems caused by such separation should be of limited relevance in Malaysia. In countries in which concentrated shareholding is the norm such as Malaysia, the shareholder-director conflict is only secondary to the controlling shareholder-minority shareholder conflict. Even though it has not been conclusively proven that companies with concentrated ownership have a higher incidence of corporate misappropriation or other forms of abuse, there is certainly more opportunity for such conduct where control rights are not matched with cash-flow rights. There will also be less incentive for controlling shareholders to maximise the interests of shareholders generally, and not merely their own or their families. There is also a persistent danger that controlling shareholders in companies with concentrated shareholding may transfer resources out of the company to benefit themselves or their associates.⁶⁸ They are able to do this because of

---

include industrial and infrastructure companies in which the state continues to hold substantial stakes (eg, the Proton group and Time group); media and communications companies (eg, Media Prima Bhd, although not directly owned, but is widely believed to be controlled by the political elites, as it is imperative to the state's control over information); and companies in industries which are the backbone of the nation's economy (eg, plantation based Guthrie group which were acquired by the government backed investment company Permodalan Nasional Berhad through a 'dawn raid' of the London Stock Exchange. Permodalan Nasional Berhad still own over 45% of Guthrie's shares).

65 The Articles of Association of the privatised national utility company Tenaga Nasional Berhad, for example, has a provision for a 'Special Share' held by a 'Special Shareholder', a representative of the state. The Special Shareholder has the right to appoint a number of directors, including the Chairman of the Board and the Managing Director. The Special Shareholder also has extensive veto rights.

66 Privatisation projects in Malaysia are examples of the politic-business nexus. See, eg, K S Jomo, 'Privatisation in Malaysia' in T Clarke and C Pitlelis (Eds), *The Political Economy of Privatisation*, Routledge, London, 1993, pp 437–54; K S Jomo, 'Overview' in K S Jomo (Ed), *Privatisation Malaysia: Rents, Rhetorics, Realities*, Westview Press, Boulder, 1994. See also generally E T Gomez and K S Jomo, *Malaysia's Political Economy: Politics, Patronage and Profits*, Cambridge UP, Cambridge, 1999; P Searle, *The Riddle of Malaysian Capitalism: Rent-Seekers or Real Capitalists*, Allen & Unwin/University of Hawai'i Press, NSW/Honolulu, 1999.

67 To be sure, it is not always the province of the majority to control, as there could well be circumstances in which the minorities could take control, although this situation would arise only in the most exceptional cases.

68 See, eg, the UEM/Renong saga discussed below. There are many other tales of misappropriation which for one reason or another was not proven simply because court actions are extremely rare. Misappropriation could be implemented through a variety of ways: 'intra-group shifting of assets, cross-lending, smoothing company decisions (inter-company transfers designed to adjust the volume or the price of inter-group trade, the level of inter-firm dividend payout, cross-lending either to avoid taxes, to exploit the government's fiscal incentives, or to lock in private benefits linked to corporate control over technological or other decisions), cross-lending and co-insurance': N Attig, K Fischer and

their influence over the board and dominion in general meeting. Also as shareholders they are under no duty to act in the interests of the company or the other shareholders. The mismatch between control rights and cash flow rights, a phenomenon which is wide-spread in East Asia,[69] and the absence of a real market for takeovers which may otherwise discipline directors,[70] exacerbates this problem.

In view of the fact that family businesses, in particular Chinese family businesses are the backbone of Malaysia's economy,[71] an understanding of these companies is vital to appreciate the underlying corporate governance issues. It has been said that kinship ties in family businesses are control relations which form the foundation of power networks.[72] In Asia, it has been repeatedly said that characteristics such as paternalism, personalism, opportunism and flexibility mean that Chinese family companies are tightly controlled by individuals or family members, even where the company is publicly listed.[73] In these companies, 'there is no real separation between family and company interests and a resulting lack of clarity as to where corporate boundaries lie'.[74] Often, the controlling families have failed to distinguish between the interests of the company and those of the family.[75]

Y Gadhoum, 'On the Determinants, Costs, and Benefits of Pyramidal Ownership: Evidence on Expropriation of Minority Interests', paper presented at the 2nd Asia Corporate Governance Conference organised by Asia Institute of Corporate Governance, 16–17 May 2002, Seoul. The lower rate of dividends paid by Asian group-affiliated companies compared to their European counterparts may also exacerbate this problem: M Faccio, L H P Lang and L Young, 'Dividends and Expropriation' (2001) 91 *American Economic Review* 54. See also D Wolfenzon, *A Theory of Pyramidal Ownership*, Mimeo, Harvard University, 1999; L H P Lang, 'Introduction' in L H P Lang (Ed), *Governance and Expropriation*, Elgar, Cheltenham, 2005.

69 Bebchuck, Kraakman and Triantis termed the use of cross-holdings, pyramids and dual-class shares which allow control though a small shareholding as 'controlling-minority structure' (or CMS). They argued that CMS insulates the controllers from the market for corporate control, a problem associated with dispersed shareholding, but further places control on an insider who holds a small fraction of the company's cash-flow rights, a problem faced by companies with concentrated shareholding. As such, they argued that CMS may possibly suffer from both incentive problems associated with both the concentrated shareholding and dispersed ownership: L A Bebchuck, R Kraakman, and G Triantis, 'Stock Pyramids, Cross-Ownership and Dual-Class Equity: The Mechanisms and Agency Costs of Separating Control From Cash-Flow Rights' in R Morck (Ed), *Concentrated Corporate Ownership*, University of Chicago Press, Chicago, 2000. However, even in countries with concentrated shareholdings, the problem is far from universal. In Japan, and to a lesser degree Germany, despite having concentrated shareholding, managers and not major shareholders wielded great powers, which are exercised not so much for the benefit of shareholders but the company's constituents, of which the most important is the company's employees. For a comparative study of the Japan/Germany and Anglo Saxon system of corporate governance, see R Dore, *Stock Market Capitalism: Welfare Capitalism: Japan and Germany versus the Anglo-Saxons*, Oxford UP, Oxford, 2000.

70 Only 25% of shares in listed companies need be in the hands of the public: Bursa Malaysia, *Listing Requirements*, para 3.05

71 See, generally, E T Gomez, *Chinese Business in Malaysia*, Curzon, Surrey, 1999.

72 See M Zeitlin and R E Ratcliff, *Landlords and Capitalists: The Dominant Class of Chile*, Princeton UP, Princeton, 1988.

73 P Lawton, 'Berle and Means, Corporate Governance and the Chinese Family Firm' (1996) 6 *Aust Jnl Corp Law* 348.

74 Lawton, ibid, at 357.

75 Lawton, ibid, at 367; R I Tricker, 'Corporate Governance: A Ripple on the Cultural

The result is a management culture which is biased towards the families' interests rather than that of the companies.[76] In view of this, there is a need for greater focus on family-based corporate governance structure as a distinct governance regime.[77]

Regardless of its relevance, Berle-Means managerialism theory has had a profound impact on corporate governance regulation in Malaysia. The powers of directors and the control of such powers have a prominent place in company law. As with the British Companies Act, Table A of the Malaysian Act provides that the company shall be managed by the directors.[78] Table A is widely adopted by Malaysian companies.[79] Even when lawyers are consulted to negotiate the respective rights of shareholders, a common occurrence when setting up 'joint venture companies', Table A is usually adopted, supplemented only by the express terms as agreed in the joint venture or shareholders agreement. Partly due to the heritage of Table A, decisions by English courts were closely followed and applied, in many cases unquestionably as if these decisions bind them.

The potential for abuses by controlling shareholders was probably the reason for the introduction of three new provisions in the Companies Act in the mid-1980s.[80] These sought to empower shareholders by giving them negative veto rights against certain transactions involving directors. The very fact that these provisions were introduced do give an indication of the presence of a problem, despite the absence of a reliable study on insider-related transactions in Malaysia or an explanation to justify the need for such provisions (such is typical in Malaysia). These provisions were however ineffective — they suffer from numerous ambiguities, leading to uncertainties (which are never welcomed by business communities) and increased costs (the increased need to consult lawyers for fear of inadvertently contravening the law).[81] More importantly, these provisions have failed to

---

Reflection' in S R Clegg and S G Redding (Eds), *Capitalism in Contrasting Cultures*, Walter de Gruyter, Berlin/New York, 1990, pp 200–1.

76 N Sang-Woo, 'Business Groups Looted by Controlling Families, and the Asian Crisis', research paper, Asian Development Bank Institute, 2001.

77 Akira Suehiro said in 1993 that research into family business is 'surprisingly small in quantity and rather shallow in its theoretical consideration': A Suehiro, 'Family Business Re-assessed: Corporate Structure and Late-starting Industrialization in Thailand' (1993) 31 *Developing Economies* 378 at 379. See also similar comments in H A Khan, 'Corporate Governance of Family Businesses in Asia', working paper, Asian Development Bank, 1999; B Tabalujan, 'Family Capitalism and Corporate Governance of Family-controlled Listed Companies in Indonesia' (2002) 25 *UNSW Law Jnl*. For other works on family companies in Asia, see M Carney and E Gedajlovic, 'Corporate Governance and Firm Capabilities: A Comparison of Managerial, Alliance and Personal Capitalisms' (2001) 18 *Asia Pacific Jnl of Management* 335; Y Yeh, T Lee and T Woidtke, 'Family Control and Corporate Governance: Evidence from Taiwan' (2001) 2 *International Review of Finance* 21.

78 Article 73.

79 This was through my personal experience during my years as a solicitor specialising in corporate law. This was confirmed by a Malaysian consultant who has more than 10 years experience in secretarial and consultancy work in Malaysia (interview conducted on 27 February 2004).

80 Sections 132C and 132D were introduced in 1985, while s 132E was enacted the following year.

81 On ambiguities, see P T N Koh, 'Principles, Practice and Prospects of Corporate Governance: The Malaysian Legal Framework' (1994) 3 *Malayan Law Jnl* 9. See also

directly confront the agency problem encountered in Malaysian companies — that is the controlling shareholder-minority shareholder conflict. It would not be difficult to overcome the shareholder consent requirement where the directors involved in a particular transaction have control over the general meeting. The Companies Act having fallen short of its objectives (this was never tacitly acknowledged), a more comprehensive provision, s 132G, was introduced in 1992. With the benefit of experience, this new provision was drafted far more comprehensively in that it prohibits outright certain transactions between related companies. This was a bold move in that it attempted to address the core of the perceived agency problem in Malaysia. Unfortunately, it creates far too many difficulties. Apart from the ambiguities, it is also unnecessarily restrictive. In many cases even bona fide transactions were caught.[82] Section 132G, however, was an indication that the authorities have come to appreciate the root of the malaise infecting corporate Malaysia. Unfortunately, the extent of this problem is unknown, in no small part due to lack of information, transparency and restraints imposed on the media and the intellectual community.[83]

Despite the unsuitability of the governance regime in addressing the controlling shareholder-minority shareholder conflict and other difficulties associated with these relatively recent innovations (especially s 132G), there has been no real effort to identify and address the governance problems inflicting Malaysian companies. The Committee on Corporate Governance did comment in its Report on 'the ability of boards to represent the interests of all shareholders' in companies 'with significant shareholder presence' and acknowledged the 'difficulties posed by ownership concentration',[84] but did not propose any recommendations to overcome these difficulties or a plan on how to tackle the issue.[85]

A sceptic may regard the reforms as nothing more than a window-dressing exercise to attract foreign investors who left in large numbers in the aftermath of the 1997 financial crisis. There is evidence that the Committee on Corporate Governance was serious at trying to address the core problems affecting Malaysian companies. However, some of its recommendations have been less than satisfactory, in particular where foreign templates (in this case primarily

---

discussion by the Malaysian Finance Committee on Corporate Governance, above n 20; J Pascoe, 'Regulation and Disclosure of Financial Benefits to Directors and Related Parties: A Comparative Analysis of the Malaysian and Australian Approaches' (1999) 3 *Sing. J Int'l & Comp L* 108.

82 Koh, ibid, and the Finance Committee on Corporate Governance, ibid. Many honest transactions are prevented, leading to more complex and innovative transactions being conceived to bypass the section. This invariably leads to increased costs in the form of lawyers and advisers costs, and wasted time.

83 For an examination of corporate transparency in Malaysia, see G Rodan, 'Do Markets Need Transparency? The Pivotal Cases of Singapore and Malaysia' (2002) 7 *New Political Economy* 23 and *Transparency and Authoritarian Rule in Southeast Asia: Singapore and Malaysia*, RoutledgeCurzon, London, 2004.

84 Malaysian Finance Committee on Corporate Governance, above n 20, p 43 para 1.8 and p 46 para 2.19.

85 The committee recommended that further studies be conducted, but no such further studies appear to have been conducted. The Corporate Law Reform Committee, established by the Companies Commission (previously Registrar of Companies) in 2003, has also failed to address this issue in any of its works.

from Britain) were used to guide local reforms. In particular, questions should be asked whether the British approach was the best approach for Malaysia. Specifically, questions should be asked whether self-regulation and non-legal sanctions are the best way to deter bad governance in Malaysian companies, especially since the efficacy of self-regulation has yet to be proven in Malaysia.[86] Also doubtful is the ability of the market to sanction state-owned or controlled companies and the ability and courage of the regulators to take action against these companies or their controllers.[87] These questions were never raised, let alone considered and addressed by the committee. Also, despite stating the need to recognise local conditions, the *Code on Corporate Governance* drew heavily on similar work done in Britain, namely, the Cadbury, Greenbury and Hampel Committees. Similarly, the Corporate Law Reform Committee's first consultative paper, the *Strategic Framework for the Corporate Law Reform Programme* borrowed extensively upon similar reform programmes in Britain, a fact which is apparent even from the title of the paper.

The Code on Corporate Governance borrowed from the Anglo-American concept of independent non-executive directors and recommended that a third of the board must be composed of these directors. The committee should be recommended for expanding the concept of 'independent' to include independent from significant shareholder as well as from management,[88] which is evidence of awareness of local conditions, but has failed to consider whether there is a sufficient pool of talents from where these directors may be recruited. The utility of independent director provisions has yet to be conclusively proven, and in Malaysia this is compounded by the scarcity of good talents who fit the definition of 'independence', brought about by the high degree of wealth concentration and the propensity for networking.[89] Additionally, there is no real market for takeovers[90] and a negligible risk of

---

86 Malaysia's capitalist class may not be as cohesive as those in advanced capitalist economies such as United States and Britain. Corporate interlocks in Malaysia were more of a pragmatic response to socio-political landscape rather than for the purpose of networking or providing the foundation of corporate powers: see Gomez, above n 71; E T Gomez, 'Governance, Affirmative Action and Enterprise Development: Ownership and Control of Corporate Malaysia' in E T Gomez (Ed), *The State of Malaysia; Ethnicity, Equity and Reform*, RoutledgeCurzon, London/New York, 2004, pp 175–6; J V Jesudason, 'Chinese Business and Ethnic Equilibrium in Malaysia' (1997) 28 *Development and Change* 119 at 138. For interlocks in the United Kingdom and Britain, see Zeitlin, above n 54 and Scott, above n 54. See also M S Mizruchi, 'What Do Interlocks Do? An Analysis, Critique, and Assessment of Research on Interlocking Directorates' (1996) 22 *Annual Review of Sociology* 271. For the Hong Kong experience, see B M Ho, 'Rethinking the System of Sanctions in the Corporate and Securities Law of Hong Kong' (1997) 42 *McGill Law Jnl* 603.
87 See above n 65 and 66 and accompanying text.
88 The *Report on Corporate Governance*, above n 20, p 83 para 4.25. Compare with the concept 'unrelated director' used in the Toronto Stock Exchange Guideline, which is defined as a director who is independent of management and is free from any interest and business which could, or could reasonably be perceived to materially interfere with the director's ability to act in the best interests of the corporation: Toronto Stock Exchange, *Corporate Governance: A Guideline to Good Disclosure*, Guideline 2.
89 For the wealth concentration and networking in Malaysia see Lim, above n 63; cf. Gomez, above n 86.
90 Hostile takeovers are almost unheard of in Malaysia due to the presence of controlling

being sued by shareholders[91] which may otherwise serve to discipline directors and senior managers. Also, the effectiveness of independent director provisions would be severely compromised in an environment where companies are run by autocratic leaders and in a culture where confrontations are generally avoided.[92] To the Chinese publicly disagreeing with a leader is scorned upon and leads to a 'loss of face', while to a Malay such behaviour may be viewed as a form of disloyalty or, in the extreme, even treason.[93] Similarly, in state-owned companies, it is very unlikely that a director, however independent, will engage in a confrontation with representatives of the state without fear of repercussions. Additionally, it was suggested that a Western-style board may not work well within a Malaysian culture.[94]

Another major limitation of the reform efforts is that much of it was directed to public listed companies through new provisions in Bursa Malaysia's *Listing Requirements*.[95] In so far as private and other unlisted companies are concerned, any changes must be in the form of changes in substantive laws, which at the moment remain largely unchanged. This has a negative effect on the efficacy of the laws.[96] It is hard to resist making an argument that behind the bustle of reforms the evidence so far shows a

---

shareholders in most companies. The last attempt was made in 2001 when Sime Darby Bhd, Malaysia's largest conglomerate, attempted to take over Palmco Holdings Bhd. It ended as an embarrassing failure for Sime Darby.

91 The derivative action in Malaysia, as in Britain, is ineffective due to numerous procedural limitations imposed by the courts. The other main remedy, the oppression remedy provided under s 181 of the Companies Act 1965, has limited use for shareholders in public companies. In the only reported case involving a public company the action was dismissed, see *Tuan Haji Ishak Ismail v Leong Hup Holdings* (1996) 1 MLJ 661.

92 See Lawton, above n 73, at 53; S G Redding, *The Spirit of Chinese Capitalism*, Walter de Gruyter, Berlin, New York, 1993, pp 218–19.

93 See M G Peletz, *Islamic Modern: Religious Courts and Cultural Politics in Malaysia*, Princeton UP, Princeton, 2002, p 262 (writing in the context of Anwar Ibrahim's challenge of the Prime Minister Mahathir Mohamed).

94 R M Haniffa and T E Cooke, 'Culture, Corporate Governance, and Disclosure in Malaysian Companies' (2002) 38 *ABACUS* 317 at 343 (suggesting that a non-executive chairperson gains greatest utility by keeping private information secret and questioning the utility of having a non-executive chairperson in Malaysia).

95 These changes were attributable to the *Code on Corporate Governance* which has resulted in some changes to Bursa Malaysia's *Listing Requirements*. Although the Code was described as a voluntary Code, changes to the Bursa Malaysia rules means that listed companies must comply. One thing which must be emphasised is that the Code and Bursa Malaysia's rules apply only to listed companies. The Securities Commission has fully implemented the Disclosure Based Regulations regime which, together with Bursa Malaysia's improved disclosure requirements, should result in better corporate transparency. A shareholder watchdog group in the form of the Minority Shareholder Watchdog Group has been established by some large institutional investors, led by EPF to establish the foundation for the growth of shareholder activism. An overview of these changes is available at the Malaysian Securities Commission's website: see <http://www.sc.com.my>. Thus, so far as listed companies are concerned, these changes should result in better shareholders protection (despite the limitations of reform efforts highlighted in this article). A joint survey by Bursa Malaysia and PricewaterhouseCoopers showed that this was indeed the case. This survey revealed a perception of a raise in Malaysia's corporate governance standards of listed companies: The Kuala Lumpur Stock Exchange and PricewaterhouseCoopers, *Malaysian Corporate Governance Survey 2002*, 2002.

96 See Pistor et al, above n 36.

shortage of political and bureaucratic determination to affect a really wholesome reform.[97]

6 Culture and corporate governance

More than anything else, racial composition in Malaysia is the key to understanding the big picture. It has helped shape the constitution, influenced the democratic processes and dictated the pattern of the economy.[98] A legacy of British colonial rule, ethnicity was so deeply institutionalised in Malaysia that it is a key factor in determining the beneficiaries to government development projects as well as educational, social and other state policies. In this environment, citizens organise themselves according to their ethnic and cultural identity. This can be seen in the corporate sector. Companies in Malaysia, including the largest listed companies, have strong ethnic identity which can often be identifiable.[99]

Cultural inclinations and value systems are important in understanding management or leadership behaviour. In fact, studies in management behaviour that ignore cultural aspects can lead to what is termed as 'sophisticated stereotyping'.[100] There is research that focuses on culture and management in Malaysia.[101] Malaysia has been described as a 'minefield of cultural sensitivities',[102] thus generalisations of Malaysians as a homogenous community with shared culture, ethics and outlook are unhelpful to

---

97 To be clear, the Committee on Corporate Governance did make some suggestions to improve some aspects in the Companies Act. In some matters, the committee did recommend a more detailed study to be conducted. For example, the committee had recommended for the removal of s 132E of the Companies Act (that allows for ratification by the general meeting of related party transactions); amendments to s 132 to extend the duties and liabilities of officers to include senior executive officers as well as directors and to s 132G (the regulation of a specific related party transaction) to require errant persons to indemnify the company, to allow innocent parties to recover their losses and to remove a certain ambiguity in the provision; and other recommendations which include the increase in penalties for breach of related party transactions; to allow voting by mail; to introduce a statutory method by which shareholders can obtain access to company records without the need to have prior approval by the board or general meeting. See also the proposals by the Companies Commission of Malaysia in its Consultative Document, *On Clarifying and Reformulating the Directors' Role and Duties*, 2006.

98 R S Milne, *Government and Politics in Malaysia*, Houghton Mifflin, Boston, 1967, p 3. See also F K W Loh and B T Khoo (Eds), *Democracy in Malaysia: Discourses and Practices*, Curzon, Surrey, 2002; A Harding, *Law, Government and the Constitution in Malaysia*, Kluwer Law International, London, 1996.

99 Chinese businesses are often closely held; therefore its ethnic identification will often persist even after the shares have been listed. Malay owned companies are a more recent phenomenon, brought about because of the state's economic policies. For discussion on these companies, see Gomez, above n 71 (a breakdown of equity ownership of Chinese companies in Malaysia is presented at 4–5); P Sloane, *Islam, Modernity and Entrepreneurship Among the Malays*, MacMillan, Hampshire, London, 1999 (an anthropological perspective of Malay entrepreneurship).

100 J Osland and A Bird, 'Beyond Sophisticated Stereotyping: Cultural Sense-making in Context' (2000) 14 *Academy of Management Executive* 65.

101 The works by Geertz Hofstede are famous examples: see, eg, G H Hofstede, *Culture's Consequences: International Differences in Work Related Values*, 2nd ed, Thousand Oaks, London, 2001; G H Hofstede, 'A Case for Comparing Apples with Oranges: International Differences in Values' (1998) 39 *International Jnl of Cultural Studies* 17.

102 A Abdullah, 'Influence of ethnic values at the Malaysian workplace' in A Abdullah and

understand cultural divergences. Focus should instead be on the cultures, values and behaviour of different ethnic groups,[103] or even sub-ethnic groups. Research that has been conducted found that the two main ethnic groups in Malaysia, the Malays and the Chinese, share some similar values but are different in other important respects.[104] They do things differently according to their 'tradition, history, values, beliefs and culture'[105] and strive to maintain their ethnic identity.[106]

Culture will have consequences for corporate governance. With regard to disclosure of information, one study hypothesised that disclosure practices may vary depending on the ethnic identity of the particular company.[107] In addition, tight control, insider domination and a heavy reliance on trust and informal rules are some of the characteristics of many Chinese companies.[108] The Chinese company in Malaysia maintains many features of the traditional Chinese corporate culture which include:

> a close overlap of ownership, control and family; centralized decision making with a heavy reliance on one dominant executive; a paternalistic organisational climate, mostly small-scale and relatively simple organizational structure; normally focused on one product or market; typically very sensitive to cost and financial efficiency; and highly adaptable to the external environment.[109]

A Low (Eds), *Understanding the Malaysian workforce: Guidelines for Managers*, Malaysian Institute of Management, Kuala Lumpur, 2001, p 1.

103 See, eg, L Lim, 'Work-related Values of Malays and Chinese Malaysians' (2001) 1 *International Jnl of Cross-Cultural Management* 229; L Lim, 'Cultural Attributes of Malays and Malaysian Chinese: Implications for Research and Practice' (1998) 33 *Malaysian Management Review* 81; R Fontaine and S Richardson, 'Cross-cultural Research in Malaysia' (2003) 10 *Cross Cultural Management: An International Jnl* 75; R Fontaine and S Richardson, 'Cultural Values in Malaysia: Chinese, Malays and Indians Compared' (2005) 12 *Cross Cultural Management: An International Jnl* 63.

104 They are both low on masculinity (being considerate, caring, shameful and preserving 'face') and high on power distance (respect for others, acceptance of social rank, loyalty to ruler and filial piety for parents). On the other hand, Malays were said to have high uncertainty avoidance (non-assertiveness, conflict avoidance, and uneasiness in dealing with ambiguities and uncertainties) compared to the Chinese who are more willing to accept new challenges and to take risks: G H Hofstede, 'Management in Multicultural Society' (1991) 26 *Malaysian Management Review* 3 and *Culture's Consequences: International Differences in Work Related Values*, 2nd ed, Thousand Oaks, London, 2001. The Chinese are also more individualistic than the Malays: A Abdullah, 'The Influence of Ethnic Values on Managerial Practices in Malaysia' (1992) 27 *Malaysian Management Review* 3.

105 S O Alhabshi, 'Corporate Ethics in Management of Corporations' (1994) *The Malaysian Accountant* 22 at 24. See also B H Chuah, 'The Unique Breed of Malaysian Managers', Management Times, NST Press, Malaysia, 1995 (asserting that the minds of Malaysian managers are influenced by race, education and type of organisation they work for).

106 H Sendut, 'Managing in Multicultural Society: The Malaysian Experience' (1991) 26 *Malaysian Management Review* 61.

107 Haniffa and Cooke, above n 94, at 325–6.

108 F C Deyo, 'Chinese Management Practices and Work Commitment in Comparative Perspective' in L Lim and L Gosling (Eds), *The Chinese in Southeast Asia*, Vol II, Maruzen Asia, Singapore, 1983; S G Redding and G Wong, 'The Psychology of Chinese Organizational Behaviour' in M H Bond (Ed), *The Psychology of Chinese People*, Oxford UP, Hong Kong/Oxford, 1986; Tricker, above n 75. The Kuok Group, which empire expands from Malaysia to Singapore and Hong Kong is the perfect example: H P Khoon and S L M Ling, 'The Chinese Business Community in Peninsular Malaysia, 1957–1999' in L Kam Hing and T Chee-Beng (Eds), *The Chinese in Malaysia*, Oxford UP, Malaysia, 2000, p 153.

109 Khoon and Ling, ibid, citing Redding, above n 92, pp 205–6. The characteristics of Overseas

It is normally closed to outsiders, hence, Chinese companies usually remain a family business with a paternalistic leader who leads the organisation with the assistance of a few trusted insiders. In these companies, the owner typically continues to retain control, especially over finance and personnel, even where the company has been publicly listed. Trust and control forms an important aspect of personnel practices: formal rules and written procedure are not extensively relied upon and delegated responsibilities are frequently rearranged.[110] In a network of family business interests, there can be little distinction between business entities and family business interests.[111] In these companies, the concept of members' rights exercised in members' meetings may not be the egalitarian, democratic meeting as in the West and minority shareholdings are merely permission to share the family's fortunes.[112]

Anthropologist Patricia Sloane's work on Malay entrepreneurship provides a valuable insight into Malay business culture in Malaysia.[113] She discovered that Malay entrepreneurship is a 'middle class; even elite, phenomenon'.[114] This, she observed, was what was intended by the state's economic policy, the New Economic Policy (or NEP, now superseded by the National Development Policy). Sloane identified one of the unique characteristics of Malays in that their self-identity is shaped so much by the religion of Islam.[115] While material self-interest serves as a powerful incentive to the Malay entrepreneur, they have a duty to share the material benefits of development with other Malays, and believe in creating a social balance. She said that the entrepreneurship of the NEP-era Malay entrepreneurs 'blurs material self-interest and socially embedded affect until they are often indistinguishable from each other'.[116] However, they do not have the same family business network as the Chinese. In particular, it is very rare for Malay brothers to engage in any kind of economic relations.[117] The Malays do try to emulate the Chinese by creating networks, but these networks are 'functional' in two senses: the first is that they seek to mobilise 'entrepreneurial possibilities', and second, have an intended effect of 'demonstrating the bonds and responsibilities of members of Malay society'.[118]

To conclude, as different ethnic groups do things differently according to their tradition, history, values, beliefs and culture, this should add a fresh but important dimension to the study of corporate governance regulation in

---

Chinese business was discussed in G S Redding and R D Whitley, 'Beyond Bureaucracy: Towards a Comparative Analysis of Forms of Economic Resource Co-ordination and Control' in Clegg and Redding, above n 75, pp 79–104.

110 Deyo, above n 108; Redding and Wong, above n 108; Tricker, above n 75; Khoon and Ling, above n 108, p 153.
111 The Economist Intelligence Unit, above n 63, p 70.
112 Tricker, above n 75, p 209; W Kirby, 'China Unincorporated: Company Law and Business Enterprise in Twentieth-Century China' (1995) 54 *Jnl of Asian Studies* 43.
113 Sloane, above n 99.
114 Ibid, pp 3, 12.
115 Ibid, p 13. This is reinforced by the Federal Constitution, which defines Malay as one 'who professes the religion of Islam': The Federal Constitution of Malaysia Art 160(2).
116 Ibid, p 23, also p 130. The sense of duty and responsibility in the Malay culture is different as it may not come with the corresponding right of others to enforce that duty: see also Peletz, above n 93.
117 Ibid, p 43.
118 Sloane, above n 99, p 130.

Malaysia. Also, the adoption of a governance structure with strict division of powers between shareholders and directors and the provisions of independent directors and independent board committees may present a certain appearance which is both familiar and comforting, but outward appearances can be misleading. A proper understanding of the 'real governance' is essential before steps can be taken to identify and solve the problems afflicting Malaysian companies.

7 Culture and conflict resolution

Malaysia is a plural but largely segregated society and its shareholding structure reflects this feature. An examination as to cultural preferences of dispute resolution should take this into account. Scholars have made some generalisations as to conflict mediation in Eastern societies, but no specific studies have been made in relation to shareholders' disputes and mediation in Malaysian companies.[119] However, one did indicate the plausibility that the 'Chinese would be more receptive to assertive mediation' while Malays 'would be more comfortable with an informal listening, opinion gathering, discussion approach'.[120] It was also said that the Chinese have a general aversion towards the judicial system as a forum for dispute settlement, which is historical baggage from the period when they were discouraged from seeking settlement by way of litigation. Therefore the existing social institutions, ie, the family, clan, village or guild, played a far more active role to help dissolve disputes.[121] Barry Hooker noted that in pre-independent Malaya no commercial disputes were ever brought to the colonial courts for adjudication based on Chinese custom.[122] Culture and history may well be the cause of this. Even today, from the frequency of shareholders' litigation it would appear that there is still an aversion towards the formal judicial system to solve disputes.[123]

---

119 See, eg, D W Augsburger, *Conflict Mediation Across Cultures: Pathways and Patterns*, Westminster/John Knox, Louisville, 1992; J P Lederach, *Preparing for Peace: Conflict Transformation Across Cultures*, Syracuse UP, Syracuse, 1995. See also W J Karim, *Emotions of Culture: A Malay Perspective*, Oxford UP, Oxford, 1990; Peletz, above n 93.
120 J A Wall Jr and R R Callister, 'Malaysian Community Mediation' (1999) 43 *Jnl of Conflict Resolution* 343 at 364. See also Geertz, above n 45.
121 G B Chan, *Law without Lawyers, Justice without Courts: On Traditional Chinese Mediation*, Ashgate, Hampshire, 2002, p 70.
122 B M Hooker, 'Law and the Chinese outside China: A Preliminary Survey of the Issues and the Literature' in B M Hooker (Ed), *Law and the Chinese in Southeast Asia*, Institute of South East Asian Studies, Singapore, 2002, pp 9–10.
123 A survey on reported decisions on shareholders remedies since the introduction of the Companies Act in 1965 to December 2004 reveal only 20 decisions, excluding those which deal solely with issues of procedure and standing. This averages to half a case a year. For comparison, an average of 2.2 cases a year was reported in Australia (for Australian data see I Ramsay, 'An Empirical Study of the Use of the Oppression Remedy' (1999) 27 *Aust Bus L Rev* 23). Another survey conducted at the Commercial Division, High Court of Malaya in Kuala Lumpur for petitions filed during a period of over four years (January 2000 to February 2004) revealed an average of 8.5 petitions a year in Kuala Lumpur (data on file with author). In contrast, an average of 78 petitions was filed a year in London: Law Commission Consultation Paper No 142, *Shareholders Remedies*, HMSO, London, 1996. It should however be noted that Malaysia has about a third the number of registered companies

8 The quality of legal institutions and access to courts

In many law reform projects, including Malaysian corporate governance reform, the emphasis is on substantive rules and regulations. However, law reforms, if not accompanied by measures to reform legal institutions, may be insufficient to create change. Legal institutions here mean the institutions that create, support and enforce laws. It therefore covers a whole range of institutions — courts, legislative bodies, law-making and drafting agencies, enforcement agencies, law schools and bar associations. A vast array of issues are involved. In relation to the courts, issues include the appointment and training of judges, independence from external interferences, court facilities (including a good library, research assistance and an organised and networked system), case management rules and court procedure.[124] There is not a lot of information and discussion on court-related issues in Malaysia, perhaps with the exception of the issue relating to judicial independence. The judiciary crisis in 1988[125] and the irregularities in the trial of the former Deputy Prime Minister Anwar Ibrahim[126] undermined the integrity of the judiciary and public administration. It also soured relations between the judiciary and the Malaysian Bar. Crucially, the strained relations affected the administration of justice. The practice of informal consultation with senior members of the Bar before appointing new judges was stopped.[127] Changes to the court system to tackle the problem of court delays were also made without prior consultation with the Bar.[128] The relations deteriorated to such an extent that a seemingly innocent suggestion by the Chief Justice for a study to be made for the implementation of an inquisitorial system drew a knee-jerk reaction from the Bar Council who warned against the intrusion of the judiciary by politicians to serve their political agenda.[129]

Another issue is the transparency in the appointment and promotion of judges, in which loyalty appears to be the overriding criteria over ability and

---

compared to Britain (Malaysia's Companies Commission Annual Report 2003 and British Companies House data, accessible at <http://www.companieshouse.gov.uk>).

124 See, generally, the World Bank's resource page for institution reforms at <http://www1.worldbank.org/publicsector/legal/index.cfm>.

125 For literature on the subject, see F A Trinidade, 'The Removal of the Malaysian Judges' (1990) 106 *LQR* 51–86; H P Lee, 'A Fragile Bastion Under Siege — the 1988 Convulsion in the Malaysian Judiciary' (1990) *MULR* 386–417; A Harding, 'The 1988 Constitutional Crisis in Malaysia' (1990) 39 *International and Comparative Law Quarterly* 57–81; R H Hickling, 'The Malaysian Judiciary Under Crisis' (1990) *Public Law* 20–7; M S Abas and K Das, *May Day For Justice*, Magnus Books, Kuala Lumpur, 1989; Lawyers' Committee on Human Rights, *Malaysia: Assault on the Judiciary* New York, 1990; T A Aziz, 'Malaysia Incorporated: Ethics on Trial' (1999) 58 *Australian Jnl of Public Administration* 19. Dato' VC George, a retired judge, said that as a result of this episode, 'standards of morality and integrity plunged': 'Interview with Dato' VC George', *Relevan*, 2004, May issue, p 16. *Relevan* is a publication of Kuala Lumpur Bar.

126 Some aspects of Anwar's trial were covered by the International Commission of Jurists at <http://www.icj.org>.

127 See C Hector, 'The Judiciary During the Mahathir Era', *Aliran Monthly*, 2003, issue 8. *Aliran Monthly* is a publication of Aliran, a Malaysian non-governmental organisation.

128 See 'Editorial: Derailed', *Relevan*, 2003, September issue.

129 Bar Council Press Statement, 'A Change to an Inquisitorial System', 13 October 2004.

competence.[130] It has been said that the best way of maintaining judicial competency is by appointing competent judges.[131] The great majority of judges in Malaysia were from the judicial and legal service, which unfortunately do not represent the cross-section of talent in the legal profession.[132] The training of judges and improved research facilities are other areas which may help improve the quality of decision making.[133]

There are perhaps several reasons for the lack of judicial independence in Malaysia. One is that judges seem to have difficulty with their role as the protector of the Constitution, especially during the early phases of the Constitution. Rais Yatim attributed the deterioration in the protection of rights immediately after independence to the judicial inability to recognise constitutional supremacy.[134] Another factor which may also contribute to a relative lack of independence is the value systems and political orientation of the judges themselves. Acceptance of social rank and loyalty to ruler are established cultural traits.[135] Harold Crouch said that the judges are 'essentially conservative custodians of a political system dominated by the Malay elite to which most judges belong', who 'rarely showed interest in reinterpreting the law in ways that might restrict the prerogatives of the government and its bureaucracy', the reason being that they 'shared the broad conservative outlook of the rest of the Malay elite'.[136]

The acute shortage of judges and support staff, backlog of cases caused by a sharp rise in the number of new cases,[137] high levels of procedural formalism[138] and poor implementation of a comprehensive computerised system have had a negative impact on efficiency.[139] The lack of an extensive

---

130 See Editorial, 'Appointment of Judges — the Way Forward', *Relevan*, 2004, September issue. See also G Seah, 'Crisis in the Judiciary, Part 5: Colonels Judging the Generals', *Aliran Monthly*, issue 8, 2004. Also, a new provision in the Federal Constitution, Art 122AB was inserted in 1994 to allow the appointment of Judicial Commissioners who had all the powers of a judge but without security of tenure. This has implications for judicial independence.

131 G J Samuels, 'Judicial Competency: How Can it be Maintained' (1980) 54 *ALJ* 581 at 585.

132 For discussion of the appointment of judges in the Australian context, see the references in M Spry, *Executive and High Court Appointments*, Research Paper, Parliament of Australia Parliamentary Library, 2000.

133 For a discussion on judicial training, see M Kirby, *Modes of Appointment and Training of Judges — A Common Law Perspective*, speech given at the ICJ/CIJL and CAJ Seminar on Legal Institutions in Transition, Belfast, 8 June 1999.

134 R Yatim, *Freedom under Executive Powers in Malaysia — A Study of Executive Supremacy*, Endowment Publications, Kuala Lumpur, 1995. One reason for this was their training in England in which parliament, and not the Constitution, is supreme. A Malaysian constitutional expert Abdul Aziz Bari openly criticised the judiciary who he said when asked to resolve a conflict between the individual and public authorities, 'invariably chose to abdicate themselves; citing lack of power and that the matter is beyond their purview': A A Bari, *Malaysian Constitution: A Critical Introduction*, The Other Press, Kuala Lumpur, 2003, p 243.

135 See, eg, G H Hofstede, *Culture's Consequences: International Differences in Work Related Values*, 2nd ed, Thousand Oaks, London, 2001.

136 H Crouch, *Government and Society in Malaysia*, Allen & Unwin, NSW, 1996, pp 138–42.

137 Bar Council Press Statement, 'Shortages of Judges and Judicial Commissioners', 13 January 2003 and 'Clearing Backlog in the Courts', 24 December 2003.

138 Djankov et al, above n 41. In this study, Malaysian courts did not perform as well as the courts in some other common law countries.

139 Although an e-court project was first announced as far back as 1996, it has yet to be

information system means that the task of compiling caseload statistics (counts of filed, pending and disposed cases) for the purposes of identifying and solving problems and improving court performance becomes a much bigger task than it should be.[140]

Some attention should also be paid to issues relating to access to justice. Rights are not very useful if not accompanied by means to enforce them. Access to courts is an important factor in determining the usefulness of a particular law. This is viewed as an important counterweight to the other key issue in judicial reform — improved court performance.[141] Leading thinkers in this area emphasise the issue of proper allocation of resources and not just merely efforts to reduce cost and delay. Anthony Jolowicz said that more effort should be made to understand and allocate priority areas to improve efficiency.[142] Adrian Zuckerman proposed that civil justice reforms employ the dual concepts of proportionality and fair allocation of resources, which depended on who benefits from litigation (public or private benefits) and that resources for the administration of justice be fairly distributed to all those who require access to justice, not only litigants.[143] Entitlement to legal aid should also reflect the allocation of resources. Britain has generous legal aid provisions, and evidence of this can be seen in the Law Commission's Consultation Paper on Shareholders Remedies where 19.2% of petitioners in the petitions surveyed received legal aid.[144] In contrast, it is very unlikely that any of the petitioners in Malaysia received any form of legal aid.[145] This aspect of reform is not on the agenda in Malaysia.

The importance of the lawmaking process cannot be underestimated. Common complaints amongst opposition parliamentarian and civil society groups includes the manner in which Bills are rushed through parliament without adequate discussion and debate, poor attendance in parliament, short supply of parliamentary committees, the ascendancy of party discipline over

---

implemented. The tender has now been awarded to a company, but irregularities in the tender process and the allegation of cronyism (due to the participation of a son of the then Prime Minister Mahathir Mohamed in the company) aroused scepticism whether the tender was appropriately awarded. See L C Wee, 'Transparency in the Creation of the Malaysian E-Court', *Relevan*, 2004, February issue, p 8.

140 For use of caseload statistics, see World Bank 'Introduction: Using Caseload Statistics', available at <http://www1.worldbank.org/publicsector/legal/CourtStatistics.pdf> (accessed 12 January 2005).

141 The World Bank, 'The Purpose of the Courts', at <http://www1.worldbank.org/publicsector/legal/purpose.htm> (accessed 13 January 2005).

142 J A Jolowicz, 'General Ideas and the Reform of Civil Procedure' (1983) 3 *Legal Studies* 295–314; *On Civil Procedure*, Cambridge UP Cambridge, 2000.

143 A Zuckerman, 'Reforming Civil Justice System: Trends in Industrial Countries' the World Bank PREM Note 46, 2000, available at <http://www1.worldbank.org/prem/PREMNotes/premnote46.pdf> (accessed 13 January 2005). See also S Shavell, 'The Fundamental Divergence between the Private and Social Motive to Use the Legal System' (1997) 26 *Jnl of Legal Studies* 575; A Zuckerman (Ed), *Civil Justice in Crisis: Comparative Perspectives of Civil Procedure*, Oxford UP, Oxford, 1999.

144 The Law Commission Report No 245, *Shareholder Remedies*, HMSO, London, 1997.

145 To qualify for state legal aid, a person's disposable income must not exceed RM3000 (approximately £450) a year. In any case, legal aid is only given for a limited range of cases (shareholder suit is not one) unless the relevant Minister gives special permission. Even then, there is the issue of competence of the legal aid solicitor to handle this type of litigation.

public interest, parliament being subservient to the Executive, the ineffectual upper house of parliament, the lack of tradition of parliament consultations with public and civil society organisations, and the lack of public hearings of parliamentary inquiries. Also lacking is the manner in which law reform projects are conducted. These are characterised by the ad-hoc manner in which committees are formed, poor communication with the public and poor transparency. Dissemination of information on their activities and public consultations has generally been limited to a select group of individuals and bodies. Poor public participation is the result of the lack of available information, the tight control over the media and an inherent lack of ability to take adverse comments and criticism. Reform committees are usually dominated by civil servants who may on occasion have had their brief on the direction they will take, making committee meetings a mere formality. The Corporate Law Reform Programme was among the first committee which bucked the trend when it published a consultation paper entitled *Strategic Framework for Corporate Law Reform Programme* in 2004. It was a move in the right direction but a sceptic may point out the necessity for greater publicity in view of the long delay in responding to the *Report on Corporate Governance* by the Corporate Governance Committee in 1999 in which the committee had pointed out the need for a revision of certain provisions in the Companies Act, and the fact that other corporate governance initiatives by the Committee on Corporate Governance, Securities Commission and Bursa Malaysia have generally been well publicised.

Limited information is compounded by poor legal resources available to the public. Most online legislation is accessible only by paid subscription, so too are case laws. University libraries charge the public for access. Newspapers do not normally report court proceedings except for cases involving public personalities or other newsworthy cases, and that too is subject to the limitations imposed upon them by the state and their ability to report court cases fairly and competently.

As to law enforcement agencies, such as the Securities Commission, the Attorney-General's Chambers, the Companies Commission and the Anti-Corruption Agency, the one common criticism directed against them is that they lacked independence and transparency. Legal enforcement is as important as the laws themselves and, furthermore, the high incidence and influence of the state in business makes independent law enforcing agencies even more important.

Quite recently the Domestic Trade and Consumer Affairs Minister and the Chief Executive Officer of the Companies Commission of Malaysia revealed that the failure to file annual returns was a common phenomenon, committed by 56% of registered companies in Malaysia. Other common offences include the failure to hold annual general meetings and filing annual accounts.[146] This gives a valuable insight into the efficacy of the commission's enforcement team. However, instead of promising to step up enforcement as one may reasonably expect, the Companies Commission recommended that all directors be required to attend a directors' training programme, without detailing how such a massive project could be implemented and the clear

---

146 The Star, 'Over half of private firms' directors breach rules', 13 July 2004.

benefits of having such a training programme.

It is not known whether resources for enforcement agencies and their enforcement powers are adequate. Most enforcement activities remain out of the public eye as they are not publicised. Prosecutions are normally made at the subordinate courts, whose judgments remain unreported. It is imperative therefore that the enforcement agencies reveal the details of their work. The Annual Report of the Commission's enforcement activities shows only data on the number of prosecutions carried out by them during the year. There is no mention what these prosecutions are for, in which court and their outcome. More significantly the Report contains no critical thought of the challenges faced by the commission in relation to their investigation and enforcement activities and how they have responded or intend to respond to these challenges.

9 Politics and business

The largest listed companies in Malaysia may be blocked into three main types: state-controlled, Chinese-controlled and Malay-controlled companies. State-controlled listed companies are in the main privatised companies in which the state retains majority shares and are controlled by the bureaucrats or dominant personalities within the ruling government. This control is exercised not only through the appointment of directors, but also on decision-making on policies and strategies.[147] As to large Chinese- and Malay-controlled listed companies, many are politically connected, which creates certain governance problems as a result of political or state involvement in these companies.[148]

Politics and business sometimes do not mix well. When political expediency influences business decisions, the interests of minority shareholders may be compromised. The purchase by United Engineers (M) Berhad (UEM) of shares in its associate company Renong Berhad (Renong) is an example of how weak institutional governance affects corporate governance.[149] This episode highlighted, among others, the importance of institutional governance in the business world. Improvement in corporate

---

147 See above n 66.
148 See Searle, above n 66; Gomez and Jomo, above n 66.
149 Both UEM and Renong were publicly listed companies. UEM brought a substantial stake in its associate company, Renong. Renong and its executive chairman Halim Saad were closely associated with UMNO and its leaders. The purchase caused uproar because Renong was during that time in dire financial difficulty (the devaluation of the local currency Ringgit Malaysia during the 1997 financial crisis caused its foreign debts to spiral) and the agreed purchase price was double the prevailing market price. The Securities Commission nevertheless allowed this transaction to go through and granted UEM a waiver from having to make a mandatory general offer for the remaining shares of Renong in accordance with the Code of Take-overs and Mergers 1987 (superseded by the Code of Take-overs and Mergers 1998). UEM was however fined a token sum of RM500 by the Registrar of Companies (now Companies Commission) for failing to give notice of a change in a substantial shareholder's interests and a public reprimand; and also fined RM100,000 by the Bursa Malaysia for breach of s 341 of its *Listing Requirements* for failing to make a 'factual, clear and succinct' statement relating to its purchase of the shares. Although UEM's purchase of Renong's shares was approved by shareholders, this was made possible by Renong's votes (the Kuala Lumpur Stock Exchange (now Bursa Malaysia) amended its *Listing Requirements* in July 1998 requiring interested parties from abstaining from voting).

governance rules, without the corresponding improvement in institutional governance, will hardly be sufficient. Institutional governance here is not limited to institutions having the control or wielding influence over companies such as the Securities Commission, the Companies Commission and Bursa Malaysia, it extends to other public bodies such as the Anti-Corruption Agency and the Attorney-General's Chambers. The independence and transparency of these two bodies has been questioned in the past.

The Anti-Corruption Agency, the body responsible for the investigation and prosecution of corruption, is organisationally structured under the Prime Minister's Department.[150] Thus, the agency is not independent from the government. So too is the Attorney-General's Chambers. Both these bodies have been criticised for lacking in transparency and exercising selected prosecutions. Some examples include the unexplained delays in the investigation involving Eric Cheah, the former chief executive officer of Perwaja Steel Berhad, a government-owned steel company, and also the mystery shrouding the investigation against former chairman of Malaysian Airlines System Berhad, Tajuddin Ramli.[151] On the other hand, many are cynical of the motivation over the relatively decisive manner in which the authorities have charged several prominent businessmen associated with the former Deputy Prime Minister Anwar Ibrahim.[152]

The price which UEM paid for Renong's shares amounts to 86.6% of the UEM's shareholders funds at that time and raised UEM's debts from RM300 million to RM2.7 billion, which the Rating Agency Malaysia said would significantly drain UEM's cash flow. UEM's share price fell 48% in the week following the announcement of the purchase. In a related event, Halim Saad failed twice to make payments for a put option he had made for Renong's shares (he agreed to re-purchase the Renong's shares bought by UEM by way of a put option in an apparent attempt to appease public anger). No action was taken against him and he appeared to have been released of his obligations without having to compensate UEM. Both companies have now been de-listed from Bursa Malaysia. See generally Searle, above n 66, pp 143–6; R Pura, 'Confidence erodes in Malaysia's ability to carry out corporate damage control', AWSJ, 21–22 September 1997, p 1; R Nathan, S L Chiew and W F Soo, 'Country Paper for Malaysia', 2nd Asian Roundtable on Corporate Governance, ADB/OECD/World Bank, 31 May–2 June 2000, Hong Kong; Far Eastern Economic Review 'Undone Deal' 11 December 1997; 'Renong Calls Draw Warning', *The Asian Wall Street Journal Weekly*, 8 December 1997; H Nesadurai, 'In Defence of National Economic Autonomy? Malaysia's Response to the Financial Crisis' (2000) 13 *The Pacific Review* 73 at 90–1.

150 The Agency is headed by a Director-General, appointed by the Yang di-Pertuan Agong on advice by the Prime Minister. Officers of the Agency are members of the general public service: Anti-Corruption Act 1997 ss 3(2) and 4(3).
151 Eric Chia was finally arrested and charged in court for corruption not long after Abdullah Badawi took over from Mahathir Mohamad as Prime Minister.
152 See Rodan (2004), above n 83, at 123. Other public bodies such as the state investment arm Khazanah Nasional Berhad, EPF, Petronas (the state oil company), MISC (the national shipping company owned by Petronas), and even Tabung Haji (National (Muslim) Pilgrims Fund) have been accused of spending public funds to rescue selected companies. For the many allegations of crony capitalism, bailouts and corruption, see Transparency International's Malaysian chapter website at <http://transparency.org.my>. Another source is the online newspaper, *Malaysiakini*, at <http://www.malaysiakini.com>. See also generally Gomez and Jomo, above n 66 and Searle, above n 66.

10 Conclusion

It is commonly accepted that transplanted laws will evolve as they interact with elements in the local environment. This evolution need not necessarily result in changes in the substantive law. Often, there will be differences in the way the law is used, administered and enforced. The Japanese corporate governance system provides a good example. The basic governance rules are borrowed from the United States. It adopts a single tier board and separates control from ownership. However, unlike the United States, the Japanese ownership structure is concentrated: banks play a major governance role, employees are given a strong voice in corporate decision-making and there exists a stable inter-organisational relationship through horizontal cross-shareholdings. The reason for this evolution was explained by Curtis Milhaupt, as the US corporate law, when imported to Japan, was 'severed from its intellectual moorings ... the atomized, depersonalized shareholder-manager relationship that animates US laws and colours our view of the corporate contract has never resonated among Japanese institutions'.[153]

When the British companies legislation was imported into Malaysia, it too was severed from its intellectual moorings. The transplanted system which has as its focus the agency problem of directors-shareholders conflict is inappropriate for the concentrated nature of Malaysia's companies.[154] This concentration is highly complex as it occurs at various levels and is enhanced by the use of interlocks. The problems caused by this, ie, the powers of controlling shareholders, be it the state, the family or even individuals, and corporate structures which enhance control rights in excess of ownership rights, should be the target of corporate governance reform in Malaysia. Additionally, questions may be asked as to the extent that cultural traits and value systems impact on corporate governance. Equally pertinent is the role and influence of the state and politicians in businesses. The importance of political and institutional transparency in corporate governance should not be underestimated. The effectiveness of the judicial and other legal institutions, including the law enforcement agencies, as well as the issue on access to courts, are also valid concerns. A proper understanding of these issues is critical for effective and comprehensive governance reform.

While learning from the experiences of others can be useful, legal transplants have their limitations. It has been said, quite rightly, that the process of lawmaking is as important as the law itself. The reform process is part of the lawmaking process. It may be stating the obvious but a good reform programme should first identify the problem and then proceed to address it. This has not been done in any meaningful way. There are also other issues which fall outside of the mandate given to the law reform committee but are imperative to an efficient and effective operation of law, such as procedural

---

153 C J Milhaupt, 'A Relational Theory of Japanese Corporate Governance: Contract, Culture, and the Rule of Law' (1996) 37 *Harv Int LJ* 3 at 14.
154 This is one reason a great deal more attention should be given to the law on shareholders' legal remedies. Brian Cheffins noted that the lack of attention received in the United Kingdom on the issue of shareholders' rights and remedies compared to other countries is because of this system of ownership and control: B R Cheffins, 'Minority Shareholders and Corporate Governance' (2000) 21 *Company Lawyer* 41.

efficiency and entitlement to legal aid. This calls for the establishment of a body with the necessary powers to affect a comprehensive law reform programme, perhaps a Law Reform Commission of Malaysia. There are also issues which fall outside of the scope of the law (using the narrow meaning of the word) while still remaining a corporate governance issue, such as the quality of legal institutions, the independence of the judiciary and the role of politics in business. These, however, require a reform programme much wider than even a Law Reform Commission can perhaps undertake.

Finally, Malaysians can draw from their own history and experiences. Mediation is more compatible to Malaysian culture compared to the inherited adversarial system. The prevalence of family businesses provides further justification for this form of dispute resolution mechanism. Mediation is not a novelty even in the formal legal system in Malaysia as it has been used in the Syaria (Islamic) courts. The system is not perfect,[155] but perhaps it is far more useful to draw from our own experiences and learn our own lessons.

---

155 See, generally, Peletz, above n 93.

[6]

Living With the IMF: A New Approach to Corporate Governance and Regulation of Financial Institutions in Korea

By
Hwa-Jin Kim*

INTRODUCTION

Improving corporate governance is not easy, particularly for newly industrialized economies. Policymakers in such economies have little experience in controlling such problems as shirking and greed when they appear in the sophisticated organizational form of the modern corporation. As a result, they must turn to the more advanced economies to find a role model for institutional reforms and improvements. Comparative corporate governance is an important area of study in this regard.

A recent study on comparative corporate governance noted that "[n]ational governance systems turned out to be more adaptable in function, and therefore more persistent in form, than the prophets of convergence expected."[1] This study also suggested that formal convergence should come as a last resort due to the substantial political and social costs involved.[2] This view delivers important messages to scholars and policy-makers of some newly industrialized countries who are struggling with corporate governance issues in order to improve the

---

* Senior Consultant, Woo, Yun, Kang, Jeong & Han, Seoul, Korea; Lecturer, Research and Training Institute of the Korean Supreme Court. Member of the New York Bar. LL.M., Harvard Law School, 1994; LL.M., Northwestern University, 1993 (Raymond Fellow); Dr. Jur., Ludwig-Maximilians-University of Munich, Germany, 1988 (Adenauer Scholar); B.S., Seoul National University, Korea, 1983. The author gratefully acknowledges the invaluable comments of Professors Kon Sik Kim and Chang Hee Lee, Seoul National University. The author also gratefully acknowledges insightful comments of Professor Ronald J. Gilson, Stanford Law School, at the *Symposium on Globalization and Law for the Twentieth Century*, sponsored by Seoul National University College of Law. The author wishes to thank Professors Lucian A. Bebchuk, Reinier Kraakman, Howell Jackson, and William P. Alford, Harvard Law School; Bruno Simma, Ludwig-Maximilians-University of Munich; Sang-Hyun Song, Seoul National University/Harvard Law School; Chul Song Lee, Hanyang University; and Judge Young-Joon Mok, Research and Training Institute of the Korean Supreme Court, for academic inspiration and support for his studies.

1. Gilson, Globalizing Corporate Governance: Convergence of Form or Function 3-4 (discussion paper for the *Symposium on Globalization and Law for the Twentieth Century*, sponsored by Seoul National University College of Law, October 10-11th, 1997) [hereinafter Gilson, Globalizing Corporate Governance].
2. *Id.* at 7.

competitiveness of their countries' enterprises in global markets.[3] In their efforts to find an optimal structural relationship between capital markets, financial institutions, and corporate governance, they must be aware of the political and social costs involved in radical institutional reforms that go beyond the path-dependent limit of their institutions. The functional approach to corporate governance issues should come first in those economies as elsewhere.

Korea, one of the most dynamic economies of the global market, should benefit from this reasoning. Korea has recently recognized the importance of the systematic improvement of its industrial organization and corporate governance practices. The globalization of Korean firms' operational and financing activities and the internationalization of its capital markets have initiated, and even greatly contributed to, recent efforts toward various reforms and reform proposals. The process of reform was hastened by the foreign exchange crisis of 1997 and the consequential involvement of the international lending agencies such as the International Monetary Fund (IMF) and the World Bank in the restructuring of Korean industries.

In this article, I will discuss the current system and developments in corporate governance in Korea and address important lessons Korea has derived from recent studies on comparative corporate governance. The issue of corporate governance of banks is given particular attention in view of the recent failures of some large Korean conglomerates and the consequential negative impact on major Korean banks.

Part I describes the traditional "Korean institution" and its problems, singling out the so-called *Chaebol*-question and representative issues of corporate governance in Korea. Recent developments in Korean markets in terms of industrial restructuring under the IMF-mandated plan are also described. Part II explains and analyzes various corporate governance mechanisms newly introduced in Korea, focusing in particular on the Korean efforts to cultivate markets for corporate control. Part III tackles the important issue of corporate governance of banks and banks' participatory investments in Korea. Part IV explores the relationship between market internationalization and globalization of financing and corporate governance with reference to the case of Korean firms. This section also describes and analyzes the influence of international regulation of financial institutions on the governance of local banks and the new role of institutional investors in the Korean market.

This article is intended to be something more than a case study. One point made throughout this article is that the internationalization of capital markets, both inbound and outbound, will greatly improve corporate governance in Korea and elsewhere. Prudential regulations, as well as active transactions in interna-

---

3. For efforts in emerging market economies, *see* Bernard Black & Reinier Kraakman, *A Self-Enforcing Model of Corporate Law*, 109 HARV. L. REV. 1911 (1996) (developing a "self-enforcing" model of corporate law for emerging markets based on a case study of the Russian Federation). *But cf.* Roberta Romano, *A Cautionary Note on Drawing Lessons from Comparative Corporate Law*, 102 YALE L. J. 2021, 2036 (1993) (noting that "no tight connection [can] be demonstrated between corporate governance institutions and international competitiveness").

tional financial markets, have strongly promoted the functional convergence of corporate governance institutions.[4] The involvement of international lending agencies in the industrial restructuring process of the Korean economy has subjected Korean firms and banks to the harsh, but fair, discipline of international financial markets. The converging process of Korean corporate governance institutions into international standards is mandated by the discipline of international financial markets. By identifying the main trends and perspectives of this convergence, Korean policy-makers may have a better idea of the way they want to lead the Korean economy in the future.

I.
PROBLEMS WITH THE "TRADITIONAL" INSTITUTION

A. The Korean Institution

The traditional corporate governance institution in Korea is characterized by large groupings of related corporations under highly concentrated family or individual control and a unique pattern of unrelated diversification.[5] In terms of finance, Korean firms are highly leveraged but do not have the harsh discipline normally associated with debt.[6] Authoritarian military governments began building Korea's economic system since the 1960s and have traditionally favored big businesses through the provision of immense bank loans ("directed lending"). The Korean populace tolerated the *Chaebol*'s rise in the belief that they greatly contributed to the competitiveness of the Korean economy in global markets.[7]

The *Chaebol*, however, cannot necessarily be understood as a pattern of corporate governance. Rather, the term *Chaebol* describes a concentration of economic power and a pattern of doing business through unrelated diversifica-

---

4. Similarly, in one of my previous studies, I suggested that market internationalization and new financial institutions' regulations of the European Union may change the traditional governance pattern and ownership structure of German corporations, roughly towards the one prevailing in the United States. *See* Hwa-Jin Kim, *Markets, Financial Institutions, and Corporate Governance: Perspectives from Germany*, 26 LAW & POL'Y INT'L BUS. 371, 394-99 (1995). *Cf.* Curtis J. Milhaupt, *Property Rights in Firms*, 84 VA. L. REV. 1145, 1185-89 (1998) (suggesting that the recent developments in Korea in terms of the currency and debt crisis support the convergence-from-competition hypothesis).

5. The Korean economy and corporate governance institutions are path dependent and are extremely sensitive to initial conditions set in the 1960s. For the concept of path dependency, see Mark J. Roe, *Chaos and Evolution in Law and Economics*, 109 HARV. L. REV. 641 (1996). The path dependency of the Korean system takes the common semi-strong form. *Cf. id.* at 648-50. Recent scholarship emphasizes the importance of path dependence in determining the ownership structure of large public companies and corporate law in general. *See id.* at 643-58; Black and Kraakman, *supra* note 3, at 1974-77; MARK J. ROE, STRONG MANAGERS, WEAK OWNERS: THE POLITICAL ROOTS OF AMERICAN CORPORATE FINANCE *passim* (1994).

6. For an excellent account of the disciplinary effects of high leverage on corporate management, *see generally* GEORGE ANDERS, MERCHANTS OF DEBT, chs. 8-9 (1992).

7. *See generally* Kon Sik Kim, Chaebol and Corporate Governance in Korea, ch.1 (University of Washington Dissertation 1995) [hereinafter KS Kim, Chaebol and Corporate Governance]; MYUNG HUN KANG, THE KOREAN BUSINESS CONGLOMERATE: CHAEBOL THEN AND NOW (1996). *See also* Meredith Woo-Cumings, *How Industrial Policy Caused South Korea's Collapse*, WALL ST. J. EUROPE, Dec. 9, 1997, at 8.

tion. The traditional Korean system can be classified as a bank-centered capital market system in which the banks lack ownership of the commercial enterprises. Most of these enterprises, even those ranked in the Fortune International 500, such as Samsung or Hyundai, are family-controlled. According to the then Korean Securities Supervisory Board, the listed Korean firms' major shareholders had an average shareholding of 33.31 percent as of the end of October 1997.[8] It has recently been reported that out of 769 listed Korean corporations, some 380 are directly controlled by their major shareholders as full-time directors.[9] These enterprises are also highly leveraged. Banks and other financial institutions have tremendous amounts of credit outstanding with these large enterprises with significant security interest in these firms' assets. Nevertheless, banks have been rather indifferent to corporate governance issues, partly because they have been under the government's influence, and partly because they have lacked motives and skills to effectively monitor these enterprises.[10]

As a result, the debt-to-equity ratios of some large Korean firms has become extremely high. The average debt to equity ratio of the 30 largest Korean conglomerates accounted for 519 percent of their shareholders' equity by the end of 1997.[11] Hanbo Steel's peak of 1,893 percent in June 1996, Sammi Steel's peak of 1,762 percent in December 1996, and Woosung Construction's peak of 3,323 percent in June 1997 are the most conspicuous examples. Such unusually high debt-to-equity ratios have been made possible through the widespread practice of "cross guarantees" between member firms within corporate groups.[12] The volume of cross guarantees within the 30 largest Korean conglomerates reached 469 percent of their shareholders' equity by April 1, 1993. The ratio decreased to 91.34 percent by April 1, 1997,[13] but this decrease was due largely to the bankruptcy of two large Korean conglomerates, Halla and Jinro, in 1997.

---

8. See KOREA HERALD, Nov. 13, 1997, at 11.

9. See JOONG-ANG ILBO, Sept. 23, 1997, at 35.

10. Although Japanese firms have long been role models for Korean *Chaebols*, the Korean system differs significantly from the Japanese in terms of commercial banks' ownership interest in and effective monitoring of borrower companies. Some view the Korean system as similar to that of the Japanese. *See, e.g.,* Alan Murray, *Asia's Financial Pain Makes U.S. System Look Like a Winner,* WALL ST. J. EUROPE, Dec. 9, 1997, at 1, 7 (arguing that the American system, with its emphasis on the short-term and shareholder activism, is doing far better than the Japanese one with long-term relationships of cross-shareholdings and preferential bank financing). *But see* Milhaupt, *supra* note 4, at 1158-84 (showing non-convergence of corporate governance systems in the United States, Japan and Korea). For the Japanese institution, see Curtis J. Milhaupt, *A Relational Theory of Japanese Corporate Governance: Contract, Culture, and the Rule of Law,* 37 HARV. INT'L L. J. 3 (1996); Ronald J. Gilson and Mark J. Roe, *Understanding the Japanese Keiretsu: Overlaps Between Corporate Governance and Industrial Organization,* 102 YALE L. J. 871 (1993); Kang, *supra* note 7, at 63-91; Masahiko Aoki, *Toward an Economic Model of the Japanese Firm,* 28 J. ECON. LIT. 1 (1990); J. Mark Ramseyer, *Takeovers in Japan: Opportunism, Ideology and Corporate Control,* 35 UCLA L. REV. 1 (1987). *See also* Mark G. Robilotti, *Codetermination, Stakeholder Rights, and Hostile Takeovers: A Reevaluation of the Evidence from Abroad,* 38 HARV. INT'L L. J. 536 (1997) (critically analyzing the stakeholder corporate governance debate in comparative perspectives).

11. See CHOSUN ILBO, April 16, 1998, at 3.

12. *See* Steve Glain and Namju Cho, *Chaebols Gasp Under Suffocating Debt,* ASIAN WALL ST. J., Dec. 23, 1997, at 1, 7 (reporting severe credit crunch of large Korean firms).

13. *See infra* p. 93 (Table 1).

These two conglomerates went into bankruptcy with cross guarantees of 891 percent and 473 percent of shareholders' equity, respectively.

As some large *Chaebols* (Hanbo, Sammi, Jinro, Dainong, Kia, New Core, Haitai, and Halla) went into bankruptcy in 1997, Korean banks lost credit in the market due to their bad loans to the failed firms. Korean commercial banks and merchant banks were saddled with 28.52 trillion won and 3.89 trillion won, respectively, in non-performing loans by October 1997.[14] The result was general skepticism about the soundness of the Korean market and system. The international financial community soon realized that the Korean economy had serious structural problems and that the government had not taken leadership in regulatory reforms.[15] As a result, foreign investors quickly withdrew from the Korean market and the Korean currency fell in international financial markets.[16] The stock market index also declined to a ten-year low. During the turmoil of 1997, the number of insolvent firms placed under the supervision of the Korea Stock Exchange reached seventy-two, representing ten percent of all listed firms. As the Korean government's emergency package for market-boosting financial stabilization measures, including the kick-off plan of Big Bang failed to satisfy markets, Korea ultimately applied for the bailout funds with the IMF on November 21, 1997, one year after joining the OECD. Korea was then forced to restructure its financial industry and industrial organization under the guidance of the IMF.[17]

---

14. *See Gov't to Allow Wider Won Price Swing*, KOREA HERALD, Nov. 20, 1997, at 1. As of the end of December 1998, total non-performing loans (loans classified as either substandard, doubtful or estimated loss), of 22 Korean commercial banks stood at 22.22 trillion won. *See* Korea Financial Supervisory Commission, *Bank Nonperforming Loans at End-December, 1998* (visited March 5, 1999) <http://www.fsc.go.kr/kfsc/board/11/pr_0303.html>.

15. *See Korean Leadership*, WALL ST. J. EUROPE, Nov. 25, 1997, at 10 (noting that the *Chaebols* are "a drag on the economy" and the Korean developmental model is "hopelessly outdated and outclassed by market forces").

16. *See* HAL S. SCOTT & PHILIP A. WELLONS, INTERNATIONAL FINANCE: TRANSACTIONS, POLICY, AND REGULATION 32-36 (5th ed. 1998).

17. *See* Mark L. Clifford, *Korea's Crisis*, BUS. WK. (Asian Edition), Nov. 24, 1997, at 18-21; Michael Hirsh, Jeffrey Bartholet and Lee Pyongchong, *Seoul Calls for Help*, NEWSWEEK, Dec. 1, 1997, at 34-37; *Seoul, IMF Agree on $55-bil. Bailout Deal*, KOREA HERALD, Dec. 4, 1997, at 1; Bob Davis, *Bitter Medicine: Korea Plays Adverse Patient to IMF's Rescue Team*, ASIAN WALL ST. J., March 3, 1998, at 1, 9. Even after the IMF bailout, Korea careened toward the catastrophe of a default. The near-bankrupt Korean economy was finally rescued by G-7 countries' decision of December 24, 1997, for advancement of the bailout package. *See* Paul Blustein & Clay Chandler, *Behind Korean Bailout*, KOREA HERALD [Washington Post Service], Dec. 30, 1997, at 6 (reporting that there had been talk [in Washington] of letting Korea fail and "pay the price for years of economic mismanagement"); David Wessel, *South Korean Bailout Evokes Some Tough Questions*, ASIAN WALL ST. J., Dec. 29, 1997, at 6 (citing some hard-liners who say world governments and the IMF are making a big mistake by insulating private investors and lenders from the discipline of the market); Michael Duffy, *The Rubin Rescue*, TIME, Jan. 12, 1998, at 12-15. Korea's total foreign debts were tallied at $156.9 billion at the end of November 1997. *See Korea's Foreign Debts Total $156.9 Bil. by IMF Standards*, KOREA HERALD, Dec. 31, 1997, at 1. Most of the country's short-term corporate foreign debts were restructured in January 1998. *See* Stephen E. Frank & Namju Cho, *Korea, Creditors Finalize Debt-Restructuring Deal*, ASIAN WALL ST. J., January 30-31, 1998, at 3.

B. Inordinate Efforts to Change Complimentary Institutions?

Even before the advent of this recent turmoil, Korean policy-makers and scholars believed that their system was relatively inefficient in comparison to those of the United States, Germany, or Japan. Korean scholars, particularly, increasingly believed that the existing Korean model could no longer effectively compete in the global market. Consequently, the Korean government's initiative towards dilution of the ownership concentration,[18] particularly in large firms, has been strongly supported by public opinion. The Berle-Means corporation, with separated ownership and control, has long been a superior ideal in the minds of the Korean public. It is widely believed that professional managers, not being the "owners,"[19] would be able to rationalize outbound corporate relationships with the government, financial institutions, securities markets and internal reform operations without a heavy conflict of interest. Furthermore, Korean law does not allow dual class voting.[20] By now, it appears that there is a consensus that the U.S. system, with its dispersed ownership structure and efficient securities market, should be imported to rationalize the Korean system. The IMF-mandated reforms will support such developments.

However, it is questionable if this is the most efficient way to achieve rationalization, especially in view of recent trends in the United States to bridge ownership and control of public companies in order to diminish agency costs. This course of action could also be tainted by the common emotional drive for "*Chaebol*-bashing."[21] Perhaps too much emphasis has been placed on institutional changes regarding ownership structure and structural relationships between capital markets and business corporations. The basic Korean approach has been to adapt the institution to fit a fixed political or social goal, no matter what the political or social costs. In such an environment, there is not much

---

18. In order to reduce the burden of servicing high-interest bearing debts, Korean firms will continuously have to increase capital. This will lead to dilution of ownership concentration and ultimately promote the separation of ownership and control. Since the cost of capital of Korean shareholders will continue to be very high because of high interest rates, new capital injections are likely to come from foreign investors.

19. This widely used term is a misnomer. No one can claim to be the owner of a public corporation unless he or she holds a 100 percent sharehold of the firm, which is not possible. Otherwise, he or she can just control the firm, identifying personal interest with that of the company in most cases. However, the agency problem still exists in view of the non-controlling shareholders' interest especially when the controlling shareholder holds less than 50 percent. In Korea, substantial agency costs already exist in such cases where the controlling shareholder-manager mismanages the firm and/or causes wealth transfer from non-controlling shareholders to himself/herself. In the latter case, the cost will be borne by non-controlling shareholders only, the controlling shareholder excluded. The term "owner" is not only a misnomer, but also contributes to distortion of reality.

20. The Korean Commercial Code accepts the one share, one vote principle. *See* Art. 369(1).

21. It should be noted that there is a widespread confusion in Korea of general corporate governance issues with the so-called "*Chaebol*-question." To be sure, the latter should be understood in terms of the unique path dependency of the Korean institution. However, the issue is better approached through the sound reasoning against concentration of economic power. It would be unfair to declare that the *Chaebols* are the source of all failures in the Korean model. Transparency and accountability of corporate management are standards applicable to any corporation in Korea. On the other hand, it would be also unfair to apply the fundamentals of the "*Chaebol*-policy" to medium or small firms. Some of the newly introduced rules in the Korean Securities and Exchange Act exemplify the confusion of the above two conceptually distinct issues.

room left for reform through functional improvements of the existing regime, whether it be political or industrial.

C. Who Replaces Poorly Performing Managers?

Will Korea be able to find a functional solution to this central question of corporate governance[22] within its path dependent limits? Although it has tried to change the ownership structure of firms through a rather formal approach, it also has tried to respond to managerial accountability problems through a functional approach. The recent general revision of the *Commercial Code* and *Securities and Exchange Act* described below evidences this. However, the point of these revisions was the protection of minority investors, not a systematic remaking of the corporate governance institution. The latter was only recently identified as an important goal since the latest involvement of the international lending agencies in reforms of the Korean economy.

Indeed, there has been no entity which has been able to replace the poorly performing managers in Korea. The managers themselves are major controlling shareholders. In most cases, Korean corporate boards are nominal organizations under direct control of these controlling shareholders. The troubling question here is: who controls the controlling shareholder-managers of Korean firms?[23] Although Korean law recognizes the concept of managers' fiduciary duty of loyalty, it falls short of the standards set in American corporate law. Derivative litigation has existed only in statute[24] until recently,[25] and its deterrence and disciplining influence will probably be nonexistent because of the absence of class action and contingency fee devices.[26] Recent developments indicate that it

---

22. For a good overview of mechanisms to replace inefficient management, *see* Park McGinty, *Replacing Hostile Takeovers*, 144 U. PA L. REV. 983, 990-99 (1996).

23. Here we come back to the question raised by Alchian and Demsetz: "[W]ho will monitor the monitor?" Armen Alchian and Harold Demsetz, *Production, Information Costs, and Economic Organization*, 62 AM. ECON. REV. 777, 782 (1972). *See also* Ronald J. Gilson, *A Structural Approach to Corporations: The Case Against Defensive Tactics in Tender Offers*, 33 STAN. L. REV. 819, 835 n. 61 (1981).

24. *See* Arts. 403-406 of the KOREAN COMMERCIAL CODE. Under Art. 403(1) of the COMMERCIAL CODE, shareholders holding 1 percent (previously 5 percent under the pre-1998 version law) of the company's issued and outstanding shares may file a derivative suit. The amount of reimbursed attorneys fees for a successful shareholder is subject to certain limits ruled by the Supreme Court. *See* Art. 99-2 of the KOREAN CODE OF CIVIL PROCEDURE.

25. The recent turmoil in the financial market has resulted in few derivative lawsuits in Korea. Further, the new practice in Japan is expected to influence the recent insurgence of derivative litigation in Korea. In Japan, shareholders derivative litigation is gaining importance in corporate governance of Japanese firms. *See* Shiro Kawashima & Susumu Sakurai, *Shareholder Derivative Litigation in Japan: Law, Practice, and Suggested Reforms*, 33 STAN. J. INT'L L. 9 (1997); Milhaupt, *supra* note 4, at 55-57.

26. For skeptical views on the benefits of derivative litigation, *see* Roberta Romano, *The Shareholder Suit: Litigation without Foundation?*, 7 J. L. ECON. & ORG. 55, 84 (1991) (finding little empirical evidence of specific deterrence and concluding that "shareholder litigation is a weak, if not ineffective, instrument of corporate governance"); Daniel R. Fischel & Michael Bradley, *The Role of Liability Rules and the Derivative Suit in Corporate Law: A Theoretical and Empirical Analysis*, 71 CORNELL L. REV. 261 (1986) (casting doubt on the assumption that liability rules enforced by derivative suits play a fundamental role in aligning the interests of managers and investors). For the mixed data on the effect of changes in laws concerning derivative suits, see Michael Bradley & Cindy A. Schipani, *The Relevance of the Duty of Care Standard in Corporate Governance*, 75 IOWA

may be the banks' role to demand accountability from management. However, Korean banks, deep in trouble themselves, have a strong voice only in those cases where their debtor firms face fatal financial failure. Would they also be active in "peace time"?

It is widely believed in Korea that the solution should be found in an active market for corporate control and with institutional investors' enhanced activism. The internationalization of the Korean capital markets, either by voluntary efforts or by the IMF-mandated plans,[27] will contribute to the shaping of the new regime. For now, Korea has decided to model its capital markets after the American system. As far as the capital market is concerned in the Korean economy, adapting to the U.S. system would not require radical institutional changes. For example, Korean efforts to seek strong venture capital markets with the opening of the Korea Securities Dealers Automated Quotation System (KOSDAQ) may be a good test for a successful adaptation.

D. Remaking of the Korean Institution Under the IMF-Mandated Plan

Immediately after its decision to seek a bailout fund from the IMF, the Korean government started to accelerate the corporate and financial restructuring process. As the IMF was expected to ask for such a restructuring anyway, and the Korean government had long been realizing its inevitability, it came as no great surprise. The *Chaebols* also started paring down businesses.[28] Throughout 1998, many Korean firms and financial institutions went through restructuring, private workouts, strategic alliance talks with foreign firms, and domestic and international mergers and acquisitions transactions.[29] In particu-

---

L. REV. 1 (1989); Elliott J. Weiss & Lawrence J. White, *Of Econometrics and Indeterminacy: A Study of Investors' Reactions to "Changes" in Corporate Law*, 75 CAL. L. REV. 551 (1987).

27. For the full text of the Korean government's Letter of Intent with the Memorandum on the Economic Program (hereinafter Korea-IMF Memorandum) submitted to the IMF, see CHOSUN ILBO, Dec. 6, 1997, at 12. For the full text of the second and third packages submitted to the IMF by the Korean government, see JOONG-ANG ILBO, Dec. 26, 1997, at 5 and MAEIL KYONGJE, Feb. 18, 1998, at 3, respectively. The implementation of the restructuring plans are coordinated by the Structural Reform Planning Unit created by the Korea Financial Supervisory Commission. For various discussions and opinions on the Korea-IMF deal, see *Korea's IMF Negotiations*, WALL ST. J. EUROPE, Dec. 3, 1997, at 8; Seong C. Gweon, *Why is IMF Bad for the Market?*, KOREA HERALD, Dec. 10, 1997, at 8; Michael Schuman and Namju Cho, *Is Korean Bailout the Right Medicine?*, WALL ST. J. EUROPE, Dec. 8, 1997, at 5; Robert J. Fouser, *Antiforeignism*, KOREA HERALD, Dec. 17, 1997, at 6; Editorial, *Hurdles Ahead for South Korea*, N.Y. TIMES, Jan. 2, 1998, at 16; Ajay Kapur, *Bad Medicine from the IMF*, ASIAN WALL ST. J., Jan. 15, 1998, at 6. *See also* George P. Shultz, William E. Simon and Walter B. Wriston, *Who Needs the IMF?*, ASIAN WALL ST. J., Feb. 4, 1998, at 8; David Sacks and Peter Thiel, *The IMF's Big Wealth Transfer*, ASIAN WALL ST. J., March 12, 1998, at 6; Lawrence Summers, *The IMF: Good for Donors Too*, ASIAN WALL ST. J., March 30, 1998, at 10; *What's an IMF For?*, ASIAN WALL ST. J., April 7, 1998, at 10; *The IMF Crisis*, ASIAN WALL ST. J., April 16, 1998, at 8; David Rockefeller, *Why We Need the IMF*, WALL ST. J. EUROPE, May 11, 1998, at 10.

28. *See* Michael Schuman, *Ssangyong's Restructuring Gives It a Fighting Chance*, ASIAN WALL ST. J., Dec. 29, 1997, at 1, 5.

29. Ninety-three merger cases among listed Korean firms have been reported in 1998. *See* MAEIL KYONGJE, Dec. 30, 1998, at 19. The following web sites provide useful data and information on recent developments in Korea in terms of industrial and corporate restructuring: *The Korea Financial Supervisory Commission* <http://www.fsc.go.kr>; *The Korea Fair Trade Commission* <http://www.ftc.go.kr>; *The Korean Ministry of Finance and Economy* <http://www.mofe.go.kr>;

lar, Korea's five largest *Chaebols* have tried to agree on so-called "Big Deals," the exchange or consolidation of big businesses under the government's guidance.[30]

Because it was believed that the Korean financial crisis was started in part by the loss of foreign investors' confidence in the governance of large Korean corporations and banks,[31] the Korean government has started to focus on this aspect and review the regulatory infrastructure again for possible reform as agreed with the IMF. As it is also widely believed that the inefficient governance of large companies and banks are one of the sources of the troubles Korea now faces,[32] various reforms in terms of industrial policy and corporate governance have been planned and are expected to be implemented.

The package developed by the IMF in consultation with the Korean government includes several measures for improving of governance institutions of Korean firms.[33] According to the Korea-IMF Memorandum ("the Memorandum"), the Korean government recognized "the need to improve corporate governance and the corporate structure."[34] Toward that end, the Korean government and the IMF agreed that: "transparency of corporate balance sheets (including profit and loss accounts) will be improved by enforcing accounting standards in line with generally accepted accounting practices, including independent external audits, full disclosure, and provision of consolidated statements for business conglomerates."[35] The Memorandum also provides that

---

and the *Korean Ministry of Commerce, Industry and Energy* <http://www.mocie.go.kr>. *Cf.* The Korea Stock Exchange <http://www.kse.or.kr>; Korea Asset Management Corporation <http://www.kamco.or.kr>; Korea Federation of Banks <http://www.kfb.or.kr>; The Korea Securities Dealers Association <http://www.ksda.or.kr>; Korea Investment Trust Companies Association <http://www.kitca.or.kr>; The Federation of Korean Industries <http://www.fki.or.kr>.

30. *See Korea Financial Supervisory Commission, Agreement for the Restructuring of the Top 5 Chaebol, December 7, 1998* (visited March 5, 1999) <http://www.fsc.go.kr/kfsc/board/11/981208-1.html>.

31. *See* HAN-GUK KYONGJE SHINMUN, Nov. 24, 1997, at 3 (analysing possible impacts of IMF bailout); *id.*, Nov. 6, 1997, at 20 (reporting foreign investors' frustration in Korean firms' ignorance of minority shareholder interest and non-transparent management and accounting practices).

32. *See, e.g.*, Tony Emerson & B. J. Lee, *Foreign Medicine*, NEWSWEEK, Dec. 15, 1997, at 41 ("To be fair, Chaebol owners were simply taking advantage of the system . . . . And to raise money by selling stock would have diluted the owners' control over family enterprises. So they borrowed and borrowed, knowing that the larger they got, the less likely the government would ever allow them to fail . . . . By forcing Chaebol to sell majority stockholdings, the IMF deal could not only topple this pyramid [of debt], but eventually the Chaebol owners themselves."); Fred Hu, *Should China Grow Chaebol?*, ASIAN WALL ST. J., Dec. 18, 1997 (Korean lessons to China).

33. The international lending agencies like the IMF and World Bank regularly extend loans with "conditionality". The concept of "conditionality" does not exist in private lending. But it is not very different from security arrangements on loans of the private sector. To be sure, it is understood that the breach of the agreement with an international lending institution does not constitute the violation of international law *per se*. However, any default in implementation of such an agreement will limit further borrowing and lower the country's credit rating, which shall exert far greater detrimental impacts on the economy than any cause of legal action might do. *See generally* HAROLD JAMES, INTERNATIONAL MONETARY COOPERATION SINCE BRETTON WOODS 322-35 (1996); WILLIAM A. MCCLEARY, THE DESIGN AND IMPLEMENTATION OF CONDITIONALITY, in RESTRUCTURING ECONOMIES IN DISTRESS: POLICY REFORM AND THE WORLD BANK 197-215 (Vinod Thomas et al. eds. 1995).

34. *See* Korea-IMF Memorandum, *supra* note 27, at No. 34.

35. *Id.*

"[t]he commercial orientation of bank lending will be fully respected and the government will not intervene in bank management and lending decisions (except for prudential regulations)."[36] Directed lending shall immediately be eliminated.[37] Further, the Korean government shall formulate, with the assistance of international lending agencies, a plan "to encourage the restructuring of corporate finances, including measures to reduce the high debt-to-equity ratio of corporations, develop capital markets to reduce the share of bank financing by corporations, and change the system of cross guarantees within conglomerates."[38] The implementation of this program began in early 1998 and has resulted in substantial regulatory changes.

II.
FUNCTIONAL APPROACHES TO CORPORATE GOVERNANCE ISSUES

A. Recent Statutory Changes

The Korean government's recent efforts towards implementing a new regulatory environment to promote an efficient function of corporate governance mechanisms and an active market for corporate control shows that the functional approach to corporate governance issues is slowly being put into place in Korea. In particular, the *Korean Securities and Exchange Act* (KSEA) and the *Commercial Code* have been amended to reflect the changed circumstances in the capital markets and to reflect Korean firms' new pattern of doing business and methods of financing. The government has also introduced numerous provisions that promote corporate restructuring and mergers and acquisition in Korea. At the same time, the new provisions are designed to protect unsophisticated investors under the changed regulatory environment. Interestingly, the new *Securities and Exchange Act* addresses many of the corporate governance issues that have traditionally been regarded as within the domain of the *Commercial Code*.

1. The New Securities and Exchange Act[39]

The KSEA, effective from April 1, 1997, has substantially improved the status of minority shareholders in listed Korean companies. To promote transparency and managerial accountability, it provides minority shareholders with the right to check and/or challenge management by less restrictive procedural requirements than those provided for in the *Commercial Code*. The requirements have been lessened further through the partial amendments to the KSEA in February and May 1998, as an implementation of the Korean government's

---

36. *Id.*
37. *Id.*
38. *See id.* at No. 37. To strengthen market discipline, the Korean bankruptcy laws shall be reformed so that their orderly function without government interference will be made possible. *Id.* at No. 35 prohibits "government subsidized support or tax privileges" to bail out individual corporations. The Korean bankruptcy laws have been amended in February 1998 to introduce more strict substantial requirements and facilitate the court proceedings.

39. For an excellent description of the Korean securities market and the (old) SECURITIES AND EXCHANGE ACT, *see* Joon Park, *Internationalization of the Korean Securities Market*, 7 INT'L TAX & BUS. LAW 1 (1989).

agreement with the IMF. Now, shareholders holding less than one percent of a listed company's issued and outstanding shares may exercise certain shareholder's rights, including the filing of a derivative suit, provided that they satisfy some technical requirements.[40] Shareholders holding 0.01% of a listed company's issued and outstanding shares may file a derivative suit, provided that they acquired their shares at least six months prior and maintained the holding continuously until the filing date.[41]

The new system has been widely welcomed by the Korean legal and academic communities. It is regarded as an advanced mechanism for a more balanced relationship between controlling and minority shareholders. Indeed, the institutional reform hastened by the recent economic crisis has initiated new shareholder activism in Korea that is led by a group of highly motivated scholars and lawyers. The advocates of minority shareholders' rights have been successful so far in raising corporate governance issues at some large Korean companies such as Samsung Electronics and SK Telecom.[42] These highly publicized victories for shareholder democracy, combined with foreign investors' active involvement,[43] is expected to greatly contribute to the improvement of corporate governance in Korea. However, it remains to be seen whether the new system can function effectively without being abused by bad-faith shareholders who want to utilize it in a control contest situation. The new provisions regarding mergers and acquisitions will be discussed separately below.

2. *The New Commercial Code*

A generally revised new *Korean Commercial Code* (KCC), went into effect on October 1, 1996. The new amendments to the KCC deal mainly with the section governing stock corporations and have a substantial impact on corporate governance. The official comments to the amendments declare that they reflect changed social and economic circumstances in Korea and are intended to promote competitiveness of Korean enterprises in an era of internationalization of business in Korea.

First of all, a quorum requirement for general shareholders' meetings is abolished. Now, no direct quorum requirement exists unless a company's Articles of Incorporation otherwise provide.[44] To be sure, new voting require-

---

40. *See* Art. 191-13 of the KSEA.
41. *See* Art. 191-13 (1) of the KSEA. Minority shareholders of the Securities Investment Companies can exercise their shareholders' rights under the rules provided by the KSEA without any regard to the listing of the stocks at the Korea Stock Exchange or KOSDAQ. Further, the 0.01% requirement is waived for the shareholders of the Securities Investment Companies, i.e., any shareholder holding at least one share can bring the derivative suit. *See* Art. 84 (3) of the SECURITIES INVESTMENT COMPANY ACT.
42. *See, e.g.*, CHOSUN ILBO, March 28, 1998, at 8 (reporting that the annual shareholders meeting of Samsung Electronics took more than 13 hours due to active discussion on corporate governance issues); CHOSUN ILBO, March 27, 1998, at 9 (reporting that SK Telecom accepted minority shareholders' request for managerial transparency).
43. *See* Part IV, B below.
44. *See* Art. 368 of the KCC.

ments[45] have the effect of imposing a *de facto* quorum requirement.[46] However, they are substantially more liberal than those imposed under the pre-1996 law. This new rule is regarded as pro-management due to the newly created flexibility for holding general shareholders' meetings.

The new KCC also allows restrictions on transfer of shares. Under the new KCC, the Articles of Incorporation of stock corporations can restrict a transfer of shares by making it subject to the approval of the board.[47] An appraisal remedy will be available to the affected shareholders. This change has significant implications for change of control of the firms with few shareholders, including joint-venture enterprises.[48] The powers of the board under the Articles of Incorporation to restrict a share transfer provide the incumbent management with a strong tool to protect its control.

Parallel with the pro-management changes to the KCC, a statutory auditor's tenure is extended from two to three years[49] to safeguard its independence and supervisory functions. Also, the statutory auditor's legal power has greatly been enhanced through, *inter alia*, the new entitlement to call an extraordinary shareholders' meeting.[50] As before, for the purpose of electing statutory auditors, a shareholder holding more than three percent of the outstanding shares having voting rights may not exercise voting rights with respect to shares held in excess of three percent.[51]

The KCC also mandates appraisal rights for dissenters in mergers or sales of businesses.[52] The appraisal remedy for dissenting shareholders in mergers or sales of businesses was not unknown in Korea; the KSEA also provides procedural rules for expressal rights, along with a valuation method.[53] There have been several instances where proposed merger transactions were aborted due to the drain on a company's liquidity. Of course, whether those deals would have been value increasing ones cannot ultimately be known.[54] Dissenting share-

---

45. *See id.*
46. The failure to meet those requirements does not invalidate the meetings held, but prevents the relevant resolutions from being adopted; normal resolutions require the vote of at least twenty-five percent of all of the issued and outstanding shares in the company voting therefor. Special resolutions for central business decisions such as mergers require the vote of at least one-third of all of the issued and outstanding shares in the company voting therefor. The Articles of Incorporation are allowed to impose more restrictive requirements than the ones stipulated in Art. 368 of the KCC, but not less restrictive ones.
47. *See* Art. 335 of the KCC.
48. It is common practice in Korea for a joint-venture agreement to have express provision prohibiting any transfer of shares without prior consent of the other partner. Although, under such contractual arrangements, no cause of action is available against the company itself, the Seoul District Court, in its decision of Nov. 20, 1997, 97pa7454, has recently ruled that shareholders who acquired shares in violation of such a prohibition are not entitled to call a shareholders' meeting.
49. *See* Art. 410 of the KCC.
50. *See* Art. 412-3 of the KCC.
51. *See* Art. 409 (2) of the KCC. Art. 409 (3) of the KCC allows more restrictive requirements in a charter provision. The three percent-limit rule applies to discharge of statutory auditors of listed companies without cause. *See* Art. 191-11 (1) of the KSEA.
52. *See* Art. 374-2 with Art. 530 (2) of the KCC.
53. *See* Art. 191 of the KSEA.
54. *Cf.* Bayless Manning, *The Shareholder's Appraisal Remedy: An Essay for Frank Coker*, 72 YALE L. J. 223, 234-36 (1962) (criticizing appraisal as a possible drain on a company's liquidity

holders in the deals reportedly were disappointed by proposed merger ratios. As they were institutional investors with significant shareholdings, they successfully blocked the transaction by announcing their intent to exercise their appraisal rights in advance.[55] Nevertheless, while approval rights can be a powerful tool of shareholders, there is little empirical evidence showing that the appraisal remedy systematically checks Korean managers' breaches of fiduciary duty.[56]

The KCC was amended again in October 1998 to comply with the IMF-mandated program. The amendments deal exclusively with the section governing stock corporations and have a direct impact on corporate governance and restructuring. The official comments to the amendments state that they are intended to support corporate restructuring and enhance managerial accountability and transparency through efficient monitoring.

The KCC has introduced the concept of directors' fiduciary duty of loyalty into the statute.[57] It has long been recognized that the director of a stock corporation is under such a duty even though the KCC did not explicitly provide for it. The current version of the KCC now imposes this statutory obligation on directors of stock corporations. Further, the current KCC also holds *de facto* directors liable for damages under certain circumstances.[58] It has been a widespread practice in Korea that the ultimate control over large firms lies in the hands of "owners" who do not hold any official corporate directorship. The KCC enhances managerial accountability by also holding them liable for mismanagement and misconduct. The status of minority shareholders is promoted through the introduction of a shareholder proposal right.[59] The KCC also introduces cumulative voting.[60] This is a quasi-default rule in the KCC

---

that may deter value-increasing deals); FRANK H. EASTERBROOK AND DANIEL R. FISCHEL, THE ECONOMIC STRUCTURE OF CORPORATE LAW 145-49 (1991) (viewing appraisal as a protective mechanism for shareholders from value-decreasing transactions).

55. *See* KS Kim, Chaebol and Corporate Governance, *supra* note 7, at 166-7. It has been reported that dissenting shareholders of 25 listed Korean companies have exercised their appraisal rights in merger or sale of business transactions for a total of 4.91 million shares in 1997. JOONG-ANG ILBO, Dec. 30, 1997, at 30.

56. *Cf.* Victor Brudney and Marvin Chirelstein, *Fair Shares in Mergers and Take-Overs*, 88 HARV. L. REV. 297, 304-07 (1974) (arguing that the appraisal remedy has limited power as a check on managers' breaches of fiduciary duty because of the rational apathy and free-rider problems).

57. *See* Art. 382-3 of the KCC.

58. *See* Art. 401-2 of the KCC.

59. *See* Art. 363-2 of the KCC.

60. *See* Art. 382-2 of the KCC. As Art. 369 (1) of the KCC (accepting the one share, one vote principle) is understood to be a mandatory rule, cumulative voting was not allowed. However, I argued elsewhere that Art. 369 (1) of the KCC can be interpreted as non-mandatory, referring to criteria developed in Jeffrey N. Gordon, *The Mandatory Structure of Corporate Law*, 89 COLUM. L. REV. 1549 (1989). *See* HWA-JIN KIM, M&A-WA KYONGYONGKWON [M&A AND CORPORATE CONTROL] ch. 6 (3rd ed. 1999) (hereinafter Kim, [M&A AND CORPORATE CONTROL]). Accordingly, cumulative voting could be adopted by charter provision. For questions of voting in emerging economies, *see generally* Black & Kraakman, *supra* note 4, at 1945-52. Black & Kraakman report that straight voting is the default rule in most emerging market jurisdictions they have studied. *See id.* at 1948, note 73. For an account of the U.S. laws, see Jeffrey N. Gordon, *Institutions as Relational Investors: A New Look at Cumulative Voting*, 94 COLUM. L. REV. 124 (1994). Many Korean corporate law scholars recognized the value of cumulative voting in protecting minority shareholders'

as it can be ruled out by charter provisions and made subject to shareholders' claims.[61]

B. A New Focus on Outside Directors

As mentioned above, Korean corporate boards are nominal organizations under the direct control of controlling shareholders in most cases. The boards of Korean firms are regularly comprised of officer-directors without the participation of outside, independent directors. Thus, the role of the board in corporate governance is minimal in Korean corporations. This is also related in part to the fact that in Korea, corporations' directors do not regularly face lawsuits for breaches of fiduciary duties.

The function of corporate boards in improving corporate governance has recently become an important point of public concern in Korea.[62] It is understood that public opinion supports the concept of active independent board members checking the controlling shareholder-managers and officer-directors. The firms themselves also have slowly realized the value of having efficient boards. Beginning in 1996, the so-called "outside director system" was adopted by several large firms including the Hyundai Group.[63] However, the new trend focusing on the board and outside directors is closely related to the *Chaebol*-policy. The Korean government sees an effective policy tool in the outside director system for its role in separating ownership and control of large public companies. The IMF also has required the Korean government to enhance the managerial accountability of Korean firms through outside directors. Accordingly, the Korean government has made it mandatory for listed companies to have a board with a ratio of three officer-directors to one outside director. The listing rule of the Korea Stock Exchange was amended in February 1998 to enforce this policy.[64]

The *Korean Banking Act* has introduced a system under which non-officer directors shall hold the majority position on corporate boards. It has been followed by the *Law for Structural Improvement and Privatization of State Enterprises*, promulgated in August 1997 and put into force on October 1, 1997.[65] This law places a ceiling of seven percent on individual ownership of shares in

---

interest. *See, e.g.*, DONG-YOON CHUNG, HOESHABUP [THE LAW OF CORPORATIONS] 363 (4th ed. 1996).

61. The new KCC has also introduced the short-form merger and the small-scale merger. In the former, the subsidiary by more than 90 percent shareholding, can be merged into the parent without the approval of the shareholders' meeting. *See* Art. 527-2 (1) of the KCC. In the latter, no approval of the shareholders' meeting of the surviving firm is required if the number of shares to be issued upon a merger amounts to less than five percent of the outstanding shares of the surviving firm. *See* Art. 527-3 (1) of the KCC. The corporate division also has been introduced in the new KCC. *See* Art. 530-2 through Art. 530-12 of the KCC.

62. *See* opinion of Kwang-Sun Chung, HAN-GUK KYONGJE SHINMIN, Sept. 30, 1997, at 10 (arguing for "corporate governance revolution" in Korea).

63. *See* HAN-GUK KYONGJE SHINMUN, Jan. 19, 1998, at 10 (reporting Hyundai Group's positive experience).

64. *See* Art. 48-5 of the Listing Rule of the Korea Stock Exchange.

65. *See* Law for Structural Improvement and Privatization of State Enterprises, Art. 5 (2) [hereinafter the Law]. This Law applies to the four giant state-invested enterprises that are planned

newly privatized state-owned enterprises. According to the official comment to this law, it is intended to enhance efficiency and accountability of professional managers.[66]

C. The Establishment of the Secondary Segment of the Korean Securities Market

The KOSDAQ was launched on July 1, 1996. This secondary segment of the Korean securities market was established mainly to support the financing efforts of new ventures and small businesses. As of November 1997, some 350 firms, including seventy-seven venture companies, were enrolled at the KOSDAQ.[67] The favorable tax treatment for securities traded on the KOSDAQ is expected to induce large numbers of investors, including foreign investors,[68] to invest in venture firms specializing in the high-tech and biotechnology areas. However, the KOSDAQ imposes the strict requirements of ownership dispersion for the firms enrolled. For a venture firm to be enrolled in the KOSDAQ, more than twenty percent of its issued and outstanding shares must be held by more than 100 minority shareholders.[69]

Korea's efforts to replicate the U.S.'s success in developing a strong venture capital industry exemplify its recognition that its current model of corporate governance and financial market fails to support newer and smaller companies. However, like some European countries,[70] Korea may not be successful in developing the institutional infrastructure necessary to support a venture capital market, unless it also introduces some complimentary institutions that are present in the U.S.[71] Merely creating a stock market in a system lacking complimentary institutions will not be sufficient to provide the necessary conditions for an active venture capital industry.[72]

---

to be privatized, i.e., Korea Tobacco & Ginseng Corporation, Korea Telecom, Korea Gas Corporation, and Korea Heavy Industries & Construction Company. *See* Art. 2 of the Law.

66. To this end, more restrictive charter provisions are allowed. *See* Art. 18 (1) of the Law. The Korean government couldn't live up to its official promise to select a foreign professional manager as CEO of one of the four firms. *See Foreign CEO Plan at State Firms Fails*, KOREA HERALD, Dec. 10, 1997, at 12.

67. *See Foreigners Allowed to Invest in KOSDAQ Venture Companies*, KOREA HERALD, Nov. 14, 1997, at 12.

68. *See id.*

69. *See* Art. 4 (1) No.3 of the KOSDAQ Rule.

70. For an overview of start-up financing in European countries, *see* Arndt Stengel and Joseph W. Marx, The Financing of Start-up Companies (General Report for AIJA Annual Congress 1997).

71. Such complimentary institutions are venture capital organizations, investment bankers, and a supply of entrepreneurs. Gilson, Globalizing Corporate Governance, *supra* note 1, at 12-13. *See also* Curtis J. Milhaupt, *The Market for Innovation in the United States and Japan: Venture Capital and the Comparative Corporate Governance Debate*, 91 Nw. U. L. REV. 865, 879-94 (1997) (singling out five traits of the institutional environment that contribute to the success of the U.S. venture capital market: "the existence of large, independent sources of venture capital funding; liquidity; highly developed legal and contractual incentive structures; labor mobility; and risk tolerance").

72. Gilson, Globalizing Corporate Governance, *supra* note 1, at 12.

D. Cultivating Markets for Corporate Control in Korea[73]

The recent hostile takeover cases in Korea exemplify some of the problems of Korean corporate governance arising from changes in Korean capital markets. They also received extensive publicity, due largely to the departure they represented from generally staid inter-corporate relations in Korea. Under the old law, there was a practical ban on hostile takeovers, which was circumvented in many cases by a loophole for certain shareholding vehicles. This ban, along with related restrictions, was lifted on April 1, 1997, and should result in a greater increase in merger and acquisition activity. In 1997 alone, eleven tender offers were launched in the market, some of them hostile. Furthermore, as will be discussed below, the lifting of the ban on hostile takeovers also applies to foreign investors. As a result, there should be an increase in foreign takeovers of Korean firms.

1. The Current Situation

The Korean business community has increasingly accepted mergers and acquisitions (M&A) as a viable strategic option for external growth and restructuring.[74] The Korean government also understands that M&A represents a useful policy tool in industrial restructuring. Although there have been no serious discussions yet in Korea about the beneficial effects of takeovers in terms of shareholder wealth,[75] the role of the market in disciplining poorly performing management[76] is slowly being recognized by the Korean academic and legal communities.

---

73. For law and practice of corporate acquisitions in Korea, see generally Kim, [M&A AND CORPORATE CONTROL], *supra* note 60.

74. *See Firms Urge Special Law on Restructuring*, KOREA HERALD, Nov. 7, 1997, at 12 (reporting that in a poll of 315 large firms about problems in industrial restructuring, about 60 percent of respondents cited the current complex procedure for M&As as the biggest hurdle to their restructuring efforts).

75. For studies of the evidence that takeovers are beneficial to shareholders and society, see Easterbrook and Fischel, *supra* note 54, at 190-205; Richard Roll, *Empirical Evidence on Takeover Activity and Shareholder Wealth*, in KNIGHTS, RAIDERS AND TARGETS: THE IMPACT OF THE HOSTILE TAKEOVER, ch.14 (John C. Coffee et al. eds. 1988). *See also* McGinty, *supra* note 22, at 992, n. 17 (informative summaries of literature). As takeovers generally benefited society, takeover defenses and anti-takeover laws of the individual States of the U.S. are viewed as detrimental to the societal wealth maximization. *See, e.g.*, Gregg A. Jarrell et al., *The Market for Corporate Control: The Empirical Evidence Since 1980*, 2 J. ECON. PERSP. 49 (1988); Jonathan M. Karpoff & Paul H. Malatesta, *The Wealth Effects of Second-Generation State Takeover Legislation*, 25 J. FIN. ECON. 291 (1989).

76. For the earliest account, *see* Henry G. Manne, *Mergers and the Market for Corporate Control*, 73 J. POL. ECON. 110 (1965) (pointing out, for the first time, the importance of the takeover threat in inducing managers to be concerned about shareholders' interests). *See also* Frank H. Easterbrook and Daniel R. Fischel, *The Proper Role of a Target's Management in Responding to a Tender Offer*, 94 HARV. L. REV. 1161, 1165-74 (1981) (emphasizing the role of tender offers in disciplining managers); Joseph A. Grundfest, *Just Vote No: A Minimalist Strategy for Dealing with the Barbarians Inside the Gates*, 45 STAN. L. REV. 857, 873-901 (1993) (collection of anecdotal evidence indicating the potential for shareholder gains from replacing incumbent management); RONALD J. GILSON & BERNARD S. BLACK, THE LAW AND FINANCE OF CORPORATE ACQUISITIONS, ch. 10 (2nd ed. 1995) (selected empirical studies). However, as American managers have successfully developed effective takeover defenses and convinced state legislatures to enact anti-takeover laws, takeovers' disciplinary threat to management has significantly weakened. Discussions about alterna-

The internationalization of Korean capital markets is likely to increase takeovers and foreign ownership of listed companies.[77] Foreign firms' acquisition of undervalued Korean firms with weak local currency is expected to increase, in particular during the industrial restructuring period guided by the IMF. This activity, along with the abolished ownership restriction, will facilitate the growth of the M&A market in Korea. An increased number of diverse M&A transactions has already been reported among listed companies since 1995. Tender offers, once viewed as a remote foreign tool, have increased recently, although usually in their most basic form. To be sure, most deals occurring in Korea so far have been friendly and consummated with the aim of restructuring the operational functions of large businesses. However, the active M&A market is expected to eventually develop a market for corporate control in Korea, which should have a wide range of impacts within Korea.

The arguably emerging market for corporate control in Korea has already impacted Korean financial markets. For instance, after the highly-publicized proxy battle for Hanwha Merchant Bank in early 1997, where the incumbent management successfully preserved control by secretly issuing convertible bonds to friendly firms,[78] many Korean companies privately placed convertible bonds or bonds with warrants in huge volumes to increase friendly shareholding. As the negative impact of this practice on the market reached the critical point in March 1997,[79] the Korean government introduced some restrictions on certain market-distorting activities. The increase of takeover activities in Korea will continuously encourage concerned firms to search for effective takeover defensive tactics, including restructuring of their capital structure.[80] The financial institutions in Korea may also be interested in entering into the lucrative busi-

---

tive mechanism are ongoing in the U.S., and increasingly focused on the new shareholder activism by institutional investors, independent directors and foreign governance institutions.

77. *See* Art. 5 of the Korean Financial Supervisory Commission Rule on Securities Transaction by Foreigners.

78. The Seoul District Court, in its decision of Feb. 6, 1997, 97kahap118, dismissed a motion to enjoin exercising voting rights attached to the converted shares in question, holding that issuing convertible bonds in the case was legitimate and legal. The Court emphasized the importance of liquidity protection for the shares. The Seoul High Court, in its decision of May 13, 1997, 97ra36, upheld the decision of first instance, but held that the convertible bonds issued in question were invalid for illegality involved in the issuing process. For the text of both decisions, *see* Kim, [M&A AND CORPORATE CONTROL], *supra* note 60, at 150-160. Such cases became moot as the merchant bank closed in February 1998.

79. In January, February, and March 1997, 46 companies issued convertible bonds and 22 companies issued bonds with warrants, all through private placement. The volume totaled 1.22 trillion won. The decision of the Seoul District Court in the Hanwha Merchant Bank Case was handed down on Feb. 6, 1997, and the 10 percent ownership restriction was abolished from April 1, 1997. *See* Kim, [M&A AND CORPORATE CONTROL], *supra* note 60, at 148-149.

80. The placement of new common shares or equity-related debt instruments on friendly hands is the most widely used, and controversial, takeover defensive tactic in Korea. Under Korean law, poison pill, in its forms prevailing in the U.S., is not allowed. Defensive stock repurchases have become fairly popular, but the 33.3 percent limit and requirement of purchase through securities exchange have been restraining factors until the recent abolishment of such limitations. Staggered boards, limiting the number of board members, proxy campaign and lock-ups are also widely used defensive tactics in Korea. For takeover defensive tactics available under Korean laws, *see* generally Kim, [M&A AND CORPORATE CONTROL], *supra* note 60, chs. 5, 6-7.

ness of takeover finance. The Korean government will focus more intensively than before on financial institutions regulation, a fundamental reform which has long been overdue.

2. The New Regulatory Framework

Under the old KSEA, there was a basic ceiling of ten percent for individual ownership of listed companies.[81] The rule generally applied to any shareholders except the founder of the company. The reasoning was to convince the controlling shareholders (founders) to let their firms go public without the fear of losing corporate control. Indeed, this policy has greatly contributed in expediting the building of Korean capital markets. This restriction, however, made less sense as the size of the Korean stock market increased. The rapid growth achieved by Korean firms compelled them to go public and, as a consequence, the incentive rule has become unnecessary. It only distorted the ordinary functioning of the capital market by imposing an anomalous barrier in securities trading. The new KSEA has abolished the restrictive rule.

Under the new KSEA, tender offers are the central mechanism for shifts in corporate control. Although some tender offers launched so far in Korea have been criticized for their questionable purposes,[82] it is widely accepted that the tender offer is the most appropriate mechanism for protection of minority shareholders from control abuses. Now, a securities transaction involving the transfer of more than a five percent (5%) shareholding out of the Korea Stock Exchange or KOSDAQ is required basically through tender offers.[83]

The old KSEA had introduced the obligation to make a bid. Any person aiming to acquire securities, which, when added to any existing holdings, gave him voting rights in a company totaling more than twenty-five percent, was obliged to make a bid by tender offer to acquire more than fifty percent of the

---

81. *See* Art. 200 of the old KSEA.
82. Some tender offers made at a price lower than market price of the shares have been successful because the tendering shareholders have already committed to tender by certain contractual arrangement with the offerer. Those shareholders were either nominal shareholders who bought the shares on offer with a simple fee arrangement or real shareholders who bought the shares upon offerer's contractual commitment to buy the shares with a fixed premium. In latter cases, agreement on voting was common. Also, there were instances where the potential acquirer entered into secret share purchase agreements with a third party and bought shares of the target in reliance on the agreement before launching a tender offer. This tactic has been used mainly to avoid the requirement of the disclosure rule. Currently, there is one reported case in Korea from which a lawsuit for damages has developed in relation to the breach of such contractual arrangements. *See* Kim, [M&A AND CORPORATE CONTROL], *supra* note 60, at 85, note 6. On the other hand, the recent high-profile tender offer for shares in Lady Furniture turned out to be part of a fraudulent scheme. This incident has raised doubt about the efficiency of current regulation. *See* HAN-GUK KYONGJE SHINMUN, Nov. 26, 1997, at 4.
83. *See* Art. 21 (1) of the KSEA. There existed a requirement for tender offer price under the pre-1998 version rule: the bid shall be made at the highest price an individual paid for any of the target company's shares within twelve months or the market price of the target company's shares on the previous day of his or her filing of application with the authority, whichever is higher (Art. 13-3 of Enforcement Decree to the pre-1998 version KSEA). Such requirement was abolished by the February 1998 revision of the rule.

issued and outstanding voting shares of that company.[84] The tender offers for 24.99 percent of Ssangyong Paper and Hankuk Electric Glass, both in November 1997, were made under the rule. This rule modified from the *British City Code on Takeovers and Mergers*[85] and the proposed *European Community 13th Directive on Company Law*,[86] was widely criticized for facilitating the concentration of economic power and setting an unreasonably high burden on value-increasing corporate acquisitions. The February 1998 amendments to the KSEA abolished this requirement.

The new KSEA has also refined "the early warning system," or five percent disclosure rule.[87] Now, the obligation to report is expanded to such equity-related debt instruments as convertible bonds, bonds with warrants, and exchangeable bonds.[88] The KSEA has widened the circle of obliged persons by introducing the concept of "holders on common purposes",[89] adopting the practical approach of the U.S. *Williams Act*.[90]

3. The Emergence of the Market for Corporate Control

The friendly acquisition of Korean firms by foreign investors was allowed, with some qualifications, under the (then) *Law on Foreign Investment and Foreign Capital Inducement*,[91] effective from February 1, 1997. However, direct hostile acquisition of Korean firms by foreign investors without the approval of incumbent management was not possible until recently. Also, the ceiling on individual foreign ownership in listed companies practically prevented foreigners from acquiring control of listed Korean firms. Nevertheless, the opening of the domestic market for foreign control has become a reality since the abolition of these restrictions.

It has been discussed whether Korea should open the domestic market for corporate control to promote competitiveness, including that of financial institutions. The proponents' view[92] has recently received much support. The issue, however, was not totally new to Korea. Since late 1996, Korea has participated

---

84. *See* Art. 21 (2) of the pre-1998 version KSEA with Art. 11-2 of Enforcement Decree to the KSEA.
85. Panel on Takeovers and Mergers, The City Code on Takeovers and Mergers and the Rules Governing Substantial Acquisitions of Shares (1993). *See* Deborah A. DeMott, *Current Issues in Tender Offer Regulation: Lessons from the British*, 58 N.Y.U. L. Rev. 945 (1983).
86. Commission Proposal for a Thirteenth Directive on Company Law Concerning Takeover and Other General Bids, 1990 O. J. (C 38) 41, 44. *See* Klaus J. Hopt, *European Takeover Regulation: Barriers to and Problems of Harmonizing Takeover Law in the European Community*, in European Takeovers – Law and Practice ch. 6 (Klaus J. Hopt & Eddy Wymeersch eds. 1992); Jeffrey P. Greenbaum, *Tender Offers in the European Community: The Playing Field Shrinks*, 22 Vand. J. Transnat'l L. 923 (1989); Nathalie Basaldua, *Towards the Harmonization of EC-Member States' Regulations on Takeover Bids: The Proposal for a Thirteenth Council Directive on Company Law*, 9 NW. J. Int'l. & Bus. 487 (1989).
87. *See* Art. 200-2 (1) of the KSEA.
88. *See* Art. 10 of Enforcement Decree to the KSEA.
89. *See id.* Art. 10-3 (4).
90. For the concept of a "group" under Section 13(d) of the Williams Act, *see* Robert Charles Clark, Corporate Law 555-57 (1986).
91. *See* Art. 8-2 Foreign Investment Promotion Act, effective from Nov. 17, 1998.
92. *See, e.g.,* Seong C. Gweon, *Fighting for What?*, Korea Herald, Nov. 19, 1997, at 8.

in negotiations on the *Multilateral Agreement on Investments* (MAI) sponsored by the OECD. The MAI would allow hostile takeovers by foreign investors in Korea as all parties to the agreement would be required to give foreigners the same treatment as their domestic counterparts. Even though most Korean companies wanted a delay in foreign investors' hostile takeover activities in Korea, it was unclear if other members of the OECD would accept such a position. The major concern of Korean companies was the lack of a level playing field for both domestic and foreign firms. The opening of the domestic market for foreign control in Korea, however, has become a reality since the abolition of restrictions on foreign ownership discussed previously.

It is anticipated that foreigners' participatory investments in large Korean companies will increase due to the weak Korean currency and undervalued stock prices.[93] Korean firms themselves have started to seek foreign partners for global strategic alliances to meet the challenges from the whole new business and regulatory environment.[94] It is widely recognized that opening of the Korean market for corporate acquisitions and strategic alliances to foreign firms will not be complete and effective without enhanced transparency of "consolidated" corporate financial statements made by generally accepted international accounting practices.[95] General deregulation on business activities, improvement of labor market flexibility, free international transfer of capital, and improvement of administrative infrastructure in the public services sector are also necessary. For the improvement of labor market flexibility, which was a key condition of the IMF bailout package,[96] the *Basic Labor Law* has been amended to allow companies to lay off workers when they face an "emergency situation."[97] According to the *Basic Labor Law*, sale of businesses or mergers and acquisitions to avoid financial trouble shall justify layoffs.[98] The new *Law Concerning Foreign Ownership of Land*, effective on June 26, 1998, has abolished various restrictions on the foreign ownership of land to promote foreign invest-

---

93. *See Listed Firms' Combined Stocks Worth Less Than World's Top 70th Company*, KOREA HERALD, Dec. 27, 1997, at 11 (reporting that, as of Dec. 24, 1997, the market value of the total amount of stocks listed on the Korea Stock Exchange stood at $33.9 billion, which was less than that of the Dutch ING).

94. *See* Steve Glain & Michael Schuman, *Seoul Looks to Foreigners for a Lifeline*, ASIAN WALL ST. J., Dec. 24, 1997, at 1, 5; *Korea's Woes Don't Deter Some Multinational Firms*, ASIAN WALL ST. J., Feb. 16, 1998, at 3; Mark Clifford et al., *Age of the Deal*, BUS. WEEK (Asian Edition), March 2, 1998, at 16-20; Martin du Bois, *Buyer's Market: As Asia's Going Gets Rough, Europe Inc. Goes Asset Shopping*, WALL ST. J. EUROPE, May 11, 1998, at 1, 11.

95. *See Chaebols Test Waters for Transparency*, KOREA HERALD, Jan. 6, 1998, at 10 (reporting that the total sales figure of a large group could be slashed by as much as 30% in consolidated financial statements). *See also Korea Financial Supervisory Commission & Korea Securities and Futures Commission, Reform of Accounting Standards in Korea, Dec. 11, 1998* (visited March 6, 1999) <http://www.fsc.go.kr/kfsc/new_e_index1.htm> (claiming that "financial accounting standards are newly born in Korea inconsistent with international best practices").

96. *See* No. 38 of the Korea-IMF Memorandum, *supra* note 27.

97. *See* Michael Schuman, *Korean Layoffs Pact Shows Union's Change in Stance*, ASIAN WALL ST. J., Feb. 9, 1998, at 3.

98. *See* Art. 31 (1) of the Law. The Law calls for management to do its best to avoid layoffs (*see id.* Art. 31 [2]) and give 60 days notice before dismissing workers (*see id.* Art. 31 [3]). Employers are also required to try to rehire dismissed workers first if business improves (*see id.* Art. 31-2).

ments in Korea. Now, acquisition of land by foreigners is not subject to government approval except for certain cases concerning military policy, environmental protection, and landmark protection.[99]

III.
CORPORATE GOVERNANCE AND BANKS IN KOREA

A. *A Need for Change of the Ownership Structure of Banks?*

One of the most contentious issues in Korea currently is corporate governance of banks. It is widely believed that many failures in Korea have been caused by bank managers' breach of their fiduciary duties. This widespread "directed lending" under governmental influence produced a huge volume of non-performing loans to highly leveraged large businesses.[100] When directed lending was the common practice, no effective monitoring system was available. As those borrower firms failed, the lender banks also lost substantial sums of money, which in turn led to the chaotic situation of the Korean financial markets. This arguably could have been prevented by closer monitoring of bank managers.

One solution to this problem is to allow non-financial firms—including those belonging to the *Chaebols*—to control commercial banks. This could be achieved by lessening ownership restrictions on bank shares. A controlling shareholder with a private business background might be able to improve the efficiency and accountability of bank management.[101] The proponents of lesser restriction on bank ownership argue that a concentration of bank ownership may be helpful in overhauling the financial system in Korea.

Others have argued that if the restrictions on the ownership of bank shares were relaxed, Korean banks would easily become the treasury of some *Chaebols*.[102] This could lead to mismanagement of those shareholder-firms because they would feel unjustifiably secure in their financing efforts. Proponents of ownership restriction argue that efficiency and accountability can be achieved by enhancing bank supervisory systems and/or introducing well-functioning outside directors. Another approach is to promote bank mergers. The Korean government has provided a separate legal regime to promote mergers of banks under the theory that such mergers increase competitiveness through enhanced operational efficiency and financial soundness. The *Korean Banking Act* also has been changed to introduce the outside director system.

---

99. Still, there are notification requirements. *See* Art. 4 (1) and Art. 5 of the Law.
100. *See* Roy Ramos & Chunsoo Lim, *Bailout or Not, Korea Needs Change*, ASIAN WALL ST. J., Dec. 1, 1997 at 20 (estimating that bad debts amount to $110 billion which would be more than the entire annual economic output of Singapore, Malaysia or the Philippines).
101. *See, e.g., Editorial*, HAN-GUK KYONGJE SHINMUN, June 26, 1997, at 11; *Opinion of Byung-Ho Kang*, MAEIL KYONGJE, Oct. 4, 1996, at 5; *Editorial*, HAN-GUK KYONGJE SHINMUN, Jan. 17, 1998, at 5.
102. *See, e.g., Opinion of Un-Chan Jung*, CHOSUN ILBO, July 2, 1997, at 5 and Chung-Lim Choi, CHOSUN ILBO, April 3, 1997, at 5.

Until recently, Korea maintained a basic ceiling of four percent for bank ownership.[103] The ceiling on bank ownership, however, has been weakened by the new *Korean Banking Act*,[104] promulgated on January 13, 1998, and partially amended again in February and May 1998 and January 1999. The *Korean Banking Act* implements the agreement of the Korean government with the IMF. Although the ceiling still formally remains, the acquisition of bank shares of more than four percent or fifteen percent may be done by the approval of the Korean government. Since the new regulation is structured in a way to favor foreign investors, it is now being discussed whether the basics should also be changed. It remains to be seen whether the IMF-mandated change of ownership structure of Korean banks will prove efficient. However, it is clear that the improvement of governance of Korean banks will also continuously be sought through functional approaches in line with such efforts for non-banking corporations.

What are the possible lessons from comparative corporate governance in terms of bank managers' accountability? Should Korea continue the efforts toward functional improvement of bank governance, even after the internationally mandated formal changes have been implemented? The answer is clearly yes. The efficiency and soundness of a banking system are too complicated to be answered by any single approach. So is the accountability of bank managers. Strict monitoring may prevent the bank managers from self-dealing and engaging in other misconduct. Nevertheless, strict monitoring may also cause conservative lending practices, which may be difficult to differentiate from self-entrenchment. Korean banks need both the changed ownership structure and the private, business-oriented, managerial minds "supported" by a well-functioning board.

B. Outside Directors Again

Under the new *Korean Banking Act*, the board of directors of Korean banks shall have more outside directors than officer-directors.[105] The outside directors are to be appointed among the candidates recommended by representatives of shareholders and the board at the elective ratio of seven to three.[106] The president of a bank shall be elected by an affirmative vote of two-thirds or more of the outside directors.[107]

This new approach to bank corporate governance has been strongly criticized for not being realistic. As in other economies, even those highly efficient economies such as Germany[108] and the U.S.,[109] the "outside" directors often

---

103. *See* Art. 17-3 of the former BANKING ACT. This restriction did not apply to the shareholding in joint venture banks and local banks with restricted regional business areas. To the local banks, the ownership ceiling of 15 percent applied. *See* Art. 17-3 (1) of the former BANKING ACT.
104. *See* Arts. 15, 16 and 17 of the Act.
105. Art. 22 (2) of the Act.
106. *See* Art. 22 (3) through (9) of the Act.
107. *Id.* Art. 24.
108. For the failure of the German two-tier system, see *Guenter H. Roth, Supervision of Corporate Management: The "Outside" Director and the German Experience,* 51 N. C. L. REV. 1369,

turn out to be not "independent" enough to contribute to managerial accountability. The complicated recommendation and appointment procedure has only made the bankers' jobs harder, with little to show for such troubles. It is, however, interesting to see that the first ever effort to rationalize corporate boards in Korea has been made by the *Banking Act*. The model suggested by the *Banking Act* has also been adopted by some newly privatized state-owned enterprises as described earlier.

C. Bank Mergers and Acquisitions

Although the M&A boom among large banks abroad[110] was well known in Korea, the concept of bank mergers has not been widely accepted until recently. This is related to the traditional view of financial institutions as quasi-public organizations rather than private business entities. It also clearly illustrates the path dependent limits of the Korean economy as it exists today. However, the argument that rising international standards and increasing competition among banks in global markets should be met by promoting mergers of banks has recently become very compelling and persuasive. Thus, in December 1996, the Korean government promulgated the *Law for Structural Improvement of Financial Industry* to facilitate mergers of Korean banks. It contains various provisions easing mergers of financial institutions, including favorable tax treatment for the merger transaction, and regulating the liquidation and reorganization process for troubled financial institutions. However, the voluntary mergers of banks as envisaged were still not feasible due largely to potential problems of layoffs that would inevitably follow any merger of banks in Korea.

The recent restructuring efforts guided by the IMF have changed the situation. As the ownership ceiling on bank shares and foreign ownership restriction

---

1378-82 (1973). Two separate and distinct bodies, i.e., the management board (Vorstand) and the supervisory board (Aufsichtsrat), govern the German stock corporation (Aktiengesellschaft). Direct control of corporate affairs is vested in the former which, in turn, is supervised by the latter. It is argued that the management boards of German corporations succeed in usurping the controlling function of the supervisory boards. *See* Josef Esser, *Bank Power in West Germany Revised*, 13 WEST EUR. POLITICS 17, 27 (1990). However, the two-tier system has been spreading throughout Europe in recent years and is presently reflected in the European Union's major legislative proposals relating to company law. *See* Kim, *supra* note 4, at 379 n. 40.

109. For recent efforts addressing the governance role of the board with increased independence of outside directors, see, e.g., The Business Roundtable, *Corporate Governance and American Competitiveness*, 46 BUS. LAW. 241 (1990); Ronald J. Gilson and Reinier Kraakman, *Reinventing the Outside Director: An Agenda for Institutional Investors*, 43 STAN. L. REV. 863 (1991) (advocating increasing the dependence of outside directors on shareholders). *But see*, Victor Brudney, *The Independent Director - Heavenly City or Potemkin Village?*, 95 HARV. L. REV. 597, 607-39 (1982) (skeptical view). For positive practical cases, see Grundfest, *supra* note 76, at 880-900. *See also* John W. Byrd and Kent A. Hickman, *Do Outside Directors Monitor Managers?: Evidence from Tender Offer Bids*, 32 J. FIN. ECON. 195, 201-05 (1992) (recognizing outside directors' role in improving managerial performance); John A. Byrne et al., *The Best BOA*, BUS. WEEK, Dec. 8, 1997, at 46-52.

110. *See, e.g.*, Thane Peterson et al., *The Big One*, BUS. WEEK, Dec. 22, 1997, at 26-29 (merger of UBS and SBC in Switzerland); Michael Siconolfi, *Citicorp Merger with Travelers Signals New Era*, ASIAN WALL ST. J., April 7, 1998, at 1, 2; *Really Big Deal*, ASIAN WALL ST. J., April 8, 1998, at 8; Steven Lipin & Anita Raghavan, *BankAmerica, NationsBank to Join in $60 Billion Deal*, ASIAN WALL ST. J., April 14, 1998, at 1, 26.

on acquisition of controlling shares of listed firms have been abolished, foreign banks are expected to acquire some Korean financial institutions, including commercial banks. The *Korea-IMF Memorandum* also provides that the financial sector restructuring could involve "mergers and acquisitions by domestic and foreign institutions"[111] and that foreign financial institutions will be allowed "to participate in mergers and acquisitions of domestic financial institutions in a friendly manner and on equal principles."[112] As the first step to honor the commitment, the Korean government agreed with the IMF to privatize to certain U.S. commercial banks the troubled Korea First Bank and Seoul Bank by November 1998.[113] The January 1998 revision of the *Korean Banking Act* accommodates, and even promotes, foreign investors' acquisition of Korean banks by allowing them to acquire bank shares without limit with the approval of the Korean government.[114] On the local level as well, bank mergers are underway as the Korean government seeks to comply with the IMF-mandated program for the restructuring of the financial industry. In June 1998, four troubled local banks have practically been merged into other local banks by relevant rules of the *Law for Structural Improvement of Financial Industry*. In August and September 1998, some local banks announced their plans for friendly merger with each other, namely, The Commercial Bank of Korea with Hanil Bank; Hana Bank with Boram Bank; and Kookmin Bank with Korea Long Term Credit Bank.

D. Banks' Participatory Investments

Contrary to the academic environment in the U.S. and Europe, banks' participatory investments in non-banking and non-financial sectors are not actively discussed in Korea.[115] At present, the *Korean Banking Act* limits bank's ownership of non-financial corporations to fifteen percent.[116] This reflects, in part, the historical reality that Korean banks have exercised far greater influence on their debtor corporations as the creditor. However, such influence does not necessar-

---

111. See No. 17 of the Korea-IMF Memorandum, *supra* note 27.
112. *Id.*, Nos. 19 and 31.
113. See HAN-GUK KYONGJE SHINMUN, Feb. 18, 1998, at 4.
114. See Art. 15 (3) of the Act.
115. The most widely studied model for banks' participatory investments is the German model because German law allows banks to hold voting shares of non-banking companies and the German firms under such a system are in fact very competitive in the global market. The literature on German corporate governance in that respect has in the mean time become very rich. *See, e.g.,* Ulrich Immenga, *Participatory Investments by Banks: A Structural Problem of the Universal Banking System in Germany*, 2 J. COMP. CORP. L. & SEC. REG. 29 (1979); Theodor Baums, *Corporate Governance in Germany: The Role of the Banks*, 40 AM. J. COMP. L. 503 (1992); Friedrich K. Kübler, *Institutional Owners and Corporate Managers: A German Dilemma*, 57 BROOK. L. REV. 97 (1991); Mark J. Roe, *Some Differences in Corporate Structure in Germany, Japan, and the United States*, 102 YALE L. J. 1927 (1993); Kim, *supra* note 4; John Cable, *Capital Market Information and Industrial Performance: The Role of West German Banks*, 95 ECON. J. 118 (1985); Hermann Kallfass, *The American Corporation and the Institutional Investor: Are There Lessons from Abroad? The German Experience*, 1988 COLUM. BUS. L. REV. 775.
116. See Art. 37 (1) of the Act.

ily contribute to the improvement of governance of the debtor firms.[117] Therefore, it is expected that the discussion on banks' participatory investments, in the form of the statutory change on the limits of ownership, will take place as the practical influence of Korean banks on their debtor firms diminishes due to the financial market internationalization.

In such anticipated discussions and studies, Koreans should also take into account the skeptical views of commercial bank involvement in corporate governance. In their recent study, Professors Macey and Miller argue that "proponents of bank involvement not only fail to address the significant costs of the Japanese and German systems of bank-dominated corporate governance, but ignore important benefits of the American system of equity-dominated corporate governance as well."[118] In their opinion, bank involvement will not cure the agency problems created by the separation of ownership and control because it carries with it an entirely new set of conflicts between equity claimants and creditors.[119] It is clear that Korean banks, having realized the importance of controlling the moral hazard of their borrowers, will actively seek the opportunity to participate in the governance of borrowers. Their stake in the borrower firms may even arise through bad debt-to-equity swaps. *The Korean Banking Act* now allows banks to transfer credits to equity even in such cases where the banks end up with a shareholding of more than fifteen percent. Such an effort, however, may have an adverse impact on the development of the securities market in Korea, which is crucial to the improvement of Korea's financial institutions.

Korean banks should also be aware that the Korean bankruptcy law accepts the principle of equitable subordination in its rather extreme form. Under the typical reorganization plan presented to Korean courts, corporate debts owed to creditors in control are completely forgiven. The Korean Supreme Court interprets the doctrine of equal treatment provided in the *Corporate Reorganization Act*[120] in terms of fairness and equity so that such treatment of creditors in control may be seen as legitimate.[121]

---

117. However, the Korean banks' influence on the governance of their borrowers is expected to increase through the "Accords for Improvement of Financial Structure" between the banks and large corporate groups. Under the accord, which was initiated by the new Korean government, large corporate groups shall appoint outside directors, cause their subsidiaries to merge, and allow banks to investigate various corporate documents and manufacturing sites. A breach of the accord will cause loan call-offs and call-ins. *See* MAEIL KYONGJE, Feb. 18, 1998, at 1, 7; Chun Sung-Woo, *Banks Seen as Key Players of Corporate Restructuring*, ASIAN WALL ST. J., Feb. 21, 1998, at 10.

118. Jonathan R. Macey & Geoffrey P. Miller, *Corporate Governance and Commercial Banking: A Comparative Examination of Germany, Japan, and the United States*, 48 STAN. L. REV. 73, 75 (1995).

119. *See id.* ("Advocates of bank influence also ignore critical differences between the monitoring incentives of equity holders and the monitoring incentives of debt holders. Much of the confusion in the current debate stems from a failure to appreciate the economics of commercial banking in general and of commercial bank lending in particular.")

120. *See* Art. 229 of the Act.

121. *See* the Court's decision of July 25, 1989, 88ma266. Further, the practice of the Korean judiciary is that once the court approves a reorganization plan, shares held by the controlling shareholder, who is responsible for the insolvency of the firm, shall in principle be redeemed in total.

IV.
MARKET INTERNATIONALIZATION AND CORPORATE GOVERNANCE

A. *International Regulation of Financial Institutions*

Bank failures, unlike those of non-financial corporations, are minimized by a different kind of safety valve. Their operational soundness and functional efficiency are also guaranteed by the regulation of financial institutions. Parallel with the improvement of corporate governance of Korean banks through structural changes, more attention should be given to the effect of banking regulations.[122] In particular, due to the rapid increase of Korean banks' activities in international financial markets, international standards for the regulation of financial institutions are expected to exert positive influences on the operation of Korean banks. These standards may enhance the bank managers' accountability.

The Korean government had already introduced the risk-adjusted capital standards recommended by the Bank for International Settlements (BIS)[123] as a prudential measure to ensure capital adequacy of Korean banks. These requirements came into force at the end of 1995 and all Korean banks are now required to maintain an equity capital position equivalent to at least eight percent as suggested by the BIS. The normative power of the BIS rules has become tremendous in the Korean financial community since the recent involvement of international lending agencies in the restructuring of the Korean financial sector. The BIS rules have been used as an important policy tool for the Korean government in its restructuring efforts for the troubled Korean financial industry, under its agreement with the IMF. The *Korea-IMF Memorandum* provides first that Korea needs "a strong and transparent financial system which operates free of political interference and according to the rules and practices of the advanced industrial countries."[124] It then makes revocation of merchant banking licenses

---

122. *See generally* Office of Bank Supervision of the Bank of Korea, Bank Supervisory System in Korea (May 1997). The LAW ON ESTABLISHMENT OF FINANCIAL SUPERVISORY AGENCY, promulgated on December 31, 1997 with effect from April 1, 1998, has set up an integrated financial supervisory agency in Korea. The new Financial Supervisory Board has resulted from the merging of financial supervisory units so far spread among the Ministry of Finance and Economy and three separate watchdogs, i.e., Office of Bank Supervision, Securities Supervisory Board, and Insurance Supervisory Board. The KSEC's jurisdiction was split and distributed to the Financial Supervisory Board and the Securities and Futures Commission.

123. Committee on Banking Regulations and Supervisory Practices, International Convergence of Capital Measurement and Capital Standards (July 1988) ("the Basle Accord"). *See* Scott & Wellons, *supra* note 16, at 256-323; Duncan E. Alford, *Basle Committee International Capital Adequacy Standards: Analysis and Implications for the Banking Industry*, 10 DICK. J. INT'L L. 189 (1992); Camille M. Caesar, *Capital-Based Regulation and U.S. Banking Reform*, 101 YALE L. J. 1525 (1992). *See also* David Fairlamb, *Beyond Capital Adequacy*, INST. INV. (International Edition), August 1997, at 22-35. *See also* <http://www.BIS.org>. The BIS standards are implemented in the European Union through its directives on its own funds and on solvency ratios. *Cf.* Council Directive 89/299 of 17 April 1989 on The Own Funds of Credit Institutions, 1989 O. J. (L 124) 16; Council Directive 89/647 of 18 December 1989 on a Solvency Ratio for Credit Institutions, 1989 O. J. (L 386) 14. For a brief account that these rules may change the traditional ownership structure of German corporations, *see* Kim, *supra* note 4, at 397-9.

124. *See* No. 2 of the Korea-IMF Memorandum, *supra* note 27.

contingent upon fulfillment of the BIS standards within a certain time frame.[125] It also envisages severe disciplinary measures to commercial banks, including liquidation, no distribution of dividends and/or freezing management payrolls, again contingent upon rehabilitation plans meeting the BIS standards.[126] Consequently, Korean commercial banks and other financial institutions have become so sensitive to the BIS standards that they almost blindly called in outstanding loans to borrowers, which has resulted in sudden bankruptcies of affected firms.[127]

It is quite interesting to see that an international standard for banking regulation may contribute to the improvement of soundness of Korean banks that in turn helps improve the governance of Korean banks. The Korean government's participation in the international supervisory system was totally voluntary in a legal sense, but undeniably motivated by the necessity for Korean banks to be recognized as credible partners in global financial markets. This clearly shows that the international financial market may exercise great influence on convergence of national institutions, including corporate governance.[128] To the extent that such regulations are successful, the use of international banking regulations to improve the banks' governance is an impressive example of functional convergence of corporate governance institutions.

B. Market Internationalization and Institutional Investors' Activism

In Korea, institutional investors will hold decisive voting blocks in many instances in Korea in the future. At the end of 1996, they held some 31.2 percent of the total shares of listed Korean companies.[129] Considering the 10.4

---

125. *See id.*, No. 22.
126. *See id.*, Nos. 23-25.
127. *See Massive Corporate Bankruptcy Looming*, KOREA HERALD, Dec. 29, 1997, at 12 (reporting banks collecting loans to meet BIS standards that would be a crucial criteria for the evaluation of their management and eventually, their M&As).
128. Professor Van Zandt views that "[i]n some respects, the banking sector is approaching a situation in which it makes sense to talk about the existence of a single international regulatory framework." David E. Van Zandt, *The Regulatory and Institutional Conditions for an International Securities Market*, 32 VA. J. INT'L L. 47, 76 (1991). It should be noted that, in contrast to the situation in banking regulation, there may be little incentive for nations to introduce an international regulatory framework to improve governance of general corporations. However, the most notable exception may be found in the European Union's efforts to harmonize company laws of the Member States. *See generally* Steven M. Schneebaum, *The Company Law Harmonization Program of the European Community*, 14 LAW & POL'Y INT'L BUS. 293 (1982); Eric Stein, HARMONIZATION OF EUROPEAN COMPANY LAWS (1971); Alfred F. Conard, *The European Alternative to Uniformity in Corporation Laws*, 89 MICH. L. REV. 2150 (1991). The European Union's efforts to harmonize Member States' company laws are also closely related to its financial market integration program. *See generally* Scott and Wellons, *supra* note 16, at 324-379; Manning Gilbert Warren, *Global Harmonization of Securities Laws: The Achievements of the European Communities*, 31 HARV. INT'L L. J. 185 (1990); Michael J. Levitin, *The Treatment of United States Financial Services Firms in Post-1992 Europe*, 31 HARV. INT'L L. J. 507 (1990); Michael Gruson & Werner Nikowitz, *The Second Banking Directive of the European Economic Community and Its Importance for Non-EEC Banks*, 12 FORDHAM INT'L L. J. 205 (1989).
129. *See* Yu-Kyung Kim, *The Growing Financial Market Importance of Institutional Investors: The Case of Korea*, in INSTITUTIONAL INVESTORS IN THE NEW FINANCIAL LANDSCAPE 159, 172-173 (OECD 1998). *See also* Je Won Lee, A Study on Institutional Investors and Their Roles in the Governance Structure of Korea's Publicly Held Companies 224 (Seoul National University Disserta-

percent held by "foreigners"—who usually are institutions—the practical number may well exceed forty percent. This could affect corporate governance, since there is a greater likelihood of a rational apathy problem where foreign investors hold a small percentage of stock in a company. Foreign investors, especially institutions, may actively involve themselves in corporate governance. However, their interest in corporate performance may be limited in that it is primarily tied to the stock price, not to the firm's long-term business prospects. Moreover, they may well prefer liquidity to control. Consequently, the inactivity and lack of interest by foreign institutional investors—who will hold substantial stakes in Korean firms—may be viewed as a problem.

Nevertheless, although the internationalization of Korean capital markets will not directly result in general improvements in corporate governance of Korean firms, many commentators argue that it is likely to introduce such American concepts as institutional investors activism,[130] shareholder value, shareholder democracy,[131] and managerial transparency. The Korean government should continue the effort to loosen its tight grip on capital markets as many other national authorities have done since the mid-1980s. The recent steps taken toward deregulation and complete opening-up of Korean capital markets have upgraded the Korean financial system and, as a consequence, created a more favorable environment for balanced development.

Also, some new laws have been promulgated to bring the Korean financial market up to international standards. For instance, in September 16, 1998, the mutual fund was introduced in Korea through the promulgation of the *Securities Investment Company Act*, which supplemented the existing *Securities Invest-*

---

tion 1997) (in Korean). Contrary to the situation in the United States, public funds in Korea have been passive in equity investments. The total assets held by some 70 public and other funds in Korea have reached 100 trillion won recently. It has been reported they invest less than two percent of their assets in the securities market. *See Editorial*, HAN-GUK KYONGJE SHINMUN, Oct. 15, 1997, at 11 (urging efficient and responsible management of public funds).

130. The literature discussing the role of institutional investors in corporate governance in the U.S. is voluminous. *See, e.g.*, John C. Coffee, *Liquidity Versus Control: The Institutional Investor as Corporate Monitor*, 91 COLUM. L. REV. 1277 (1991); Thomas A. Smith, *Institutions and Entrepreneurs in American Corporate Finance*, 85 CAL. L. REV. 1 (1997); Bernard S. Black, *The Value of Institutional Investor Monitoring: The Empirical Evidence*, 39 UCLA L. REV. 895 (1992); Edward B. Rock, *The Logic and (Uncertain) Significance of Institutional Shareholder Activism*, 79 GEO. L. J. 445 (1991); Bernard S. Black, *Agents Watching Agents: The Promise of Institutional Investor Voice*, 39 UCLA L. REV. 811 (1992); Bernard S. Black, *Shareholder Passivity Reexamined*, 89 MICH. L. REV. 520 (1990); John C. Coffee, *The Folklore of Investor Capitalism*, 95 MICH. L. REV. 1970 (1997) (book review article). For studies in a more comparative style, *see* INSTITUTIONAL INVESTORS AND CORPORATE GOVERNANCE (Theodor Baums, Richard M. Buxbaum and Klaus J. Hopt eds., 1994); Bernard S. Black & John C. Coffee, *Hail Britannia?: Institutional Investor Behavior Under Limited Regulation*, 92 MICH. L. REV. 1997 (1994); G. P. Stapledon, INSTITUTIONAL SHAREHOLDERS AND CORPORATE GOVERNANCE (1996); Ronald J. Gilson and Reinier Kraakman, *Investment Companies as Guardian Shareholders: The Place of the MSIC in the Corporate Governance Debate*, 45 STAN. L. REV. 985 (1993); Thomas Christian Paefgen, *Institutional Investors Ante Portas: A Comparative Analysis of an Emergent Force in Corporate America and Germany*, 26 INT'L LAW. 327 (1992); James A. Fanto, *The Transformation of French Corporate Governance and United States Institutional Investors*, 21 BROOK. J. INT'L L. 1 (1995).

131. For recent developments in Europe, *see* Paula Dwyer et al., *Shareholder Revolt*, BUS. WEEK (International Edition), Sept. 18, 1995, at 16-21 (reporting new shareholder activism in European countries).

ment Trust Business Act.[132] Mutual funds may have significant impact on the corporate governance of Korean firms, in particular in the control contest context, if aggressive managers oversee them with long-term perspectives. Thus far, securities investment trust companies in Korea exercise voting rights that they hold by the shadow voting rule. This rule, however, has been changed to the extent that the securities investment trust companies may now exercise their voting rights without restriction unless such exercise is to acquire the control over the portfolio companies.[133] The new *Securities Investment Company Act* has the same provision.[134]

The developments in the Korean market so far have resulted in some foreign institutions becoming increasingly active and aggressive[135] in corporate governance issues towards the firms in which they are investing.[136] One can expect that the influence of foreign institutions will become more visible as the ceiling on foreign stock ownership is abolished and Korean capital markets become more global. Future occurrences of this kind of activism may well provoke a reaction among the Korean public and invite government action. In March 1998, Tiger Management successfully forced SK Telecom, Korea's largest mobile-phone operator, to give outsiders two seats on its board and consult in advance with such outside directors for certain large overseas investments and transactions.[137]

It will be very interesting to see how financial institutions in Korea— both domestic and foreign—view their role in corporate governance as the capital market develops. The discussion of these issues has only just begun in Korea, and will continue to draw keen attention in the future. Recent developments still seem to promote the separation of ownership and control. In Korea, the Berle-Means corporation is part of the future, not just the past.

C. Globalization of Financing and Corporate Governance

Due largely to high interest rates in the domestic financial market, an increasing number of Korean firms now raise funds abroad, often by issuing Depository Receipts (DRs) and equity-related debt instruments such as Convertible Bonds in the Euromarket. By the end of 1996, Korean firms raised $10.6 billion

---

132. Other new financial regulations include the LAW CONCERNING ASSET-BACKED SECURITIZATION, which was promulgated and went into effect on September 16, 1998, and the HOME MORTGAGE LOAN SECURITIZATION COMPANY LAW, promulgated on January 29, 1999, effective from April 30, 1999. *See* Hwa-Jin Kim, *The New Special Purpose Companies in Korea*, forthcoming in RECENT TRANSFORMATION OF KOREAN SOCIETY AND LAW (1999).
133. *See* Art. 25-2 of the Act.
134. Art. 31 of the Act.
135. *See, e.g.,* CHOSUN ILBO, Feb. 1, 1997, at 11 (reporting that the Korea Investment Trust indicated its intent to support hostile takeover of Midopa should Midopa issue convertible bonds for defensive purposes).
136. *See* CHOSUN ILBO, Feb. 29, 1997, at 11 (reporting Tiger Management's plan to raise voice in the management of Chosun Brewery); MAEIL KYONGJE, Jan. 17, 1998, at 1 (reporting that three foreign investment funds have exercised their minority shareholders' rights).
137. CHOSUN ILBO, March 21, 1998, at 9; Jon E. Hilsenrath, *Tiger Won Telecom Fight, But Locals May Win War,* ASIAN WALL ST. J., March 23, 1998, at 19, 28.

by issuing equity-related overseas securities.[138] Korean involvment in the U.S. market has also increased, due to the easy access afforded by *SEC Regulation S* and *Regulation 144A*.[139] As the restrictions on raising capital abroad have been abolished on implementation of the agreement with the IMF,[140] the Korean firms' practice of international financing with securities is expected to increase further. In 1997, Korean listed firms financed nearly $2 billion by issuing securities abroad. Of this amount, 64.7 percent were convertible bonds and 31.5 percent were DRs.[141]

These developments may have significant implications for corporate governance in Korea. In particular, many Korean firms have accessed the U.S. capital markets through the issuance of DRs. In order to get their shares admitted to the U.S. securities markets, corporate governance related requirements must be met.[142] In order to keep their shares listed and traded on NYSE or NASDAQ (as of May 1999, ADRs of four Korean companies were listed on NYSE - Pohang Iron & Steel, Korea Electric Power, Korean Telecom and SK Telecom), the strict periodic reporting requirements must also be fulfilled. In practice, they may face pressure from their foreign owners in the global markets to disclose more information to investors[143] and manage in their interests. According to a report, Merrill Lynch considered suing some Korean commercial banks that issued DRs for their possible acquisition of bad assets from troubled merchant banks.[144] Further, Korean managers can be sued by U.S. investors even in the

---

138. *See* Ho-Yun Chang, *International Listing of Korean Stocks and Stock-related Securities and Its Impact on the Korean Stock Market* (Korean), 8 KUJHE KYONGYONG YONGU 151, 152, 185-88 (1997).

139. Samsung Electronics was the first Korean issuer placing GDRs under Regulation S and Rule 144A in December 1990, followed by numerous other companies. Regulation S was adopted by the SEC on April 24, 1990 in order to provide safe harbors for offshore distributions and resales of unregistered securities of U.S and foreign issuers. It clarifies the non-applicability of the registration requirements of the SECURITIES ACT OF 1933 to offers and sales of securities that occur outside the United States. *See* JAMES D. COX ET AL., SECURITIES REGULATION: CASES AND MATERIALS 329-39 (1991). Rule 144A was adopted by the SEC on April 23, 1990 in order to provide a safe harbor exemption from the registration requirements of the SECURITIES ACT OF 1933 for resales of restricted securities to "qualified institutional buyers." *See id.*, at 479-85. Despite SEC's attempts to increase access and to eliminate barriers to foreign participants in U.S. markets, foreign issuers still regard the American market as highly restrictive. *See generally* Roberta S. Karmel & Mary S. Head, *Barriers to Foreign Issuer Entry Into U.S. Markets*, 24 LAW & POL'Y INT'L BUS. 1207 (1993); Andreas J. Roquette & Christoph W. Stanger, *Das Engagement ausländischer Gesellschaften im US-amerikanischen Kapitalmarkt*, 48 WERTPAPIER MITTEILUNGEN 137 (1994). For non-U.S. companies listed on the NYSE, see <http://www.nyse.com/international>.

140. *See* No. 33 of the Korea-IMF Memorandum, *supra* note 27 ("[A] timetable will be set by end-February 1998 to eliminate restrictions on foreign borrowing by corporations").

141. Due to the sluggish domestic stock market and plunging credit ratings, 42 firms canceled or deferred issuance worth $3,231.8 million. From January to October 1998, Korean firms financed only $663.6 million by issuing securities abroad. *See Korea Financial Supervisory Commission, Overseas Securities Offerings by Type* (visited March 5, 1999) <http://www.fsc.go.kr/kfsc/static/12/0107.htm>. In 1996, Korean listed firms financed $2,586.9 million by floating securities abroad. *See* KOREA HERALD, Dec. 31, 1997, at 13. *See also Local Firms Issue 23 Overseas Securities Worth $2 Bil. in '97*, KOREA HERALD, Jan. 17, 1998, at 11.

142. *Cf.* New York Stock Exchange Listed Company Manual, section 3.

143. *Cf.* Merritt B. Fox, *Securities Disclosure in a Globalizing Market: Who Should Regulate Whom*, 95 MICH. L. REV. 2498 (1997).

144. *See, e.g.*, CHOSUN ILBO, Nov. 29, 1997, at 11.

U.S. courts. It is well known that the U.S. courts traditionally exercise wide extraterritorial jurisdiction in securities law cases based upon effects and/or conduct tests.[145] The monetary interest of holders of DRs in the United States may easily establish U.S. courts' jurisdiction in such cases where a violation of U.S. securities laws by a Korean firm is alleged.[146] This corporate manager's nightmare is becoming reality, as is evidenced by the recent solicitation of an American insurance company to Korean managers advertising their D&O liability insurance package.[147]

V.

CONCLUSION

Will we be still discussing the convergence of corporate governance institutions ten years from now? Either functionally or formally, the national corporate governance institutions may converge by that time due to globalization of firms' operational and financing activities, as is evidenced by recent developments in Korea. Still, the answer to the question above may be yes. The dynamics of economic development and changes in the competitive environment of the global markets will continuously require private enterprises to innovate and adapt to new economic circumstances. Methods of doing business will constantly evolve dependent upon each economy's path dependency and/or political decisions; the search for the most efficient system will continue. Comparative corporate governance will matter, especially for emerging market economies.[148] The focus will also move from the comparative study of the problems of monitoring and disciplining corporate managers to that of assessing various systems "in terms of their ability to encourage and find economic innovation and to promote corporate adaptability."[149]

---

145. *See, e.g.*, Schoenbaum v. Firstbrook, 405 F. 2d 200 (2d Cir. 1968), cert. denied, 395 U.S. 906 (1969); Leasco Data Processing Equipment Corp. v. Maxwell, 468 F. 2d 1326 (2d Cir. 1972). *See also* COX ET AL., *supra* note 139, at 1333-70; Louis Loss, *Extra-territoriality in the Federal Securities Code*, 20 HARV. INT'L L. J. 305 (1979).

146. On the other hand, it is not unthinkable that Korean firms with their ADRs issued in the United States will request a U.S. court to enjoin hostile tender offer claiming a violation of the WILLIAMS ACT. But *cf.*, Plessey Company Plc. v. General Electric Company Plc., 628 F.Supp. 477 (D. Del. 1986) (dismissing plaintiff's motion for injunctive relief based upon comity and application of the balancing of interests test). For extraterritorial application of tender offer rules, see generally GUNNAR SCHUSTER, DIE INTERNATIONALE ANWENDUNG DES BÖRSENRECHTS 557-89 (1996).

147. The major Korean corporate groups have recently been reported to purchase such insurance for their key managers to protect them from minority shareholders' lawsuit for damages. *See* HAN-GUK KYONGJE SHINMUN, Feb. 19, 1998, at 11; MAEIL KYONGJE, Feb. 19, 1998, at 1. According to the Korea Financial Supervisory Commission, a total D&O insurance premium of 22.5 billion won was paid by them in 1998.

148. Commenting on Roe, Professor Romano points out that "the lesson to be drawn from the mutability of the corporate form is opaque" because "the legal and institutional differences across the three nations [Germany, Japan, and the United States] make it difficult to ascertain whether one approach to corporate governance is superior to another and whether a superior organizational form could be successfully transplanted into another setting." Romano, *supra* note 3, at 2021. However, in my opinion, her view cannot be interpreted as negating the necessity of learning the advanced institutional and organizational wisdom from efficient corporate governance institutions by emerging market economies.

149. Milhaupt, *supra* note 71, at 867.

As far as Korean firms are concerned, the globalization of financing may enhance the efficiency of corporate governance without radical formal changes in its structural relationships with capital markets and financial institutions. The rules of international financial markets and/or the desire and necessity to be recognized as credible participants in global markets will cause Korean firms to innovate their governance structure and endeavor towards more transparent and responsible management. The functional approaches to corporate governance issues described above should be promoted through the opening of capital markets and continuous efforts to reform the infrastructure of domestic capital markets.[150] The international lending agencies involved in the restructuring of Korea's industrial organization and corporate governance should encourage the functional improvements of the Korean system by introducing fair market discipline to the Korean market and refraining from "recommending" sweeping formal changes in the structural relationships between capital markets, financial institutions, and corporate governance. Both market internationalization and the globalization of Korean firms' financing activities can assure effective market discipline in Korea. Active involvement in international financial markets will facilitate functional convergence of corporate governance institutions.

---

150. Professor Gilson observes a functional rather than a formal convergence of major (U.S., German, and Japanese) systems because "each system's governance institutions have sufficient flexibility to find a solution [to the question of replacing poorly-performing senior management] within their path dependent limits." According to Professor Gilson, "[the] functional convergence is driven by selection: [a] system that allows poor managers to remain in control will not succeed." Gilson, Globalizing Corporate Governance, *supra* note 1, at 8.

TABLE 1. THIRTY LARGEST *CHAEBOLS* IN KOREA (1997)

(billion won, %, as of April 1, 1997)

	Member Firms:	Shareholders' Equity (A)	Cross Guarantees(B):	B/A:
Hyundai	57	9,842	10,085	102.47
Samsung	80	14,070	2,474	17.59
LG	49	8,314	2,338	28.13
Daewoo	30	7,824	10,123	129.38
Sunkyoung	46	4,702	790	16.80
Ssangyoung	25	3,217	2,974	92.47
Hanjin	24	2,119	8,178	385.92
Kia	28	2,289	2,535	110.77
Hanwha	31	1,243	1,982	159.34
Lotte	30	2,658	553	20.81
Kumho	26	1,281	1,555	121.37
Halla	18	306	2,727	891.01
Dongah	19	1,383	2,799	202.39
Doosan	25	807	711	88.07
Dealim	21	1,117	863	256.18
Hansol	23	1,234	627	50.82
Hyosung	18	878	369	42.11
Dongkuk Steel	17	1,117	626	56.06
Jinro	24	109	518	473.31
Kolon	24	918	778	84.80
Kohap	13	529	425	80.28
Dongbu	34	946	878	92.82
Tongyang	24	663	609	91.91
Haitai	15	465	265	57.02
New Core	18	211	364	172.48
Anam	21	464	1,677	361.31
Hanil	7	383	827	215.76
Keopyung	22	527	1,867	354.27
Miwon	25	444	667	150.41
Shinho	25	387	1,162	300.12
Total	819	70,460	64,361	91.34

Source: Korea Fair Trade Commission

TABLE 2. MAJOR EVENTS IN THE TURMOIL (NOV. 97–FEB. 98)

11.21	Korea applied for the bailout funds with the IMF
12.02	Business at 9 merchant banks suspended
12.03	Korea-IMF agreement
12.05	Coryo Securities suspended
12.06	Halla Group filed for court protection
12.08	Daewoo's takeover of Ssangyong Motor announced
12.10	Business at 5 additional merchant banks suspended Mandatory tender offer requirements lessened
12.11	Foreign ownership ceiling raised to 50 percent
12.12	Dongsuh Securities suspended, filed for court protection
12.15	Guidelines for financial-sector M&A unveiled
12.16	Currency fluctuation restrictions removed
12.18	Presidential election
12.19	Shinsegi Investment Trust suspended
12.22	Moody's and S & P's downgraded the foreign currency credit rating of Korea to Ba1 and B+, respectively
12.24	Moratorium speculated in financial sector Korea-IMF first supplementary agreement
12.25	G-7 countries' advancement of the bailout package announced
12.26	Chong-gu Group filed for court protection
12.29	18 financial reform bills passed, including amendments to the "real name" system in financial transactions
12.30	Foreign ownership ceiling raised to 55 percent Domestic bond markets fully opened to foreigners
01.13	President-elect met CEOs of 4 largest *Chaebols* for reform talks
01.14	Nasan Group filed for court protection
01.15	Labor-Reform Committee organized to discuss a layoff bill
01.29	New York agreement for the rescheduling of Korea's short-term corporate foreign debts
02.06	Labor law reform accord
02.14	17 "IMF reform bills" passed, including layoff bill
02.17	Korea-IMF second supplementary agreement

[7]

Legal Transplants through Private Contracting: Codes of Vendor Conduct in Global Supply Chains as an Example

LI-WEN LIN*

The legal transplant literature typically focuses on legal transplants through governmental channels (e.g., legislative or judiciary processes). This Article, however, directs attention to a generally ignored phenomenon: legal transplants through private contracting in the globalization age. Private actors have transplanted a variety of private and public laws across jurisdictions through contracting for over a decade. This Article argues that codes of vendor conduct in global supply chains are a vivid example of this type of legal transplantation. Given that these vendor codes can be interpreted as legal transplants through private contracting, this Article further examines the transplant effects in China, one of the many receiving countries. Finally, this Article proffers a theoretical analysis of the comparative advantages and disadvantages of legal transplants through private contracting.

I. INTRODUCTION

The history of legal transplants can be traced back thousands of years.[1] An early wave of large-scale legal transplants was driven by colonialism. Legal transplants could be viewed as a tool for colonists to control their new settlements. In the post-World War II period, a large number of newly independent states borrowed laws from western countries. To a great extent, such borrowings still reflected the legacy of colonialism. The legal transplants during the colonial and the post-World War II periods tended to be blanket transplants of a certain legal system, which facilitated the formation of legal families. In the late 1980s, the legal reforms of former socialist countries initiated another wave of legal transplants. More recently, global

---

* Paul F. Lazarsfeld Fellow, Department of Sociology, Columbia University; JSD (2008), LLM (2005), University of Illinois at Urbana-Champaign. I am grateful to Professors Cynthia Williams and Margaret Blair for giving me inspiration. I also appreciate comments by Professors Tom Ginsburg, Mathias Reimann, and anonymous reviewers. Errors remain my own.

1. *See* ALAN WATSON, LEGAL TRANSPLANTS: AN APPROACH TO COMPARATIVE LAW 22-24 (1974) (taking the ancient Near Eastern provisions concerning a goring ox around eighteenth century B.C. as a legal transplant example).

economic integration has become a powerful engine pushing the wave of legal transplants to its apex.

In the era of globalization, legal reforms at the individual state level usually transfer fragments of rules from various legal systems and integrate the fragments into a single law.[2] The concept of legal families that may be deemed a colonial legacy is expected to diminish. A parallel idea to the combination of fragmented rules from different foreign sources into a single law in a national legal reform is the legal standardization or harmonization, particularly in the global finance and trade arena. International governmental, semi-governmental, and non-governmental organizations (NGOs) are the major contributors to legal standardization and harmonization today. At present, there are hard and soft approaches to facilitate that goal.[3] The hard approach is notably illustrated by the legal interactions between the WTO and its members, or between the EU and its Member States. The soft approach can be seen in examples such as OECD Corporate Governance Principles, UNCITRAL Model Law on International Commercial Arbitration, and UNIDROIT Principles of International Commercial Contracts. The impetus behind these projects is to reduce transaction costs for international market participants as well as the hope to improve the institutional environments of receiving countries. The transplanted laws under the standardization or harmonization movement are usually products of international negotiation and conciliation, rather than wholesale adoptions of any particular legal system. For example, the OECD Principles on Corporate Governance contain elements of the Anglo-American shareholder model and the European stakeholder model. States generally play a key role in this transplant process because the standardized rules are made by states at the international level, and the laws usually need to be incorporated into a legal system through legislative processes at the national level. Given that standardized or harmonized laws are usually mixtures of different legal sources, every country, whether developed or developing, subject to these laws may treat them as legal transplants to a certain extent.[4] However, the transplant aspect tends to be more striking for

---

2. *See* Takao Tanase, *Global Markets and the Evolution of Law in China and Japan*, 27 MICH. J. INT'L L. 873, 876 (2006).

3. Legal standardization and harmonization cover a wide range of approaches with variations of coerciveness: legally-binding agreements backed by enforcement mechanisms, economic enticement, non-binding principles intended to provide guidance, and foreign technical assistance programs. The hard approach refers to measures backed by legal enforcement, while the soft approach refers to measures not backed by legal enforcement.

4. Developed countries may treat harmonized laws as legal transplants, *see e.g.,* Gunther Teubner, *Legal Irritants: Good Faith in British Law or How Unifying Law Ends Up in New Divergences*, 61 MOD. L. REV. 11 (1998) (analyzing the transplant of the European continental principle of *bona fides* into the British contract law through the EU Directive on Unfair Terms in Consumer Contracts).

developing countries because they usually have a weak voice in the international lawmaking process and relatively limited development of their legal institutions. Some scholars caution against the possible dangers of overzealous legal standardization and harmonization to developing countries.[5] Professor Katharina Pistor in particular envisions the potentially harmful effects resulting from ignorance of the interdependence of legal rules embedded in a legal system and the adaptation process operated by local law users.[6]

According to contemporary legal transplant scholarship, the state (the governmental organs, particularly the legislative branch) is the major conveyor of foreign law, holding the power over whether and how to transplant. The transplanted objects are usually formal law codified in a legal system. The transplant motivations are normally associated with political or governmental functions, such as regulating a new national problem, pursuing foreign policy interests, or gaining governmental legitimacy.[7]

A much less noticed phenomenon occurring in the globalization age is that law can be transplanted by non-state actors. Some non-state actors also play an important transplant role in the legal standardization and harmonization movement. For example, the International Accounting Standards Board (IASB), a non-profit, private sector organization, develops international standards for financial reporting; the International Organization of Securities Commissions (IOSCO), which includes public and private securities regulators, develops international principles of securities regulation.[8] But these non-state actors usually still follow the typical transplant method, which involves government legislation/regulation processes at the national level. This Article discusses another type of legal transplants through private actors: borrowing law through private contacting. Through the channel of contracting, private transactors have been "smuggling" tons of regulatory law across borders for over

---

5. *See, e.g.*, Katharina Pistor, *The Standardization of Law and Its Effect on Developing Economies*, 50 AM. J. COMP. L. 97 (2002); Graham Mayeda, *Developing Disharmony? The SPS and TBT Agreements and The Impact of Harmonization on Developing Countries*, 7 J. INT'L ECON. L. 737 (2004); Michael Trebilcock & Robert Howse, *A Cautious View of International Harmonization: Implications from Breton's Theory of Competitive Governments*, *in* COMPETITION AND STRUCTURE: THE POLITICAL ECONOMY OF COLLECTIVE DECISION (Gianluigi Galeotti et al. eds., 2000) (arguing that policy diversity is important to promote competitive governments).

6. *See* Pistor, *supra* note 5.

7. *See* Jonathan M. Miller, *A Typology of Legal Transplants: Using Sociology, Legal History and Argentina Examples to Explain the Transplant Process*, 51 AM. J. COMP. L. 839, 847 (2003) (analyzing why a receiving country would decide to make a legal transplant).

8. *See* International Accounting Standards Board (IASB), About Us, at http://www.iasb.org/About+Us/International+Accounting+Standards+Board+-+About+Us.htm; International Organization of Securities Commissions (IOSCO), Applications for Membership, at http://www.iosco.org/about/index.cfm?section=memberapps (last visited Aug. 25, 2008).

a decade. This phenomenon is rarely detected by the radar of legal transplantation. The purpose of this Article is to direct attention to this specific type of legal transplantation.

International commercial arbitration may be put into this category. Arbitration as a dispute resolution mechanism is increasingly popular with international commercial actors. By virtue of arbitration or through choice of law clauses in private contracts, foreign legal rules that would be otherwise inapplicable may be contractually transmitted in a given dispute. An advantage of arbitration is that it can largely, though not completely, circumvent local legal institutions that are incapable of delivering acceptable adjudicatory outcomes to the contracting parties.[9] This is an important advantage, especially for contracts to be enforced in countries where rule of law is weak or lacking. Professor Inga Markovits names this kind of legal transplantation "the potted transplant": "self-contained organisms that carry their own foundation and substance with them and that, like a houseplant, can be placed anywhere the purchaser desires (and the light is right)."[10] The potted transplant is a form of "private ordering as an alternative to public law reform."[11] Note that although arbitration law appears neutral in that it gives contracting parties great latitude regarding their choice of procedural and substantive rules, the international arbitration practices between western and nonwestern transactors usually show a tendency toward westernization.[12] This makes the legal transplant feature of international arbitration more prominent in the eyes of nonwestern parties.

This Article proffers another example of legal transplants via private contracting: multinational companies' codes of vendor conduct in their global procurement contracts. Codes of vendor conduct refer to a set of supplier eligibility criteria structured with social and environmental standards established internally by a buyer company itself or externally by NGOs; they are usually accompanied by an internal or external auditing system. Examples of such codes of vendor

---

9. The reason why it is not a complete circumvention is that if a contracting party does not voluntarily comply with an arbitration award, the other party may seek enforcement by local courts. When the award is to be enforced by local courts, the quality of local legal institutions affects contract enforcement. *See* Randall Peerenboom, *Seek Truth From Facts: An Empirical Study of Enforcement of Arbitration Awards in the PRC*, 49 AM. J. COMP. L. 249 (2001) (using the enforcement of arbitration awards by the Chinese courts to test the development of rule of law in China); Daniel Berkowitz et al., *Legal Institutions and International Trade Flows*, 26 MICH. J. INT'L L. 163 (2004) (arguing that domestic institutions remain important in the global trade because global traders still rely on local legal systems when contracts or arbitration awards are not voluntarily complied; based on the incomplete contract theory, complex goods exporters suffer more when the local legal institutions are weak).

10. *See* Inga Markovits, *Exporting Law Reform – But Will it Travel?*, 37 CORNELL INT'L L.J. 95, 99 (2004).

11. *See id.*

12. *See* Philip J. McConnaughay, *Rethinking the Role of Law and Contracts in East-West Commercial Relationships*, 41 VA. J. INT'L L. 427 (2001).

conduct in global supply chains include the Gap Code of Vendor Conduct, Wal-Mart Standards for Vendor Partners, HP Supplier Code of Conduct, and many corporations' procurement policies that refer to standards such as SA8000 or ISO 14001. Although a great body of literature on global labor and environmental governance discusses at length the potential and limitations of such private codes as a transnational and nongovernmental regulatory mechanism, no study has yet looked at the codes from a legal transplant perspective.[13] Therefore, a major purpose of this Article is to explain how the private codes in global commerce can be interpreted as a form of legal transplantation through private contracting.

Currently, a large and growing number of multinational companies adopt codes of vendor conduct into their supplier selection requirements. At first glance, the proliferation of such codes running through global supply chains and getting to developing countries may simply be deemed a replication and transmission of business strategies between corporations, which are a result of private economic competition. The typical notion of legal transplantation, which contains sovereignty and legitimacy elements, seems irrelevant to the proliferation of such business practices. But the underlying configuration of business transactions in global supply chains is more complex than that. As this Article shows, multinational companies transform international as well as their home-country laws into concrete legal obligations by contracting with companies in developing countries. Although it is well-known that many business strategies have been turned into contractual obligations, in the eyes of suppliers especially in developing countries, codes of vendor conduct have regulatory features that other business strategies do not possess. From the perspective of these suppliers, the regulatory features of vendor codes derive from the combination of the following arrangements: a contractual obligation of implementing the social and environmental

---

13. The volume of the literature on corporate codes of conduct is huge. *See, e.g.*, Dara O'Rourke, *Outsourcing Regulation: Analyzing Nongovernmental Systems of Labor Standards and Monitoring*, 31 POL'Y STUD. J. 1 (2003); Sean Murphy, *Taking Multinational Corporate Codes of Conduct to the Next Level*, 43 COLUM. J. TRANSNAT'L L. 389 (2005) (arguing that governments should provide carrots and sticks for corporate codes of conduct to be effective); David Kinley & Junko Tadaki, *From Talk to Walk: The Emergence of Human Rights Responsibilities for Corporations at International Law*, 44 VA. J. INT'L L. 931, 952-60 (2004); Thomas F. McInerney, *Putting Regulation Before Responsibility: The Limits of Voluntary Corporate Social Responsibility*, (Gwu Law School Public Law Research Paper No.123 Oct. 10, 2005), *available at* SSRN: http://ssrn.com/abstract=658081; Beth Stephens, *The Amorality of Profit: Transnational Corporations and Human Rights*, 20 BERKELEY J. INT'L L. 45, 78-81 (2002); Mark B. Baker, *Tightening the Toothless Vise: Codes of Conduct and the American Multinational Enterprise*, 20 WIS. INT'L L.J. 89 (2001); Lance Compa & Tashia Hinchliffe-Darricarrere, *Enforcing International Labor Rights Through Corporate Codes of Conduct*, 33 COLUM. J. TRANSNAT'L L. 663 (1995); Charles Sabel et al., *Ratcheting Labor Standards: Regulation for Continuous Improvement in the Global Workplace* (2000), *available at* http://papers.ssrn.com/paper.taf?absttract_id=262178.

standards that used to be within the sphere of public regulation; the designated contract enforcement mechanisms that are independent from weak legal institutions in many developing countries, and; the sanction of losing business, which is ultimately judged by multinational companies.

The thesis in this Article is that multinational companies, backed by their strong bargaining power, have transmitted a new legal order to developing countries through contracting with local suppliers and that such transmission may be interpreted as a form of legal transplantation. This kind of legal transplantation is different from the usual type in several aspects. First, it is multinational companies (non-state actors) rather than states playing a key role in the transplant process. Multinational companies' strong bargaining power as the source of authority and non-legal institutions as contract enforcement mechanisms make the transplants possible. Second, the vendor codes themselves are not government-mandated laws. Yet, they have an effect of approximately reflecting international law or multinational companies' home-country law or even the already transplanted but poorly enforced law in receiving countries. Third, this kind of transplantation is a response primarily to market demands rather than to political considerations. Economic and social pressures in the multinational companies' home countries are the ultimate forces behind this type of legal transplantation.

When a law is transplanted from one state to another, the viability of the law in the new environment depends on numerous factors external to the quality of the transplanted law itself. Basically, the outcome of a legal transplant can be mutation, withering, or, albeit rarely, unscathed survival. Looking at vendor codes in global supply chains as a form of legal transplantation raises the question of what the results of such legal transplants are. Since vendor codes in global supply chains are mainly implemented at factories in developing countries, this Article takes China, characterized as "the world's factory," as a case study. China provides interesting perspectives on the circumstances under which vendor codes in global supply chains can be easily assimilated into a receiving country and on the extent to which the legal transplants may be regarded as successful in terms of the intended purposes.

As Alan Watson argues, human history is full of works recording the importance of legal transplants in the development of law.[14] Globalization unquestionably makes these works much more conspicuous than ever. The revolution of manufacturing modes in the globalization age has brought about innovations in legal transplant methods. More research is necessary to examine the various kinds of legal transplant methods and to compare their advantages and disad-

---

14. *See generally* WATSON, *supra* note 1.

vantages in different settings. This Article draws attention to these issues which are of increasing importance in the globalization age. Such a study is important and useful for international and national policymakers when making legal reforms.

This Article is arranged as follows: Section I? explains why vendor codes in global supply chains can be interpreted as a form of legal transplantation through private contracting. It considers the transplant motivation, objects, and process. Based on the understanding that vendor codes in global supply chains are legal transplants, Section III takes China, a major receiving country, as a case study to illustrate how the transplanted legal order interacts with the local environments. This Article particularly compares the different results of the imported social and environmental standards, i.e., SA8000 and ISO 14001. Section IV proffers some theoretical contributions to the literature on legal transplantation.

II. The Basic Structure of Vendor Codes in Global Supply Chains as Legal Transplants

Although there are a large number of academic studies examining vendor codes in global supply chains, none considers the vendor codes as legal transplants. Therefore, it is important to explain why vendor codes in global procurement contracts square with the concept of legal transplantation through private contracting. To illustrate the structure of the vendor codes as legal transplants through private contacting, this section analyzes the transplant motivation, objects, and process.

A. The Transplant Motivation

Codes of vendor conduct require suppliers to meet certain labor and environmental protection standards in the production process. The labor standards generally include topics concerning child labor, forced labor, health and safety measures in workplaces, freedom of association and right to collective bargaining, discrimination, working hours, and compensation. The environmental standards usually involve hazardous substance management (e.g., safe handling, shipping, storage, recycling, and disposal of hazardous materials), waste management, air emission management, energy efficiency measures, and other pollution prevention requirements.

But why do multinational companies require suppliers to meet labor and environmental standards in the production process? These standards seem irrelevant to the tangible quality of products themselves. The answer to the question has social, economic, and business management aspects.

The social aspect relates to the changes in consumer expectation in developed markets. Prior to globalization, companies only ran a race with domestic competitors who were subject to the same cost basis and regulatory environment. In the globalization age, however, the competition is ruthless, pushing every company to compete regardless of its size, origin, and industry. In order to survive in the competitive global market, companies have adopted new business management methods, one of which is to reshape supply chains for cost reduction. An important aspect of the reshaping is the extension of supply sources from domestic to global, particularly in order to tap into the reservoir of cheap labor and natural resources in developing countries. The supply manufacturers in developing countries that contract with multinational businesses are usually companies that are small when measured on an international scale. These small manufacturers profit from the multinationals' cost-reduction strategy. They make profits not from selling advanced knowledge, but from selling cheap labor and materials. To be competitive and profitable, these suppliers do not pay much attention to labor and environmental protection concerns and sometimes even egregiously violate laws, gaining profits at the expense of workers' health and local environments. Moreover, the regulatory institutions in developing countries are usually incapable, or unwilling because of the national comparative advantage concern, to control these harmful practices. Meanwhile, product competition in developed markets has become so fierce that multinational companies are pressed to squeeze every penny out of their operations, including their supply chains. Therefore, multinational companies do not have strong incentives to consider the production processes of their suppliers in developing countries. Price is their primary, if not only, concern. Workers and environments in developing countries suffer in this unregulated global supply chain. Since the 1990s, a large number of news reports have revealed multinational companies' massive labor exploitation and environmental destruction in developing countries.[15] The revelations of corporate irresponsibility have caused consumers and NGOs in developed markets to boycott the companies and to initiate the movement of corporate social responsibility (CSR).[16] The CSR movement signals that corporations are expected not only to provide goods, services, and employment, but also to undertake social and environmental obligations in proportion to their economic power. Codes of vendor conduct in global supply chains constitute an important

---

15. *See, e.g.*, Philip Shenon, *Made in the U.S.A.? — Hard Labor on a Pacific Island/A Special Report.; Saipan Sweatshops Are No American Dream*, N.Y. TIMES, July 18, 1993, § 1, at 1 (reporting that labor exploitations were found in the suppliers of Arrow, Liz Claiborne, Gap, Montgomery Ward, Geoffrey Beene, Eddie Bauer, and Levi-Strauss).

16. For the anti-sweatshop movement since 1990s, see KIMBERLY ANN ELLIOTT & RICHARD B. FREEMAN, CAN LABOR STANDARDS IMPROVE UNDER GLOBALIZATION? 147-50 (2003) (including a timeline of anti-sweatshop activities in the 1990s).

branch of the CSR movement. They are a response to social change, and social change has practical economic and business significance.

In economic terms, although outsourcing to suppliers in developing countries where cheap labor and loose regulatory control can reduce certain costs, it does not guarantee reduction in total production costs. In economic parlance, "the costs of production are the sum of transformation costs and transaction costs."[17] Global outsourcing may reduce transformation costs (e.g., labor wages); however, it may also increase transaction costs. The transaction costs including how to control the quality of production processes (including labor and environmental conditions) would be very likely to surge given that the exchanges are between parties in markets with great distance in space, business culture, and institutions. Therefore, it is important to ensure that, for a profitable outsourcing, if there is any increase in transaction costs, such increase would not eliminate the benefits derived from reduction in transformation costs.

In business terms, it is a question about supply chain management—how to manage risks in the lengthened supply chains. Since companies do not have direct control over their suppliers' factories, the core mission of supply chain management is to ensure the smooth flow of supply. Price, delivery speed, quality, and reliability are the typical focuses of supply chain management. From a multinational company's standpoint, there are multiple layers of suppliers, from its first-tier suppliers, with which it has direct relationships, to its suppliers' suppliers with which it has no contact at all. Multinational buyers may very well argue that they are incapable of controlling their suppliers, in particular those hidden under the multiple layers of contracting. Ostensibly, the shift of manufacturing to suppliers in developing countries and the invisibility of suppliers may justify shifting labor and environmental protection costs associated with manufacturing processes to the suppliers. This is an important economic reason for multinational buyers to extensively utilize suppliers in developing countries. However, sweatshop practices and adverse environmental impacts hidden in the extended and entangled supply chains and traced back to multinational companies have become increasingly known throughout the world. This has brought a deluge of condemnation by consumers in their major markets. This indicates that supply chain management must obtain not only high quality products with low prices by timely delivery but also do so in a socially and environmentally responsible manner.

In short, multinational companies adopt codes of vendor conduct in their global supply chains because of social and economic pressures in their major markets. Codes of vendor conduct in global supply

---

17. *See* DOUGLASS C. NORTH, INSTITUTIONS, INSTITUTIONAL CHANGE AND ECONOMIC PERFORMANCE 27-28 (1990).

chains are a tool to satisfy social demands and to control transaction costs and risks arising from socially or environmentally irresponsible conduct by their suppliers. The transplant motivation is driven by multinational companies' enlightened self-interest—responsively to repair their tarnished images, or preventively to maintain customer goodwill.[18]

B. The Transplanted Law

By reviewing codes of vendor conduct in global supply chains, it is easy to find that the contents of such codes usually refer to three categories of legal texts: international law, the multinational company's home-country law, and the supplier's country law. The former two types agree with the notion of legal transplantation. The scope of "international law" in this section includes hard and soft law. The distinction between them lies in whether the law can be enforced by formal legal sanction, though sometimes it may be proper to interpret the relationship between hard and soft law as a spectrum rather than a dichotomy.[19]

With regard to social standards, codes of vendor conduct frequently refer to International Labor Organization (ILO) Labor Conventions, the Universal Declaration of Human Rights, and the UN Convention on the Rights of the Child.[20] These international conventions and declarations aim at setting up internationally minimum labor standards. One may argue that vendor codes citing these international laws cannot be treated as legal transplants because many developing countries have already signed and ratified these international laws. This argument is true only to a limited extent. A large number of vendor codes refer to the ILO conventions on hours of work and freedom of association, but these conventions are not ratified by

---

18. *See, e.g.,* Robert J. Liubicic, *Corporate Codes of Conduct and Product Labeling Schemes: The Limits and Possibilities of Promoting International Labor Rights Through Private Initiatives,* 30 LAW & POL'Y INT'L BUS 111, 114-15 (1998) (arguing that self-interest motivation is the predominant reason multinational companies adopt codes of conduct); Harvey L. Pitt & Karl A. Groskaufmanis, *Minimizing Corporate Civil and Criminal Liability: A Second Look at Corporate Codes of Conduct,* 78 GEO. L.J. 1559, 1573-1600 (1990) (providing a historical review of the growth of codes of conducts fostered by scandals); Murphy, *supra* note 13, at 397-403 (explaining the impetus for the proliferation of codes of conduct); ELLIOTT & FREEMAN, *supra* note 16, 42-46 (2003) (describing firms' practice of adopting codes of conduct because they believe that "consumers will penalize them if they do not undertake corrective action" and analyzing firms' cost-benefit calculation of adopting higher labor standards).

19. *See* John J. Kirton & Michael J. Trebilcock, *Introduction: Hard Choices and Soft Law in Sustainable Global Governance, in* HARD CHOICE, SOFT LAW 9 (Kirton & Trebilcock eds., 2004).

20. *See, e.g.,* Social Accountability 8000, *available at* http://www.sa-intl.org/; Apple Supplier Code of Conduct, *available at* http://www.apple.com/; The IKEA Way on Purchasing Home Furnishing Products, *available at* http://www.ikea.com/.

major exporting countries such as Brazil, China, and Thailand.[21] More importantly, signatory states may not actually implement these international conventions at the national level. According to the orthodoxy of international law, these laws have no direct application to corporations and individuals when the state is not a signatory or when the state is a signatory but does not incorporate the respective conventions into domestic law.[22] Therefore, when international labor law is incorporated into vendor codes and further transformed into contractual obligations, it can be deemed a direct application of international law to private entities in developing countries.

In addition to the reference to the international legal instruments of which states are the addressees, codes of vendor conduct also consult international instruments that target corporations, such as the UN Global Compact.[23] The contents of these standards usually link back to the ILO conventions and UN declarations previously mentioned.

With regard to environmental issues, frequent references include the ISO 14001 Environmental Management System and the EU Eco-Management and Audit Scheme (EMAS).[24] In contrast to the international labor standards dictating substantive requirements, the international environmental instruments referred to in the codes of conduct are procedural rules. They offer standardized environmental management process and auditing principles. Vendor codes in global supply chains therefore transplant the internationally-standardized environmental procedural rules.

Codes of vendor conduct also incorporate multinational companies' home-country laws. When a multinational company adopts a set of universal standards for its worldwide operations, the multinational company's home-country law is an important reference. An explicit example can be seen in the code of vendor conduct of New

---

21. For example, major developing countries that export labor-intensive products, such as Brazil, China, Thailand, Malaysia, and Vietnam do not ratify Convention 1 (hours of work for industry) and Convention 87 (freedom of association). India does not ratify Convention 87. Indonesia and Russia do not ratify Convention 1. *See* International Labour Organization Database of International Labour Standards Country Profiles, *at* http://www.ilo.org/ilolex/english/newcountryframeE.htm (last visited Sept. 3, 2007).

22. *See* David Kinley & Junko Tadaki, *From Talk to Walk: The Emergence of Human Rights Responsibilities for Corporations at International Law*, 44 VA. J. INT'L L. 931, 947-51 (2004).

23. The UN Global Compact is an international initiative with an objective to promote corporate social responsibility and to advance ten universal principles in the areas of human rights, labor, environments, and anti-corruption. *See* www.unglobalcompact.org/.

24. For detailed discussion about ISO 14000, see Section III of this Article. The EU Eco-Management and Audit Scheme (EMAS) is a management tool for companies and other organizations to evaluate, report, and improve their environmental performance. For more information, see http://ec.europa.eu/environment/emas/index_en.htm (last visited Sept. 3, 2007).

Balance, a U.S.-based branded athletic shoe company. In New Balance's Supplier Code of Conduct, the safety and sanitary conditions of workplaces are measured against the benchmark set by the United States Occupational Safety and Health Administration (OSHA).[25] Nike, a U.S.-based branded sportswear giant, also requires its footwear suppliers to provide indoor air quality equal to or better than the limits established by U.S. OSHA.[26]

The standards set forth in codes of vendor conduct may differ from applicable laws in countries where suppliers operate their factories. A typical resolution to the conflict is to choose the stricter standard.[27] Therefore, foreign law (including international law and multinational companies' home-country law) adopted by codes of vendor conduct may actually control a given labor or environmental issue.

Note that the transplanted law here is public law and regulatory in nature. Part of the transplanted law involves human rights such as freedom of association and prohibition on forced labor. This is an important point that we should bear in mind, given that business and commercial laws are generally assumed more easily to transplant than human rights law because of the differences in their institutional sensitivity.[28] This nature of the transplanted law may significantly affect transplant outcomes.

C. *The Transplant Process*

1. Private Contracting

Codes of vendor conduct are real legal obligations in global supply contracts. Although supply contracts are usually confidential and not accessible to the public, publicly available information, such as corporate statements posted on companies' websites and material contracts filed with SEC, has demonstrated the prevalence of codes of vendor conduct as contractual obligations. Professor Michael Vandenbergh recently conducted a study concerning the pervasiveness of environmental standards in the procurement policies of the

---

25. *See* New Balance Supplier Code of Conduct, *available at* http://www.newbalance.com/ (last visited Mar. 10, 2007).
26. See Nike's press releases about corporate responsibility initiatives in 2000 and 2001 (on file with author).
27. *See, e.g.,* Article II of SA8000, *available at* http://www.sa-intl.org/; the Ethical Trading Initiative Base Code, http://www.ethicaltrade.org/Z/lib/base/code_en.shtml; Nike Code of Conduct (e.g., hours of work/overtime); IBM Supplier Conduct Principles (e.g., child labor, working hours, etc.).
28. *See* Frederick Schauer, *The Politics and Incentives of Legal Transplantation,* (Center for International Development at Harvard University, Working Paper No. 44, Apr. 2000) (arguing that "political, social, and cultural factors are more important in determining the patterns of legal migration for constitutional and human rights laws, ideas, and institutions than they are for business, commercial and economic laws, ideas, and institutions").

top ten companies in various sectors as identified by Hoovers, a Dun & Bradstreet affiliate.[29] He found that, based on the policies and statements disclosed by the companies themselves, at least half of the top ten companies in various sectors have imposed some type of environmental requirements on their suppliers. He also found that eleven of the fifty-two supply agreements (21%) filed with the SEC during the fourth quarter of 2001 include environmental requirements for suppliers, and some of the environmental standards imposed are not even required by the environmental law in the suppliers' countries.

According to the information found with the phrases "code of vendor conduct" and "supplier code of conduct" in the LexisNexis SEC EDGARPlus Exhibits database, a number of companies such as Tommy Hilfiger, a premium apparel company, also include labor standards (e.g., SA8000) in the contracts with their suppliers.[30] Hewlett-Packard, a well-known computer equipment company, openly discloses its standard contract concerning HP's code of vendor conduct on its corporate website. The contract is called "the Supplier Social and Environmental Responsibility Agreement," which requires all of its suppliers to sign the agreement and comply with HP's supplier code of conduct.[31]

2. Contract Enforcement

Contract enforcement plays an important role in the legal transplant process. Legal scholarship commonly finds gaps between the law on the books and the law in practice after transplants. Codes of vendor conduct confront the same problem. Multinational companies such as Nike, Gap, and Wal-Mart, provide vivid case examples showing that simply transforming codes of vendor conduct into contractual obligations does not warrant compliance by suppliers in developing countries.[32] Therefore, how to ensure that suppliers actually respect

---

29. *See* Michael P. Vandenbergh, *The Wal-Mart Effect: The Role of Private Contracting in Global Governance,* 54 UCLA L. REV. 913 (2007).

30. *See, e.g.,* Tommy Hilfiger Corp. (Form 10-K, Exhibit 10. Material Contracts, filed on June 26, 2001), Phoenix Footwear Group Inc. (Form 10-Q, Exhibit 10. Material Contracts, filed on Nov. 15, 2005), Stride Rite Corp. (Form 10-K, Exhibit 10. Material Contracts, filed on Mar. 1, 2000), Marvel Entertainment Group Inc. (Form 10-Q, Exhibit 10. Material Contracts, filed on Aug. 21 1998). This author does not argue that the information found here was complete.

31. *See* HP's Supplier Social and Environmental Responsibility Agreement, *available at* http://www.hp.com/hpinfo/globalcitizenship/environment/pdf/supagree.pdf.

32. Nike established the code of conduct for its suppliers in 1992, but in the late 1990s, Nike was seriously charged for its suppliers' labor exploitation despite the code's existence. The famous case is Kasky v. Nike Inc., 79 Cal. App. 4th 16; 27 Cal. 4th 939. Wal-Mart also adopts a code of conduct for its suppliers but is still infamous for its suppliers' poor labor performance. *See also* Leslie Kaufman & David Gonzalez, *Made in Squalor: Reform has Limits: Labor Standards Clash with Global Reality,* N.Y. TIMES, Apr. 24, 2001, at A1 (reporting Gap intensified monitoring efforts because suppliers failed to comply with Gap's code).

the social and environmental standards in the production process has been a challenging question for global buyers. A prevailing solution by global buyers is to use internal and external auditing systems to enforce the contractual obligations.

An internal audit is conducted by trained employee auditors of a buyer company. There is a trend, however, that global buyers are also using external auditing by specialist auditing firms or NGOs.[33] The typical audit includes three main aspects: a physical inspection (a factory tour); interviews with employees; and a review of records concerning payroll, tax, insurance coverage, and environmental protection processes.[34] Whether audits are announced or unannounced depends on different audit purposes and strategies. They are periodically conducted. After the audit, a report and corresponding corrective action plans are produced. The audited supplier would be given some time to correct identified problems.

There is an interesting question why global buyers use internal and external auditing to ensure suppliers' performance of the social and environmental obligations in global procurement contracts. Typically, there are three alternatives to enforce international commercial contracts, including formal procedures (i.e., in courts), informal mechanisms (e.g., reputation, networks, barter), and international arbitration.[35] Based on this understanding, why do multinational companies favor internal and/or external auditing systems over the conventional enforcement mechanisms to enforce the social and environmental terms in supply contracts? This question may also be translated into a general inquiry of why state courts as a legal institution for dispute resolution are avoided and a new extralegal enforcement institution is favored. The point of looking at the relationship between legal and extra-legal contract enforcement mechanisms is not to find systematic superiority of one over the other. Rather, scholars have recognized that each enforcement mechanism has its strengths and weaknesses for different kinds of transactions.[36] Thus, we should examine each contract enforcement

---

33. For detailed discussion on the rise of such external auditing in the global supply chain and its theoretical implications, see Margaret M. Blair et al., *The New Role for Assurance Services in Global Commerce*, 33 J. CORP. L. 325 (2008).

34. For detailed discussion about how the audits are conducted, see e.g., Ivanka Mamic, IMPLEMENTING CODES OF CONDUCT: HOW BUSINESSES MANAGE SOCIAL PERFORMANCE IN GLOBAL SUPPLY CHAIN 127-31, 202-20, 276-94 (2004); JILL ESBENSHADE, MONITORING SWEATSHOPS 69-82 (2004); Nike, Inc., NIKE FY04 Corporate Social Responsibility Report (disclosing how Nike's M inspection, SHAPE audit and FLA independent audit are conducted).

35. *See* Michael Trebilcock & Jing Leng, *The Role of Formal Contract Law and Enforcement in Economic Development*, 92 VA. L. REV. 1517 (2006) (giving a review of formal and informal contract enforcement mechanisms).

36. *See, e.g.*, Barak D. Richman, *Firms, Courts, and Reputation Mechanisms: Towards a Positive Theory of Private Ordering*, 104 COLUM. L. REV. 2328, 2338 (2004) (arguing that "the nature of the underlying transaction will consistently determine

mechanism in the specific context of codes of vendor conduct in global supply chains; this will reveal the comparative advantages of using auditing systems.

Courts are not a favored enforcement institution because they have intrinsic and extrinsic limitations in the specific context of enforcing vendor codes. Although codes of vendor conduct adopted by multinational companies bear much resemblance to each other, the social and environmental standards are very industry- or even firm-specific.[37] They vary depending on types of products, production procedures, and locations of factories. To determine whether a supplier's measures meet the standards set forth in the vendor code requires professional knowledge and experience. The standards in the vendor codes are more like regulations administered by labor and environmental agencies, which are somewhat outside courts' expertise. Moreover, disputes in courts over irresponsible outsourcing may attract public attention, and global buyers cannot easily disconnect themselves from the irresponsibility label attached by the public. This certainly spells trouble for their businesses. Global buyers prefer a way that they can retain confidentiality of production processes and have a chance to correct the problem before it becomes exposed to the public. Besides these inherent limitations, courts may not be available or reliable in many developing countries where suppliers mainly locate.

Global buyers may also turn to reputation to enforce the social and environmental standards in supply contracts. However, reputation as a contract enforcement mechanism is effective only under certain conditions.[38] For example, reputation can work only where transactors can communicate the information accurately and inexpensively to other transactors in the business circle.[39] Most of the pertinent scholarship builds on examples where certain ethnic ties, closely knit communities, and trade associations in certain industries facilitate the transmission of reputation information; such mechanisms are usually constrained by geography.[40] However, buyers and

---

the superior method of enforcement"); Ariel Porat, *Enforcing Contracts in Dysfunctional Legal Systems: The Close Relationship between Public and Private Orders*, 98 MICH. L. REV. 2459 (2000) (arguing responses in private ordering differ according to the underlying reasons for a dysfunctional public order).

37. *See generally* MAMIC, *supra* note 34; *see also* Gare Smith & Dan Feldman, *Company Codes of Conduct and International Standards: An Analytical Comparison* Vol. 1 (2003-2004) (a report published by the World Bank Group Corporate Social Responsibility Practice), *available at* the World Bank Document & Reports Database, http://www.worldbank.org/reference/.

38. *See* OLIVER E. WILLIAMSON, THE MECHANISMS OF GOVERNANCE 151-58 (1996).

39. *See id.* at 153.

40. *See, e.g.*, Barak D. Richman, *How Communities Create Economic Advantages: Jewish Diamond Merchants in New York*, 31 LAW & SOC. INQUIRY 383 (2006) (arguing that the combination of family-based reputation mechanisms and community-based enforcement institutions allows the trading of valuable and portable articles); Lisa

suppliers in the complex global supply chains are generally on different continents and comprise different ethnic groups, languages, and business cultures. Also, reputation works well only when transactors have reputation at stake. Some small suppliers in developing countries may not take reputation seriously because the expectation of ongoing business relationships may be diminished by uncertainties in macroeconomic, political, and legal environments. Thus, reputation is a possible but not a sufficient enforcement mechanism in the specific content of vendor codes in global supply chains.

Arbitration seems to be a suitable enforcement mechanism for vendor codes in the supply chains given that it offers confidentiality, specialized substantive and procedural rules, and expert decision-makers. But arbitration involves situations where a dispute has already occurred. In other words, it is a remedial mechanism. Implementation of vendor codes, however, does not only have a remedial dimension but a preventive one. Since NGOs and media have shown their ability to peek into global buyers' supply factories, global buyers do not want to risk their reputation by solving problems *ex post facto*. In this regard, the typical arbitration model does not satisfy the prevention demand. To be sure, that does not mean arbitration plays no role in this transplant process. For example, when a buyer requires a supplier to be certified under SA8000 or ISO 14001 by an auditing firm, there is a contractual relationship between the audited party (usually a supplier) and the auditing firm. Disputes between the audited and the auditor concerning how to interpret and implement the contractual terms (including performance and auditing standards/measures) may still be subject to arbitration.[41] But this is a derivative question. This Article focuses on how to enforce vendor codes between a buyer and a supplier.

Thus, neither courts, nor reputation, nor arbitration provides a timely, proactive, and preventive solution to the compliance problem. Global buyers, therefore, resort to a tailored enforcement mechanism—internal and external auditing. Such auditing offers confidentiality, proactive monitoring, and preventive measures.

Bernstein, *Opting Out of the Legal System: Extralegal Contractual Relations in the Diamond Industry*, 21 J. LEGAL STUD. 115 (1992); Lisa Bernstein, *Private Commercial Law in the Cotton Industry: Creating Cooperation Through Rules, Norms and Institutions*, 99 MICH. L. REV. 1724 (2001); John McMillan & Christopher Woodruff, *Private Order Under Dysfunctional Public Order*, 98 MICH. L. REV. 2421 (2000) (giving a literature review of examples on how business and social networks facilitate the dissemination of reputation information).

41. Such dispute resolution can be found in contracts provided by certification firms. See the contracts disclosed by two global prominent certification bodies—RINA (Rules for the Certification of Social Accountability Management Systems, *available at* http://www.rina.org/eng/management_system/responsabilita_sociale.asp) and SGS (General Conditions for Certification Services, *available at* http://www.sgs.com/terms_and_conditions.htm) (last visited Sept. 3, 2007).

Internal and external auditing keeps production processes confidential and avoids unfavorable and uncontrollable exposure to the public. The information produced in internal auditing is not publicly accessible because the auditing process is conducted by the employees of a buyer for internal use. Unless the law mandates disclosure, the buyer can decide whether and how to disclose the information to the public, though the discretion has been challenged in recent years by the rising transparency demand from consumers and NGOs. For external auditing where a buyer uses outsiders, still only limited information is disclosed to the public. For example, when a company uses an auditing firm to ensure social and environmental performance, the auditing firm cannot disclose confidential information acquired in the audit without the consent of the audited.[42] Even NGOs that provide accreditation and/or certification services such as Worldwide Responsible Apparel Production (WRAP), Social Accountability International (SAI), and the member organizations of Standardization Organization International (ISO) disclose information only about applicant factories that pass audits but not those that fail.[43] From the global buyers' view, such confidential treatment helps to correct the enforcement problem without paying a reputational price.

In addition, internal and external auditing is conducted periodically and sometimes with no advance notice to suppliers. Periodic auditing and unannounced investigation are important for proactive and preventive purposes. This is because labor and environmental conditions can vary from moment to moment and may be temporarily fixed if a specific date for investigation is known in advance.

Finally, besides the comparative advantages of auditing, the role of external auditing in particular helps the operation of reputation as contract enforcement in the global market. The external auditing services providers, including auditing firms and NGOs, may be deemed reputation intermediaries facilitating the collection, verification, and dissemination of reputation information about suppliers' social and environmental performance to global buyers.[44]

---

42. *See id.* (confidentiality clauses in the contracts).

43. The list of certified facilities released by WRAP can be found at http://www.wrapapparel.org/; WRAP even contains a statement: "We keep all information supplied by participating factories confidential unless instructed otherwise. Therefore, the list generated below contains only those factories that have provided express authorization to be mentioned. As such, not all WRAP certified factories in this country may be included." The list of certified factories released by SAI can be found at http://www.sa-intl.org/. ISO itself does not retain a list of certified facilities; it is the concern of organizations in each member country to provide such information. For example, China Quality Certification Center maintains a database to search certified facilities and check the validity of ISO 9000 and ISO 140000 certifications issued in China. *See* http://www.cqc.com.cn/Chinese/search/index.asp (last visited Sept. 3, 2007).

44. *See* Blair et al., *supra* note 33.

3. Imbalance of Power

In the transplant process, it is important to consider the relationship between the donors (multinational companies/global buyers based in developed countries) and the receivers (suppliers, particularly in developing countries). Based on the assumption that a contract is a result of negotiation, what are the dynamics in the negotiation process? In order to protect their corporate images, multinational companies require suppliers to comply with codes of vendor conduct. If the implementation of vendor codes is a gain without cost for both parties, there is no question that both sides (buyers and suppliers) would agree to incorporate the codes into contracts without any bitter discussion. Implementation of such codes, however, entails a non-negligible increase in production costs. For example, enhanced standards in wages, working hours, and working conditions would certainly raise production costs. Therefore, whether to adopt social and environmental standards into contracts and who should be responsible for the implementation are contested between buyers and suppliers, as these questions involve allocation of costs and benefits between the parties.

Power is an important factor influencing the outcome of the battle. As recognized in the business and sociological literature, power is an influential factor in defining the inter-firm relationships in supply chains.[45] These structures are rarely balanced and may vary in different types of supply chains. Suppliers in developing countries usually have weaker bargaining power than multinational companies based in developed countries. This is particularly true for suppliers in apparel, footwear, toy, and other industries, in which codes of vendor conduct are very common. These industries are classic examples of buyer-driven commodity chains. "Buyer-driven commodity chains refer to those industries in which large retailers, branded marketers, and branded manufacturers play the pivotal roles in setting up de-

---

45. A number of early research articles on marketing channels have examined the power relationships between firms. *See, e.g.*, Shelby D. Hunt & John R. Nevin, *Power in Channels of Distribution: Sources and Consequences*, 11 J. MKTG. RES. 186 (1974); Jack Kasulis & Robert E. Spekman, *A Framework of the Use of Power*, 14 EUR. J. MKTG. 180 (1980). The research specifically on the power factor in the supply chain is of more recent vintage. *See, e.g.*, Michael Maloli & W.C. Benton, *Power Influences in the Supply Chain*, 21 J. BUS. LOGISTICS 49 (2000). These studies primarily develop on the typology of social power proposed by French and Raven. *See* John R.P. French, Jr. & Bertram Raven, *The Bases of Social Power*, *in* STUDIES IN SOCIAL POWER 150-65 (Dorwin Cartwright ed., 1959). French and Raven propose five types of social power: reward, coercive (ability to punish), legitimate (a person internalizes values because of an obligation to accept the external influence, e.g., power from cultural values, social structure), referent (a person desires association with another person, a role or a group), and expert (knowledge and information). Another important idea related to the role of power between firms is the resource dependence theory proposed by Pfeffer and Salancik. *See* JEFFREY PFEFFER & GERALD R. SALANCIK, THE EXTERNAL CONTROL OF ORGANIZATIONS (2003).

centralized production networks in a variety of exporting countries," particularly developing counties.[46] Profits in the buyer-driven chains are gained from the "unique combination of high value research, design, sales, marketing and financial services that allow the retailers, branded marketers and branded manufacturers to act as strategic brokers in linking overseas factories with evolving product niches in the main consumer markets."[47] With the power to shape consumer demand in markets through the use of brand names and strategic networks, the buyers (retailers, branded marketers, and branded manufacturers) have leverage in price bargaining with suppliers[48] and in setting business conditions (e.g., vendor codes) with suppliers in developing countries. Although a global buyer with strong bargaining power may have good reasons to forgo the use of power and share gains from a cooperative relationship with its suppliers, practical experience in developing countries suggests that global buyers in buyer-driven commodity chains tend to maximize their bargaining power over suppliers when inserting codes of vendor conduct in supply relationships.[49]

In other words, from the view of suppliers in developing countries, codes of vendor conduct in global supply contracts match the externally-dictated transplant under Professor Jonathan Miller's typology of legal transplants. The externally-dictated transplant involves "a foreign individual, entity or government that indicates the adoption of a foreign legal model as a condition for doing business or for allowing the dominated country a measure of political autonomy."[50] "If one understands this type of transplant to include all

---

46. See Gary Gereffi, *International Trade and Industrial Upgrading in the Apparel Commodity Chain*, 48 J. INT'L ECON. 37, 46 (1999).

47. See id. As opposed to buyer-driven commodity chains, producer-driven commodity chains refer to "those in which large, usually transnational, manufacturers play the central roles in coordinating production networks." The typical example of producer-driven commodity chains is the automobile industry. Profits in the producer commodity chain are gained from "scale, volume and technological advances."

48. See id.

49. See MAMIC, *supra* note 34, 102-04, 260-62 (reporting multinational companies' insistence on vendor codes and low prices based on the 147 interviews with suppliers in countries including Cambodia, China, Guatemala, Honduras, Sri Lanka, Thailand, Turkey, United Kingdom, United States, and Vietnam); KUAGUO GONGSI DE SHEHUI ZEREN YU ZHONGGUO SHEHUI [SOCIAL RESPONSIBILITY OF TRANSNATIONAL CORPORATIONS & THE CHINESE SOCIETY] 1-91 (Shen Tan & Kaiming Liu eds., 2003) (reporting multinational companies' insistence on vendor codes and low prices based on interviews with suppliers in China); Helle Bank Jørgensen et al., *Strengthening Implementation of Corporate Social Responsibility in Global Supply Chains*, prepared for the Corporate Social Responsibility Practice in the Investment Climate Department of the World Bank Group (2003) (reporting global buyers demand responsible production and low prices); Dexter Roberts & Pete Engardio, *Secrets, Lies and Sweatshop*, BUSINESSWEEK ONLINE Nov. 27, 2006, *available at* http://www.businessweek.com/magazine/content/06_48/b4011001.htm (reporting Chinese suppliers' compliant about multinational companies' responsible production and low prices strategies).

50. See Miller, *supra* note 7, at 847.

transplants whose acceptance is motivated by the desire to please foreign states, individuals or entities—whether in acquiescence to their demands, or to take advantage of opportunities and enticements that they offer—many different situations involve this type."[51] Under the externally-dictated transplant, the degree of the external pressure affects the extent of acceptance in the receiving country. The transplanted law is doomed to be abandoned as soon as the external pressure disappears, unless the law has been internalized by the receiving country.[52] The following section examines how a receiving country (society) reacts to the externally-dictated transplant.

III. The Transplant Effects: China as a Case Study

What are the effects of such transplants on the receiving country (or society)? This section examines two examples of social and environmental standards that are usually mentioned in multinational companies' codes of vendor conduct: SA8000 and ISO 14001. The two standards are representative because of their worldwide applicability and popularity. They produce different outcomes after being transported by multinational companies to China. The China case study also indicates the potential and limitations of legal transplants through private contracting.

A. Socially Responsible Production Standards: SA8000

SA8000 is a set of auditable labor standards established by the Council on Economic Priorities Accreditation Association (CEPAA) in 1997 and now administered by SAI. SA8000 addresses compliance with national law, International Labor Organization Conventions, the UN's Universal Declaration of Human Rights, and the Convention of the Rights of the Child.[53] To measure a company's labor protection performance, SA8000 provides criteria for nine areas including child labor, forced labor, health and safety, freedom of association and rights to collective bargaining, discrimination, discipline, working hours, compensation, and management systems. To be certified under SA8000, a facility must first conduct a preliminary internal assessment of compliance with SA8000 and make any changes to conditions and policies required by the standard. Then an auditing company accredited by the SAI conducts an initial assessment and provides corrective action requests for the applicant facility. After making changes in accordance with the corrective action requests, the facility contacts the auditing company to arrange a full certification audit. If it passes the audit, the facility will be certified. Surveillance audits periodically occur thereafter. The cost of

---

51. *See id.*
52. *See id.* at 868.
53. *See* Article II of SA8000 Standard.

obtaining a SA8000 certification can be categorized into two types: the certification fees and the corrective/compliance costs. As to the corrective/compliance costs, the amount can vary from facility to facility depending on factors such as the degree of non-compliance and the number of workers.

As of March 31, 2008, China ranked as the third largest country in terms of the number of SA8000-certified facilities and the second largest country in terms of the number of workers covered under the standard.[54] The growth of SA8000 in China is attributable to the external pressure from foreign buyers.[55] I have discussed elsewhere in great detail the SA8000 development in China so that a short summary may suffice here.[56] Briefly speaking, the Chinese government and suppliers generally resist SA8000. They suspect that the ulterior motive of SA8000 and similar standards is to undercut developing countries' competitiveness by raising their labor costs. Moreover, the chaotic certification market in China makes Chinese suppliers believe that SA8000 is an extortion scheme, paying off auditors in exchange for a responsible production label. Also, they charge that SA8000 and other similar standards ignore the reality that most of the indigenous companies are still in early stages of development and accumulation of capital. During this stage, many companies lack the resources for labor protection. Finally, and most importantly, global buyers refuse to bear the costs of improving labor conditions, which places suppliers in developing countries in a very difficult economic situation.

As Professor Jonathan Miller argues, in an externally-dictated transplant, the receiving party would focus in particular on the costs and benefits of compliance and noncompliance.[57] The development of SA8000 and other similar standards in China in recent years is consistent with this theory. Since global buyers with strong bargaining power condition business on implementation of vendor codes, in order to obtain business, suppliers accept the condition. However, it is very difficult for suppliers to faithfully implement the codes because their implementation (in particular wages, work hours, insurance, and

---

54. *See* Social Accountability Accreditation Services, Certified Facilities List, *available at* http://www.saasaccreditation.org/certfacilitieslist.htm#summary (last visited July 11, 2008). As of Mar. 31, 2008, the number of certified facilities by country: Italy (795), India (267), China (214), Brazil (94), Pakistan (52), Vietnam (38), Thailand (24), Spain (20), Portugal (11), Taiwan (11), Greece (9), Indonesia (9), and the Philippines (9). Under SA8000, 872,052 workers were covered (200,215 workers in India and 186,761in China).
55. *See* KUAGUO GONGSI DE SHEHUI ZEREN YU ZHONGGUO SHEHUI [SOCIAL RESPONSIBILITY OF TRANSNATIONAL CORPORATIONS & THE CHINESE SOCIETY] 1-91 (Shen Tan & Kaiming Liu eds., 2003).
56. For a detailed discussion, see Li-Wen Lin, *Corporate Social Accountability Standards in the Global Supply Chain: Resistance, Reconsideration and Resolution in China*, 15 CARDOZO J. INT'L & COMP. L. 321 (2007).
57. *See* Miller, *supra* note 7, at 876.

pension) incurs substantial costs and because, as many Chinese suppliers claim, they cannot demand increased prices from foreign buyers to reflect the costs.[58] Therefore, it is no surprise that many suppliers falsify labor protection records to get business.[59] The suppliers calculate the compliance level based on a cost-benefit analysis. In response to the compliance problem, global buyers usually intensify auditing, making code implementation like a cat and mouse game.[60]

Moreover, as Professor Miller notes, when a transplant is driven by foreign pressure, it may produce an unintended or counterproductive response from the receiving country, and such a response may depend on political and cultural factors prevailing there.[61] The development of SA8000 and similar standards in China offers a concrete example. Some Chinese suppliers have taken unanticipated measures to respond to the legal transplant by global buyers. Since Chinese suppliers individually cannot reject the import of vendor codes by their foreign buyers, some suppliers in the textile and apparel industries, where foreign vendor codes are common, have tried to gain leverage against foreign vendor codes by forming associations and developing their own standards. A prominent example is CSC9000T, which was developed by the China National and Textile and Apparel Council and other representatives of Chinese corporations.[62] CSC9000T is a social management system. It sets forth objectives in the areas of management systems, employment contracts, child workers, forced or compulsory labor, working hours, wages and welfare, trade unions and collective bargaining, discrimination, harassment and abuse, and occupational health and safety.

At first glance, CSC9000T looks very similar to SA8000. Yet, CSC9000T is not a set of standards designed for certification. It builds on a model in which third-party evaluation organizations evaluate the suppliers' social performance and give advice on how to improve it. Therefore, CSC9000T takes a much softer approach than SA8000. The standards set forth in CSC9000T are long-term goals

---

58. See Lin, *supra* note 56; *see also* Poland Li, *CSR in the Supply China*, CSR ASIA WEEKLY, Vol. 24, Week 28, July 2008, at 12 (reporting interviews with suppliers in China and finding that it seems true that no suppliers really can fully comply with the standards because suppliers cannot pass the costs to global buyers). CSR Asia is the leading NGO with a focus of promoting corporate social responsibility in China.

59. See Lin, *supra* note 56; *see also* Wal-Mart 2005 Report on Ethical Sourcing (finding the frequent use of "double books" to hide the numbers of hours worked or wages/benefits paid by suppliers); Gap, Inc. 2004 Social Responsibility Report (finding cases of record falsification in 2003 and 2004); Nike FY04 Corporate Social Responsibility Report (finding record falsification is an obstacle in China).

60. See, e.g., Leslie Kaufman & David Gonzalez, *Made in Squalor: Reform Has Limits: Labor Standards Clash with Global Reality*, N.Y. TIMES, Apr. 24, 2001, at A1 (reporting Gap intensified monitoring when finding suppliers' violations).

61. See Miller, *supra* note 7.

62. See CSC9000T, at http://www.csc9000.org.cn/.

but do not require immediate compliance. The Chinese suppliers further soften the stiffness of social performance by maintaining control over the whole evaluation process. This process is controlled by the Responsible Supply Chain Association (RSCA) whose members are essentially the very companies that are subject to the evaluation process. Given the softness of CSC9000T, western buyers and NGOs may suspect that CSC9000T is merely a contrivance to forge a responsible production label for Chinese suppliers rather than a genuine device to protect labor rights. While it may be too early to tell the true motive behind CSC9000T, based on the 2006 CSC9000T Annual Report, it seems that CSC9000T may herald a Chinese way of implementing socially responsible standards.[63] The Annual Report discloses the identity of ten companies that participated in the experimental program under CSC9000T. It also discloses the preliminary evaluation results, showing serious and prevalent violations of minimum wages, working hours, and health protection. Such a disclosure may weaken the suspicion of deception. It also addresses in particular the harmonious and cooperative interaction between the evaluated companies and the evaluators during the evaluation process, the importance of training and technical support, and the flexibility of correcting problems with different urgency levels. Although CSC9000T uses so-called "third party evaluation organizations," it does not stress the independent or adversarial dimension that is typically associated with a third-party auditor. Rather, according to the Report, it is the "cooperative and harmonious" relationship between the CSC9000T evaluators and the evaluated companies that inspires corporate commitment to labor rights improvement.[64] The emphasis on such a cooperative and harmonious relationship may have its root in the Chinese cultural preference for non-adversarial mechanisms such as mediation and conciliatory negotiation to resolve disputes,[65] but it also strongly reflects the cross-country finding that capacity-building assistance to suppliers in developing countries is an important complement to adversarial monitoring for effective implementation of socially responsible production.[66] In short, faced with SA8000 and similar

---

63. *See* CSC9000T, 2006 CSC9000T Annual Reports, Chinese and English versions *available at* http://www.csc9000.org.cn/ (released on Jan. 18, 2007, last visited Apr. 25, 2007).
64. *See id.*
65. *See* Carlos de Vera, *Arbitrating Harmony: 'Med-Arb' and the Confluence of Culture and Rule of Law in the Resolution of International Commercial Disputes in China*, 18 COLUM. J. ASIAN L. 149 (2004) (arguing the Chinese arbitration system that intermingles the conflicting roles of arbitration and mediation, which undermines the impartiality of arbitrators from a western view, has its root in the Chinese cultural preference for harmony).
66. *See* Richard Locke et al., *Does Monitoring Improve Labor Standards?: Lessons from Nike* (MIT Sloan School of Management Working Paper No. 4612-06, July 2006) (arguing that after surveying over 800 of Nike's suppliers in fifty-one countries, moni-

standards imposed by global buyers, Chinese suppliers are trying to find their own way to strike a balance between satisfactory working conditions and cruel business reality.

B. Environmentally Responsible Production Standards: ISO 14001

ISO 14001 is a set of environmental management standards developed by the ISO.[67] ISO14001 was first published in 1996 and revised in 2004. ISO 14001 is a management tool for an organization to control the impact of its activities, products, or services on the natural environment. The environmental management system under ISO 14001 is process-focused rather than substance-oriented. As a result, an organization in compliance with ISO 14001 does not itself guarantee environmentally responsible performance. Still, ISO14001 accompanied by auditing mechanisms provides an important tool for a firm that wants to demonstrate its commitment to environmental protection.

As of December 2006, China ranked as the second largest country in the number of ISO14001 certificates.[68] Empirical studies have shown that multinational companies' procurement policies presses Chinese suppliers to be certified under ISO 14001.[69] Foreign pressure, however, is not a sufficient account of the rapid growth of ISO 14001 in China because implementation of SA8000 is also encouraged by foreign buyers but has so far received limited acceptance.[70]

In contrast to the SA8000's difficult acclimatization to Chinese society, ISO 14001 enjoys relatively easy acceptance in China. These

---

toring combined with capacity building supports to suppliers is more conducive to improving working conditions than monitoring alone); Richard Locke & Monica Romis, *Beyond Corporate Codes of Conduct: Work Organization and Labor Standards in Two Mexican Garment Factories* (MIT Sloan School of Management Working Paper No. 4617-06, Aug. 2006) (arguing that monitoring plus technical and organizational assistance helps suppliers to improve working conditions).

67. See the website of ISO, at http://www.iso.org/.
68. The top ten countries are as follows: Japan (22,825), China (18,842), Spain (11,125), Italy (9825), United Kingdom (6070), South Korea (5893), United States (5585), Germany (5415), Sweden (4411), and France (3047). See ISO, *The ISO Survey-2006*, available at http://www.iso.org/iso/survey2006.pdf (last visited Aug. 21, 2008).
69. See Petra Christmann & Glen Taylor, *Globalization and the Environment: Determinants of Firm Self-Regulation in China*, 32 J. INT'L BUS. STUDIES 439 (2001); Petra Christmann & Glen Taylor, *Firm Self-Regulation Through International Certifiable Standards: Determinants of Symbolic versus Substantive implementation*, 37 J. INT'L BUS. STUDIES 863 (2006).
70. There has been a rapid growth of ISO 14001 in China over the last decade, from only 9 certified facilities as of Dec. 1996 to 8,862 certified facilities as of Dec. 2004. See ISO, *The ISO Survey of ISO 9000 and ISO 14000 Certificates: Tenth Cycle (2000)*, available at http://www.iso.org/iso/en/iso9000-14000/certification/isosurvey.html; *The ISO Survey of Certifications 2005*, available at http://www.iso.org/iso/en/iso9000-14000/certification/isosurvey.html. Although SA8000 has developed approximately over the same period (since 1997), there were only 140 certified companies in China as of Dec. 2006.

different fates can be attributed to four factors: the content of the standard, the standard setting process, the goal of the standard, and the local policy in China.

As to the content, SA8000 is a set of substantive standards, while ISO 14001 is a set of management process standards. Compared with the rigidity of substantive standards, the process-oriented feature offers flexibility for different business entities at different development stages in different regulatory environments.[71] This flexibility allows them to take local circumstances into account and thus reduces irritation. But it may also indicate that suppliers have more authorized discretion in maneuvering environmental performance without incurring the charge of "falsification."

As to the standard setting process, ISO 14001 is produced through international negotiation. ISO is composed of national standardization institutes from 157 countries, comprising of one member per country.[72] Each member body is represented by the most representative standardization institution in its country. The representative institution may be in the public or private sector. The representative institution of China has always been part of the government.[73] China has participated in the ISO 14001 standard-setting process since the very beginning.[74] This participation may tone down the sharp foreign image of the standard. In contrast, the socially responsible production standards are currently developed either by western organizations or companies without substantial input from developing countries in which the standards are actually implemented. This also implies the great potential of ISO 26000, a new set of socially responsible production standards that will be completed in

---

71. According to the explanation provided by ISO, ISO 14001 is known as "generic management system standards." "Generic" means the standard can be applied to any organization, large or small, whatever its product, in any sector of activities, whether it is a business enterprise, a public administration, or a government department. *See* ISO, *ISO 9000 and ISO 14000 – in brief*, *available at* http://www.iso.org/iso/en/iso 9000-14000/understand/inbrief.html.

72. *See* ISO, *Overview of the ISO System*, *available at* http://www.iso.org/iso/en/aboutiso/introduction/index.html#two (last visited May 3, 2007).

73. The People's Republic of China became a member of ISO in 1978 with China Association for Standardization (CAS) as the representative institution. CAS was replaced by China National Standardization Institute (CNSI) in 1985. CNSI was replaced by the General Administration of Quality Supervision, Inspection and Quarantine of the People's Republic of China in 1989. Because the governmental organization reform in China, now Standardization Administration of China (SAC) established by the State Council of China in 2001, is the representative institution for China. *See* http://www.sac.gov.cn/english/cnorg/index2.asp (last visited Aug. 25, 2006).

74. The delegation of the State Environmental Protection Administration of China participated in the meetings concerning environmental protection (ISO/IEC SAGE) held by ISO in 1991 and 1992. China also has participated in the meetings later held by ISO/TC207 since 1993.

2010 by the ISO.[75] The participants in the ISO 26000 standard-setting process include not only developed but also many developing countries such as China. However, ISO 26000 will only be a set of guidelines rather than certifiable standards. The guideline model limits the potential of ISO 26000, but it also reflects the actual disagreement on labor standards among countries that bring their local concerns into the negotiation.

With regard to its goal, ISO 14001 is designed with a view to facilitate trade and remove non-trade barriers.[76] The WTO has affirmed the link between trade and environment and recognized that each member country has the right to take measures for environmental protection so long as they are not arbitrary and discriminatory.[77] Therefore, when countries have conditioned import on diverse environmental standards, which may create compliance difficulties for international traders, ISO 14001 can be seen as a mechanism to coordinate conflicting environmental requirements and international trade. However, SA8000 does not share the same background. The trade and labor protection linkage has been hotly debated in recent years and decisively thrown out of the Doha negotiation agenda.[78]

---

75. *See* ISO Social Responsibility, *at* http://isotc.iso.org/livelink/livelink/fetch/2000/2122/830949/3934883/3935096/home.html (last visited May 3, 2007).

76. ISO/TC207, the technical committee for ISO 14000 of the ISO, declares that "ISO/TC 207's vision is the worldwide acceptance and use of the ISO 14000 series of standards which will provide an effective means to improve the environmental performance of organizations and their products, facilitate world trade and ultimately contribute to sustainable development" and "TC 207 has tried to create a positive mechanism for improving trade, while encouraging improvements in environmental performance. Its challenge now is to help ensure that the standards are used as intended, and not as a barrier to trade." *See* http://www.tc207.org/about207.asp#background and http://www.tc207.org/faq.asp?Question=15 (last visited May 4, 2007). ISO has also reached an agreement with WTO with the common goal of promoting a free and fair global trading system, in which standardizing bodies subject to the agreement are required to develop standards based on the Code of Good Practice for the Preparation in the WTO's Agreement on Technical Barriers to Trade (TBT) and follow certain notice procedures. *See* ISO, *ISO and Trade*, at http://www.iso.org/iso/en/aboutiso/introduction/index.html#eight (last visited May 4, 2007).

77. At the end of Uruguay Round in 1994, trade ministers from participating countries created Trade and Environmental Committee, bringing the environmental and sustainable issues into the mainstream of the WTO. The Doha negotiation round also has included environmental issues such as the coordination between the WTO and multilateral environmental agreements. See also the prominent "Shrimp-Turtle" case, in which the Appellate Body affirmed countries have the right to take trade actions to protect environments so long as certain requirements, such as non-discrimination, are met. *See* Appellate Body Report, United States—Import Prohibition of Certain Shrimp and Shrimp Products, WT/DS58/AB/R (Oct. 12, 1998).

78. For the literature on trade-labor linkage, see, e.g., Clyde Summers, *The Battle in Seattle: Free Trade, Labor Standards, and Societal Values*, 22 U. PA. J. INT'L ECON. L. 61, 87 (2001) (arguing that "[d]eveloping countries can retain their legitimate comparative advantages while recognizing at least minimum fundamental values"); Michael J. Trebilcock & Robert Howse, *Trade Policy & Labor Standards*, 14 MINN. J. GLOBAL TRADE 261, 279 (2005) (arguing that trade sanction should apply to violation of core labor standards and some generally accepted human rights, e.g., genocide, torture, and detention without trial); Daniel S. Ehrenberg, *The Labor Link: Applying the*

This means that trade-labor barriers imposed by governments are hard to defend under the scrutiny of international trade law. SA8000 itself seems to be a trade barrier when adopted by multinational companies in supply chains.

The governmental policy in China also gives a profound account of the different acceptability of ISO 14001 on the one hand and SA8000 on the other by Chinese suppliers. ISO 14001 has been transformed into its national legal system and into concrete measures. The State Environmental Protection Administration of China (SEPA) started to implement ISO 14001 in several cities in 1996. In 1997, the SEPA instituted the China Steering Committee for Environmental Management System Certification (CSCEC) to formally construct the implementation platform for ISO 14001 in China.[79] The responsibilities of CSCEC include administering consultation, certification, and training. The SEPA also had approved thirty-two National Model Areas for ISO 14001 by the end of January 2007.[80] Furthermore, the SEPA has formalized the establishment procedure of National Model Areas for ISO 14001 to systematically promote ISO 14001.[81] The Chinese government's support is particularly helpful to create a policy climate that is friendly to ISO 14001. In such a climate, Chinese suppliers do not have a strong position to argue that ISO 14001 is an unreasonable burden imposed by powerful global buyers. In fact, the promotion of ISO 14001 is a domestic state policy in China. Even if Chinese suppliers are not really willing to accept ISO 14001, their complaint would be suppressed in such a political climate.

C. Evaluation

It is difficult to claim that vendor codes in global supply chains are successful legal transplants in China if success is measured by the gap between the law in contracts and the law in implementation. But the impact of a legal transplant may be an issue much broader

---

International Trading System to Enforce Violations of Forced and Child Labor, 20 YALE J. INT'L L. 361 (1995).

In the 1996 Singapore Ministerial Declaration, the WTO rejected the use of labor standards for protectionist purposes and believed the competent organization for labor issues should be ILO. The 2001 Doha Ministerial Conference reaffirmed the Singapore declaration on labor without any specific discussion. *See* WTO, *Labor Standards: Consensus, Coherence and Controversy*, at http://www.wto.org/english/thewto_e/whatis_e/tif_e/bey5_e.htm (last visited May 4, 2007).

79. See the official documents concerning the establishment of CSCEC (State Council [1997] No. 27; Environment [1997] No. 379) issued by the State Council and the State Environmental Protection Administration of China (on file with author).

80. See the official directory of the model areas issued by SEPA (or ZHB, in Chinese), at http://www.zhb.gov.cn/tech/ISO14000/rkjx/200405/t20040531_90316.htm (last visited May 4, 2007).

81. *See* ISO 14000 Guojia Shifan qu Guanli Banfa [Regulations on ISO 14000 National Model Areas], effective as of Sept. 1, 2006. The official document (Environment Development [2006] No. 68) issued by SEPA, *available at* http://www.sepa.gov.cn/info/gw/huangfa/200605/t20060517_76735.htm (last visited May 4, 2007).

than the question concerning the implementation/compliance degree of the transplanted law itself. In fact, the proliferation of vendor codes in global supply chains creates an opportunity for Chinese policymakers to reconsider the role of corporations in economic development. In other words, legal transplants via private contracting help some changes in government policy, which in turn affects the acceptability of the privately transplanted law.

For years, Chinese scholars and policymakers have debated the reasonableness of vendor codes in global supply chains and the rationality of CSR, the core idea underlying the vendor codes. The Chinese literature on CSR topics has grown noticeably in the recent few years, and it generally assumes vendor codes in global supply chain trigger the CSR discussion in China.[82] The idea of CSR imported in the vendor codes helps to create a focus of the discussion. The debate has very recently settled on accepting the idea of CSR and of responsible production standards, though with some qualifications as shown below. The discussion has also resulted in some important legal reforms. The leading example can be seen in the recently revised Chinese Company Law, which took effect on January 1, 2006. The law clearly requires Chinese companies to "undertake social responsibility" in the course of business.[83] It thus provides a legal foundation for vendor codes in China.

Also, following the recognition of CSR in the 2006 Company Law, a number of state-driven CSR initiatives have recently emerged in China. An important example is the Guide Opinion on the Social Responsibility Implementation by the Central-Government-Controlled State-Owned Enterprises ("Guide Opinion") released by the State-Owned Assets Supervision and Administration of the State Council (SASAC).[84] The SASAC supervises 150 Chinese state-owned companies, all of which are large and important. According to the SASAC's statement, the organization recognizes that there is a proliferation of CSR initiatives at the global level, including the UN Global Compact, ISO 26000, and multinational companies' codes of conduct.[85] But in the SASAC's view, the contents and measures of CSR in China were

---

82. By using the term "gongsi shehui zeren" [corporate social responsibility] for title search in the China Academic Journals Full Text Database, this author found only 1 article published in 1994, 2 in 1998, 1 in 1999, 1 in 2001. But since 2002, the literature has grown noticeably: 8 articles in 2002, 15 in 2003, 21 in 2004, 39 in 2005, 172 in 2006, 104 in 2007, and 57 in 2008 (as of Aug.). For an overview of the discussion path, see YOHUAN LI, QIYE SHEHUI ZEREN ZAI ZHONGGUO [CORPORATE SOCIAL RESPONSIBILITY IN CHINA] 4-7 (2007).
83. Article 5 of the 2006 Company Law of the People's Republic of China.
84. See SASAC, Guanyu Zhongyang Qiye Luxing Shehui Zeren de Zhidao Yijian [The Guide Opinion on the Social Responsibility Implementation by the Central-Government-Controlled State-Owned Enterprises], available at http://www.sasac.gov.cn/n1180/n1566/n259760/n264851/3621925.html.
85. See SASAC, Press Release, Q&A between the SASAC Official and News Reporters, at http://www.sasac.gov.cn/n1180/n1566/n259760/n264866/3621552.html.

not clear, so the SASAC conducted a two-year study and produced the Guide Opinion for the Chinese state-owned enterprises to follow.[86] The SASAC also intends to encourage the Chinese state-owned enterprises to set CSR examples for all Chinese companies to follow suit.[87] It declared that the Guide Opinion is consistent with international standards but also compatible with the national and organizational reality in China.[88] The Guide Opinion lays out the basic contents of CSR in China requiring the companies to fulfill a long list of requirements: comply with the law; improve product quality; reduce emission and waste; provide safe, healthy, and clean working conditions and living environments for workers, and; protect workers' legal rights (such as signing and implementing employment contracts, launching pay-raise mechanisms, paying the full amount of social insurance in a timely manner, strengthening employee training, and avoiding discrimination, etc.). It also suggests that the companies establish CSR management and reporting systems. Partly because of SASAC's promotion, some important Chinese state-owned enterprises have already engaged in CSR reporting.[89] All of these measures are consistent with vendor codes in global supply chains. This is not to say that China fully accepts CSR as generally understood in western countries. The SASAC explicitly refers to the UN Global Compact, which requires companies to "support and respect the protection of internationally proclaimed human rights; and make sure they are not complicit in human rights abuses," while the Guide Opinion implicitly excludes human rights issues from the Chinese CSR agenda. The exclusion of human rights may be one of the SASAC's so-called "CSR with Chinese characteristics." In short, the Chinese government accepts the labor and environmental aspects of CSR and vendor codes, but it rejects the human rights aspect. In a political climate where human rights issues are strictly controlled by the government, it is no surprise to find that no Chinese private CSR initiatives (e.g., CSC 9000T and the Social Responsibility Guide that was launched by the Chinese Industrial Companies and Industrial Associations) cross the red line; none of them include human rights issues.[90]

---

86. *See id.*
87. *See id.*
88. *See id.*
89. The companies include China National Petroleum Corporation, State Grid, China Mobile, China Ocean Shipping Group (COSCO), China Huaneng, China Datang, Sinochem Corporation, Sinopec, SinoSteel, Aluminum Corporation of China, Bao Steel, CNOOC, etc.
90. *Zhongguo Gongye Qiye ji Gongye Xiehui Shehui Zeren Zhinan* [*The Social Responsibility Guide of the China Industrial Companies and Industrial Associations*], full text *available at* CHINA INDUSTRY NEWS, Apr. 16, 2008, at A3, http://www.cinn.cn/show.asp?ClassID=33&id=44792. The guide was launched in Apr. 2008 by eleven industrial associations in coal, mechanics, steel, petroleum and chemicals, light

China has multiple motives for adopting the Chinese version of CSR. As some Chinese commentators advocate, adopting specifically Chinese CSR standards can prevent SA8000 or other similar western standards from becoming universal.[91] In other words, the construction of Chinese CSR standards can be a defense against the imposition of western norms.

The reason behind adopting CSR standards in China is not simply that global buyers require them but also, and probably more importantly, the Chinese government's domestic economic and political interests in adopting the modified version of CSR. The Chinese government has recognized that the labor-exploitation and environment-pollution production model has reached a bottleneck in economic development so that a redirection of macroeconomic development strategy is necessary. The Chinese government has recently employed an array of tax measures and export regulations to force companies to move up the value chain, from low-skilled and labor-intensive to high-skilled and technology-intensive work. For example, it has taken tough measures on labor-intensive and low-technology manufacturers in export processing zones, including export restrictions on nearly 2000 kinds of labor-intensive/low-technology products, substantial increases in tax rates, and elimination of other regulatory exemptions.[92] These measures have caused a large wave of shutdowns or relocations of companies in the economically developed areas (e.g., the Pearl River Delta), according to scores of major Chinese news reports. CSR and vendor codes are consistent with the new economic development policy, helping to purge companies that cannot meet good social and environmental performance.

Moreover, in the past few years, domestic social and environmental problems have become serious and even resulted in social unrest, which may eventually threaten the Chinese Communist Party's ruling authority. In October 2006, the Sixth General Meeting of the Sixteenth Central Commission of the Chinese Communist Party made an important declaration that "building a harmonious society"

---

industry, textiles, building materials, non-ferrous metals, electricity, and mining industries.

91. *See, e.g.,* YOHUAN LI, QIYE SHEHUI ZEREN ZAI ZHONGGUO [CORPORATE SOCIAL RESPONSIBILITY IN CHINA] 31 (2007) (arguing that China should take actions to prevent SA8000 from becoming a universal standard); Le-Zhen Huang, *Qiye Gongming Yundong [Corporate Citizenship Movement]*, CHINA ECON. WEEKLY (P.R.C.) Vol. 41, Oct. 24, 2005 (reporting that Yu-Ling Ren, Counsellor of the State Council, said that China has to speed up its research and establish its own corporate social responsibility standards in order to prevent China from being constrained by the standards set up by the western countries) (on file with author).

92. *See* Jiagong Maoyi Xianzhilei Chukou Chanpin Mulu [The Directory of Export Products in the Restricted Category], Public Notice No. 44 of the China Customs of the Ministry of Commerce, issued on July 23, 2007 and effective as of Aug. 23, 2007, the full text of the Notice, *available at* http://finance.sina.com.cn/g/20070724/1127381 4818.shtml.

is a long-term goal of Chinese socialism. According to the declaration, there are many existing problems that can cause conflicts and damage social harmony, mainly including inequality in regional development, population pressure and environmental pollution, unemployment, income inequality, and low accessibility and low quality of health care and social security. The declaration also makes clear that solving these problems is currently the principal agenda of the Chinese Communist Party. CSR and vendor codes in fact address many of these problems. In this regard, the Chinese government's adoption of CSR and vendor codes is a measure to implement this newly-minted political ideology ("social harmony") in China.

In summary, vendor codes in global supply chains have caused two transplant results in China. First, they have made some Chinese companies improve their social and environmental performance, although many Chinese suppliers are still struggling to honestly implement the codes. The gap between the law in contracts and the law in practice seems still large. Second, the code proliferation in global supply chains has successfully triggered policy discussion in China, facilitating some changes in government policy. In other words, the bottom-up legal transplant has brought about top-down CSR measures in China that are an important factor influencing the acceptability of the transplanted law through private contracting.

IV. Theoretical Discussion and Future Research

The existing legal transplant literature generally focuses on relocation of law across jurisdictions through governmental channels (e.g., legislatures or courts). This Article has directed attention to a generally ignored phenomenon: law can also be transplanted through contracting between private parties. Arbitration clauses and codes of vendor conduct in global commercial contracts are great examples. The transplanted law in private contracting may include not only private law but also, more importantly, public law (e.g., human rights, labor, and environmental law).

Given that there are alternative ways of legal transplantation, future research might focus on the differences between legal transplants via governmental and private channels and on the comparative advantages of each channel in a given context. Let us here consider some possible advantages of legal transplants through private contracting.

First, sometimes it may be easier to transplant through private contracting than through governmental legislation because it may avoid political or bureaucratic obstacles. It may be easier for two business parties to reach an agreement than for a large number of political representatives to reach a consensus. Second, legal transplants through private contracting can be a potential bottom-up approach of legal reform. For example, since some types of law, such as human rights, are politically-sensitive, some governments may not be willing to transplant because it may threaten their political power. But when a transplant is attached to a lucrative commercial transaction, private actors may be well-motivated to transplant the law despite its political implications. For private parties, business interests in everyday life are usually far more important than political ideology enshrined in the political forum. Third, legal transplants through private contracting may be more likely to take real effect because private actors in a real business world may know better what transplants fit their needs and to what extent they would be effective. When a party to the contract fails to implement the transplanted law, the other party who is negatively affected by the implementation gap may have strong incentives to quickly correct the problem through renegotiation or other remedial measures. For example, when Gap and Nike were publicly criticized for their suppliers' labor exploitation practices in developing countries, these companies quickly intensified monitoring their suppliers to ensure compliance with the transplanted law and therefore to protect their corporate images.

But the possible advantages of legal transplants through private contracting also imply important risks. For example, although legal transplants through private contracting may avoid inefficient political discussions, they also raise accountability concerns. When a legal transplant is through governmental legislation, different interested parties have a chance in the legislative process to air their views, at least theoretically and in democratic countries. The legislative process may serve as a filter to control the suitability of the transplanted law. The legislative body is held accountable for the result of the transplant. When a legal transplant occurs through the judiciary, the courts assume responsibility for the result. The quality and suitability of the transplanted law may be assured by the appeal system. But who is held accountable for the transplant effect when it is the result of private contracting? Does the private contracting process offer comparable deliberation and quality control? This is a particularly acute issue when the transplanted law is regulatory in nature and has an impact on the interests of third parties who probably do not have a chance to air their opinions in the contracting process. In the example of vendor codes in global supply chains, the greatest beneficiaries of the legal transplants are the workers at the factory and the local communities around the factory. But worker and local community participation in the contracting process is usually none or at best minimal.[93] Multinational companies are pressured by their major

---

93. The lack of participation by workers and local communities in developing countries has been criticized by NGOs. Therefore, more and more multinational companies now begin to take a so-called "stakeholder dialogues" approach to bring the

markets, mainly in developed countries, to maintain a reputation of responsibility, but they are also pushed by the same markets to offer competitive prices. Since suppliers with relatively weak bargaining power have a narrow profit margin, some of them will falsify labor and environmental records to protect their profits. This, in turn, will undercut the function of the transplanted law, i.e., the protection of workers and environments in the production process. In other words, the legal transplant through private contracting is extremely vulnerable to the economic interests of the contracting parties. When these economic interests do not support the transplanted law, the transplant may be quickly eliminated from the contract, even though the legal transplant can bring crucial benefits to non-contracting parties (e.g., workers). Although there is a possibility that non-contracting parties who have interests in the contract may make claims as "intended third-party beneficiaries" to protect their interests, the Wal-Mart and GUESS? cases suggest that non-contracting parties stand little chance to succeed in this regard.[94] It is not uncommon that supply contracts even include a "no third-party beneficiaries" clause to prevent non-contracting parties from making such a claim to begin with. All this raises serious questions about the reliability of a legal transplant attached to a private commercial contract as an alternative to public legal reform.

Also, legal transplants through private contracting may be much less transparent than transplants through legislative or judicial processes. Contracts between private entities are usually confidential. In the vendor code example, the details of the transplanted law (i.e., the implementation details of vendor codes) are usually confidential and not released to the public. In this fashion, commercial/trade secrets may be a barrier to transparency.

It is also important to consider the role of lawyers in the contracting process. The major, if not the only, legal experts in the process are lawyers representing the contracting parties. Do these

---

stakeholders in the discussion process. But the process is still mainly controlled by multinational companies and western NGOs.

94. In Aug. 1996, a group of workers filed a law suit against GUESS? for violations of minimum wages and work hours. One of the workers' claims was based on the theory of intended third-party beneficiaries. But GUESS? urged workers in the contracting shops to waive their rights to participate in the lawsuit. *See* ESBENSHADE, *supra* note 34, at 2. On Sept. 3, 2005, a group of Bangladeshi, Chinese, Indonesian, Nicaraguan, and Swazilander workers also launched a suit against Wal-Mart for alleged violations of Wal-Mart's vendor code, based on the theory of intended third-party beneficiaries. But the court dismissed the plaintiff's claim based on the reasons that third-party beneficiaries can only enforce a contract against the promisor, which is the suppliers, not Wal-Mart in this case, and Wal-Mart has the right—not the obligation—to inspect the factories. Moreover, when making claims across borders, the plaintiff in developing countries may also confront the problems such as *forum non conveniens* and failure of showing exhaustion of remedies in the plaintiff's home country.

lawyers consider the local circumstances on a case-by-case basis, or do they just copy and paste standard contracts? To find an answer requires further research. But at least in the case of vendor codes, the latter alternative seems to be more likely.

Besides the accountability and quality concerns, legal transplants through private contracting also raise efficiency concerns from a legal reform perspective. The transplanted law in private contracting usually applies to a limited number of parties—Nike's code of conduct only applies to Nike's suppliers. To effectuate a legal reform in a jurisdiction (e.g., setting up safety standards in workplaces in China) would require numerous negotiations and contracts among a large number of private parties. In addition, a private legal transplant initiator is unlikely to reach all entities that should be subject to the transplanted law; it is impossible, and does not make any sense, for Nike to contract with all manufacturers in China. But the coexistence of many private initiators to transplant a certain kind of law through contracting involves the risk of inconsistency, unless there is coordination between them. For example, although many multinational companies have adopted vendor codes referring to the same international law, their codes still vary greatly in detail. Legal transplants through private contracting therefore may create multiple, and conflicting, legal orders concerning the same issue in the same jurisdiction. While this is not necessarily bad, as multiple orders may reflect the need for flexibility—different companies may just need different standards—it is a reason for concern and caution. It shows that legal transplants through private contracting may not be an efficient way to carry out a large-scale legal reform.

Still, legal transplants through private contracting may play an experimental role in the legal reform process. A legal transplant through private contracting can test on a small scale whether the transplanted law is compatible with the institutional environments of a receiving country and allow quick modifications through renegotiation. If the experimentation succeeds, a legal transplant through private contracting may be upgraded to a legal transplant through legislation, and based on the information gained by the experiment, it may be easier for the government in the receiving country to choose a transplant that is compatible with the local environment.

Part II
Case Studies

[8]
Cultivating *Guanxi* as a Foreign Investor Strategy

John A. Pearce II and Richard B. Robinson, Jr.

The success of the joint venture involving three enterprises—New Jersey's North Sea Shipping, Inc., privately held China United Oil Refinery, and state-owned Sino Chemical—is due to the tightly fitted strengths of its partners. It is a near-classic example of how a Western firm can enter a profitable and growing Chinese market. Western expertise from North Sea Shipping, established supply and distribution channels from China United Oil, and, perhaps most critically, highly influential collaborators arranged through Sino Chemical's socio-political network—its *guanxi*—have produced a highly successful strategic alliance.

Many Western companies, like North Sea Shipping, are eager to enter the most populous market on earth with its 1.2 billion citizens. But doing business in China is complicated by the profound differences between Western and Chinese cultures. Success requires an understanding of China's unique business environment. Its most striking feature and the one that is most likely to undermine the efforts of foreign managers is *guanxi*.

Guanxi is a network of relationships a person cultivates through the exchange of gifts and favors to attain mutual benefits. It is based on friendship and affection, and on a reciprocal obligation to respond to requests for assistance. People who share a *guanxi* network are committed to one another by an unwritten code. Disregarding this commitment can destroy a business executive's prestige and social reputation.

Guanxi networks bind millions of Chinese firms into social and business webs, largely dictating their success. In China, enterprises are built on long-lasting links with political party, administrative leaders, and executives in other companies. Through connections with people who are empowered to make decisions, Chinese executives obtain vital information and assistance. Many Chinese entrepreneurs rely almost exclusively on their "old friends" to obtain material and financial resources, skilled personnel, and even tax considerations.

Because *guanxi* is based on reciprocity, executives implicitly accept an obligation to "return a favor" in the unspecified future whenever they benefit from the *guanxi* network. Thus, developing and expanding *guanxi* is a form of social investment that enriches the executive's current resources and future potential. To aid Western managers in gaining a perspective on how they can cultivate the *guanxi* necessary to succeed in China, we conducted an email survey in the Chinese language with nine Chinese business executives who have partnered with Western companies attempting to operate in China. With their permission, their experiences are reported here.[1]

Guanxi and Business Networking

Personal relationships are the quintessential basis for all business transactions in China. People do business only with those they know and trust. Negotiations are undertaken more obliquely than in the West, often focusing on long-term goals rather than specific current objectives. Negotiators take longer to gather information about the other party and evaluate the trustworthiness of a potential partner. The focus is rarely on closing a business deal as soon as possible. Business relationships are designed to enhance *guanxi* and thereby lead to other opportunities.

> **Developing and maintaining guanxi, say these executives, goes beyond gift-giving and favor exchanges. It requires building long-term mutual benefits, friendships, and trust.**

Foreign managers can be confused and irritated by this long negotiation process and regard it as inefficient. However, being impatient, impersonal, and critical impedes the development of effective *guanxi*. Chinese executives believe in the long-term benefits of *guanxi* and are committed to investing time and resources to cultivating it. Foreign managers can benefit by working to establish their own *guanxi*, which requires looking beyond the transaction at hand to its implications for the development of a personal relationship.

Business Transactions Depend on *Guanxi*

The ability to initiate and maintain social contacts in the Chinese culture is one of the most important traits that expatriates can develop. While Westerners' business communications emphasize the exchange of facts and information, Chinese use communication primarily to enhance *guanxi*. So Western executives need to be sensitive to the communication style of the Chinese and try to adapt to this cultural difference. Sunny Zhou, General Manager of Kunming Lida Wood and Bamboo Products, concedes that this adaptation is difficult:

> *"Favor exchanges among members of a guanxi network are not just commercial, but also social, involving the exchange both of favor and affection."*

I have to suppress my tendency to be impatient. The Chinese way of making decisions begins with socialization and initiation of personal *guanxi* rather than business discussion. The focus is not market research, statistical analysis, facts, Power Point presentations, or to-the-point business discussion. My focus must be on fostering *guanxi*.

I devote, on average, two-thirds of my work time to developing *guanxi* with important people I meet. For example, we travel to remote areas in Yunnan province to buy lumber every month. The lumber price varies drastically, depending on whether one has strong *guanxi* with the local administrators. The government owns the land and the forest, the selling price is under the discretion of the local officials. The better the *guanxi*, the cheaper the price.

When I go there to meet them, I never talk about business for the first couple of days even if I'm eager to close the deal and go home. It is just not the Chinese way of doing business. Instead, I invite them to dinner, drink with them, play with their children, and chat with their spouses to develop friendship and trust. Once we know each other on a personal level, then they feel comfortable enough to talk about the price and quality of lumber.

Corporate networking is not a new phenomenon. It is critical to most business success in our global society. Western management literature reflects executives' appreciation for the value of networking and for the need to develop corporate links. Networking is now believed to enhance a firm's competitive advantage by providing access to the resources of other network members. It is used to bridge the gap between business people of different nations and cultures, stimulating trade that might not otherwise occur.

Guanxi embodies these networking attributes. However, favor exchanges among members of a *guanxi* network are not just commercial, but also social, involving the exchange both of favor and affection. This feature makes *guanxi* a form of social investment. In slight contrast, networking is the Western management term associated with commercial relations. Because of this difference, many Western businesspeople are in danger of overemphasizing the gift-giving component of *guanxi* to the neglect of the long-term Chinese goal of building trust.

***Guanxi* Marketing**

The success of relationship marketing in China is based on *guanxi* networks. In fact, a new term has arisen in China: *guanxihu*, a term now applied to specially connected firms. It refers to the bond between *guanxi* members that leads them to give highly preferential treatment to other members of their network. Relationship marketing is predicated on this requirement.* Australian Sydney Corporation, a lubricant manufacturing company operating in China, had difficulty finding distributors because of the country's newly developing market infrastructure and the resistance of Chinese to doing business with strangers. Wang Li, marketing manager of the China Division, described the experience:

> In the beginning, we advertised heavily in newspapers and magazines, but nothing came of it. We then tried to send sales agents to various cities to push our products. But because we had no established

---

*Editor's note: See the article by Yau et al., "Relationship Marketing the Chinese Way," on page 16 of this issue.

guanxi, the effort was in vain, even though we spent a lot of money on the operation.

Later, we developed *guanxi* with a person in charge of a division in the Department of Commerce in Beijing and hired him as a consultant. He introduced us to a local distributor who is his *guanxihu*. Subsequently, the distributor agreed to put our products on the market, but only because of his *guanxi* with the consultant. His personal assessment of the quality of our products was largely immaterial.

Guanxi and Lending

Credit extension for businesses that operate in China is closely associated with *guanxi*. *Guanxihu* can facilitate favorable loan terms and flexible payment schedules through the respect of network members and the provision of assistance to those partners who need help. Because there are no credit report agencies or standard credit lending policies in China, credit is granted based on the level of trust and reputation in the *guanxi* network. Because banks in China are government-controlled and operated, one's *guanxi* with higher government officials can also be crucial for obtaining loans.

Guanxi and Employee Relations

Whereas executives in other cultures prefer to keep relationships with business partners and employees on a strict business basis, the Chinese emphasize a simultaneous development of social and business relationships. Strong interpersonal relations facilitate favorable business results. As a consequence, Chinese managers are encouraged to develop and maintain *guanxi* with staff members. They take time to mentor and demonstrate concern for employees to secure their subordinates' loyalty. This process is so successful that many Chinese employees become allied with specific managers, whom they consider their friends.

One of the biggest problems confronting Western managers of joint ventures (JVs) involves recognizing the unique value system and work ethic of the Chinese. Employees form tightly knit teams based on personal relationships. Western managers who encounter employee difficulties can frequently trace their problems to having ignored or disrupted these informal groups. When difficulties occur, employee morale drops and public conflicts erupt. In a related way, expatriates learn that employees need attention. Managers who take time to interact and socialize with employees gain their respect and trust, and find that Chinese employees are extremely loyal once *guanxi* has been established.

The leadership problem is exacerbated by the relatively low numbers of available Chinese who are prepared to assume new management positions. The shortage of skilled personnel results in part from the phenomenal success of early entrants who formed an estimated 80,000 foreign JVs in China and hired or developed a quarter of a million Chinese managers. Local talent is claimed. Adding to the problem in the short term is the fact that Chinese universities graduate only a few hundred MBA students annually, although thousands are seeking collegiate business educations overseas. These conditions make the retention and motivation of talented staff a critical priority for foreign executives.

Establishing *Guanxi*

In the West, information can be obtained through phone books, newspapers, magazines, TV, radio, Web sites, and other channels. In China, information is frequently passed through noncommercial media, a process that is very people-intensive. Thus, to establish *guanxi* with the important people, one must be extremely sociable, because the preferred way to meet prospective *guanxi* partners is through personal introductions. Meeting friends and becoming engaged in their *guanxi* webs leads to business opportunities.

Wang Li, Marketing Manager of the China Division, Australian Sydney Corp., had such an experience:

> We tried to market our products through aggressive marketing campaigns. We sent our best sales agents to push the products but nothing came of it. Because in China, you must have *guanxi* and develop friendships with your potential clients first, then you can think about selling your products.

From Wang Li's perspective, product quality, market demand, and pricing are secondary issues to be considered only once *guanxi* has been established.

Sunny Zhou concurs, saying that Chinese rely more on *guanxi* than facts, figures, and information in their decision-making. He explains:

> *Guanxi* played a very important role when we tried to bid on a construction project in Kunming. The person in charge of the project would not schedule an appointment with us because we did not have *guanxi* with him. It did not matter to him that we had the best lumber, the best engineers, and the lowest

bid. He refused even to meet us. We had to find an intermediary who had *guanxi* with him to get an appointment to discuss the project. In China, one simply does not barge into someone's office and start making a presentation. One must have a guide in order to get to know the other party first.

Fortunately for newcomers, *guanxi* networks have a transferable quality. If an executive wants to ask a favor of someone with whom he does not have *guanxi*, he can establish himself through a third person whose influence overlaps the two networks. Thus, *guanxi* can be established by bridging the gaps of personal relationships. Ming Xu of Golden Enterprises adds that in China, executives sometimes pay commissions to intermediaries who use their personal relationships to help foreign investors link with critical *guanxi* networks. The intermediaries may or may not be directly involved in the business deal but they can facilitate the essential introductions that bring potential partners together.

Foreign companies can adopt this tactic of employing intermediaries to expand their *guanxi*. Cosmetics manufacturer Yamei initially failed to gain market share by direct marketing even though the company spent heavily on advertising. The firm later obtained assistance from a consultant who was well known for his *guanxi* with government officials, local distributors, and major TV network executives. The consultant opened doors for Yamei by transferring his valuable *guanxi* to his friend Li Zhang, public relations director of Yamei. Li Zhang acknowledges, "This *guanxi* helped Yamei get free TV time and preferred shelf space in government-owned stores, thus reducing the need for much of its advertising."

Time, money, and effort are required to maintain *guanxi* once it has been achieved. One needs to bestow favors, cultivate personal relationships, build trust, and nurture long-term mutual benefits. Although gifts are essential, they are not sufficient as a basis for long-term *guanxi*. It is important to develop a personal relationship with the other party that is deeper than mutual tangible benefits. To merit *guanxi*, executives should understand the needs and priorities of their Chinese contacts, topics they like to talk about, their background, and even their food preferences.

Thus, in general, an executive can demonstrate the good faith that forms the basis for the gradual transition from outsider to insider by bestowing favors in the form of considerate and sensitive gift-giving, hosting dinners in the honor of the Chinese partner, and, most important, giving personal attention. Nurturing long-term mutual benefits creates an interdependence between the two parties in the relationship, thus making *guanxi* more productive and long-lasting.

A Company's Ability to Cultivate *Guanxi*

Several factors affect a firm's ability to cultivate *guanxi*, including company size, organizational design, mode of entry, and experience in China. The apparent size of the firm is an important factor when its managers try to develop a *guanxi* network. In China, small firms have an advantage stemming from their cultural heritage. Because *guanxi* is sustained by family and intimate personal ties, the Chinese rely on close friends and relatives in building their business networks. Central to these relationships is the notion that *guanxi* members must be supported even at the cost of business efficiency. Consequently, many Chinese believe that personal *guanxi* loyalties, and the organizational inefficiencies they spawn, are likely to undermine business objectives in large firms that subordinate the well-being of individuals to the good of the firm. Understandably, people are suspicious of the implementation capabilities of large firms, which are thought to lack the ability to tap the *guanxi* of their workers.

When large foreign firms enter China, they gain from exhibiting attributes of small size and intimacy, such as flexible organizational structures and a minimization of rules and regulations. A learning organization that is fluid, decentralized, and team-oriented seems best suited to China's business environment.

Regardless of a company's mode of entry into China, the development of its *guanxi* network plays an important role in helping it gain a commercial foothold. Foreign investors most often enter China's markets through a JV or a wholly foreign-owned subsidiary. Under either option, they must be able to gain access to the appropriate *guanxi* webs, either through their JV partners or by recruiting targeted *guanxi* members as key personnel. Understandably, JVs remain the dominant entry mode because local Chinese partners, who provide access to the powerful *guanxi* networks, can facilitate quick acceptance of the foreign investor.

The advantages of JVs can include preferential access to government services and contracts, favorable tax treatment, and private sector priority for raw material supplies and market access. However, the Chinese culture that values relationships based on trust makes JVs hard to dissolve. If foreign investors find themselves in unhappy situations or in conflict with their partners, *guanxi* can backfire and make divorce from the venture extremely difficult.

The problems for the foreign investor can range from the loss of *guanxi*, to the forfeiture of assets, to an inability to attract future JV partners in China. Audi, Chrysler, and Daimler-Benz have all risked forfeiting access to China's automobile market by withdrawing from JVs with Chinese partners. In the most celebrated example, Audi's decision to terminate its JV prompted its Chinese partner, First Automobile Works, to expropriate its car design and manufacturing processes. The result was an enormously successful, unauthorized Audi clone, with a Chrysler engine and a First Automobile Works nameplate.

As opposed to a simple pull-out when a JV sours, other foreign partners have pursued more successful strategies. Kimberly-Clark bought out its Chinese partner, gaining control and profitability. Siemens streamlined its complex and costly government relations by consolidating its JVs, thereby simplifying its Chinese approval requirements and its *guanxi* needs.

In recent years, foreign investors have begun to use Wholly Foreign-Owned Enterprises as an entry mode. A WFOE is a foreign subsidiary over which a company has complete control. Its creation requires the firm's local managers to have a heightened awareness of economic, cultural, and political conditions. Many WFOEs are successful because they actively recruit educated and talented Chinese managers with valuable personal *guanxi* networks. Foreign investors can then design strategies to transform personal *guanxi* into organizational *guanxi*—through personal introductions, meetings, and social activities—in order to engage the new partner. A WFOE can also recruit overseas and return ethnic Chinese to assignments in their homeland. In this way, the firm benefits from the employees' cultural knowledge, language skills, and *guanxi* networks, as well as their capacity to develop further *guanxi*.

The process of building an effective *guanxi* network is extremely time-consuming. Foreign executives must identify potential key contacts, arrange meaningful introductions, and develop trust in personal and professional relationships. The more experience they have in China, the more likely they will develop a *guanxi* network that is extensive and of good quality. Foreigners need time to become familiar with local business practices and build networks. Dining with business associates serves a very important function. Chinese like to treat people to extravagant meals as a way to develop *guanxi*. Many business deals are negotiated and closed at the dinner table.

Lee Qiang, Chinese General Manager of DALI-Cola Joint Venture, offers this advice:

> When foreign investors first enter China, they need to get to know and develop *guanxi* with many people. It is important for them to identify the most useful *guanxi* from the complicated *guanxi* web. They have to focus their time, energy, and resources on further reinforcing these *guanxi* so they can benefit immediately from them.

Guanxi in Social Context

The Chinese culture provides a tightly knit social framework in which individuals are protective of one another and organizations safeguard their members' interests. It projects a preference for cooperation, group decision-making, and relationships. Thus, the importance of networks lies in their emphasis on collectivism and group harmony. Social status is determined largely by the *guanxi* system to which one belongs—a determination often preordained by the composite membership of one's extended family. The Chinese strive to keep relationships among *guanxi* members stable and harmonious because *guanxi* is the basis on which they exchange a lifetime of favors, resources, and business leverage.

> "Chinese like to treat people to extravagant meals as a way to develop guanxi. Many business deals are negotiated and closed at the dinner table."

Guanxi in the Legal Context

Guanxi is a key to resolving disputes and conflicts. The legal system in China is not well-developed and Chinese are not litigious. Although the country has enacted thousands of laws, rules, and regulations, they are rarely enforced in a consistent or comprehensive way. Justice in China is imposed less by courts than by appointed individuals who are in positions to make decisions.

In China, rules, regulations, and policies are open to interpretation by those who occupy positions of authority or power. Whereas Westerners depend on contractual law, Chinese use personal contacts and negotiations to resolve disputes. They believe this approach is a much more effective and efficient way to resolve disagreements and disputes than is the judicial system. Foreign investors accustomed to relationships based on legally enforceable contracts may not anticipate how legal matters can be put on hold almost indefinitely in the Chinese legal system. Yet, for better or worse, these same problems can be resolved quickly through friendly discussions and consultation if one has a well-developed *guanxi* network.

The Chinese partner who has *guanxi* with powerful people in the justice department and other government agencies can escape contractual commitments without retribution. When a deal sours, the courts in China generally offer little assurance to foreign partners. A Kimberly-Clark venture turned into a tale of legal frustration when its Chinese partner set up a rival firm to manufacture an identical product. The contract between the partners was not upheld after a multi-year legal entanglement.

Chinese managers and Western expatriates approach deal-making from different perspectives. Western executives are legalistic and contract-oriented; they feel comfortable with the certainty that enforceable commitments place on them and their partners. Commercial law is ingrained in Western thinking. In contrast, China's commercial law has historically been undeveloped, in part because its inclusion in negotiations is thought to be indicative of bad faith. Obligations from *guanxi* take precedence over contractual mandates.

Despite having a contract, McDonald's was forced to relocate in Beijing to accommodate real estate development by Hong Kong billionaire Li Ka Shing. Because of his strong *guanxi* with high-ranking officials in China, Shing successfully bought rights to property where McDonald's had been given permits to operate under a contract with the Beijing government. McDonald's ended up losing the legal battle, even though it was in full compliance under the contract.

Understanding the differences in business laws and practices between China and the West can help foreign expatriates gain perspective on the importance of *guanxi* in the legal context. Chinese laws and regulations are often purposely vague. They can change quickly and without warning, and are rarely enforced in a consistent or comprehensive way. Chinese executives therefore pay more attention to cultivating *guanxi* with policy-makers and enforcers to help ensure fair or favorable treatment than they do to creating legal advantage. Similarly, to protect their rights, foreign executives must both study the Chinese legal system and gain support from its laws' enforcers.

> "Major financial and economic resources are controlled by a relatively few power figures who can allocate resources with considerable personal discretion."

Guanxi in the Political Context

China's political foundation rests on the principle of public ownership. Top-down control by government agencies characterizes every aspect of business activity. So *guanxi* with government officials is often essential for business success.

The starting point for building social bridges is an in-depth understanding of how the government functions. As great as the need is to study and understand governmental policies, rules, and regulations, foreign investors need to understand the roles government officials play in China's economy. Hiring retired officials as consultants is a tactic foreign companies have adopted successfully to facilitate their company's orientation.

China is moving toward becoming a market-driven economy that allows decentralization. The government has relinquished its dominant role in managing firms as a result of this reform. However, bureaucrats retain control over resource distribution, bank loans, and business formations. Major financial and economic resources are controlled by a relatively few power figures who can allocate resources with considerable personal discretion. Firms thus have strong incentives to cultivate *guanxi* with those in power to provide opportunities and ensure fair, if not preferential, treatment.

The dark side of *guanxi* in the political context is corruption. Many bureaucrats in China are not well-paid. To supplement their income, they often use their power to help individuals or firms in their *guanxi* networks in exchange for monetary gifts. Thus, some Western executives think giving bribes is a quick way to establish *guanxi*. However, such an approach grossly overemphasizes the gift-giving element of *guanxi*. While a *quid pro quo* cash payment may facilitate a single business transaction, it creates neither friendship nor trust, two essential elements of *guanxi*. Further dulling the appeal of such a tactic, the Chinese government periodically initiates action to stem such corruption, and the penalties are severe for both the individuals and companies that get caught.

Establishing *guanxi* with the multilevel and fractionalized Chinese government is complicated. For example, selling valuable technology and equipment to government bodies or state enterprises in China requires possessing *guanxi* with more than just the end user. Approvals from local and provincial authorities are also commonly required, and decision-makers at every level have their own agendas and are free to interpret rules and regulations according to their own priorities. Making the decision process even more complicated is the fact that rules, tariffs, and policies change often, and with little warning. Thus, the smooth conduct of commerce often relies on *guanxi*. Network members can keep a vendor apprised of requirements and facilitate the movement of various paperwork through the approval system.

Foreign investors must understand that if they rely principally on rules and regulations to get things done, they may never be able to achieve their objectives. Wu Bing of the Pangtong Real Estate Joint Venture explains that "to get a business permit one usually has to go through at least ten officials and get ten stamps of approval on the application." Each of these approvals can be expedited by support from *guanxi* members.

There are few rigid deadlines on the government for making decisions. So without *guanxi*, the bureaucratic process of obtaining an approval can be painfully long. When a poorly connected executive inquires about an application status, officials often inform him that the matter is being discussed. Such discussions preclude decisions. A range of transparent excuses will be given if the applicant is persistent. However, if an individual has strong *guanxi* with a government official who is in a position to make decisions, the long and difficult process can be short-circuited. After many years as an executive in China, Wu Bing reports with a sense of accomplishment that he can now "make a phone call to his *guanxi* members in the government and get an application approved in a few days."

Firms that have strong *guanxi* with local governments can use their connections to bypass bureaucratic channels of the central government. Ho Zhu, General Manager of D&D Pharmaceuticals, was eager to enter the huge Chinese pharmaceutical market. However, the industry is tightly controlled by the Chinese Drug Administration of the central government. It is very difficult for foreign companies or private enterprises to obtain approval to sell their products in China because of strict government regulations. After numerous applications to and denials from the administration, D&D executives realized they would never be able to market their products in China if they followed the normal bureaucratic channels.

Ho Zhu was then introduced to the mayor of a small town. They socialized frequently and, over time, developed strong *guanxi*. The mayor helped D&D executives find a way to bypass the rules of the Chinese Drug Administration. Ho Zhu explains:

> He served as an intermediary for us in forming a partnership with the government-owned pharmaceutical company in his town, since such companies can obtain approval from the Drug Administration without scrutiny. This partnership allowed our products to be approved and sold in the Chinese market.

Local governments have been granted authority to approve projects with investments up to $30 million. They exercise control over resource distribution, investment size, construction permits, bank loans, and business formations. Local governments have the power to make operations easier for a company, or they can scrutinize a company into a state of paralysis. For example, local governments can impose energy and environmental assessments on any firm, at any time, and for any amount. Li Qiang, Chinese General Manager of the DALI-Cola Joint Venture, related his experience. At the early stage of the JV, DALI-Cola encountered many obstacles because its executives neglected to develop strong *guanxi* with officials in the local government. The officials in charge of issuing construction permits to DALI-Cola delayed construction for several months. Li Qiang recalls:

> Even after we broke ground, the local officials excessively scrutinized our quality control process and the construction was not able to move forward because they refused to authorize inspection approvals. As a result, we were not able to get our products to the market during the high season. Direct and indirect losses for our JV reached millions of dollars.

Foreign executives benefit when they understand the needs of the local government and establish a presence in the community. Local officials in many regions welcome foreign investors who are willing to contribute to the prosperity of their cities and towns. Investors who organize community activities and undertake goodwill projects, such as funding schools and renovating historical buildings, appeal to local officials and their constituencies. These efforts help companies establish *guanxi*. Executives also need to establish personal *guanxi* with top local officials who ultimately determine which companies can market products in their cities.

All nine of the Chinese business executives who participated in this research stressed the importance of developing *guanxi* with Chinese government officials. Understanding *guanxi* in the political context is an important step for expatriates. Public ownership and top-down control by government agencies continue to characterize business activity. *Guanxi* can help expatriates function within the bureaucratic system and ensure the smooth transaction of commerce.

The conduct of business differs strikingly between China and the West. Understandably, then, business success in China may be jeopardized if attention is not paid to its peoples' cultural preferences. Understanding the role of *guanxi* and how to develop and maintain it will help foreign executives adapt to and accommodate the differences.

Guanxi can be a source of frustration for expatriates who are not accustomed to developing close personal relationships with their customers and clients before conducting business. It also takes a great deal of time and energy for Western managers to maneuver among the complicated *guanxi* webs. Nevertheless, the energies put into developing *guanxi* are well invested. Even in China's new, dynamic business environment, *guanxi* retains its traditional position of prominence. According to Sunny Zhou, "Competition is intensifying in China. With limited resources and increasingly congested markets, companies are relying on their *guanxi* networks to survive."

Having recognized the vast market opportunities created by China's recent receptivity to foreign corporate investors, Western executives must now formulate and implement strategies for competing in China's distinctive cultural environment. Central to these strategic management efforts is the cultivation of strong *guanxi* networks, which are proving to be a critical correlate of success for Western companies in China. ❐

Notes

1. To ensure understanding in the survey, we used a double-translation methodology. We wish to thank Helen Deng for using her *guanxi* to develop the list of surveyed executives, as well as for her translations of their responses and her assistance in the initial stages of the project.

The executives who participated were A. Chou, Vice President of Alston, Inc.; Ho Zhu, General Manager of D&D Pharmaceutical; Li Qiang, Chinese General Manager of the DALI-Cola; Ms. Li Zhang, Public Relations Director of Yamei; Liu Jingming, Manufacturing Chief of Global Media, Inc.; Ming Xu, Vice President of Golden Enterprise, Inc.; Wang Li, Marketing Manager of the China Division of Sydney Australia; Wu Bing, General Manager of the Pangtong Real Estate Joint Venture; and Sunny Zhou, General Manager of Kunming Lida Wood and Bamboo Products.

References

L. Beamer, "Bridging Business Cultures," *The China Business Review*, May-June 1998, pp. 54-58.

M. Chen, "*Guanxi* and the Chinese Art of Network Building," *New Asia Review*, Summer 1994, pp. 40-43.

K. Hanes, "Divorce in China," *Global Finance*, 12, 4 (1998): 44-48.

B. Hendrischke, "China's Rural Entrepreneurs: Ten Case Studies," *Journal of Contemporary Asia*, 26, 4 (1996): 544-546.

Y. Luo, "Business Strategy, Market Structure, and Performance of International Joint Ventures: The Case of Joint Ventures in China," *Management International Review*, 35, 3 (1995): 241-264.

Y. Luo, "*Guanxi*: Principles, Philosophies, and Implications," *Human Systems Management*, 16, 1 (1997): 43-51.

Y. Luo, "*Guanxi* and Performance of Foreign-Invested Enterprises in China: An Empirical Inquiry," *Management International Review*, 37, 1 (1997): 51-70.

Y. Luo and M. Chen, "Financial Performance Comparison Between International Joint Ventures and Wholly Foreign-Owned Enterprises in China," *The International Executive*, 37, 6 (1995): 599-613.

D. Meyers, "Open for Business, World's Largest Market Offers Risks, Rewards," *Denver Post*, February 8, 1998, p. 1J.

J. Micklethwait, "The Search for the Asian Manager," *Economist*, March 9, 1996, Survey insert, pp. 3-5.

J.A. Pearce II, "Selecting Among Alternative Grand Strategies," *California Management Review*, Spring 1982, pp. 23-31.

D. Roberts, C. Power, and S. Forest, "Cheated in China?" *Business Week*, October 6, 1997, pp. 142-144.

E.W.K. Tsang, "Can *Guanxi* Be a Source of Sustained Competitive Advantage for Doing Business in China?" *Academy of Management Executive*, May 1998, pp. 64-73.

W. Vanhonacker, "Entering China: An Unconventional Approach," *Harvard Business Review*, March-April 1997, pp. 130-140.

I. Yeung and R. Tung, "Achieving Business Success in Confucian Societies: The Importance of *Guanxi*," *Organizational Dynamics*, Autumn 1996, pp. 54-65.

John A. Pearce II is a professor of management and holds the Endowed Chair in Strategic Management and Entrepreneurship at Villanova University, Villanova, Pennsylvania. **Richard B. Robinson, Jr.**, is a professor of entrepreneurship and strategic management at the University of South Carolina, Columbia.

[9]

Caveats for Cross-Border Negotiators

James K. Sebenius

Scholars and practitioners have detailed a number of ways that differences in national culture can affect bargaining behavior: from surface etiquette and protocol to deeper cultural characteristics and to systematic variations in decision making and governance. Such cross-national analysis can be quite useful but is prone to at least four hazardous fallacies described in this article and illustrated, in some cases, by probabilistic reasoning. Along with suggestions for avoiding them, these fallacies include: (1) "The John Wayne v. Charlie Chan Fallacy" (stereotyping); (2) "The Rosetta Stone Fallacy" (overattribution); (3) The Visual Flight Rules Fallacy (skewed perceptions and information processing); and (4) "St. Augustine's Fallacy" ("When in Rome...").

A virtual cottage industry has grown up in and around the academic community to analyze cross-border negotiations and provide culturally relevant advice to the involved parties.[1] Some authors (e.g., Axtell 1998) focus on gestures and body language. Others dissect systematic differences in surface etiquette, deportment, and protocol (e.g., Acuff 1993; Morrison, Conaway, and Borden 1994; or Leaptrott 1996). Others delve into deeper cultural characteristics that may give rise to more specific behaviors (e.g., Hall 1959; Hofstede 1984 and 1991; and Trompenaars and Hampden-Turner 1998). Still others probe differences in organizational decision processes and corporate governance across national borders to uncover their tight links to dealmaking practice (see Sebenius, 1998, 2001, and 2002). And finally, some scholars link current research to explicit frameworks for international negotiation (e.g., Brett 2001; Salacuse 1991; and Weiss 1994a and 1994b). These areas of focus overlap, but collectively form an impressive edifice touching major elements that distinguish cross-cultural negotiations from those that take place within the same culture.

While some of the work on culture and negotiation is at best superficial, much of the relevant academic literature is well grounded and accompanied by careful statements as to its limits and the conditions under which it should apply. While holding on to the truth that some characteristics do systematically vary across national borders, however, there is often a general uneasiness about unwarranted use of purported cross-cultural insight.

To help address this set of concerns, some years ago Frank Sander and the late Jeff Rubin wrote a brief and wise cautionary article in the *Negotiation Journal* entitled "Culture, Negotiation, and the Eye of the Beholder" (Rubin and Sander 1991). My purpose in this essay is to further their mission, in part by drawing on new insights, in part by using simple probabilistic examples to make certain points more precise, and in part by gathering their caveats and those of others from the many places they are now scattered into one place for useful reference. My objective is to make analysts and negotiators more sophisticated consumers of this advice by suggesting four classes of caveat, each with a slightly tongue-in-cheek name that will, I hope, be usefully evocative.

1. The John Wayne v. Charlie Chan Fallacy: Stereotyping National Cultures

Start with the obvious: All American negotiators are not like John Wayne and all Chinese negotiators are not like Charlie Chan. Or Bill Gates and Mao Zedong. Or Michael Jordan and Zhu Chen, the phenomenal women's world chess champion who recently also defeated the world men's champion. We also know that some negotiators in southeastern France may bear more resemblance to northern Italian negotiators than to their Parisian compatriots. Likewise, the culture of western Chinese Uighers is far more akin to neighbors in Pakistan than comrades in Beijing. On another front, what is distinctively "Canadian" when its citizens vary from francophone Québecois to traditional anglophone Torontonians and to transplanted Hong Kong tycoons now living in Vancouver? In the face of such internal variation, we wisely caution ourselves against mindless stereotyping by nationality (as well as by gender, religion, race, profession, or age). Even so, in many situations it remains all-too-common to hear offhand remarks such as "all Chinese negotiators..." (as well as generalizations about "women..." or "engineers"). To combat this, a strong version of the anti-stereotyping prescription calls for ignoring nationality altogether in preparing for negotiation.

That advice by itself is too strong. Nationality often does have a great deal to do with cultural characteristics, particularly in relatively homogeneous countries like Japan. The careful work of many researchers confirms significant associations between nationality and a range of traits and outcomes (see, e.g., Brett 2001 and Salacuse 1998). It would be foolish to throw away potentially valuable information. But what does information on a particular group's behavioral expectations or deeper cultural characteristics really convey? Typically, cultural descriptions are about *central tendencies* of populations that also exhibit considerable "within-group" variation. Suppose that a trait like "cooperativeness" (versus "competitiveness") is carefully measured by a psychological testing instrument for the citizens of Country X. The results will be a *distribution* with a few citizens rating highly cooperative, a few rating highly uncooperative, and the majority clustered around a more middle range.

Suppose that this distribution was a normal or bell-shaped curve with the most likely value equal to the mean of the distribution (see Figure One). Extremely homogeneous cultures would be characterized by a "tight" distribution around the mean; the greater the heterogeneity on the cooperative-competitive dimension, the more "spread out" the distribution would be.

Figure One
Cooperative and Competitive Negotiators of Country X

Less cooperative   *More cooperative*

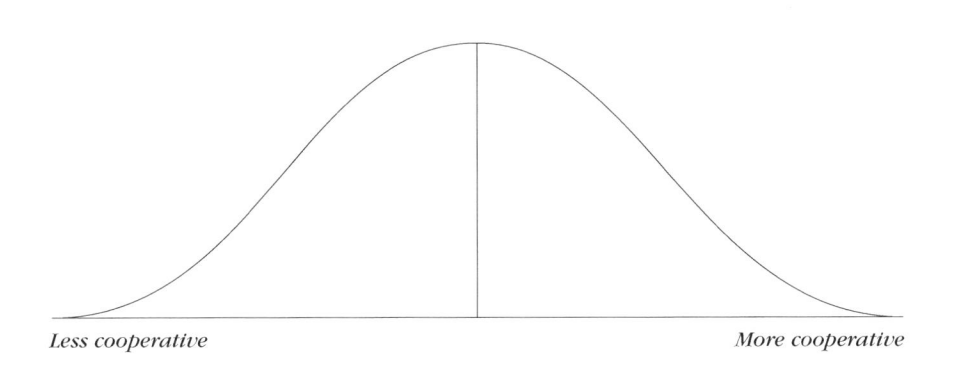

Figure One offers useful information that can, nonetheless, be easily misinterpreted. Social psychologists describe the "prototypicality error" or tendency to treat people from a given population group as if they would exhibit the group's most likely tendencies; that is, knowing that someone is from Country X, one naturally assumes that this person is about as cooperative as the mean or most likely point in that distribution. Yet a bit of statistical reasoning exposes some of the dangers of this common-sense approach. Take a randomly chosen citizen of Country X whose distribution of cooperativeness is accurately portrayed by Figure Two. Question: How likely is it that this randomly chosen citizen displays a level of cooperativeness somewhere within the range of 20 percentile points above or below the mean, which is the most probable description? (See Figure Two.) Answer: There is only a 40 percent chance that this person exhibits cooperativeness 20 percentile points above or below the most likely value for Country X. Equivalently, there is a 60 percent chance — more than even odds — that this person displays a level of cooperativeness *outside* this centrally representative, most likely, range.

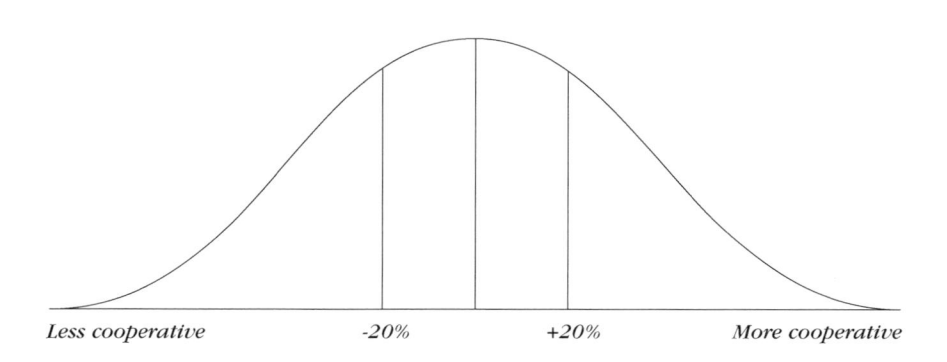

Figure Two
The Individual Country X Citizen

Less cooperative   -20%   +20%   More cooperative

This means that even the most likely trait for a population as described in Figure Two will not likely apply to a given individual from that group. Remember, you negotiate with individuals, not averages.

What does it actually mean for one culture to be, for example, more oriented to interdependence than another? Take for example the bell curves shown in Figure Three, gleaned from Hofstede's (1980) study, representing the independent vs. interdependent nature of Americans and Guatemalans. This chart[2] reflects that the average American is more independent-minded than the average Guatemalan. Yet both cultures exhibit a range of orientations, and there is considerable overlap between them.

Figure Three
Hypothetical Distributions of Independent/Interdependent Value Scores in an Individualist and a Collectivist National Culture

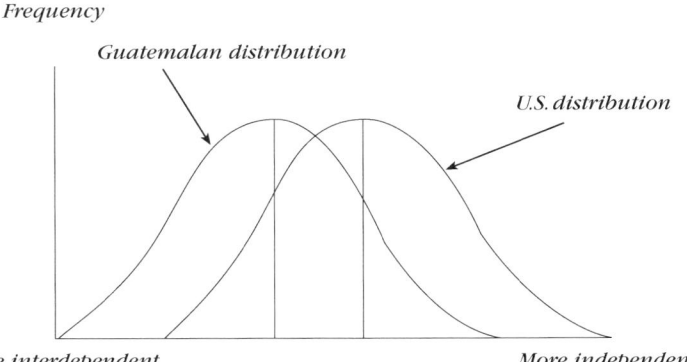

Frequency

Guatemalan distribution

U.S. distribution

More interdependent   *More independent*

Even though the central tendencies of two different national groups for given traits may systematically differ, correct inferences about how given individuals from the two countries compare can be quite tricky. Consider a second thought experiment comparing individuals from two countries, which we'll call COOP and COMPET. Say that, on average, citizens from COOP are twice as cooperative as those from COMPET. To make this more precise, suppose that we represent the two countries by a pair of dice, each with six sides. Say that a green side represents a cooperative personality while a red side represents a competitive one. Therefore, the die representing COOP has four green sides (and two red ones) while the COMPET die has four red sides (and two green ones). Thus to be from COOP is, on average, to be twice as likely to be cooperative as your COMPET counterpart.

Question: If a randomly chosen citizen from each country were going to negotiate, what are the odds that the citizen from COOP is more cooperative than the one from COMPET? This is equivalent to saying that you roll the dice and ask what the odds are that the COOP die ends up green while the COMPET die ends up red. Despite the overall likelihoods, and the fact that there are *twice* as many competitors in COMPET than in COOP, the answer is *"less than half"* (4/9 to be precise). To see this, remember that there are 36 possible combinations of reds and greens when two dice are rolled. The cases in which a COOP is strictly more cooperative than a COMPET correspond to the dice rolls in which COOP comes up green while COMPET is red. There are four green sides to the COOP die and four red sides to a COMPET die implying 4x4 (or 16) possible outcomes with a green COOP die and a red COMPET die. 16/36 (or 4/9) is, therefore, the right answer.

The broader point? Inferences about individuals from central tendencies are often misleading or wrong. *You negotiate with individuals, not averages.*

But viewing the world without the aid of stereotypes is difficult. Forming stereotypes is a natural reflex that helps order the overflow of information that barrages people. Social psychologist Ellen Langer (1989) argues that a solution to the negative effects of stereotyping is "mindfulness," which she defines as a willingness to create new categories, an openness to new information, and an awareness that more than one perspective exists. Rather than straining against forming stereotypes, a more realistic strategy is to allow stereotypes room to change, multiply, and adapt to new information.

In sum, remember that "national traits" — as well as traits supposedly associated with gender, ethnicity, etc. — are *distributions* of characteristics across populations, not blanket descriptions applicable to each individual. Be very cautious about making inferences about characteristics of specific individuals from different groups — even where the groups are, on average, sharply different. Avoid stereotyping and the "prototypicality" error of assuming an individual will exhibit the most likely group characteristic. Even if U.S. negotiators are on average more impatient, deal-focused, and individually oriented than their Chinese counterparts, be careful not to help amplify that stereotype in the mind of the other side. It is highly unlikely that many U.S.-Chinese negotiations will feature the equivalent of John Wayne pitted against Charlie Chan. Or Bill Gates against Mao Zedong. Or Michael Jordan against Zhu Chen.

2. The Rosetta Stone Fallacy: Overattribution to National Culture

National culture clearly matters. But there is a tendency to see it as the Rosetta Stone, the indispensable key to describe, explain, and predict the behavior of the other side. Of course there are many possible "cultures" operating within a given individual. Beyond her French citizenship, an ABB executive may well be from Alsace, have a Danish parent, feel staunchly European, have studied electrical engineering, and have earned an MBA from the University of Chicago. National culture can be highly visible but, obviously, it is only one of many possible influences. For example, Jeswald Salacuse (1998) surveyed executives from a dozen countries to determine national tendencies on ten important bargaining characteristics, such as negotiating goal (contract v. relationship), orientation (win-win v. win-lose), formality level, communication style, risk-taking, etc. While his results showed significant national differences, he also analyzed the data according to profession and occupations of the respondents such as law, engineering, marketing, the military, diplomacy, accounting, etc. These categories, too, showed systematic association with different bargaining styles. Finally, Salacuse could also differentiate many of these style characteristics by gender. Other extensive studies extend and elaborate analogous findings: Nationality often matters when considering someone's bargaining characteristics but so too does gender, ethnicity, functional specialty, etc.[3] Figure Four reminds us that national culture is but one of many "cultures" that can influence bargaining behavior.

**Figure Four
The Many "Cultures" that Influence Bargaining Behavior**

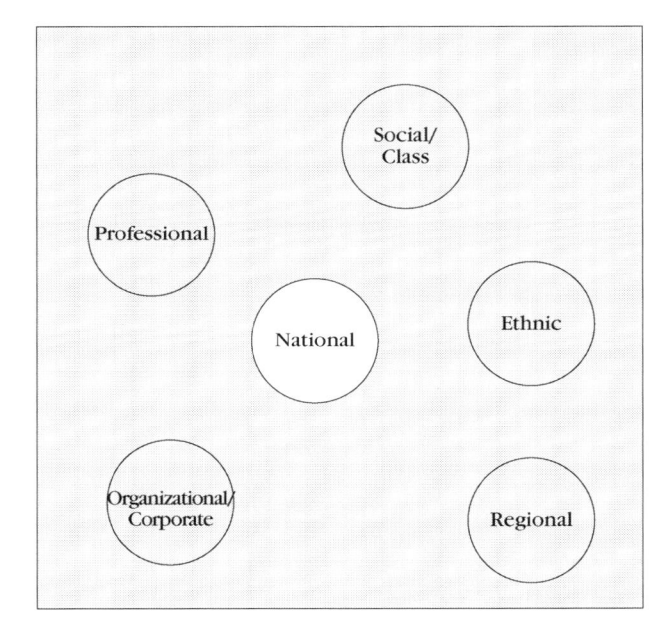

[Figure Four: Diagram showing circles labeled "Social/Class," "Professional," "National," "Ethnic," "Organizational/Corporate," and "Regional."]

Just as there are many cultures influencing bargaining behavior, there are many other potential contributing factors such as personality, finance, business fit, politics, and strategy. Figure Five makes this point graphically. In a study of the performance of a number of companies that had been acquired by "foreign" entities, Rosabeth Moss Kanter and Ian Corn (1994) carefully sought to account for post-acquisition outcomes. While business and technical factors were often determined to be the dominant factor, the first explanation advanced by managers of the target firms was "cultural."

**Figure Five
Other Factors Affecting Bargaining Behavior**

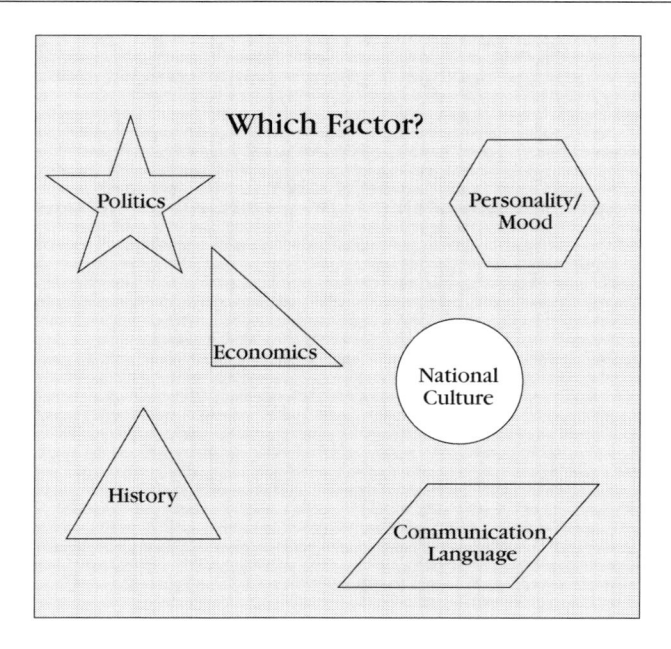

Which Factor?
- Politics
- Personality/Mood
- Economics
- National Culture
- History
- Communication, Language

Attribution bias. Cultural differences, often evident in surface behavior, are easy to see; richer contextual factors frequently are not. In unfamiliar cross-border settings, factors like strategic incompatibility, politics, or even individual personality are less likely to be "blamed" for undesirable outcomes. The powerful but unconscious tendency to overattribute behavior to culture, all too often clouds negotiators' vision of the full range of factors that can affect a negotiation (Gilbert and Malone 1995). Psychologists have extensively documented this dynamic, a systematic tendency to focus on supposed characteristics of the person on the other side of the table, rather than on the economic or other powerful contextual factors.[4] The antidotes? First, remember that "culture" doesn't just mean nationality; instead there are many potentially influential "cultures" at work. Second, beyond "culture" are many other factors that have potential to affect negotiation behavior. Nationality can carry important information, but with many other cultures and many other factors at work, you should be careful not to treat your counterpart's passport as the Rosetta Stone.

3. The "Visual Flying Rules" at Night Fallacy: Falling Prey to Potent Psychological Biases

Just as trying to pilot by "visual flight rules" (VFR) at night or in a storm is hazardous, the psychology of cross-cultural perception can be treacherous. Beware the witches' brew of biases and psychological dynamics that can bubble up when one begins to label "other" groups, attribute characteristics to them, and act on these perceptions.

Self-serving perceptions of our own side. There is a powerful tendency, formally studied as "biased assimilation," for people to interpret information in negotiation self-servingly (see Robinson 1997a). For example, experimenters give a number of people identical information about a pending court case but randomly assign them to the role of plaintiff or defendant. When each person is asked for his or her private assessment of the probability that the plaintiff will win, those assigned the role of plaintiff on average give much higher odds than those (randomly) assigned to the role of defendant (but, again, on the basis of *identical* information). People tend to "believe their own lines" or self-servingly interpret information. Similar results have been found for corporate valuation results — done on the basis of the same data — by randomly assigned buyers and sellers. And this tendency runs deep: Back in the 1950s, researchers[5] conducted an experiment at a boy's camp, sponsoring a jelly bean hunt among the campers. After the hunt, the boys were shown an identical picture of a jar of jelly beans. Each boy evaluated the total number of beans in the jar according to whether he was told the jar belonged to his own team or to the other side. The same photograph was estimated to contain many more beans when it was presented as "your team's" and far fewer when it was alleged to be the "other side's."

Partisan perceptions of the other side. If our capacity to process information critical of our own side is flawed, it is even more the case for our assessments of the other side in a conflict or negotiation. In part, this stems from the in-group/out-group phenomenon.[6] Persons from different cultures, especially on the opposite side of the bargaining table, are more readily identified as belonging to an out-group, or the *Other*. Once that labeling is in place, powerful perceptual dynamics kick in (beyond the tendencies toward stereotyping and overattribution). Robert Robinson (1997b:2) describes extensive research over the last 40 years, documenting an unconscious mechanism that enhances "one's own side, portraying it as more talented, honest, and morally upright" while simultaneous vilifying the *Other*. This leads to a systematic exaggeration of the other side's position and an overestimation of the extent of the actual conflict. As a result, negotiators are often unduly pessimistic about their ability to find common ground, and can be unwilling to pursue it (Robinson et al. 1995: 416).

Self-fulfilling prophesies. Such partisan perceptions hold the power to change reality by becoming self-fulfilling prophesies. The effects of labeling and stereotyping have been documented thoroughly to show that perceptions have the power to shape reality. Experiments testing the effects of teachers' expectations of students; diagnoses on mental patients; and platoon leaders' expectations of their trainees are only a few of many studies confirming that expectations prod behavior.[7] At the negotiating table, the same principle holds true: clinging firmly to the idea that one's counterpart is stubborn, for example, is likely to yield intransigence on both sides, precluding the possibility of a compromise that might have occurred had the label of "obstinacy" not been so rigorously affixed (see Rubin and Sander 1991).

In short, just as a pilot trying to navigate by visual flight rules at night or in a storm is prone to dangerous misjudgments, the psychology of perception in cross-cultural situations is rife with biases. Not only do we stereotype and overattribute to nationality, we are also poor at interpreting information on our own situation, vulnerable to partisan perceptions of the other side, and likely to act in ways that become dangerously self-fulfilling.

4. St. Augustine's Fallacy: "When in Rome..."

Assume that you have undertaken a full analysis of the culture of the person you will meet on the other side of the bargaining table. St. Augustine gave the classic cross-cultural advice: When in Rome, do as the Romans do. While this admonition certainly has merit, it is not always good advice. Steven Weiss (1994a and 1994b) has extensively developed the point that much better options may be available. For example, learning that the Chinese, on average, are more hesitant than North Americans to take risks is only a first step. Clearly, a responsive strategy would not mimic this hesitancy, but effectively anticipate it.

Rather than learning to behave as the Romans do (while in Rome or elsewhere), strategies should accommodate the degree of cross-table understanding each side has of the other. For example, consider the best approach for a U.S. manager on his first visit to Japan dealing with a Yale-educated Japanese executive who has worked extensively in Europe and North America. Here it would be sensible to let the Japanese take the lead. If a negotiator is far more familiar with a counterpart's culture than vice versa, the best strategy might be to embrace the counterpart's negotiating "script." If both sides are equally "literate," an improvisational and mutually-accommodating approach might be most appropriate. A lower degree of familiarity dictates bringing in locally familiar expertise, perhaps on your side and perhaps even as a mediator (Weiss 1994a: 54).

A great deal depends on how familiar you are with "Roman" culture and how familiar your "Roman" counterpart is with your culture. And of course you want to avoid the previous fallacies as well. The nationalities across the table from each other may be Chinese and U.S., but both players may be regulars on the international business circuit, which has its own, increasingly global negotiating culture. Again, assess — etiquette, deeper traits, negotiation-specific expectations, and caveats; do not assume and project your assumption onto your counterpart.

In Conclusion

Cross-cultural negotiation analyses offer insight as to systematic differences in gestures and body language, etiquette and deportment, deeper behavioral traits, as well as organizational decision-making processes and forms of corporate and public governance. Accurately applying the very real insights from such studies can be challenging, but the difficulties perhaps lessened by thinking of four unlikely categories that themselves derive from cultures most dissimilar: John Wayne and Charlie Chan, the Rosetta Stone, VFR at night, and St. Augustine.

NOTES

I would like to acknowledge the energetic and insightful research assistance of Rebecca Hulse and Ron Fortgang as well as the useful suggestions of David Lax, Guhan Subramanian, and Rob Robinson. This essay was adapted from part of my Harvard Business School Working Paper, "Assess, Don't Assume, Part I: Etiquette and National Culture," August 2001.

1. Standards in this field include Edward Hall's (1960) *Harvard Business Review* essay, "The Silent Language of Oversees Business" and his (1959) book of the same name, as well as Edward Hall and Mildred Reed Hall's (1990) book, *Understanding Cultural Differences*. Major empirical survey studies by Geert Hofstede have become staples of this area, including Hofstede (1984 and 1991) and Hofstede and Usunier (1996). A particularly well-presented, recent survey book is by Fons Trompenaars and Charles Hampden-Turner (1998), *Riding the Waves of Culture*. Theoretically-focused works include Janosik (1991) and Faure and Rubin (1993). Several excellent, practice-oriented sources on negotiation include Jeswald Salacuse's (1991) book, *Making Global Deals*; Jeanne Brett's (2001) book, *Negotiating Globally*; Raymond Cohen's (1991) book *Negotiating Across Cultures*; and two *Sloan Management Review* essays by Stephen Weiss (1994a and 1994b). A large number of books and articles targeting specific countries or regions exist; very nice examples include Hodgson, Sano, and Graham (2000) and Chen (2001).

2. Based on Smith and Bond (1993: 41). This graph is only indicative, not precise.

3. See, for example, Chapter 15 of Fons Trompenaars and Charles Hampden-Turner's (1998) book, *Riding the Waves of Culture*.

4. Discussed in Rubin and Sander (1991).

5. Sherif and Sherif (1953), as cited by Rubin, Pruitt, and Kim (1994: 103).

6. For more in-depth explanation see Tajfel (1982) and Howard and Rothbart (1980).

7. E.g., see Rubin, Pruitt, and Kim 1994: 100-101; Rosenthaul and Jacobson 1968; Rosenhan 1979; and Eden 1990.

REFERENCES

Acuff, F. 1993. *How to negotiate anything with anyone anywhere in the world.* New York: American Management Association.

Axtell, R. 1998. *Gestures: The do's and taboos of body language around the world.* New York: John Wiley & Sons.

Brett, J. M. 2001. *Negotiating globally: How to negotiate deals, resolve disputes, and make decisions across cultural boundaries.* San Francisco: Jossey-Bass.

Chen, M-J. 2001. *Inside Chinese business.* Boston: Harvard Business School Press.

Cohen, R. 1991. *Negotiating across cultures.* Washington: U.S. Institute of Peace Press.

Eden, D. 1990. Pygmalion without interpersonal contrast effects: Whole groups gain from raising manager expectations. *Journal of Applied Psychology* 75(4): 394-398.

Faure, G.O. and J. Z. Rubin, eds. 1993. *Culture and negotiation: The resolution of water disputes.* Newbury Park, Calif.: Sage Publications.

Gilbert, D.T. and P.S. Malone. 1995. The correspondence bias. *Psychological Bulletin* 117(1): 30.

Hall, Edward T., 1959. *The silent language.* New York: Doubleday & Co.

———. 1960. The silent language of oversees business. *Harvard Business Review* 38, no. 3 (May-June): 87-96.

Hall, E.T. and M. R. Hall. 1990. *Understanding cultural differences.* Yarmouth, Maine: Intercultural Press.

Hodgson, J.D., Y. Sano, and J.L. Graham. 2000. *Doing business with the new Japan.* London and Lanham, Md.: Rowman & Littlefield.

Hofstede, G. 1984. *Culture's consequences: International differences in work-related values.* London: Sage Publications.

———. 1991. *Cultures and organizations: Software of the mind.* London: McGraw-Hill.

Hofstede, G. and J-C. Usunier. 1996. Hofstede's dimensions of culture and their influence on international business negotiations. In *International business negotiations*, edited by P. Ghauri and J-C. Usunier. Oxford: Pergamon.

Howard, J. W. and M. Rothbart. 1980. Social categorization and memory for in-group and out-group behavior. *Journal of Personality and Social Psychology* 38(2): 301-310.

Janosik, R. J. 1991. Rethinking the culture-negotiation link. In *Negotiation theory and practice*, edited by J. W. Breslin and J.Z. Rubin. Cambridge, Mass.: PON Books (The Program on Negotiation at Harvard Law School).

Kanter, R.M. and R.I. Corn. 1994. Do cultural differences make a business difference?: Contextual factors affecting cross-cultural relationship success. *Journal of Management Development* 13(2): 5-23.

Langer, E. 1989. *Mindfulness.* Reading, Mass.: Addison-Wesley.

Leaptrott, N. 1996. *Rules of the game: Global business protocol.* Cincinnati: Thomson Executive Press.

Morrison, T., W.A. Conaway; and G. A. Borden. 1994. *Kiss, bow, or shake hands: How to do business in sixty countries.* Holbrook, Mass.: Adams Media Corporation.

Robinson, R.J. 1997a. Errors in social judgement: Implications for negotiation and conflict resolution. Part I: Biased assimilation of information. Harvard Business School.

———. 1997b. Errors in social judgement: Implications for negotiation and conflict resolution. Part II: Partisan perceptions. Harvard Business School.

Robinson, R.J., A. Ward, L. Ross, and D. Keltner. 1995. Actual versus assumed differences in construal: "Naive realism" in intergroup perception and conflict. *Journal of Personality and Social Psychology* 68(3): 416.

Rosenhan, D.L. 1979. On being sane in insane places. *Science* 179: 250-258.

Rosenthaul, R. and L.F. Jacobson. 1968. *Pygmalion in the classroom.* New York: Holt, Rinehart & Winston.

Rubin, J. Z., D.G. Pruitt, and S.H. Kim. 1994. *Social conflict: Escalation, stalemate, and settlement.* New York: McGraw Hill.

Rubin, J. Z. and F.E.A. Sander. 1991. Culture, negotiation, and the eye of the beholder. *Negotiation Journal* 7(3): 249-254.

Salacuse, J.W. 1991. *Making global deals: What every executive should know about negotiating abroad.* New York: Times Business, Random House.

———. 1998. Ten ways that culture affects negotiation: Survey results. *Negotiation Journal* 14(3): 221-240.

Sebenius, J.K. 1998. Negotiating cross-border acquisitions. *Sloan Management Review* 39(2): 27-41.

———. 2001. Assess, don't assume, part II: Decision making, corporate governance, and political economy. Harvard Business School Working Paper, August 2001.

———. 2002. The hidden challenge of cross-border negotiations. *Harvard Business Review* March: 76-85.

Sherif, M and C.W. Sherif. 1953. *Groups in harmony and tension*. New York: Harper & Row.

Smith, P.B. and M.H.Bond. 1993. *Social psychology across cultures: Analysis and perspectives*. New York: Harvester Wheatsheaf..

Tajfel, H. 1982. Social psychology of intergroup relations. *Annual Review of Psychology* 33: 1-39.

Trompenaars, F. and C. Hampden-Turner. 1998. *Riding the waves of culture*. New York: McGraw-Hill.

Weiss, S.E. 1994a. Negotiating with the Romans, Part I. *Sloan Management Review* 35(2): 51-61.

———. 1994b. Negotiating with the Romans, Part II. *Sloan Management Review* 35(3): 85-99.

[10]

The Norms and Incentive Structures of Relational Contracting in Vietnam – Two Surveys

Quan H Nguyen[*]

Economists have often stated that, without adequate systems of contract law, an economy will be unable to flourish. This assumption has been challenged by legal realists, who contend that contract law may not be the only way to ensure promises are kept. This article examines this assumption through the perspective of business and contract practices in Vietnam. This is done through in-depth interviews and case studies of the interactions of business, human relationships and the law in the market. The article first sets out the different types of participants involved in this study and their professional, ethnic and social backgrounds. Second, the protocol used in interviews is explained. Third, the data from the interviews is analysed and an explanation for certain behaviours of participants in contracting and business practices is offered. Fourth, the article examines how participants view certain contractual concepts, including the contract itself, negotiation, performance and enforcement. Finally, the article looks at McMillan and Woodruff's previous scholarship on mapping contractual behaviour in Vietnam. It critiques the iterative game theory hypothesis of relational contracts, arguing that it is institutional social norms, rather than the nature of persons, which determine contractual behaviour.

Since the early 20th century, legal realists have questioned whether contract law is more powerful than social norms in regulating contracts (Llewellyn, 1931). More recently, challenges to the relevance of contract law to real-life contracts have been increasing in number and have emanated from a wider base of literature that now includes contract law in action, relational contract theory and law, and economic analysis of contract law.[1] In 1974, Grant Gilmore, a professor of contract at Yale Law School, published a book in which he declared the death of what is now called 'classical contract law'. Although contract law continues to be a core subject for undergraduate law students in law schools, contract law scholars have not provided satisfactory theoretical foundations for contract law in regulating real life contracts (Scott, 2004).

This article provides an empirical account of how merchants arrange their contractual relationships in the Vietnamese market and how real-life contractual arrangements respond to contract law reform modelled after contract laws of developed market economies. Drawing on two surveys of contract practice in the Vietnamese market, one conducted by

McMillan and Woodruff in 1995-97 and the other by myself during field trips in 2003-04, I argue that the governance structures of real-life contractual arrangements in the Vietnamese market are very much determined by institutional structures of the market. Contract behaviour is a kind of social behaviour and can be shaped by social institutions in the market as much as, if not more than, contract law and the court system.

My study confirms the contract law-in-action hypothesis, but amends this hypothesis to stress the role of social structures within the market in shaping contract behaviour.

My Survey

An inquiry into the nexus between contract law reform and real-life contractual arrangements in the Vietnamese market is necessary to understand how local merchants contract and resolve their contractual disputes. I pursued this inquiry by a survey of contract behaviour and employed a sociological approach, in which law is considered a 'social factor' that is influenced by 'the interactions, motivations and beliefs' of the members in the society (Cotterrell, 1992: 11). There were several reasons for selecting such an approach. First, a key objective of this project was to gain an in-depth understanding of contract practices in Vietnam. A socio-legal perspective provides an effective means of explaining the institutional structures that give rise to the social phenomena studied (Cotterrell, 1992: 11). Second, case studies can provide an enhanced understanding and explanatory insights into a particular inquiry, which, in this case, is the contract law-in-action hypothesis (Babbie, 2001). Another strength of case studies is that they provide examples of 'real people in real situations' (Cohen, Manion & Morrison, 2000: 181). Investigating the questions raised by this research through these means enables the exploration of the complex interactions of business norms, human relationships and the law in the particular context of contract governance. This enables an empirical picture to be formed of the role of contract law in real life contractual arrangements (Macaulay, 1963; Cohen, Manion and Morrison, 2000).

The Sample

Participants in the study operated in many different industries, but all had a history of at least four years in their current business at the time of the interview, and had therefore accumulated experience in entering certain kinds of contracts in the area of their business.

The majority of them were business-owners or the main shareholders in their businesses. All of them were at managerial levels of firms with full responsibility for contracting with their firm's clients. The merchants surveyed were categorised into four groups: Vietnamese merchants operating in Vietnam; ethnic Chinese merchants operating in Vietnam; Vietnamese merchants operating in Cambodia; and foreign merchants operating in Vietnam.

Ho Chi Minh City was chosen as the location of the interviews because the city is usually referred to as the most dynamic hub in the Vietnamese economy (Gainsborough, 2003). Surveyed merchants in Ho Chi Minh City were exposed to complex transactional structures in manufacturing and service industries. Can Tho City, although not as dynamic an economic hub as Ho Chi Minh City, offered a traditional manufacturing and trading centre in the Mekong Delta, together with established business communities of Vietnamese and ethnic Chinese groups to study. Phnom Penh was selected as a comparative market place where a contract law system virtually does not exist.

The ethnic Chinese merchants make up a surveyed group because they are usually described as loyal to their traditional business ethics and institutions (Redding, 1990; Reid, 1993). Ethnic Chinese merchants generally have strong reliance on their ethnic group in developing client bases, procuring credits and resolving disputes. Strong family structures maintain their way of life, by upholding their traditional philosophies about life, business, and medicine. Surveyed merchants in this group were from the Chaozhu and Cantonese language groups, which are the two most populous ethnic Chinese groups in Vietnam (Barton, 1983).[2]

Vietnamese merchants doing business in Phnom Penh made up a surveyed group, because, as mentioned, they did business in a market virtually without a contract law system at the time of the survey. Some of them are local traders of Vietnamese origin who have retail networks in Cambodia. Many still have relatives in Vietnam and travel back and forth between the two countries for holidays and businesses. Trade representatives of Vietnamese manufacturers in Cambodia are generally staff members of the firm assigned to act as the wholesaler of the company's products within the Cambodian market. Vietnamese merchants doing business in Phnom Penh were asked to comment on their contract practice in Phnom Penh, compared with their contract practice back in Vietnam.

Three foreign merchants were selected as a comparative group to highlight differences between Vietnamese and other (Western) contract practice, at least anecdotally. One of these merchants came from Western Europe, the other two from Australia, where formal contract law systems are well developed compared with the contract law system in Vietnam. The merchants worked at managerial levels for transnational companies in Vietnam and two of them had set up their own businesses in Vietnam.

All had worked, or had been doing business, in Vietnam for more than 10 years. Most of their contracting was with local merchants, but before coming to Vietnam they received education and business training in Europe and Australia. They had also acquired business experience in Europe or Australia before going to Vietnam. Their backgrounds allow them to comment on contract practice in the Vietnamese market by comparing it with the contract practice experienced in Europe and Australia. They were therefore interviewed in order to gain an 'outsiders' view' of the characteristics of contract practice of local merchants.

Interviews

The interviews in this study were conducted on the basis of a protocol. An interview pro-forma served as a guideline to establish the direction of the dialogue and assisted in ensuring the consistency and objectivity of the conduct of the interviews. The interviews were conducted in a conversational manner and care was taken to undertake the interview as smoothly and naturally as possible, to reduce respondents' inhibitions (Babbie, 2001). Follow-up questions were posed on the basis of responses to previous questions, providing flexibility and space for both the interviewer and the interviewee to discuss the questions and answers and to ensure effective communication. Some interviews lasted about 20 minutes, but most lasted for more than half an hour. Some interviewees were interested in the questions and were willing to explain more about their contractual arrangements. The focus of the interviews was the contracting practice of local firms and possible influences on the structures of their business relationships, given the unattractiveness of the court process as a mechanism to resolve commercial disputes. The interviews sought to elicit the strategies used by merchants in their contract governance and the rationale for their use.

Thirty-two in-depth interviews were conducted with local merchants during my two field trips during 2003-04. Single interview sessions were undertaken with each participating merchant and were conducted individually. The participants were introduced to me through business networks with which I have contact, beginning with my friends who are now doing business in Ho Chi Minh City and Can Tho. I also approached persons not previously known to me at social gatherings of business people. Most local merchants I approached at business gatherings declined my invitation to take part in my research. Some merchants who had received education in Western countries were, however, interested in my research and agreed to participate.

I was introduced to one foreign merchant in Ho Chi Minh City by one of my relations who was a business partner with that merchant. Another foreign participant was introduced to me by an academic colleague during that participant's short trip back home in Australia. That merchant then introduced me to another merchant in Melbourne. They had met each other while doing business in Vietnam. All interviewees explicitly consented to be interviewed after I had explained to them the purpose of the interview. Most of the interviews were tape-recorded with the interviewees' consent, but some participants refused to have their conversations recorded. Those interviews were recorded exclusively in the form of field notes.

Data Analysis

The data from interviews covered a wide range of contract types including:

- material supply contracts between manufacturers and material suppliers to plan input for production (Merchants 1, 6, 7, 8 and 10);
- distributorship contracts between manufacturers and wholesalers to plan production output and financial issues (Merchants 1, 8 and 10);
- service contracts between service providers and service users to provide a one-off job, or an ongoing consulting service (Merchants 2, 4 and 16);
- sale of real estate contracts between real estate investors and households (Merchant 8);
- agricultural contracts between fertilizer, insecticide and agricultural machinery traders and farmers, which usually require the trader to sell fertilizers, insecticides and other agricultural machineries to farmers on credit – payments are usually collected by the end of the harvest, sometimes in the products harvested (Merchants 6 and 9);
- principal-agent contracts between principals and agents to perform a specific task, such as marketing a product (Merchants 2 and 4);
- trade agency contracts between wholesalers and retailers to plan the supply of a product during a certain period (Merchants 9, 10, 11, 12, 13, 14 and 15).

Across the spectrum of relational contract theory, these contract types vary from one-off, discrete, impersonal contracts to those heavily reliant on a relationship history (Macneil, 1978). According to my observations and interviews with local merchants in the Vietnamese market, sales of real estate contracts are usually negotiated between strangers. A buyer reads a classified advertisement offering a house for sale in a newspaper, calls the seller for an appointment to inspect the house and negotiates the price. If agreement is struck, full payment is usually made in a few weeks. The buyer and the seller do not rely on either past or future relations once the consideration is paid in full. Hence, contracts for sale of real estate commonly take the form of discrete contracts.

Distributorship contracts and agricultural contracts, however, are usually reliant on past and future relations between the contractors. A manufacturer usually tests a wholesaler's sales volume and credit worthiness over a period of time before entering a distributorship contract, as the whole production chain may be geared to or be dependent on the wholesaler's sale volume. In addition, the manufacturer may need to extend extensive credit to the wholesaler for marketing and promotion of a new product. There may also be arrangements on after-sale services that require ongoing cooperation between the manufacturer and the wholesaler.

In agricultural contracts, the trader usually sells fertilizer, insecticide, and agricultural machinery to farmers on credit. The ability to collect debts from farmers very much depends on ongoing cooperation between the trader and the farmer throughout the season. This may be influenced by unpredictable variables such as changes in the weather which may require on-time supply of additional fertilizer or insecticide to rescue the harvest. In the event of a poor harvest, the ability of the trader to call-in debts depends on the ongoing relationship with the farmer, whereas credit is extended during lean periods and recouped during bountiful seasons.

My data analysis is followed by an institutional approach, which postulates that the structure of formal and informal institutions influence the way humans interact in efforts to maximise their wealth (North, 1997). Creating contracts is one of the key means for humans to maximise their wealth and the formal institutions for forming contracts are contract law and the processes of the court. Contract law and court processes influence contract practice, especially through reducing transaction costs. The court is a legal institution and legal institutions are designed to reduce the transaction costs of enforcing contracts. This institutional approach assumes that merchants respond to legal institutions of the market in ways that maximise their self-interest (Korobkin, 2004). Merchants maximise their self-interest by designing their contractual relationship in such a way that maximises their expected value from the transaction. In this sense, relational contracting is a practice that arguably maximises the expected value of a business transaction by minimising the transaction costs of the market.

An Institutional View of Relational Contracts

In August 2004, Thai Vinh Truong (the fabric tycoon of Soai Kinh Lam textile and fabric market in Ho Chi Minh City) disappeared, leaving behind debts from unexecuted contracts to the value of USD $5 million (Anh, 2004). Most of these debts were advances from corporate and individual fabric wholesalers in Ho Chi Minh City to Kim Vien (Truong's company) for fabric shipment imports.

According to local newspapers, most individual and corporate fabric wholesalers in Soai Kinh Lam market (the largest wholesale market of fabric in Southern Vietnam) bought fabric from Kim Vien (Anh, 2004). Truong's clients also included many big state-owned enterprises in the textile and fabric industry, which relied on the tycoon for large volume and reliable supplies of fabric. According to several newspaper reports, few of Truong's clients had written contracts to prove their transactions with Kim Vien or their ownership of fabric left in Kim Vien's warehouses, with the exception of some handwritten receipts issued by Truong's two brothers, who assisted Truong in the family business. Some buyers reported to the police that they had negotiated transactions valued up to a million US dollars on the telephone or orally during face-to-face meetings, which were evidenced only by handwritten notes of money received.

Kim Vien is neither the first, nor probably the last, case where local merchants relying on relational institutions in the market to safeguard even high-value transactions are exploited by rogue merchants. Similar cases include the Toan Gia Phuc and Ngoc Loan supermarkets in 1998, when the owners of these markets simply disappeared. These cases predictably shook local business communities and the lack of contractual evidence presented insurmountable obstacles for many creditors seeking remedies from the court (Doanh & Luat, 1998: 10). These cases reveal the risks attached to the common practice in Vietnam of undocumented relational contracting by the local business community, which may exclude the safeguards afforded by the contract law and court systems. They also raise questions of how local merchants enter and execute contractual arrangements in real-life business and what they do to secure these transactions.

What do 'Contracts' Mean to Local Merchants?

The concept of a contract under the law contains four basic elements: an offer, an acceptance, an intention to create a binding agreement and the payment of consideration. In textbooks, these concepts are commonly characterised in a more formal way: 'an agreement which is either enforced by law or recognized by law as affecting the legal rights or duties of the parties' (Treitel, 1979: 1). This legal conceptualisation of 'contracts' suggests a formal structure of property rights and obligations, voluntarily created by contracting parties according to prescribed procedures, formalities and conditions to govern their exchange relations, and which is legally enforceable by the state under a more encompassing contract type – the social contract (Hart, 1961; Hobbes, 2002).

One key issue to be investigated in this research is the very real possibility that the concept of contract in real-life exchange relations in the Vietnamese market may not conform to this model. The research for this thesis undertaken in Vietnam indicated a common attitude among surveyed merchants that requesting a detailed contract reflected a lack of trust between business partners. When surveyed merchants were asked whether they used contracts for everyday business transactions, a common response was: 'Well, people here don't usually need contracts to do business'. The reason for this common attitude, as one merchant further explained, is that 'trust is the most important. If you trust someone, you don't need contracts to do business with that person' (Merchant 4).

What can we conclude from this response? When merchants transact on the basis of trust, negotiating a contract becomes a redundant activity (Williamson, 1985).[3] Beyond this, negotiating a contract may even jeopardise business activity because many local merchants may refuse to do business with someone who insists on formal contracting. A merchant who runs a business consultant company in Ho Chi Minh City remarked: 'Here people don't like contracts. If you show them a carefully drafted contract, they may not do business with you' (Merchant 4). This perspective strongly suggests that the creation of a structure of legal rights and obligations based on formal contracts is not a popular practice for contracting in this market.

During a lunch with a group of young entrepreneurs in Ho Chi Minh City, the researcher asked the CEO of a private telecommunications company whether he preferred formal contracting or trust-based business deals. The CEO, who had extensive business experience in multinational Western companies,[4] responded that the choice between formal contracting and trust-based business dealing was one of his daily headaches (Merchant 24). He related that one of his staff was a dynamic ethnic Chinese-Vietnamese executive, who had created a number of key business opportunities for the firm but relied heavily on personal relations to seek assurance for the firm's investments. These business opportunities arose largely through the executive's networks within the Chinese community, who are traditionally averse to formal contracting and enforcement procedures. The CEO faced a dilemma as to whether the company's resources should be invested in trust-based business deals or whether to insist on written formal contracts that would increase the CEO's ability to manage the risks of non-performance, but would do so at the risk of upsetting Chinese clients and potentially jeopardising the deals.

The CEO admitted that he was personally more comfortable with the practice of written formal contracts, to which he had grown accustomed while working for multinational corporations. Business for multinational corporations can, however, be easily distinguished from local trade, as large transnational corporations often have the position and market power to demand that their local clients follow their ways of contracting that fit their organisational structures and transactional disciplines. The CEO further related that, in running a private company that mainly deals with local businesses, it is difficult for him to reject the relational contract practice which is so dominant in the local market (Merchant 24). As suggested in this entrepreneur's story, relational business dealings therefore appear to be the mainstay of daily contracting between local merchants.

For those foreign to local social norms that govern local contractual behaviour, local merchants may appear to be inefficient and overly casual in their contract practice. One common criticism of local merchants by Western merchants in Vietnam is that they operate as a 'closed shop', sometimes refusing to deal with a stranger despite the stranger offering a profitable business deal (McMillan and Woodruff, 1999a: 1315).[5] 'I met some local merchants who would clearly have a lot of benefit from doing business with us. But the way they behave makes us think that they want to chase us away', a European furniture importer in Ho Chi Minh City complained (Merchant 20). His comments highlight how local contracting practices have a tendency to prioritise the development of locally based/familiar relationships even over profits, operating as a constraint on the 'free' operation of the market.

Looking more deeply into the rationale for prioritising relationships in contracting, many local merchants feel the risks of doing business with a stranger, considered an unknown quantity, may outweigh the potential profits as they are not comfortable using formal institutions to support their contracts. One local manager said he would visit his customers to investigate not only their financial capacity, but also their personality (McMillan and Woodruff, 1999a). A pre-existing personal relationship allows both parties to identify the internalised norms or codes of conduct of each other in their contractual behaviours with regard to facilitating, planning and cooperation – making future exchanges between the two parties more predictable and, therefore, more desirable. The potential to build a long-term relationship is considered a prerequisite for the bonds necessary to achieve good contracting behaviour. Finite resources are concentrated on building long-term relationships, at the expense of short-lived business opportunities.

While Vietnamese merchants are generally averse to formal contracting, some surveyed merchants were aware of how they could use contract law and the enforcement mechanisms offered by courts as tactics in contract governance (Merchants 2 and 5). Two surveyed merchants had actually lodged complaints with the courts to pressure their clients to pay debts when negotiation processes had been exhausted. One was the head of the legal department of a large state-owned enterprise, the other the director of a door-to-door logistics company. It is interesting to note that, in the second case, almost all clients of the logistics company were foreigners moving in and out of the country who needed the company's services to move their belongings. Perhaps in this market, an adversarial reputation may not be as negative for the company's image as it is in a market where clients are local merchants.

The research indicated that ethnic Chinese merchants are more averse to formal contracting than their Vietnamese counterparts. All the ethnic Chinese merchants interviewed in Can Tho City and Ho Chi Minh City stated that they had never relied on the court system, either to overcome negotiation impasses in contractual disputes, or to strengthen their bargaining position for enforcement of contracts. The key strategy utilised by ethnic Chinese merchants for minimising the risk of contractual non-performance was, instead, insistence on a deeper understanding, and approval, of the personality of the business partner.

A general conclusion that can be drawn from the survey of local merchants undertaken is that contracts are founded on personal relationships of trust and harmony between the merchants. A contract does not have the meaning of a 'sharp in, sharp out' deal. Instead, it is embedded within social relationships built between family members, friends, or social networks.

As the Australian entrepreneur remarked, contracts in the Vietnamese market are 'a very, very relational thing' (Merchant 33). He related that, in Australia, contracting is usually an adversarial process where parties would try to get as much as possible out of the contract. Companies often have a contract administrator, who would study every clause of a contract and ensure that it is strictly adhered to. By contrast, in the Vietnamese market, the contracting process may include visits to workplaces, residential houses, or meetings on tennis courts, in restaurants and tea houses for dinners, lunches and drinks, during which contracting parties seek to learn about the personal norms of the other parties to help predict contractual behaviours and renegotiate contractual positions when the market changes (McMillan and Woodruff, 1999a: 1287).[6] The conventional functions of contracts as tools to plan future exchanges between parties, as devices to allocate risks and costs and as instruments to guarantee against non-performance fade into insignificance against the priority of developing business relationships supported by more holistic human relations.

The research supports the view that Vietnamese local merchants generally do not draft contracts for planning purposes. Those merchants who used written contracts described their contracts as brief and containing only general terms (Merchants 3, 4 and 5). Some who did write contracts said that they used a written contract to keep a record of what had been agreed to, rather than for the purpose of planning to achieve contractual efficiency (Merchant 21).

One participating merchant further explained that implicit in the relational norms practised in this market was the notion that client relationships naturally evolve from good interpersonal relationships. Careful drafting of contracts to govern a business relationship may signal that the merchant does not value the relationship highly and that therefore there will be fewer opportunities for cooperation.

An alternative perspective offered by some merchants was that the Vietnamese market was still unstable due to institutional reform – hence the best business strategy was to refrain from long-term contracting (Merchant 3). Planning an exchange into the future is not as important as planting a good relationship, which is seen as a more secure way to ground future opportunities for profitable cooperation.

The merchants surveyed who did write contracts generally viewed the dominant function of a contract as a mechanism for reducing disputes, rather than a process for planning future exchanges. Similarly, merchants who participated described the verbal exchange of offer and acceptance in the everyday course of their business less as a contracting issue and more as an issue of personal integrity: the need to save face or maintain *chữ tín*,[7] seen as an essential norm of business transactions.

Given the superiority of relational institutions over contract law in managing the risk of local merchant contract practice, 'contracting' in this context may be better described as transactional governance, rather than contract governance. As vividly put by a European merchant who runs a furniture business in Ho Chi Minh City, contracting in Vietnam can be featured as 'beer' and 'handshake' contracts: European merchants work hard during the negotiation of the contract, and then go out for dinner to celebrate the successful negotiation. Vietnamese merchants go out for dinner first, chat about personal things during the dinner, and then negotiate the basic terms of the contract over a beer, concluding the contract with a handshake in the office (Merchant 20).

The next sections look in greater detail at how surveyed merchants structure their contracts into relational institutions that support their business relationships.

How do Local Merchants Negotiate their 'Contracts'?

The traditional wisdom of contract theories predicts that when contracting parties plan an exchange into the future, they extend resources to predict market contingencies and ensure that contractual terms adequately cover their interests should those contingencies arise. The terms of the contract also structure the rights and obligations of the parties in the event of default and establish the mandatory rules if legal enforcement becomes necessary.

Contract law in Vietnam appears to loosen the role of legal frameworks for setting and enforcing norms to project exchange into the future. Most merchants interviewed did not have contract law in mind when they entered transactions.[8] In Ho Chi Minh City, where economic activities are most concentrated, contracts are normally entered into when a merchant picks up the telephone to call a friend to place an order, or to ask a friend out for a lunch, a dinner or an occasional drink to place an order in more detail (Merchants 2, 4 and 9). *Ex ante* contracting – exchange of information, processing of information, bargaining on the allocation of benefits and costs – is usually a process that takes place during intervals in a tennis match after office hours or during other social meetings, rather than in the office with lawyers and secretaries assisting to pin down the terms (Merchants 2, 4, 9, 20 and 21). Usually, the relational norms that support the preceding and ongoing background relationship become implicit norms for the contract regarding risk-sharing and lineage of incentives.

Generally, the Vietnamese merchants surveyed do not purposefully set norms in formal contracts with a view to later seeking reliance on court orders for long-term exchange. Although the contract law system in Vietnam generally fails to enforce business contracts without written evidence of contracts (Ordinance on Economic Contracts, art 1),[9] many interviewed merchants said that they usually did not write down their oral agreements. One merchant surveyed said he provided regular logistics services to a friend's company without any evidence in writing about their transactions. Negotiations and renegotiations are memorised for the purpose of performance (Merchant 27). The merchants who did not write down their oral agreements explained that they did not concern themselves very much with providing for uncalculated-for contingencies or the risks of their partners behaving opportunistically by breaching promises. They said they trusted their partners and believed that they could renegotiate with their partners for adjustments to contracts when regretful contingencies arose. Despite the risk that courts may reject claims of contractual rights without evidence in writing to substantiate those claims, the common practice which ignores any need for legal evidence to substantiate contractual claims suggests that merchants do not consider the setting of norms through formal contracting or court ordering assurance for their exchange to be important.

Bargaining for contractual terms 'in the shadow of contract law' in order to secure access to legal remedies and sanctions is a common conventional contract law strategy to deter opportunism and to ensure contractual rights in the case of non-performance or if disputes arise – however, most surveyed merchants did not use this strategy. More than two-thirds of merchants surveyed reported that they never used written contracts in their business transactions. The other one-third, who used written contracts, stated they did not draft contracts with legal remedies and sanctions in mind and that they intentionally limited the use of written contracts by keeping terms to a minimum level to avoid 'stiffening' business relationships. Those who used some form of written contract were mostly firms based in Ho Chi Minh City, where the market is much larger, transactions are more complicated, alternative clients are easier to find and where the court is easier to access.

In contrast with Western contract practices, a European merchant in Ho Chi Minh City describes contract negotiation in the Vietnamese market as flexible, renegotiable and 'about compromise'. European merchants expect the contract to be executed according to a strict interpretation of the contract, word by word. Penalties are automatically applied when delivery is late, quality or quantity varied, or when there are minor breaches of contract. For example, when goods are delivered with some minor defects, the best that the seller can expect is a discounted payment into its account. Contrary to Western practice, local merchants telephone their business partners to renegotiate the contract when contingencies arise. Contract terms and conditions are interpreted loosely, according to the underlying relationship. Compromise during renegotiation is expected and necessary for the survival of the underlying relationship (Merchant 20).

How do Local Merchants Monitor Performance and Enforce their 'Contract'?

The rationale underlying iterative game theory suggests that the key sanction against reneging in relational contracting is the loss of future gains from trade if the partner quits the relationship in retaliation (McMillan and Woodruff, 1999b). Cooperation is stable if the discount rate is not too high and if it is understood that retaliation will follow the tit-for-tat rule (Axelrod, 1990). In the world of local merchants, renegotiation during the performance of a contract is not only accepted practice, but sometimes required by accepted business morality. When asked how they would respond to a client who insisted on revising the terms and conditions agreed to earlier in the transaction, most surveyed merchants said that they would agree to renegotiate with their clients.

Surveyed merchants indicated that it was not uncommon for trading partners to telephone them to report unexpected contingencies and to suggest changes to what had been negotiated.[10] As some surveyed merchants explained to me, the norm in the market which shapes this practice indicates that if a client has difficulties living up to his or her obligations, the merchant should generally agree to renegotiate and should compromise if necessary to help the client, and maintain the merchant's *chữ tín* (prestige) in the market (Merchants 10 and 15). 'Keeping a good reputation is the most important thing', noted one local merchant. 'In Vietnam if you treat customers fairly when they have difficulties you will have that reputation. People will do business with you because they think you will not kill them when they have difficulties' (McMillan and Woodruff, 2000: 126). This norm is particularly appealing when there is a pre-existing relationship between the merchant and the client. This practice is commonly applied by family businesses as a way to reward loyal clients, and to secure their future loyalty in the market. Some merchants who practise Buddhism quoted the Buddhist concept of the impermanence of life and of possession to explain why they think it is necessary to accept renegotiation and compromise during contract execution if their clients face hardship, reflecting a much more flexible and forgiving framework than under conventional contract doctrine (Merchant 20).

Contract law is rarely used as a basis for resisting renegotiation requests. A merchant in the garment industry, who engages local contractors to supply products that he sells to foreign buyers, said he had often acceded to his contractors' requests to renegotiate a deal, even though it leaves him vulnerable to breaching his contract with his foreign clients as it is very difficult for him to renegotiate with foreign buyers. Despite this difficulty, he stated that he had never used contract law as the basis for resisting requests for renegotiation by local contractors, even though he was entitled to do so. He explained: 'What can I do? If I don't agree [to renegotiate], they would say 'OK, if you don't like, you can take your materials back'. It is difficult for me to find another contractor, and we don't do one deal only, we still have to work with them in the future' (Merchant 17). Local merchants often try to keep the relationship going despite non-performance or deficiencies in performance. Disputes are generally resolved by amicable negotiation and within a framework that places a high premium on maintaining relationships wherever possible (McMillan and Woodruff, 1999b: 642).

Surveyed merchants were also reluctant to threaten the court action to break negotiation impasses or to push for remedies. Local merchants expressed the common concern that suing trading partners may give them a bad reputation in the market as a person who is difficult to deal with (Merchant 28). Non-performance of a contract is not sufficient in the eyes of other traders to justify the use or threat of court action against a merchant. It must also be clear to the merchant's other customers or potential customers that the reneging partner cheated or behaved dishonestly.

In line with these sentiments, litigation or the threat of litigation is not a common endgame strategy for contract disputes either (Bernstein, 1996). Even a director of a consulting firm in Ho Chi Minh City (who has an MBA from a European institution and a law degree from Ho Chi Minh City Law School) said that he never mentions courts and contract laws with his clients when he tries to recover overdue debts (Merchant 4). Most of his clients were from Asian countries such as Indonesia, Malaysia, Singapore, Japan and Hong Kong, usually with ethnic Chinese backgrounds (except for some Japanese clients). To explain their attitudes towards contract law and court processes, local merchants usually quote the Vietnamese proverb: *vô phúc đáo tụng đình* (to be involved in court is a misfortune) (Merchant 5).

All merchants surveyed answered in the negative to a question asking whether using legal sanctions in carefully drafted contracts to induce compliance with the norms of their exchange is good for business (Merchants 4, 5 and 21). Not only is litigation not favoured, but rights-based adversarial solutions to enforce contracts are seen as selfish and generally not considered desirable. One surveyed merchant said that 'in order to keep long-term relationships with other customers, the firm must be very careful in dealing with disputes' (McMillan and Woodruff, 1999a).

Among the 31 local merchants interviewed, only one said that he sometimes mentioned courts and contract laws to overcome impasses during negotiations to resolve contractual disputes between his company and clients.[11] He is the head of the legal department of a large state-owned company running a port in Ho Chi Minh City (Merchant 4). Given his position as an in-house counsel of the company, it is clearly his duty, as well as in his personal interest, to advance legal solutions to commercial disputes. However, as he also explained during the interview, managers of state-owned companies sometimes choose to follow the legal process to avoid personal responsibility (Merchant 4). When a transaction turns out to be inefficient, having a court decide that their contracting partner is responsible for the inefficiency of the transaction can help them to clear their responsibility for the transaction and to maintain their position in the company.

The distinctiveness of contractual practice of local merchants has been noted by foreign merchants doing business in Vietnam, particularly those from Western-trained contract backgrounds. A surveyed European merchant who had lived in Vietnam for nearly a decade, when asked to compare contract dispute resolution practice in Vietnam with contract practice in Europe, characterised this practice as the 'beautiful face' relationship: even when the deal goes sour because of impasses in renegotiation, Vietnamese merchants try to maintain friendliness and civility. Business disputes should not deteriorate into expressions of anger between the parties. Where they do, the impact is usually irreversible and a good indication that the relationship will terminate (Merchant 20).

These behavioural patterns, although unlikely to be universal in contract practice of all local merchants in Vietnam, nevertheless suggest that there are distinctive features of contract practice in Vietnam.

McMillan and Woodruff's Survey: A Standard Iterative Game View of Relational Contracts

For the purpose of mapping contractual behaviour in Vietnam, it is necessary to introduce the work of economists John McMillan and Christopher Woodruff. They surveyed trading relationships in Vietnam during 1995-97 and provide an additional source of empirical data for my analysis of relational contracting in Vietnam. McMillan, of Stanford Business School, and Woodruff, of the University of California, conducted a survey of 259 private firms in Hanoi and Ho Chi Minh City (McMillan and Woodruff, 1999a). They asked local merchants how they developed and maintained trading relationships in the absence of legal enforcement of contracts and assumed that the incentive structures of repeated dealings between local merchants played the main role in inducing cooperation in contracting in the market (McMillan and Woodruff, 1999a). They explained this ordering mechanism as an ad hoc strategy, devised to compensate for the absence of a contract law system to enforce contracts in Vietnam. With data from the survey, they ran a regression with variables borrowed from the repeated-game theory exploring economic factors that determine the success of trading relationships in Vietnam market.

Two key conclusions were drawn: first, that trading relationships in Vietnam fit the standard repeated game theory of relational contracts pattern; and, second, that local merchants do not contract and resolve contract disputes in 'the shadow of the law'.

McMillan and Woodruff's survey offers a rich empirical source for the study of contractual behaviours in Vietnam (McMillan and Woodruff, 1999b). Nearly a decade, however, has elapsed since their fieldwork. As a result of economic and legal reform, the commercial law context in which McMillan and Woodruff conducted their survey has changed significantly. Arguably, the market frictions that McMillan and Woodruff identified as key shapers of local contract practice have also significantly changed. During McMillan and Woodruff's survey, the private sector in Vietnam had virtually no access to the court system to enforce contracts, because the Economic Court was in a nascent stage, having been established only one year earlier in 1994 (McMillan and Woodruff, 1999a). In addition to the weak court system, government policies at that time were not favourable to the private sector (McMillan and Woodruff, 1999a: 1285).

The Nobel Laureate economist Joseph E Stiglitz recently observed how, during the past decade, Vietnam has dramatically transformed its economy into a market economy at a pace that ranks it among the two most successful transitional economies in the world, the other being China (Stiglitz, 2003). Given the rate and exchange within the Vietnamese economy, the business environment and market frictions that shaped contract practice in the 1990s cannot be assumed to be the same as now. This then raises further questions as to whether, and if so how, contractual behaviours in Vietnam adapt and respond to the changing business environment.

A Critique on the Iterative Game Hypothesis of Relational Contracts

As noted, contract practice in Vietnam challenges the traditional view of contract law. In Vietnam, contractual relationships are not characterised by clear terms for a deal. Local merchants expect contract terms to be interpreted flexibly as the market unfolds during contract performance and do not expect themselves or their business partners to abide strictly by the terms. They tolerate demands to renegotiate contractual terms during contract performance stage. They avoid adversarial mechanisms to resolve disputes. They avoid threatening sanctions for breach of contract in order to maintain the higher value of a cooperative image in the market. They prefer to negotiate amicably when a partner fails to perform their part of a deal. And they avoid making the opponent 'lose face'. Local merchants neither contract 'in the shadow of the law', nor use litigation as the usual endgame strategy to seek remedies for their losses when bargaining fails (McMillan and Woodruff, 1999b: 637).[12] To this extent, my survey confirms some key findings about relational contract practices in the Vietnamese market of McMillan and Woodruff.

Iterative game theory explains an incentive structure of relational contracting. In this view, relational contracting is a governance structure that punishes breach of contract by the loss of future deals. Where relational contracting works smoothly to deter opportunism, that is, where the loss of future deals outweighs the benefit of opportunistic breach of contract, merchants may have no need for a contract law system.

The hypothesis of iterative game theory with regard to relational contracting does not, however, fully explain contractual behaviour in Vietnam. In order to sanction a breach of contract, one first needs to know whether a breach has occurred, regardless of whether the parties are dealing through formal contracting or relational contracting. How does one identify a breach if there was never a clear agreement as to contractual terms? Further, how can breaches be sanctioned if one does not expect one's partners to abide strictly by their commitments as the market unfolds? Iterative game theory also suggests that to induce cooperation, contracting parties have necessarily to follow a tit-for-tat strategy in response to contractual breach, which means that violation of contracts should instantly result in retaliation (Axelrod, 1990).

In the Vietnamese market, as my survey found, renegotiation of contracts is an accepted practice and local merchants are reluctant to retaliate when contracts are breached (McMillan and Woodruff, 1999b).[13] My survey also found that local merchants sometimes tolerated unreasonable demands for renegotiation of contracts, even where it exposed the victim merchant to the risk of breaching an inflexible contract with another party.[14] These findings confirm a point not explained in McMillan and Woodruff's study, namely that, in many aspects, iterative game theory does not reflect real-life business contractual practice in Vietnam (McMillan and Woodruff, 1999b: 637).[15]

Some empirical studies in other markets suggest that merchants habitually follow the practices in these markets to conduct economic exchanges rather than wealth-maximising norms for each and every transaction (Macaulay, 1963). Empiricists admit that economic variables do not always explain why contract practice differs in different markets.[16] Further, economists have also observed that contract practices in the market do not always produce outcomes that achieve wealth-maximisation. Hernando de Soto, for example, observed that in the informal business sector in Peru, merchants create and maintain trust, deal primarily with family members and fashion long-term continuing relationships (Soto, 1989). These practices, which are aimed at ensuring contractual performance, impose unnecessary transaction costs on the merchants, de Soto (1989) argued. In the realm of relational contracting, merchants may behave differently in different markets (Soto, 1989). McMillan and Woodruff perceived this when they decided to go to Vietnam to collect data in the field, instead of relying on universal theories and American data. The question why successful trading relationships in Vietnam have their own determinant factors that differ from successful trading relationships in other markets cannot be answered by regression. It is here that my analysis differs from that of McMillan and Woodruff.

In my opinion, the answer comes from what game theorists call 'nature' and relational contract theorists call 'social matrix' (Macneil, 2000: 189). It is the matrix of social institutions in the market, legal and informal institutions, that determine contract behaviour. The institutional matrix influences contractual behaviours in the market by setting the preferences of the players – inducing them to adopt a strategy that may not be optimal for the player in a specific deal, but which is considered optimal for the players in their overall performance within the market. As Douglass North (1993) put it, it is 'only under the conditions of costless bargaining will the actors reach the solution that maximises aggregate income regardless of the institutional arrangement. When it is costly to transact, institutions matter. And it is costly to transact'.

Vietnam is a developing market. Transaction costs in developing markets are usually high because these markets are usually not yet well-structured, or they may lack conventional institutions to support transactions (McMillan, 2002). Institutions therefore take on heightened importance in the study of contract practice in Vietnam: the features of local institutions are critical in understanding the features of local contract practice. To overlook the characteristics of local institutions would lead to the misleading assumption that there exists a universal model of relational contracting.

Relational contracting in Vietnam is best described as a web of business transactions and non-business relationships that are interwoven into an ongoing relationship. As this research has demonstrated, it is difficult to separate business deals from non-business deals in relational contracts in Vietnam. Local merchants in their pursuit of economic ends invest resources not only in negotiating, monitoring and enforcing business deals but also in numerous relational commitments in the social realm which are considered part of the business relationship. The relational contract depicted in this research is therefore not merely about the establishment of repeated business transactions with an implicit norm for readjustment, but also involves interwoven multi-faceted relationships that support a business deal. Accordingly, an optimal governance structure of contracting in the Vietnamese market aims not only to achieve the economic ends of a profitable one-off transaction, but also the efficiency and overall improved performance of the merchant in the web of relationships.

In game theory jargon, the preferences of players in games reflect the social norms in the market. No study of the function of a contract law system can ignore the role of powerful social norms. Legal realists have long warned us of powerful social norms that compete with contract law as the 'rule of the game' for contracting (Llewellyn, 1931; Llewellyn, 1936a; Llewellyn, 1936b). The role of powerful social norms may also be used to explain some inconsistencies between the iterative game theory hypothesis of relational contracting, and real relational contracting in Vietnam. My hypothesis here is that contract practice in Vietnam not only responds to the incentive structures of the standard iterative game theory, but also to the social matrix in which parties contract. A distinctive feature of contract practice in Vietnam is the outcome of a complex process of interaction between merchants – the players in the market – and the institutional framework in the market. Ideally then, relational contracting in Vietnam should be explained using an institutional approach that takes into account the existence of other social institutions in the market beside the contract law system.

Following the institutional approach, relational contracting in the Vietnam market should be studied not only in the light of the iterative game theory scenario of contracting in the absence of legal institutions, but also in light of the interaction between court ordering and other social institutions in Vietnam. This raises the question of what institutional structures induce the behavioural patterns of relational contracting in the Vietnamese market. A further question is how these structures emerge. These are questions I am seeking to address in my current research.

Notes

* LLB (Vietnam), MCL (UQ), PhD (Melb), Lecturer in Business Law at Swinburne University of Technology and Managing Consultant, Quan Consulting (<www.contractvietnam.com>). Special thanks to Professor Tim Lindsey and Dr Pip Nicholson at the Asian Law Centre, University of Melbourne for their help in the development of this article.

1 For discussions on the crisis of contract law in the relational contract literature and evidence from the contract law in action literature, see articles in the Faculty Symposium: Relational Contract Theory: Unanswered Questions, Northwestern University Law Faculty, January 1999, published in 94(3) *Northwestern University Law Review*.

2 *The Chinese in Vietnam and Ho Chi Minh City* Chinese Affairs Department of Ho Chi Minh City, <http://www.nguoihoa.hochiminhcity.gov.vn/vietnamese/xemtin.asp?idcha=814&ID=949&cap=2>.

3 Oliver Williamson offered an explanation on this point: in the absence of opportunism, there is no need for contract enforcement, because whenever cooperation is efficient, parties will honestly cooperate and perform their parts to carry out the transaction and to split the profit fairly. Readjustment during contract performance is a matter of course to ensure efficiency of the transaction. When unexpected contingencies cause the transaction to be inefficient, parties would release themselves from the cooperation and honestly split the loss. In the absence of opportunism, there is no need to contract.

4 He had worked in the sale department of Nisso Iwai and Ericssons in Ho Chi Minh City for many years, then several years as a consultant to a state-owned telecommunication giant in Ho Chi Minh City.

5 McMillan and Woodruff survey also noted this hesitance of local merchants to deal with strangers.

6 It is a common practice in the market that merchants visit their clients' shops to learn about the personality, work habits and business acumen of their clients.

7 A simplified interpretation of *chữ tín* is trust, but local merchants interpret *chữ tín* as compliance with a moral code rather than simply keeping promises.

8   Exceptions include Merchants 2,3,4, and 23, who actually have a law background.
9   'Economic contracts are agreements in writing or exchange of documents …' (Ordinance on Economic Contracts, art 1). The Commercial Code 1997 left untouched this requirement on contract formality because art 49 of this Code said that contracts required in writing by other laws (that is, the Ordinance on Economic Contracts) still need to be in writing.
10 All merchants agree that this is a received practice. Particularly, Merchants 10, 15, 17 and 21 have stressed that they followed this practice in their daily business contracting.
11 Merchant 23 also mentions courts and contract laws to overcome impasses during negotiations. He has been excluded from this analysis, however, as he is the managing lawyer of a large law firm in Ho Chi Minh City.
12 'Vietnam's firms contract without the shadow of the law and only partly in the shadow of the future. Although contracting rests in part on the threat of loss of future business, firms often are willing to re-negotiate following a breach, so the retaliation is not as forceful as in the standard repeated-game theory and not as effective a sanction. To ensure agreements are kept, firms rely on other devices to supplement repeated-game incentives. Firms scrutinize their trading partners. Community sanctions are occasionally invoked. Transactions with greater risk of reneging are supported by more elaborate governance structure': McMillan and Woodruff, 1999b: 637.
13 For example, Merchant 10 referred to Buddhist principles of tolerance when she was asked if she ever threatened retaliation against business partners who wrongly breached contracts with her company.
14 For example, Merchant 17 faced the risk of legal action from foreign buyers when his local contractors demanded to renegotiate contracts, but said that he did not intend to retaliate, in order to keep good ongoing relationships with them.
15 'Although contracting rests in part on the threat of loss of future business, firms often are willing to re-negotiate following a breach, so the retaliation is not as forceful as in the standard repeated-game story and not as effective a sanction. To ensure agreements are kept, firms rely on other devices to supplement repeated game incentives. Firms scrutinize their trading partners. Community sanctions are occasionally invoked. Transactions with greater risk of reneging are supported by more elaborate governance structures': McMillan and Woodruff, 1999b: 637.
16 For an empirical study that reveals differences in contract practice in different markets, see Bigsten et al, 1998: 8 – the authors admit 'that there are significant differences in contract practice across studied countries and sectors but also that these differences are not well captured by contract environment variables'.

References

Anh, Phi (2004) 'Vụ trùm vải Thái Vĩnh Trương bỏ trốn: Nợ 21 tỷ đồng và gần nửa triệu USD! (The disappearance of fabric tycoon Thai Vinh Truong: More than 21 billions VND and half a million of USD in debts!)' *Pháp Luật (The Law Newspaper)*, 13 September, <www.nhandan.org.vn>.

Axelrod, Robert (1990) *The Evolution Of Co-operation*. London: Penguin Books.

Babbie, Earl (2001) *The Practice of Social Research*. 9th ed, Belmont, CA: Wadsworth Thomson Learning.

Barton, Clifton (1983) 'Trust and credit: some observations regarding business strategies of Overseas Chinese traders in Vietnam' in Linda YL Lim and LAP Gosling (eds), *The Chinese in Southeast Asia*. Singapore: Maruzen Asia.

Bernstein, Lisa (1996) 'Merchant Law in a Merchant Court: Rethinking the Code's Search for Immanent Business Norms' 144 *University of Pennsylvania Law Review* 1765.

Bigsten, Arne et al (1998) 'Contract Flexibility and Conflict Resolution: Evidence from African Manufacturing', Working Paper No WPS/98-21, Centre for the Study of African Economies, Department of Economics, University of Oxford, <http://www.csae.ox.ac.uk/workingpapers/pdfs/9821text.pdf>.

Cohen, L Manion, L and Morrison, K (2000) *Research Methods in Education.* London: RoutledgeFalmer.

Cotterrell, Roger (1992) *The Sociology of Law: An Introduction.* London: Butterworths.

Doanh, Kinh and Luat, Phap (1998) *Business & Law*, 29 October, 10.

Gainsborough, Martin (2003) *Changing Political Economy of Vietnam – The Case of Ho Chi Minh City.* London: Routledge Curzon.

Gilmore, Grant (1974) *The Death of Contract.* Columbus: Ohio State University Press.

Hart, HLA (1961) *The Concept of Law.* Oxford: Clarendon Press.

Hobbes, Thomas (2002) *Leviathan*, edited by AP Martinich, Ontario: Broadview Press.

Korobkin, Russell B (2004) 'A "Traditional" and "Behavioural" Law-and-Economics Analysis of *Williams v Walker-Thomas Furniture Company*' 26 *University of Hawaii Law Review* 441.

Llewellyn, Karl (1931) 'What Price Contract? – An Essay in Perspective' 40 *Yale Law Journal* 704.

Llewellyn, Karl (1936a) 'On Warranty of Quality and Society 1' 36 *Columbia Law Review* 699.

Llewellyn, Karl (1936b) 'On Warranty of Quality and Society 2' 37 *Columbia Law Review* 341.

Macaulay, Stewart (1963) 'Non-Contractual Relations in Business: A Preliminary Study' 28 *American Sociological Review* 55.

McMillan, John (2002) *Reinventing the Bazaar: A Natural History of Markets.* New York: WW Norton.

McMillan, John and Woodruff, Christopher (1999a) 'Interim Relationships and Informal Credit in Vietnam' 114 *Quarterly Journal of Economics* 1285.

McMillan, John and Woodruff, Christopher (1999b) 'Dispute Prevention Without Courts in Vietnam' 15 *Journal of Law, Economics, and Organization* 637.

McMillan, John and Woodruff, Christopher (2000) 'Private Order Under Dysfunctioning Public Order' 98 *Michigan Law Review* 101.

Macneil, Ian R (1978) 'Contracts: Adjustment Of Long-term Economic Relations Under Classical, Neoclassical, And Relational Contract Law' 72 *Northwestern University Law Review* 854.

Macneil, Ian (2000) 'Relational Contract Theory: Challenges and Queries' 94 *Northwestern University Law Review* 877.

North, Douglass C (1997) *Where Have We Been and Where are We Going*, Social Science Research Network, <http://ssrn.com/abstract=1494>.

North, Douglass C (1993) 'Prize Lecture', Speech delivered at the Nobel Prize Award Ceremony, Stockholm, 9 December), <http://nobelprize.org/economics/laureates/1993/north-lecture.html>.

Redding, S Gordon (1990) *The Spirit of Chinese Capitalism.* Berlin: W de Gruyter.

Reid, Anthony (1993) *Southeast Asia in the Age of Commerce 1450 – 1680.* New Haven: Yale University Press.

Scott, Robert E (2004) 'The Death of Contract Law' 54 *University of Toronto Law Journal* 369.

Soto, Hernando de (1989) *The Other Path: The Invisible Revolution in the Third World.* New York: Harper & Row.

Stiglitz, Joseph E (2003) 'Ethics, Market and Government Failure, and Globalisation', Paper presented at the Vatican Conference at the Ninth Plenary Session of the Pontifical Academy of Social Sciences, Casina Pio IV, 2–6 May.

Treitel, GH (1979) *An Outline of The Law of Contract.* 2nd ed, London: Butterworths.

Williamson, Oliver E (1985) *The Economic Institutions Of Capitalism: Firms, Markets, Relational Contracting.* London: Collier Macmillan Publishers.

Legislation

Ordinance on Economic Contracts (Vietnam)

Commercial Code, 1997

[11]

RETHINKING RELATIONSHIP-SPECIFIC INVESTMENTS: SUBCONTRACTING IN THE JAPANESE AUTOMOBILE INDUSTRY

Yoshiro Miwa*
J. Mark Ramseyer**

Longer ago than either of us cares to remember, one of us attended junior high in Tokyo. On Saturdays, he worked at a printed circuit factory. Or maybe "factory" makes it all sound too grand. A small building in back of a gas station, it had three or four punch presses. The "president" supervised matters (though he actually spent more time hanging out at the gas station), together with a sidekick who did assorted odd jobs besides. Several middle-aged women with no apparent technical education or skill ran the presses.

The junior high kid spent his time trimming the sheets to which others would eventually attach the transistors. The women then punched the holes and margins onto the boards, and the president's sidekick loaded the finished boards onto a truck. Periodically, he returned them to the firm that had ordered the work and brought more sheets to punch along with any press dies the firm needed. The punch presses were standard generic affairs, and the buyer seems to have kept title to the dies.

Thirty years later, the other one of us knows the president of a factory near Nagoya. For many years, the firm has done machining work for a first-tier Toyota subcontractor. Unfortunately for the firm, Toyota has increasingly substituted integrated plastic units for the steel shock absorber parts the firm machines. Worried that the Toyota-bound work might disappear, the president has begun to move the firm toward machining materials for computer hard disks on the side.

A machining firm can make a wide variety of products, the president seemed to explain. His firm could make products for the automobile industry or otherwise, Toyota-bound or otherwise. If the demand for shock-absorber parts fell, well then it would simply make computer disks instead.

---

* Professor of Economics, University of Tokyo. B.A., Ph.D., University of Tokyo. — Ed. We received helpful comments and suggestions from Eric Feldman, Tomotaka Fujita, Yoshitaka Fukui, William Grimes, John Haley, Shuichi Hashimoto, Hideki Kanda, Yoshitsugu Kanemoto, William Klein, Motonari Kurasawa, Richard Lempert, Scott Masten, Toshihiro Matsumura, Curtis Milhaupt, Kazuro Saguchi, Kazuo Wada, Mark West, Noriyuki Yanagawa, and participants at workshops at Harvard University, the University of Michigan, and the University of Tokyo. We gratefully acknowledge the generous financial assistance of the Sloan Foundation (Miwa and Ramseyer) and the John M. Olin Center for Law, Economics & Business at the Harvard Law School (Ramseyer). We thank the many officials of various suppliers who permitted and facilitated Miwa's interviews and on-site visits.

** Mitsubishi Professor of Japanese Legal Studies, Harvard University. B.A. 1976, Goshen College; A.M. 1978, University of Michigan; J.D. 1982, Harvard University. — Ed.

What neither of us saw in either firm was any evidence of investments that were specific to the firm's trading partners. Yet whether such relationship-specific investments ("RSIs") structure the arrangements firms make matters. Indeed, for at least two independent reasons, whether they structure the Japanese automobile industry matters crucially.

Within law and economics, the prevalence of RSIs matters because of the way the issue goes to the heart of market contracting. At root, RSI theory challenges our routine assumption that straightforward market contracting produces something close to socially optimal arrangements. Although the theory is clear, the empirics are less so. Scholars have looked hard for evidence of governance arrangements driven by large relationship-specific investments. To date, they have reached only mixed conclusions. They find substantial evidence of the relation between RSIs and governance within idiosyncratic industries like public utilities, aerospace, and defense. Although they find some evidence of the relation within "ordinary" industries, they find considerably less. In that empirical vacuum, the Japanese automobile industry has stood as a prominent exception — an important example of RSI-driven extra-contractual governance arrangements in an "ordinary" industry.

Within Japanese studies, RSIs provide a convenient theoretical rationale for taking the conventional tales of "socially embedded" contracts and relational stability at face value. To date, all too many scholars have been all too happy to "explain" these tales by citing strong cultural norms of integrity or obligation. The theoretically more astute justifiably find the "explanations" hollow. For them, RSIs have offered an analytically coherent incentive-compatible rationale for exactly the same tales.

In this Article, we argue that the usual accounts of the industry are myth. Notwithstanding those accounts, the industry does not contain widespread, substantial physical-asset or human-capital RSIs. To the extent that we are right, theorists might do well to rethink the empirical role RSI theory has played over the past two decades. We do not argue that firms never make RSIs or that contracts will always solve incentive problems. Far be it from us to make such a claim, especially since this Article is only about one industry in one country. Neither do we claim that RSI theory is wrong as theory. Neither of us is a theorist, this is not a theoretical paper, and the intuition behind RSI theory has generally made sense to us anyway. Instead, we make a more modest point: that modern production may require lower levels of idiosyncratic investment than we have usually supposed; that market contracting may work better than usually asserted; and that, as a result, RSI theory may explain less of the contracting and governance patterns in place than scholars have often asserted.

In this Article, we argue that RSIs in the Japanese automobile industry are usually quite small and usually play a minor role. Toward that end, we begin by summarizing the implications RSI theory poses for contract theory (Section I.A) and surveying the empirical evidence (Section I.B-.C). We then turn to the Japanese automobile industry. First, we anecdotally canvass the practices at Honda (Section II.B), and provide a background to the industry as a whole (Section II.C). Second, we examine the evidence of RSIs among second- and third-tier suppliers (Section III.A). Finally, we examine the evidence among first-tier suppliers (Section III.B).

I. Specific-Investment Theory

A. *The Idea:*

Relationship-specific investments matter — and matter deeply — argue Oliver Williamson, Benjamin Klein, Robert Crawford, and Armen Alchian.[1] Dozens of scholars have since repeated the logic they pioneered, and today it graces such mainstream sources as the industrial organization text of Dennis Carlton and Jeffrey Perloff and the management text of Paul Milgrom and John Roberts.[2] According to this intuition, the scope and size of RSIs can directly affect the governance arrangements firms choose. Whether business partners negotiate long-term contracts, spot contracts, equity investments, franchise arrangements, or even mergers can depend vitally on the RSIs at stake.

Crucially, investments specific to a relationship generate appropriable quasi rents. In a world of incomplete contracting, as Scott Masten, James Meehan, Jr., and Edward Snyder put it, that appropriability may increase the "resources expended attempting to negotiate a favorable distribution of the gains from trade."[3] In the words of Klein, Crawford, and Alchian themselves, "[a]fter a specific investment is made and such quasi rents are created, the possibility of opportunistic behavior is very real."[4] To avoid such rent-seeking and

---

1. *See* Oliver E. Williamson, The Economic Institutions of Capitalism: Firms, Markets, Relational Contracting (1985) [hereinafter Williamson, The Economic Institutions of Capitalism]; Benjamin Klein et al., *Vertical Integration, Appropriable Rents, and the Competitive Contracting Process*, 21 J.L. & Econ. 297 (1978); Oliver E. Williamson, *Transaction-Cost Economics: The Governance of Contractual Relations*, 22 J.L. & Econ. 233 (1979) [hereinafter Williamson, *Transaction-Cost Economics*].

2. Dennis W. Carlton & Jeffrey M. Perloff, Modern Industrial Organization chs. 2, 13 (2d ed. 1994); Paul Milgrom & John Roberts, Economics, Organization and Management ch. 9 (1992). The theory plays an even more pronounced role in David Besanko et al., The Economics of Strategy pt. I (1996).

3. Scott E. Masten et al., *The Costs of Organization*, 7 J.L. Econ. & Org. 1, 6 (1991).

4. Klein et al., *supra* note 1, at 298.

rent-avoidance costs, firms may sometimes introduce governance arrangements that are otherwise unnecessary (and probably problematic, given the way most of them weaken market incentives). RSIs can potentially transform a competitive market exchange into a bilateral monopoly, in other words. When appropriate contractual arrangements are infeasible, that transformation may call forth arrangements that otherwise would be superfluous at best.[5] Or as Klein, Crawford, and Alchian write:

> The crucial assumption underlying the analysis of this Article is that, as assets become more specific and more appropriable quasi rents are created (and therefore the possible gains from opportunistic behavior increases [sic]), the costs of contracting will generally increase more than the costs of vertical integration. Hence, *ceteris paribus*, we are more likely to observe vertical integration.[6]

B. *The Evidence*

1. *GM-Fisher Body*[7]

Consider a short summary of the anecdote Klein, Crawford, and Alchian used to popularize this analysis: the 1926 merger between General Motors and Fisher Body. Before 1919, claim Klein, Crawford, and Alchian, car companies used wooden or wood-and-metal coaches. Making these early coaches involved standard tools and standard knowledge. Making a good one took skill, but it was a skill a coachmaker could use as easily to fit a coach onto a frame by assembler A as onto one by assembler B. Conversely, assembler A could as easily use a coach from coachmaker X as from coachmaker Y.

In this pre-1919 world, continue Klein, Crawford, and Alchian, assemblers and coachmakers traded on what was virtually a spot market. In doing so, they took little risk. If a coachmaker stopped selling, the assembler could buy its coaches elsewhere. If an assembler stopped buying, the coachmaker could sell its coaches elsewhere. As neither had invested much in either assets or skills that were specific to the relationship, neither had much to lose from switching contract partners.

By the next decade, Klein, Crawford, and Alchian write, car makers started to make standardized coaches out of steel. Fashioning these steel coaches required dies. In turn, these dies cost large sums,

---

5. *See* Williamson, *Transaction-Cost Economics, supra* note 1, at 241-42.

6. Klein et al., *supra* note 1, at 298.

7. After this Article was written but before it went to press, we received a copy of Ramon Casadesus-Masanell & Daniel F. Spulber, *The Fable of Fisher Body,* 43 J.L. & ECON. 67 (2000). We urge readers interested in the Fisher Body example to consult the extremely careful account in Casadesus-Masanell & Spulber. Many of our own conclusions about the relevance of RSI theory track their conclusions.

and could be used only for specific models. Now, the assembler and coachmaker faced the prospect of investing in an asset that paid off only within the relationship. As such, the asset generated appropriable quasi rents: if the coachmaker bought the die, the assembler could threaten to end the relationship in order to shift the terms of the deal in its favor.[8]

Rather than risk this opportunism, reason Klein, Crawford, and Alchian, assemblers and coachmakers integrated vertically. In 1919, Fisher Body and General Motors entered into a long-term contract. Alas, given the problems inherent in long-term contracts in the real world, opportunism-related problems persisted. By 1926, GM simply acquired Fisher Body outright. Given the large RSIs involved, the two firms found it paid to eliminate the risk through vertical integration.

2. RSI Taxonomy

To Klein, Crawford, and Alchian, the risk of opportunism in the GM-Fisher Body relationship lay in the investment in large stamp dies: "The manufacture of dies for stamping parts in accordance with the above specifications gives a value to these dies specialized to [the assembler], which implies an appropriable quasi rent in those dies. Therefore, the die owner would not want to be separate from [the assembler]."[9] Yet such physical assets are not the only RSIs that theorists identify. Oliver Williamson, for example, cites several types of RSIs, of which we consider three here:

site specificity — e.g. successive stations that are located in a cheek-by-jowl relation to each other so as to economize on inventory or transportation expenses;

physical asset specificity — e.g. specialized dies that are required to produce a component; [and]

human asset specificity that arises in a learning-by-doing fashion . . . .[10]

The evidence of occasional site specificity may well be the strongest. If a utility company builds a generating plant near a coal mine, for example, the utility and mine lock themselves into a relation close to a bilateral monopoly. Sometimes, this affects the governance structures they choose.[11]

---

8. In fact, Casadesus-Masanell & Spurber, *supra* note 7, at 84-86, point out that Fisher Body did not begin to produce exclusively metal bodies until the late 1930s.

9. Klein et al., *supra* note 1, at 308.

10. WILLIAMSON, THE ECONOMIC INSTITUTIONS OF CAPITALISM, *supra* note 1, at 95 (emphasis added). Williamson also discusses a fourth category of "dedicated assets." *See id.*; *see also* Williamson, *Transaction-Cost Economics*, *supra* note 1.

11. *See* Keith J. Crocker & Scott E. Masten, *Mitigating Contractual Hazards: Unilateral Options and Contract Length*, 19 RAND J. ECON. 327 (1988); Stephen J. DeCanio & H.E. Frech III, *Vertical Contracts: A Natural Experiment in Gas Pipeline Regulation*, 149 J. INSTITUTIONAL & THEORETICAL ECON. 149, 370 (1993); C. Paul Hallwood, *On Choosing*

The evidence of human-capital specificity is more tenuous, though here too some scholars claim to find evidence on point. Marketing scholars, for example, argue that employees sometimes invest in brand-specific knowledge in ways that affect the governance choices firms make.[12] Others claim that employees invest in relation-specific manufacturing know-how to similar effect.[13]

By contrast, observers tend to find less evidence (though more than zero, to be sure) of the sort of physical-asset specificity Klein-Crawford-Alchian use to explain the GM-Fisher Body merger. Granted, Keith Crocker and Kenneth Reynolds conclude that physical-asset specificity affects the structure of defense procurement decisions.[14] Scott Masten makes the same point about government aerospace purchases.[15] Yet if ever there were idiosyncratic procedures, the defense and aerospace industries would be the place to find them. In

---

Organizational Arrangements: The Example of Offshore Oil Gathering, 38 SCOT. J. POL. ECON. 227 (1991); Jean-Francois Hennart, *Upstream Vertical Integration in the Aluminum and Tin Industries*, 9 J. ECON. BEHAV. & ORG. 281 (1988); Paul L. Joskow, *Contract Duration and Relationship-Specific Investments: Empirical Evidence from Coal Markets*, 77 AM. ECON. REV. 168 (1987); Paul L. Joskow, *Price Adjustment in Long-term Contracts: The Case of Coal*, 31 J.L. & ECON. 47 (1988); Paul L. Joskow, *Vertical Integration and Long-term Contracts: The Case of Coal-burning Electric Generating Plants*, 1 J.L. ECON. & ORG. 33 (1985); Scott E. Masten & Keith J. Crocker, *Efficient Adaptation in Long-Term Contracts: Take-or-Pay Provisions for Natural Gas*, 75 AM. ECON. REV. 1083 (1985); J. Harold Mulherin, *Complexity in Long-term Contracts: An Analysis of Natural Gas Contractual Provisions*, 2 J.L. ECON. & ORG. 105 (1986); Russell Pittman, *Specific Investments, Contracts, and Opportunism: The Evolution of Railroad Sidetrack Agreements*, 34 J.L. & ECON. 565 (1991); Pablo T. Spiller, *On Vertical Mergers*, 1 J.L. ECON. & ORG. 285 (1985).

12. *See* Erin Anderson, *Transaction Costs as Determinants of Opportunism in Integrated and Independent Sales Forces*, 9 J. ECON. BEHAV. & ORG. 247 (1988); Erin Anderson & Anne T. Coughlan, *International Market Entry and Expansion via Independent or Integrated Channels of Distribution*, 51 J. MARKETING 71 (1987); Erin Anderson & David C. Schmittlein, *Integration of the Sales Force: An Empirical Examination*, 15 RAND J. ECON. 385 (1984); Jan B. Heide & George John, *The Role of Dependence Balancing in Safeguarding Transaction-Specific Assets in Conventional Channels*, 52 J. MARKETING 20 (1988); George John & Barton A. Weitz, *Forward Integration into Distribution: An Empirical Test of Transaction Cost Analysis*, 4 J.L. ECON. & ORG. 337 (1988); Gary L. Lilien, *Advisor 2: Modeling the Marketing Mix Decision for Industrial Products*, 25 MGMT. SCI. 191 (1979).

13. *See* Henry Ogden Armour & David J. Teece, *Vertical Integration and Technological Innovation*, 62 REV. ECON. & STAT. 470 (1980); Marvin B. Lieberman, *Determinants of Vertical Integration: An Empirical Test*, 39 J. INDUS. ECON. 451 (1991); Scott E. Masten et al., *Vertical Integration in the U.S. Auto Industry: A Note on the Influence of Transaction Specific Assets*, 12 J. ECON. BEHAV. & ORG. 265 (1989); Kirk Monteverde & David J. Teece, *Supplier Switching Costs and Vertical Integration in the Automobile Industry*, 13 BELL J. ECON. 206 (1982); Gary P. Pisano, *Using Equity Participation to Support Exchange: Evidence from the Biotechnology Industry*, 5 J.L. ECON. & ORG. 109 (1989).

14. *See* Keith J. Crocker & Kenneth J. Reynolds, *The Efficiency of Incomplete Contracts: An Empirical Analysis of Air Force Engine Procurement*, 24 RAND J. ECON. 126 (1993).

15. *See* Scott E. Masten, *The Organization of Production: Evidence from the Aerospace Industry*, 27 J.L. & ECON. 403 (1984).

more ordinary industries, however, observers have found much less evidence of physical-asset specificity.[16]

Consistent with the difficulty in finding widespread evidence of the ties between physical-asset specificity and governance, the GM-Fisher Body story raises its own problems as well. If relation-specific dies were the problem, GM could have mitigated it contractually by owning the dies itself — a tactic modern car companies routinely use.[17] So long as it owned and could repossess the dies, it faced little more risk through contract than it did through vertical integration.

More basically, by 1919 GM already held a majority interest in Fisher Body anyway.[18] Absent any unusual arrangement, as a controlling shareholder, GM could have appointed the entire board and, through the board, could have mandated all policy.[19] Whether the coaches were steel or wood and whether GM owned the dies or Fisher Body did, neither GM nor Fisher Body would have faced the risk of any opportunism justifying an otherwise *non*-cost-justified merger between of the two firms.

Indeed, GM seems to have done perfectly well with independent suppliers for other specialized products. A.O. Smith, for example, was already making automobile frames for GM and others in the early 1930s. Half a century later, A.O. Smith was still the largest automobile frame manufacturer, was still independent, and still had GM as a principal customer. "Major model changes involve[d] substantial ex-

---

16. See Kirk Monteverde & David J. Teece, *Appropriable Rents and Quasi-Vertical Integration*, 25 J.L. & ECON. 321 (1982), however, find that it does lead the buyer to retain title to the dedicated physical asset used in the production process. Other studies claiming to locate evidence of physical-asset specificity include David T. Levy, *The Transactions Cost Approach to Vertical Integration: An Empirical Examination*, 67 REV. ECON. & STAT. 438 (1985) (claiming that advertising intensity proxies for RSIs); Ian C. MacMillan et al., *Uncertainty Reduction and the Threat of Supplier Retaliation: Two Views of the Backward Integration Decision*, 7 ORG. STUD. 263 (1986) (using multi-industry "Profit Impact of Market Strategies" database); Thomas M. Palay, *Comparative Institutional Economics: The Governance of Rail Freight Contracting*, 13 J. LEGAL STUD. 265 (1984) (discussing idiosyncratic freight cars).

17. On the GM-owning-the-die tactic, see, for example, WILLIAMSON, THE ECONOMIC INSTITUTIONS OF CAPITALISM, *supra* note 1, at 95; Masten et al., *supra* note 3; Monteverde & Teece, *supra* note 16. Klein himself acknowledges this point in Benjamin Klein, *Vertical Integration as Organizational Ownership: The Fisher Body-General Motors Relationship Revisited*, 4 J.L. ECON. & ORG. 199, 205 (1988).

18. See R. H. Coase, *The Nature of the Firm: Influence*, in THE NATURE OF THE ORIGINS, EVOLUTION, AND DEVELOPMENT 61 (Williamson & Winter eds., 1991); Klein et al., *supra* note 1, at 308 n.25.

19. Others have claimed that the Fisher brothers controlled this stock through a voting trust. Although that would indeed have removed GM's voting control, in most states the disability would have been temporary. State statutes generally limit the terms of voting trusts to 10 years or less, which would have ended the Fisher Body trust by 1929 at the latest. See ROBERT CHARLES CLARK, CORPORATE LAW 777 (1986); HARRY G. HENN & JOHN R. ALEXANDER, LAWS OF CORPORATIONS AND OTHER BUSINESS ENTERPRISES 531-32 (1983). In fact, Casadesus-Masanell & Spurber, *supra* note 7, at 80, point out that the actual Fisher Body voting trust ended in 1924.

penses by A.O. Smith for new tooling, the arrangement of production lines and learning time for production employees," reports Ronald Coase, but contractual and reputational constraints kept opportunism to manageable levels.[20]

C. Japan

Despite the apparent shortage of evidence showing widespread extra-contractual governance mechanisms driven by large physical-asset specificities, RSIs have played an increasingly prominent part in academic discussions of Japan. The story begins with the late Banri Asanuma. Asanuma devoted much of the 1980s to studying the automobile industry, and throughout the decade reported his results in both Japanese and English. He also maintained a long-standing interest in Williamson's work, translating *Markets and Hierarchies* into Japanese.[21]

According to Asanuma, the relationship between Japanese automobile assemblers and suppliers is long-standing, and long-standing for reasons that closely reflect the Williamson-Klein-Crawford-Alchian logic. First, the parties trade in "customized parts." Second, the parties can produce these customized parts efficiently only by investing in "relation-specific skills." Third, through those skills they produce a "relational quasi rent" and — to return to the original point — that rent creates an incentive to maintain the relationship long-term. How the parties prevent the rent-seeking and rent-avoidance activities that trouble Williamson and Klein-Crawford-Alchian, Asanuma seems not to have addressed.[22]

Relying in part on Asanuma's field work, Masahiko Aoki similarly argues that Japanese manufacturers and subcontractors rely on RSIs.[23] Subcontractors invest heavily, explains Aoki, in skills that are specific to their relationship with a given manufacturer. To make money on such investments, a subcontractor must be able to expect long-term returns. By the logic of Williamson and Klein-Crawford-Alchian, the insecurity inherent in the appropriability of the quasi rents should

---

20. *See* Coase, *supra* note 18, at 71-72. Perhaps reflecting some of these issues, Klein switched much of his explanation for the 1926 merger to human-capital investments ten years after the original article. *See* Klein, *supra* note 17, at 208.

21. *See* Banri Asanuma, *Nihon ni okeru meekaa to sapuraiyaa to no kankei [The Manufacturer-Supplier Relationship in Japan]*, in SAPURAIYAA SHISUTEMU [SUPPLIER SYSTEM] 1, 37 n.* (Takahiro Fujimoto et al. eds., 1998). The translation appeared as SHIJO TO KIGYO SOSHIKI [MARKETS AND FIRM ORGANIZATION] (1980).

22. *See* Banri Asanuma, *Manufacturer-Supplier Relationships in Japan and the Concept of Relation-Specific Skill*, 3 J. JAPANESE & INT'L ECON. 1 (1989).

23. *See* MASAHIKO AOKI, INFORMATION, INCENTIVES, AND BARGAINING IN THE JAPANESE ECONOMY 216-17 (1988); *see also* Masahiko Aoki, *Toward an Economic Model of the Japanese Firm*, 28 J. ECON. LIT. 1 (1990).

drive the subcontractor to merge with the manufacturer. In Japan, they do not. This presents a puzzle to Aoki, who solves it by arguing that Williamson and Klein-Crawford-Alchian overstate the problem of opportunism and that, generally, a firm will keep its promises out of concern for its own reputation.

Jeffrey H. Dyer finds the extensive use of RSIs crucial to the very success of the automobile industry in Japan, since they lead to "lower costs, higher quality, and greater profits":

> [A] key to the success of Japanese network relationships is the practice of dedicating supplier assets to the customer. That is, Japanese auto-parts suppliers send engineers to work at the customer's site, locate plants near the customer, or invest in customized physical assets.[24]

All told, concludes Dyer, "dedicated assets provide Japanese manufacturers with substantial competitive advantages."[25]

This analysis also appears in legal scholarship. In an intriguing recent study of Japanese cross-shareholdings, leading corporate law scholars Ronald Gilson and Mark Roe argue that firms buy stock in each other when they make heavy RSIs in each other.[26] Where Aoki primarily stresses the relationship-specific human capital investments, Gilson-Roe suggest that Japanese production (including the automobile industry) involves high degrees of all three Williamsonian RSIs: human-capital specificity, site specificity, and even physical-asset specificity.

Like other scholars in this tradition, Gilson and Roe note that RSIs generate appropriable quasi rents. Where Aoki argued that reputational effects largely prevent opportunism, however, Gilson and Roe turn to the cross-shareholdings. Because (they argue) Japanese business groups (namely, the *keiretsu*) often own controlling interests in manufacturing firms, groups can collectively control their members. Should any one member behave opportunistically, the group can collectively intervene. The RSIs in the industry are large, in short, and generate distinctive extra-contractual governance arrangements.[27]

---

24. Jeffrey H. Dyer, *Dedicated Assets: Japan's Manufacturing Edge*, HARV. BUS. REV. Nov.-Dec. 1994, at 174, 174.

25. *Id.*

26. *See* Ronald J. Gilson & Mark J. Roe, *Understanding the Japanese Keiretsu: Overlaps Between Corporate Governance and Industrial Organization*, 102 YALE L.J. 871, 884 (1993). A similar argument is made in David Flath, *The Keiretsu Puzzle*, 10 J. JAPANESE & INT'L ECON. 101 (1996). An assertion similar to that made by Gilson & Roe is also made in J. Mark Ramseyer, *Cross-shareholding in the Japanese Keiretsu*, in CONVERGENCE IN CORPORATE LAW: THE EMERGING QUESTIONS (forthcoming 2000). Not to put too fine a point on it, the claim here is that the argument about the automobile industry in Ramseyer, *supra*, is wrong.

27. *See* Gilson & Rose, *supra* note 26.

II. The Industry

A. *Introduction*

Such is the theory. The question is how much of the governance patterns in the Japanese automobile industry it actually explains. We confess to being skeptical. What we know of the industry suggests that RSIs are modest, and what we know of Japanese contracting practice suggests that the parties could solve most of their problems by contract.[28] RSI theory, however, posits that parties will negotiate extra-contractual governance mechanisms primarily when they find large RSIs juxtaposed with significant barriers to contract.

To begin to examine these issues, we pose two necessarily interrelated empirical questions: (a) whether assemblers and suppliers make large RSIs; and (b) whether any RSIs they make lead to extra-contractual governance arrangements. We are the first to admit that we lack direct measures of RSIs. We do, however, have a variety of indirect measures (however imperfect). In this Article, we combine them with an investigation of when and how the parties negotiate what sort of extra-contractual governance mechanisms.

B. *Subcontracting at Honda*[29]

1. *Introduction*

To give a feel for the industry, we begin this analysis of Japanese subcontracting by describing five firms in the Honda network. We realize that the statistically inclined will be impatient with the discursive account. Because much of the misunderstanding about the industry results from the way most scholars understandably lack an intuitive sense of the "shop floor," however, we begin with some anecdotes.

---

28. Contracts could potentially solve the problems whether enforced through the courts or through reputational mechanisms. On reputational sanctions in the industry, see YOSHIRO MIWA, FIRMS AND INDUSTRIAL ORGANIZATION IN JAPAN 75-76 (1996).

29. Generally in this Section, we rely on NIHON RODO KENKYU KIKO, SANGYO BUNGYO KOZO TO RODO SHIJO NO KAISO SEI [THE STRUCTURE OF THE DIVISION OF LABOR IN PRODUCTION, AND THE CLASS STRUCTURE OF THE LABOR MARKET] (1992), as well as conversations with the original investigators. We update the data through FUYUMI MIYOSHI, JIDOSHA GYOKAI HAYAWAKARI MAPPU [EASY-TO-READ MAP OF THE AUTOMOBILE INDUSTRY] (1999); NIHON KEIZAI SHIMBUN SHA, NIKKEI KAISHA JOHO [NIKKEI COMPANY INFORMATION] (relevant years); and SHUKAN TOYO KEIZAI, KIGYO KEIRETSU SORAN [OVERVIEW OF FIRM KEIRETSU] (relevant years) where appropriate. For information on the supplier system generally, see MIWA, *supra* note 28, at § 4.2. On the lack of important government aid to the industry, see John Creighton Campbell, *The Automobile Industry and Public Policy*, *in* THE AMERICAN AND JAPANESE AUTO INDUSTRIES IN TRANSITION 79 (Robert E. Cole & Taizo Yakushiji eds., 1984).

The points we make are not unique to Honda. Instead, they apply to contracting relationships in other manufacturing networks as well.[30]

Founded a half century ago, Honda conquered the motorcycle world in the 1960s.[31] It remains near the apex of that industry, and now stands as Japan's third largest automobile producer. Where Toyota sold 3.2 million cars in 1998 and Nissan 1.6 million cars, Honda sold 1.2 million. Where Toyota had 1998 sales of 7.8 trillion yen and Nissan 3.5 trillion yen, Honda had sales of 3.1 trillion yen. Where Toyota had a workforce of 70,000 and Nissan 40,000, Honda had a workforce of 29,000.

Honda buys components from approximately 280 firms. It maintains long-term ties with about eighty of these, and has equity stakes in a third of the eighty. It pays its suppliers amounts equal to about 80% of its sales. In many cases, these subcontractors are substantial firms in their own right: Keihin (carburetors, fuel injection systems; sales of 144 billion yen and 4,000 employees), for example, or Nippon seiki (gauges; 87 billion sales and 1,700 employees), and Yutaka giken (exhaust systems; 72 billion sales and 1,100 employees).

Honda buys shock absorbers from three firms, but relies most heavily on A_1.[32] With sales of 103 billion yen and 2,800 employees, A_1 is one of Honda's largest subcontractors. In turn, A_1 buys from over 200 suppliers. Many of A_1's suppliers (the steel producers, for instance, or rubber) are large and do not rely heavily on A_1 sales. Others (like the stamping and machining firms that make peripheral products) are much smaller.

Generally, A_1 buys peripherals from eight stamping and thirteen machining companies. Of the eight stamping firms, three sell less than 20% of their output to A_1, two sell 40-60%, and three sell over 60%. Of eleven machining firms (we lack data on two), three sell under 10% of their output to A_1, two sell 10-30%, three sell 50-60%, and three sell over 70%.

Among these second-tier subcontractors, B_1 runs stamping operations and B_2 machining operations. In turn, B_1 buys from sixty-two suppliers, and B_2 from fifteen. Among these third-tier subcontractors, C_1 does spot-welding jobs and C_2 stamping work, both for B_1. We begin with these third-tier firms and turn then to the second- and finally the first-tier.

---

30. Discussions of the Nissan network in RODO, *supra* note 29, reflect this, and Miwa's own interviews confirm this. Contrary to many claims, the contracting practices by the firms in the industry (including Toyota) are standard and used routinely by firms in a variety of other industries as well. *See* MIWA, *supra* note 28, at 64-68. To test the common Toyota-is-different hypothesis, we add a Toyota dummy in the regressions below.

31. *See* MIWA, *supra* note 28, at 64.

32. Because of the assurances of confidentiality the original researchers gave their interviewees, we do not identify the firms involved in the following examples.

2. Third-tier Subcontractors

C_1. Established in 1968 as a welding operation, C_1 initially consisted of the president, his wife, and two part-time employees. Together, they produced television parts. They started selling to B_1 in 1985, and by 1989 had annual sales of 78 million yen, eleven workers, and seventeen welding machines. The firm now sells half its output to B_1. The rest of its output involves electrical equipment, water heaters, and automobile accessories like audio and lighter parts.

On the 27th or 28th of each month, B_1 gives C_1 the next month's order plan. Twice a day, it sends a truck with the materials for C_1 to weld and picks up any finished work.

For all practical purposes, only the president at C_1 has any engineering expertise. Of the eleven workers, three are family members and eight are nonfamily employees with less than ten years' experience. When faced with a new product from B_1, the president personally determines the technical specifications of the manufacturing process: what voltage to set for the weld, for instance, how much time to use, and what pressure to apply. After he does, the employees follow his instructions.

C_2. Firm C_2 began in 1973 with five workers. For several years, it did stamping work for air conditioners and vending machines. As demand fell the president asked B_1 for work. When B_1 agreed, C_2 bought the new equipment necessary. Within a year, it had fifteen employees and sent 70% of its work to B_1.

Of the fifteen people at C_2, three are family members, five are full-time employees, and seven are part-time. The work is sufficiently simple that virtually any employee can do it with little experience. B_1 pays C_2 on a piece-rate basis, and charges it for the supplies and stamping dies it needs.

C_2 sends some of its work (10-20% of its sales) to four other firms. These fourth-tier subcontractors too are mostly family operations. Typically, they have one or two non-family employees.

3. Second-tier Subcontractors

B_1. The creation of an ex-Nakajima Aircraft employee, B_1 began in 1947. Initially, it produced agricultural machines, but in 1954 took up stamping work. It adopted its current corporate status in 1962, and began selling door-handle parts two years later.

In 1971, B_1 began doing stamp work for A_1. By 1984, it had eighty-five employees (including seven part-time) and sales of 2.13 billion yen. It pays its suppliers amounts equal to 40% of its sales. It sells two-fifths of its output to A_1 and two-fifths to another firm that incorporates the work into brake assemblies bound for Honda. The remaining fifth it sells elsewhere. It owns its own stamp presses.

When A_1 and B_1 negotiate a new job, they set the expected quantity and price, and calculate a depreciation charge for the stamp dies. On the 20th of each month, A_1 announces its projected demand for the next ninety days. Within each month, when necessary, it can change orders on five days' notice.

B_2. As of 1987, second-tier subcontractor B_2 had fifty-five employees and 667 million yen in sales. Established in 1964, it had started as a machining firm for a textile machine producer. Because the president knew the president of first-tier subcontractor, X, it shifted to automobile parts the next year.

In 1970, with fifteen to sixteen employees, B_2 began trading with A_1. At the time, X had no objection to its doing so. When B_2's orders from A_1 began to rival its sales to X, X still did not object. By 1987, B_2 sold half of its output to A_1.

B_2 specializes in precision machining. Of its fifty-five employees, thirty-seven are "regular" employees (twenty-seven male and ten female; twenty-seven full-time and ten part-time). Of the twenty-seven full-time regular employees, twenty have less than ten years' experience.

The part-time employees are primarily housewives from nearby farms. They do the same labor-intensive manufacturing work as their full-time counterparts. Although the company would prefer that they worked full-time, they remain part-time to preserve the option of staying home during the peak agricultural work season.

In 1987, B_2 hired a retired A_1 director as a technical advisor. He advised the firm twice a week on equipment investment, negotiations with A_1, and assorted other managerial issues. B_2 holds title to its own equipment. It buys from its own subcontractors products worth a quarter of its total sales.

4. *First-tier Subcontractor A_1*

Founded in 1938, A_1 began by manufacturing aircraft parts. In 1953, it switched to motorcycle shock absorbers for the young Honda firm. When Honda moved into automobiles, A_1 followed. In 1970, it experienced financial problems, and Honda responded by buying an equity stake (now 35.8%). It has since listed its stock on the Tokyo Stock Exchange. Its president and about half its directors are from Honda.

A_1 currently makes shock absorbers and a variety of other air- and oil-pressure-related goods. By product, 61% of its 1998 sales go to cars or trucks, 33% to motorcycles, and 8% to boats. By buyer, 72% of its sales go to Honda, 8% to Suzuki, and smaller amounts to such firms as Kawasaki, Yamaha, Fuji Heavy Industries (maker of Subarus), Mazda, and Mitsubishi Auto. Purchases from its own suppliers count for about 63% of its sales.

A_1 regularly designs products in collaboration with Honda and sends its people to Honda as guest engineers. In developing these new products, A_1 and Honda generally ignore the lower-tier subcontractors (who, as the discussion above suggests, lack much engineering expertise anyway).

Honda models are subject to a four-year product cycle, with minor annual changes. Many of A_1's products are subject to the annual changes.

C. Industry-wide Data[33]

1. Firm Size

We turn now from this discursive account to aggregate statistics on the industry and consider first some information on firm size (Section 1) and supplier associations (Section 2). Although (as the account above implies) many second- and third-tier suppliers are small, some first-tier suppliers are larger even than a few of the assemblers.[34] As noted earlier, Toyota has 70,000 employees and annual sales of 7.8 trillion yen. Mazda has only 24,000 employees and 1.5 trillion yen in sales; Suzuki has 14,000 employees and 1.2 trillion yen sales; and Daihatsu has 11,000 employees and 783 billion yen sales.

By comparison, Denso (maker of air-conditioning and other automobile-industry electrical units) has 40,000 employees and sales of 1.3 trillion yen. Asahi Glass has 8,000 employees and 855 billion yen in sales; Aishin seiki (running gear) has 12,000 employees and 521 billion yen sales; and Kyocera (high-tech ceramics) has 13,000 employees and 492 billion yen in sales. Indeed, several first-tier suppliers are multinational conglomerates that swamp the smaller automobile assemblers: Hitachi (69,000 employees and annual sales of 4.1 trillion yen), Toshiba (66,000 employees and 3.7 trillion yen in sales), and Matsushita Electric (46,000 employees and 4.9 trillion yen in sales).

Nor should one think suppliers simply make ashtrays and brakes for Toyota and Honda to bolt onto their cars. Sometimes the "assembler" out-sources even the assembly itself. A "Toyota" car, for example, might well have been assembled by Toyoda Automatic Loom,

---

33. In this Section and elsewhere, we obtain general information on firm sales, employees, and the like from NIHON KEIZAI, *supra* note 29; TOYO KEIZAI, *supra* note 29; NIHON KEIZAI SHIMBUN SHA, KAISHA SORAN [ANNUAL CORPORATION REPORTS] (relevant volumes and years); NIHON NO JIDOSHA BUHIN KOGYO (1998 NEN BAN) [JAPANESE AUTOMOTIVE PARTS INDUSTRY ASSOCIATION, 1998] (Nihon jidosha buhin kogyo kai & Oto toreedo jaaneru eds., 1998) [hereinafter JAPIA]; TOYO KEIZAI SHIMPOSHA, SHIKIHO: MIJOJO GAISHA BAN [SEASONAL REPORTS: UNLISTED COMPANIES] (relevant years).

34. These are not mutually exclusive categories. The same supplier may be a first-tier supplier with respect to one assembler but a second- or third-tier supplier with respect to another. Teikei kikaki sells both to Aisan kogyo (a supplier) and to Yamaha (an assembler); Aisan sells directly to Toyota (an assembler) but also to Denso (a supplier).

Toyota Auto Body, or Kanto Automobile Works. All told, Toyota consigns the entire assembly of nearly half its cars. At times in its history, Toyota even consigned the development of some of its cars to other firms.[35]

We have less data on the second-, third-, or fourth-tier suppliers. The Japan Automotive Parts Industry Association ("JAPIA") does not maintain a list of these suppliers, and even if it did their small size would make information on them hard to collect. The annual government *Census of Manufactures*, however, does collect data on manufacturing establishments (each plant within a firm is a separate unit), and this census confirms the small size of most automobile supplier plants. In Table 1, we give plant size in the transportation equipment sector. Of the 7,533 establishments, 4,236 (56%) have ten to twenty-nine employees. Only 128 establishments (1.7%) have more than 1,000.[36]

2. *Supplier Associations*

Most assemblers maintain associations of first-tier suppliers.[37] The suppliers in these associations meet from time to time to exchange information with each other and with the assembler. Obviously, suppliers will find membership most worthwhile if they are producing customized goods for the supplier. Toyota, for example, has 189 suppliers in its network, Nissan has 234, and Mitsubishi 377.

---

35. *See* Haruhito Shiomi, *The Formation of Assembler Networks in the Automobile Industry: The Case of Toyota Motor Company (1955-1980)*, *in* FORDISM TRANSFORMED: THE DEVELOPMENT OF PRODUCTION METHODS IN THE AUTOMOBILE INDUSTRY 28, 30-31 (Haruhito Shiomi & Kazuo Wada eds., 1995); KANTO JIDOSHA KOGYO, KANTO JIDOSHA KOGYO 40 NEN SHI [40-YEAR HISTORY OF KANTO JIDOSHA KOGYO] 118, 153 (1986).

36. HEISEI 9 NEN, KOGYO TOKEI HYO: SANGYO HEN [CENSUS OF MANUFACTURES: REPORT BY INDUSTRY, 1997] (Tsusho sangyo sho ed., 1999). Not all data are available broken down at the three-digit sectors. However, of the 13,518 establishments in the two-digit transportation equipment sector, 9,964 are from the three-digit automotive sector; of the 907,000 employees in the two-digit sector, 770,476 are in the three-digit automotive sector. The correlation coefficients between the two-digit transportation and three-digit automotive sectors are: (a) for distribution of employees, by establishment size — 99.96%; and (b) for distribution of establishments, by establishment size — 99.97%.

37. On supplier associations, see MIWA, *supra* note 28, at 70-72. In several cases, the assembler maintains more than one association. Toyota, for example, has three associations divided on the basis of geography. Honda does not maintain a formal association; here, we use its list of suppliers instead. For our database, we rely on the 1998 JAPIA list of 1,649 firms. *See* JAPIA, *supra* note 33. The list primarily includes JAPIA members but includes some prominent non-member parts manufacturers and excludes some members who do not make parts (*e.g.*, scrap dealers) or wholesalers who deal primarily in other goods. *See id.* at 251.

TABLE 1: ESTABLISHMENT SIZE AND INVESTMENT LEVELS IN THE TRANSPORTATION EQUIPMENT SECTOR (1997)

A Estab. size (emp's)	B Capital	C Employees	D Establishments	B/C	B/D
10-29	302,800	76,410	4,236	3.96	71.5
30-49	192,900	39,093	1,000	4.93	192.9
50-99	421,900	72,251	1,032	5.84	408.8
100-199	547,900	80,549	589	6.80	930.2
200-299	373,700	48,422	198	7.72	1,887.4
300-499	637,400	72,940	186	8.74	3,426.9
500-999	1,160,700	116,503	164	9.96	7,077.4
1000-	3,766,900	363,618	128	10.36	29,428.9

Notes: Capital is in million yen, excluding land.
Establishments are those in the 2-digit transportation equipment sector.

Source: HEISEI 9 NEN, KOGYO TOKEI HYO: SANGYO HEN [CENSUS OF MANUFACTURES: REPORT BY INDUSTRY, 1997] (Tsusho sangyo sho ed., 1999).

Observers frequently cite these associations as evidence of automobile industry "keiretsu," and assume that the groups are exclusive. In fact, they are anything but. Consider a simple correlation matrix of association membership. Yamaha, Suzuki, and Honda also make motorcycles, and thus draw on a different set of suppliers. Among the other assemblers, however, all correlation coefficients except one are above 0.20, and among Subaru, Daihatsu, and Mazda all coefficients are above 0.50. Even the membership correlation coefficient for archrivals Toyota and Nissan is 0.22. Put another way, of the 189 Toyota and 234 Nissan association members, sixty-eight suppliers are in both associations.[38]

Or consider the following: 1,098 firms are in one or more of the Toyota, Nissan, Mitsubishi, Subaru, Mazda, Daihatsu, Hino, Isuzu, Yamaha, Suzuki, and Honda networks.[39] Among these firms, the mean association membership is 1.91. Seven hundred thirty-eight firms are in only one association; 135 are in two associations; 135 are in three-to-five associations; sixty-two are in six-to-eight associations, and twenty-eight are in nine or more.

Nor are these associations peculiar to the assemblers. Many suppliers also maintain associations of *their* suppliers. For example, Denso (air conditioners; 40,000 employees and 1,375 billion yen in sales) has an association of sixty-seven suppliers; Koito (lighting

---

38. Toyota has a 20% equity interest in Hino and a 34% interest in Daihatsu. As one might expect given this equity network, the correlation coefficients among the supplier associations for these three firms are higher — ranging from 0.30 to 0.44

39. The Honda network is not a formal organization like the others. However, we follow the categorization of JAPIA, *supra* note 33, which lists some firms as regular suppliers to Honda.

equipment; 4,600 employees and 148 billion yen in sales) has an association of sixty-eight suppliers; Akebono Brake (2,900 employees and 108 billion yen in sales) has an association of seventy-nine suppliers; and Kayaba (oil pressure equipment; 4,200 employees and 177 billion yen in sales) has an association of 270 suppliers.[40] More generally, of the 373 firms on which the JAPIA provides data, 188 (50%) maintained their own supplier associations. Among the firms with 500 or fewer employees, the figure was 39% (sixty-two firms); among those with 501-1,000 employees, 53% (forty-six firms); among those with 1,001-5,000 employees 67% (seventy-two firms); and among those with 5,001 or more employees, 40% (eight firms).

III. Relation-Specific Investments

A. *Smaller Firms*

The discussion of the Honda network suggests two preliminary points about the level of RSIs at the smaller suppliers. First, they invest very little in relationship-specific human capital. We know they invest little in relationship-specific human capital because they invest little in human capital at all. In many of these firms, only one or two people know any engineering. The other employees are so new that if they did have any expertise, it would be general rather than specific to the firm or its partners.

Second, small as they are, the firms can and do sell to buyers in several distinct industries. Not only do they not sell to a single firm, they do not even sell to a single industry. Depending on their niche, they stamp, they machine, they assemble, they weld. If the price is right, they will stamp, machine, assemble, and weld Honda-bound products. But they can apparently do the same for aircraft, air conditioners, boats, textile equipment, television sets, and vending machines.

Loosely to be sure, industry-wide data confirm these impressions. First, employee tenure at the small firms is notoriously short. Consider data from the government's annual census of wages (Figure 1).[41] Among the smallest firms (those in the two-digit transportation equipment sector with ten to ninety-nine employees), nearly 40% of

---

40. *See* Nihon Denso, Nihon Denso 25 nen shi [A 25-Year History of Nihon Denso] 243-44 (1974); Koito Seisakusho, Koito Seisakusho 70 nen shi [A 70-Year History of Koito Seisakusho] 42 (1985); Akebono Bureeki, Hanseiki no Ayumi [A Half Century of Progress] 347 (1979); Kayaba Kogyo, Kayaba Kogyo 50 nen shi [A 50-Year History of Kayaba Kogyo] 284-86 (1986).

41. *See* Rodosho, Chingin Sensasu, Heisei 9 nen Chingin Kozo Kihon Tokei Chosa [Basic Survey on Wage Structure 1997] (1998). In compiling this figure, we use data provided to us by the ministry, which breaks down industry into smaller categories than those used for the final published survey.

the workers have been at the firm for less than four years. Another 20-odd percent have worked there five to ten years. Even among the firms with 100-999 employees, half have less than ten years' tenure.

Second, the small firms lack substantial physical-asset investments of any sort, much less relationship-specific physical assets (Table 1). At the smallest plants, capital investment per employee is a mere 4 million yen — at 120 yen/dollar, about $33,000. Even among plants with 200-300 employees, the figure approaches only 7.8 million yen, or about $65,000.

Finally, as we explain in more detail immediately below, among automobile suppliers of all sizes, most technology is general rather than specific. Those investments that are specific, in turn, are specific not to a relationship but to a model. As such, they necessarily have, at most, four years' duration.

FIGURE 1: EMPLOYEE TENURE IN THE TRANSPORTATION EQUIPMENT SECTOR (1997)

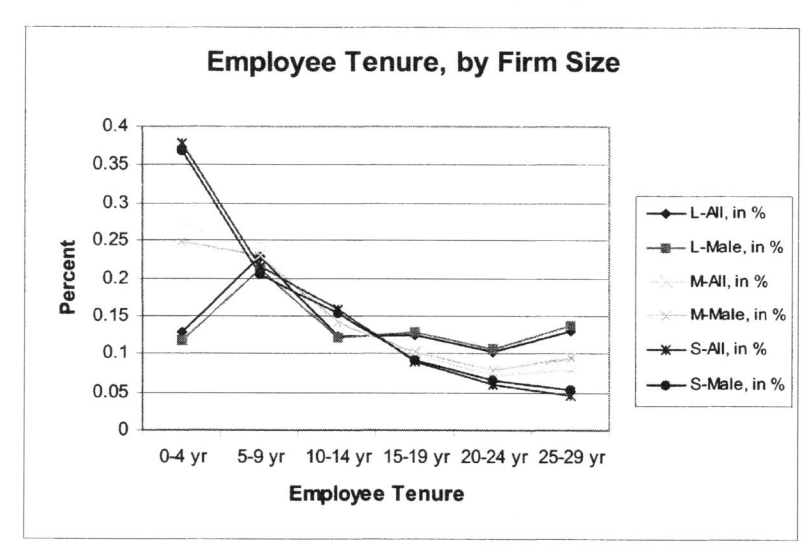

Note: L — firms with 1,000 or more employees; M — firms with 100-999 employees; S — firms with 10-99 employees.

Source: RODOSHO, CHINGIN SENSASU, HEISEI 9 NEN CHINGIN KOZO KIHON TOKEI CHOSA [BASIC SURVEY ON WAGE STRUCTURE 1997] (1998). In compiling this figure, we use data provided to us by the ministry that disaggregate the industry into categories smaller than those used for the final published survey.

B. *Larger Firms*

1. *The Logic*

Given this lack of substantial investments among second- and third-tier suppliers, if any suppliers in the Japanese automobile industry have large RSIs, they must be among the larger first-tier suppliers. At least there, according to Table 1 and Figure 1, the levels of capital investment are relatively high and employee tenures long. At least there, physical assets *could* be substantial and relationship-specific, employees *could* have significant relationship-specific expertise, and those investments *could* affect the governance arrangements the firms adopt. And at least there, the assemblers sometimes make equity investments: as we show in Table 4, the probability that an assembler invests in a supplier increases with supplier size.

Yet even here, basic logic should give one pause. First, these firms make products common to all cars everywhere. All cars have windshields, shock absorbers, headlights, seats, piston rings, and cigarette lighters. They may come in different sizes and different shapes, but if a supplier can make these sorts of products for one assembler, it could probably make them for another assembler.

Put another way, any asset-specificity in production seems model-specific rather than relationship-specific. Suppose a supplier needs to invest in idiosyncratic equipment or training to make Camry-bound tail lights. If those investments would not transfer to Accord-bound tail lights, they probably would not transfer to Corolla-bound ones either.[42]

Second, any model-specific investments are short-lived. For most assemblers, a model lasts only four years. As a result, even if a subcontractor does own a specialized asset, it usually will not generate quasi rents long-term. Instead, it will generate them for four years at most. Yet the subcontractors sign contracts with the assembler that last for the term of the model. If any firm earns model-specific quasi rents on its investments, it can readily protect them by contract and by the prospect of market competition at the end of the model cycle.

Third, by simple geography and component size, even any site specificities should be minor. Japan is small, and so are most components. The entire country covers roughly the size of California, and Toyota city is a scant 200 miles from Tokyo. Other than car bodies and completed engines, moreover, most automobile parts are easy to ship. Given the elaborate networks of railroads and super highways,

---

42. As implied in Asanuma's own discussion. *See* Asanuma, *supra* note 22, at 4.

suppliers everywhere should be able cost-effectively to deliver components to assemblers anywhere.[43]

Fourth, if the biggest companies potentially have the largest RSIs, they are also the ones least likely to let that specificity affect fundamental aspects of governance like equity ownership. They are simply too big and too diversified. Among the suppliers, take the 248 stock-exchange listed firms. These firms maintain memberships in a mean 3.2 supplier associations. Or take the firms for which we have data on sales to automobile assemblers (again, about 250). On average, these firms sell about half their output to their lead customers in the automobile industry. Even if such firms did make large RSIs, they would rarely want to structure their basic governance mechanisms to deal with firms buying only half their output.

2. *Cross-shareholdings*

a. Introduction. Turn from these broad impressions to firm-level data on the first-tier suppliers. To explore the role that RSIs play in this environment, we first identify those contractual ties where logic predicts large RSIs would most likely exist, if they exist anywhere. We then ask whether the parties to those ties negotiate the extra-contractual governance mechanisms (like equity investments) that RSI theory dictates.

Note the limits inherent in this exercise. Necessarily, we examine a composite hypothesis: (i) that RSIs are large enough to create significant problems of opportunism, (ii) that contractual solutions to such problems are infeasible, and (iii) that the RSIs and contracting problems lead to the predicted governance mechanisms. Suppose that, despite having good proxies for RSIs, we fail to observe the predicted governance mechanisms. In itself, that result would not tell us whether the hypothesis failed because RSIs were small, because contracts worked, or because RSI theory did not apply. Note too that we ask readers to table the social scientific custom of focusing on regressions as the key test in an article. To us at least, the most relevant material on RSIs is the least technical: that which we obtain by observation and industry-wide data. We present the regressions below only as supplementary evidence.

We reason that in the automobile industry, as in most industries, large RSIs most likely will exist in transactions in which suppliers have close, exclusive (or nearly exclusive) ties to a given assembler. Sup-

---

43. The high cost to consumers of shipping materials around Japan through the commercial transportation industry is irrelevant. Automobile assemblers are large enough that if such shippers (whether because of regulatory restrictions or because of cartelization) charge more than the average cost of transportation (a function only of tolls, fuel, driver wages, and truck maintenance and repair), the assembler can provide the transportation services in-house.

pose that to produce a given part for Assembler *A* requires heavy, idiosyncratic equipment. *A* could itself pay for the equipment, or Supplier S could pay. Either way, in order to plan for the investment *A* and S will communicate with each other extensively. Provided the idiosyncratic investment generates returns to scale, they will also try to maximize S's sales to *A*.

If production involves large RSIs for which S pays, then by RSI theory S will need protection against *A*'s ex post opportunism. *Inter alia*, it could try to obtain a controlling equity interest in *A*. This does not happen. Even the largest Japanese suppliers do not buy controlling interests in Toyota, Nissan, or even Suzuki.[44] Neither do they seem to negotiate other controls over *A*'s governance.

Alternatively, assembler *A* could pay for the RSI. To prevent opportunistic action by S, it might then negotiate a controlling equity interest in (or other control mechanisms over) S. Our testable hypothesis follows: if large RSIs structure the Japanese automobile industry, assemblers will tend to negotiate control over those suppliers who have the closest ties with them.

b. The Test. To examine whether suppliers with the closest ties to an assembler are subject to extra-contractual governance mechanisms, we regress:

an assembler's equity investment in a supplier (both a dummy for investments of 10% or more [**SubEqInv**] and a continuous variable [**Eq%**]), *on*

(i) the fraction of its output which that supplier sells to the assembler (both a dummy for sales of 50% or more [**SubSales**] and a continuous variable [**Sales%**]), *and*

(ii) whether the supplier is a member only of that assembler's supplier association (**LoneClub**).

For controls, we include:

(x) a dummy for whether S lists its stock on an exchange (**Listed**),

(y) a dummy for whether S is a member of no supplier association (**NoClub**), *and*

(z) as a measure of firm size, the number of employees at S (**Employees**).[45]

---

44. The exception may be Toyoda Automatic Loom, which assembles some Toyota automobiles. This firm (founded by the father of the founder of Toyota Motor) antedates Toyota Motor. It initially specialized in producing automated weaving machines for Japan's booming pre-war cotton textile industry. With 5.1% of the stock, it is the largest shareholder of Toyota Motor; and Toyota Motor owns 24.7% of Toyoda Automatic Loom. In January 1999, Toyoda Automatic Loom's interest in Toyota Motor was worth about 560 billion yen; Toyota Motor's interest in Automatic Loom was worth about 140 billion yen.

45. We also used total sales by the firm but did not generate substantially different results.

Because many observers claim that Toyota maintains unusually close ties with its suppliers, we add a dummy for whether the assembler involved is Toyota (**Toyota**).[46] We include more precise definitions of the variables in Table 2, summary statistics and sources in Table 3, and regression results in Table 4.

TABLE 2: REGRESSION VARIABLES — DEFINITIONS

Dir: 1 if the assembler that buys the largest fraction of a supplier's output has a seat (including a seat held by a former assembler employee) on the supplier's board of directors; 0 otherwise.

Employees: The number of full-time employees at a supplier.

Eq%: The percentage of a supplier's stock held by the assembler that buys the largest fraction of the supplier's output.

Listed: 1 if a supplier lists its stock on either the Tokyo or Osaka Stock Exchange; 0 otherwise.

LoneClub: 1 if a supplier is listed in JAPIA data as a member of only one assembler's supplier association; 0 otherwise.

NoClub: 1 if a supplier is listed in JAPIA data as a member of no supplier association; 0 otherwise.

NumDir: The number of directors that the assembler buying the largest fraction of a supplier's output has on the supplier's board (including seats held by former assembler employees).

Sales%: The percentage of a supplier's output bought by the assembler that buys the largest fraction of the supplier's output.

SubSales: 1 if a supplier sells 50% or more of its output to a single assembler; 0 otherwise.

SubEqInv: 1 if the assembler that buys the largest fraction of a supplier's output owns 10% or more of the supplier's stock; 0 otherwise.

Toyota: 1 if the assembler that buys the largest fraction of the supplier's output is Toyota; 0 otherwise.

c. The Results. Perhaps the biggest surprise in Table 4 involves the radically different effects that **SubSales** (and **Sales%**) and **LoneClub** have. On the one hand, the coefficients to **SubSales** (and **Sales%**) suggest that the parties do adopt extra-contractual governance mechanisms: the coefficients are consistently positive and significant in regressions (a), (c), (d), and (f). On the other hand, the coefficients on **LoneClub** suggest nothing of the sort: the coefficients are insignificant in all specifications and do not even consistently have the same sign.

---

46. According to Table 4, Toyota is distinctive only in that it is located in the same prefecture (Aichi) as many of its suppliers.

TABLE 3: REGRESSION VARIABLES — SUMMARY STATISTICS

	n	Min	Mean	Max
Dir	209	0	0.368	1
Employees	700	7	1,848	68,947
Eq%	462	0	11.750	100
Listed	1,648	0	0.150	1
LoneClub	1,648	0	0.447	1
NoClub	1,648	0	0.346	1
NumDir	209	0	1.536	14
Sales%	249	0.6	48.7	99.8
SamePref	477	0	0.344	1
SubSales	249	0	0.510	1
SubEqInv	462	0	0.286	1
Toyota	479	0	0.251	1

Sources: The data — when possible from 1998 — is variously assembled from the relevant years of NIHON KEIZAI SHIMBUN SHA, *NIKKEI KAISHA JOHO [NIKKEI COMPANY INFORMATION]* (1998); SHUKAN TOYO KEIZAI, *KIGYO KEIRETSU SORAN [OVERVIEW OF FIRM KEIRETSU]* (1998); TOYO KEIZAI SHIMPOSHA, *SHIKIHO: MIJOJO GAISHA BAN [SEASONAL REPORTS: UNLISTED COMPANIES]* (relevant years); NIHON KEIZAI SHIMBUN SHA, *KAISHA SORAN [ANNUAL CORPORATION REPORTS]* (1998); *NIHON NO JIDOSHA BUHIN KOGYO (1998 NEN BAN) [JAPANESE AUTOMOTIVE PARTS INDUSTRY, 1998]* (Nihon jidosha buhin kogyo kai & Oto toreedo jaaneru eds., 1998).

The difference between **SubSales** and **LoneClub** is surprising, because one might have thought that the variables would identify roughly the same suppliers. One would have thought, for example, that if S were affiliated only with A's supplier association (**LoneClub**) it would disproportionately sell to A (**SubSales**). The suppliers in these associations meet from time to time to exchange information with each other and with the assembler. Obviously, suppliers will find membership most worthwhile if they are producing customized goods for the supplier. If so, then the two variables would be heavily correlated and generate similar results in Table 4. In fact, the correlation coefficient between the two is only 0.13.[47]

For our purposes, the resulting question becomes: If there were significant RSIs in the industry, would **SubSales** or **LoneClub** more likely signify their presence? If the answer is **SubSales**, then Table 4 suggests that the transactions involve substantial RSIs. If the answer is **LoneClub**, then the very absence of equity investments suggests either that large RSIs do not exist or that they do not structure governance patterns.

---

47. Adding a variable interacting **LoneClub** and **SubSales** results in a significant, positive coefficient on **SubSales** but insignificant coefficients for both **LoneClub** and the interaction term.

TABLE 4: SALES DIVERSIFICATION AND EQUITY INVESTMENTS

RHS:	SubEqInv			Eq%		
	(a)	(b)	(c)	(d)	(e)	(f)
SubSales	.421		.435			
	(6.02)		(6.02)			
Sales%				.361		.358
				(7.65)		(7.39)
LoneClub		.011	-.067		2.716	.736
		(0.22)	(0.85)		(1.24)	(0.26)
Employees	.0001	.00001	.0001	.002	.0005	.002
	(3.48)	(2.07)	(3.30)	(2.49)	(1.57)	(2.50)
Listed	.061	-.089	.054	.860	-5.678	.938
	(0.74)	(1.86)	(0.65)	(0.29)	(2.55)	(0.31)
NoClub	-.031	-.124	-.067	1.86	-3.667	2.239
	(0.19)	(1.53)	(0.42)	(0.35)	(0.97)	(0.41)
Toyota	.052	.085	.039	2.298	3.116	2.447
	(0.71)	(1.67)	(0.52)	(0.82)	(1.34)	(0.86)
Constant				-6.261	11.340	-6.554
				(1.91)	(5.93)	(1.89)
Adjusted R^2	0.19	0.02	0.19	0.23	0.02	0.22
n	248	462	248	248	462	248
	Probit	Probit	Probit	OLS	OLS	OLS

Notes: For the OLS regressions, we give the coefficients, followed by the absolute value of the t-statistics on the line below.

For probit regressions, we give the probability of a change in the dependent variable given a one-unit change in the independent variable. We give the absolute value of the z values for the underlying coefficients on the line below.

For probit regressions, we give the pseudo-R^2 rather than the adjusted R^2.

Sources: See Table 3.

Reasons linked to technological innovation suggest that **LoneClub** more plausibly proxies for RSIs than does **SubSales**. We discuss that hypothesis in Subsection 3 below. We turn to the possibility that **SubSales** better proxies for RSIs in Subsection 4.

3. *RSIs and Technological Innovation*

a. Introduction. Firms that invest heavily in RSIs will prefer to deal with suppliers who avoid selling customized components to their competitors. All else equal, off-the-shelf technology is cheaper than new. As a result, firms will not invest in idiosyncratic technology unless doing so generates a competitive advantage. If it does generate that advantage, they (the investing firms) will want to do what they can to keep that technology from their rivals.

Once an investing firm's supplier sells similarly sophisticated products to the investing firm's competitors, however, the odds increase dramatically that the technology will leak. After all, given the new improved technology, the supplier has an incentive to adapt the technology in a way that will let it win business from those competitors. Only by limiting its ties to suppliers who restrict their other customized sales to buyers outside the industry can the investing firm slow the technological leak. The conclusion: large RSIs most likely will exist (if they exist anywhere) in situations where the supplier sells customized components only to one automobile assembler.

b. An Example. Perhaps an illustration would help. Suppose a subcontractor, with the aid of Toyota engineers, develops a new, more cost-effective Camry shock absorber. Given that Nissan and Honda do not use such a shock absorber (the technology is still secret, after all), the production process is, by definition, specific to Toyota trades. Like virtually all automobile parts, though, shock absorbers themselves are common to all assemblers, and many technological innovations are not patentable. As a result, even if only Toyota cars were to use this improved technology, the supplier could potentially win orders from Honda and Nissan by adapting it to Accords and Maximas. Often, Toyota would want to keep this technology from its competitors.[48] To lower the risk of a technological leak, in turn, it may have an incentive to develop the new technology only with suppliers who do not make customized components for those competitors.

What this logic ignores, of course, are those RSIs that are simple adaptations to model size and shape rather than real technological improvements. For those RSIs, the assembler will not worry about technological leaks to competitors. No matter how mundane a shock absorber it may be, a Maxima shock absorber will not fit an Accord. In this sense, the technology behind any Maxima shock absorber is specific to trades with Nissan, but it is also technology that Nissan will not try to keep secret.

Crucially, however, for such size and shape specificities, the amount of the RSI is also quite small. Given the essential interchangeability of most shock-absorber technology, most suppliers who now make Maxima shock absorbers will be able to shift production to Accord shock absorbers with relative ease. They will incur some transitional costs, to be sure, but probably little more than they would incur in shifting among Toyota models — from, for instance, a Camry shock absorber to a Corolla shock absorber.

c. Technology and Table 4. Consider, then, the implications of this analysis for the importance of **SubSales** and **LoneClub**. Firm size held

---

48. Not always, of course. Sometimes Toyota is happy to let the supplier market it elsewhere, in exchange for a lower price on the new technology.

constant (as in Table 4), when **SubSales** and **LoneClub** firms differ, they will differ primarily in whether they:

(a) sell customized products to multiple automobile assemblers, *or*

(b) sell customized products only to one automobile assembler and fill the rest of their output with either general open-market products within the automobile industry or products for buyers outside the industry.

To see this, consider several possibilities:

(i) *SubSales = 1, LoneClub = 1 (30 firms)*. If most suppliers sold primarily to one assembler and no one else, then for most suppliers both **SubSales** and **LoneClub** would equal one. In Table 4, the two variables would then have similar coefficients. They do not.

(ii) *SubSales = 1, LoneClub = 0 (58 firms)*. Suppose a supplier sells more than half its output to one assembler, but is a member of multiple supplier associations (**SubSales** = 1, **LoneClub** = 0). That it has ties to other assemblers sufficiently close to justify association membership indicates that it probably sells significant amounts (even if less than half) of sophisticated, customized goods to others in the industry.

(iii) *SubSales = 0, LoneClub = 1 (69 firms)*. By contrast, suppose a supplier sells a low fraction of its sales to its principal automobile assembler buyer, but is a member only of one supplier association (**SubSales** = 0, **LoneClub** = 1). That it has joined only one association suggests it produces few customized products for other assemblers in the industry. That it nonetheless sells a high fraction of its output to other firms suggests that it must either (i) be selling outside the industry, or (ii) be selling non-customized goods to other assemblers.

(iv) *The Result.* Consequently, the factor driving the different coefficients on **SubSales** and **LoneClub** in Table 4 would seem to lie in the degree of extra-industry (or noncustomized, intra-industry) sales. If a supplier sells to firms other than its lead assembler buyer, does it sell customized goods to other buyers in the industry? Or does it instead sell only either generally available open-market goods or customized goods to those outside the automobile industry? If production involves large RSIs, then the assembler should prefer the latter group of suppliers over the former. If so, the key variable for our purposes would be **LoneClub** rather than **SubSales**. From the coefficients to **LoneClub** in Table 4, a simple bottom line then follows: RSIs do not explain equity cross-holdings in the automobile industry.

4. *Sales Diversification and RSIs*

We hesitate to push this interpretation too hard. Readers of earlier versions complained (perhaps justifiably) that in doing so we were belittling inconvenient results. Might it not be, they asked, that the lack of sales diversification *did* signal the presence of RSIs, while the supplier associations were trivial social clubs? If the associations performed no significant information-transmission function, might the lack of sales diversification not signal the presence of RSIs after all? And is not the stability of the relationships itself evidence of large RSIs?

   a. Equity Investments. Perhaps — but in pursuing this line of attack one can easily miss several key bits of evidence. Most basically, one can exaggerate the pervasiveness of the extra-contractual governance mechanisms in place. More specifically, one can exaggerate the pervasiveness of the cross-shareholdings in the industry. For in truth, the level of cross-shareholdings is low.

We have equity ownership data on 462 suppliers (162 listed firms and 300 unlisted). In 57% of the suppliers (262 firms) the lead automobile assembler buyer owns no equity. In an additional 15% (sixty-eight firms), it owns under 10%. In only a quarter of the suppliers does it have at least a 10% interest, and in only 5% does it own a majority interest.

One might plausibly ask whether equity investments are not more pervasive in the suppliers on whom we lack the data. After all, we have data disproportionately on the larger firms. And yet, stock exchange listing held constant, the assemblers are more likely to invest in the larger firms than the smaller (as we will show in Table 4, regressions (a)-(c)). Thus our data, though they disproportionately derive from the larger firms, give us reason to doubt that equity investments are more common among suppliers as a whole.[49]

   b. Sales diversification. One can also exaggerate the extent to which suppliers fail to diversify their sales. We have sales data on 249 suppliers (firms with 67 to 11,574 employees; mean employees of 1,260). In only 127 of these firms (51%) did the lead assembler buyer buy 50% or more of the supplier's output. In only seventy-four (30%) did it buy 70% or more.

Given that we disproportionately have information on the larger, listed firms, here too we should worry about sample bias. Curiously, stock listing held constant, the bigger firms are less likely to diversify sales; more predictably, firm size held constant, the listed firms are more likely to diversify sales:

$$\text{Sales\%} = 55.00 + 0.0011 \text{Employees} - 24.35 \text{Listed} + e,$$
$$(23.92) \quad\quad (2.48) \quad\quad\quad (6.49)$$

where n = 249, the absolute value of the t-statistics are in parentheses, and the adjusted R^2 is 0.14.

---

49. Note, however, that the effect is still ambiguous: disproportionately, we have information on the listed firms, and regressions (b) and (d) suggest that, size held constant, the assemblers are more likely to invest in unlisted firms.

Because we have data disproportionately on the larger, listed firms, the effect among suppliers as a whole is hard to predict. Other surveys (Table 5) indicate that the smaller, unlisted firms tend to diversify less than the larger firms. Bear in mind, however, both that these smaller firms produce a relatively minor fraction of the industry output and that even they diversify significantly. According to Table 5, for instance, firms with less than 10 billion yen in sales constitute the smallest 40% of the firms but produce less than 7% of the industry total. Even these firms, however, still diversify: only a quarter sold all their output to one firm, and over half sold to three or more firms.

c. Relational Stability. Nor does the stability of these relationships reflect large RSIs. First, so long as switching costs are not zero, people generally expect most relations to be stable. This holds in a wide variety of settings and for a wide variety of reasons — whether employment contracts, marriages, or a businessman's loyalty to his barber. In equilibrium, stability will be the norm.

Second, Japanese subcontracting relations are ruthlessly competitive. To the extent that they are stable, they are stable only because — in equilibrium — the existing trading partners will be the firms that do the job better than their potential rivals. As one Toyota director explained:

> Our policy of maintaining double- and multiple-sources is not an opportunistic one. It follows from the notion that a reasonable level of competition is good. We're all human, after all. It's through competition that we'll get improvements in quality, in price, in managerial coordination.[50]

Suppliers understand this. Only by winning the perpetual tournament will they maintain — let alone expand — their business with any given assembler. Take one stamp press firm in the Toyota network. It sold a variety of stamped and plastic products to Toyota, and had for years. But it did not wait for Toyota to place orders. At its own cost, on its own initiative, and with no explicit or implicit commitment from Toyota, it regularly and aggressively explored new technologies. When the supplier found something it thought Toyota might want, it proposed the product to Toyota. If Toyota liked the idea, the supplier obtained a contract. If Toyota did not, it went back to the lab.[51]

---

50. Shoichi Matsuo, *Buhin seisaku wa ikkan shita "koyzon kyoei" [Consistency Turns Parts Policy into One of "Co-existence and Co-prosperity"]*, in JAPIA, *supra* note 33, at 138-39.

51. Interview by Yoshiro Miwa with president of a 20-employee stamping firm, fall 1999 (identity not disclosed for reasons of confidentiality).

TABLE 5: SALES DIVERSIFICATION IN THE AUTOMOBILE SECTOR, BY FIRM SIZE (1996)

Firms, by Sales Vol. (billion yen)	A	B	C	D	E	F Output
	\multicolumn{5}{c}{Number of Domestic Buyers to Whom Firm Sells}	
	1	2	3-4	5 or more	Total firms	
10 or less	42 (27.1%)	23 (14.8%)	40 (25.8%)	50 (32.3%)	155 (40.9%)	920 (6.8%)
10-30	21 (18.9)	12 (10.8)	24 (21.6)	54 (48.6)	111 (29.3)	2,101 (15.5)
30-50	3 (6.3)	3 (6.3)	4 (8.3)	38 (79.2)	48 (12.7)	1,916 (14.2)
50-100	1 (2.4)	0 (0)	7 (16.7)	34 (81.0)	42 (11.1)	3,158 (23.3)
100-200	0 (0)	1 (7.1)	0 (0)	13 (92.9)	14 (3.7)	2,007 (14.8)
over 200	0 (0)	0 (0)	0 (0)	9 (100)	9 (2.4)	3,436 (25.4)
Total firms	67 (17.7)	39 (10.3)	75 (19.8)	198 (52.2)	379 (100)	13,538 (100.0)

Notes: For all but the numbers in the two far-right columns, the table gives the number of firms in each row (firm size) that sell to the number of sellers given at the top of each column, followed by the percentage of all firms in that row. Column E gives the number and percentage of all firms (379) in that size category. Column F gives the output in billion yen (and percentage of total industry output) produced by firms it that row.

For reasons of data availability, Column F includes firms that do not directly sell to assemblers. This distinction is primarily relevant only to the top two rows. Thus, Column F row 1 includes data on 237 firms rather than 155 firms; row 2 on 121 firms; row 3 on 50 firms, row 4 on 43 firms, row 4 on 15 firms, and row 5 on the same 9 firms.

Source: NIHON NO JIDOSHA BUHIN KOGYO (1998 NEN BAN) [JAPANESE AUTOMOTIVE PARTS INDUSTRY, 1998] 16-17 (Nihon jidosha buhin kogyo kai & Oto toreedo jaaneru, eds., 1998).

Third, in the end, the relationships are not necessarily stable anyway. Although firms often do keep their existing trading partners, often does not mean always — or even nearly always. Second- and third-tier firms are particularly prone to shifting partners. These firms are frequently family firms. Like family firms everywhere, they come and go as the talents and interests of family members ebb and flow in generational cycles. Even first-tier contractors shift subcontracting ties. In 1998, the JAPIA listed 189 suppliers in the Toyota supplier network. Of these, only 122 (65%) had been members in 1973. Conversely, of the 150 firms in the association in 1973, twenty-eight (19%) had disappeared by 1998.

5. Board Seats

Equity investments are not the only extra-contractual governance mechanisms that assemblers can use. They can also take positions on their suppliers' boards. Primarily, however, whether an assembler obtains such a seat depends on its equity investment.

Again, one can exaggerate the prevalence of assembler representatives: only exceptionally do assemblers put their representatives on supplier boards. Among Japanese automobile parts suppliers, we have information on the board composition of 209 firms. In 132 of these firms (63%), the assemblers had no board representative. When an assembler did have a board member, the modal number was one (twenty-six firms, or 12%). At only twenty-seven of the suppliers (13%) did the principal buyer among the automobile assemblers have five to nine board members, and at only five (2%) did it have ten or more.

Whether an assembler has a representative on a supplier's board depends critically on the equity stake that the assembler holds in the supplier. If we compare the predictive effect on the number of assembler representatives (**NumDir**) of (i) the fraction of S's sales made to A (**Sales%**) and (ii) A's equity investment in S (**Eq%**), the latter predicts far better:

NumDir=-2.85+0.090Eq%+0.019Sales%+0.0003Employees+2.89Listed+e,
         (4.96)   (5.79)   (1.93)   (2.99)   5.79

where n=120, the absolute value of the t-statistics are in parentheses, and the adjusted R^2 = 0.55.[52] Moreover, a regression of **NumDir** on **Eq%** yields a coefficient of 0.10, a t-statistic of 12.25, and an adjusted R^2 of 0.42; a regression on **Sales%** yields a coefficient of 0.05, a t-statistic of 6.01, and an adjusted R^2 of 0.23. For predicting the presence of assembler representatives on a supplier board, the investment an assembler makes in a supplier's stock matters greatly. The fraction of its output the supplier sells to the assembler matters far less. Obviously, one does not need RSI theory to explain why director seats should correlate with stock holdings.

IV. Conclusions

Within industrial organization, scholars increasingly integrate RSI theory into their analysis of the way firms structure their affairs with each other. Suppose that production requires large idiosyncratic investments and that detailed contracts are infeasible. In such a world, production would generate quasi rents, and the quasi rents would in

---

52. Running the same regression with the Toyota dummy as well does not substantially change the results; the t-statistic on Toyota is 0.018.

turn create the risk of ex post opportunism. To mitigate that risk, scholars reason, firms may negotiate governance mechanisms they would otherwise avoid.

Although the theory sparked a promising research program, scholars generally have found less evidence of large-scale RSIs than one might suppose — particularly of physical-asset specificity, and particularly in industries outside of aerospace, defense, or public utilities. Accordingly, Ramon Casadesus-Masanell and Daniel F. Spulber recently concluded that "asset specificity and opportunism in contracts fail in a fundamental way to explain vertical integration."[53] Pierre-Andre Chiappori and Bernard Salanie observe that "[i]n the last 20 years contract theory has developed at a rapid pace..., [but] empirical applications have lagged behind."[54] They then suggest that scholars have exaggerated the more general problem of asymmetric information in contracting: studying the French insurance market, for example, they find "no evidence of asymmetric information."[55] These findings are consistent with our findings that standard competitive market models apply straightforwardly to developing economies.[56]

Within this empirical context, the Japanese automobile industry has offered hope. There, at least, observers thought they would find the combination of large RSIs and extra-contractual governance mechanisms (particularly equity cross-holdings) that RSI theory had suggested.

Not so. In the Japanese automobile industry RSIs are low, and so are equity cross-holdings. We make this point with a mix of indirect evidence. We are the first to admit that we lack firm-level direct measures of RSIs. Instead, we bring to the enterprise a wide-ranging mix of observational evidence and industry data. To that mix, we add a set of supplementary regressions.

From this evidence, two points stand out. First, among the smaller firms (which is to say, most firms), the levels of RSIs are low for a simple reason: all investment levels are low. This simply is not a capital intensive sector. Second, among the larger firms (which is to say, the most productive firms), investment levels are higher — but these investments seem not to be idiosyncratic, and cross-holdings are low. These larger suppliers broadly diversify their sales outlets, and seldom issue significant equity blocks to assemblers.

---

53. Casadesus-Masanett & Spurber, *supra* note 7, at 69-70.

54. Pierre-Andre Chiappori & Bernard Salanie, *Testing for Asymmetric Information in the Insurance Markets*, 108 J. POL. ECON. 56, 56-57 (2000).

55. *Id.*

56. *See* Yoshiro Miwa & J. Mark Ramseyer, *Corporate Governance in Transitional Economies: Lessons from the Prewar Japanese Cotton Textile Industry*, 29 J. LEGAL STUD. 171 (2000).

Through this, we do not purport to disprove RSI theory as theory. After all, the theory predicts that firms will create distinctive governance mechanisms when RSIs are large and contractual solutions infeasible. If production technology is standard and contracting straightforward, they will solve any problems by contract. And in the end, that is pretty much what we show in Japan. Our claim is instead more modest: that perhaps RSI theory explains a narrower band of phenomena than we have thought.

[12]

Aggressive Legalism: The Rules of the WTO and Japan's Emerging Trade Strategy

Saadia M. Pekkanen

1. INTRODUCTION

ONE of the most significant trends in Japan's trade strategy in the last decade has unfortunately been either overlooked or glossed over by most observers. In part, this is because both the academic and media attention has concentrated on the doom and gloom of Japan's economic turmoil or the volatility of its political changes. In greater part, however, this is because the Japanese government has, thus far, characteristically kept a low profile on the matter.[1]

The heart of this emerging new strategy is not about the oft-heard distinction between bilateral and multilateral approaches to dispute resolution. Rather, it is far more precise and constraining, because it is about the use of international

---

SAADIA M. PEKKANEN is Assistant Professor of Political Science at Middlebury College, Vermont. He wishes to thank the many government officials as well as lawyers in Tokyo for their assistance and input into this project, especially Noboru Hatakeyama, Jiro Kodera, Makoto Kuroda, Mitsuo Matsushita, Naoko Munakata, Yoshiji Nogami, Sozaburo Okamatsu, Yoshihiro Sakamoto, Akitaka Saiki, Naoko Saiki, Masakazu Toyoda, Koji Tsuruoka, Kazuyoshi Umemoto and Bunroku Yoshino. An earlier version of this paper was presented at the New England Political Science Association (NEPSA), 5–6 May, 2000, Hartford, CT. The author is solely responsible for the opinions, as well as the errors, in this essay.

[1] The issue of US-Japan trade, in fact, has lost much of its political salience and has certainly dropped in visibility in both popular and academic attention. One of the few exceptions to this trend is the recent work by Edward Lincoln (1999) who has attempted to keep attention focused on the crucial issue of US trade relations with Japan. Lincoln, however, while recognising the importance of the WTO to the future of US-Japan trade relations, continues to stress the bilateral context as the main means for pressuring Japan. His underlying assumption is that the WTO-based international context, while clearly important, has not had much of an impact on Japan's trade diplomacy, and that therefore the only way for the US to proceed is to pressure the Japanese directly. But much has changed already. As I will explain, given the significant emerging changes in Japan's external trade diplomacy, the utility of a unilateral approach is dubious in a world where Japan is increasingly willing to use the rules of the WTO to its advantage.

legal rules. More specifically, Japan's emerging trade strategy is about the use of the substantive rules of the World Trade Organisation (WTO) to counter what the Japanese government deems to be the unreasonable acts, requests, and practices of its major trade partners. Legal rules, in short, are deliberately and strategically being made to matter to the results and outcomes of major trade disputes involving Japan. And in a very short time, the Japanese government has made abundantly clear how the legal rules in the treaties and agreements overseen by the WTO can be turned into instruments of power and means of persuasion against others in a legitimate way. This is the essence of what I call aggressive legalism – a conscious strategy where a substantive set of international legal rules can be made to serve as both 'shield' and 'sword' in trade disputes among sovereign states. This is the strategy that Japan has embraced as the principal means of dealing with its major trade partners. And this transition is especially remarkable given the non-legalistic and non-confrontational character of Japan's postwar trade diplomacy. Understanding this unfolding strategy reveals much about both a new Japan and the power of international law.

This paper is both thematic and chronological, with the goal of tracing out and analysing the increasing use of WTO rules by the Japanese government. It is organised as follows. Firstly it briefly sets out Japan's historical relationship with the GATT/WTO system, and shows how there has been a marked shift in both the attitudes and perceptions regarding the utility of a rule-based approach. It then analyses some of the more prominent legal cases involving Japan, with a view to exposing how legal rules affect and constrain trade relations. It focuses more closely on the period after the birth of the WTO in 1995 when the contours of this strategy, as well as its costs and advantages, became clearer. Following this it sets out the implications of Japan's emerging new strategy – best characterised as 'aggressive legalism' at its core – for both the rule of WTO law and the future of trade diplomacy among the major global players.

2. EMERGENCE AND EVOLUTION OF JAPAN'S LEGALISED STRATEGY

After several years of negotiation, Japan finally acceded to the GATT on 7 June, 1955.[2] This section sets out the changes that have taken place over time in terms of Japan's use of legal remedies centred on the GATT, and now the WTO, system.

In the early postwar period, the legal rules of the GATT had a negligible impact on Japan's foreign trade diplomacy, and this remained largely true until the late 1980s. In fact, from the time of Japan's accession in 1955 to the start of the Uruguay Round in 1986, Japan actually avoided using the GATT dispute-

---

[2] GATT *Basic Instruments and Selected Documents 4th Supplement 1956* (hereafter BISD [No.] Suppl. [year]), pp. 7–10.

THE WTO AND JAPAN'S EMERGING TRADE STRATEGY 709

settlement machinery altogether. During this period, if there were GATT-related complaints against Japan, the Japanese government almost always tried to reach a bilateral settlement with the complainant before a formal panel conclusion could take place.[3]

Before 1986, there were 11 cases involving Japan as a defendant at the GATT. As a result of Japan's emphasis on settling cases bilaterally outside the legal framework only one of them, namely the leather case, ever led to a public panel ruling. Japan also avoided legal actions as a complainant. Up until 1988, it had filed only four formal complaints at the GATT.[4] Japan's participation in the GATT system remained, in fact, so meagre that the GATT leadership tried to encourage greater involvement on the part of the Japanese government by launching a major trade round in Tokyo in 1973. But Japan remained largely uninterested in the GATT.[5] Why?

There were two principal reasons. First, the uninterest can be attributed to the legal weaknesses and loopholes in the GATT machinery in the early years. The Japanese government was no different from most others in refraining from the use of GATT's legal processes, and the reluctance may well have stemmed from fears of exposing Japan's many visible trade barriers and restrictive practices to legal scrutiny. Second, perhaps a more crucial factor in the uninterest lay in the terms of accession, which restrained Japan from being a 'full' member of the GATT club. This refers to the invocation of Article XXXV – the non-application of the agreement between Contracting Parties – by fourteen countries against Japan, with the primary justification that up-and-coming Japanese exports would overwhelm traditional sectors like textiles.[6] As a result, Japan's GATT diplomacy in the early years was concentrated on bilateral negotiations with the relevant countries to dislodge the use of Article XXXV so that Japan could achieve full MFN status.[7]

It was not until the late 1980s that perceptions of the GATT began to change in the Japanese foreign trade policy establishment. The turning point came in 1988, when Japan won a case against Canada. Canada had charged that Japan was levying a tariff of eight per cent on Canadian exports of SPF (spruce-pine-fir) lumber while letting 'like wood products' from the US enter Japan duty-free – a direct violation of GATT Article I (General Most-Favoured-Nation

---

[3] Komatsu (1992, esp. pp. 35–37).
[4] Japan's four complaints involved French restrictions on VCRs (no panel ruling; ended up with Japanese VER), US retaliation in semiconductors (no panel ruling; ended up with continuing VIE), a US Customs Court decision on Japan's border tax adjustments as countervailable subsidies (panel upheld Japan's claim; Customs Court decision overruled by US appellate court; appellate ruling further upheld by US Supreme Court), and an EC anti-dumping regulation (panel upheld Japan's claim; EC forestalled compliance).
[5] Hudec (1993 [1991], pp. 21–22, 212, 256).
[6] See GATT *GATT Activities in 1961/62* (hereafter GA [year]), pp. 31–32; and also GATT BISD 10th Suppl. (1962, pp. 69, 71).
[7] Interview, Yoshino Bunroku, Ex-Vice Minister for Economic Affairs, Ministry of Foreign Affairs, Tokyo, 1998.

Treatment), the MFN clause.⁸ For the first time ever, the dispute-settlement procedures ended up ruling in favour of Japan. The GATT panel established to judge the case found that the Canadian legal basis for establishing 'like products' was unsound. Furthermore, Canada did not provide sufficient legal evidence that the Japanese tariff classification had been specifically designed to discriminate against its SPF platform lumber exports. The favourable panel ruling had a profound effect on domestic Japanese perceptions of the GATT at two levels. It affected domestic perceptions about the GATT's fairness towards all its members, and also about the GATT's utility as a legal weapon against foreign complaints and pressures.⁹

The foreign trade policy establishment, primarily located in the Ministry of International Trade and Industry (MITI) and also the Ministry of Foreign Affairs (MOFA), then turned its full diplomatic attention to the then ongoing Uruguay Round talks. According to leading Japanese negotiators at the Uruguay Round, Japan was especially keen on the dispute settlement processes.¹⁰ At one level, Japan's new interest in a more strengthened GATT went hand in hand with its overall ambition to take on a high-profile role internationally, one commensurate with its great economic power status. In the early 1990s, Japan made a big push to upgrade its status, as well as push its vision, in many international organisations, like the IMF and the World Bank.¹¹ But the perceptions concerning the GATT,

---

⁸ For details of the case, see GATT (GA 1988, pp. 79–80); and GATT (BISD 36th Suppl. 1988–1989), pp. 186–93, 198–199). Japan also won a 'first-ever' case against the EC when a panel upheld Japanese complaints in 1990 that EC anti-circumvention dumping duties violated, among other things, GATT Article III, the national treatment clause. Although the Council adopted the panel report, a legal victory for Japan, the EC stalled compliance by arguing that the anti-dumping measures were then under discussion at the Uruguay Round. On the EC case, see GATT (GA 1990, pp. 55–57); and also GATT (BISD 37th Suppl. 1990, pp. 132–199).

⁹ Interview Makoto Kuroda, Ex-Vice Minister for International Affairs, Ministry of International Trade and Industry, Tokyo, 1997. Kuroda is widely considered to be one of the earlier proponents of using a GATT-based strategy to deal with the US.

¹⁰ Interview, Naoko Saiki, Director, International Peace Cooperation Division, Ministry of Foreign Affairs, Tokyo, 1998. Saiki was responsible for heading up six of the fifteen negotiating groups at the Uruguay Round talks, including that on dispute settlement. The emphasis on dispute settlement, based on the specific legal rules of the GATT, was also raised by a Japan representative in 1990 just after Japan had undergone the process of a Trade Policy Review Mechanism (TPRM). In response to criticisms that, even at that point, Japan had a propensity to deal with trade problems in the context of bilateral relations, the representative stressed that Japan intended to use the GATT dispute settlement whenever specific trade problems could be resolved through them. To that end, Japan was committed to making the Uruguay Round negotiations on making the dispute settlement procedures more credible and reliable. At this stage, Japan's more legalised trade strategy was just getting under way. For an overview see, GATT (GA Activities 1990, esp. pp. 93–95).

¹¹ Throughout the 1980s, Japan's financial muscle allowed it to move up the ranks in prominent multilateral organisations. In 1981, Japan became the number two shareholder in the International Development Agency (IDA) at the World Bank, and by 1984 it had become the second largest shareholder in the World Bank itself. By 1992 Japan was on par with Germany as the number two shareholder in the International Monetary Fund. The high-profile rise of Japan in these Western-dominated organisations was also accompanied by some ideological clashes. In the early 1990s,

THE WTO AND JAPAN'S EMERGING TRADE STRATEGY 711

and the negotiations in the Uruguay Round, were unique in that they were not about money, status, or representation but rather about the letter of the law.[12] The realisation of key Japanese officials that international legal rules could be a strategic source of national power, and could serve as both 'shield' and 'sword' for Japan then began to take concrete shape domestically. The vision of these officials was entirely legal, and one that was to have enormous implications for Japan's ability to exercise power at the international level.

The first domestic indication that Japan was moving into high legal gear came in 1992 with the start of an annual publication on the WTO 'consistency' of Japan's trade partners. This report is produced by the Subcommittee on Unfair Trade Policies and Measures under the WTO Committee of the Industrial Structure Council, which is itself an advisory body attached to MITI.[13] Drawing on the talent and expertise of the leading legal specialists and trade experts in Japan, the goal of this report is to evaluate foreign trade policies and measures on the basis of rules in the treaties (such as the GATT) and agreements (such as that on Anti-dumping) now overseen by the WTO.[14] Some key officials draw a contrast between the Japanese report which justifies its complaints based on the WTO rules versus the USTR report on foreign trade barriers which, it is believed, simply catalogues complaints.[15] In addition, administrative changes, such as

---

Japanese officials took on the prevailing non-interventionist orthodoxy of economic development espoused by the World Bank, and stressed their own vision of state-guided industrialisation. This reportedly was the impetus behind the Japanese government's desire to fund and support the World Bank's study entitled *The East Asian Miracle: Economic Growth and Public Policy* (1993) which at least attempted to grapple with the role of public policy or government intervention.

[12] In fact Japan's contributions to and representation in the WTO are hardly commanding. Financially, the US is by far the largest contributor to the WTO with about 15 per cent of the total, followed by Germany at about 10 per cent. Japan has consistently been the third largest contributor to the WTO since its inception, and has provided about 8 per cent of the total annual operating budget between 1995 and 2000. In 1997/98, just as the legalised trade strategy was in full swing domestically, Japan's contribution actually dropped slightly whereas those of both Germany and the US increased modestly. Even more telling, Japan's representation in terms of professional Japanese personnel in the WTO thus far remains meagre. Since 1995 to the present day there have been only 3–4 professional Japanese nationals in the WTO, none of them in senior management, i.e. at the Director-General, Deputies Director-General, and Division Director levels. One Japanese national has thus far continuously been on the WTO Appellate Body, Mitsuo Matsushita 1996–2000, and more recently appointed, Yasuhei Taniguchi 2000–2003 (replacement for a deceased Appellate Body member). As yet, overall, there are no visible signs that Japan is interested in taking on a high-profile leadership role in the immediate future within the WTO itself. Eventually, however, commensurate with its emphasis on a legalised trade strategy, Japan will need to devote greater financial and human resources to the WTO to be considered an even more effective player in the international legal game. See www.ustr.gov/reports/tpa for more details on the comparative statistics on budget contributions by member states.

[13] This report is published simultaneously in both Japanese and English.

[14] Interview, Mitsuo Matsushita, Member of WTO Appellate Body 1996–2000, Nagashima & Ohno (Law Firm), Tokyo, 1998.

[15] Interview, Masakazu Toyoda, Director-General of International Economic Affairs Department, Ministry of International Trade and Industry, Tokyo, 1997 and 1998. Toyoda is considered to be one of the key architects of this new legalised trade strategy both by his peers and, perhaps even

devoting more human resources to WTO-legal analyses across divisions or setting up specific 'WTO-Divisions' for cases involving Japan, also point towards the institutionalisation of a legalised trade strategy.[16]

The first external indication that Japan's trade strategy was taking a legalistic turn came on the heels of the formation of the WTO in January 1995. Earlier, one leading economist had astutely observed – and was unfortunately ignored – that the US was now dealing with a 'new' Japan, and that, one way or another, the US method of being both judge and jury in controversial trade disputes had to be laid to rest.[17] Just how 'new' became clear slowly but surely in the ways Japan chose to deal with the US, its most important trading partner bar none, in the few years after the birth of the WTO.

Again Japan's actions and reactions towards the US, as well as its other major trade partners, have little to do with bilateralism versus multilateralism. As top diplomats in Japan point out pragmatically, the process of settling disputes at the WTO is quintessentially bilateral in nature because it pits one sovereign trade partner (or partners) against another.[18] Rather, Japan's actions have to do with what officials now call the 'strategic use' of international legal rules.[19] While political realities continue to matter even in the WTO setting, and perhaps do so even in the processes leading up to the establishment of a panel, the fact is that the existing rules level the playing field for all concerned, making even the

---

more importantly, by his seniors. At least one ex-vice minister of international affairs from MITI has called him the 'original ideologist' of the rule-based approach. He is presently the lead WTO negotiator for MITI.

[16] Interviews, various deputy-director level officials in the European and North America Divisions at both MITI and MOFA, 1997 and 1998. Although an emphasis on the WTO legal rules is commonly seen as the most important means of dealing with Japan's trade partners, officials are quick to point out some important constraints. One commonly cited constraint is the lack of legal resources, with many officials pointing out that Japan only has 16,000 trained lawyers compared to about 900,000 in the US. Another is the continued security dependence of Japan on the US which, according to a surprisingly few, may induce Japan to be more cautious in its trade dealings with the US even in the WTO since bilateral negotiations precede the initiation of formal dispute settlement mechanisms. Finally, some officials point to the jurisdictional disputes between MITI and MOFA that have become even more important. While the basic laws of both ministries give them jurisdiction over foreign matters, the issue of 'who' rules in the WTO-legal realm affects their power and status domestically. The issue has become even more prominent because international or WTO treaties (considered the preserve of diplomats at MOFA) have significant consequences for domestic industries (almost always supervised by MITI). Whatever the truth of such jurisdictional claims, almost all officials agree that eventually some sort of administrative integration will be required – perhaps along the lines of the Canadian 'Ministry of Foreign and Trade Affairs.' This would not only help reduce the tremendous amounts of duplication across ministries but also allow Japan to confront its trading partners more effectively.

[17] Bhagwati (1994, pp. 7–12).

[18] Interview, Yoshiji Nogami, Deputy Minister for Foreign Affairs, Ministry of Foreign Affairs, Tokyo, 1997.

[19] Interview, Naoko Munakata, Deputy Director, General Affairs Division, International Trade Policy Bureau, Ministry of International Trade and Industry, Tokyo, 1998.

impotent the legal equal of the strong.[20] This level 'legal playing field' is what Japan has gambled on as a strategy and, while it has distinct costs as well, so far it is paying off as a number of notable victories make clear.

The strategy itself is two-fold. First, the Japanese government uses the legal rules as a 'shield' which provide a cover for domestic measures and institutions no matter how controversial they may appear to Japan's trade partners. Two cases stand out in this particular instance, the long-running dispute over leather, and the more recent row over consumer photographic film. Second, the Japanese government uses the WTO legal rules as a 'sword' which allow it to challenge foreign measures and practices that it deems to be controversial – a marked departure from its usual low-profile, behind-the-scenes diplomacy in trade. Here several concluded as well as ongoing cases stand out, namely automobiles, semiconductors, and anti-dumping. Let me discuss both aspects of the strategy in more detail using these two sets of cases.

a. Prominent GATT/WTO Cases Involving Japan[21]

This sub-section examines the processes and outcomes in both the 'shield' and 'sword' aspects of the strategy a little more closely. The goal is to show how the legal rules are effectively becoming a powerful tool in the hands of the Japanese government, and how, perhaps more importantly, they are making the idea of aggressive legalism a reality with which Japan's trade partners will have to contend in the future.

(i) The 'shield' aspect at work

Leather: One of the earliest and still ongoing disputes concerns the restrictions in the Japanese leather industry, and it is an important case for showing how the GATT/WTO rules came to be used as an effective shield for Japanese government measures.[22] Between 1952 and 1963, Japan was able to justify quantitative

---

[20] Both Articles XXII (Consultation) and XXIII (Nullification and Impairment) emphasise the importance of direct bilateral talks and negotiations between any two contracting parties to resolve issues of concern to one of them before more formal dispute settlement processes are set in motion. A similar point is made in Article 4 (Consultations) of the Understanding on Rules and Procedures Governing the Settlement of Disputes.

[21] Unless otherwise indicated, the discussion of the cases in the section below relies directly on materials published by the GATT and now the WTO. Where appropriate, it is also supplemented with the relevant synopsis of GATT cases between 1948 and 1989 found in Hudec (1993 [1991]), Appendix I. Information on Section 301 cases is drawn from the official website of the USTR at www.ustr.gov/reports/301report/act301.htm. More up-to-date information on WTO dispute settlement cases is drawn from the official WTO website at www.wto.org.

[22] The procedural and substantive facts in the leather dispute are drawn from GATT (BISD 26th Suppl. 1978–1979, pp. 320–321); GATT (BISD 27th Suppl. 1979–1980, pp. 118–119); and the panel report as published in GATT (BISD 31st Suppl. 1983–1984, pp. 94–114).

import restrictions on certain leather products using the balance of payments safeguard provisions cited in Article XII. As Japan rose in economic prominence, however, the balance of payments justification was no longer valid and expired in 1963. From then on Japan claimed that the restrictions were justified on social grounds, namely regard for an underprivileged and poor 'Dowa' minority.

It was the US which first brought charges against Japan.[23] The US claimed that the Japanese restrictions both violated Article XI (General Elimination of Quantitative Restrictions) and were nullifying and impairing American benefits under the GATT. But the US did not move to initiate formal GATT proceedings until 1978, at which point it engaged in serious bilateral consultations with Japan provided for under Article XXIII. Initially the two sides failed to come to an agreement, and the US moved to have a panel established in late 1978. But in keeping with Japan's early diplomacy centred on bilateral settlements, Japan then engaged in serious efforts to settle the dispute without going through the GATT panel process. On 26 February, 1979, the US withdrew its complaint, saying that the bilateral consultations had reached a 'successful conclusion.'

Eight months later on 16 November, 1979, the Canadians filed their own complaint, and requested the establishment of a panel. Again, the charge was that Japan was violating Article XI, and that its quantitative restrictions, including that of the earlier preferential US-Japan settlement, nullified and impaired Canadian benefits under the GATT. Again, also, Japan engaged in serious bilateral consultations, and on 30 June, 1980, the panel was informed that Canada and Japan had also reached a satisfactory conclusion.

On 31 March, 1982, the bilateral US-Japan settlement, which was essentially an increased quota for the US, expired. This time, despite Japan's best efforts at a bilateral settlement in specific leather products, the US proved unwilling to settle for further quota increases. From the perspective of the US, the 1979 understanding did not improve market access for the US, one of its main objectives. This time the US based its nullification and impairment claim on several grounds. It not only charged that Japan's import quota on leather was a clear and continuing infringement of Article XI, but also that Japan's failure to publish the total amount of the import quota violated provisions in Article X (Publication and Administration of Trade Regulations) and Article XIII (Non-discriminatory Administration of Quantitative Restrictions). The panel was established on 20 April, 1983, and during the proceedings, five other parties also presented statements that their economic interests were adversely affected by the Japanese quantitative restrictions on leather imports.[24] Much in line with the arguments made in the US case, these parties also asserted that the import

---

[23] The Tanners Council of America first filed a petition with the USTR in August 1977 (301-13, and also 301-35/36), protesting both high tariffs and quantitative restrictions which hurt US exports to Japan. Notably, this organisation based its case on Japan's violation of GATT XI.

[24] The five parties were Australia, the European Communities, India, New Zealand, and Pakistan.

restrictions were not justified under GATT provisions, and as such violated Japan's GATT obligations.

For the first time, Japan found itself embroiled in a legal game from which there was going to be no bilateral way out. Its initial reaction was to claim that other developed countries also maintained residual import restrictions that were specific to each item. Thus keeping the import restrictions on leather and leather footwear could be justified under the unique and complex socio-economic situation found in the Japanese industry. Japan further pleaded that despite these domestic considerations it had increased the quota over the years especially since 1979, which had benefited the US directly. In keeping with its non-legalistic emphasis, Japan further stated that it was not realistic to seek 'only a legal judgment.'

But an entirely legal judgment is what emerged, with the panel noting that Japan had used 'social' arguments to respond to the US's essentially 'legal' case. In fact, Japan's tactic of relying on social arguments backfired because the panel's terms of reference only allowed it to examine the matter in the light of specific GATT provisions. And the existing provisions, especially in Article XI, made it clear that Japan's import restrictions in the leather industry could not be justified. In short, the panel concluded that Japan's restrictions constituted a *prima facie* case of nullification or impairment, and had to be brought in conformity with GATT provisions. Further, the issue that the restrictions did not cause nullification and impairments of US benefits, as the Japanese side claimed and the panel also agreed to some degree, was moot. The conclusion was still that Japan intentionally maintained import restrictions in order to restrict leather imports, including those of the US. The hindrance of US trade was all that counted in the eyes of the GATT panel at the time. The report of the panel was adopted in May 1984, and its recommendations constituted a distinct legal obligation for Japan.

At first Japan refused to budge on the issue of eliminating its quantitative restrictions. This state of affairs could not continue because technically Japan was violating its GATT obligations. Although Japan removed some restrictions promptly, it took about a year for more serious efforts at liberalisation in which the quantitative restrictions were replaced with GATT-legal tariff quotas. The US, however, found these changes inadequate, and in September 1985 the President directed the USTR to recommend retaliation unless there were substantial reductions in the Japanese leather industry. In December 1985, Japan agreed to provide the US with about $236 million in compensation through reduced tariffs, but the US still raised tariffs on $24 million worth of Japanese leather imports.

All in all, this was a hard lesson for Japan in terms of a legal game. In April 1986, Japan questioned the GATT legality of the continued US tariff increases but, in keeping with its non-legalistic emphasis, did not take up the issue formally or with any conviction. Things have changed, however. Japan learned its lesson well, and there is a substantial difference in the way that Japan handled its case in the earlier leather disputes and how it may do so in the future. For in fact, Japan's legal troubles in the leather industry are far from over. MOFA officials have been aware for some time that the continued restrictions in the leather industry are still a great source of concern to the EU.[25]

From 1986 to 1996, the EU did not overtly protest the tariff-quota system because the quotas continued to increase. But according to MOFA officials, the problem started in 1997, when the quotas stopped increasing due to the recession, and consequently weak demand, in Japan. At that point the EU complained informally to Japan through diplomatic channels that its leather imports had been decreasing under both the first and second rates, and that the lack of quota expansion presented a particular problem. Since the EU was aware that Japan's tariff quotas are consistent with WTO rules – a fact that Japan counts on should there be a formal panel – it was reluctant to initiate formal dispute settlement processes at the WTO. Confident that Japan's measures in the industry would withstand WTO legal scrutiny, Japan rebuffed initial EU claims for quota expansion. As a result, in October 1998, the EU Commission ended up taking the case before the WTO, less it appears to butt legal heads with Japan and more to appease internal political pressures especially from Spanish and Italian producers. The case is still pending consultations, and Japanese officials, while hopeful that the EU will back down, are still markedly willing to undergo a formal panel process at the WTO. There is of course no question that Japan would be under obligation to eventually bring its protectionist measures in line with the WTO rules if it comes to that. But in the meantime it is clear that Japan can play by the existing rules to shield its internal measures to the maximum extent of the WTO rules possible.[26]

---

[25] Interview, Jiro Kodera, Director, First International Economic Affairs Division, Economic Relations with Europe, MOFA, Tokyo, 1998. The following discussion draws on the interview.

[26] There are several interpretations on the nature of international legal obligations under the dispute settlement understanding of the WTO, epitomised in an exchange between Bello (1996) and Jackson (1997). Bello tries to head off American cries of eroding sovereignty by suggesting that in cases of violation the WTO dispute settlement is flexible because, rather than creating an overarching obligation, it gives sovereign members choices: comply by withdrawing the violating measure, or compensate the aggrieved party, or simply face retaliation by that party. In this way, she is fundamentally questioning whether the WTO rules are binding in the traditional sense and whether there is any international law obligation to comply. Examining specific clauses, however, Jackson points out, among other things, that the DSU clearly establishes compliance as the highest priority, that compensation can only be resorted to if the immediate withdrawal of the measure is not possible, and that furthermore the violating measure shall be kept under surveillance until compliance has occurred – all of which points to definite international law obligations to perform the recommendation of the panel report at the earliest possible time. Should the Japanese leather case go through another panel process at the WTO, and Japan's measures are found to be inconsistent with WTO obligations, it will have no choice but to comply.

THE WTO AND JAPAN'S EMERGING TRADE STRATEGY

Consumer Photographic Film and Paper: This more recent case, popularly known as the Fuji-Kodak dispute, is another important one for showing how Japan can potentially use the WTO rules to shield its domestic institutions and practices from foreign criticisms.[27] This is also a case that is about competition policy, one where presumably the market, not government measures as the Japanese side asserted throughout, determine outcomes in the marketplace.

In May 1995, the Eastman Kodak company filed a complaint with the USTR, alleging that specific Japanese practices were causing it market access problems. While it conducted its own investigation, the USTR turned to consultations with Japan directly, in the hope no doubt of coming to a bilateral settlement. But, according to Japanese officials, this case was a matter of pure competition policy, which meant that the Japanese government had nothing to do with the workings of the marketplace.[28] In fact, rather than getting into detailed negotiations and consultations, government officials urged the US to approach the Japanese Fair Trade Commission (JFTC) concerning anti-competitive practices in this sector. When the US side proved sceptical of the JFTC, it was urged instead to go to the WTO. The Japanese side, in short, refused to negotiate bilaterally on any but their own terms – something they could afford to do in a WTO world.[29]

The legal game was afoot in June 1996 when the US invoked Article 4.4 of the Dispute Settlement Understanding and Article XXIII:1 of the GATT on the same day that it released its Section 301 investigation determinations.[30] Consultations proved unsatisfactory to both sides, and three months later, the US requested the establishment of a panel claiming that its benefits were being nullified and impaired within the meaning of Article XXIII because of the combined effect of a set of Japanese measures. The US pinpointed the implementation and maintenance of Japanese *government* 'laws, regulations, requirements and measures' that affected the distribution and sale of imported consumer photographic film and paper. Specifically, these referred to three items, distribution countermeasures, the Large Stores Law, and promotion countermeasures.

These were collectively termed 'liberalisation countermeasures,' and the US

---

[27] The procedural and substantive facts in this case are drawn exclusively from the WTO Report of the Panel published as Document WT/DS44/R (31 March, 1998). Additional information and details are based on Komuro (1998).
[28] Interview, Kazuyoshi Umemoto, Director, First International Organisation Division, WTO Division, Economic Affairs Bureau, MOFA, Tokyo, 1998.
[29] Interview, Yoshihiro Sakamoto, Ex-Vice Minister for International Affairs, MITI, Tokyo, 1997 and 1998. Kodak did eventually submit evidence to the JFTC in August 1996, which was not dealt with independently of the JFTC's own investigation of the conditions in the photographic film industry. The results of this investigation, which concluded that there were no anti-competitive practices in the Japanese industry, were released during the panel proceedings in July 1997.
[30] In fact, the US invoked three separate WTO dispute settlement procedures, namely GATT Article XXIII, GATS Article XXIII, and the 1960 Arrangement by the GATT Contracting Parties for consultation on restrictive business practices. However, only the procedures under GATT Article XXIII:1 led to the establishment of a formal panel.

laid out how they constituted an 'organic whole' that contravened GATT articles. Distribution countermeasures contravened provisions in Article III (National Treatment on Internal Taxation and Regulation). Unpublished enforcement actions by the JFTC, and unpublished guidance by the Japanese government in the actual operation of the Large Scale law violated Article X (Publication and Administration of Trade Regulations). In short, Japanese government measures were not only discriminatory they also lacked transparency. The US also took the extraordinary step of asserting a 'non-violation' claim, in which a member asserts that its benefits are being nullified or impaired by a measure that does not conflict with WTO provisions. The non-violation claim was based especially on what the US side termed 'distribution countermeasures,' a series of government actions and policy processes that either encouraged or facilitated the creation of an exclusionary domestic market. As Japan pointed out, such claims are not normally considered until the alleged violations have been addressed. Moreover, the US could not make distribution countermeasures, which allegedly led to the creation of an exclusionary distribution system for consumer photographic materials, the centrepiece of both its violation and non-violation claims.

Japan's legal tactics began with the consultations phase of the dispute settlement process. Cleverly using the arguments raised by the US itself in other dispute panels, Japan pointed out that certain measures at issue in the present case needed to be identified with clarity and specificity so that the panel's terms of reference could be plainly confined to the legal benefit of all concerned. From the start, Japan claimed that this was something the US had not done. More importantly, the Japanese side staunchly maintained that the so-called 'liberalisation countermeasures' were too general and ambiguous, and since they were a generic term they could hardly be termed 'specific measures' as required by the rules of Article 6.2 (Establishment of Panels).

In more detailed arguments presented by the parties, Japan questioned the fundamental US claim that the Japanese market structure for consumer photographic film and paper was exclusionary and closed, and that this must have resulted because of government measures and policies. In fact, as it claimed time and again, there were no government measures at play in this sector, and certainly none that could be considered to lie within the scope of Article XXIII.[31]

---

[31] As Japan pointed out, there were no current *government* measures that stood in the way of a foreign producer intent on improving its competitive lot in the Japanese market. There were no restrictions on hiring more sales people, reducing prices, increasing advertising spending, acquiring distributors or photofinishing laboratories for sale, expanding distribution networks, or establishing relationships with independent primary wholesalers. At this point, the US switched to a weaker claim, namely that a distribution set up by government measures in the 1960s and 1970s was self-sustaining. But if so, this played right into the Japanese government's claim there were no *present* government measures that could be pinpointed with any specificity. In its findings, the panel also acknowledged that many of the 'measures' cited by the US were very old with an unclear current status. In addition, they appeared to be neutral with respect to the origin of the products. These facts also made it difficult to justify a non-violation claim.

THE WTO AND JAPAN'S EMERGING TRADE STRATEGY

Nor was there any formal or visible coordination between the government and private sector to exclude foreigners. Whatever problems Kodak was having could perhaps be attributed less to its distribution and pricing tactics, and more perhaps to its severe 'brand image problems.' Moreover, if a key fact was the degree of foreign shares of the domestic market, then both Kodak and Fuji had similar shares in third markets and an equally large share of their respective domestic markets.[32]

Perhaps even more clever was Japan's stinging response to charges of a lack of transparency in government notifications. After all, the US had provided vast amounts of translated copies of reports and other items on Japan's measures; and as such the US did not seem to have had any trouble identifying and reproducing everything it considered relevant with 'perfect specificity' after drafting its panel request. Thus, as far as Japan was concerned, in the WTO-legal context not only were there no government measures that affected imports adversely the very idea that they were somehow opaque in their operation was ludicrous. As to the key US claim that it was not so much the individual but rather the collective effect of the measures that led to nullification and impairment, Japan rebutted that 'combining nothing with nothing still produces nothing.'

The panel, however, was not so convinced by Japan's narrow emphasis on formal and visible government regulations within the meaning of Article XXIII. In fact, by using an incentive-disincentive test, the panel opted for a broad interpretation of the word 'measure.' That is, if there were government actions, such as administrative guidance, that created incentives or disincentives for private parties to act, and their compliance depended largely on the government action itself, then any such government action constituted a satisfactory meaning of the word measure under Article XXIII. Moreover, several earlier GATT cases had made it clear that what appeared to be purely private market behaviour did not rule out the possibility of informal government involvement.[33] But the panel also made it clear that the burden of proof, with respect to Japanese government actions that nullified or impaired benefits, was on the US. Establishing that something fell legally within the scope of a GATT measure and then causally proving that it in fact harmed or impaired trade benefits were two different matters.

And the latter is where the US failed more miserably, both on claims of non-violation nullification and impairment under Article XXIII:1(b), and also under violation claims under Article III:4 and Article X:1. In the non-violation claims,

---

[32] According to Japan, foreign market shares for black and white paper ranged between 31 and 55 per cent, and stood at about 15 per cent for colour film.

[33] The panel used the 1988 semiconductor case to actually chide Japan. During those proceedings Japan had claimed that there were no governmental measures affecting the prices and exports of semiconductors, and that decisions about such matters were a function of private actors. However, in that case, the panel concluded that there was indeed an 'administrative structure' created by the government of Japan that affected such decisions.

the US could not satisfy the requirements of nullification and impairment as set out in Article XXIII for any of the three sets of measures that formed the centrepiece of its case. Of the eight 'distribution measures' cited by the US and examined by the panel, only half were accepted as measures for the purposes of Article XXIII:1(b). None of them could be shown to have led to a nullification or impairment of US benefits. In large part this was because the measures could not even be shown to promote vertical integration or single-brand distribution as the US claimed, making the claim for nullification and impairment even more dubious. On the restrictions stemming from the 'Large Stores Law,' the panel found not only that there was substantial liberalisation in the application of the law but also that it was clearly neutral as to products and the origin of products. It was less clear to the panel, however, whether large stores did indeed carry more imported film as the US claimed or whether it was high-volume sellers of film that were more likely to carry imported film as Japan maintained. Nevertheless, given the record, the panel concluded that the US did not sufficiently demonstrate that the Large Stores Law impaired or nullified benefits accruing to it. Finally, of the eight 'promotion measures' that the US pinpointed, the panel found them all to constitute measures for the purposes of Article XXIII:1(b). But here too, while these measures were alleged to disadvantage imports by restricting sales promotion, the panel concluded that the US did not demonstrate that they caused nullification and impairment of benefits. In fact, overall the panel concluded that the cited Japanese measures did not, either individually or collectively, nullify or impair US benefits.

On the violation claims, the US also bore the burden of proof. Here too it was unable to prove its more straightforward case. On the violation of Article III:4, the national treatment clause, the US had claimed that the same eight distribution measures, that formed the heart of the non-violation claims, also led to less favourable treatment for imported products. Again the panel concluded that only four of those cited constituted measures, and only three could be examined since one of them had expired. Here too the panel found that of the distribution measures examined, none could be found to accord less favourable treatment to imported film and paper than to film and paper of Japanese origin. On the violation of Article X:1, the transparency clause, the US had claimed that Japanese government agencies failed to publish materials such as administrative rulings establishing or modifying criteria applicable in future cases, or those relating to the administration of the Large Stores Law and relevant local regulations. The panel, however, found that the US did not demonstrate sufficient violation of the transparency rule in any one of the cited instances.

With both the non-violation and violation claims essentially dismissed by the panel, the case against Japan was over by March 1998. A strict legal analysis had vindicated Japan's claims that its consumer photographic and film sector was not exclusionary and did not discriminate against imported products. In fact, despite the broad interpretation of 'measures' employed by the panel, many of the measures or practices the US pinpointed could not be legally ascertained for the purposes of Article XXIII. Even more importantly, none could be satisfactorily shown to cause nullification or impairment of benefits to the US. To the extent that there were any exclusionary measures in the sector – which the Japanese government denied throughout but to which even third parties such as the EU and Mexico attested – they had been *legally* shielded from blame and criticism. A high-profile rule-based system had ruled in favour of Japan and against the US.[34]

Little did the US side know that it was setting in motion a historic legal episode in 1998 – one that would go on to become as important a milestone in Japan's legalisation strategy as the 1988 Canadian panel decision a decade earlier. The fact that the Japanese side 'won' worked wonders for boosting greater interest in the Japanese foreign trade policy establishment with respect to the WTO dispute settlement system. The widespread perception was that such a system would 'render fair and impartial judgments according to objective rules.'[35] The fact also that, despite 'strong disagreement' with the panel's legal findings and conclusion, the US did not appeal against the panel decision, even further bolstered Japanese confidence in the power and efficacy of WTO rules.[36]

As both the leather and consumer photographic materials cases show, the WTO rules can be used to provide a legal shield for Japanese measures and practices – a conscious strategy which, while controversial, is nevertheless legally legitimate. But Japan is no longer simply reactive with respect to trade pressures and complaints. In fact, it now appears set to dish them out as well.

(ii) The 'sword' aspect at play

The Japanese government has recently started demonstrating how the WTO rules can also be used as a sword to challenge or thwart Japan's trade partners directly – a confrontational strategy that Japan has avoided for most of the postwar period. Armed with a substantive set of rules in the WTO treaties and agreements, Japan is now becoming visibly active in terms of the legal evaluations and indictments of its major trade partners. And, as the following cases suggest, this is where the trend towards aggressive legalism is even clearer.

Automobiles: One of the earliest indications of Japan's commitment to the legalised trade strategy appeared forcefully in early 1994, just a few months before

---

[34] Curiously, the USTR has yet to update the negative outcome of this particular case (301–99) on its website location for Section 301 cases.
[35] Industrial Structure Council (1998, p. 327).
[36] Both the US and Japan expressed their comments on the panel report in April 1998. Despite its serious qualms, the US did not formally engage in the appeals process. This was significant both because the US still obviously believed in the validity of its claims, and also because this was the only case that was not appealed since the inception of the WTO in 1995. All previous twelve cases had seen formal appeals go through.

the Uruguay Round agreements were to be finally signed after seven controversial years of global negotiations. At that point then Prime Minister Hosokawa made headline news around the world by saying a very definitive 'no' to US demands for numerical targets as a means to open the Japanese market, especially in automobiles and auto parts, as well as government procurement, insurance, and medical equipment markets.[37] This was a high-profile rejection by the Japanese side of the results-oriented approach during the Framework Agreement talks, and marked a fairly significant departure from Japan's usual behind-the-scenes trade diplomacy with respect to the US.[38] Since the 1930s, Japan had agreed to a series of bilateral quantitative restrictions with the US, and in fact the Framework Agreement in 1993 itself stressed explicit changes in economic indicators.[39] But at first blush, despite Hosokawa's flamboyant no, it seemed that the nature of trade diplomacy between the US and Japan had not changed very much. President Clinton revived Super 301 in March. And a few weeks later, the American side was claiming a negotiation victory concerning access to the Japanese cellular phone market, since Motorola finally got access to the Tokyo-Nagoya corridor.[40]

But this results-oriented path was not one that Japan wanted to continue down on. And, in a post-Cold War world, what better way to challenge the US than to use the legal rules of the WTO to legitimately push back American pressures and demands.[41] And this is exactly what the Japanese side did as American frustration continued to grow about market access issues in Japan that then had about a $60 billion trade surplus with the US. In May 1995, four months after the birth of the WTO, the USTR targeted the market access issue in the Japanese auto market in a highly public confrontation, designed to draw political attention and sympathy.

---

[37] *Nihon Keisai Shinbun* (13 February, 1994).

[38] Lincoln (1999, pp. 125–66). The Framework Agreement was signed on 10 July, 1993, and allowed the US and Japan to consult, negotiate, and monitor issues at the macroeconomic, microeconomic, and global levels. Although numerical targets were not specifically mentioned, the language of the agreement nevertheless emphasised the importance of change in specific economic variables, as well as the process of monitoring to assess outcomes.

[39] Product by product, US bilateral quantitative restrictions (QRs) with Japan have had a long history. See, for example, Finger and Harrison (1996, pp. 201–3), Destler, Sato, Clapp and Fukui (1979) and Hufbauer, Berliner and Elliott (1986). The earliest QRs against Japan were based on Section 3(e) of the short-lived National Industrial Recovery Act (NIRA) between 1933 and 1935. Of the ten completed investigations by the Tariff Commission, all the four cases involving Japan resulted in VERs, specifically in wood-cased lead pencils, cotton chenille rugs, hit-and-miss rag rugs, and other rugs. QRs with Japan were especially prominent in textiles. They began with the VER in cotton textiles in 1935, a VRA on cotton textiles in 1957 (which later continued under the more global Long-Term Arrangement on Cotton Textiles from 1962 onwards), and a bilateral agreement on synthetic fibres in 1971. Other bilateral QRs have included a tariff-rate quota on canned tuna (1956), a VER in carbon steel (1982), an OMA in speciality steel and alloy tools steel (1976), an OMA in colour television (1977), a VER in automobiles (1981), and, perhaps most controversial of all, a VIE in semiconductors (1986).

[40] *The Boston Globe* (13 March, 1994). See also ACCJ (1997) for the very high marks given by American industry representatives to the Cellular Telephone Agreement (12 March, 1994, pp. 28–9).

[41] Interview, Sozaburo Okamatsu, Ex-Vice Minister for International Affairs, MITI, Tokyo, 1997.

THE WTO AND JAPAN'S EMERGING TRADE STRATEGY

At first, the USTR claimed that it would challenge the collusive business practices in Japan by filing a case at the WTO.[42] Later, more directly, President Clinton threatened the imposition of 100 per cent retaliatory tariffs on about $5.9 billion worth of 13 models of Japanese luxury cars by the end of June if no progress was made in the talks.

But the international context had changed, and this time around Japan had a fully functional and hard-hitting strategy in mind, with the full support of some of its other trade partners.[43] First, the Japanese government presented its case at an OECD Ministerial meeting, where almost all parties agreed with the Japanese position.[44] And second, within days of that agreeable outcome, Japan filed its first case at the WTO, charging that the US imposition of import duties on automobiles from Japan violated GATT Articles I and II. Once the formal dispute settlement process was set in motion it took less than a month for the two sides to reach a conclusion, and on 19 July, 1995, both parties notified settlement without further seeking to escalate the process to a panel stage. In part, this quick result can be attributed to the fact that while there is no formal legal constraint on domestic US legislation such as Section 301, its use nevertheless violates both the language and spirit of the WTO Agreements except when it is explicitly authorised by the WTO.[45] In part also, both parties were encouraged to come to a bilateral agreement without jeopardising the new and still-fragile dispute settlement system.[46]

---

[42] *The Washington Post* (11 May, 1995).

[43] *The Daily Yomiuri* (21 May, 1995); and also *The Times* (26 June, 1995). Some unnamed senior officials of the EU both encouraged and supported Japan's decision to take the auto and auto parts dispute to the WTO, making it clear that they themselves reserved the right to appeal to the WTO should Japan reach a preferential agreement with the US.

[44] Okamatsu was asked by then MITI minister Ryutaro Hashimoto to present this case at the meeting.

[45] Abels (1998, pp. 484–502). Article 22 of the Understanding on Rules and Procedures Governing the Settlement of Disputes deals with the compensation and suspension of concessions. But in my reading as Article 22.2 states clearly, members first have to engage in the formal dispute settlement process with a view to developing mutually acceptable compensation and only then to request suspension of concessions or other obligations. In this case, the US had imposed unilateral measures without going through the WTO process. This fact also constrained the US side from making an effective case for itself in the WTO system because it is not the mere fact of the existence of Section 301 but rather the legitimacy of its unilateral use that is at issue. See USTR, Press Release 00–06, 'WTO Adopts Panel Findings Upholding Section 301,' 27 January, 2000. Contrary to EU claims, a WTO panel formally confirmed that Section 301 is consistent with US WTO obligations. It therefore remains the main statutory means by which the US can assert its international trade rights, including those under the WTO Agreements.

[46] Maswood (1997–1998, pp. 542–43). Some sources point out that the WTO head, Renato Ruggiero, was himself involved in urging the two countries to come to a bilateral agreement. In large part, this was because of concerns about the ambiguity of the status of the WTO and US sovereignty especially at that early stage, and the possibility of a US withdrawal if the WTO ruled against it persistently. See, for example, Senate majority leader, Bob Dole's comment in *The New York Times* (24 November, 1994), that the major point which had led him to a deal favourable to the WTO was the Administration's concession to give Congress a 'trigger mechanism.' Presumably, this mechanism would enable the US to withdraw from the WTO if there were unfair rulings by the newly created court of international trade against the US.

When the Japanese side finally negotiated the auto agreement in August 1995, it stressed that the qualitative and quantitative criteria set out did not constitute numerical targets, and for this reason very few actual figures, percentage or otherwise, exist in the text of the agreement.[47] The Japanese government also stressed the importance of the private sector, rather than the government, in ultimately resolving what the Americans perceived to be the problem of market access. Moreover, all measures were to be implemented with due regard for consistency with international law (WTO law) and the most-favoured-nation clause. While the US side claimed the negotiations as a victory, it was actually Japan that emerged as the legal winner.[48] The presence of the WTO had allowed the Japanese government to not only effectively push back US Section 301 measures, but also to resist numerical targets in its domestic market altogether.

Nor was Japan merely content to push back only US pressures and measures in the automobile industry. In a bold subsequent move, it also initiated an indirect challenge by questioning the legality of Canadian import measures that favoured especially the big three US automobile manufacturers.[49] Japan filed a complaint on 3 July, 1998, alleging that the duty-free treatment violated, among other rules, the key MFN and national treatment clauses of GATT 1994. Failure at the consultation stage led Japan to unhesitatingly request the establishment of a panel on 12 November, 1998, and by February of the following year a panel was established. In the process, Japan's legal challenge received an additional moral boost when the EU also filed a separate complaint on the same issue on 17 August, 1998. Since the EU cited essentially the same Canadian measures to be in violation of the rules and agreements overseen by the WTO, both parties requested on 15 March, 1999, that a single panel be charged with the responsibility of examining the case.

Under the 1965 Auto Pact between the US and Canada, a limited number of auto manufacturers could import vehicles into Canada with an exemption from the generally applicable customs duty, and distribute them at both the wholesale

---

[47] ACCJ (1997, p. 101). A copy of the 'Measures by the Government of Japan and the Government of the United States of America regarding Autos and Auto Parts' can be found in Appendix B, Lincoln (1999).

[48] See also Maswood (1997–1998, esp. pp. 549–51), who attempts to account for the Japanese government's obduracy on numerical targets for several reasons such as the desire to break the precedent of the results-oriented approach, the triumph of a 'nationalist' faction at MITI etc. However, he does not account for the new international legal context in which the auto dispute unfolded. The most important factor, as I am stressing here, was the presence of the WTO rules that allowed the Japanese side to both articulate and legitimise its obduracy.

[49] The procedural and substantive facts in this case are drawn directly from the WTO Report of the Panel published as Document WT/DS139/R and WT/DS142/R (11 February, 2000), and the Report of the Appellate Body published as Document WT/DS139/AB/R and WT/DS142/AB/R (31 May, 2000). This panel proceeding was initiated by both Japan and the EU, but I will concentrate on the legal arguments and facts pertaining to Japan since it was the first of the two to start the formal complaint process at the WTO.

THE WTO AND JAPAN'S EMERGING TRADE STRATEGY

and retail level.[50] More specifically, Japan took issue with what it collectively termed the Canadian 'Duty Waiver,' claiming that the measure generally violated the MFN and national treatment rules in both the GATT and the GATS, as well as rules in the Agreements overseen by the WTO.[51] In elaborating its legal arguments, Japan also claimed that successively the Auto Pact, the Canada-US Free Trade Agreement of 1 January, 1989 (CUSFTA), and the North American Free Trade Agreement of 1 January, 1994 (CUSFTA) exacerbated and deepened the discriminatory effects of the original measure.[52]

In October 1999, the WTO panel ruled comprehensively against the Canadian measures at an interim review, upholding almost all the Japanese claims that the Canadian measures were inconsistent with WTO rules and agreements. Specifically the panel found that, by reserving the import duty exemption in the MVTO 1998 and various SROs for certain importers, Canada accorded an advantage to products originating in certain countries. This advantage was not accorded immediately and unconditionally to like products

---

[50] More formally the 'Auto Pact' refers to the Agreement Concerning Automotive Products Between the Government of Canada and the Government of the United States. This was a treaty signed by both parties in January 1965. Canada agreed to duty-free treatment for US vehicles and original equipment manufacturers under specific conditions. Chief among them was the criterion of the base year (i.e. an Auto Pact manufacturer must have produced in Canada in the base year 1963–64 vehicles similar to the one it was importing), although this criterion could be waived by the Canadians. In addition, the conditions stipulated that eligible manufacturers had to maintain a minimum ratio of production-to-sales ratio between their local and Canadian production, and also had to maintain a minimum amount of Canadian value added in their local production. Domestically, in Canada, the provisions of eligibility for the Auto Pact manufacturers were given effect through the Motor Vehicles Tariff Order (MVTO) 1965, later replaced by MVTO 1988 and then MVTO 1998 which is the measure in effect today. Canada also extended eligibility through the Special Remission Order (SRO) to other auto manufacturers who had not qualified under the MVTO 1965.

[51] Specifically at issue were Article I:1 (General Most-Favoured-Nation Treatment) of GATT 1994, Article II (Most-Favoured-Nation Treatment) and XVII (National Treatment) of the GATS, the General Agreement on Trade in Services. In addition, Japan claimed that Canada's domestic content requirements violated Article III:4 (National Treatment) of GATT 1994, Article 2.1 (National Treatment and Quantitative Restrictions) of the TRIMs (Trade-Related Investment Measures) Agreement, Articles 3.1 and 3.2 (Prohibition) of the Subsidies and Countervailing Measures (SCM) Agreement, and Article XVII (Market Access) of the GATS. Finally Japan also maintained that because of the manufacturing requirement, the Canadian measure was also inconsistent with Articles 3.1 and 3.2 of the SCM Agreement.

[52] A GATT Working Party was established in March 1965 to examine the Auto Pact. At that point the US admitted that its obligations under the Auto Pact were inconsistent with GATT Article I:1 (MFN), and ended up requesting a waiver under Article XXV:5 (Joint Action by the Contracting Parties). Unlike the US, however, Canada maintained that its obligations under the Auto Pact were fully consistent with the GATT and did not request a waiver. A few members of the Working Party openly questioned the compatibility of Canada's obligations under the Auto Pact with Articles I (MFN) and III (National Treatment) of the GATT. To assuage their concerns, Canada gave assurances that the benefits under the Auto Pact would be extended to all and that the Auto Pact would not lead to discrimination against new entrants. But both Japan and the EC claimed that these assurances were broken by Canada.

originating from other WTO members, and this meant that Canadian measures were inconsistent with Canada's obligations under Article I:1 of the GATT.[53] The panel also ruled that Canada was in violation of Article III:4 of the GATT, and that the application of the CVA requirements, as well as conditions contained in Letters of Undertaking with respect to Canadian value-added, led to less favourable treatment of imported materials in comparison to domestic materials. This, in turn, had an adverse effect on the equality of competitive opportunities for imported products in relation to domestic ones.[54] Finally, the panel also upheld charges that the Canadian measures were inconsistent with some aspects of the SCM Agreement, as well as Article II:1 and Article XVII of the GATS. In short, the Canadian measures violated both the MFN and the national treatment rules. The panel therefore recommended that the Dispute Settlement Body request Canada to withdraw the export subsidy without delay, allowing a mere 90 days to remove the offending measures since they were acts of the executive and not legislative branch of government. In doing so, the panel struck at the heart of the production-sharing agreement between the US and Canada.[55]

The report of the panel was circulated to WTO members on 11 February, 2000, and constituted a clear legal victory for Japan. Almost immediately after the ruling, however, on 2 March, 2000, Canada announced that it would appeal against the panel decision. It did not take the Appellate Body long to return its ruling. On 31 May, 2000, it upheld the panel's, and thereby Japan's, complaints that Canada was violating its MFN obligations under Article I:1 and national treatment obligations in both Article III:4 of the GATT and Article XVII of GATS.[56] As such, Canada stands in violation of its WTO obligations, very much in line with Japan's legal case against it.[57]

---

[53] Moreover, contrary to Canadian defensive claims with respect to NAFTA, the panel also found that Article XXIV (Territorial Application – Frontier Traffic – Customs Unions and Free-Trade Areas) of the GATT did not provide a justification for being inconsistent with Article I with respect to the import duty exemptions.

[54] Notably, the panel rejected the EU's claim that the production-to-sales ratio violated Article III:4 on the basis of insufficient evidence.

[55] *Financial Times* (15 October, 1999).

[56] The Canadian measures were also found to be inconsistent with Article 3.1 (Prohibition) of the SCM Agreement. The Appellate Body did not, however, find Canada to be in violation of Article II (Most-Favoured-Nation) of the GATS and thereby reversed the panel's findings. It appears that the Appellate Body was almost reluctant to reverse this aspect of the panel's findings, because it also concluded that given the newness of the GATS itself much closer analysis needed to be done in the future. After all, as it noted, the GATS is a new agreement under the WTO, and this case represented only the second time that the Appellate Body had been involved in reviewing a panel's findings on provisions of the GATS.

[57] I have concentrated here on Japan's aggressive legalism with respect to the advanced industrial countries, although this does not mean that Japan's legal tactics can be ignored in its trade relations with less developed countries. To give one example: Along with the US and the EU, Japan also won a case against Indonesia's 1996 National Car Programme (both February and June). Japan filed a

THE WTO AND JAPAN'S EMERGING TRADE STRATEGY 727

Semiconductors: A similar controversy over market access had led Japan to file a GATT case in semiconductors against the US in April 1987. Here also Japan charged that the US had imposed discriminatory tariffs that violated Articles I and II but, in keeping with its non-confrontational strategy, did not at that point go on to request the establishment of a panel.[58] After some extra-GATT negotiations, on 4 June, 1991, Japan extended the controversial 1986 agreement with the explicit assurance that it 'recognised' that the US semiconductor industry expected the foreign market share in Japan to grow more than 20 per cent.[59] Irrespective of evaluations of the success of the first and second agreements on the basis of numeric indicators, the Japanese side was unwilling to conclude a third agreement that followed any sort of a quantitative emphasis.[60] In fact, the Japanese side was reluctant to conclude any agreement whatsoever, especially since the 20 per cent target was surpassed in late 1992 and allegedly went about as high as 30 per cent at the end of 1995.[61]

But as events began to move towards a new agreement in 1996, the topmost priority for the Japanese side was to shatter the precedent of a results-oriented and a strictly bilateral approach.[62] This priority was made clear both rhetorically and textually, and acquired a sheen of legitimacy with a repeated emphasis by the

---

complaint on 4 October, 1996, charging that by granting luxury sales taxes and import duty exemptions to automobiles which met certain local content requirements, Indonesia was violating rules against non-discrimination and national treatment in the GATT as well as the Agreement on Trade Related Investment Measures (TRIMs). In addition, the measures were not promptly published and so violated rules of GATT transparency. In April 1997 Japan requested the establishment of a panel. And in April 1998, a WTO panel essentially ruled that Indonesia was indeed in violation of its MFN and national treatment obligations. The report was adopted by the WTO Dispute Settlement Body on 23 July, 1998. The Arbitrator determined that, given Indonesia's social and economic problems as a developing country during the financial crisis, it could have 12 months from 23 July, 1998, to implement the rulings and recommendations. And on 15 July, 1999, Indonesia informed the Dispute Settlement Body that it had done so by instituting the 1999 Automotive Policy. For the legal case, see the single WTO Document numbered WT/DS54/R, WT/DS55/R, WT/DS59/R and WT/DS64/R (2 July, 1998), as well as the Arbitration report published as a single WTO Document numbered WT/DS54/15, WT/DS55/14, WT/DS59/13, and WT/DS64/12 (7 December, 1998).

[58] The US increased its tariffs because it alleged that Japan had violated the 1986 Semiconductor Agreement.

[59] Irwin (1996, pp. 56–64). The recognition of the 20 per cent market share was expressed in a not-so-secret side-letter to the 1986 Agreement, but became an explicit part of the text in the 1991 Agreement. In fact, Irwin contends that the whole emphasis on results had become so institutionalised on both sides that the second agreement was not as difficult to negotiate as the first one. But Japan rejected further institutionalisation of any such emphasis in the later agreements and arrangements.

[60] ACCJ (1997, pp. 58–63).

[61] *The New York Times* (21 December, 1996). I say allegedly because the Japanese government had significantly overstated the share of its market held by foreign semiconductor companies in early 1996 as the negotiations and talks over the agreement got under way. At that point, the Japanese claimed that the foreign share stood at 30.6 per cent, but along with the American government at the end of the year, it conceded that the foreign share was actually 26.9 per cent. Some American critics complained that this led the new agreement to be far weaker than it could have been.

[62] *The New York Times* (28 May, 1996); and *The New York Times* (30 July, 1996).

Japanese side that this was now a WTO world in which many interested players would baulk at a US-Japan agreement. The EU had already set a precedent by successfully challenging key aspects of the agreement at a GATT panel in 1987, and was moreover keen not to be left out of any future agreement.[63] Speaking at the Foreign Correspondents' Club of Japan, the vice minister for international affairs at MITI, Yoshihiro Sakamoto, made a high-profile statement that was guaranteed to make headline news at a crucial episode early in the talks.[64] Sakamoto said plainly that there was no longer any raison d'être for such an agreement and that, moreover, the 'era of bilateralism' itself was over.[65]

When the US and Japan reached the three-year Semiconductor Accord on 2 August, 1996, there were no specific numerical targets mentioned in the text, which constituted a victory for the Japanese side.[66] More importantly, the

---

[63] See GATT (GA 1987, pp. 63–65); and GATT (BISD 35th Suppl. 1987–1988, pp. 116–63). The key complaint raised by the Europeans concerned the Japanese government's agreement to undertake a Third Country Market Monitoring provision in countries other than the US. Since the 1986 Agreement had increased prices in the US market and disadvantaged US competitiveness in third markets, the EU claimed that the purpose of this monitoring was to help increase prices artificially in third markets through an elaborate system of restrictions maintained by the Japanese government. These restrictions included both export approvals and also the close monitoring of costs and export prices by the various Japanese producers, thereby ensuring that prices were higher to wherever Japan was exporting. Thus the EU claimed that this monitoring system violated Article VI (Anti-dumping and Countervailing duties) since only an importing country could decide whether, on balance, a product was being dumped and thereby causing harm or benefit to its interests. In addition, it violated Article XI:1 (General Elimination of Quantitative Restrictions), because the net effect of the restrictive policies was to keep up export prices artificially in third markets. The panel essentially concluded that the monitoring system had led the Japanese government to maintain an administrative structure that forced the private sector to cease exporting at prices below company-specific costs. While Japan was to be lauded for acting in the spirit of upholding Article VI which condemned dumping, this did not mean that it could thereby justify restricting the sale of exports of semiconductor products in violation of Article XI:1. The panel focused its legal reasoning on the Japanese violation of Article XI:1 which, according to GATT practice, was presumed to have nullified or impaired benefits accruing to the EU under the General Agreement. Separately, in another major claim, the EU maintained that the 1986 Agreement was worded in a way to grant preferential market access in Japan for US producers and exporters of semiconductors, and as such it violated Article I (General Most-Favoured Nation Treatment). Notably, the panel did not find that to be the case based on the evidence presented. The GATT Council adopted the panel report in May 1988.
[64] *The Daily Yomiuri* (16 March, 1996).
[65] Interview, Yoshihiro Sakamoto, Ex-Vice Minister for International Affairs, MITI, Tokyo, 1997, 1998. In his personal interviews, Sakamoto emphasised that his statement had been taken out of context, and that he had meant more that it would be difficult to justify such agreements in a WTO world. Semiconductors was now a global industry with many players, and a limited bilateral context could be very controversial from the point of view of the other players. He pointed especially to the legal obligation Japan had under the GATT to avoid quantitative or artificial restrictions, which had been challenged successfully by the EU at the GATT earlier as discussed above. The main point is that his statement signalled a shift in Japan's trade strategy towards a more rule-oriented approach.
[66] See USTR, Press Release 96-65, 'U.S. and Japan Reach Semiconductor Accord' (2 August, 1996); and also the brief commentary by ACCJ (1997, pp. 62–63), which suggests that the hitherto success of American semiconductor-related companies in Japan has been based on the controversial numeric indicators.

THE WTO AND JAPAN'S EMERGING TRADE STRATEGY 729

agreement transferred much of the responsibility for data collection and analysis primarily to both the US and Japanese industries through a World Semiconductor Council (WSC), thus minimising the role of both governments. In keeping with Japan's emphasis throughout on third parties, as well as the legal challenge issued by the EU at the GATT in 1987, both sides also committed to the creation of a Global Governmental Forum (GGF) where all interested parties could jointly assess the challenges in the semiconductor industry. This was clearly meant to be a mini-multilateralised talking forum that helped push attention away even further from the strict bilateral precedent set by US-Japan negotiations in the semiconductor industry since the mid-1980s.[67]

With the US-Japan Accord set to expire in the middle of 1999, both sides agreed to continue with the emphasis on the multilateral framework on consultations. This time there was a stronger emphasis on the role the WSC, not government-to-government negotiations, could play in resolving conflicts and concerns in the industry. In fact, according to the joint multilateral announcement by the US, Japan, EU, Korea, and Taiwan released on 10 June, 1999, the related governments and authorities would meet only once a year to discuss the recommendations of the WSC about any government policies or measures affecting competitive conditions in the global semiconductor industry.[68] In many ways, as Sakamoto had prophesised, the era of bilateralism was indeed over at least in the semiconductor industry. And in any event, as the Japanese government kept emphasising repeatedly, and conveniently so by legal standards, strictly bilateral arrangements were difficult to justify and maintain in a WTO world.

Anti-dumping: At least two other recent WTO cases demonstrate how the Japanese government intends to challenge or thwart foreign pressures outright using the WTO, and both have to do with anti-dumping concerns. In fact, anti-dumping is one of the most important agenda for the 'millennium' round as far as the Japanese side is concerned, in conjunction with both the EU and other developing countries.[69] If rhetoric alone is not convincing enough then Japan's

---

[67] *Financial Times* (9 July, 1996).

[68] See USTR, Press Release 99-50, 'United States, Japan, European Union, Korea and Taiwan Announce New Accord on Semiconductor Trade Practices' (10 June, 1999). The joint statement will be subject to review after five years (1 August, 2004), and may be modified in part or whole by mutual consent of the relevant parties. The WSC consists of electronic or semiconductor industry associations from each of the five countries.

[69] Letter of 22 October, 1999 from Vice-Minister for International Affairs, Hisamitsu Arai, to Undersecretary of Commerce for International Trade, David L. Aaron, regarding Mr. Aaron's Remarks Made at the National Press Club in Washington DC on 19 October, MITI, Tokyo (1999). Drawing a parallel in terms of the number of cases against both Japan (76) and the US (65), Arai urges that this alone should be incentive enough for the US to focus on the issue of preventing anti-dumping abuses in the new round. More importantly, he also drives home the point that the US, with an outstanding amount of 326 anti-dumping cases (of which 53 stand against Japan), is the largest user of the anti-dumping provisions – a point perhaps intended to put the US diplomatically on notification that Japan intends to do something about such rampant usage. See also MOFA, Preparations for the 1999 Ministerial Conference: Proposal on Anti-dumping, MOFA, Tokyo (1999).

active use of the WTO dispute settlement system concerning anti-dumping measures should be proof enough of the seriousness with which it takes the matter.

Once again the cases concern the US. On 20 October, 1999, Japan issued a public statement that the US imposition of anti-dumping duties ranging from 17 to 67 per cent on certain hot-rolled steel from Japan was inconsistent with US obligations under both the GATT and the Agreement on Anti-dumping.[70] Japan further claimed that with the rise of anti-dumping petitions in the US since 1997, as much as 80 per cent of Japan's steel exports to the US had become subject to anti-dumping actions, either in terms of investigations or actual duties imposed. While anti-dumping duties are one of the trade remedies permitted under the WTO rules, their implementation is allowed for under certain conditions.[71] The danger, ever present, is that anti-dumping measures can become the 'protectionist weapon of choice' in the WTO system much as they have done in the US.[72] Using this as the key argument, the Japanese side stepped up the legal onslaught on this front most recently.

On 18 November, 1999, Japan challenged both the preliminary and final determinations of the US Department of Commerce and the US International Trade Commission on about five anti-dumping investigations of certain Japanese steel products between 1998 and 1999. Among other things, Japan charged that the US measures violated Article VI (Anti-dumping and Countervailing Duties), Article X (Publication and Administration of Trade Regulations), and various provisions in the Anti-dumping Agreement. While consulting directly with the US, Japan also reserved its third-party rights in a similar anti-dumping steel case filed by Korea against the US – a tactic which would allow the Japanese side to gain access to information on opinions in that dispute which it could potentially use to its advantage and also allow it to present its own opinions on the issue of anti-dumping.[73] Japan also no doubt received some amount of satisfaction in light

---

[70] Statement of Mr. Takashi Fukaya, Minister of International Trade and Industry, On Request for Consultation with the United States Regarding the Imposition of Anti-dumping Duties on Certain Hot-rolled Steel from Japan, MITI, Tokyo (1999).

[71] Article VI (Anti-dumping and Countervailing Duties) of GATT 1994 deals formally with anti-dumping provisions, which are further elaborated in the Agreement on Implementation of Article VI of the General Agreement on Tariffs and Trade 1994, informally known as the Agreement on Anti-dumping. Article VI:1 states that dumping is to be 'condemned' if it causes or threatens material injury or materially retards the establishment of a domestic industry. Once a determination of dumping has been made along specified criteria, a country can levy anti-dumping duties 'not greater in amount than the margin of dumping' in the product concerned.

[72] Krueger (1996, pp. 2, 8). In the US, 'administered protection' is used to refer to the processes through which anti-dumping (to offset price below cost or sales price in other markets) and countervailing duties (to offset foreign subsidies) can be imposed. Here firms approach the protection process through US 'fair trade laws.'

[73] Korea filed this case on 30 July, 1999, charging that the US determinations of anti-dumping duties during 1998–1999 were erroneous and also incompatible with the US's WTO obligations. Failure at the bilateral consultation stage led Korea to request the establishment of a panel, which was formally instituted on 19 November, 1999. Some press reports suggested that these tactics

THE WTO AND JAPAN'S EMERGING TRADE STRATEGY 731

of the EU's successful legal challenge to US administered protection in the case of countervailing duties, which were found to be in violation of the WTO rules and thereby responsible for nullifying and impairing benefits to the EU.[74]

Most recently, on 29 May, 2000, Japan followed the successful lead of the EU in challenging a little-used US provision, namely the Anti-dumping Act of 1916, and also in obtaining a favourable legal ruling.[75] In both cases, two WTO panels came to nearly identical conclusions and recommendations. Both found that the 1916 Act, which allows for civil and criminal penalties in US federal courts in the event of price dumping undertaken with specific intent, violated various provisions of Article VI (Anti-dumping and Countervailing Duties) of the GATT and the Anti-dumping Agreement.[76] As a result, the panels concluded that benefits accruing to the EU and Japan under the WTO Agreement had been nullified or impaired. Despite US protestations that the 1916 Act is not justiciable under the WTO anti-dumping measures, the fact stands that both panels have recommended that the US bring the 1916 Act into conformity with its obligations under the WTO Agreement.[77]

With the cases against US administered protection in various guises increasing from all quarters, Japan too, almost without hesitation on 24 February, 2000, requested the establishment of a formal WTO panel to review the legality of US determinations of anti-dumping on Japanese steel imports.[78] This panel is

---

would allow Japan to get a favourable legal ruling in its own case. See *Jiji Press Ticker Service*, 20 November, 1999.

[74] Specifically, this case concerned the imposition of countervailing duties on certain British steel exports. In that case, a WTO panel concluded that the US had failed to show that there were British subsidies bestowed directly or indirectly on the production of the steel imports. As such it concluded that the US imposition of countervailing duties violated Article 10 (Application of Article VI of GATT 1994) of the Agreement on Subsidies and Countervailing Measures. The Appellate Body upheld the same conclusion in terms of the violation charges. See conclusions and findings in the WTO Documents numbered WT/DS138/R (23 December, 1999) and WT/DS138/AB/R (10 May, 2000).

[75] Japan had requested enhanced third party rights during the US-EU dispute concerning the 1916 Anti-dumping Act. While the EU supported Japan's request, the US objected strongly because it claimed that the 'apparent purpose' of this request was to give third parties an opportunity to make additional submissions in their own panel process. The panel eventually did not grant Japan's request.

[76] The violated provisions in the Anti-dumping Agreement included Articles 1 (Principles), 4 (Definition of Domestic Industry) and 5.5 (Initiation and Subsequent Investigation) of the Anti-dumping Agreement. In the US-Japan dispute, the panel also expanded the list of violations to include additional provision of Article 5, as well as Article 18 (Final Provisions). The panels also found the US Act to be in violation of Article XVI:4 (Miscellaneous Provisions) of the Agreement Establishing the WTO. See WTO Document WT/DS136/R (31 March, 2000) for the US-EU dispute, and WT/DS162/R (29 May, 2000) for the US-Japan dispute.

[77] See USTR, Press Release 00-23-A, 'U.S. Disagrees with WTO Dispute Settlement Ruling on Antidumping Act of 1916' (31 March, 2000).

[78] In keeping with its emphasis on aggressive legalism across both developed and developing countries, Japan also took up the issue of anti-dumping with India. In February 1999, Japan explicitly warned India about the possibility of a WTO panel concerning the imposition of Indian

presently under way and while the prospects look good for the Japanese side, given the legal precedents that have been set in the various cases, it remains to be seen what the Panel and possibly the Appellate Body will conclude more formally in this specific case. The important point is not simply about winning or losing. Rather the point is that Japan is no longer hesitant about using the WTO legal rules and processes to challenge its trade partners in a visibly confrontational manner irrespective of the legal outcomes.

3. FUTURE TRENDS AND IMPLICATIONS

Japan's aggressive legalism is here to stay. As the cases in this essay make clear, the core idea behind aggressive legalism is the active use of the legal rules in the treaties and agreements overseen by the WTO to stake out positions, to advance and rebut claims, and to embroil all concerned in an intricate legal game. This is hardly dramatic. But then, characteristic of most Japanese foreign policy initiatives, it is not meant to be. It is meant to be measured, slow, and cautious, carefully trapping everything within the legitimate game of legal tactics. It is also deliberately meant as a way to use the legal rules as both 'shield' and 'sword' in Japan's disputes with its principal trade partners, most notably but not exclusively the US.

From controversial and long-standing disputes over market-access in Japan to concerns with the treatment of Japanese firms in other markets, this two-fold legal strategy is at play across a number of specific cases. In shielding its *domestic* measures and practices, as in the leather and consumer photographic film cases, strict legal analyses have vindicated Japan's claims that its markets are not exclusionary and do not discriminate against imported products. In challenging *foreign* demands and practices, as in the automobiles, semiconductors, and most recently anti-dumping cases, the same legal rules have allowed Japan to thwart both what it deems to be unreasonable pressures and also what it deems to be discriminatory measures towards its exported products. Legal rules matter, and will matter increasingly more as Japan continues down this path. Japan's strategy of aggressive legalism has of course its advantages but also important costs that could be a boon to its trade partners. It would be helpful to end by discussing what these are.

---

anti-dumping duties in December 1998 on acrylic fibre, EPDM rubber (a synthetic polymer used in automotive applications), and industrial sewing needles. The Japanese ambassador to India, Hiroshi Hirabayashi, was quoted in the Indian press as saying that Japan expected the Indian government not to follow the 'bad precedent' set by the US and EU in matters of anti-dumping. See *The Financial Express* (12 February, 1999). The course of this anti-dumping-related dispute remains open.

THE WTO AND JAPAN'S EMERGING TRADE STRATEGY 733

From the perspective of the Japanese government the advantages are many. First, and perhaps foremost, a clear advantage is that Japan now has a legitimate way of saying no to pressures and requests from its major trade partners that it deems to be unreasonable or against its interests. This ability is perhaps most evident with respect to the US, which still remains Japan's most important trading partner.

Second, by latching onto rules as an ally in trade disputes Japan is able to exercise marked independence in its foreign trade policy – an independence that is not as previously constrained by military alliances or considerations as it has been with the US in the past. For this reason alone, Japan is not as beholden to the bilateral prism through which the US still continues to see Japan.

Third, because of the presence of a substantive set of rules, Japan now has an open and transparent way of dealing with its trade partners. By embarking on a strategy of aggressive legalism, it has clearly signalled its strong interest in rule-oriented approaches to resolving disputes whether in a bilateral arena or under the auspices of the WTO. It is not important whether Japanese officials fundamentally believe in the procedural and substantive fairness of the legal rules of the WTO. Rather, the important point is that they are willing to use them to buttress their positions and arguments in confronting their trade partners.

Fourth, following on, the power of using a substantive set of international legal rules cannot be denied, conferring as it does an aura of legitimacy over Japan's actions. Perhaps for the first time in its postwar history, Japan now has a vision, considered legitimate by all, of how to achieve its foreign trade policy ends in a highly legalised multilateral setting. Once Japan's trade partners fully understand the essence of aggressive legalism, this will have the added effect of helping to both set and stabilise expectations about Japanese trade diplomacy in the future.

Recently there have been concerns that Japan's trade diplomacy is moving in the direction of regional pacts with Korea and Singapore, perhaps in keeping with the trend towards regionalism in the major economic centres of the world.[79] Notwithstanding issues of where this rhetoric will actually end up going, this move towards regional pacts does not constitute an about-face with respect to Japan's keen interest in using the legal rules of the WTO to its advantage in trade disputes with the rest of the world. In fact, for the foreseeable future, it is a safe bet that Japan will continue to channel its disputes with partners like the US, EU, Canada, and perhaps even China in the near future, through the WTO system as much as possible. This is because, given the checkered and volatile bilateral past with the US, Japan's ability to be able to influence its partners' behaviour depends heavily on sustaining the legal validity of its claims in the WTO system. Stripped of the procedural, substantive, and legitimate weight of the WTO rules, the Japanese government is more likely to flounder in

---

[79] See *Financial Times* (12 May, 2000, and 17 May, 2000).

confronting its major, as well as its minor, trade partners. For this reason, it should be recognised that Japan's emerging ambitions regarding regionalism stand in addition to, *not* instead of, its present emphasis on utilising legal rules in a multilateral setting.

But aggressive legalism is a double-edged sword. And there are costs to this strategy, which may well become distinct advantages for Japan's trade partners. For one thing, playing legal hardball with trade partners means that they too can then turn around and expose controversial aspects of Japan's political economy to the full glare of the WTO dispute settlement system. Again, the point here is not that they may win or lose based on the existing legal rules and their scope, but rather that they may be able to create legal obligations that Japan must comply with and also legal precedents that can come back to haunt Japan.

Important examples of both of these can be found in the agricultural sector, long the most protected and still as yet the least likely to be liberalised in Japan.[80] In 1987 Japan lost a GATT case to the US concerning restrictions on imports of twelve agricultural products.[81] The US had claimed that the Japanese import quotas violated Article XI:1 (General Elimination of Quantitative Restrictions), and that the restrictions on each of the twelve products did not meet the criteria for exception set out in later provisions of the same article. The panel upheld this claim on ten of the twelve products. This created a precedential effect which worked to the advantage of the US in that it was key to the 1988 liberalisation of the beef and citrus quotas.[82] Japan's more recent legal loss to the US concerning quarantine procedures for agricultural imports may well also create similar precedential effects in the future.[83] At the very least the findings and conclusions

---

[80] There are now fears, for instance, that Japan will be using the popular arguments concerning genetically modified organisms (GMOs) to restrict agricultural produce from the US. See *Financial Times* (26 April, 2000).

[81] The actual case is summarised in GATT (GA 1987, pp. 65–8). The panel report, adopted on 22 March, 1988, can be found in GATT (BISD 35th Suppl. 1987–1988, pp. 163–243).

[82] Porges (1991, pp. 313–14).

[83] In 1998, Japan lost a case to the US at the WTO concerning quarantine procedures for imports of agricultural products. Specifically the US complained that in products requiring quarantine treatment, Japan prohibited the importation of each variety of that product until it was tested. Furthermore, the US complained that Japan conducted the quarantine treatment even when the treatment had proven effective with respect to other varieties of the same product. Japan did not contest that the so-called varietal testing requirement was in effect or that it was applied. Moreover, it acknowledged that the provisions relating to this requirement had not been published. The panel found these measures to be inconsistent with, *inter alia*, Japan's obligations under the Agreement on the Application of Sanitary and Phytosanitary Measures (SPS). Upon appeal, the Appellate Body upheld the panel's conclusions that Japan's varietal testing of apples, cherries, nectarines and walnuts was inconsistent with, again *inter alia*, some of its obligations under the SPS Agreement. In December 1999, Japan abolished its varietal testing requirements, and began consulting with the US to come up with a new quarantine methodology. See introduction and conclusions in the panel report number WT/DS76/R (27 October, 1998) and also in the Appellate Body report number WT/DS76/AB/R (22 February, 1999).

in these cases mean that Japan will proceed with caution regarding import restrictions in the agricultural sector, and other sectors as well, that can be scrutinised and challenged under the WTO agreements from various quarters.

There may also be costs from the institutional perspective of the WTO. These are most often expressed as fears that something like aggressive legalism on the part of the major economic powers could seriously jeopardise the future of the WTO system as a whole.[84] The argument, in short, is that the reality of great powers going head-to-head in the WTO, and then refusing to comply with panel or Appellate Body decisions bodes ill for the future viability of the multilateral rule-based system. There is surely truth in that. But much worse perhaps is a neglect of the rules altogether as there was in the GATT's past, and an avoidance of the still relatively new dispute settlement machinery of the WTO. More importantly at a practical level, this consideration does not appear to have stopped the US, which is by far one of the biggest users of the new WTO processes, from challenging other countries. It has also certainly not stopped Japan as demonstrated in this essay. In fact, the actions of these great economic powers, has the effect of drawing all concerned into the legalised system of the WTO, and inadvertently strengthening, not weakening, the dispute settlement processes. Rational calculations should make it clear to them also that their individual reputation matters in this multilateral system, and that among equals the reputation may matter more because they have equal capability to do harm as well as good. As an additional bonus, by going through the WTO, the actions of these powers can avoid a negative power-oriented imagery when they charge weaker, less developed countries, with violating their obligations under the WTO agreements.

Finally, strategic considerations should also be paramount in the minds of Japan's trade partners. The way they choose to deal with Japan in the present will have repercussions for how they may deal with other Asian countries in the future. With China poised to join the WTO, setting the importance of the rule of the WTO now will help to interject greater calm and certitude with respect to resolution processes when trade disputes with China arise – and there is no question that they will arise – later down the line. From the US perspective, it is important to know now that China is not Japan, and that China will not succumb to high-profile bilateral pressures in the way that Japan has done in many cases. The only way to deal with China, as with Japan, is to embroil it hard and fast in the legal game of the WTO at an early stage.

---

[84] Schoppa (1997, pp. 308–9). See also Lincoln (1999, p. 227), who suggests that while the coverage of the WTO has expanded, it simply does not apply to all sectors. But this can only mean that in the so-called 'millennium' round, the US should devote considerable attention to strengthening existing rules, especially those concerning competition policy which are key to unlocking Japan. Moreover, as it did in the Uruguay Round, the US should take the lead in helping to expand the coverage of the rules to areas it deems vital to its national economic security.

In conclusion, what Japan has done through its deliberate strategy of aggressive legalism is to show the world the power of international law. By virtue of its economic status, it has helped set in motion the diffusion of international legal rules across both developed and developing countries. To be sure there are important and sensitive considerations stemming from this strategy, whether at the domestic level in Japan, the regional level in Asia, or even at the international level in the WTO. But despite these considerations, and especially the costs, the message from Japan is increasingly clear: Let the rules of the WTO fall where they will. The message from the US, and others such as the EU, should be equally forceful, equally clear.

REFERENCES

Abels, T.M. (1998), 'The World Trade Organization's First Test: The United States-Japan Auto Dispute', *UCLA Law Review*, **44**, 467–526.

ACCJ (1997), *Making Trade Talks Work: Lessons from Recent History* (Tokyo: The American Chamber of Commerce in Japan).

Bello, J.H. (1996), 'The WTO Dispute Settlement Understanding: Less is More', *American Journal of International Law*, **90**, 416–18.

Bhagwati, J. (1994), 'Samurais No More', *Foreign Affairs*, **73**, 7–12.

Destler, I.M., H. Sato, P. Clapp and H. Fukui (1979), *Managing an Alliance: The Politics of U.S.-Japanese Relations* (Ithaca: Cornell University Press).

Finger, J.M. and A. Harrison (1996), 'The MFA Paradox: More Protection and More Trade', in A.O. Krueger (ed.), *The Political Economy of American Trade Policy* (Chicago: The University of Chicago Press for the National Bureau of Economic Research).

GATT. *GATT Activities*. Various issues (Geneva).

GATT. *Basic Instruments and Selected Documents*. Various issues (Geneva).

Hufbauer, G.C., D.T. Berliner and K.A. Elliott (1986), *Trade Protectionism in the United States: 31 Case Studies* (Washington, DC: Institute for International Economics).

Industrial Structure Council (1998), *1998 Report on the WTO Consistency of Trade Policies of Major Trading Partners* (Tokyo: Ministry of International Trade and Industry).

Irwin, D.A. (1996), 'Trade Politics and the Semiconductor Industry', in A.O. Krueger (ed.), *The Political Economy of American Trade Policy* (Chicago: The University of Chicago Press for the National Bureau of Economic Research).

Jackson, J.H. (1997), 'The WTO Dispute Settlement Understanding – Misunderstanding on the Nature of Legal Obligation', *American Journal of International Law*, **91**, 60–64.

Komatsu, I. (1992), 'Japan and the GATT Dispute-Settlement Rules and Procedures', *The Japanese Annual of International Law*, **35**, 33–61.

Komuro, N. (1998), 'Kodak-Fuji Film Dispute and the WTO Panel Ruling', *Journal of World Trade*, **32**, 161–217.

Krueger, A.O. (1996), 'Introduction', in A.O. Krueger (ed.), *The Political Economy of American Trade Policy* (Chicago: The University of Chicago Press for the National Bureau of Economic Research).

Lincoln, E.J. (1999), *Troubled Times: U.S.-Japan Trade Relations in the 1990s* (Washington, DC: Brookings Institution Press).

Maswood, S.J. (1997–1998), 'Does Revisionism Work? U.S. Trade Strategy and the 1995 U.S.-Japan Auto Dispute', *Pacific Affairs*, **70**, 533–54.

Porges, A. (1991), 'U.S.-Japan Trade Negotiations: Paradigms Lost', in P. Krugman (ed.), *Trade*

With Japan: Has the Door Opened Wider? (Chicago: The University of Chicago Press for the National Bureau of Economic Research).

Schoppa, L.J. (1997), *Bargaining With Japan: What American Pressure Can and Cannot Do* (New York: Columbia University Press).

WTO. *Report of the Appellate Body*, Various cases (Geneva).

WTO. *Report of the Panel*, Various cases (Geneva).

[13]

NO MORE NEGOTIATED DEALS?: SETTLEMENT OF TRADE AND INVESTMENT DISPUTES IN EAST ASIA

*Junji Nakagawa**

ABSTRACT

Many argue that East Asian countries have come to adopt 'aggressive legalism' in trade and investment policy, in the sense that they have come to settle their trade and investment disputes through the dispute settlement mechanism (DSM) of the WTO and the other third-party procedures. Scrutiny of the dispute cases of these countries shows, however, that East Asian legalism is not so aggressive, that it varies country by country, and that there still exists room for negotiated deals in settling trade and investment disputes among them. On the other hand, the recent move toward regional integration through free trade agreements (FTAs), economic partnership agreements (EPAs), and bilateral investment treaties (BITs) in East Asia may lead to the adoption of a more aggressive legalism in the region, in particular in settling investment disputes, disputes relating to intellectual property rights, and trade remedies.

INTRODUCTION: HOW FAR HAS LEGALIZATION REACHED IN EAST ASIAN TRADE AND INVESTMENT?

Legalization of the international economic relationship, and particularly the trade relationship, has drawn much academic attention in the past few years.[1]

---

* Professor of International Economic Law, Institute of Social Science, University of Tokyo. 7-3-1 Hongo, Bunkyo-ku, Tokyo 113-0033 Japan, E-mail: nakagawa@iss.u-tokyo.ac.jp. The earlier version of this article was presented at the 2007 Annual Conference of the International Studies Association (Chicago) in February 2007. Special thanks go to Saadia Pekkanen for inviting me to the panel on 'The Legalism in East Asia'. Thanks also go to those who kindly commented on the earlier drafts, in particular, Joel P. Trachtman, Tomer Broude, Marcia Harpaz, Shun Kaku, Armand de Mestral, Aya Iino, Tomohiko Kobayashi, Kazuyori Ito, Meredith Lewis, and Yongshik Lee.

[1] See, for instance, Yuji Iwasawa, 'WTO Dispute Settlement and Japan', in Marco BronckersandReinhard Quick (eds), *New Directions in International Economic Law: Essays in Honor of John H. Jackson* (The Hague, Boston: Kluwer Law International, 2000) 473 ff; Judith Goldstein, Miles Kahler, Robert O. Keohane, andAnne-Marie Slaughter (eds), *Legalization and World Politics* (Cambridge, MA: The MIT Press, 2001); Judith Goldstein and Lisa Martin, 'Legalization, Trade Liberalization, and Domestic Politics: A Cautionary Note', in ibid (2001)

Following the argument of Abbott and others,[2] by legalization I mean a relationship which possesses the following three characteristics: obligation – states are bound by rules or commitments; precision – rules unambiguously define the conduct they require, authorize, or proscribe; and delegation – third parties have been granted authority to implement, interpret, and apply the rules, to resolve disputes, and (possibly) to make further rules. As many have argued,[3] the WTO and its highly judicialized dispute settlement mechanism (hereinafter the 'DSM') are at the center of the current legalization of the international trade and, to some extent, investment relationship.

East Asia is no exception. As Pekkanen,[4] Kawashima,[5] Araki,[6] and Iida[7] thoroughly describe, Japan seems to have adopted 'aggressive legalism', in the sense that Japan has come to settle its trade disputes through application of the WTO rules (obligation and precision) by the WTO DSM (delegation). Ahn points out that Korea has also adopted a similar policy stance.[8] Thailand, the Philippines, and Indonesia have followed suit. Finally, China seems to be moving in the same direction, as exemplified by the enactment of the Chinese version of Section 301 of the US Trade Act

---

at 219–48; Miles Kahler, 'Legaliation as Strategy: The Asia-Pacific Case', in ibid, at 165–87; Saadia Pekkanen, 'Aggressive Legalism: The Rules of the WTO and Japan's Emerging Trade Strategy', 24 The World Economy 707 (2001) [hereinafter 'Pekkanen (2001)']; Saadia Pekkanen, 'Sword and Shield: The WTO Dispute Settlement System and Japan' in Ulricke Schaede and William Grimes (eds), *Japan's Managed Globalization: Adapting to the Twenty-first Century* (Armonk, NY: M.E.Sharpe, 2003) [hereinafter 'Pekkanen (2003)'], at 77–100; Dukgeun Ahn, 'Korea in the GATT/WTO Dispute Settlement System: Legal Battle for Economic Development', 6 Journal of International Economic Law 597 (2003) [hereinafter 'Ahn (2003a)']; Dukgeun Ahn, 'WTO Dispute Settlements in East Asia', NBER Working Paper 10178, Cambridge, MA: National Bureau of Economic Research, http://www.nber.org/papers/w10178 [herein after 'Ahn (2003b)'] (visited 14 May 2007); Ichiro Araki, 'Higashi Asia no keizai kankei ni okeru houteki seidoka no genjou' (The current situation of the legalization of East Asian economic relations), 77(6) Houritsu Jihou (Law Journal) 60 (2005) [hereinafter 'Araki (2005)']; Fujio Kawashima, 'Wagakuni no WTO funsou kaiketsu tetsuzuki no katsuyou jisseki to kongo no kadai' (Japan's utilization of the WTO dispute settlement procedure and its challenges for the future) 77(6) Houritsu Jihou (Law Journal) 46 (2005); Henry Gao, 'Aggressive Legalism: The East Asian Experience and Lessons for China', in Henry Gao and Donald Lewis (eds), *China's Participation in the WTO* (London: Cameron May, 2005), 315–351; Ichiro Araki, 'The Evolution of Japan's Aggressive Legalism', 29 The World Economy 783 (2006) [hereinafter 'Araki (2006)']; Keisuke Iida, *Legalization and Japan: The Politics of WTO Dispute Settlement* (London: Cameron May, 2006).

[2] Kenneth W. Abbott, Robert O. Keohane, Andrew Moravcsik, Annne-Marie Slaughter and Dunkan Snidal, 'The Concept of Legalization', in Goldstein et al. (eds) n 1, 17–35, at 17.

[3] See above n 1.

[4] Pekkanen (2001) and Pekkanen (2003), above n 1.

[5] Kawashima, above n 1.

[6] Araki (2006), above n 1,

[7] Iida, above n 1.

[8] Ahn (2003a), above n 1.

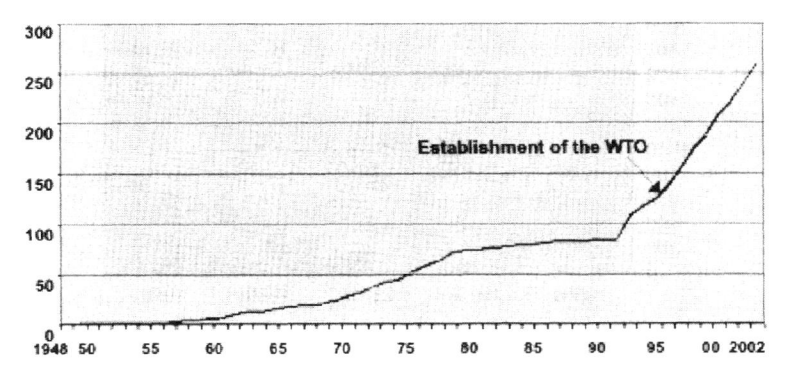

Figure 1. Number of FTAs and EPAs notified to the GATT and the WTO.
Source: WTO Secretariat, Evolution of Regional Trade Agreements in the world, 1948–2006, http://www.wto.org/english/tratop_e/region_e/regfac_e.htm (visited 17 May2007).

of 1974.[9] These East Asian countries are fairly active users of the DSM – either as complainants, respondents, or third parties. With the exception of Japan, they also have made frequent use of trade remedies (anti-dumping and countervailing duties, and safeguards).[10]

In parallel with such legalization within the multilateral framework, East Asian countries are zealously seeking regional economic integration by means of FTAs, EPAs, and BITs.[11] Regional economic integration through FTAs and EPAs and BITs has been a global trend for the past decade, and East Asia is no exception (Figures 1 and 2).

From the viewpoint of legalization of the international economic relationship, this trend seems to accelerate legalization, because it will enhance more obligation, precision, and delegation in the region. Are these observations well founded?

This article examines these observations by answering the following three sets of questions: First, how aggressive is legalism in East Asia? Why is it so? Is there any change expected in the near future?; Second, which is closely related to the first, does the tendency toward legalization in East Asia lead to decrease of negotiated deals in settling trade (and investment) disputes

---

[9] Provisional Investigation Rules on Foreign Trade Barrier, implemented 1 November 2002, as amended by Investigation Rules on Foreign Trade Barrier, implemented 1 March 2005. http://policy.mofcom.gov.cn/simplesearch_en.aspx (visited 18 February 2007).

[10] See Junji Nakagawa (ed.), *Anti-Dumping Laws and Practices of the New Users* (London: Cameron May, 2007), Chapters 2 (China), 3 (Taiwan), 4 (Korea) and 5 (Thailand).

[11] For a general overview of the East Asian trend toward regional economic integration, see Trade Policies Bureau, Ministry of Economy, Trade and Industry (METI) (ed.), *Report on the WTO Consistency of Trade Policies by Major Trading Partners*. (Tokyo: Keizai Sangyou Chousakai, 2006) http://www.meti.go.jp/policy/trade_policy/wto_consistency_report/html/f_y2006e.html (visited 14 May 2007), at 457–86.

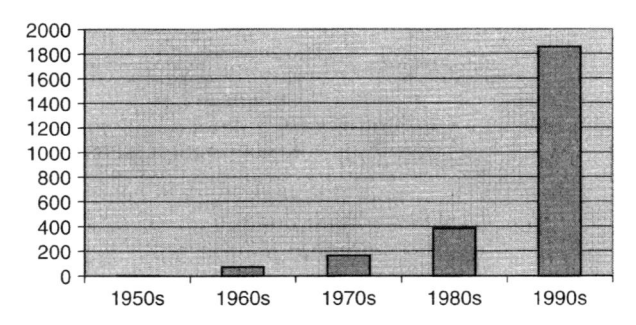

Figure 2. Growth of the Number of BITs (1959–1999).
Source: UNCTAD, Bilateral Investment Treaties 1959–1999, U.N.Doc. UNCTAD/ITE/IIA/2 (New York and Geneva: United Nations, 2000), at 1.

within the region?; Third, how can we assess the East Asian regional economic integration from the viewpoint of legalization of the international economic relationship? With regard to the first set of questions, this article examines the adequacy of the arguments of Pekkanen[12] and other researchers through observation of the behavior of three major East Asian countries (Japan, Korea, and China) in WTO litigation and their domestic politico-economic and institutional contexts. My conclusion is slightly different from that of Pekkanen. I argue that East Asian legalism has, for mainly politico-economic and institutional reasons, been fairly moderate, though the moderateness (or aggressiveness) varies country by country. Addressing the second question, this article traces a few precedents of negotiated deals in settling trade and investment disputes in East Asia. The conclusion is that there still is and will continue to be room for negotiated deals whose contents may not be WTO-consistent in the region. Finally, with regard to the third question, the analysis is rather speculative than empirical, as there has been no formal trade and investment disputes settled within the framework of FTAs, EPAs, and BITs in the region. Here, again, I make arguments similar to those in the first and second questions, namely that the legalism in East Asian regional economic integration will be of a modest kind and there will continue to be room for negotiated deals. There is, however, a possibility that legalism may become more aggressive in settling investment disputes[13] and those disputes relating to intellectual

---

[12] Pekkanen (2001) and Pekkanen (2003), above n 1.

[13] By 'investment disputes' I refer to any legal disputes between foreign investors and the government of host states. See, for instance, Article 25.1 of the Convention on the Settlement of Investment Disputes between States and Nationals of Other States (ICSID Convention), done 18 March 1965, entered into force 14 October 1965, http://www.worldbank.org/icsid/basicdoc/basicdoc.htm (visited 14 May 2007).

property protection and trade remedies. The following three sections deal with each set of questions, respectively. Section V concludes the analysis.

I. HOW 'AGGRESSIVE' IS EAST ASIAN LEGALISM?

A. East Asian Members' utilization of the WTO DSM

Let us first take a look at the performance of East Asian Members under the WTO DSM.

Table 1 shows the 12 most frequent complainants of the WTO DSM. It is noted that three East Asian countries are among them, with Korea ranked 8th with 13 complaints, and Japan and Thailand both ranked 9th with 12 complaints. Though included in the category of 'others', considering their volume of trade, the Philippines, and Indonesia have also been fairly active complainants with four and three complaints, respectively. Judging from their utilization of the WTO DSM as complainants, these East Asian countries may be regarded as having adopted 'aggressive legalism'. However, the extent of aggressiveness is different among them. In what follows, I will analyze the case records of Japan, Korea, and China, and assess the extent of aggressiveness of their legalism.

B. Japan's 'moderate legalism'

Of these five East Asian countries, Japan's ostensibly 'aggressive legalism' has been well analyzed. Pekkanen, in her pioneering article of 2001,[14] depicted Japan's new strategy of increasing use of the WTO DSM and coined the phrase 'aggressive legalism' to describe it. Araki analyzed Japan's WTO litigation behavior up to June 2004 and generally supported Pekkanen's argument, though with a modest caveat ('moderately active'[15] or 'moderately aggressive'[16]). Iida also affirms Japan's legalism under the WTO, but named it 'tactical' or 'shallow' legalism, as contrasted with 'deep' legalism.[17] Kawashima implicitly shares Iida's assessment, as he argues that Japan should expand beneficiaries of the DSM (private sector) and enlarge the list of target Members (Table 2).[18]

As they make their assessments on basically the same category of data (number of WTO DSM cases in which Japan participated

---

[14] Pekkanen (2001), above n 1.
[15] Araki (2006), above n 1, at 784.
[16] Ibid, at 799.
[17] Iida, above n 1, at 31–45.
[18] Kawashima, above n 1, at 50.

Table 1. State-of-play of WTO Dispute Settlement, 15 February 2007

Respondent	Complainant													
	US	EC	Canada	Brazil	India	Mexico	Argentina	Korea	Japan	Thailand	Chile	Australia	Others	Total Resp.
US		31	14	8	7	7	3	7	8	4	2	2	16	109
EC	32		7	6	5	3	3	3	0	4	2	2	15	82
Canada	5	5		3	0	0	0	0	1	0	0	0	1	15
Brazil	4	4	1		1	0	1	0	1	0	0	0	2	14
India	3	9	1	0		0	0	0	0	0	0	1	4	18
Mexico	6	3	0	1	0		0	0	0	0	1	0	3	14
Argentina	4	7	0	2	1	0		0	0	0	1	1	1	16
Korea	6	4	1	0	0	0	0		0	0	0	1	1	13
Japan	6	6	1	0	0	0	0	2		0	0	0	0	15
Thailand	0	0	0	0	0	0	0	0	0		0	0	1	1
Chile	1	3	0	0	0	0	5	0	0	0		0	3	12
Australia	4	1	1	0	0	0	0	0	0	0	0		3	9
Others	14	3	2	2	3	6	2	1	2	4	4	1	24	68
Total	85	76	28	22	17	16	14	13	12	12	10	7	74	386

Source: WTO Secretariat, Update of WTO Dispute Settlement Cases, WT/DS/OV/29, 9 January 2007; WTO, Chronological List of Cases, available online http://www.wto.org/english/tratop_e/dispu_e/dispu_status_e.htm (accessed 15 February 2007).

Table 2. WTO Cases Initiated by Japan as of 23 April 2007

	Filing date	Case Title	DS #
1	May 1995	US – Imposition of Import Duties on Automobiles from Japan under Section 301 and 304 of the Trade Act of 1974	DS6
2	July 1996	Brazil – Certain Automotive Investment Measures	DS51
3	October 1996	Indonesia – Certain Measures Affecting the Automobile Industy	DS55
4	November 1996	Indonesia – Certain Measures Affecting the Automobile Industy	DS64
5	July 1997	US – Measure Affecting Government Procurement	DS95
6	July 1998	Canada – Certain Measures Affecting the Automobile Industry	DS139
7	February 1999	United States – Anti-Dumping Act of 1916	DS162
8	November 1999	US – Anti-Dumping Measures on Certain Hot-Rolled Steel Products from Japan	DS184
9	December 2000	US – Continued Dumping and Subsidy Offset Act of 2000	DS217
10	January 2002	US – Sunset Review of Anti-Dumping Duties on Corrosion-Resistent Carbon Steel Flat Products from Japan	DS244
11	March 2002	US – Definitive Safeguard Measures on Imports of Certain Steel Products	DS249
12	November 2004	US – Measures Relating to Zeroing and Suset Reviews	DS322

as a complainant),[19] the difference among them may largely be that of characterization. At any rate, I would like to describe Japan's legalism as modest for the following reasons: first, considering its amount of trade and taken from the number of its complaints (12), Japan, the world's fourth largest trading country behind Germany, the US, and China, is far less aggressive than the US (88 complaints) and EC (76) (see Table 1 above);[20] second, although Japan has become far more aggressive than it used to be

---

[19] Pekkanen used the term 'aggressive legalism' to refer to the strategy to use international trade rules in settling trade disputes both as 'swords' (as complainant) and 'shields' (as respondent). See Pekkanen (2001), above n 1, at 708. However, I will focus here to only those cases where East Asian countries became complainants ('swords') to gauge aggressiveness of legalism, because becoming a respondent is a rather passive and often unavoidable policy, given the automaticity of the DSM under the negative consensus formula.

[20] As Araki points out (Araki (2006), above n 1, at 784), Japan's Ministry of Economy, Trade and Industry (METI), in its *2004 Report on the WTO Consistency of Trade Policies by Major Trading Partners*, laments a 'significant gap' between the performance of the US and the EC on the one hand and that of Japan on the other 'regarding the active use of international economic rules toward securing compliance with WTO obligations' (Trade Policies Bureau, Ministry of Economy, Trade and Industry (METI) (ed.), *2004 nenban fukousei boueki houkokusho* (2004 Report on the WTO Consistency of Trade Policies by Major Trading Partners). Tokyo: Keizai Sangyou Chousakai (in Japanese), http://www.meti.go.jp/policy/trade_policy/wto_consistency_report/html/f_y2004.html (visited 14 May 2007), 351). Oddly enough, the chapter containing this passage, titled 'The current situation of Japan's utilization of international economic rules and the challenges', is not contained in its English version on the website of the METI.

in the GATT era,[21] its litigation pattern has not much changed since the late 1980s in particular, namely, (i) anti-dumping measures as the major subject matter of complaints[22] and (ii) the US (and the EC) as a major target.[23] Given the wide coverage of the subject matter of the WTO rules and Japan's global trade and investment presence, there are many potential subject matters and target countries that Japan could take up under the WTO DSM. It may be because Japan has been careful in selecting only absolutely winnable cases.[24] Or, it may simply because Japan has not found many foreign policies and measures whose WTO-consistency was disputable. Neither of these explanations is convincing. For instance, the METI's *2006 Report on the WTO Consistency of Trade Policies by Major Trading Partners* devotes 75 pages to explain China's policies whose WTO consistency are at least problematic,[25] but Japan has never filed complaint against China

---

[21] Authors concur on this. See Pekkanen (2001), above n 1, Araki (2006), above n 1, at 796–99, and Iida, above n 1, at 31.

[22] Five out of 13 complaints challenged foreign anti-dumping laws and/or their implementation under the WTO DSM, while 4 out of 11 complaints challenged the same subject matter under the GATT DSM.

[23] Eight out of 12 complaints challenged the US laws and/or their implementation under the WTO DSM, while 10 out of 11 complaints were against the US and the EC (or its Member countries) under the GATT DSM.

[24] Araki argues that 'Japan seems to have been highly selective in filing cases, carefully avoiding frivolous claims and focusing on winnable cases'. See Araki (2006), above n 1, at 794.

[25] See above n 11, at 73–147. The measures and practices whose WTO consistency are allegedly problematic covers the following subject matters: transparency of trade policies and measures (GATT Article X:1); uniform administration of laws and administrative orders [GATT Article X:3(a)]; judicial review [GATT Article X:3(b)]; national treatment in the sales of imported automobiles (GATT Article III:4); import prohibition of second-hand cloths [GATT Articles XI and XX(b)]; export licenses [GATT Article XI and XX(g)]; failure to fulfill tariff concessions for photographic film (GATT Article II); the system for certifying finished vehicle characteristics (GATT Articles II and III, TRIMS Agreement); tariff classification decisions [GATT Article X:3(a)]; the initiation of an anti-dumping investigation can occur without complete review of the details of the application (Article 5.3 of the AD Agreement); injury analysis can be unclear and not enough grounds can be disclosed in injury determination (Articles 3.1, 3.4, and 3.5 of the AD Agreement); Chinese authorities do not give notification of the reasons for not using evidence submitted by an interested party and do not grant opportunities for complainants to make comments on when the authorities use facts available (FA) (Article 6.8, Annex II, Clauses 5 and 6 of the AD Agreement); failure to notify the SCM Committee of the details of its value-added tax refund regime to domestic copper refineries (Article 25 of the SCM Agreement); local content requirements for automobiles (GATT Article III:4 and TRIMS Agreement); export requirements to certain categories of foreign investment projects (GATT Article XI and TRIMS Agreement); administration of the Compulsory Commodity Certification (CCC) Mark system to electric appliances (Article 2.2 of the TBT Agreement); measures for controlling pollution by electronic information products (Article 2.2 of the TBT Agreement); system for environmental management on the import and export of toxic chemicals (Articles 2.9 and 2.12 of the TBT Agreement); distribution services (wholesaling, retailing, and franchising) (Schedule of Commitments); construction, architecture, and engineering services (Schedule of Commitments); freight forwarding agency services (Schedule of Commitments); telecommunication services

on any of them.[26] Last but not least, Japan has rarely filed complaints under its own initiatives. In two of the three early settlement cases,[27] and in eight out of ten paneled cases, Japan was co-complainant, almost always with the EC. In the remaining two cases,[28] Japan also followed the lead of other complainant(s). Japan filed only one complaint independently, *US – Auto* (DS6).[29] This 'herd behavior or bandwagoning' [30] can hardly be called aggressive.

Why then has Japan taken 'not so aggressive' or 'moderate' legalism? I argue that it has done so due to several constraints on both demand side (private sector) and supply side (Japanese government).

WTO law, while formally a domain of public international law, benefits the private sector,[31] particularly the competitive exporting industries. They are the direct beneficiaries of trade liberalization and complaints through the WTO DSM. They are also in a good position to detect WTO-inconsistent laws and/or measures in importing countries, because they are the direct victims of such laws and/or measures. In sum, they are 'enforcement constituencies'[32] of the WTO, and they demand aggressive legalism. They are also familiar with the WTO rules and their domestic implementation (and lacks thereof) in importing countries. Therefore, it is no coincidence that automobile and steel industries have practically been the sole beneficiaries of Japan's WTO complaints.[33] These industrial sectors are highly

---

(Schedule of Commitments); postal/courier services (Schedule of Commitments); inadequate administrative, civil and criminal remedies for intellectual property rights (IPR) infringements (Article 41, 45, 46, 59, and 61 of the TRIPS Agreement); lax control of plagiarized invention/design (Article 41.1 of the TRIPS Agreement); lax control of IPR infringements by local authorities ('local protectionism') (Articles 3.1 and 41.1 of the TRIPS Agreement); licensing regulations on patents and know-how (Articles 3 and 28.2 of the TRIPS Agreement).

[26] Some of China's laws, practices and measures mentioned in n 25 above were subject to recent WTO complaints (*China – Certain Measures Granting Refunds, Reductions or Exemptions from Taxes and Other Payments* [WT/DS358 (complainant: U.S.), 359 (complainant: Mexico)], *China – Measures Affecting the Protection and Enforcement of Intellectual Property Rights* [WT/DS362 (complainant: U.S.)], *China – Measures Affecting Trading Rights and Distribution Services for Certain Publications and Audiovisual Entertainment Products* [WT/DS363 (complainant: U.S.)]. However, Japan did not join them as complainant but as interested third party.

[27] *Brazil – Autos* (DS51) and *US – Government Procurement* (DS95).

[28] *US – Hot-Rolled Steel* (DS184) and *US - Sunset Review* (DS244).

[29] Even in this case, backing of the EC and other powers through such forum as the OECD and the G7 Summit was critical for the success of Japan's WTO litigation strategy. See Iida, above n 1, at 44 and 96.

[30] Ibid, at 45.

[31] Gregory C. Shaffer, *Defending Interests: Public-Private Partnership in WTO Litigation* (Washington, D.C.: The Brookings Institution, 2003) at 3.

[32] Iida, above n 1, at 29.

[33] Automobile industry was the major beneficiary in five out of Japan's first six complaints. Steel industry was the major beneficiary in practically all the last six complaints. See Table 2 above.

competitive in the global market and are heavily dependent on export earnings. They are well organized with an oligopolistic industrial structure and have strong influence in business world and Japanese politics.[34] They have also accumulated knowledge of and expertise in international trade law and foreign-trade remedy laws and practices.

This explains Japan's moderate legalism as well. Besides automobile and steel industries, few industrial sectors are influential and informed enough to build strong coalition for aggressive legalism. They may simply not know how useful the WTO DSM is, or they may be reluctant to press the Japanese government to take action.[35] Or, they may prefer adapting their businesses to the laws and practices of their trading partners, regardless of whether they are WTO consistent or not.

On the supply side, the Japanese government has so far been rather reluctant to take active steps in WTO litigation. It has been highly selective in filing cases, choosing to focus on winnable cases.[36] The Ministry of Economy, Trade and Industry (METI) began to publish its annual 'Report on the WTO Consistency of Trade Policies by Major Trading Partners' in 1991. The Report is analogous to the *National Trade Estimate Report* by the USTR. However, despite its consistent emphasis on the 'rule-oriented approach' in contrast to the allegedly 'result-oriented approach' of the US, the Report has no formal linkage to WTO litigation. In contrast to the Section 301 of the US Trade Act and the EC's Trade Barriers Regulations, Japan has not established a formal procedure through which private sector can petition its government to make complaints challenging WTO-inconsistent laws and practices of trading partners. It was only in May 2004 that METI opened an inquiry point for compliance with WTO rules by Japan's trading partners on its website.[37] The inquiry point, however, has hardly ever been utilized by Japanese companies.[38] It is an informal contact

---

[34] It is noted that both sectors are oligopolistic, and led by Japan's most influential companies, Toyota and Shin Nippon Seitetsu (Nippon Steel Corporation), whose former CEOs recently occupied the Presidency of the Nippon Keidanren (Japan Business Federation).

[35] In 2004, METI published the result of an inquiry to Japan's major exporting companies concerning their assessment and utilization of international economic rules (METI, above n 19, at 351–55). The majority of the respondents admitted the importance of the international economic rules, but they had rarely consulted the competent Japanese governmental authorities with respect to dubious foreign laws and practices, nor did they have enough staffs skilled in international economic rules. Again, this part of the *2004 Report on the WTO Consistency of Trade Policies by Major Trading Partners* was not included in its English version on the website of the METI. See above n.19.

[36] Araki (2006), above n 1, at 794.

[37] 'On the opening of the homepage inquiry point for compliance with WTO rules by foreign governments', 21 May 2004, http://www.meti.go.jp/policy/trade_policy/wto/compliance/soudan.html (visited 14 May 2007).

[38] Kawashima reports that the service had accepted only one request for consultation during its first year, and the request ended up without any WTO action (Kawashima, above n 1, at 53, n 30).

procedure and there is no legal assurance that an inquiry, if proved well founded, will trigger Japan's WTO complaint. Despite calls for the establishment of a formal procedure from academia[39] and private sector,[40] Araki believes that 'it is extremely unlikely that government agencies would voluntarily give up their jurisdiction over trade matters'.[41] The term 'jurisdiction' can be described as the 'discretionary power to decide whether or not to take cases' and this is exactly the essence of governmental power. It should be noted here that even under the formal complaint procedure such as US Section 301, the USTR has maintained such discretionary power at different stages of the procedure, particularly at its early stages.[42]

With respect to China, the Japanese government may have been reluctant to take strong stance against it for political and diplomatic reasons. It is reported that when the US made a complaint against Chinese IPR protection in April 2007[43] it invited Japan to join as co-complainant, but Japan declined it and joined the procedure as a third party.[44] The Japanese Minister of Economy, Trade and Industry explained this decision as an extension of Japan–China bilateral cooperation in strengthening China's IPR protection.[45] However, it must be noted that it was just one day before the Chinese Prime Minister's official visit to Japan for the first time in six and half years that the US made the complaint. It is reasonable to infer from this that Japan declined to join the US as co-complainant mainly for diplomatic reasons.

Finally, resource constraints, particularly human resource constraints, have thwarted Japan's legalism. WTO litigation has become increasingly complicated and successful litigation requires high level of legal expertise not only in WTO law but also in international law on treaty interpretation and civil litigation rules (burden of proof, evidence, etc.) of domestic,

---

[39] See, for instance, Iwasawa, above n 1, at 485 and Kawashima, above n 1, at 51.

[40] See, for instance, Nippon Keidanren, 'Call for a Petition System for Initiation of Investigations Regarding the Unfair Trade Practices of Foreign Nations', 13 February 2004, http://www.keidanren.or.jp/english/policy/2004/016.html (visited 14 May 2007).

[41] Araki (2006), above n 1, at 801.

[42] Under Section 301 as amended (19 U.S.C.s411), the USTR, once it accepts a petition from private sector on account of an allegedly WTO-inconsistent foreign practice, shall determine within forty-five days whether the petition is appropriate. It is only when the USTR makes an affirmative determination that it starts investigation. Moreover, the USTR has a power to decide whether or not it accepts a petition as *prima facie* well founded, and it frequently makes a negative determination and declines to accept it. Hearing at the General Counsel's Office, USTR, March 2004.

[43] *China – Measures Affecting the Protection and Enforcement of Intellectual Property Rights* (WT/DS362).

[44] Asahi Shimbun, 20 April 2007.

[45] Ibid.

largely Anglo-American, legal system. Although the METI and the Ministry of Foreign Affairs (MOFA) has been reinforcing the staff members for WTO litigation,[46] they are still outsourcing substantial amount of the litigation work (preparation of written submissions, etc.) to leading US trade law firms.[47] Recent policy focus on negotiating regional trade and investment agreements has put an additional burden on the Japanese government because both Ministries have reassigned their staff members from WTO litigation to the negotiation of FTAs, EPAs, and BITs.

C. Korea's more aggressive legalism

Korea has so far been the most frequent complainant in East Asia (see Table 1 above). As Ahn eloquently puts it, 'the Korean government changed from a dispute aversion attitude[48] and has become considerably more active in asserting its rights through the dispute settlement mechanism' of the WTO.[49] Considering its amount of trade (about half the size of Japan, both in exports and imports), we may coin Korean legalism more aggressive than that of Japan (Table 3).

Reviewing Korea's case record in WTO litigation, however, we must add a few caveats to Ahn's assessment. First, Korea's complaints are concentrated in foreign trade remedies (five against anti-dumping law and practices, three against countervailing duties, and two against safeguards). Second, the US has been its major target (seven complaints), though the EC (three complaints) and Japan (two complaints) recently became targets. Third, only a few competitive exporting sectors were the main beneficiaries of the complaints, namely, semiconductor (four complaints), steel (three complaints), chemical (two complaints), and shipbuilding (two complaints).[50] Judging from these, Korea's WTO litigation strategy has been fairly similar to that of Japan and it is hard to coin it as full-fledged aggressive legalism. The factors on demand and supply sides constraining Japan's aggressive legalism (limited enforcement constituencies, reluctance of the government to establish formal procedure for private

---

[46] The reinforcement has been through (i) personnel shift within the Ministries, and (ii) recruiting a small number of Japanese trade lawyers and young scholars of international trade law for a definite term (usually two years).

[47] Iida, above n 1, at 41–42.

[48] Since its accession to the GATT in 1967, Korea made only one complaint under the GATT DSM (*EC – Article XIX Action on Imports to the U.K. of Television Sets from Korea* [GATT, C/M/124 (1978)], while it became the target of as many as 291 trade remedy actions abroad from 1960 to 1994. See Ahn (2003a), above n 1, at 602–7.

[49] Ibid, at 609.

[50] These do not include *US – Continued Dumping and Subsidy Offset Act of 2000* (DS217), but all of these competitive exporting industries were the beneficiaries of this complaint.

Table 3. WTO Cases Initiated by Korea as of 23 April 2007

	Filing date	Case Title	DS #
1	July 1997	US – Imposition of Anti-Dumping Duties on Imports of Color Television Receivers from Korea	DS89
2	August 1997	US – Anti-Dumping Duty on Dynamic Random Access Memory Semiconductors (DRAMs) of One Megabit or Above from Korea	DS99
3	July 1999	US – Anti-Dumping Measures on Stainless Steel Plate in Coils and Stainless Steel Sheet and Strip from Korea	DS179
4	June 2000	US – Definitive Safeguard Measures on Imports of Circular Welded Carbon Quality Line Pipe from Korea	DS202
5	December 2000	Philippines – Anti-Dumping Measures regarding Polypropylene Resins from Korea	DS215
6	December 2000	US – Continued Dumping and Subsidy Offset Act of 2000	DS217
7	March 2002	US – Definitive Safeguard Measures on Imports of Certain Steel Products	DS251
8	June 2003	US – Countervailing Duty Investigation on Dynamic Random Access Memory Semiconductors (DRAMs) from Korea	DS296
9	July 2003	EC – Countervailing Measures on Dynamic Random Access Memory Chips from Korea	DS299
10	September 2003	EC – Measures Affecting Trade in Commercial Vessels	DS301
11	February 2004	EC – Aid for Commercial Vessels	DS307
12	December 2004	Japan – Import Quotas on Dried Laver and Seasoned Laver	DS323
13	March 2006	Japan – Countervailing Duties on Dynamic Random Access Memories from Korea	DS336

sector complaint,[51] and human resource constraints[52]) also apply in the case of Korea.

Nevertheless, there is one notable difference in the litigation strategies of Korea and Japan. In contrast to Japan, Korea has made most of its complaints on its own and 'herd behavior or bandwagoning' was observed in only two cases: *US – Continued Dumping and Subsidy Offset Act of 2000* ('Byrd Amendment') (DS217);[53] and *US – Definitive Safeguard Measures on Imports of Certain Steel Products* (DS251).[54] One possible reason for this 'independent' behavior is the success of an earlier complaint [*US – Anti-Dumping Duty on Dynamic Random Access Memory Semiconductors (DRAMS) of One Megabit or Above from Korea* (DS99)]. Since the GATT era, Korea has

---

[51] Korean Ministry of Foreign Affairs and Trade began to publish annual report titled *A Comprehensive Survey of the Trade Environment* in 1998. This can be viewed as a Korean version of *National Trade Estimate Report* by the USTR, but without Section 301 linkage. See Ahn (2003a), above n 1, at 630, n 153.

[52] Ahn points out that Korean government has relied heavily on foreign private counsels in WTO litigation. See ibid, at 630.

[53] Eleven Members were the co-complainants of this case.

[54] Eight Members were the co-complainants of this case.

been the frequent target of foreign trade remedy actions,[55] but the standard solution during the GATT era used to be voluntary export restraints (VERs). *US – DRAMS* case was one of the earliest complaints that Korea made under the WTO DSM.[56] Its first 'win' through the WTO DSM 'led the Korean government to move to the direction of "aggressive legalism" in handling subsequent trade disputes'.[57] This overlaps Japan's first 'win' through the GATT DSM in *EEC – Regulation on Imports of Parts and Components*,[58] which, as some have argued, led the Japanese government in the direction of 'aggressive legalism'.[59] As was seen in II.B above, Japan has since been focusing on foreign anti-dumping laws and practices in its WTO litigation. But it has preferred 'bandwagoning', and focused on so-called 'law as such' cases [for instance, *US – AD Act of 1916* (DS162), *US – Byrd Amendment* (DS217) and *US – Zeroing* (DS322)] rather than targeting individual anti-dumping measures against Japanese exports. In that sense, we may call Korea's legalism 'more aggressive' or 'less moderate' than that of Japan.

D. China's legalism: en route to aggressiveness

China seems to be less conspicuous than the other two East Asian countries with only one complaint, which was a bandwagon litigation against the US steel safeguards with seven co-complainants.[60] Considering its status as the world's third largest trading country next to Germany and the US, this is a very small number and we should coin it as far from aggressive legalism(Table 4).

One possible explanation is China's status in the WTO as a newcomer. Since its accession in December 2001, China hasn't had enough time to become aggressive in WTO litigation. Gao points out 'a clear reluctance of China to make use of the WTO dispute settlement system' in 2005.[61] This also holds true for China's trading partners. It was only in March 2004,

---

[55] See above n 48.

[56] Korea's first WTO complaint, *US – Imposition of Anti-Dumping Duties on Imports of Color Television Receivers from Korea* (DS89), also targeted a US anti-dumping measure, filed on 10 July 1997, was settled through bilateral consultation by the revocation of the measure by the US in August 1998, which terminated the anti-dumping duty that had been imposed since 1984. Korea withdrew its complaint in September 1998. See Ahn (2003a), above n 1, at 681.

[57] Ibid, at 620.

[58] Request for consultations, 29 July 1988. L.6381. Report of the panel adopted 16 May 1990. L/6657; *BISD 37S*/132.

[59] Iwasawa, above n 1, at 449.

[60] *US – Definitive Safeguard Measures on Imports of Certain Steel Products* (DS252). Other co-complainants were EC (DS248), Japan (DS249), Korea (DS251), Switzerland (DS253), Norway (DS254), New Zealand (DS258), and Brazil (DS259).

[61] Gao, above n 1, 344.

Table 4. WTO Cases Initiated by China as of 23 April 2007

	Filing Date	Case Title	DS #
1	March 2002	US – Definitive Safeguard Measures on Imports of Certain Steel Products	DS252

more than two years after China's accession, that the US filed the first complaint against China.[62] The start-up, wait-and-see period seems to have been over, however, and China's major trading partners including US and EC, with the exception of Japan, have cautiously been moving in the direction of aggressive legalism against China.[63]

It must be noted, however, that China's fairly moderate record in WTO litigation does not mean it will continue to be so in the future. There are a few symptoms of policy change. As I mentioned earlier, China enacted the Chinese version of Section 301 in November 2002,[64] less than one year after its accession to the WTO. As will be seen in III.B below, the first application for foreign trade barrier investigation was filed against Japan's laver import quota in 25 February 2004. Furthermore, China began to participate in WTO litigation as a third party in a great number of cases soon after its succession (Table 5).

This long list of cases which China joined as a third party suggests that China has been utilizing third-party participation as a means of learning WTO litigation and enhancing its legal expertise (including training its trade officials and Chinese international trade lawyers), rather than as a means of addressing its trade concerns.[65] These suggest that China is currently learning how to utilize the WTO DSM, and that it may become more aggressive in the future.[66]

---

[62] *China – Measures Affecting Imports of Automobile Parts* (WT/DS339, 340, 342).

[63] See above n 25. The USTR, in its *2006 Report to Congress on China's WTO Compliance*, states that 'when bilateral dialogue fails to succeed in addressing US concerns, the United States will not hesitate to exercise its WTO rights through the initiation of dispute settlement *against China, as it would with any other mature WTO trading partner*'. (emphasis added by the author) United States Trade Representative (USTR), *2006 Report to Congress on China's WTO Compliance*, http://www.ustr.gov/assets/Document_Library/Reports_Publications/2006/asset_upload_file688_10223.pdf (visited 14 May 2007), at 5.

[64] See above n 9 and the corresponding text.

[65] Hearing from a Chinese international trade lawyer, Beijing, March 2004. Gao (above n 1, at 350) also emphasizes the importance of building up the expertise of WTO legal system for China to adopt aggressive legalism through outsourcing (hiring foreign trade lawyers) and in-house training, in particular encouraging its citizens to work in the WTO Secretariat.

[66] Jung came to the similar conclusion. See Youngjin Jung, 'China's Aggressive Legalism: China's First Safeguard Measure', 36 Journal of World Trade 1037 (2002), at 1056. However, his reasoning is not based on China's aggressive third-party participation but on its first bandwagon WTO complaint on US steel safeguards.

Table 5. WTO Cases where China joined as a third party as of 23 April 2007[a,b]

	Filing Date	Case Title	DS #	Complainant(s)
1	January 2002	US – Rules of Origin for Textiles and Apparel Products	DS243	India
2	September 2002	EC – Export Subsidies on Sugar	DS265/,266/283	Australia, Brazil Thailand
3	September 2002	US – Subsidies on Upland Cotton	DS267	Brazil
4	October 2002	EC – Customs Classification of Frozen Boneless Chicken Cuts	DS269/286	Brazil, Thailand
5	October 2002	Korea – Measures Affecting Trade in Commercial Vessels	DS273	EC
6	December 2002	Canada – Measures Relating to Exports of Wheat and Treatment of Imported Grain	DS276	US
7	February 2003	US – Anti-Dumping Measures on Oil Country Tubular Goods (OCTG) from Mexico	DS282	Mexico
8	May 2003	EC – Measures Affecting the Approval and Marketing of Biotech Products	DS291/292/293	US, Canada, Argentina
9	June 2003	Mexico – Definitive Anti-Dumping Measures on Beef and Rice	DS295	US
10	June 2003	US – Laws, Regulations and Methodology for Calculating Dumping Margins (Zeroing)	DS294	EC
11	August 2003	US – Countervailing Duty Investigations on Dynamic Random Access Memory Semiconductors (DRAMs) from Korea	DS296	Korea
12	July 2003	EC – Countervailing Measures on Dynamic Random Access Memory Chips from Korea	DS299	Korea
13	September 2003	EC – Measures Affecting Trade in Commercial Vessels	DS301	Korea
14	October 2003	Dominican Republic – Measures Affecting the Importation and Internal Sale of Cigarettes	DS302	Honduras
15	March 2004	Mexico – Tax Measures on Soft Drinks and Other Beverages	DS308	US
16	June 2004	Korea – Anti-Dumping Duties on Imports of Certain Paper from Indonesia	DS312	Indonesia
17	September 2004	EC – Selected Customs Matters	DS315	US[b]
18	November 2004	US – Measures Relating to Zeroing and Sunset Reviews	DS322	Japan
19	October 2002	Australia – Certain Measures Affecting the Importation of Fresh Fruit and Vegetables	DS270	Philippines
20	January 2003	US – Countervailing Duties on Steel Plate from Mexico	DS280	Mexico

(Continued)

Table 5. Continued

	Filing Date	Case Title	DS #	Complainant(s)
21	February 2003	US – Anti-Dumping Measures on Cement from Mexico	DS281	Mexico
22	April 2003	Australia – Quarantine Regime for Imports	DS287	EC
23	October 2004	EC et al. – Measures Affecting Trade in Large Civil Aircraft	DS316	US
24	October 2004	US – Measures Affecting Trade in Large Civil Aircraft	DS317	EC
25	November 2004	US – Continued Suspension of Obligations in the EC-Hormones Dispute	DS320	EC
26	November 2004	Canada – Continued Suspension of Obligations in the EC-Hormones Dispute	DS321	EC
27	June 2005	Mexico – Anti-Dumping Duties on Steel Pipes and Tubes from Guatemala	DS331	Guatemala
28	June 2005	Brazil – Measures Affecting Imports of Retreated Tyres	DS332	EC
29	November 2005	Turkey – Measures Affecting the Importation of Rice	DS334	US
30	November 2005	US – Anti-Dumping Measures on Shrimp from Ecuador	DS335	Ecuador
31	March 2006	Japan – Countervailing Duties on Dynamic Random Access Memories from Korea	DS336	Korea
32	March 2006	EC – Anti-Dumping Measure on Farmed Salmon from Norway	DS337	Norway
33	April 2006	US – Measures Relating to Shrimp from Thailand	DS343	Thailand
34	May 2006	US – Final Anti-Dumping Measures on Stainless Steel from Mexico	DS344	Mexico
35	June 2006	US – Customs Bond Directive for Merchandise subject to Anti-Dumping/Counter- vailing Duties	DS345	India
36	January 2006	EC et al. – Measures Affecting Trade in Large Civil Aircraft (Second Complaint)	DS347	US
37	January 2006	US – Measures Affecting Trade in Large Civil Aircraft (Second Complaint)	DS353	EC

Notes: [a]This covers only original panel/AB cases, and does not include compliance cases relating to Article 21.5 and 22.6 of the DSU.
[b]Cases #1 through 17 are completed. Case #18 is under appeal. Cases #19 through 37 are under panel procedure.

II. NEGOTIATED DEALS IN EAST ASIAN TRADE (AND INVESTMENT) DISPUTES

Legalism in WTO, whether aggressive or moderate, does not mean that every dispute under the WTO must be solved through the panel/Appellate Body procedure. The Understanding on Rules and Procedures Governing the Settlement of Disputes (DSU) encourages Members to reach '(a) solution mutually acceptable to the parties to a dispute and consistent with the covered agreements' as a 'preferred' solution (Article 3.7). Such solution is encouraged not only before the establishment of a panel but also during the panel procedure.[67] In fact, from 1 January 1995 to 23 April 2007, 58 complaints have been settled by mutually agreed solutions and 30 complaints have been settled otherwise or inactive, while 102 complaints have been settled by the adoption of panel/Appellate Body reports.[68]

Therefore, negotiated deals have their place in the WTO DSM, on condition that it be (i) mutually satisfactory among the parties to the dispute, and (ii) consistent with the covered agreements. From the viewpoint of legalism, the latter condition is important because a negotiated deal which is WTO-inconsistent would be detrimental to the integrity of the WTO system as a legal order, even though it might be mutually satisfactory to the parties. It must be noted here that the Agreement on Safeguards definitely prohibits and eliminates voluntary export restraints or any other similar measures on exports or imports. [Articles 11.1(b) and 11.3].

The problem is that the above conditions are not strictly legal obligations, nor are they adequately monitored. They are only encouraged as 'preferred' solution (DSU, Article 3.7). Consultations shall be confidential (Article 4.6),[69] and the contents of the solution are not reported to the Dispute Settlement Body (Articles 3.6 and 12.7). There is still room for negotiated deals which are not consistent with WTO rules, in particular the Safeguard Agreement. The following two recent dispute cases among East Asian countries support this argument.

A. Shiitake safeguards (Japan–China)

As I have traced the factual aspects of this case elsewhere,[70] it will suffice to make a few remarks which are relevant here. First, although the dispute

---

[67] Article 12.7 of the DSU provides that a panel shall submit its findings only '(w)here the parties to the dispute have failed to develop a mutually satisfactory solution' during the panel procedure. It continues that '(w)here a settlement of the matter among the parties to the dispute has been found, the report of the panel shall be confined to a brief description of the case and to reporting that a solution has been reached'.

[68] WTO, Update of WTO Dispute Settlement Cases, WT/DSOV/30, 25 April 2007, p.ii.

[69] Panel deliberations shall also be confidential (DSU, Article 14.1)

[70] Junji Nakagawa, 'Lessons from the Japan-China "Welsh Onion War"', 36 Journal of World Trade 1019 (2002).

started in November 2000 by the initiation of a safeguard investigation by Japan, the final settlement was reached on 21 December 2001, shortly after China's accession to the WTO. The aforementioned rules of the WTO were therefore applicable to the final settlement.[71] Second, the gist of the solution was (i) Japan's pledge not to apply definitive safeguard measures, (ii) China's pledge to withdraw the retaliatory special customs duties,[72] and (iii) the establishment of 'an information exchange scheme for the three targeted agricultural products'.[73] As a follow-up of (iii), the 1st meeting of the Japan–China Agricultural Products Trade Council (hereinafter the 'Council') was convened in February 2002, and it has held 19 meetings by the end of April 2007.[74]

It is important to clarify the structure and function of the Council for an assessment of the WTO-consistency of the solution. According to the Memorandum of Understanding (MOU) of 21 December 2001, the private sectors of Japan and China would establish a forum for consultations and information exchange on market demand, production, prices, etc. of the three agricultural products at issue.[75] The Council is, therefore, *prima facie* a private forum. Representatives of Japan's producers' associations and importers' associations and China's exporters' associations are the members of the Council. Nonetheless, the relevant governmental authorities of both countries have been attending the Council as 'observers'.[76] They have been providing information and advice for the purpose of securing smooth consultations and enhancing the effectiveness of such information exchange among private members.[77] In addition, the Japanese government has been monitoring the quantity of production (both in Japan and China) and imports, and price (both import price and domestic price in

---

[71] Ibid, at 1032.

[72] China imposed 100% special customs duties on imports of Japanese automobiles, cellular and car phones, and air conditioners on 22 June 2001 in response to Japan's discriminatory treatment of Chinese shiitake and the other agricultural products. It based this countermeasure on Article 6 of the Regulations on Imports and Export Duties, which empowers Chinese customs authorities to impose such duty on imports originating in a country that applies 'discriminatory rates of duty or other types of discriminatory treatment' to Chinese products. Ibid, at 1023. Though Article XIX of the GATT does not allow such countermeasure against provisional safeguards, this prohibition was not applied to China, as it was not a member of the GATT then.

[73] Ibid, at 1024.

[74] Japan, Ministry of Agriculture, Forestry and Fisheries (MAFF), Press Release, On the Result of the 19th Meeting of the Japan–China Agricultural Products Trade Conference. 30 January 2007, http://www.maff.go.jp/www/press/2007/20070130_press4.html (visited 14 May 2007).

[75] MOU between Japan and China, item 3, para.3, http://www.kantei.go.jp/jp/koizumispeech/2001/1221oboegaki.html (visited 14 May 2007). (in Japanese)

[76] From Japan, officials of the MAFF, METI, the Ministry of Finance (MOF), and the Ministry of Foreign Affairs (MOFA) attend the Council. From China, official of the Ministry of Commerce (MOFCOM) attend it. See Nakagawa, above n 70, at 1024 and 1033.

[77] Ibid.

the Japanese market of the like products) of the three products on a weekly basis.[78]

Judging from these, the consistency of the Council with the Safeguard Agreement is dubious. It should be noted that the prohibition and elimination under Article 11 of the Agreement is across-the-board. It covers a wide range of governmental 'measures' that have a trade-restrictive effect [Art.11.1(b)]. In addition, as Article 11.3 prohibits Members to 'encourage or support measures or maintenance by public and private enterprises of non-governmental measures equivalent to those referred to in paragraph 1', governmental encouragement or support of private measures is also prohibited. One may still defend for the WTO-consistency of the Council by focusing on its function as a 'forum for consultation and information exchange'. However, as was stated in the MOU of 21 December 2001,[79] consultations and information exchange was not an end in itself, but a means to achieve the goal of 'orderly trade'. Regardless of whether the Council is characterized as a VER under Article 11.1(b) of the Safeguards Agreement or as containing governmental encouragement or supporting private measures under Article 11.3, it is inconsistent with the Safeguards Agreement.[80]

B. Laver import quota (Japan–China–Korea)

This case concerns Japan's import quota for dried and seasoned laver (*nori*) from China and Korea. After having briefly traced the facts of the case,[81] I will analyze its implications, focusing on two questions: (i) was the solution WTO-inconsistent? or (ii) was it an example of legalism in East Asia?

The case can be divided into two phases. Phase one was China's investigation under the aforementioned Provisional Investigation Rules of 2002 against Japan's laver import quota allocated exclusively to Korea (initiated in April 2004).[82] This dispute was settled through bilateral consultation in October 2004, as a result of which Japan promised to replace the exclusive import quota to Korea with a 'global quota', which practically meant allocating a certain amount of import quota to China, the sole exporting country of laver products to Japan besides Korea.[83] This solution triggered the next phase of the dispute. In December 2004, Korea requested consultations under Article 4 of the DSU, alleging that (i) Japan's 'global'

---

[78] See, for instance, the MOF, Press Release, On the Result of the Monitoring of Imports of Three Products including Welsh Onion. 21 February 2007, http://www.mof.go.jp/jouhou/kanzei/ka3m190221.htm (visited 14 May 2007).

[79] See above, n 75.

[80] Nakagawa, above n 70, at 1033.

[81] See Araki (2005), supra n 1 for the detailed facts of the case.

[82] Ibid, at 62.

[83] Ibid.

import quota violates Article XI.1 of the GATT 1994, which prohibits quantitative restriction of imports, and (ii) it violates Article 4.2 of the WTO Agreement on Agriculture, which requires 'tariffication' with respect to the products which were subject to quantitative restrictions.[84] A panel was established in March 2005, but on 23 January 2006 Korea and Japan notified the DSB of a mutually agreed solution under Article 3.6 of the DSU.[85] A brief report of the panel noting the settlement was circulated to Members on 1 February 2006, in accordance with Article 12.7 of the DSU.[86] The report of the panel does not disclose the contents of the mutually agreed solution. It was reported, however, that Japan had promised to increase the import quota of laver from Korea from 240 million sheets in 2004 to 1.5 billion sheets by 2015.[87]

It must be noted that the solution of the dispute in both phases contains some elements of legalism, in particular 'delegation'. In phase one of the case, China's investigation was conducted under the Provisional Investigation Rules of 2002, which, in case of the failure of a negotiated solution, would lead to China's complaint under the WTO DSM. In phase two, Korea filed a formal complaint under the WTO DSM. This seems to allow us to conclude that both phases were settled under the framework of the WTO DSM, and that the laver import quota case can be claimed as an example of aggressive legalism among East Asian countries.

On the other hand, the WTO consistency of the solution in both phases ('obligation' and 'precision') was dubious. Both phases were settled through the increase in the quantity of import quota, which, Korea argued, was inconsistent with Article XI.1 of the GATT 1994 and Article 4.2 of the Agreement Agriculture. The Panel in *Japan – Laver* did not make findings on the substantive issues of the case, and it is still unclear whether such a solution is consistent with the WTO rules. As was seen earlier in the introductory paragraph of this section, the deliberation of the parties in the Panel procedure is confidential (DSU, Article 14.1). However, Araki disclosed the gist of the Japanese government's argument: (i) Article XI.2(c) of the GATT 1994 allows quantitative restrictions on agricultural or fisheries products to the extent that it is necessary for the enforcement of governmental measures which operate to restrict the quantities of the like domestic products permitted to be marketed or produced, and (ii) *arguendo* it is not justified under Article XI.1 of the GATT 1994, it can be justified under

---

[84] Ibid, at 63.
[85] *Japan – Import Quotas on Dried Laver and Seasoned Laver*, Notification of Mutually Agreed Solution. WT/DS323/5, 27 January 2006.
[86] *Japan – Import Quotas on Dried Laver and Seasoned Laver*, Report of the Panel. WT/DS323/R, 1 February 2006.
[87] MOFA, Recent cases of the WTO DSM to which Japan is the party as of 31 July 2006, http://www.mofa.go.jp/mofaj/gaiko/wto/funso/funsou.html (visited 14 May 2007).

Article XX(g) of the GATT 1994 as measures relating to the conservation of natural resources.[88] Yamashita, a MAFF (Ministry of Agriculture, Forestry, and Fisheries) expert on the WTO rules on agricultural trade, argues that the solution does not violate Article 4.2 of the Agreement on Agriculture because the negotiators of the Agreement agreed not to apply that Article to fishery products.[89] As he admits, however, recent reports of the panel and the Appellate Body in *EC – Export Subsidy on Sugar* (DS265, 266, 283) and *US – Subsidies on Upland Cotton* (DS267), based principally on textual interpretation of the covered agreements according to Article 31 of the Vienna Convention on the Law of Treaties, refuted the respondents' argument that the negotiators had agreed not to prohibit the measures at issue as a result of the Uruguay Round negotiation of the Agreement on Agriculture.[90] It is, therefore, not realistic to expect that the Panel in *Japan – Laver* would have accepted the Japan's arguments.

In sum, the solution in these two cases is classified as a 'negotiated deal through (or in the guise of) legalism', whose consistency with the WTO rules is dubious.[91] Why, then, did the parties strike such deals? There are two reasons, one being systemic and the other being case specific. The former relates to the inherent limits of securing compliance with the WTO rules under the current DSM. As was seen above, the DSU practically tolerates such negotiated deals among the disputing parties even after a panel has been established. It is only when a third Member, whose benefit under the WTO has been allegedly nullified or impaired by such deals, takes action under the WTO DSM against it that the WTO-consistency of the deal will be reviewed under the WTO DSM. But as the content of the mutually satisfactory solution is not disclosed, there is a small chance for an interested third Member to detect it and take action against it under the WTO DSM. Likewise, as in the case of shiitake safeguards, the negotiated deal which is prohibited under Article 11 of the Agreement on Safeguards is viable insofar as the parties to the dispute have agreed and no other Member takes action under the WTO DSM against it.

---

[88] Araki (2005), above n 1, at 64.

[89] Remark of Kazuhito Yamashita in Junji Nakagawa et al., 'Zadankai: Henkakuki no kokusai tsūshouhou to Nihon – WTO, FTA, EPA wo chūshin ni' (Round-table: International trade law in times of transformation and Japan – Focusing on the WTO, FTA, and EPA), 77(6) Houritsu Jihou (Law Journal) 4 (2005), at 22.

[90] Ibid, at 22–23.

[91] It should be noted here, however, that the Protocol on the Accession of the People's Republic of China provides for transitional product-specific safeguard mechanism, under which China is required to take action to prevent or remedy the market disruption, including VERs. (Article 16.2 of the Protocol of Accession of the People's Republic of China. WT/L/432, 23 November 2001.) This provisional permission of VERs shall be terminated twelve years after the date of China's accession, namely, in November 2013 (Article 16.9).

No third Member took such action against the negotiated deal in both cases. It was largely because of the specific trade (and investment) relationship of the cases. In both cases, the complaining party (China and Korea) was practically the sole exporter of the products at issue, so no third interested Member existed. Therefore, the disputing parties could agree on negotiated deals without any fear of being complained against by a third Member.

There was an additional factor in the shiitake safeguards case that contributed to the negotiated deal. The vast majority of the product's imports at issue were conducted within the framework of the so-called 'develop-and-import scheme' (*kaihatsu yunyū*), where Japanese trading companies and large scale consumers (supermarkets, fast food restaurants) consign the cultivation of the products to their affiliated firms in China and/or Chinese farmers and farmers' associations or Chinese-affiliated companies, which then export the products to Japan. Therefore, the gist of this trade (and investment) dispute was not China (exporting country) against Japan (import countries), but the conflict of interests between Japanese farmers and Japanese trading companies and their large-scale clients (and Japanese consumers). Thus the solution required political compromise both at the international (Japan v China) and domestic (agricultural protection v traders' and consumers' interests) levels.[92]

As the Japanese develop-and-import scheme has been proliferating beyond the range of the three products at issue in Japan–China trade, both in terms of product coverage and trading partner in East Asia (for instance, poultry products in Thailand), a similar trade (and investment) dispute is likely to occur in East Asia. Negotiated deals will be the most likely solution.

Finally, it must be noted that the most recent trade dispute between Japan and Korea, *Japan – Countervailing Duties on Dynamic Random Access Memories from Korea* (DS336) has so far been dealt with along the lines of 'aggressive legalism'. On 24 August 2006, a panel was established. There has so far been no mutually satisfactory solution reached between the parties. On the contrary, judging from the conflicting views adopted by panel's rulings and the Appellate Body on the interpretation of the term 'entrusts or directs' as used in Article 1.1(a)(1)(iv) of the WTO Agreement on Subsidies and Countervailing Measures (SCM Agreement) in the similar complaints by the US and the EC,[93] both the complainant (Korea) and the respondent (Japan) seem to have decided to thoroughly pursue the

---

[92] For a slightly different but basically politico-economic assessment of the shiitake safeguards case, see Arata Kuno, 'An Evaluation of Japan's First Sefeguards Actions', 29 The World Economy 763 (2006).

[93] *US – Countervailing Duty Investigation on Dynamic Random Access Memory Semiconductoirs (DRAMS) from Korea*, Report of the Panel, WT/DS296/R, 21 February 2005, Report of the Appellate Body, WT/DS296/AB/R, 27 June 2005; *EC – Countervailing Measures on Dynamic Random Access Memory Chips from Korea*, Report of the Panel, WT/DS299/R, 17 June 2005.

WTO litigation. In that sense, legalism (moderate or aggressive) and negotiated deals may coexist in East Asia, depending on the subject matter, demand (private sector) and supply (governments) situation, and the specific situation of the case.

III. LEGALISM IN EAST ASIAN REGIONAL ECONOMIC INTEGRATION

Movements toward East Asian regional economic integration are still in their early stages, and it may be too early to draw definitive conclusions to the questions posed here. However, judging from the experiences of the past and existing frameworks for regional economic integration in Asia and elsewhere, we may speculate on what might occur in East Asia with regard to the settlement of disputes within such a regional framework.

The two major existing frameworks for regional economic integration in Asia – ASEAN and APEC – have low profiles from the viewpoint of legalism. As Lawan puts it, 'ASEAN has not created any judicial or monitoring institutions to ensure the coordination of legal norms relevant to regional commerce'.[94] The APEC, started as a forum for consultations and dialogue rather than as binding commitments among the Members, has kept its informal and non-legalistic characteristics, failing to move toward binding commitments, deadlines, extensive monitoring, or the application of sanctions. The APEC Economic Leaders' Declaration of Common Resolve 15 November 1994 (Bogor Declaration) stated that the Members 'agree to examine the possibility of a voluntary consultative dispute mediation service, to supplement the WTO dispute settlement mechanism, which should continue to be the primary channel for resolving disputes'.[95] Even this fairly moderate agreement was not realized, however, due to strong opposition from the Asian members of APEC, in particular China and ASEAN members.[96]

Based on these two precedents in the region, there seems to be little chance of legalization in East Asian regional economic integration, and still less chance of full-fledged legalization akin to the European Court of Justice.[97] I argue, however, that none of these should be an appropriate reference point in forecasting legalism in East Asian regional

---

[94] Lawan, Thanadsillapakul, 'Legal and Institutional Frameworks for Open Regionalism in Asia: A Case Study of ASEAN', in Tamio Nakamura (ed.), *The Dynamics of East Asian Regionalism in Comparative Perspective*, ISS Research Series No.24 (Tokyo: Institute of Social Science, University of Tokyo, 2007), 189–210, at 203. Kahler calls this 'ASEAN Way' as 'collaboration without legalization'. See Kahler, above n 1, at 167.

[95] Bogor Declaration, s9, http://www.apec.org/apec/leaders__declarations/1994.html (visited 14 May 2007).

[96] Kahler, above n 1, at 172–75.

[97] Takao Suami, 'Regional Integration and the Role of the International Court: Experience of the European Court of Justice', in Nakamura, above n 94, at 239–60.

economic integration. We should instead refer to recent FTAs and BITs elsewhere in the world, in particular in North America, because these agreements are quite similar to those which have been, and are being negotiated in East Asia in both their substance and institutional/procedural settings. In what follows, I will speculate on the extent to which East Asian regional economic integration will be moving toward legalism, referring mainly to the NAFTA (North American Free Trade Agreement) because of its abundance of legalization in trade and investment disputes.

NAFTA has several different DSMs.[98] For the purpose of this article, it suffices to refer to two of them and two substantive subject matters, as these are common to the FTAs, EPAs, and BITs in East Asia: (i) investor-state dispute arbitration; (ii) inter-state DSM whose subject matter overlaps that of the WTO; (iii) protection of intellectual property rights (IPR); and (iv) trade remedies.

A. Legalization of investment disputes through arbitration

One feature of the NAFTA that is distinct from the WTO is that it covers investment and provides for a formal procedure for the settlement of investment disputes. NAFTA's Chapter 11 endowed private investors with a right to obtain relief directly against host states for a violation of NAFTA investment rules stipulated in the Chapter through arbitration according to, among others, the ICSID Convention[99] (NAFTA, Articles 1115–1138). Remedies for violations of NAFTA investment rules include monetary damages and restitution (Article 1135.1). Although an arbitration panel cannot enforce these remedies by itself, the investor can bring the arbitral award to a court in any NAFTA Party and seek its enforcement under the ICSID Convention, the New York Convention[100] or the Inter-American Convention[101] (Article 1136.6).

The NAFTA Chapter 11 arbitration procedure has been utilized fairly frequently, with 47 cases (finished and pending cases combined) from January 1994 to April 2007.[102] The long list of Chapter 11 cases

---

[98] Junji Nakagawa, 'In Search of an Optimal Legal/Institutional Framework for the Americas; Dispute Settlement Mechanisms of NAFTA and MERCOSUR', in Nakamura, above n 94, 223–37.

[99] See above n 13.

[100] Convention on the Recognition and Enforcement of Foreign Arbitral Awards, adopted on 10 June 1958, entered into force on 7 June 1959, http://www.uncitral.org/uncitral/en/uncitral_texts/arbitration/NYConvention.html (visited 14 May 2007).

[101] The Inter-American Convention on International Commercial Arbitration, adopted on 30 January 1975, entered into force on 16 June 1976, http://www.sice.oas.org/dispute/comarb/iacac/iacac2e.asp (visited 14 May 2007).

[102] Of the 47 cases, 17 claims were against the US, and 15 claims each were against Canada and Mexico. See http://www.naftaclaims.com/cop.htm (visited 14 May 2007).

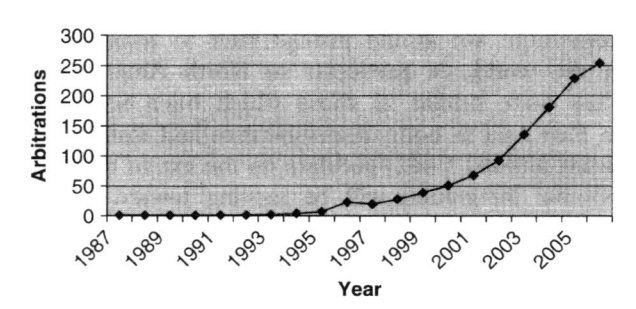

Figure 3. Known investment treaty arbitration (1987–November 2006).
Source: UNCTAD, Latest Developments in Investor-State Dispute Settlement, http://UNCTAD/WEB/ITE/IIA/2006/11 (visited 14 May 2007), at 2.

is a reflection of the global trend of settling investment disputes through investor-state arbitration. Since the mid-1990s, a growing number of BITs (and FTAs and EPAs which contain a chapter on investment, as does NAFTA) have been concluded, most of which provide for investor-state arbitration procedures under the ICSID Convention, UNCITRAL Arbitration Rules,[103] or ICC Rules of Arbitration.[104] Many developing countries and former socialist countries, after having kept themselves aloof from such procedures for a long time, have come to conclude BITs (and FTAs and EPAs) to attract foreign investment. Settlement of investment disputes through arbitration, as opposed to settlement through domestic litigation or diplomatic intervention, is an almost universal characteristic of these BITs (and FTAs and EPAs).[105] The reason for the prevalence is that these mechanisms are considered to secure the interests of foreign investors more effectively than domestic litigation or diplomatic intervention, and thus to attract foreign investors (Figure 3).

East Asia is no exception. Most BITs, FTAs, and EPAs concluded within the region provide for investor-state arbitration procedure quite similar

---

[103] United Nations Commission on International Trade Law (UNCITRAL), UNCITRAL Arbitration Rules, U.N. General Assembly Resolution 31/98, adopted on 15 December 1976, http://www.uncitral.org/uncitral/en/uncitral_texts/arbitration/1976Arbitration_rules.html (visited 14 May 2007).

[104] International Chamber of Commerce (ICC), ICC Rules of Arbitration, entered into force on 1 January 1998, http://www.iccwbo.org/court/english/arbitration/pdf_documents/rules/rules_arb_english.pdf (visited 14 May 2007).

[105] Akira Kotera, 'Keizai renkei kyoutei no igi to kadai' (The significance and challenges of economic partnership agreements (EPAs) 77(6) Houritsu Jihou (Law Journal) 27 (2005).

to that of the NAFTA.[106] So far, there have been no arbitration cases reported in the region. It is, however, highly speculative from this as to whether investor-state arbitration will proliferate in the region. The lack of arbitration cases may be simply because most of these agreements in the region were concluded fairly recently. Or, it may be because of conflict aversive culture of the region, where negotiated deals are preferred to formal dispute settlement. It is still early to speculate on the future use of investor-state arbitration in the region.[107]

B. Overlapping jurisdiction of the DSMs under the WTO and the FTAs, EPAs, and BITs

While FTAs and EPAs cover a wide range of subject matter beyond trade in goods and services, such as investment, competition law and policy, government procurement,[108] and trade facilitation, they also contain rules and commitments on liberalization of trade in goods and services. When a dispute occurs with respect to these subject matters also covered by the WTO, there is a need to coordinate the jurisdiction of the DSMs between these treaties and the WTO. A similar issue may be raised with respect to BITs on investment provisions in services sector.

Here, again, NAFTA is a good reference. Its Article 2005.1 provides that disputes regarding any matter arising under both this Agreement and the WTO may be settled in either forum at the discretion of the complaining Party. Once a dispute settlement procedure has been initiated under either forum, the forum chosen shall be used to the exclusion of the other (Article 2005.6).[109]

---

[106] See, for instance, the Japan–Singapore Economic Partnership Agreement (EPA), signed 13 January 2002, entered into force 30 November 2002, Chapter 8: Investment, http://www.mofa.go.jp/region/asia-paci/singapore/sjepa-1.pdf (visited 14 May 2007).

[107] Japan has concluded 11 BITs, but there has been no arbitration under them. On the other hand, a Dutch affiliate company of Nomura Securities, Co., Japan's largest securities company, won an arbitration against Czech government according to the UNCITRAL Arbitration Rules (see above n 103) under the BIT between the Netherlands and the Czech Republic (Saluka Investments B.V. (The Netherlands) v The Czech Republic, Partial Award, 17 March 2006). See Akira Koreta and Kayo Matsumoto, 'Toushi kyoutei no shin sokumen to Nihon, Dai 2 kai, Saluka jiken' (New era of investment treaties and Japan, No. 2, Saluka case), 34 Kokusai Shouji Houmu (International Legal Transaction) 1141 (2006).

[108] The WTO Agreement on Government Procurement (hereinafter the 'GPA') is a plurilateral agreement with a limited number of signatories. From East Asia, only Hong Kong, Japan, Korea, and Singapore are the parties to the GPA. When an EPA or an FTA is concluded by one of them with an East Asian country which is not a party to the GPA, and it contains rules on government procurement, these rules are outside of the coverage of the GPA. See Kotera, above n 105, at 30.

[109] The NAFTA provides for three exceptions to this general principle, where the Chapter 20 DSM shall be exclusive: (i) where the responding Party claims that its action is subject to the NAFTA Article 104 Concerning Environmental and Conservation Treaties; (ii) where the dispute arises under Section B of Chapter Seven (Sanitary and Phytosanitary Measures) or Chapter Nine (Standards-Related Measures); and (iii) the third Party wishes to have recourse to dispute procedures under the NAFTA. See the NAFTA Articles 2005.2–4.

This method is fairly common in contemporary FTAs and EPAs.[110] This is also common in East Asia. For instance, Article 139.3 of the Japan–Singapore EPA[111] provides that once a dispute settlement procedure has been initiated under the DSM of the EPA or the WTO, the procedure shall be used to the exclusion of other DSM for that particular dispute. Such coordination is needed to avoid 'double jeopardy', as was the case of the panel report in *Argentina – Definitive Anti-Dumping Duties on Poultry from Brazil* (DS241), which practically repealed the judgment of the MERCOSUR Ad Hoc Tribunal on the same subject matter.[112]

On the other hand, this method, namely, the combination of (i) forum choice and (ii) exclusive jurisdiction of the forum chosen, might cause a disturbing effect on WTO law. If the Parties to the FTAs and EPAs choose DSM under these agreements, and the judgments of these forums provide divergent interpretations on the subject matters which are covered by the WTO as well, the result might undermine the obligation and precision of the WTO law. Such 'fragmentation' of the DSM might also cause forum shopping, which would undermine the obligation and precision of the FTAs and EPAs as well. This might be detrimental to legalization in international trade (and investment). It is, therefore, desirable to adopt the principle of exclusive jurisdiction of the WTO DSM with respect to the disputes which might arise under both the WTO and the FTAs and EPAs.

C. Stringent protection of intellectual property rights

Some FTAs and EPAs provide for higher (and wider) level of protection of intellectual property rights (IPRs) than the one provided by the WTO Agreement on Trade-Related Aspects of Intellectual Property Rights (TRIPS Agreement). For instance, Article 98.1 of the Japan–Singapore EPA requires Singapore to take appropriate measures to facilitate the patenting process of an application filed in Singapore that corresponds to an application filed in Japan. Article 16.7.7 of the US–Singapore FTA[113] requires both parties to extend the term of a patent to compensate for unreasonable delays in the granting of the patent.

Provisions of FTAs and EPAs for such 'TRIPS plus' protection will be enforced either through the WTO DSM or through the DSM of FTAs and

---

[110] James McCall Smith, 'The Politics of Dispute Settlement Design: Explaining Legalism in Regional Trade Pacts', 54 International Organization 137 (2000), at 156–57.

[111] See above n 106.

[112] After this WTO case, a new Protocol for the DSM (Protocol of Olivos) was concluded among the MERCOSUR members in 2002. Its Article 1.2 provides for forum choice between the DSMs of the MERCOSUR and the WTO and exclusive jurisdiction of the forum after it has been chosen. See Nakagawa, above n 98, at 230.

[113] United States–Singapore Free Trade Agreement, signed 6 May 2003, entered into force 1 January 2004, http://www.ustr.gov/assets/Trade_Agreements/Bilateral/Singapore_FTA/Final-Texts/asset_upload_file708_4036.pdf (visited 14 May 2007).

EPAs because they are applied to the other Members of the WTO on a most favored nation basis under Article 4 of the TRIPS agreement. As among the subject matters which are covered by both the FTAs and EPAs and the TRIPS Agreement, there is a risk of 'double jeopardy' or forum shopping. Here again, instead of the formula of (i) forum choice and (ii) exclusive jurisdiction of the forum chosen in most FTAs and EPAs in the region, the author would like to argue for the WTO DSM as a preferred forum, for the reasons mentioned above.

Regardless of whether to settle a dispute through the DSM of FTAs and EPAs or through the WTO DSM, the effectiveness of the dispute settlement largely depends on the clarity of obligation (precision). From this viewpoint, the effectiveness of the aforementioned provision of the Japan–Singapore EPA is dubious, because the obligation of Singapore under Article 98.1 is only to 'take appropriate measures to facilitate the patenting process' 'in accordance with its laws and regulations'. This practically creates no new international obligation owed by Singapore. By contrast, the provisions of the US–Singapore FTA are much more detailed,[114] and can be enforced through the DSM. From the viewpoint of legalization, one lesson to be learned from these examples is that FTAs and EPAs will have to provide 'TRIPS plus' protection which is as detailed and clear as possible.

D. Prospective increase in the number of trade remedies

FTAs and EPAs will enhance trade liberalization between the Parties. This may increase the application of trade remedy measures to rescue less competitive domestic industries, which might be seriously or substantially injured by the increased imports from the other Party. The aforementioned shiitake safeguards and *Japan – DRAM* (countervailing duty) cases are the symptom of what will happen in a more regionally integrated East Asia.

When Japan and Korea concluded their first FTA (EPA) with Singapore and Chile, respectively, they adopted the same approach for anti-dumping and countervailing measures. They decided to use the WTO rules and its DSM, instead of establishing independent disciplinary measures. The Japan–Singapore EPA[115] does not include specific provisions concerning anti-dumping and countervailing measures, implying that these matters would be addressed solely by the WTO Agreements. The Korea–Chile

---

[114] On the terms of patent application, Article 16.7.7 of the Agreement (see ibid.) provides that '(e)ach Party, at the request of the patent owner, shall extend the term of a patent to compensate for unreasonable delays that occur in the granting of the patent. For the purposes of this paragraph, an unreasonable delay shall at least include a delay in the issuance of the patent of more than four years from the date of filing of the application with the Party, or two years after a request for examination of the application has been made, whichever is later, provided that periods attributable to actions of the patent applicant need not be included in the determination of such delays'.

[115] See above n 106.

FTA[116] provides in Chapter Seven that the parties maintain the same rights and obligations as under the WTO Anti-Dumping and Subsidy Agreements, and that anti-dumping or countervailing measures taken pursuant to them shall not be subject to the DSM of the FTA.

Although many recent FTAs and EPAs follow this policy, some FTAs modified the WTO discipline. For instance, Article 9 of the Singapore–New Zealand EPA[117] stipulates additional requirements to the WTO Anti-Dumping Agreement 'in order to bring greater discipline to anti-dumping investigations and to minimize the opportunities to use anti-dumping in an arbitrary or protectionist manner'. Under this EPA, the *de minimis* margin was increased to 5% for both new investigations and review procedures.[118] The sunset period was also shortened to three years.[119] To take another example, the Korea–Singapore FTA[120] adopted the following additional disciplines on anti-dumping measures: (i) the prohibition of 'zeroing' [Article 6.2.3(a)], and (ii) the lesser duty rule [Article 6.2.3(b)].[121]

East Asian countries have been frequent targets of trade-remedy actions abroad. Enhanced trade through FTAs and EPAs may increase the risk of their exports being challenged by trade-remedy actions, particularly anti-dumping measures. The potential risk of abusive trade-remedy actions may be mitigated by incorporating such additional disciplines into the FTAs and EPAs.[122]

---

[116] Free Trade Agreement between the Government of the Republic of Korea and the Government of the Republic of Chile, signed 15 February 2003, entered into force 1 April 2004, http://www.bilaterals.org/IMG/pdf/Korea_Chile_FTA.pdf (visited 14 May 2007).

[117] Agreement between New Zealand and Singapore on a Closer Economic Partnership, signed 14 November 2000, entered into force 1 January 2001, http://www.mfat.govt.nz/Trade-and-Economic-Relations/0-Trade-archive/0-Trade-agreements/Singapore/0-cep-part1.php (visited 14 May 2007).

[118] Article 5.8 of the WTO Anti-Dumping Agreement provides for a *de minimis* dumping margin of 2%.

[119] Article 11.3 of the WTO Anti-Dumping Agreement provides for a maximum sunset period of five years.

[120] Free Trade Agreement between the Government of the Republic of Korea and the Government of the Republic of Singapore, signed 4 August 2005, entered into force 2 March 2006, http://www.iesingapore.gov.sg/wps/portal/!ut/p/kcxml/04_Sj9SPykssy0xPLMn Mz0vM0Y_QjzKLN4g3Cw0GSYGY5oFm-pFoYo4YImah3phiIWEIMV-P_NxU_SB9b_0A_ YLc0NDQiHJHAKO0wuk!/delta/base64xml/L0lDU0lKQ1RPN29na21BISEvb0VvUUFBS VFnakZJQUFRaENFSVFqR0VBLzRKRmlDbzBlaDFpY29uUVZHaGQtc0lRIS83XzBfOU 1MLzUzNDkwMA!!?WCM_PORTLET=PC_7_0_9ML_WCM&WCM_GLOBAL_ CONTEXT=/wps/wcm/connect/FTA/Singapore%27s+FTAs/Concluded+FTAs/Korea/ General/Legal+Text (visited 14 May 2007).

[121] For the details, see Dukgeun Ahn, 'Emerging Diversity in Trade Remedy Systems: The Case of East Asian FTAs', in Nakamura, above n 94, 211–21, at 214–15.

[122] Given the stagnated Rules Negotiation in the Doha Development Agenda, and the persistent opposition of the US to introducing more stringent discipline to the WTO Anti-Dumping Agreement, incorporating additional disciplines to FTAs and EPAs may be far more feasible than doing so to the WTO Anti-Dumping Agreement.

IV. CONCLUDING REMARKS

East Asian 'legalism' in WTO DSM should not be overemphasized. It should be characterized as a moderate use of WTO DSM with diversity. East Asian modest legalism has its roots in both demand and supply sides of WTO litigation. Many industries do not have sufficient knowledge and expertise with respect to the rules and the DSM of the WTO. They tend to accept the local rules and regulations as given, and construct its trade and investment strategy accordingly, regardless of whether they are WTO consistent or not. On the supply side, governments of East Asia tend to maintain discretionary power to decide whether or not to bring cases. There are, however, signs that East Asian legalism may move in the direction of more aggressive use of the WTO DSM. Korea and China might take the lead. In terms of the frequent use of trade-remedy actions pursuant to the WTO rules, East Asian countries, with the exception of Japan, may be moving in this direction.

The second main argument of this article is that settlement of trade (and investment) disputes through negotiated deals has survived the WTO discipline and will continue to survive in East Asia. The reasons are both systemic (limitation of the WTO DSM) and case-specific, particularly the Japan-led 'development-and-import' scheme that is becoming increasingly prevalent in the region. Insofar as the 'development-and-import' scheme continues to prevail in the region, negotiated deals will persist – to the detriment of legalism, either aggressive or moderate.

It is too early to draw any definitive conclusions from the recent movements toward East Asian economic integration in terms of legalization, but one may speculate that (i) most trade disputes between the Parties to the FTAs and EPAs may preferably be brought to the WTO DSM, rather than to those of the regional agreements, (ii) the investor-state disputes will be brought to arbitration under the ICSID Convention, etc., though the frequency of such resort is yet to be seen, (iii) 'TRIPS plus' protection of IPRs will be prevailing, though the effectiveness of which depends largely on the precision of the rules, and (iv) enhanced trade liberalization within the region may increase the number of trade remedy actions, which will most probably be regulated by the WTO rules and the 'WTO plus' disciplines of the regional agreements.

Finally, I must admit that these are the 'snapshots' of legalism in East Asian trade and investment based on the observation of the first decade of the WTO and a shorter period of the FTAs, EPAs, and BITs of the region. East Asian economy is dynamically developing, so are its legal and institutional infrastructure and human resources for dealing with trade and investment disputes. In particular, China's 'learning curve' is amazing. Maybe ten years from now, we will witness a fairly different picture of legalism in East Asia – a combination of more aggressive legalism in trade and investment and the persistent negotiated deal.

[14]

THE ESTABLISHMENT AND DEVELOPMENT OF THE CHINESE ECONOMIC LEGAL SYSTEM IN THE PAST SIXTY YEARS

CHEN SU[*]
TRANSLATED BY XIE ZENGYI[**]

I. CHINA'S ECONOMIC LEGAL SYSTEM WITHIN A HIGHLY CENTRALIZED PLANNED ECONOMIC SYSTEM (1949–1978) 110
II. THE ECONOMIC LEGAL SYSTEM IN THE EARLY STAGE AFTER THE POLICY OF REFORM AND OPENING (1978–1992) 116
III. THE ECONOMIC LEGAL SYSTEM UNDER THE SOCIALIST MARKET ECONOMY SYSTEM (1992–2009) 124

---

[*] The Author is a Professor of Law and Deputy Director of the Chinese Academy of Social Sciences Institute of Law.
[**] The Translator is an Associate Professor of Law at the Chinese Academy of Social Sciences Institute of Law.

Since the establishment of the People's Republic of China (PRC) in 1949, the Chinese economic legal system has gone through multiple transformative stages, exhibiting different characteristics at each stage as a result of the interaction between the changing economic system and legal ideology of the time. Due to the differences between the prevailing economic systems and legal ideologies at different stages, the structural concepts, content, governing systems, implementation mechanisms and effects of the economic legal system vary significantly at each stage.

I. CHINA'S ECONOMIC LEGAL SYSTEM WITHIN A HIGHLY CENTRALIZED PLANNED ECONOMIC SYSTEM (1949–1978)

Before the implementation of the Reform and Opening Up policy in 1978, China had a highly centralized planned economic system. Under the planned economic system, the formulation and implementation of state plans resembling administrative orders were the essence of the economy. "The essential feature of economic activities was state planning," which meant that "the economic activities were to be implemented according to the state plans."[1] Because economic activities were based on the plans formulated by government agencies, the enterprises carrying out specific business operations were actually affiliates of government agencies. As a result, laws were basically unnecessary in the governing of economic activities, and played little part throughout the formation, existence, and evolution of the planned economic system, which was initiated in the early 1950s, took shape in the late 1950s and declined by the mid- to late-1970s.

The laws, legal institutions and legal interpretation of the former government were abolished at the time of the establishment of the PRC.[2] In particular, the old civil laws were dismantled.[3] Thus, without inheriting any legal tradition from the past, the economic legal system of the PRC was reestablished over time in an inconsistent and unsystematic manner. In the early 1950s, several major economic regulations and rules were formulated, including the Decision on Unifying the State's Financial and

---

[1] 王家福、谢怀栻等著, 合同法 [WANG JIAFU, XIE HUAISHI ET AL., CONTRACT LAW] 8 (中国社会科学出版社 [China Social Science Press] 1986).

[2] See 中共中央关于废除国民党的六法全书与确定解放区的司法原则的指示 [Instruction of the Central Committee of the CPC Regarding the Repeal of "The Complete Book of Six Codes" of the Kuomintang and the Establishment of Judicial Principle in the Liberated Areas] (1949), *available at* http://www.dffy.com/sifashijian/jj/200809/20080921204129.htm (last visited Nov. 4, 2009).

[3] See 中国法学四十年 [FORTY YEARS OF LEGAL STUDIES IN CHINA] 327 (张友渔 [Zhang Youyu] ed., 上海人民出版社 [Shanghai People's Press] 1989).

Economic Work, the Provisional Regulations on Budget and Final Accounts, the Provisional Rules on Infrastructure Work, the Agrarian Reform Law, the Model Articles for Higher-Stage Agricultural Producers' Cooperatives, and the Provisional Regulations on Industrial Enterprises of Joint Public and Private Ownership. Meanwhile, economic legal institutions, such as the Economic Protection Tribunal, were also established.[4] However, very few economic laws were enacted in the following thirty years, and the ones which were enacted were vague and general in content, consisting mostly of administrative orders rather than laws passed by the legislature. With the exception of certain specific statutes, such as the Agrarian Reform Law, only a small number of these economic laws were consistently and effectively enforced.

The Common Program of the Chinese People's Political Consultative Conference adopted in 1949 effectively served as the interim Constitution for the country,[5] which stipulated that the state should coordinate and regulate the state-owned economy, the cooperative economy, the individual economy of peasants and manual laborers, the private capitalist economy and the state capitalist economy. In this way, all components of the social economy could, under the leadership of the state-owned economy, carry out division and coordination, and play their respective parts in promoting the development of the social economy as a whole.[6] Such provisions dealing with the basic Chinese economic system were further confirmed in the Constitution of 1954.[7] However, this policy was soon changed. From 1953 to 1956, China carried out a large-scale socialist transformation of the private economy, including the individual economy of peasants and manual laborers, private capitalist industry and commerce. This approach consisted mainly of directing individual agriculture and manual laborers towards cooperative economy, and to purchase capitalist industries and businesses.[8] This conversion from an individual agriculture to cooperative economy was implemented through the adoption of three economic institutions, namely, the mutual aid group, the lower-stage agricultural pro-

---

[4] *See* 经济法 [ECONOMIC LAW] 25 (王家福 [Wang Jiafu] ed., 中国经济出版社 [China Economic Press] 1988).

[5] 宪法学 [CONSTITUTIONAL LAW] 92 (吴家麟 [Wu Jianlin] ed., 群众出版社 [Qunzhong Press] 1983).

[6] 中国人民政治协商会议共同纲领 [Common Program of the Chinese People's Political Consultative Conference] (1949) art. 26, *available at* http://china.findlaw.cn/fagui/gj/21/2.html (last visited Nov. 4, 2009).

[7] 1954年宪法 [The Constitution of 1954] (promulgated by the Nat'l People's Cong., Sept. 20, 1954, effective Sept. 20, 1954) NAT'L PEOPLE'S CONG. GAZ. (P.R.C.), art. 5.

[8] *See* 张卓元, 从百年积弱到经济大国的跨越 [Zhang Zhuoyuan, *Leap From a Century of Weakness to Economic Power*], 光明日报 [GUANGMING DAILY], Aug. 27, 2009, at 11, *available at* http://www.gmw.cn/01gmrb/2009-08/27/content_970632.htm (last visited Nov. 4, 2009).

ducers' cooperative and the higher-stage agricultural producers' cooperative.⁹ The higher-stage agricultural producers' cooperatives were mostly established by the end of 1956, which marked the completion of the socialist transformation of rural areas and agriculture in China. The movement of people's communes was launched in September 1958, and communization was completed by the end of that year. The people's communes in the rural areas were a form of collective ownership economy,¹⁰ an "integration of the administrative and the economic entity."¹¹ The collective economy in cities and towns formed gradually, starting from the 1950s,¹² and was formed mainly as a result of the cooperativization of individual manual laborers enterprises in urban districts. The state-owned economy was the dominant economic system. All enterprises of national economic significance or wielding a controlling influence over people's livelihoods were under the centralized operation of the state.¹³ However, there were no comprehensive legal regulations governing the organization of enterprises during this period. It was not until more than a decade after the end of this period that the Law of the People's Republic of China on Industrial Enterprises Owned by the Whole People (1988), the Regulation on Collective Ownership Enterprises in Rural Areas (1990), and the Regulation on Collective Ownership Enterprises in Urban Areas (1991) were enacted, though all these enterprises were then faced with the challenges posed by the new wave of reform.

The importance of the legal system in regulating economic activity diminished after China established a highly centralized planned economy based on state ownership. The contract law of economic transactions provides an example of this. The Finance and Economy Committee of the Government Administrative Council promulgated the Provisional Regulations on Concluding Contracts Between Government Agencies, State-Owned Enterprises and Cooperatives in 1950 (the first contract law in the

---

⁹ "Mutual aid groups" refers to the mutual assistance of farmers who owned the means of production; "lower-stage agricultural producers' cooperative" involves the unified operation of agriculture with private ownership of the means of production; "higher-stage agricultural producers' cooperative" means the unified operation of agriculture with public ownership of the means of production. See 农业合作化运动 [The Agricultural Cooperativization Movement], *available at* http://news.xinhuanet.com/ziliao/2003-01/20/content_697957.htm (last visited Nov. 4, 2009).

¹⁰ 1975 年宪法 [The Constitution of 1975] (promulgated by the Nat'l People's Cong., Jan. 17, 1975, effective Sept. 20, 1954) NAT'L PEOPLE'S CONG. GAZ. (P.R.C.), art. 7.

¹¹ The integration of the administrative and the economic entity means the combination of political power at the town level and at the level of economic organizations.

¹² *See* 王兆国, 在第十届全国人民代表大会第五次会议上的《关于<中华人民共和国物权法(草案)>的说明》[Wang Zhaoguo, Speech at the Fifth Session of the Tenth National People's Congress: Explanation on the Draft of the Property Law of the PRC] (2007), at section 3(4).

¹³ 中国人民政治协商会议共同纲领 [Common Program of The Chinese People's Political Consultative Conference] (1949) art. 28.

PRC), and more than forty further regulations concerning contracts were adopted by relevant authorities by 1956. However, the contract system was abolished from the late 1950s until the early 1960s due to the prohibition on free production and exchange of goods. The contract system was reestablished temporarily from 1962 to 1966, but it was abandoned again at the start of the Cultural Revolution before ever being generally implemented.[14] In fact, the definition of "contract" during this period was fundamentally different from that under a market economy. Contracts in this period were executed and performed according to state plans, instead of being the product of the freedom of contract exercised by the relevant parties. Rather, they served as tools and mechanisms for the implementation of state plans. As late as 1978, policy makers saw breach of contract as prejudicing the socialist planned economy.[15] Since the economy during this period was basically limited to the state-owned economy, most production and consumption goods were assigned and distributed according to state plans. Trade credit was limited or abolished. After 1952, individuals could not write checks, and both promissory notes and bills of exchange were forbidden domestically. Bills of exchange could be used only for international trade.[16] Furthermore, free trade of goods that violated or evaded state plans (so-called "speculation") continued to be regarded as criminal offenses for a prolonged period of time, even after the commencement of reform and opening.[17]

There had long been a lack of a basic civil law system in China under the planned economy. Although the Standing Committee of the National People's Congress organized the drafting of the Civil Law in 1954 and finished a draft Civil Law in December 1956, the drafting process was suspended soon thereafter due to political unrest. The drafting process of the Civil Law resumed in 1962 when China attempted to develop the basis for the production and exchange of goods. A proposed draft was completed in July 1964, but the drafting process was suspended again due to the political movement that started in 1964.[18] Also, the property law in China during this period was underdeveloped. The Constitution of 1954 provided that the state should protect peasants' land ownership and the

---

[14] See WANG JIAFU, XIE HUAISHI ET AL, *supra* note 3, at 142–46.
[15] *Id.* at 146.
[16] See 谢怀栻, 票据法概论 [XIE HUAISHI, THE LAW OF NEGOTIABLE BILLS OF EXCHANGE] 27 (法律出版社 [Law Press] 1990).
[17] 刑法 [Criminal Law] (1979), 1979–1984 法律汇编 [COLLECTED LAWS] 98, *translated in* 1 P.R.C. LAWS 87, arts. 117, 118. 刑法 [Criminal Law] (1997), 1997 法律汇编 [COLLECTED LAWS] 87, *translated in* 9 P.R.C. LAWS.
[18] See 梁慧星, 制定民法典的设想 [Liang Huixing, *Thoughts on the Making of Civil Law Code*], 现代法学 [MODERN LAW SCIENCE], Vol. 2, 2001, at 3.

ownership of other means of production.[19] However, due to the socialist transformation and the movement for communization, peasants as well as other individuals had no ownership stakes in land or major means of production. The state only protected "the ownership of the labor income, savings, housing and other consumption goods."[20] Other types of property, such as shares, and intellectual property, were almost non-existent in economic life. China had not yet established an intellectual property legal system at this time. Although there were several regulations that could be categorized as laws relating to intellectual property, the content thereof was simple and not comprehensive. For instance, the trademark system was incomplete and the patent system essentially did not exist. Only four patents were granted from the adoption of the Provisional Regulations on Protecting the Right of Invention and Patents in July 1950 until its abandonment in November 1963.[21] The protection of copyrights mainly relied on certain administrative legal rules, which were general in content, such as the Rules on Combating the Copying of Books Without Authorization (1953), the Draft Provisional Rules on the Remuneration of Authors of Literature and Social Science Books.[22]

With regard to the financial and taxation system, the distribution of financial resources between central and local governments had long been the key to the reform of the financial system. The Regulations on the Reform of the Financial Administration System, adopted in 1957, stipulated the scope, allocation and type of financial revenue and expenditure for the central and local governments. The Key Principles of the National Tax Administration, promulgated in 1950, marked the unification of the Chinese tax administration and the establishment of a new tax system.[23] The Regulation on the Agricultural Tax, promulgated in 1958, set up a proportional tax system for agricultural taxation. The Regulations on the Consolidated Industrial and Commercial Tax, promulgated in 1958, was the second major reform of industrial and commercial tax.[24] In 1973, a trial implementation of industrial and commercial tax was carried out, marking the third major reform of industrial and commercial tax. Thereafter, only the industrial and commercial tax was levied on state-owned en-

---

[19] The Constitution of 1954, *supra* note 7, art. 8.
[20] *Id.* art. 9.
[21] *See* 李顺德, 知识产权法律基础 [LI SHUNDE, FUNDAMENTALS OF INTELLECTUAL PROPERTY LAW] 69 (知识产权出版社 [Intellectual Property Press] 2005).
[22] 知识产权法 [INTELLECTUAL PROPERTY LAW] 64 (李明德 [Li Mingde] ed., 社会科学文献出版社 [Social Science Academic Press] 2007).
[23] 北京经济学院财政金融教研室, 新中国税制演变 [FINANCE DEPARTMENT OF THE BEIJING ECONOMY ACADEMY, REFORM OF THE TAXATION SYSTEM IN CHINA] 7 (天津人民出版社 [Tianjin People's Press] 1985).
[24] *Id.* at 35.

terprises, while the industrial and commercial tax and the industrial-commercial income tax were levied on collective enterprises. The basic feature of tax reform at this stage was that the number of different taxes was reduced and the tax system was simplified.[25] China had also tried to increase financial revenue by issuing public debt. For instance, the Decision on Issuing People's Victory Parity Bonds in Kind, which approved the issuance of such bonds in 1950, was passed in December 1949.[26] To accelerate national economic development, China adopted specific regulations on the issuance of public debt for national economic development each year from 1954 to 1958. However, the issuance of public debt was suspended at the end of the 1950s, due to China's policy of having "neither international debt nor domestic debt."[27]

Overall, the economic legal system at this stage fluctuated significantly. It received much attention from 1949 to 1956, was ignored from 1957 to 1961, was on the verge of resumption from 1962 to 1964, and was then abolished from 1965 to 1978. The rise and fall of the economic legal system during this period can be attributed to several factors. First, from the standpoint of legal ideology, legal nihilism and legal instrumentalism gained popularity in turn, with legal nihilism prevailing.[28] Even though for a short period, considerable attention was paid to the economic legal system, this was merely a reflection of legal instrumentalism. Second, in connection with the social governance system, the "rule of man" prevailed over the rule of law. Often, leaders' words were regarded as law and thus the so-called law changed with leaders' pronouncements.[29] Third, with regard to economic administration policies, the political doctrines of "policy can replace law," "only policies, no laws" and "policy itself is law" were the dominant values.[30] Finally, in the economic system, the operational mechanism of the planned economy system left little room for the functioning of laws.

---

[25] *Id.* at 51–53.
[26] "In kind" means that the par value of the People's Victory Parity Bonds was calculated on the basis of the prices of daily necessities.
[27] 周恩来, 在第四届全国人民代表大会上的《政府工作报告》 [Zhou Enlai, Speech at the Fourth National People's Congress: Government Work Report] (1975), *translated in* DOCUMENTS OF THE FIRST SESSION OF THE FOURTH NATIONAL PEOPLE'S CONGRESS OF THE PEOPLE'S REPUBLIC OF CHINA 45–65 (Foreign Languages Press 1975).
[28] 当代中国法学研究 [CONTEMPORARY CHINESE LEGAL RESEARCH] 26–32 (陈甦 [Chen Su] ed., 中国社会科学出版社 [China Social Science Press] 2009).
[29] 邓小平文选第 2 卷 [SELECTED WORKS OF DENG XIAOPING VOL. 2] 146 (人民出版社 [People's Press] 1994).
[30] *See* FORTY YEARS OF LEGAL STUDIES IN CHINA, *supra* note 3, at 90.

II. THE ECONOMIC LEGAL SYSTEM IN THE EARLY STAGE AFTER THE POLICY OF REFORM AND OPENING (1978–1992)

Starting in 1978, China abandoned the political theme of "using class struggle as a principle" and decided instead to focus on economic development. It thus began to implement the Reform and Opening-Up Policy[31] that is still ongoing to date. Since the adoption of this new policy, with deepened knowledge obtained through experience and implementation, the economic system underwent a number of vital changes. In 1982, the economic system was described as a "planned economy supplemented by market mechanism"; in 1984, as a "planned commodity economy based on public ownership"; in 1987, the principle was that "the socialist planned commodity economy shall be the internal unification of the planned and market mechanisms"; in 1989, it was "the establishment of an economic system and operational mechanism that combines planned economy and market mechanisms, and capable of adapting to the socialist planned commodity economy"; and in 1992, China put forward a new aim for its economic system reform: the creation of a "socialist market economy."[32] Generally, the basic approach underpinning the Chinese Reform and Opening Up Policy consisted of three major themes: firstly, in terms of its foreign economic policy, attracting foreign capital and expanding exports; secondly, in terms of its domestic policy in rural areas, the key to reform was the policy of "a contract system with remuneration linked to output";[33] thirdly, in terms of its domestic policy in urban areas, the key was to increase the independence and vitality of enterprises and to adjust the relationship between the state and enterprises (most of which were state-owned).[34] The economic legal system at this stage was also based on the three policies above.

In order to expand international economic cooperation and technological exchange, China enacted the Law on Chinese-Foreign Equity Joint Ventures, allowing foreign companies, enterprises and other economic

---

[31] See 中共中央十一届三中全会决议 [Resolution of the Third Session of the Eleventh Central Committee of Chinese Communist Party] (1978).
[32] See 江泽民, 在第十四届全国人民代表大会上的《加快改革开放和现代化建设步伐，夺取有中国特色社会主义事业的更大胜利》谈话 [Jiang Zemin, Speech at the Fourteenth National People's Congress: Accelerate Opening Up Reform and the Pace of Modernization, Strive for the Success of Socialism with Chinese Characteristics] (1992), available at http://news.xinhuanet.com/ziliao/2003-01/20/content_697148.htm (last visited Oct. 18, 2009).
[33] The "contract system with remuneration linked to output" was a form of production used in the Chinese rural collective economy, under which individuals or families contracted for the use of land or other means of production, and enjoyed autonomy in operation and management.
[34] 厉以宁, 社会主义政治经济学 [LI YINING, SOCIALIST POLITICAL ECONOMICS] 45 (商务印书馆 [Commercial Press] 1986).

organizations or individuals to establish joint ventures with their counterparts in China.[35] This law established the legal status of Chinese-foreign joint ventures and the protection of their property. From a legal perspective, these are important landmarks of the Opening Up policy. In 1980 and 1981, China passed the Law on Income Tax on Chinese-Foreign Equity Joint Ventures and the Law on Income Tax on Foreign Enterprises respectively, which provided exemptions or other favorable tax treatment for foreign enterprises that needed encouragement and development. By the end of 1986, there were more than 3,000 Chinese-foreign equity joint ventures in China.[36] At the same time, to further improve the investment environment, protect the legitimate interests of foreign investors, and enrich the organizational forms of foreign enterprises as a means of attracting more foreign investment, China passed the Foreign-Invested Enterprise Law in 1986 and the Law on Chinese-Foreign Contractual Joint Ventures in 1988, and revised its Law on Chinese-Foreign Equity Joint Ventures in April 1990. By means of these laws, a comprehensive legal system regarding foreign enterprises was established.

In August 1980, the Fifteenth Session of the Fifth Standing Committee of the National People's Congress ratified the Regulation on Special Economic Zones in Guangdong Province, which set up three special economic zones in Shenzhen, Zhuhai and Shantou in Guangdong Province. In October of the same year, the State Council also granted approval to the city of Xiamen to set up its special economic zone. The legal basis for the special economic zones system with Chinese characteristics was thereby established. These special economic zones were designed with reference to the experiences of free trade zones and export processing zones in other countries, where more favorable policies, including exemption and reduction of taxes, were implemented in international economic activities.[37]

Beginning in the spring of 1979, different forms of the agricultural production responsibility system appeared in rural China and the "contract system with remuneration linked to output" eventually became the major form of agricultural production. Although there was considerable political controversy in the intervening period, 99.5%[38] of farmers' pro-

---

[35] 中国合资经营企业法 [Law on Chinese-Foreign Equity Joint Ventures] (promulgated by the Standing Comm. Nat'l People's Cong., July 8, 1979, effective July 8, 1979) STANDING COMM. NAT'L PEOPLE'S CONG. GAZ. (P.R.C.), art. 1.

[36] 经济法要义 [UNDERSTANDING ECONOMIC LAW] 605 (王家福 [Wang Jiafu] ed., 中国财政经济出版社 [China Finance and Economy Press] 1988).

[37] Id. at 637–38.

[38] The "farmer's production team" was the basic unit of rural production during the period of the movement for communization.

duction teams[39] had adopted the "contract system with remuneration linked to output" by November 1982. The "contract system with remuneration linked to output" was not only a form of production—more importantly, it served as a framework for property rights and legal relationships. Based on this contractual system, individual peasants and their families would enjoy autonomy of agricultural production and property rights in their means of production. The implementation of the "contract system with remuneration linked to output" not only increased the income of peasants and promoted economic development in rural areas, but also made the people's communes redundant. The Constitution of 1982 changed the system of "integration of administrative and economic entities" into a system based on the separation of political and economic entities. While people's communes were solely preserved as economic organizations, local governments were established at the town level.[40] By the end of 1984, the people's communes that had existed in China for more than twenty years had disappeared.[41] However, it was not until the amendment of Constitution of 1993 that the people's communes were abolished as a matter of law.[42] The establishment and expansion of the "contract system with remuneration linked to output" not only benefited rural China, but served as a pioneering example for the reform of urban China. In particular, the framework for property rights and obligations within that system helped to provide the conceptual foundation and practical experiences for creating further civil and commercial laws, which focused on property relationships. The development of agriculture was strongly influenced by national policy rather than law,[43] and so the rural reforms relating to major legal issues and property rights were also mostly determined by policy. Except for a handful of administrative rules, such as the Regulation on Collective Ownership Enterprises in Rural Areas, legislation concerning agriculture lagged behind.[44]

---

[39] *See* 罗汉平, 农村人民公社史 [LUO HANPING, THE HISTORY OF PEOPLE'S COMMUNES IN RURAL CHINA] 387–400 (福建人民出版社 [Fujian People's Press] 2003).
[40] 1982 年宪法 [Constitution of 1982] (promulgated by the Nat'l People's Cong., Dec. 4, 1982, effective Dec. 4, 1982) NAT'L PEOPLE'S CONG. GAZ. (P.R.C.), arts. 8, 95.
[41] *See* LUO HANPING, *supra* note 39, at 413.
[42] 1993 年宪法修正案 [Amendment to the Constitution 1993] (promulgated by the Nat'l People's Cong., Mar. 29, 1993, effective Mar. 29, 1993) NAT'L PEOPLE'S CONG. GAZ. (P.R.C.), art. 6.
[43] 李成贵, 中国农业政策—理论框架与应用分析 [LI CHENGGUI, CHINA'S AGRICULTURAL POLICY: THEORETICAL FRAMEWORK AND ANALYSIS OF APPLICATION] 3 (社会科学文献出版社 [Social Science Academic Press] 1999).
[44] 王存学、骆友生, 中国农村经济法律基本问题 [WANG CUNXUE & LUO YOUSHENG, FUNDAMENTAL LEGAL ISSUES OF THE CHINESE RURAL ECONOMY] 11 (法律出版社 [Law Press] 1998).

Serving as the focus of urban reform during this period, the reform of state-owned enterprises followed the basic principles of separating enterprises and government and expanding the autonomy of enterprises. In 1979, the State Council issued certain regulations including the Rules on the Expansion of the State-Owned Enterprises' Autonomy of Operation and Management and launched pilot projects in a few state-owned enterprises within the public transportation sector. To promote state-owned enterprise reform, several relevant regulations were issued, including the Provisional Regulation on Worker Representative Congresses in State-Owned Industrial Enterprises (1981), the Provisional Regulation on Factory Managers of State-Owned Enterprises (1982), the Regulation on Rewards and Penalties for Enterprise Employees (1982), and the Provisional Regulation on State-Owned Industrial Enterprises (1983). The Law on Industrial Enterprises Owned by the Whole People was enacted in 1998 based on practical experience gained from prior reforms, paying particular attention to the actual situation and the need for reform of the then more than 90,000 "industrial enterprises owned by the whole people" (which accounted for over 70% of the gross industrial domestic product).[45] This law abolished the relationship of non-separation between government and enterprises and recognized the autonomy of enterprises. It also gave them independent property rights through the separation of ownership rights and management rights. At the same time, the law overcame the disadvantages of enterprises "eating from the same pot"[46] as the state.[47]

During the process of state-owned enterprise reform, another important trend in the Chinese economy was gaining momentum: the emergence and development of private economy. At the time of the enactment of the Constitution of 1982, the only individual economy that was allowed was the individual economy of urban laborers.[48] However, a large number of private enterprises which owned assets and hired workers did

---

[45] *See* 吕东, 在第七届全国人民代表大会第一次会议上的《关于<全民所有制工业企业法(草案)>的说明》 [Lü Dong, Speech at the Seventh Session of the First National People's Congress: Explanation on the "Draft Law on Industrial Enterprises Owned by The Whole People"] (1988), *available at* http://www.law-lib.com/fzdt/newshtml/20/20050721212402.htm (last visited Oct. 18, 2009).

[46] "Eating from the same pot" is a metaphor for the extreme egalitarianism characteristic of the Chinese income system, wherein the people's income was not determined by the operation of enterprises or the performance of workers. This was considered analogous to a situation where each person shared the same amount of food from the same pot.

[47] *See* ECONOMIC LAW, *supra* note 6, at 34–36.

[48] Constitution of 1982, *supra* note 40, art. 11.

emerge.⁴⁹ Under Article 1 of the Constitution as amended in 1988, "[t]he state permits the private sector of the economy to exist and develop within the limits prescribed by law. The private sector of the economy is a complement to the socialist public economy. The state protects the lawful rights and interests of the private sector of the economy, and exercises guidance, supervision and control over the private sector of the economy." Accordingly, the Provisional Regulation on Private Enterprises was passed in 1988 to stimulate and regulate private enterprises as well as to protect their legal interests.⁵⁰

The country's Reform and Opening Up Policy led to the adoption of foreign-inspired mechanisms regarding production and the exchange of goods. As a result, the enactment of laws regarding property and transactions was placed on the agenda of the legislature. In November 1979, which marked the beginning of the Reform and Opening Up, a drafting group was set up to draft the Civil Law Code.⁵¹ Considering the difficulties in enacting a comprehensive civil law code within a short period of time, the legislature adopted an approach of enacting separate, specific civil laws first, and then consolidating them in a comprehensive civil law code when conditions permitted.⁵² The *General Principles of the Civil Law* passed in 1986 included nine chapters: Basic Principles (Chapter I), Citizens (Natural Persons) (Chapter II), Legal Persons (Chapter III), Civil Law Acts and Agency (Chapter IV), Civil Rights (Chapter V), Civil Liability (Chapter VI), Limitation of Action (Chapter VII), Choice of Law in Civil Relations with Foreigners (Chapter VIII), and Supplementary Provisions (Chapter IX). This law laid down the basic principles and institutions of civil law and served as the fundamental civil law in China before the Civil Law Code was enacted.⁵³

---

⁴⁹ According to statistics, in 1988 there were more than 90,000 private enterprises with about 1,640,000 employees, *see* 聚焦共和国第一个宪法修正案 [*Report on the First Amendment of the Constitution*], 检察日报 [PROSECUTION DAILY], Apr. 12, 2008.

⁵⁰ 私营企业暂行条例 [The Provisional Regulations on Private Enterprises] (promulgated by the St. Council, June 25, 1988, effective July 1, 1988) ST. COUNCIL GAZ. (P.R.C.), art. 1.

⁵¹ For example, on Dec. 23, 2002, the draft of the Civil Law Code was submitted to the Standing Committee of the National People's Congress for deliberation. There were nine chapters in this draft, namely, General Principles, Property Law, Contract Law, Personal Right Law, Marriage Law, Adoption Law, Inheritance Law, Torts Liabilities Law, and Choice of Law for Foreign-Related Civil Activities. *See* 新华网 [XinhuaNet.com], 民法草案首次提请人大常委会审议 [The Draft of the Civil Law Code First Submitted for NPC Standing Committee's Review], *available at* http://news.xinhuanet.com/newscenter/2002-12/23/content_667932.htm (last visited Oct. 18, 2009).

⁵² 梁慧星, 民法总论 [LIANG HUIXING, FUNDAMENTALS OF CIVIL LAW] 19 (法律出版社 [Law Press] 1996).

⁵³ 梁慧星, 民法 [LIANG HUIXING, CIVIL LAW] 10 (四川人民出版社 [Sichuan People's Press] 1998).

Within civil law legislation, the evolution of land law was particularly notable. The forms of the ownership of land in China at the time included state ownership and collective ownership. Before the reform of the economic system, the law stipulated that no organization or individual may appropriate, buy, sell, or lease land or otherwise engage in the transfer of land by unlawful means.[54] But in reality, Article 5 of the Law on Chinese-Foreign Equity Joint Ventures (1979) provided that the "right to the use of a site" could be a form of contribution to joint ventures. The law did not specify whether the "right to the use of a site" contributed to a joint venture was a "contractual right" or a "property right." However, since the term of a joint venture was generally ten to thirty years, or even fifty years or more for special projects, this "right to the use of a site" could be regarded as an early form of "land use rights" in the nature of "property rights."[55] Due to the subsequent diversification and extension in the terms of the use of land, China adjusted its land law and created "land use rights" based on the idea of the separation of the ownership right in land and the right to use the land.[56] Such an arrangement laid the institutional foundation for the subsequent rapid development of the Chinese real estate market.

With the implementation of the policy of "revitalizing the domestic economy, and opening up to the outside world," the production and exchange of goods inevitably became important drivers of the economy. As a result, contract law gradually came to play a leading role in economic transactions. In 1981, the Economic Contract Law was enacted, which represented a significant development in the field of Chinese contract law. Thereafter, given the differences which existed between foreign-related contracts and domestic contracts, China passed its Foreign-Related Economic Contract Law in order to promote foreign trade. In 1987, to advance the development of science and technology and to control increasingly significant technological development, technology transfer, technology consulting and technology services, China passed the Law on Technology Contracts. By then, China had essentially laid the foundations of its contract law.[57]

---

[54] Constitution of 1982, *supra* note 40, art. 10.

[55] 中国物权法研究 [STUDIES IN CHINESE PROPERTY LAW] 599 (梁慧星 [Liang Huixing] ed., 法律出版社 [Law Press] 1998).

[56] 城镇国有土地使用权出让和转让暂行条例 [The Interim Regulations Concerning the Assignment and Transfer of the Right to the Use of the State-Owned Land in the Urban Areas] (promulgated by the St. Council, May 19, 1990, effective May 19, 1990) ST. COUNCIL GAZ. (P.R.C.), art. 1.

[57] 王利明、崔建远, 合同法新论·总则 [WANG LIMING & CUI JIANYUAN, CONTRACT LAW: GENERAL PROVISIONS] 94–95 (中国政法大学出版社 [China University of Political Science and Law Press] 1996).

For the purpose of fair adjudication of economic disputes, the Chinese courts at all levels began to set up economic tribunals in the second half of 1979. All intermediate courts (with the exception of some courts in remote areas) and 93% of lower courts had set up economic tribunals by April 1985.[58]

The emergence of the Chinese securities market was another notable economic development during this period. Starting in 1981, China promulgated several Regulations on the Treasury Bonds of the People's Republic of China in consecutive years and issued treasury bonds to the public. The purpose of the treasury bond issuances was to cut the financial deficit and to maintain fiscal balance. The treasury bonds were not transferable. The issuances of treasury bonds marked the reappearance of securities in China after three decades, and marked also the emergence of the modern Chinese securities market. In November 1984, the Shanghai Feiyue Audio Company issued public shares, which was the first public offering in China since the initiation of the Reform and Opening Up Policy. In September 1986, the Shanghai Trust Investment Company, which was affiliated with the Industrial and Commercial Bank of China, began to operate the first stock exchange counter in China. In December 1990, the Shanghai Stock Exchange was established. Soon after that, the Shenzhen Stock Exchange was established in July 1991. The Chinese securities market developed rapidly thereafter.[59]

The establishment of the intellectual property system was initiated at the end of the 1970s and started to develop with the implementation of the Reform and Opening Up Policy.[60] In 1979, the registration of trademarks was resumed and approximately 26,000 trademarks were registered in 1980 alone.[61] In 1984, the *Patent Law* was enacted. By April 1, 1985, the day on which the *Patent Law* came into effect, a total of 3,455 applications had been received, setting a new world record in patent history at the time, according to the World Intellectual Property Organization (WIPO).[62] The General Principles of the Civil Law for the first time stipulated that "[c]itizens and legal persons shall enjoy rights of authorship (copyrights) and shall be entitled to sign their names as authors, issue and publish their works and obtain remuneration in accordance with the

---

[58] *See* UNDERSTANDING ECONOMIC LAW, *supra* note 36, at 731.
[59] *See* 新证券法论 [SECURITIES LAW] 12–13 (周友苏 [Zhou Yousu] ed., 法律出版社 [Law Press] 2007).
[60] *See* LI SHUNDE, *supra* note 21, at 69.
[61] *See* 中国商标局 [Chinese Trademark Bureau], 历年商标注册申请及核准注册商标统计表 [*Statistics for Trademark Applications and Trademarks Approved in Force over Previous Years*], *available at* http://sbj.saic.gov.cn/tjxx/TJTableLNSBTJ.asp?BM=09 (last visited Nov. 5, 2009).
[62] *See* 熊志云, 浅谈专利档案及其管理 [Xiong Zhiyun, *Trademark Documents and Management*], 档案学研究 [RESEARCH IN ARCHIVAL SCIENCE], No. 1 1988, at 58.

law."[63] In 1990, the Copyright Law was passed, and in 1991, the Regulation for the Protection of Computer Software was adopted. With the Reform and Opening Up Policy, the integration of the Chinese intellectual property system into the global system proceeded at an unprecedented pace. As early as 1980, China had submitted its application for membership to WIPO and became a member of the organization that same year. In 1984, China also submitted its application to join the Paris Convention for the Protection of Industrial Property and has been a member since 1985. In 1989, China submitted its application to WIPO to join the Madrid Agreement Concerning the International Registration of Marks, and has been a member since 1989. In July 1992, China submitted applications to WIPO and the United Nations Educational, Scientific and Cultural Organization to join the Berne Convention for the Protection of Literary and Artistic Works and the Universal Copyright Convention, respectively. In October of that year, China was accepted as a member of those two conventions.[64]

Before the reform of the economic system, China lacked a clear conception of modern environmental protection, as well as a system of environmental law.[65] However, contrary to common belief, China's approach was not one of "development first, environment later." Rather, it adopted a new environmental policy around the same time as the Reform and Opening Up Policy, and maintained a heavy emphasis on environmental legislation even as it developed its economy. Numerous laws and regulations in this field were enacted during this period, including the Environmental Protection Law (For Trial Implementation) (1979), the Marine Environment Protection Law (1982), the Provisional Regulation on Pollutant Discharge Fee Collection (1982), the Regulations of the People's Republic of China Concerning Environmental Protection in Offshore Oil Exploration and Exploitation (1983), the Regulations of the People's Republic of China on the Control over Prevention of Pollution by Vessels in Sea Waters (1983), the Law on Prevention and Control of Water Pollution (1984), and the Law on Prevention and Control of Atmospheric Pollution (1987). For all of this legislation, however, China's current environmental laws remain far from ideal, and these laws have not been enforced in a

---

[63] 民法通则 [General Principles of Civil Law] (promulgated by the President of the People's Republic of China, Apr. 12, 1986, effective Jan. 1, 1987), art. 94.
[64] See INTELLECTUAL PROPERTY LAW, *supra* note 22, at 511, 518, 532, 538.
[65] 马骧聪、蔡守秋，中国环境法制通论 [MA XIONGCONG & CAI SHOUQIU, GENERAL INTRODUCTION TO CHINESE ENVIRONMENTAL LAW] 42–43 (学苑出版社 [Xueyuan Press] 1990).

uniform and rigorous manner. These remain issues to be solved by Chinese environmental law.[66]

Generally, China made significant progress in the construction of its economic legal system during this stage. Firstly, the laws became integrated into the country's economy in all aspects. The legal system played an important role in protecting the rights of individuals in economic activities, maintaining economic order and promoting economic development. Secondly, legal ideology changed substantially during this period. The importance and necessity of the law in the economy was recognized and legal nihilism was abandoned. Thirdly, although certain economic laws remained general and incomplete, and their contents inconsistent with one another, the basic content and direction of the economic legal system were properly established. This foundation would promote the further development and reform of the Chinese economy.

III. THE ECONOMIC LEGAL SYSTEM UNDER THE SOCIALIST MARKET ECONOMY SYSTEM (1992–2009)

In 1992, China proposed the establishment of a socialist market economy system, which had long been a goal of the country's reform.[67] In 1993, Article 15 of the Constitution was amended. The Article had formerly stated that "the country will implement a planned economy on the basis of socialist public ownership," and this was now amended to state that "the country will implement a socialist market economy."[68] In order to develop the socialist market economy, China comprehensively strengthened the construction of its economic legal system, which went through a significant expansion during this period.[69] This development was marked by the following trends: firstly, the legislation and standards set by the economic legal system were designed to focus on practicality, in order to reflect the practices and inherent requirements of China's market

---

[66] See 李恒远、常纪文, 现状、问题与走向：中国环境法治 30 年之评析 [Li Henyuan & Chang Jiwen, *Current Situation, Problems and Future: Thirty Years of Chinese Environmental Law*], in 中国环境法治 (2007 年卷) [CHINESE ENVIRONMENTAL LAW (2007)] 12–13 (法律出版社 [Law Press] 2008).

[67] See JIANG ZEMIN, *supra* note 32.

[68] Amendment to the Constitution 1993, *supra* note 42, art. 7.

[69] By March 2008, China had 229 currently effective laws in total, nearly 600 administrative regulations, and more than 7,000 local regulations, among which economic laws and regulations account for a large proportion. See 吴邦国, 在第十一届全国人民代表大會第一次会议上的《常务委员会工作报告》 [Wu Bangguo, Standing Committee Work Report at the First Session of the Eleventh National People's Congress] (2008), *available at* http://www.jconline.cn/Contents/Channel_4095/2008/0321/74363/content_74363.htm.

economy.⁷⁰ Secondly, an emphasis was placed on the democratization of the economic legal system. Numerous measures were taken to increase democracy within the legislative process, particularly after 2000. In the creation of several major economic laws, such as the country's property law, labor contract law and social insurance law, actors in relevant sectors and fields were asked to comment on the draft laws. These drafts were also published in order to solicit opinions from the public.⁷¹ Thirdly, the economic legal system focused on making systematic changes. In 2001, China proposed the development of a "socialist legal system with Chinese characteristics" to be completed by 2010, which would include seven bodies of law, namely, the Constitution and relevant laws, civil and commercial law, administrative law, economic law, social law, criminal law, litigation and non-litigation procedural law.⁷² Fourthly, the economic legal system was built with a focus on globalization. In particular, emphasis was placed on making domestic laws conform with international rules in the period immediately preceding and following China's accession to the World Trade Organization (WTO). For example, in order to join the WTO, China adopted, revised and abolished a large number of laws, administrative regulations, rules and other legal documents that were not in accordance with WTO rules and various other international obligations that the country had undertaken.⁷³

One distinctive feature during this period was that theoretical studies of law began to have a direct and significant impact on the economic legal system. For example, the Chinese Academy of Social Sciences Institute of Law first put forward the theory that "a socialist market economy is an

---

⁷⁰ *E.g.*, the "CPC Central Committee's Decision on the Establishment of a Socialist Market Economic System" (1993) pointed out that great importance should be attached to the legal system, and to laws and regulations incompatible with the establishment of a socialist market, which should be abolished or amended. *See* 中共中央关于建立社会主义市场经济体制若干问题的决定(1993) [CPC Central Committee Decision on the Establishment of a Socialist Market Economic System (1993)], *available at* http://www.china.com.cn/chinese/archive/131747.htm.

⁷¹ *E.g.*, in 2005, the full version of the Draft Property Law was published. From July 10th to August 20th, citizens sent in 11,543 opinions, in the form of both online and written letters. The Standing Committees in twenty-six provinces (including autonomous regions and cities with provincial status), as well as fifteen large cities, forty-seven governmental agencies, sixteen large companies, twenty-two legal teaching and research institutions also expressed their views on the draft. *See* 全国人民代表大会法律委员会 [NAT'L PEOPLE'S CONG. LAW COMM.], 关于物权法(草案)修改情况的汇报 [*Report on the Revision of the Draft Property Law*] (Oct. 22, 2005), *available at* http://www.cctv.com/news/china/20051022/100618.shtml.

⁷² *See* 李鹏, 在第九届全国人民代表大会第四次会议上的《常务委员会工作报告》 [Li Peng, Standing Committee Work Report at the Forth Session of the Ninth National People's Congress] (2001).

⁷³ By the end of 2001, China had formulated, revised and repealed about 1,150 laws in its process of legal reform. *See* 新华网 [XINHUANET], 履行入世承诺, 我国清理法规 1150 余件 [Reviewing 1150 Regulations to Fulfill Our Promise under WTO Laws], Dec. 28, 2001, *available at* http://news.xinhuanet.com/fortune/2001-12/28/content_216380.htm (last visited Oct. 18, 2009).

economy that is under the rule of law" in 1993, stating that China should establish a socialist market economic legal system. The Institute also detailed the ideologies and basic structure that the socialist market economic legal system should adopt.[74] This work provided an important theoretical basis as well as policy suggestions for the development of the economic legal system that China subsequently undertook. In another example, legal scholars proposed in 1995 the legislation of a nationwide property law, while scholars in civil law also drafted proposals for a property law.[75] The country's Property Law was finally adopted in 2007, twelve years after these proposals were first made, with much effort and participation from academics.[76] As a third example, after China initiated the drafting of its Contract Law in 1993, scholars from twelve law schools around the country drafted proposals in 1995 which, after extensive discussion, served as the basis of the official draft prepared by the legislature and submitted to the Standing Committee of the National People's Congress.[77] Since then, the field of Chinese legal theory has continued to draw from numerous legal theories and the experiences of legal construction from different jurisdictions (including those from outside the country).[78] This absorption of various theories and experiences has served as

---

[74] 中国社会科学院法学研究所课题组, 建立社会主义市场经济法律体系的理论思考和对策建议 [Chinese Academy of Social Sciences, Institute of Law Research Group, *Theories and Policy Proposals for the Construction of a Socialist Market Economy Legal System*], 法学研究 [CHINESE JOURNAL OF LAW], No. 6, 1993, at 3.

[75] 中国社会科学院法学研究所课题组, 制定物权法的基本思路 [Chinese Academy of Social Sciences Institute of Law Research Group, *General Thinking on the Making of Property Law*], 法学研究 [CHINESE JOURNAL OF LAW], No. 3, 1995.

[76] *See* 中国物权法草案建议稿 [SUGGESTED DRAFT OF PROPERTY LAW OF CHINA] (梁慧星 [Liang Huixing] ed., 社会科学文献出版社 [Social Science Academic Press] 2000); 中国物权法草案建议稿及说明 [DRAFT OF PROPERTY LAW OF CHINA AND EXPLANATION] (王利明 [Wang Liming] ed., 中国法制出版社 [China Legal Press] 2001).

[77] *See* 合同法 [CONTRACT LAW] 10 (崔建远 [Cui Jianyuan], ed., 法律出版社 [Law Press] 2003).

[78] The "Chinese Journal of Law" is China's most authoritative legal journal. Chang Peng'ao has compiled statistics on the citations of articles on civil law published in the "Chinese Journal of Law" in the thirty years from 1978 to 2007, which illustrate, to a certain extent, changes in Chinese legal research that reflect the influence of foreign theories. In civil law articles published in the "Chinese Journal of Law" between 1978–1986, a total of 127 citations were to the works of Marx and Engels, thirty-five to the works of Lenin, thirteen to Soviet sources, four to Yugoslav sources, eleven to Anglo-American legal sources, six to German sources, six to French sources, four to Japanese sources, fourteen to pre-1949 or Taiwan Province sources, and four to Roman legal literature. In the papers published in 1987–1999, 468 citations were to pre-1949 and Taiwan Province sources, 296 to Anglo-American law, 214 to Japanese sources, sixty-four to German sources, thirty-five to the works of Marx and Engels, thirty to Roman law, twenty to French sources, and twenty-seven to Soviet sources. In 2000–2007, 595 citations referred to pre-1949 Chinese sources of Taiwan Province sources, 585 to German sources, 290 to Anglo-American law, 225 to Roman Law, 190 to Japanese law, fifty-nine to French sources, and 113 from other countries (including Italy, the Nether-Netherlands, Russia, and Argentina). *See* 常鹏翱,《法学研究》三十年: 民法学 [Chang Peng'ao,

one of the most powerful driving forces behind the development of the Chinese economic legal system.

During this period, China's public-owned economy continued to develop in accordance with the reform policy, but the traditional state-owned enterprise development policy of simply increasing the number and scale of enterprises was replaced by policies aimed at improving the quality of corporate governance and management. By the end of March 2009, there were 97,177,000 enterprises, of which 541,600 were state-owned enterprises.[79] State-owned enterprises accounted for only 5.57% of the total number of enterprises, but the operational mechanisms and corporate governance structures of such enterprises saw greater improvement during this stage than those of non-state-owned enterprises. In order to protect state assets and the state-owned economy's leading role in the national economy, and to promote the development of the socialist market economy, China adopted the State-Owned Assets Law in 2008. Along with the deepening of China's economic reform and the development of its market economy, the law increasingly warmed up towards the idea of a non-public ownership economy. With the Constitutional Amendment of 1999, the original provisions stipulating that "the private economy is a complement to the socialist public economy" were revised to state that "the non-public ownership economy is an important component of the socialist market economy."[80] The 2004 Constitutional Amendment also amended the original provision stating that "[t]he individual economy and private economy should be under guidance, supervision and management" to state that "the country encourages, supports and guides the development of the non-public ownership economy."[81] Abolishing or changing laws, regulations and policies limiting the development of the non-public economy became one of the key policies for stimulating the development of this sector.[82] With such welcoming laws and policies, China saw the rapid development of its private economy. By the end of

---

Thirty Years of the "Chinese Journal of Law": Civil Law Studies], 法学研究 [CHINESE JOURNAL OF LAW], No. 3, 2008, at 19, 24, 31, 38.

[79] *See* 国家工商总局 [STATE ADMIN. OF INDUSTRY AND COM.], 统计分析发布: 2009 年一季度全国市场主体发展情况报告 [*Statistical Analysis: Report on the Main Development of National Economic Organizations in the First Quarter of 2009*] (May 11, 2009), *available at* http://www.saic.gov.cn/zwgk/tjzl/zhtj/bgt/200905/t20090511_47153.html (last visited at Oct. 18, 2009).

[80] 1999 年宪法修正案 [Amendment to the Constitution 1999] (promulgated by the Nat'l People's Cong., Mar. 15, 1999, effective Mar. 15, 1999) NAT'L PEOPLE'S CONG. GAZ. (P.R.C.), art. 16.

[81] 2004 年宪法修正案 [Amendment to the Constitution 2004] (promulgated by the Nat'l People's Cong., Mar. 14, 2004, effective Mar. 14, 2004) NAT'L PEOPLE'S CONG. GAZ. (P.R.C.), art. 21.

[82] *See* 中共中央关于完善市场经济体制若干问题的决定 [CPC Central Committee Decision on Improving the Market Economy System] (Oct. 14, 2003), *available at* http://www.china.com.cn/chinese/zhuanti/sljszqh/426675.htm#1 (last visited Oct. 18, 2009).

March 2009, there were a total of approximately 6,642,700 private enterprises and 29,480,000 individual businesses.[83]

In the early stages of reform, there was a period of confusion in the area of Chinese enterprise legislation, but gradually two approaches to such legislation developed.[84] Under one approach, laws were enacted according to the different types of enterprise ownership. For example, in the cases of the Law on Industrial Enterprises Owned by the Whole People (1988), the Rural Collective Enterprises Regulation (1990), the Urban Collective Enterprises Regulation (1991), the Provisional Private Enterprises Regulation (1988), the Law on Chinese-Foreign Equity Joint Ventures (1979), the Foreign Enterprise Law (1986), the Law on Chinese-Foreign Contractual Joint Ventures (1988), all of these laws were formulated before the market economy policy.[85] Although they are still legally in force, the scope of application of these laws has been reduced.[86] Under the second approach, laws were created based on the legal forms of enterprises and investors' liability. Examples include the Company Law (1993), the Partnership Enterprise Law (1997), the Individually-Owned Enterprise Law (1999), and the Farmers Professional Cooperatives Law (2006). These laws were revised and improved along with the deepening of economic reform and an increased awareness of the function of enterprise laws.[87] They have since become the main legal norms governing the organization and operation of enterprises, and effectively promote the development of the economy and the flourishing of business.[88]

The enactment and revision of the Company Law is illustrative of the evolution in Chinese enterprise laws. After China's socialist economic transformation in 1956, the company as a corporate legal form disappeared for the following twenty-three years.[89] But after China enacted its

---

[83] *See* STATE ADMIN. OF INDUSTRY AND COM., *supra* note 79.

[84] *See* 赵旭东, 企业与公司法纵论 [ZHAO XUDONG, BUSINESS AND COMPANY LAW] 61–65 (法律出版社 [Law Press] 2003).

[85] *See* 经济法 [ECONOMIC LAW] 162 (史际春 [Shi Jichun], ed., 中国人民大学出版社 [China Renmin University Press] 2005).

[86] *E.g.*, transforming state-owned enterprises into companies in order to establish a modern enterprise system has been the main thrust of state-owned enterprise reform after 1992. *See* CPC Central Committee Decision on the Establishment of a Socialist Market Economic System, *supra* note 70. If state-owned enterprises were reorganized into corporations, the *Company Law* would apply.

[87] *E.g.*, the *Company Law* and *Partnership Enterprise Law* were modified significantly in 2005 and 2007, respectively.

[88] As of the end of March 2009, there were 125,500 stock corporations, 6,336,700 limited liability companies, 123,100 partnership enterprises, 1,078,900 individual wholly-owned enterprises and 139,100 farmers' cooperatives. *See* STATE ADMIN. OF INDUSTRY AND COM., *supra* note 79.

[89] *See* 王保树、崔勤之, 中国公司法原理 [WANG BAOSHU & CUI QIUZHI, CHINA'S COMPANY LAW THEORY] 10–15 (社会科学文献出版社 [Social Science Academic Press] 2000). In fact, the word "company" did exist at that time, but had no strict legal definitions. Often, it was used to name

Reform and Opening Up Policy, a large number of "companies" emerged within this freer economic environment, particularly after China adopted the socialist market economy policy. Companies spread rapidly across the country, with their numbers increasing from about 480,000 in 1992 to over 1,000,000 by the end of 1993.[90] In order to regulate the form of enterprises and to safeguard the economic order, China formulated the Company Law in December 1993. However, with the continued development of economic reform and the improvement of the market economy system, it became clear that the Company Law could not fully meet the needs of the new situation. Various problems began to emerge as a result of this inadequacy: for example, conditions that were too stringent on the incorporation of companies, inadequate corporate governance in some companies, insufficient protection mechanisms for shareholders (especially minority shareholders), and the lack of liabilities and fiduciary duties for company directors, supervisors and management.[91] Thus, in 2005, China enacted major changes to its Company Law.[92]

After the adoption of the market economy system, the development of a basic civil and commercial law, as well as economic law, became China's most pressing legislative task. With regards to transactional law, the formulation of contract law came as the first priority. Due to the existence of three separate contract laws, namely, the Economic Contract Law, the Foreign-Related Economic Contract Law and the Technology Contract Law, there were repeated, inconsistent and sometimes even contradictory provisions in these three laws, but no basic system governing all contracts, and no regulations for new and emerging forms of contract (such as the sale leaseback contract).[93] China therefore embarked on drawing up a new contract law in 1993, which underwent multiple drafts and revisions. In 1999, the Contract Law was promulgated, while the Economic Contract Law, the Foreign-Related Economic Contract Law and the

---

those commercial enterprises that could not be called "factories," such as department stores and public transport companies.

[90] See 全国人民代表大会法律委员会 [NAT'L PEOPLE'S CONG. LAW COMM.],《关于<公司法(草案)>审议结果的报告》[Report on the Result of Deliberation on the Draft Company Law] (Dec. 20, 1993).

[91] See 曹康泰, 在第十届全国人民代表大会第十四次会议上的《关于<公司法(修订草案)>的说明》[Cao Kangtai, Speech at the Fourteenth Session of the Tenth National People's Congress: Explanation on the Draft of the Revision of Company Law] (2005), available at http://www.5izy.cn/articles/h000/h01/1143710658d1198.html (last visited Oct. 18, 2009).

[92] There were 230 articles in the Company Law at its adoption in 1993. In the National People's Congress amendment to the law in 2005, forty-six of the original articles in the law were deleted, forty-one new articles were inserted, and 137 articles were revised. See 周友苏, 新公司法论 [ZHOU YOUSU, NEW SURVEY ON CORPORATION LAW] 3 (法律出版社 [Law Press] 2006).

[93] See CONTRACT LAW, supra note 77, at 10.

Technology Contract Law were abolished.[94] The Contract Law provides a basic set of rules for contracts in its "General Provisions," and specific rules for fifteen types of commonly-seen contracts in its "Specific Provisions."[95] This law comprehensively and accurately reflects the essential requirements of the market economy, establishing a complete structure for a contracts system and advanced legislation techniques.[96] Some scholars believe that the Contract Law is one of the best examples of civil legislation in China.[97]

As the foundation of the country's market economy, China's property system also became one of the main focuses for legislative changes during this period. In order to regulate the utilization of land and to promote the development of real estate, China formulated the Urban Real Estate Administration Law in 1994, made revisions to the Land Administration Law in 1998, and adopted the Rural Land Contracting Law in 2002. The system for the legal protection of personal property was consistently improved: in 2004, Article 13 of the Constitution was amended from stating that "the country protects the lawfully earned income, saving, housing and other property rights of citizens" to stating that "the property rights of citizens are inviolable."[98] The individual's legal right to private property is enshrined in the Constitution, and the property protected is no longer limited only to the materials necessary for subsistence, but also those needed for production. It became widely recognized in China that under the conditions of a socialist market economy, all market players should work together and operate on equal footing. They should all enjoy the same rights, observe the same rules and bear the same responsibilities.[99] Thus, as the country's basic property protection law, the Property Law established the principle of equal protection of property rights, stating that "[t]he state adopts a socialist market economy, and guarantees equal legal status and the right to develop to all market players," and that "[s]tate, collective and private property rights, as well as the property rights of other rights holders, are protected by law, which no unit or individual

---

[94] 合同法 [Contract Law] (promulgated by the Nat'l People's Cong., Mar. 15, 1999, effective Oct. 1, 1999) NAT'L PEOPLE'S CONG. GAZ. (P.R.C.), art. 428.
[95] *Id.*
[96] *See* CONTRACT LAW, *supra* note 77, at 10–11.
[97] 韩世远, 合同法总论 [HAN SHIYUAN, CONTRACT LAW] 27 (法律出版社 [Law Press] 2008).
[98] Amendment to the Constitution 2004, *supra* note 81, art. 24.
[99] 王兆国, 在第十届全国人民代表大会第五次会议上的关于《关于<中华人民共和国物权法（草案）>的说明》 [Wang Zhaoguo, Speech at the Fifth Session of the Tenth National People's Congress: Explanation on the Draft of the Property Law of the PRC] (Mar. 8, 2007), at section 3(4), *available at* www.gov.cn/2007lh/content_545775.htm (last visited Oct. 18, 2008).

shall violate."[100] The principle confirmed in the Property Law that public and private properties are "both recognized and equally protected" was a milestone in China's legislative history.[101]

After the establishment of the market economy system, China further reinforced its intellectual property legislation, which had significant social and economic impact. For example, in 1993, the year that China made its first revisions to the Trademark Law, the number of trademark applications swelled to over 130,000.[102] Since 2002, the annual number of trademark applications has grown by almost 100,000 applications per year, making China the world leader in this respect for the past seven years.[103] According to the latest statistics released by the National Intellectual Property Bureau, by the end of July 2009, China had accepted 5,341,000 patent applications, of which approximately 4,457,000 were domestic applications, and 884,000 of which were foreign applications.[104] China also continues to actively participate in numerous international conventions relating to intellectual property rights: in 1994, the country joined the Patent Cooperation Treaty, and in 1995, it became a member of the Protocol on Madrid Agreement for International Registration of Trademarks. In 2001, China formally signed the Agreement on Trade Related Aspects of Intellectual Property Rights (TRIPS). In addition, China has continuously strengthened its efforts in the enforcement of intellectual property rights. For example, in the area of copyright protection, copyright administrative departments confiscated a total of 350,000,000 pirated copies of copyright-infringing materials between the years of 1995 to 2004. During that period, 51,368 tort cases were accepted for hearing by courts, of which 49,983 were decided.[105] To improve the quality of the trials in intellectual property rights cases, China has placed an emphasis on the consultation of intellectual property rights experts in particularly technical and difficult cases. By December 2006, there were sixty-two intermediate courts empowered to deal with

---

[100] 物权法 [Property Law] (promulgated by the Nat'l People's Cong., Mar. 16, 2007, effective Oct. 1, 2007), arts. 3, 4.

[101] 孙宪忠, 中国物权法总论 [SUN XIANZHONG, CHINESE PROPERTY LAW] 15–17 (法律出版社 [Law Press] 2009).

[102] See 曹中强、黄晖, 中国商标报告(第四卷) [CAO ZHONGQIANG & HUANG HUI, CHINA TRADEMARK REPORT VOL. IV] 300 (中信出版社 [Citic Press] 2005).

[103] See 中国商标局 [Chinese Trademark Bureau], 商标申请与注册概况表 [Table of Trademark Applications and Registration], available at http://sbj.saic.gov.cn/tjxx/tjxx.asp (last visited Oct. 18, 2009).

[104] See statistics on the website of 国家知识产权局 [State Intellectual Property Office], http://www.sipo.gov.cn/sipo2008/tjxx (last visited Oct. 18, 2009).

[105] See 国务院新闻办公室, 中国知识产权的新进展(白皮书)[STATE COUNCIL INFO. OFFICE, WHITE PAPER ON NEW PROGRESS IN CHINA'S INTELLECTUAL PROPERTY] (2005).

patent disputes in the first instance, thirty-one courts for the patent disputes in the second instance, forty-three intermediate courts for integrated circuit layout and design cases in the first instance, and thirty-eight intermediate courts for new plant variety cases in the first instance.[106]

During this period, China paid heightened attention to the legal structures underpinning its market system, and in particular to legislation governing financial markets. In accordance with the development of financial market conditions, China successively enacted the People's Bank of China Law (1995), Commercial Bank Law (1995), Negotiable Instruments Law (1995), Insurance Law (1995), Securities Law (1998), and Trust Law (2001). The enactment of these laws provided basic rules for the maintenance of order and the effective regulation of the financial market. Existing financial laws continued to be frequently modified with the rapid development of China's financial markets, in order to adapt to ongoing changes.[107] As a result, the adoption and implementation of such laws protected and promoted the development of the financial markets. By the end of September 2006, there were 1396 listed companies in mainland China, with a security market value of over RMB 5.2 trillion. The number of accounts opened by investors totaled over 76 million, making China the third-largest securities market in Asia.[108]

Since 1992, China's financial regulatory system has undergone frequent changes. Following the State Council's Decision on Financial System Reform of 1993, China established an independent macro-control system for the People's Bank of China, as well as a financial institution system separating policy-oriented finance and commercial finance, where state-owned commercial banks coexist with multiple financial institutions. Prior to 1994, the People's Bank of China served as the sole regulatory body for financial institutions and financial markets (with the exception of the China Securities Regulatory Commission, which was partly in charge of securities market regulation).[109] In 1998, China made significant alterations to its finance regulatory system, one of which was to begin constructing separate sub-sector regulatory regimes. The

---

[106] *See* 中国知识产权保护体系改革研究 [CHINA'S IPR PROTECTION SYSTEM REFORM] 227–28 (中国社会科学院知识产权中心 [Chinese Academy of Social Sciences Intellectual Property Center] ed., 知识产权出版社 [Intellectual Property Press] 2008).

[107] *See, e.g.*, 证券法 [Securities Law] (2005); 保险法 [Insurance Law] (2002); 保险法 [Insurance Law] (2009); 中国人民银行法 [Law on the People's Bank of China] (2003); and 商业银行法 [Commercial Bank Law] (2003), which all underwent substantial changes.

[108] 陈洁, 证券法 [CHEN JIE, SECURITIES LAW] 25 (社会科学文献出版社 [Social Science Academic Press] 2006).

[109] 中国金融法治报告 (2009) [Chinese Financial Law Report 2009] 5 (胡滨、全先银 [Hu Bin, Quan Xianyin] eds., 社会科学文献出版社 [Social Science Academic Press] 2009).

People's Bank of China transferred its authority with regards to the securities market to the China Securities Regulatory Commission, and its supervision of the insurance market to the China Insurance Regulatory Commission, thus creating the basis for separate financial regulatory systems. In 2003, China reformed its financial system yet again by revising the Law on the People's Bank of China, which provides that the Bank's role is to ensure the formulation and implementation of national monetary policy, to establish and improve the Central Bank macro-control regulatory system, and to maintain financial stability.[110] At the same time, the government enacted the Banking Supervision Law, which clarified the authority of the banking regulatory body to monitor and regulate banking institutions and their business operations.[111]

The State Council's Decision on the Implementation of the Revenue-Sharing System of the Fiscal System was enacted in 1993 with regard to changes in China's taxation system. In accordance with the principle of combining financial revenue and financial expenditure, taxes were classified into three categories: central tax, local tax and shared tax. In addition, separate central and local taxation systems were established, with separate collection agencies for the two systems. Prior to the 2007 adoption of the new Enterprise Income Tax Law, estimates based on surveys of sources of corporate income tax showed that domestically funded enterprises had an average actual tax rate of approximately 25%, a figure which was 10% higher than foreign capital enterprises with a tax rate of approximately 15%. As such, there was high demand for a uniform tax rate in order to foster fair competition.[112] As a result of the enactment of the new Enterprise Income Tax Law in 2007, the enterprise income tax rate was uniformly set at 25% to advance equal treatment and fair competition. In addition, China revised the Tax Collection and Administration Law in 2001, which further improved the tax management system.

One legislative milestone during this phase was the enactment of the Anti-Monopoly Law. Before that, there were various rules prohibiting monopoly in the Anti-Unfair Competition Law (1993), the Price Law (1997), the Bidding Law (1999), and the Telecommunications Regulation (2000), but these rules proved insufficient in dealing with the changes in

---

[110] 中国人民银行法 [Law on the People's Bank of China] (promulgated by the Nat'l People's Cong., Mar. 18, 1995, effective Mar. 18, 1995) NAT'L PEOPLE'S CONG. GAZ. (P.R.C.), art. 1.

[111] 中华人民共和国银行业监督管理法 [Banking Supervision Law] (promulgated by the Standing Comm. Nat'l People's Cong., Dec. 27, 2003, effective Feb. 1, 2004) STANDING COMM. NAT'L PEOPLE'S CONG. GAZ. (P.R.C.), art. 1.

[112] 金人庆, 在第十届全国人民代表大会第五次会议上的《关于<中华人民共和国企业所得税法(草案)>的说明》[Jin Renqing, Speech at the Fifth Session of the Tenth National People's Congress: Explanation on the Draft Enterprise Income Tax Law] (2007), § 1, *available at* http://www.law-lib.com/fzdt/newshtml/20/20070308112435.htm (last visited Nov. 4, 2009).

the socialist market economy and meeting the growing demands of international competition.[113] Although there were rules meant to curb monopolistic behavior dispersed throughout various laws and regulations, without a separate anti-monopoly law operating as a complete and uniform system of administrative sanctions, such scattered rules could not effectively combat anti-competitive behavior. These rules ultimately did not serve their purposes well, due to the lack of an independent and authoritative enforcement agency, amongst other reasons.[114] After over ten years of research and repeated rounds of revisions, China enacted the Anti-Monopoly Law in 2007, addressing issues such as monopoly agreements, abuses of dominant market positions, abuses of administrative power to eliminate or restrict competition, and the investigation of suspected monopolistic conduct. The enactment of the Anti-Monopoly Law had far-reaching importance in preventing and restraining monopolistic behavior, protecting fair competition in the market, enhancing economic efficiency, safeguarding the interests of consumers and the general public, and promoting the healthy development of the socialist market economy.

China has continued to pursue economic development while advancing the notion of building a harmonious society according to the principles of democracy and rule of law, fairness and justice, honesty and friendliness, dynamism, safety and good order, and coexistence between mankind and nature.[115] As such, China's economic legal system has placed a strong emphasis on promoting intrapersonal harmony, and on harmony between nature and mankind. Moreover, the government has taken into account the growing income disparity brought by the country's rapid economic growth. Thus, the government has attempted to balance the different interests of the people and deal adequately with potential social conflicts in drafting economic legislation. Statistics show that in the twelve years between 1995 and 2006, the number of labor dispute cases in China multiplied by approximately thirteen times; in particular, the figure for collective labor disputes grew fivefold.[116] Because emphasis

---

[113] 曹康泰，在第十届全国人民代表大会常务委员会第二十二次会议上做的《〈反垄断法(草案)〉说明》 [Cao Kangtai, Speech at the Standing Committee of the Tenth National People's Congress: Explanation on the Draft Anti-Monopoly Law] (2006), *available at* http://www.npc.gov.cn/wxzl/gongbao/2007-10/09/content_5374671.htm (last visited Nov. 4, 2009).

[114] *See* 王晓晔，竞争法学 [WANG XIAOYE, COMPETITION LAW] 195–97 (社会科学文献出版社 [Social Science Academic Press] 2007).

[115] *See* 中国共产党中央委员会，中共中央关于构建社会主义和谐社会若干重大问题的决定 [CPC CENT. COMM., DECISION ON ESTABLISHING A SOCIALIST HARMONIOUS SOCIETY] (2006), *available at* http://news.xinhuanet.com/politics/2006-10/18/content_5218639.htm (last visited Nov. 4, 2009).

[116] 全国人大法律委员会主任委员，解读劳动合同法 [CHAIRMAN OF THE LAW COMM. OF THE NAT'L PEOPLE'S CONG., INTERPRETATION OF THE LABOR CONTRACT LAW] (2007), *available at* http://www.xinhuanet.com/zhibo/20070723/wz.htm (last visited Nov. 4, 2009).

has long been placed on the speed of economic growth, social legislation in China has lagged behind economic legislation for the past two decades.[117] However, since the notion of constructing a socialist harmonious society was first proposed in 2006,[118] China has reinforced legislation in the areas of labor relations and social security, by enacting and implementing the Labor Contract Law (2007), the Law on Employment Promotion (2007), the Law on Labor Dispute Mediation and Arbitration (2007), the Regulations on Paid Annual Leave of Workers (2007), and the Regulations on Labor Contact Law Enforcement (2008). These laws and regulations provide rules for the effective resolution of labor disputes. After the promulgation of the Labor Contract Law in 2008, the number of labor dispute cases submitted for arbitration increased by more than 98% compared with the number filed in 2007; these cases involved over 1.21 million workers.[119] In 2008, courts at all levels handled as many as 286,000 labor cases, 93.9% more than the number of cases handled in 2007.[120]

China has not neglected its efforts in environmental protection while developing its market economy, and has enacted a number of environmental laws and regulations such as the Law on the Prevention and Control of Atmospheric Pollution (as amended in 1995 and 2000), Law on Prevention of Environmental Pollution Caused by Solid Waste (as amended in 2004), Law on Prevention and Control of Environmental Noise Pollution (1996), Law on Anti-Desertification (2001), Law on Environmental Impact Assessment (2002), Law on the Promotion of Cleaner Production (2002), and the Law on Water Pollution Prevention and Control (as amended in 2008). Moreover, the country has established a relatively comprehensive legal system for environmental protection. With the latest scientific developments serving as a guide, China will seek to further balance the demands of both economic development and environmental protection, and strive to build an ecological and environment-friendly society.[121]

---

[117] 史探径, 社会法学 [SHI TANJING, SOCIAL LAW] 35 (中国社会保障出版社 [China Labor and Social Security Press] 2007).
[118] See CPC CENT. COMM., *supra* note 115.
[119] 人力资源社会保障部、国家统计局, 2008年人力资源和社会保障失业发展统计公报 (DEPT. OF HUM. RES. AND SOC. SEC. & NAT'L BUREAU OF STAT., STATISTICAL BULLETIN OF THE DEVELOPMENT OF HUMAN RESOURCES AND SOCIAL SECURITY IN 2008) (May 19, 2009), *available at* http://www.stats.gov.cn/tjgb/qttjgb/qgqttjgb/t20090519_402559984.htm (last visited Oct. 18, 2009).
[120] 王胜俊, 2008 年最高人民法院工作报告 [WANG SHENGJUN, SUPREME PEOPLE'S COURT WORK REPORT 2008] (2009).
[121] See 蔡守秋、王欢欢, 论加强环境法治文化建设的重要性和迫切性 [Cai Shouqiu & Wang Huanhuan, *The Importance and Urgency of Strengthening the Foundations of Environmental Law*], *in* 中国环境法治 (2007 年卷) [CHINESE ENVIRONMENTAL LAW (2007)] 27–33 (法律出版社 [Law Press] 2008).

Despite all the ups and downs experienced over the past six decades in the construction of China's economic legal system, the overall trend is a positive one, pointing towards progress and prosperity.

[15]

Berle and Means, Corporate Governance and the Chinese Family Firm

*Philip Lawton**

While concentrating primarily on the Hong Kong experience this paper will analyse the nature of the Hong Kong Chinese corporation from the point of view of corporate governance. Only in very exceptional circumstances do Chinese business organisations in corporate form develop into anything like the traditional model of the Anglo-American Berle-Means corporation characterised by a separation of ownership and management. Rather, they have strong, culturally based, characteristics which determine a particular type of hierarchical structure and often a tendency, as elsewhere, for a relatively short life cycle of two to three generations. For those, often family dominated, companies which do become listed, problems of compliance with standards of corporate governance imposed by the corporate law and listing rules regimes are common. One of the problem areas which will be explored in this paper is the recent attempt to introduce independent non executive directors, as an example of the imposition of a corporate governance norm which may not be easily accepted in the context of the Chinese family dominated listed company. The corporate and securities regime of Hong Kong is about to undergo a major review. This paper will argue that any review which fails to consider and take account of the cultural context in which legal business vehicles, including registered companies, operate, is liable to exacerbate rather than remedy the compliance and governance problems currently encountered. Before doing so I wish to make some points concerning recent research on the Berle-Means corporation and the influence of history, politics and culture on the various types of governance structure prevalent on today's worldwide corporate scene.

Economics, Politics and Culture as Influences on Corporate Structures

The idea that the Anglo American Berle/Means type of public listed company, characterised by a separation of ownership and management resulting from the need of growing enterprises for capital and the specialisation of management, is the most economically rational of large business organisational forms has been increasingly questioned in recent work. Roe argues that an important part of the Berle-Means corporation is the product of American politics, not just economic necessity.[1] He argues that the political element has two parts. The first being that powerful laws barred or restricted intermediaries in governance roles during most of the 20th century, a century which has been essentially one of growth for large firms. The second element according to Roe is that there is enough similarity in the pattern behind some

---

* Associate Professor of Law, City University of Hong Kong
1 M J Roe, "A Political Theory of American Corporate Finance", (1991) 91 *Colum L Rev* 10; M J Roe, "Political and Legal Restraints on Ownership and Control of Public Companies", (1990) 27 *J Fin Econ* 7. M J Roe, *Strong Managers Weak Owners: The Political Roots of American Corporate Finance*, Princeton University Press 1994.

of these laws to challenge whether economic evolution alone explains the shape of the large public firm. His thesis is that if the political system fragments intermediaries (and American populism, federalism, and interest groups in fighting did fragment them) then the Berle-Means corporation is inevitable.[2]

The classical economic explanation would, if it were universal in application, tend to predict that nations with similar economics would have similar corporate structures. Just as there may be a best way to manufacture a particular product such as steel, on this approach there is a best way to organise large steel firms. Therefore, managerial incentive compensation schemes, proxy fights, conglomerates takeovers, and boards of independent outsiders, all of which reflect the attempt to reduce the agency costs of organising the large American public firm should play a role in corporate governance in Germany and Japan. According to Roe, the absence of these features in the structures prevalent in Germany and Japan poses a challenge in that it shows that there is more than one way to deal with the large firm's organisational problems.[3] These differences in corporate structure indicate that differences in political histories, cultures and paths of economic development have a part to play in explaining the different structures.[4] The purely economic model, although important, must be considered in the context of these other factors and their no doubt complex interrelationships better understood. Therefore, much more research is required to understand and explain the relative role and interaction of each of these and possibly other factors in the development of corporate structures and modes of governance.

In the modern global economy competition exists not only among products, but also among governance systems. It is argued by some that the Chinese family business has a rationality of its own.[5] According to the Columbian school of thought real world competition has obliged business scholarship to focus on comparative corporate governance and in the light of the sometimes, if not often, better performance of other systems understanding the differences has become urgent.[6] However, models of governance elsewhere do not simply have the purpose, like the American system of solving the Berle-Means monitoring problem but often serve additional functions. Gilson and Roe have, for example, developed a model of the Japanese Keiretsu as involving

---

2 Roe, supra, n 1, *Strong Managers Weak Owners*, at 53.
3 M J Roe, "Some Differences in Corporate Structure in Germany, Japan, and the United States", (1993) 102 *Yale Law Journal* 1927 at 1929.
4 J Charkham, *Keeping Good Company: A Study of Corporate Governance in Five Countries*, Clarendon Press Oxford (1994) at 1-2, 249; Roe supra, n 3 at 1929.
5 This viewpoint seeks to explain the growth and strength of family business in Asia by focusing on family structure and affiliation networks. It opposes the joint stock company control concept (which presumes a linear type growth and expansion of enterprise organisation) insisting that the family business is not an early capitalist management form that will necessarily wither away in the midst of the advance of a modern joint stock company system but that the Asian, particularly the Chinese family business, has a rationality all its own: cf A Suehiro, "Family Business Reassessed: Corporate Structure and Late Starting Industrialisation in Thailand", (1993) 31 *The Developing Economies* 378 at 380.
6 Business Roundtable, "Corporate Governance and American Competitiveness" (1990) 46 *Bus Law* 241, 242-3; Charkham, n 4 at 1 cf n 1 supra.

not only governance, but also the need to support production and exchange, a system for which they coin the term "contractual governance".[7] I will return to this approach in the context of the Chinese family corporation later, when exploring the concept of networks of personalistic relationships which are often both internal and external to the Chinese firm.

Nevertheless, the Columbian analysis and the role of comparative governance studies has its detractors. In particular, Romano emphasises that without a means to make comparative judgments, truly helpful lessons cannot be drawn from other nations' experiences for the purpose of reforming corporate governance or at least the possibility of doing so is diminished. This undermines the rationale for making comparisons in the first place. Why, for example, should the corporate organisational form produced by a political process that empowers banks be viewed as preferable to a process that does not, without evidence of the superiority of the former organisational form? In reviewing extensive data on relative competitiveness she argues that the assumption of the superior competitiveness of German and Japanese firms over US firms is mistaken.[8] Other recent work by Edwards and Fischer on the merits of the bank based system in Germany, shows that the positive view of that system is not supported by the evidence. The supposed advantages of the bank's control of voting rights and representation on supervisory boards which, inter alia, allow for reduced asymmetric information problems thereby enabling banks to supply more external finance to firms at a lower cost and increase investment; and the control of management of firms on behalf of shareholders ensuring efficiency in terms of agency costs and outputs are overrated, according to Edwards and Fischer.[9]

They do however emphasise that there are many other respects in which Germany differs from eg, the UK or indeed other economies, which may be relevant for relative economic performance since 1945. These other factors could include: Germany's system of education and training, its structure of industrial democracy reducing confrontation between labour and management or contributing to overall efficiency as well as the country's macro economic policy. It is recognised therefore that it is impossible to conclude anything about the contribution of the German financial system to German economic performance on the basis of simple correlations which do not take account of other possible influences.[10] Nevertheless, problems of comparative study aside, the point is well made that other factors are relevant in the

---

7 R J Gilson and M J Roe, "Understanding the Japanese Kieretsu: Overlaps Between Corporate Governance and Industrial Organisation", (1993) 102 *Yale Law Journal* 871.

8 R Romano, "A Cautionary Note on Drawing Lessons from Comparative Corporate law", (1993) 102 *Yale Law Journal* 2021; J M Ramseyer, "Columbian Cartel Launches Bid for Japanese Firms", (1993) 102 *Yale Law Journal* 2005.

9 J Edwards and K Fischer, *Banks, Finance and Investment in Germany*, Cambridge University Press, 1994. A new law has recently been proposed which will eliminate German Banks' most powerful weapon at companies' annual general meetings: their right to cast proxy votes for other investors whose shares they manage. In future, German bankers will need explicit consent from clients to vote their shares, making it harder for them to use the proxies for their own ends, see "Banks and Industry Unburdening", *The Economist* 20 July 1996, at 67.

10 Ibid at 6.

understanding of economic competitiveness, the development of corporate structures and their legal regimes.

In this regard three basic points may be made about Hong Kong's economy and the nature of its largely family dominated businesses. They are first that its economy has some crucial differences particularly in its use of capital. Redding has argued that when comparing the overseas Chinese economies at large including Hong Kong's, with those of Japan, Europe and North America, the way capital is used in those Chinese contexts is different. There is a different strategic tendency, indicated by (a) the proliferation of small firms among the overseas Chinese, (b) the avoidance of highly complex, integrated, capital intensive structures such as are needed in car manufacture and heavy industry and (c) the tendency to concentrate in property, banking, commercial trading, and small scale manufacture.[11] This facet is closely interrelated with the second point namely the nature of the Chinese family firm, its strengths and problems in relation to its patrimonialistic control, the close relationship between authority and ownership and the firms external relationships being largely dependant on personalistic networks with suppliers, customers and other third parties.[12] This in turn leads to the third proposition which is also closely related to the first two, namely the relatively short life cycle of Chinese businesses and the fact that few Chinese companies in Hong Kong have reached the stage of separation of ownership and management. When they do there is a strong tendency to split up rather than successfully negotiate such a separation for a number of reasons which are partly cultural in nature.[13] The Berle-Means type corporation has simply not developed as a common type to date.[14]

I now propose to examine some key elements of the Chinese family firm and weave in, where appropriate, relevant similarities and differences in mainland China since, post 1997, the influence of business practice and corporate governance between Hong Kong's SAR and China will increasingly become a two way traffic.

---

11 S G Redding, *The Spirit of Chinese Capitalism*, Walter de Gruyter, Berlin, New York, 1993 at 216.
12 Ibid at 213, 221; S L Wong, "Chinese Entrepreneurs and Business Trust", *Business Networks and Economic Development in East and Southeast Asia*, ed G Hamilton, Centre of Asian Studies University of Hong Kong, 1991; C Tseng, "Uncovering the Asian Web", *World Executive Digest*, July 1996, 25-46.
13 S L Wong, "The Chinese Family Firm: A Model" (1985) 36 *The British Journal of Sociology* 58 at 67. Redding, supra, n 11 at 106-7, 178 and 216. See generally S L Wong, *Emigrant Entrepreneurs*, OUP, Hong Kong, 1988; V F S Sit, R D Cremer and S L Wong, *Entrepreneurs and Enterprises in Macau*, Hong Kong University Press, 1991.
14 The evidence that the managerial thesis of a separation of ownership and control as a corporation grows applies to, for example Britain and the USA, is at best tendentious, contrast the findings of E S Herman, *Corporate Control, Corporate Power* (1981), Cambridge University Press, New York, 1981 with those of P H Burch, *The Managerial Revolution Reassessed: Family Control in American Large Corporations*, Lexington Books, Lexington Mass, 1972 in relation to the USA; and P S Florence, *Ownership, Control and Success of Large Companies*, Sweet and Maxwell, London, 1961 with J P Scott, "Corporate Control and Corporate Rule: Britain in an International Perspective" (1990) 41 *British Journal of Sociology* 351.

Hong Kong's "Chinese family" corporations

Before considering Hong Kong it is important to note that according to Kirby[15] the history of company law in the first half of the twentieth century in China tends to show that the assumption of early reformers regarding the anonymous private corporation on a Western model as the essential means to "facilitate commerce and help industries", proved over optimistic. The record shows that with its own organisational structures and values rooted in networks of family and regional ties, what may be termed a "capitalism with Chinese characteristics" resisted the corporate structure even in the period of its dynamic growth in the first half of the twentieth century. However leery of government, China's capitalists appeared even more suspicious of the public, finding the idea that they would be invited to share in one's business's control and profits most dislikeable.[16]

A similar tendency is discernible in Hong Kong where Chinese businessmen initially rejected the partnership and corporate law imported from the UK, which they found quite alien, insisting on their Chinese partnership legal regime. Apart from the Western educated elite,[17] only after the second world war did local Chinese businessmen take to using the corporate form as a legal vehicle for business activity. So successful has the adoption of this legal form been that almost two thirds of all business registrations today are registered in the name of corporate bodies.[18]

The Legal Regime

The Law of Hong Kong is primarily influenced by that of England and Wales and to a lesser extent by that of Australia.[19] Hong Kong public companies, are in the main incorporated for a non commercial or quasi charitable purpose.[20] Those which are of a purely commercial or business nature are usually listed and quite closely controlled, since the minimum percentage of equity

---

15 W C Kirby, "China Unincorporated: Company Law and Business Enterprise in Twentieth Century China" (1995) 54 *Journal of Asian Studies* 43.
16 Li Chun, "The King-SSu-Uy of 1904 and the Modernisation of Chinese Company Law" (1974) 10 *Chengchi University Legal Review*, 17-21, continued (1974) 11 ibid at 163-209.
17 Research on the Japanese re-registration of companies during the Japanese occupation indicates that circa 254 limited companies were registered of which 218 have complete files. With only a couple of exceptions, all companies on the list are Chinese businesses, both managed and owned by Chinese. As a consequence of a fire that destroyed the British records, the Japanese re-registration constitutes the only surviving firm level data for the Hong Kong economy before the 1950's, Chung Wai Kung, "The Organisation of Chinese Businesses in Hong Kong During 1940s", presented at *The Rise of Business Corporations in China from Ming to Present at the Centre of Asian Studies*, The University of Hong Kong, 12-13 July 1996.
18 By March 1995 there were 636,312 businesses registered under the Registration of Businesses Ordinance and in excess of 470,000 registered companies.
19 The Hong Kong Companies Ordinance was until recently based on the UK Companies Act 1929. In 1984 it underwent substantial updating which has continued on an almost annual basis since. Similarly the Hong Kong Securities Ordinance bears a remarkable resemblance to the New South Wales Securities Industry Act 1975.
20 As at 31 December 1995 there were 6322 public companies on the register of companies in Hong Kong. Of these, 5655 were companies limited by guarantee: Company Registry Statistics 1995.

securities which must be in public hands may be between 10% and 25% depending on the market value of the applicant, and this is only exceptionally exceeded.[21] The vast majority of companies (both large and small) are private in nature.[22] From approximately 2000 companies registered in 1948 the number has risen to 471,883 by December 1995. To this must be added the increasing number of offshore incorporations which for political and fiscal reasons are often situated in tax havens such as the Bahamas or the British Virgin Islands.[23] Indeed the majority of Hong Kong's listed companies have, post 1989, incorporated their ultimate holding companies offshore.[24]

Many public listed and private Hong Kong companies retain many of the characteristics of small scale family businesses, such as paternalism, personalism, opportunism and flexibility, even when conducting a very large scale of operations. They do not display the characteristics of separation of ownership and control, professionalisation, bureaucratisation and neutralisation to anywhere near the same extent as their Western equivalents.[25]

There are even more fundamental differences in Hong Kong in relation to the core nature of the Chinese controlled corporation. In the Chinese context personal connections or guangxi have remained a key element of Chinese organisation. Law was never really available in China as a practical recourse for the merchant, and without such a backing all relationships remained personalised.[26] This in turn produced a barrier to the scale of enterprise, as important transactions would only be made face to face, and it made redundant any need for the professional executive who would rationally pursue goals on the part of others as part of a contractual exchange.[27] As Faure points out, for a long period of Chinese history, lineage and family connections were, and were recognised to be, the most fundamental relationships in economic organisation, not only for consumption but also for production and trade.[28] By placing a heavy emphasis on the family form of society, Confucianism sanctioned a family based economic system.[29]

---

21 See Rules Governing the Listing of Securities on the Stock Exchange of Hong Kong Ltd, r 8.08 and 8.09.
22 As at 31 December 1995 there were 465,561 private companies on the register: Company Registry Statistics 1995.
23 E L G Tyler, "Some Comments on Recent Hong Kong Incorporation Figures" HKICSA (1996) Company Secretary, Forthcoming.
24 By the end of 1995 of the 544 listed companies, 203 were registered in Hong Kong, 263 in Bermuda and 51 in the Cayman Islands.
25 S G Redding, supra n 11 at 3.
26 This is not to say that the "contract" the most common form of business institution was unknown in China, quite the contrary for the common use of contracts, in land transfer and partnership agreements suggests that contracts were widely used, D Faure, "Capitalism and the History of Chinese Business", presented at *The Rise of Business Corporations in China From Ming to Present*, Centre of Asian Studies, The University of Hong Kong, 12-13 July 1996.
27 S G Redding, supra n 11 at 136-7, 213-7; S L Wong, supra n 12.
28 D Faure, "The Lineage as Business Company: Patronage Versus Law in the Development of Chinese Business". Paper presented at the *Second Conference on Modern Chinese Economic History*, The Institute of Economics, Academic Sinica, Taipei, Taiwan, 5-7 January 1989, pp 347-76.
29 The role of Asian religion representing core societal values played a central role in economic development. For Weber the "tension" between religious ideals and practical reality was important. Its capacity to explain why some cultures strive to change the world and others

In China "law" was traditionally an expression of the rule of heaven (tianli or tiandao) and from this concept came the idea of gongdao which may roughly be translated as "justice" and is a term usually used when people think that a result is unacceptable or unjust and that something should be done to put it right. In theory law should be in harmony with, or in case of contradiction subordinate to, "the people's feeling" (renquing) following the view that "the rule of heaven is great because it is in line with people's feelings".[30] As the dominant school confucianism placed emphasis on "people's feeling" (renquing). Individuals are therefore more concerned about the feelings of those with whom closer personalistic ties (guanxi) exist. Since the family was conceived by Confucius as the basic social unit, family ties or feelings are strongest. From these basic units a network of class is formed and degrees of relationship with people from the same village or locality (tongxiang).[31] As a general rule, the combined effects of this emphasis on "people's feeling" and confucianism are that the closer the relationship the better the treatment will be: generally family members should be trusted and treated best, secondly your clansmen, then friends and colleagues and those who live in the same village, bear the same surname[32] or come from the same locality or province, and finally those who have no relationship with you.[33] There remain however some metatheoretical issues in the study of Chinese social interaction one of which is that the distinction between ideology, "ideal culture", or "big traditions" and on the ground behaviour, "real culture", or "little traditions", is insufficiently drawn. This encourages an overly enthusiastic application of confucian precepts to modern chinese life.[34]

According to Hamilton[35] one of the most successful attempts to envision the patterned differences between Western and Chinese societies is that of Fei Xiaotong originally published in 1947.[36] Explaining the organisational and social psychological differences between China and the West, Fei uses two

---

(those without the tension) see the world as unchangeable. For Weber Protestantism particularly was all about change and control, whereas Confucianism was all about the preservation of the status quo: M Weber, *The Religion of China*, 1951, pp 237, 241, 277. See generally R N Bellah, *Religion and Progress in Modern Asia*, 1965, p 145, Redding, supra, n 11 at 139-41.

30 Yinwenzi: Yinxun; cf n 36 infra.
31 For a positive view and examples of the influence of Confucianism, expressed in the form of clan or tongxiang relationships, on economic developments in Japan and the "Four Little Dragons", see Du Xuncheng *Zhong Guo Chuan Tong Lun Li Yu Jin Dai Zi Ben Zhu Yi (Traditional Chinese Ethics and Recent Capitalism)* Shanghai: Shanghai She Hui Ke Xue Yuen Press, 1993 56-61; for an illustration of the tongxiang phenomenon in the traditional Chinese commercial community, ibid 133-43. Contrast Redding supra n 11 at 111.
32 On the ground that if two persons have the same surname, they may be descendants of the same ancestor.
33 For a consideration of this phenomenon in the context of the enforcement of foreign arbitral awards in China see K Y Wong and D Roebuck, "The Influence of Traditional Morality on the Enforcement of Foreign Arbitral Awards in China", (1995) 5 *AJCL* 342.
34 W K Gabrenyu, Jr and K K Hwang "Chinese Social Interaction: Harmony and Hierarchy on the Good Earth" in *The Handbook of Chinese Psychology*, M H Bond, OUP, Hong Kong 1996 at 319.
35 G Hamilton, "Patriarchy, Patrimonialism and Filial Piety: A Comparison of China and Western Europe", (1990) 41 *British Journal of Sociology* 77.
36 Fei Xiatung, Xiangtu Zhongguo (Rural China), Hong Kong, Joint Publishing Co 1986 chs 4 and 5.

extended metaphors to explain the distinctive patterning in each society. Western society is compared to the way rice straw is gathered to build a haystack. Individuals obtain their identities from the organisation to which they belong or are affiliated to. These organisations have clearly defined boundaries. Organisations such as a club, or the office or a division of a corporation in which one works fit into other organisations, such as a city and so on, until the highest level subsuming organisation is reached. Fei believes this to be the Western state. In Hamilton's terms individuals fall under specific and distinct jurisdictions and take their rights and duties accordingly. Organisations from the club to the corporate workplace to the state legitimately constrain individual actions in separate but distinct ways.[37]

Chinese society in contrast does not build upon distinct basic social units. Fei demonstrates that even the Chinese family (jia) is not a clear social unit in the way it is in the West, but is ambiguous as to which relatives are included within this definition. The metaphor he uses for Chinese society is that of concentric rings flowing out from the centre when a stone is thrown into a lake. A Chinese person stands at the centre of the circles produced by his or her own social influence. The rings near the centre are those of kinship relations which are many and varied but they do take precedence over other more distant relationships as indicated above. Everyone's circles of influence or rings of relationship are interrelated, but no one person has exactly the same set. Unlike the clearly "organisational" jurisdictions in the West, Chinese relationships are ranked and the duties for each relationship are publicly known and to some extent codified. Fei suggests that individuals calculate their actions by knowing, not where they are organisationally, but rather by knowing with whom they are dealing and knowing the relationship that prevails.

Recent work on the role of personalistic relationships in China and the development of its new legal system has emphasised the continuing importance of such patterns of behaviour[38] and these are often mirrored in the internal management function and decision making process of mainland enterprises even at board level. As Child observes of senior mainland managers:

> The cultural tradition within which they work leads to an expectation that managers will attempt to accommodate the demands placed upon them through personal relations in which they endeavour to establish some tolerance based upon trust and negotiate in a relatively harmonious fashion some space within which to operate.[39]

In China the influence of renzhi and its direct counterpart guanxi inevitably lead to the "rule of the virtuous man", rather than the rule of law. However,

---

37 Hamilton, supra n 35 at 99.
38 Gabrenya and Hwang, supra, n 34, P B Smith and Z M Wang, "Chinese Leadership and Organisation Structures" in *The Handbook of Chinese Psychology* ed M H Bond, OUP, Hong Kong 1996 at 322-37; cf C A G Jones, "Capitalism, Globalisation and Rule of Law: An Alternative Trajectory of Legal Change in China", (1994) *Social Legal Studies* 195; A Smart, "Gifts, Bribes and Guanxi: a Reconsideration of Bourdieu's Social Capital" (1993) 8 *Cultural Anthropology* 388; R Tomasic, "Company Law and the Limits of the Rule of Law in China" (1995) 4 *AJCL* 470; Redding, supra n 11, ch 5.
39 J Child, *Management in China During the Age of Reform*, Cambridge University Press, 1994, at 145.

renzhi often results in government by whim or caprice. There are numerous examples of this, which when combined with government and justice by guanxi, often lead to attempts to nullify the rules which do exist or pervert the course of justice. This is also reflected to some extent in Hong Kong.[40] It has serious implications for regulatory compliance and enforcement.

Culture and Governance

The role of culture in the Hong Kong corporate governance context has also been examined by Tricker. He points out that the word "man" with all of its overtones of separateness, free will and individualism does not overlap in meaning with the Chinese word yan with all its overtones of connectedness and reciprocal relations. This has important implications for corporate governance. The original Western concept of the corporate entity creates a juristic person separate and distinct from its members. That juristic entity in law takes on the attributes of a person, a Western person. By way of contrast the Chinese perception of the nature of man as not being "separate" but connected and imbued with overtones of reciprocal relations "entails correspondingly different expectations of the corporate entity".[41] There is no real separation between family and company interests and a resulting lack of clarity as to where corporate boundaries lie. Furthermore, the question has been posed whether, given the lack of abstracts in the Chinese language and underlying differences in thought processes, the basic abstract concepts necessary for the development of modern Western corporations, and not only the concept of "separate legal personality", but also "marketing function", "financial control" and "divisionalisation", are not just foreign but somehow unnatural to Chinese organisations.[42]

Officials of Western origin in the Hong Kong Securities and Futures Commission (SFC) have expressed concern that the controllers of local listed companies sometimes fail to grasp the distinction between corporate and family property.[43] Perhaps the real concern is that in importing Western

---

40 For several anecdotal examples see N D Kristoff and S Wudunn, *China Wakes*, Nicholas Brealey Publishing, London, 1994, in particular the cases of Tang Rimei and Boss Wong at pp 27-30; Wang Chaoru and Grandma Zhang at 94-103; Wang Zhiqiang and fake medicine at 188-91; the case of the recycled hypodermic needles at 356-8 and for an overseas chinese entrepreneur allegedly using political contacts to circumvent the law see A L Neuman, "Who Loves Lucio" *Asia Inc* Vol 5 No 8 August 1996 at 21-6; cf A H Yee, *A People Misruled: The Chinese Stepping Stone Syndrome* 2nd ed, Heinemann Asia, Singapore, 1992, at 160-1; T W Lo, *Corruption and Politics in Hong Kong and China*, Open University Press, Buckingham 1993; R P L Lee (ed), *Corruption and its Control in Hong Kong*, Chinese University Press, Hong Kong, 1981.
41 R I Tricker, "Corporate Governance: A Ripple on the Cultural Reflection" in *Capitalism in Contrasting Cultures*, eds S R Clegg and S G Redding, Walter de Gruyter, 1990.
42 Redding, supra n 11 at 141. As to problem of translation, see D Roebuck and K K Sin, "The Ego and I and Ngo: Theoretical Problems in the Translation of the Common Law into Chinese" in *Hong Kong, China and 1997: Essays in Legal Theory*, ed R Wacks, Hong Kong University Press 1993; cf, J T Wu and I M Liu "Chinese Lexical Access"; H C Chen, "Chinese Reading and Comprehension: A Cognitive Psychology Perspective", C K Leong and S Hsiu "Cross Linguistic Constraints on Chinese Students Learning English" in *The Handbook of Chinese Psychology*, ed M H Bond, OUP, Hong Kong 1996.
43 Discussion with former SFC officials and members of the HK Company Law Reform Committee.

corporate concepts regulators have failed to realise the significance of local culture and that the local perspective of and use of the corporate form is in some ways fundamentally different. The problem is exacerbated by the ambiguities of relationships in relation to property which is exemplified by the following quotes:

> You have to understand a Chinese family. There is no difference between my father's personal investments versus my personal investments. Its one. It is called family investment and that is it.[44]

And in contrast:

> Capital accumulation is to keep the company running. That was my father's philosophy. It is not personal property. It belongs to all contributors, the staff included.[45]

The latter quote may be viewed in terms of a family estate not being personal property in the sense of belonging to an individual but as family property in the sense that the family estate is a business and the family is notionally extended to include loyal staff.[46]

This attitude to property may also be reflected in the patterns of corporate control. As Scott has commented:

> Any comparative account of corporate control must recognise that while there are certain uniformities of technology and business practice in all of the major capitalist economies there are equally important divergencies arising from specific historical experiences and differing cultural and legal systems. These national variations shape the constraints which operate on the actions and orientation of business leaders and result in the existence of a number of alternative patterns of capitalist development. The pattern taken by impersonal possession in Britain, the USA, Australia, Canada and New Zealand is to be seen as the outcome of a specific convergence of national and international forces in the Anglo-American, English speaking world. In other parts of the world, and under the impact of other forces, different patterns of impersonal possession are apparent.[47]

The separate juristic nature of the corporation and its economic counterpart the concept of personal property represented by shares in the corporation as distinct from industrial property represented by the property owned by the registered company does not fit well with the cultural milieu of the Chinese family firm.

Although the Western based legal business system in Hong Kong gave Chinese entrepreneurs a freedom of opportunity which they seized, it was adapted to their cultural context.[48] Incorporation is used and limited liability

---

44 Victor Li (son of Li Ka Shing) quoted in D Gutslein, *The New Landlords: Asian Investment in Canadian Real Estate*, Press Parcepic, Vancouver, 1990.
45 Redding, supra n 11 at 195.
46 S L Wong, "The Chinese Family Firm: A Model" (1985) 36 *The British Journal of Sociology* 58 at 64.
47 J P Scott, "Corporate Control and Corporate Rule: Britain in an International Perspective" (1990) 41 *British Journal of Sociology* 351 at 371.
48 For a discussion of this adaptation in a historical context see E L G Tyler, "Does the Complexity of Companies Legislation Impede Entrepreneurship? The Hong Kong Experience" delivered at the *Conference on Market Forces and the Law*, Beijing University 21-2 October 1994.

welcomed, but the underlying nature of a Chinese family owned business has significant implications for a Western concept of corporate governance. Chinese family based organisations are described as being imbued with "patrimonialism", which includes features such as paternalism, hierarchy, responsibility, mutual obligation, family atmosphere, personalism and protectionism. Redding identifies three related themes which flow from these and are in some senses expressions of patrimonialism: the idea that power cannot really exist unless it is connected to ownership; a distinct style of benevolently autocratic leadership and personalised as opposed to neutral relations.[49]

A distinct and particularly Chinese organisational characteristic, viewed from a Western managerial perspective as a defect, arises because corporate power derives from ownership which is vested in a family rather than an individual. Nobody outside the owning group can generate for himself truly legitimate authority. Chinese family businesses are often unable to escape autocratic control because of a common inability to delegate and inherent mistrust (especially of professionals) makes it very difficult to graft into the organisation a middle and senior management group made up of competent professionals.[50]

Wong identifies various instances when a Chinese family business comes under breakup stresses. One of these is the third generation problem which clearly reflects a major difficulty in pushing a Chinese family business through a Western style managerial revolution to transfer power to professional executives and divorce, to some extent, ownership and control.[51] Resistance to the competent non family executive remains strong and is potentially dangerous for him if he is perceived as a threat. Given the endemic leaning towards secrecy in Chinese family businesses, as in other aspects of life,

---

49 Redding, supra n 11 at 155. It has been argued that authority relations identified by the terms patriarchy, patrimonialism, and filial piety represent very different complexes of action in Imperial China and Western Europe, G Hamilton, "Patriarchy, Patrimonialism, and Filial Piety: A Comparison of China and Western Europe" (1990) 41 *British Journal of Sociology* 77.

50 Redding, supra n 11 at 158, 159. Exceptional examples include Mr Li Ka Shing, Sir Y K Pao, Mr Fung King Hey, Mr Liem Sioe Liong. See generally Redding, supra n 11 at 165, 207-12. See also Child, supra n 39 at chs 5, 8. It may be noted that Li Ka Shing's delegation of management responsibilities may be out of necessity. Amongst the largest Chinese family owned or controlled enterprises in Hong Kong both listed and unlisted his holdings are amongst the small minority in which the founder has so few blood relatives in control. He has no brother and no sister in Hong Kong. His sons are young for a man of his age although both of them are in the family business. In the years of business expansion Lee simply had to delegate. There are numerous examples of family managed second and third generation companies: eg the Garden Co Ltd (known as the baker to Hong Kong) is run now by three sons and two daughters of the founder; the Lui Chong Hing Bank is now run by the Lui Brothers, sons of the founder. Lee Kam Kee Ltd, the oyster sauce company, Wing On Co Ltd, the merchandiser, are run by the sons and grandsons of their founders. The Bank of East Asia and the Wing Lung Bank are still run by the sons and daughters of the founding families. Cf the study of the Sincere Co Ltd in P Lawton, "Expanding Shareholder Control in Hong Kong" in *Legal Developments in China: Market Economy and the Law*, ed G G Wang and Z Y Wei, Sweet and Maxwell, Hong Kong 1996, at 88-9. For a changing perspective see "Like Father, Unlike Son", *World Executive Digest* August 1996, 26.

51 Cf supra n 13.

simply knowing too much about the business could constitute such a threat.[52] This has serious implications for any attempt to introduce non executive directors.

There are however Chinese corporations in south east Asia which have to some extent evolved beyond the concept of guanxi and developed non particularistic ties as a major factor in their business strategy, but they remain few and far between.[53] Reliance on personal ties within and without the Chinese family firm give it the special advantages that enable it to be so successful in the context and on the terms in which it operates. Networks of external personal relationships and an autocratic span of control within allow the Chinese family business to prosper and respond to challenges such as, for example, the need to retool with almost acrobatic flexibility. The other side of the coin, however, relates to limitations on the growth in size of the business and potential break up stresses. When an organisation begins to grow the Chinese capacity for mistrust "begins to weaken the seams in the fabric".[54] Companies do not cope well with the maintenance of control as they expand into new markets, new products and new technologies. In fact such challenges are often avoided and the vast majority of companies remain small.[55]

As regards the issue of maintaining control and venturing into large scale operations Redding identifies two possibilities, particularly in the context of Hong Kong.[56] One route is to graft on professional management and build a conglomerate. Strategic thinking may still be retained by family members, while divisional operations are left in the hands of professional managers. According to Redding the few conglomerates that have emerged tend to suffer from power disputes dividing the professionals and the owning entrepreneurial strategists. This type of large operation remains very much the exception remarkable for their rarity.[57]

One company which might be regarded as an example of a relatively successful conglomerate is Hutchinson which is involved in property, shops and store chains such as "Watsons" and "Park and Shop" and general trading. The company was originally founded by a flamboyant Australian Douglas Clague.[58] In the business recession of 1974 Hong Kong Bank invested in the company and obtained equity control, showing Clague the door. After turning

---

52 Redding, supra n 11 at 178.
53 Cf L Sunyadinata, "Chinese Economic Elites in Indonesia: A Preliminary Study" in *Changing Identities of the Southeast Asian Chinese since World War II*, ed J Cushman and G W Wang, HKU Press (1988); J Cushman, "The Khaw Group: Chinese Business in Early Twentieth Century Penang", (1986) 17 *Journal of Southeast Asia Studies* 58-79.
54 Redding, supra n 11 at 214.
55 See generally ibid, ch 9 "Sources of efficiency and failure".
56 Ibid at 219-20.
57 In other South East Asian countries there are examples of successful conglomerates see for example Y Sato "The Salim Group in Indonesia: The Development and Behaviour of the Largest Conglomerate in Southeast Asia" (1993) 31 *The Developing Economies* 408-41; and for a successful conglomerate along the lines described by Redding see I Numazaki, "The Tainanbary: The Rise and Growth of a Banana-Bunch-Shaped Business Group in Taiwan" (1993) 31 *The Developing Economies* 485-509, and for the Chinese family business in Thailand see A Suehiro, "Family Business Reassessed: Corporate Structure and Late Starting Industrialisation in Thailand", (1993) 31 *The Developing Economies* 378-407.
58 Douglas Clague was also responsible for building the first cross harbour tunnel in HK, cf D Wilson, *Hong Kong* Unwin Hyman London, 1990 at 186.

the company around, the bank sold its controlling share to Li Ka Shing. He is one of the few Hong Kong entrepreneurs recognised for an ability to trust and delegate to professional management.

The alternative, more successful route is to choose a business or industry which has the following characteristics:
  (a) large but relatively infrequent judgemental decisions, as for example in property;
  (b) day to day operations which can be replicated using a standardised formula, and easily controlled or managed contractually, as for example in shipping or hotel management.
  (c) financing which can be based in the headquarters city on an individual's reputation.

In such a context to extend the influence of the key executive group or individual is much more feasible. Hong Kong examples of Chinese companies with these characteristics include Cheung Kong Holdings based on the skills of Mr Li Ka Shing and World Wide Shipping, based on the skills of the late Sir Y K Pao.

At this point it is perhaps important to note the role of banks in the development of these larger businesses. Wong has dispelled the view that overseas Chinese businesses do not use banks as a source of finance.[59] Simple pragmatism dictates that they will when appropriate and business historians have extensively documented these relationships.[60] The Hong Kong Bank, in particular played an important role in the development of a number of Hong Kong businesses particularly in times of crisis as indicated in the Hutchinson example referred to above. Their equity investments were often used in some of the boardroom struggles and intercompany rivalries, especially where these allowed the bank to tip the scales in favour of Hong Kong Chinese entrepreneurs of proven ability (eg Sir Y K Pao and Li Ka Shing) at the expense of older British companies which appeared to have lost their way or become overstretched. In this sense the bank fulfilled a politico-sociological as well as a financial function. At one point the bank held a half of Pao's shipping companies and a fifth of Hutchinson Whampoa and Eastern Asia Navigation as well as a quarter of Cathay Pacific Airways and almost half of the South China Morning Post.[61] Banks have therefore played an important if not crucial role in relatively recent times, by means of equity investments, in the development and survival of Hong Kong's larger listed companies. Similarly, in earlier periods, networking in Chinese business was strongly characterised by internal banking in the sense that the banker would enter into businesses as a partner, and that he would do so in a wide range of businesses in the search of good returns and in order to spread his risk.[62]

---

[59] See Generally Sources in n 13 supra.
[60] See Faure, supra, n 26; R A Brown, "Chinese banking Networks in SE Asia"; presented at *The Rise of Business Corporations in China From Ming to Present*, Centre of Asian Studies, The University of Hong Kong 12-13 July 1996.
[61] Wilson, supra n 58 at 164 and see generally ch 17.
[62] Faure, supra n 26 at 22. The only competition in later periods, for example the late nineteenth and early twentieth century was from Western capital, but even here the institution of the compradore assisted in funnelling Western capital into Chinese "mixed" banking cartels; Brown, supra n 60; cf P T Lee, "Business Networks and Patterns of

Vertical Cooperation, Meetings and Management style: The Problem of Governance and Control

One of the perceived weaknesses of the strong paternalistic Confucian style of management is the limitation of the strong vertical cooperation which gives strength on a small scale of operation but is a source of inefficiency and failure in the context of large size and growth. The key question is how far one person's decision making can be stretched. There are examples of Western and Japanese CEOs who have extensive influence throughout their corporations but it may be emphasised that they establish a system and a culture which expresses their policies, and then other people can make large decisions within that framework.[63] In the context of the Hong Kong Chinese corporation the issue is the extent of the authority of the paternalistic controller, that person's decision making, his or her direct involvement. Successful large organisations have devised a formula for gearing up on the strategic intelligence of the dominant individual. Examples from shipping and property have been referred to above. In other spheres particularly product markets this is more difficult because a greater variety of factors need to be considered and in such circumstances, a one man decision making process will eventually lead to inadequately informed and late decisions leading to decline in the fortunes of the business.

Personalistic methods of control do have advantages in terms of internal transaction costs due to less paperwork and fewer formalities just as the external trust networks of personalistic social/business relationships lends to efficiency of transaction costs in economic exchanges. This is because transactions may be dealt with reliably and quickly by telephone or handshake or over dim sum whereas in a Western context they would require lawyers, contracts, guarantees, wide opinion seeking and investigation all accompanied by inevitable delay.[64] Such an approach is mirrored in mainland China where foreign businessmen often complain bitterly about the delays associated with establishing such relationships and the shifting sands of Chinese negotiation tactics.[65]

While in recent years delayering and re-engineering has eliminated much of middle management in listed corporations in the Western world, Chinese family controlled listed and unlisted corporations have relatively little middle management if only because management and strategic decisions are made at the highest levels of the corporation and executed by staff who report directly to the corporate "management person" (who will also often be CEO/MD) or management team. As a result these corporations rarely have retainers such as legal, accounting and marketing management save and except what may be characterised as support staff.[66]

Cantonese Compradors and Merchants in Nineteenth Century Hong Kong (1995) *Journal of the Hong Kong Branch of the Royal Asiatic Society* 1.

63 Redding, supra n 11 at 212.
64 Ibid at 213 and 219.
65 Child supra n 39, ch 11.
66 Contrast the development of the British Brewing Industry where after incorporation in the later 1890s and early 1900s, many brewing companies operated much as they had done before, ie as Family businesses, but many made the transition from a family based to a more

All of this has important implications for the role of meetings and the decision making process in governance structures. The Western format of the structured meeting with the occasional expression of differences of opinion is often viewed with anathema in a culture based on the avoidance of conflict, consensus and personalistic relations in the overall context of what is often an autocratic leadership or management system imbued with deference to authority.[67]

A perusal of the annual reports of many listed companies in Hong Kong will reveal the extent to which a large number of such companies farm out their compliance work to service companies and individuals who provide company secretarial services.[68] Several years ago the Carrian affair was the subject of criminal proceedings. During those proceedings one of the senior partners of a leading law firm gave evidence to the effect that his company secretarial staff would prepare minutes of Carrian Group company meetings in one of three ways. These were either by having someone present (which he admitted was rare); or by asking the directors to recount what was discussed and decided; or by using their sense of imagination.[69] This is indicative of the local style where decisions are made and then lawyers etc approached where appropriate. I have discussed the technical and often disastrous legal consequences of such decision making elsewhere with graphic Hong Kong case examples.[70] Suffice it to say that it is a reflection of the reality of the Hong Kong situation, namely that its corporate law regime is often little more than the formal clothing for, what in substance remains, essentially a familiar and personalistic Chinese organisation.

In the view of one Western educated local management consultant, board meetings are hardly ever confrontational unless there is a serious breakdown in personal relationships. Where a difference of opinion on, for example, a proposed course of action exists, the parties will simply state their positions. There is no attempt to openly debate and resolve a conflict. A compromise will be reached or decision made behind the scenes without an open loss of face

---

professional top management in the period 1914-55. The introduction of trained brewers, company secretaries, lawyers and later, accountants, to brewing boards gave companies more of the skills necessary to the effective supervision of a modern business enterprise. This helped with problems of succession. T R Gourvish and R G Wilson, *The British Brewing Industry 1830-1980*, CUP, Cambridge, 1994, at 389 et seq.

67 In one Securities and Futures Commission investigation into the affairs of a Hong Kong listed company it was discovered that the head of the company often made a decision which would then be communicated, inter alia, by telephone message to board members as a de facto decision of the board. Interview with former SFC official.

68 According to one recent report into the role of the company secretary in Hong Kong up to 67% of listed companies delegate shareholder registration and relations to outside firms, Tricker et al, *The Company Secretary in Hong Kong's Listed Companies*, HKICSA, 1995 at 6-9.

69 Cf paper by John Brewer FCIS, Chief Executive HKICSA, "The Legal Liabilities of the Company Secretary" at the *Asian Law Journals Conference on Company Secretaries Legal Liabilities*, 28 October 1994 Century Hotel Hong Kong. Cf "Share transfers to names of nominees" *South China Morning Post (SCMP)* 18 April 1996.

70 P Lawton, "Corporate Governance and Informal Decision Making: The Theoretical and Practical Limits of Hong Kong's Legal Regime", (1995) 1 *Corporate Governance Quarterly* (Issue 1) 17-24; (Issue 2) 29-41.

which is potentially damaging for both sides.[71] This is not very different from the situation in the boardrooms of many UK listed companies according to the work of Hill.[72] The evidence there is similar. The majority of executive directors prefer not to disagree openly in public. Disagreements are voiced privately. A board meeting is a decision making event not a debate. Any debate will usually have taken place prior to the meeting. It is therefore most likely that any cultural differences will impact at that earlier stage. The greater power-distance relationship in Hong Kong Chinese society and, for example, differences in humour will affect the extent to which dissent is expressed as well as the manner and force with which it is done.[73] Similar observations have been made in relation to the operation of boards of directors in Sino-Western joint ventures but with the importance of the impact of culture on this phenomenon emphasised. Björkman, notes that the risk of losing face, the tendency of the "superior" to talk for most of the time inhibiting input from directors and the need for permission from superiors before being able to support a board decision (which is difficult to obtain during a meeting) all militate against open debate and discussion in board meetings. Also, in the context of a joint venture, the trust and general relationship between the foreign partner and the Chinese is likely to deteriorate if they openly show that they have conflicting ideas. A failure to realise this on the part of the foreign partner has led to total deadlock at both board and operational level in the initial stages of several joint ventures. Later, several stages of consultation were adopted resulting in a smooth formal board meeting for which the minutes have often been written in advance.[74]

The Hong Kong scenario of an avoidance of structured meetings and a preference for unscheduled, unstructured meetings, cultivating informal personal contacts therefore appears to be even more accentuated in studies of mainland Chinese enterprises. Stewart suggests that one reason for this is the limited experience and competence of mainland Chinese managers in the use of formal scheduled meetings:

> in the Western world schedule meetings as a communication medium have been fully developed and practised with sets of structured, formal and commonly accepted meeting procedures, and their actions in information dissemination and problem solving are well exploited. However, these procedures and functions are still somewhat lacking in China. Instead, the PRC managers tend to attach different values to attending scheduled meetings (cultivating interpersonal relationships,

---

71 Interview with management consultant.
72 S Hill, "The Social Organisation of Boards of Directors", (1995) 46 *British Journal of Sociology* 245 at 253.
73 Note the differences between British and German managers in this respect. The latter have a relatively low power distance score like the British but a high uncertainty avoidance score, cf G Hofstede, *Culture and Organisations: Software of the Mind*, McGraw Hill (Europe), 1991 at 109-17. Their differences in attitudes to and use of meetings are markedly different as are their attitude to the tolerance for ambiguity and use of humour to ease relationships and conflict and note the marked British practice of injecting humour into most mundane requests to cancel any hint of authoritarianism; R Stewart, J L Barsoux et al, *Managing in Britain and Germany*, St Martins Press, New York, 1994, at 97-8 and 168-71.
74 I Björkman, "The Board of Directors in Sino-Western Joint Ventures", (1995) 3 *Corporate Governance* 156 at 164.

showing one's commitment, diligence and fishing for unsystematic information) but these aims are more easily achieved in unscheduled meetings.[75]

The traditional approach and its value to mainland Chinese managers is also emphasised by Stewart:

> the value of unscheduled meetings in the PRC is due to another factor. The importance of Guanxi, or personal connections, in China is well known ... The unscheduled meetings provide ways in which to cultivate valuable interpersonal relationships more easily than during formal occasions. Most managers interviewed stressed the need to develop and maintain good working relationships with colleagues and environmental contacts: they saw this as the chief factor in their career success.[76]

Child also makes similar and forceful points concerning the conduct of high level scheduled meetings in China:

> It is rare for such meetings to have a formal agenda or for papers to be presented to members in advance. Discussion defers very much to the most senior person present, who is generally more concerned to establish a climate of consensus around general principles or directions of policy than to raise specific issues. His or her approach looks to securing agreement on these general lines, which can then serve as the justification for arrangements and deals that are later struck through informal personal discussions. The outcome of these meetings is sometimes left so vague that it is not even clear what has been agreed. Normally, no minutes are taken though various clerks will take copious notes which are then filed away primarily to protect the heads of their departments or units should any dispute or criticism later arise. This means that follow up action has to be initiated personally by the senior manager and that the next meeting does not necessarily review progress on any systematic basis. It all reinforces the ever continuing need of Chinese senior managers, and directors in particular, to deal with matters on a personal basis.[77]

Child goes on to pose the question whether Chinese senior managers' reluctance to delegate and their inclination to handle matters personally can be viewed as a response to the system of industrial governance within which they operate (particularly the power structure and informational environment), to the competencies at their disposal, or to their cultural context.[78] It is reasonable to assume that the cultural characteristics discussed earlier will reinforce the hierarchical top down command structure that China's economy acquired under socialism and from which it is slowly retreating.[79]

One might step back at this point and contrast the approach in the UK, for long the model of Hong Kong's Corporate legal regime and governance system. As Charkham points out, boards of UK quoted companies take meetings seriously and this is reflected by Hill.[80] However, "any chairman can 'fix' the composition of the board or the agenda or the information or the meeting. It is no wonder that two boards with identical structures may be quite different in their effectiveness. It is the possibility of such extreme variation that underlines the importance of the role of the non executive directors and

---

75 S Stewart, "China's Managers", (1992) 34 *The International Executive* 165 at 176.
76 Ibid at 178.
77 Child, supra n 39 at 152-3.
78 Ibid, at 153.
79 Ibid, at 39.
80 Charkham, supra n 4 at 264, Hill, supra n 72.

... requires the active vigilance of the shareholders."[81] Charkham's acid test of the effectiveness of non executive directors is the "say 'No' test".[82] In the consensus and high power-distance context of Hong Kong Chinese firms this poses serious problems, but as Charkham points out the test is not as negative as it sounds because it is based on the important principle, in a Western context, of reciprocal respect. If a CEO and the board do not respect each other the system will not work as it should. Failing this acid test means that boards are not boards at all but merely advisory committees. This poses serious questions concerning the recent Hong Kong Stock Exchange introduction of a requirement for listed companies to appoint independent non executive directors.

The cultural aspects of interlocking directorships and their impact on the introduction of non executive directors in Hong Kong

I have briefly examined the introduction and role of independent non executive directors (NEDs) in Hong Kong in the context of directors' remuneration in an earlier volume of this journal.[83] I now, wish to re-examine that issue emphasising the cultural aspects of interlocking directorships and the implications for independent NEDs in Hong Kong.

The significance of interlocking directorships has been interpreted in the context of several models, each postulating distinct mechanisms and processes in the exercise of economic power. There are also a number of contending perspectives often associated with rival political positions.[84] However, the fundamental question remains, irrespective of the perspective or position within which interlock researchers work, namely what does an interlocking directorship signify? Scott asserts that the majority of researchers have gradually come to realise that interlocks are most usefully treated as indicators of social relations.[85] Given the importance of social and personal relations in the Hong Kong business context the introduction of independent NEDs was bound to meet with some resistance.

In fact many listed companies had problems complying with the deadline. At an executive conference organised by HKICSA, Mr Keniel Wong a director of the HKSE listing division stated in his speech that as of 1 December 1994, one month before the deadline for the appointment of the second NED, 6 listed companies had not yet appointed their first NED and over 100 had not appointed their second. The deadline was subsequently extended by 3 months.[86] This is not surprising. The work of Gilbert Wong on interlocking directorships in Hong Kong demonstrates a distinctive

---

81 Ibid at 267.
82 Ibid at 268.
83 P Lawton, "Directors' Remuneration, Benefits and Extractions, an Analysis of their Uses, Abuses and Controls in the Corporate Government Context of Hong Kong" (1995) 4 *AJCL* 430, at 452-5.
84 J Scott, "Theoretical Framework and Research Design" in *Networks of Corporate Power*, eds F N Stokman, R Zeigler and J Scott, Polity Press, Cambridge, 1985.
85 Scott, supra n 84 at 13.
86 Speech given at HKICSA Conference "Advice to Directors and the Board - the Critical Issues" 3 December 1994.

interlocking behaviour in the nature of Chinese firms in Hong Kong. His research demonstrates that the ownership and control of the top 100 largest corporations in Hong Kong has actually become more concentrated and personalised in recent years and more of the boards were controlled by family members of the major shareholders. Many characteristics of the traditional small Chinese family firms were brought into large corporations which were once controlled by British owners and managements. Given the high degree of personalism in the management of Chinese family businesses, inter corporate relationships became more personal and informal. According to Wong, formal business networking ties in the form of outside directors appointed to created corporate interlocks, is not a major ingredient in the Chinese business recipe. When Chinese business relationships are often based on personal trust it may well be regarded as an affront to the integrity of the businessmen concerned to force them to accept the Western method of using outside directors to safeguard investment interests.

In this context of listed companies characterised by concentrated ownership relying on personalised trust and control the emphasis is on the use of multiple executive directorships. This fosters an inward orientation based an inter corporate relationships generally limited to the in group of businesses which are possessed of strong associations with each other based on ownership ties, family and other traditional linkages. According to Wong therefore:

> The intense and personal commitment of executive directors to the family firms also means that it would be unlikely for other business to invite them to serve as non executive directors. Their independence, in the context of the competitive environment of Hong Kong, would be questionable. In this situation, directorate linkages, if required at all, will be effected through outsiders who are not executives of either of the connected businesses. In consequence, executive and non executive directors take up different roles in the Chinese businesses and this leads to a sharper differentiation in the roles of the strong and weak ties in the interlocking directorates.[87]

Wong emphasises the importance of the cultural factor in shaping business behaviour in Hong Kong and highlights the limitations of applying "Western" theoretical models straightforwardly in the Asian societal context. Therefore the configuration of directorates ties, must be explicated in the context of the social culture in which they are found irrespective of whether they follow resource interdependence, ownership, family relation or some other social and economic pathway.

The emphasis in both the Cadbury and Bosch reports tends to be on the monitoring role of executive directors. A polarisation of attitudes between family executive directors and NEDs may well result from such an approach in the context of the Chinese family dominated listed company. As Redding observes: "The grafting on of new outsiders at a senior level in such organisations is particularly difficult, given the lengthy socialisation needed for understanding the organisation's core and often concealed features, but

---

87 G Wong, "The Changing Patterns of Interlocking Directorates in Hong Kong - The Effects of the Rise of Chinese Big Business in the Period 1976-1986", paper presented at the conference *The Last Half Century of the Chinese Overseas (1945-1994): Comparative Perspectives*, University of Hong Kong, 19-21 December 1994 at 9-10.

more particularly given the problem of time needed for the essential networking, not just outside but also inside the company."[88] Although NEDs are not executive managers or directors in the personalistic context of Hong Kong they must be, acceptable to the "governing" family and gain their trust. This will erode their independence and capacity to say "No". Problems have emerged of access to information and the use of informal channels upsetting the delicate relationship of trust, confidence, and in the words of Charkham "reciprocal respect" that must exist between a managing director and the board. It has been reported that in one Hong Kong listed company non executive directors are allowed to see relevant papers at the start of board meetings and have them taken away at the end.[89] This reflects the initial lack of trust which may well arise in the context of a Chinese family controlled listed company when they are forced to accept relative outsiders. Yet issues of confidentiality if not secrecy are also of importance in the Western context. All directors whether executive, nominee executive or non executive, and independent NEDs owe a duty of confidentiality to the board and case law has confirmed this.[90] Indeed the report of the UK Committee of Public Accounts on the role and responsibilities of nominee directors emphasised that nominee directors could not assist government departments and non departmental public bodies directly in the monitoring process, or pass confidential company information to them, without the prior agreement of companies or unless special arrangements such as contractual conditions of financial assistance permitted them to do so.[91]

Perhaps the better approach to boards as whole, is that of the Hilmer Committee's "Strictly Boardroom". That emphasises the theme that formal rules which are imposed on boards to ensure conformance with external requirements, must not be allowed to prevent directors from achieving the main goal which boards must serve. The boards key role is defined as ensuring that corporate management is continuously and effectively striving for above average performance taking account of risk.[92] This does not deny the boards additional role with respect to shareholder protection. In relation to strategy and policy, Hilmer felt that the board of a large public company is an inappropriate body for developing strategy, setting corporate culture and policy and initiating major decisions. Instead the board should concentrate on the critical review of proposals, with management having the primary duty to formulate and then implement proposals.[93] NEDs should concentrate on keeping the board's primary performance responsibility at the top of the agenda. Such an approach may be received more positively in Hong Kong and would certainly leave the controlling family heads free to devise strategy and policy. The problem of allowing that strategy to be reviewed by relative

---

88 Redding, supra n 11 at 218-19.
89 S Fluendy, "Call for Action on Directors", *South China Morning Post (SCMP)* 18 October 1994.
90 *Bell v Lever Bros Ltd* [1932] AC 161, HL at 194; *Harkness v Commonwealth Bank of Australia Ltd* (1993) 32 NSWLR 543.
91 House of Commons, First Report from the Committee of Public Accounts Session 1985-6, "Role and Responsibilities of Nominee Directors", vii.
92 Hilmer Committee, Strictly Boardroom at 33.
93 Ibid ch 3.

outsiders would however remain difficult to surmount.

Non executive directors have recently played a key role in the removal of members of a founding family from the board of a listed property developer, Keng Fong Sin Kee Construction & Investment Co after perceived abuses on their part. The managing director was quoted as saying "Having two independent non executive directors on the board is the best thing the stock exchange has done in the market". In that case it was other members of the extended family which voted the directors out of office. Where the situation is one of a united controlling family versus the investing public the task of NEDs may not be so easy.[94]

One issue which over time may prove of significance is the increase in and demand for well educated and professionally trained managers. In recent years Hong Kong has expanded its tertiary education sector and courses in business studies and related fields have mushroomed in response to a high level of demand.[95] Much the same has happened in the context of legal studies. A similar phenomenon has occurred in China with the demand for trained management not only in the state sector but in the ever increasing number of joint venture projects in China. A large number of mainland Chinese are increasingly opting for business and management studies particularly in the USA.[96] The extent to which this will influence business, management and to some extent corporate governance practices in future remains to be seen. One important aspect is the cross cultural influence of joint ventures in both Hong Kong and China. I will now turn to a brief consideration of this issue.

The impact of joint ventures on management and governance style

There are many examples in Hong Kong of equity joint ventures between Western companies, with a desire to manufacture and sell in Southeast Asia Region and local Chinese companies with extensive distribution networks throughout the region.[97] Mainland China has also encouraged the growth of numerous joint ventures with Western, Japanese, Hong Kong and Taiwanese business in its bid to develop its economy. Indeed, the development of China Post 1979 owes much to the overseas Chinese Diaspora.

In both contexts, as explained above, the Hong Kong and Chinese manager has been imbued with a different system of management norms which are even more marked in the mainland Chinese context because of the political economic system. As Child points out, in the mainland context these

---

94 See Noel Fung, "Shareholders Vote Family Out of Group" *South China Morning Post* 29 September 1995. Excessive remuneration and large unsecured loans to associated companies were some of the causes of the split in the family. This is a modern Hong Kong example of Cohen's description of the processes by which a joint family's sense of harmony (du wo) is sabotaged from within: "it seems clear that a deliberate effort to force partition is involved when a family's sharing practices are increasingly compromised by the refusal of some individuals to contribute their labour and time or by the outright embezzlement of family funds", M L Cohen, *House United, House Divided: The Chinese Family in Taiwan*, Columbia University Press, New York, 1976 at 204.

95 Cf Redding, supra n 11 at 133.

96 Cf D Devoes, "A Major Business Asset", Asia Inc (1994) Vol 3 No 9 at 33-9.

97 Cf T Dobson, "Equity Joint Ventures' in Trade and Investment Law in Hong Kong, eds P Smart and A Halkyard Butterworth Asia 1993.

differences create problems of mutual comprehension and present both sides with the need for considerable adjustment and learning.[98] Joint ventures also have other problems. They are often regarded as second best compared to wholly owned subsidiaries because of concern over the limits to the control that a parent company can exercise. As Schaan points out, they have all the control problems of subsidiaries plus those which arise from joint ownership.[99] But in the context of South East Asia and China the need to tap into the existing personalistic business networks of a joint venture partner is immediate, for otherwise a Western company may spend years building up the same trust relationships and a competitor who taps into those of a joint venture partner has a considerable advantage. According to Child both partners are bringing complementary strengths to the joint ventures. In order to realise these an agreed basis of cooperation must be found. Even the holding of a majority equity position cannot be used to enforce control over the venture without jeopardising the basis for its success. Therefore some limitation of control is the price to be paid for securing the advantages of a joint venture.[100]

The evidence from joint ventures on changes in management and boardroom practices introduced by foreign parties identifies the different approaches of the various foreign partners and discerns the modes by which foreign and Chinese managers relate and adjust to each other. Some of these have already been referred to in the context of board meetings.[101]

American and European companies tend to introduce formalised systems for transmitting key information and for defining the framework of managerial authority and responsibility. This helps to clarify managerial roles and obligations while at the same time establishing a framework within which operational decisions could potentially be delegated and responsibility for those decisions be clearly identified.[102] When this is combined with substantial management training programmes evidence from longer established joint ventures suggests that after a while local managers, at least on the mainland, develop to the point where the foreign partner is confident about delegating responsibility to them. However, in this context it is important to note that the American joint ventures in particular tended to recruit the most highly educated workforce.[103]

Formalisation is found to be much less developed in the Japanese and Hong Kong partnered ventures. The approach among the latter was to control through personal intervention while the Japanese, as one Japanese vice chairman of a Shanghai venture put it, "want to change their minds". They attempt, not wholly successfully, to fashion Chinese work behaviour through creating organisational cultures with strong collective norms.[104] American

---

98 Child, supra n 39 at 241.
99 J L Schaan, "How to Control a Joint Venture even as a Minority Partner", (1988) 14 *Journal of General Management* 4 at 4-5.
100 Child, supra n 39 at 243.
101 Bjorkman, supra n 74. See also P B Smith and Z M Wang, "Chinese Leadership and Organisational Structures" in *The handbook of Chinese Psychology* ed M H Bond, OUP, Hong Kong, 1996.
102 Child, surpa, n 39, at 261, 267 and 269.
103 Ibid, at 269 and 271.
104 Ibid, at 270 and 275.

joint venture partners tend also to push for change more aggressively, but do not require so much a re-culturalisation as an understanding of how to conduct business and to use the modern techniques associated with this although they sometimes fail to give their local colleagues much opportunity to get involved in the strategic process.[105] In this context, however, it is important to note Child's point that when Chinese managers hold a different orientation this is not necessary born out of a poor strategic understanding but is rather founded upon a realistic perception of different interests between partners: it is inextricably bound up with the issue of control.[106] A second issue becomes relevant here namely that when "forced" to adopt new methods or practices the behaviour of the Chinese may be modified but the reasoning behind the changes they are obliged to accept is not internalised.[107] The extent to which Western organisational norms influence behaviour, particularly in relation to the issue of open discussions, delegation and questions of control is debatable. With the advent of organisational behaviour texts which emphasise the South East Asian context the cultural tendencies of managers and directors of future Hong Kong companies are arguably being reinforced rather than diluted by Western style training.[108] The cultural implications for the internal organisation and style of corporate governance of Chinese family controlled businesses remains therefore an important part of the equation which, if ignored in any corporate law reform, will be ignored at the peril of that reforms success including any reform relating to securities markets, control and accountability and transparency. With this in mind I now wish to explore some cultural aspects and Wong Sui Lin's Model of the Chinese family firm, its life cycle and the possible separation of ownership and control.

Some cultural and psychological insights

The importance of "national" cultural traits and their impact on organisational behaviour has been emphasised by the work, inter alia, of Hofstede[109] and more recently Trompenaars.[110] I will refer briefly to some of the factors identified by these and other writers which may prove relevant to the corporate governance issues as well as the expanding research in the field of Chinese psychology. The two elements which I wish to draw attention to here are those of power distance and uncertainty avoidance.

Although there are some similarities between British social hierarchies and those of the Hong Kong Chinese one major difference is in their "power

---

105 Ibid, at 273.
106 Ibid, at 280.
107 Ibid, at 277.
108 See eg R I Westwood (ed) *Organisational Behaviour: Southeast Asian Perspectives*, Longman Far East (1992). The cultural bias is very difficult for Anglo-American researchers, and those influenced by them, to avoid, given that nearly all of their constructs and theories for understanding and categorising management emanate from the highly individualistic Anglo-American countries, Stewart et al, supra, n 73 at 197.
109 G Hofstede, *Cultures and Organisations: Software of the Mind*, McGraw Hill (Europe), 1991.
110 F Trompenaars, *Riding the Waves of Culture*, Nicholas Brealey Publishing, London, 1993.

distance score".¹¹¹ According to some writers there is little remaining today beyond lip service to Confucian thought in Chinese behaviour except in hierarchial authority and power.¹¹² According to Hofstede and Trompenaars the Chinese (including Hong Kong) have a much higher power distance score than the British. In large power distance countries there is considerable dependence by subordinates on bosses. The response of subordinates is either to prefer an autocratic or paternalistic boss ie accepting or preferring dependence, or to reject it entirely. The latter is called counterdependance (in psychology a form of dependence with a negative sign). In both cases, the emotional distance between bosses and their subordinates is large: subordinates are unlikely to approach and contradict their bosses directly. This factor when combined with the other cultural elements referred to earlier has a significant impact on decision making, for example, within the cultural context of high power distance, Chinese managers are likely to spend much more of their time with their superiors and much less of it with outsiders and their peers than say American or British managers.¹¹³ It is likely that Chinese directors/managers give more orders and spend more time checking on their implementation than do their Western counterparts. Similarly, making short term decisions involves senior directors/managers much more in China than it does for example in the UK, whereas in the case of long term decisions, the pattern is often reversed. Substantially different results have been observed in different economic sectors for example manufacturing as compared to service industries. This underlines many findings that effective leadership behaviours are not dependant solely on cultural issues, but are driven by an interaction between culture and the logic of each organisation's commercial and political environment.¹¹⁴ To the latter might be added its legal and regulatory regime. There are, of course, numerous other aspects of a large power distance factor and its impact and interaction with other elements both cultural and non cultural. In particular the interaction with "in group" (including the family) and "out group" relationships, assertiveness¹¹⁵ and decision making in high and low risk contexts.¹¹⁶

A lower uncertainty avoidance score for Hong Kong and Singapore Chinese is in some aspects difficult to explain.¹¹⁷ The scores for Taiwan for example are much higher.¹¹⁸ But both the British and Hong Kong scores are relatively low. This ability to accept and deal with ambiguity in both cultures may

---

111 For an explanation of this concept see Hofstede, supra n 109 at 24-28. For a comparison with Trompenaars see Smith and Wang, supra n 101 at 324-7.
112 Yee, supra n 40 at 162-3.
113 M Baisot and X G Liang, "The Nature of Managerial Work in the Chinese Enterprise Reforms: A Study of Six Directors", (1992) 13 *Organisation Studies* 161-84, cf Smith and Wang, supra n 101 at 327.
114 Smith and Wang, supra n 101 at 331, see also J F Yates and J W Lee, "Chinese Decision Making" in *The Handbook of Chinese Psychology*, ed M H Bond, OUP, Hong Kong. 1996.
115 Gabrenya and Hwang, supra n 34 at 314-6, 319.
116 Yates and Lee, supra n 114 at 344-7.
117 For an explanation of this concept see Hofstede, supra n 109, ch 5. For a consideration of this issue see Smith and Wang supra n 101 at 325.
118 The original score for Taiwan is 69, Hong Kong 29 and Singapore 8, Hofstede supra n 109 at 113. The table on p 324 for Hofstede's scores of Smith and Wang supra, n 101 appears to be inaccurate and does not correspond with the text on p 325. For insight into the

provide some answers for the successful adoption of the UK corporate form in Hong Kong.

A corporation is no less an invention than a steam engine. It is an institutional invention developed in a particular historical and cultural context. Therefore, it may take considerably more time for businessmen from another culture to appreciate its advantages whereas those of a steam engine are more obvious.[119] According to Faure, the Chinese have their own very clear ideas of corporations which are described by a wide range of terms for which translation is often at best approximate. Nevertheless, the Chinese concept, whether voluntary or not gave the appearance that its existence extended beyond the individual and allowed for the illusion that property rights could be maintained for generations if not perpetuity.[120] However, by the latter part of the nineteenth century merchants conducting business on the China coast and South East Asia were served in part by sophisticated institution that had their origins outside China particularly Western banks, shipping and insurance companies.[121] Over the years that followed and increasingly after the second world war those institutions were used by the Hong Kong Chinese merchants themselves but adopted to the context of their business culture.[122] That context was the Chinese family firm with its extended business networks.

The Chinese family firm and its lifecycle

According to Wong in order to understand the characteristics of a Chinese family firm it is important to identify the stage of its development and the social dynamics involved at each stage.[123] He identifies four important stages, the emergent, centralised, segmented and disintegrative. The emergent stage may be bypassed where an entrepreneur has sufficient capital, but as Wong points out many corporate businesses, eg textiles and banks, do not start simply as a family concern "because it is unlikely that the funds mastered by an individual and his jia (family estate) alone are sufficient to set up an enterprise other than a very modest one".[124] Where "partnerships" are used albeit in corporate form jockeying for control will occur and an asymmetrical

---

philosophical ambiguity of the Chinese mind see R E Allison, "An Overview of The Chinese Mind" in *Understanding the Chinese Mind: The Philosophical Roots* ed R E Allison, OUP, Hong Kong 1989.

119 For the luddicism of Chinese craftsmen and guilds in the nineteenth century, see D J MacGowan, "Chinese Guilds or Chambers of Commerce and Trade Unions", (1886) 21 *Journal of the North China Branch of the Royal Asiatic Society* 8, discussed in Kristoff and Wudunn, supra n 40 at 321. See also P T Ho, "Economic and Institutional Factors in the Decline of the Chinese Empire" in *The Economic Decline of Empires* ed Cippola, Meuthen, 1980; J Y Lin, "The Needham Puzzle: Why the Industrial Revolution Did not Originate in China" (1995) *Journal of Economic Development and Cultural Changes* 264.

120 Faure, supra n 26 at 13.

121 J Wang, "Chijiu shiji waiguo qinhau qiye zhong de naushang fugu huodong" (1965), *Lishi Yanjiu*, 4, discussed in Faure supra n 26 at 21.

122 For a consideration of the increased use of registered companies by Hong Kong Chinese Businessmen Post 1948 see E L G Tyler, "Does the complexity of Companies Legislation Impede Entrepreneurship? The Hong Kong Experience" paper delivered at the *Conference on Market Forces and the Law*, Beijing University 21-2 October 1994.

123 S L Wong, "The Chinese Family: Firm a Model", (1985) 36 *The British Journal of Sociology* 58.

124 Ibid, at 62.

growth in the distribution of shares. Similar evidence is provided by Suehiro in relation to Chinese firms in Thailand[125] and by Hattori in relation to family control of Chaebol in Korea.[126] Eventually, a shareholder and his jia ultimately attain majority ownership. In the centralised stage, the managerial and structural aspects of which have been considered earlier, profits are often used to finance expansion which may also include transfer of assets from one line of business to another for lateral expansion and mutual sustenance. Capital is mobile within the family group of businesses because it belongs to a common unified family budget. Although the father entrepreneur has absolute authority in utilising the capital of the family firm it is not his person property. He is almost, in Western terms, a trustee of the family estate which belongs to his children. The more he enriches that endowment the greater his social recognition. This can often lead to a tug of war between the father entrepreneur and sons inheritors which usually drags on while the father tries to contain the centripetal tendency of his sons and maintain his social recognition.[127]

After the demise of the father entrepreneur the firm enters the segmented stage. Unlike land which must be divided equally between inheritors a business is more amenable to surviving intact in the later phases of the centralised stage and early phases of the segmented stage because profits can be shared. Also the typical restrictions in a private company's constitution on the transfer of shares such as a pre-emption clause or directors' discretion to register transferee as members help to contain the business intact as a family business. The likelihood of splintering the estate of the family firm at this stage is not great.[128]

The situation as regards management and control is however different. Brothers may attempt to foster their own distinct spheres of influence and consensus among them cannot be taken for granted which curtails the power of the chief executive. This in turn gives rise to characteristics of outward expansion of the enterprise owing to segmentation, and a reduction in the flexibility for reinvestment and risk taking as the CEO increasingly takes on the role of caretaker of the family estate instead of innovator. There is some similarity with the emergent stage and one of the brothers, if not the CEO, may take over the business securing control for his family unit or fang. Otherwise there is an increasing tendency to split.[129] The latter is accentuated in the third "disintegrative" stage. Brothers' sons, ie first cousins have more divergent interests because unlike their fathers, who begin on an equal footing as regards inheritance of shares in the family company, they will not have equal shares because of different fertility among various fang. This third generation situation leads to less identification with the original family business for economic and personal reasons and therefore to a greater potential for fission.[130] Redding has also emphasised that even at this stage

---

125 Suehiro, supra n 57 at 380.
126 T Hattori, "Ownership and Management of Contemporary Korean Enterprises" (1984) 25 *Ajia Keizai* Nos 5-6, May-June.
127 Wong, supra, n 123, at 64.
128 Ibid, at 65.
129 Ibid, at 66-7.
130 Ibid, at 67-8.

there is unwillingness to rely on outside professional management.[131]

Before leaving the life cycle of the Chinese family firm one other sociological element needs to be considered which is not dealt with directly by either Wong or Redding. The stages in the development of the Chinese family firm may well be mirrored in Western firms. The case law on minority shareholder protection in the UK has many examples of breakdowns in relationships between partners, eg *Re Westbourne Galleries Ltd*[132] and *Re Cummana*[133] and between fathers and sons as in *Re H R Harmer Ltd*[134] or even brothers or other inheritors of the family business such as *Re Cuthbert Cooper Ltd*[135] and *Clemens v Clemens & Sons Ltd*.[136] But in the context of the Chinese family firm and the important role of the family estate the concubine or second and even third wife can, and often does have, an additional disintegrative effect, just as extended polygamous business families also have inherent strengths.[137]

Many wealthier, and some not so wealthy, Chinese businessman take several wives or concubines. The practice of taking more than one wife was made illegal in Hong Kong in 1971.[138] That does not stop the practice continuing on a more informal basis. One current social problem in Hong Kong is the practice, for example, of taking a second wife or mistress on the mainland by the increasing number of businessmen and managers or lorry drivers who spend a significant amount of their working time there.[139]

Concubinage was fairly well sanctioned in Chinese culture by the need to have male descendants.[140] The practice often led to greater opportunity for discord and disjunctions. The acquisition of concubines as an outlet for sexual desires and a source of affectional response gave concubines the opportunity to take advantage of their primacy in the affection of the husband.[141] They could exercise considerable informal power in the family; so much so that one late Ming dynasty lineage rules from the Miu lineage in Guangdong province had the following to say on the matter:

---

131 Redding, supra n 11 at 158 and 178.
132 [1973] AC 360.
133 [1980] BCLC 430.
134 [1959] 1 WLR 62.
135 [1937] Ch 392.
136 [1976] 2 All ER 268.
137 Suehiro, supra n 57, has emphasised the success of extended polygamous family businesses giving each other mutual support, in a pro industrial context, observing a "clear intent on the part of family business to maintain intact and even expand the family's enterprises and assets over a number of generations" at 403 in contrast to the anti-industrial pro gentrification thesis of Useem in relation to Britain and the USA, cf M Useem, *The Inner Circle*, OUP, New York, Oxford 1984.
138 Chinese Marriages Ordinance 1971.
139 Cf L F So, "Plea on Concubines" SCMP 30 January 1995 and E Ng and I Cheung, "Concubine Negates Registry Marriage", SCMP 31 December 1994.
140 See generally A P Wolf and C S Huang, *Marriage and Adoption in China, 1845-1945*, Stanford University Press, California 1980; M Jaschok, *Concubines and Bondservants: The Social History of a Chinese Custom*, OUP, Hong Kong, 1988.
141 S A Queen, R W Habenstein and J S Quadagno, *The Family in Various Cultures* at p 82; S C Lee, "China's Traditional Family, Its Characteristics and Disintegration" (1953) 18 *American Sociological Review* 272.

Taking concubines in order to beget heirs should be a last resort, for the sons of the legal wife and the sons of the concubine are never of one mind, causing innumerable conflicts between half brothers. If the parents are in the least partial, problems will multiply, creating misfortunes in later generations. Since families have been ruined because of this, it should often not be taken lightly.[142]

This has been reflected in some recent case law in Hong Kong where the sons of the first wife have attempted to disinherit the children of concubines.[143] Similarly, although Hong Kong's minority shareholder law is very similar to that of the UK's there are relatively few minority shareholder cases which get to court, either at an interlocutory stage or for a full hearing.[144] Many more writs are however issued.[145] These are currently under investigation by a research project in my department which, although in its early stages, does indicate that splits in Chinese family businesses often involve disputes between concubines and their children on the one hand and the children of the first wife on the other, often at the segmented stage of a family business' development. One Barrister for example, who had dealt with seven such cases in the last four years, all of which settled out of court, confirmed that in two of them the disputes involved concubine scenarios.

One case which did get to court is *Re Shiu Fook Ltd*.[146] In that case a concubine argued for just and equitable winding up on the basis of deadlock with the son of the first wife. There was evidence that she desired to emigrate to Australia and take part of the family estate with her. She failed to establish deadlock on the facts or that she had acted reasonably in not pursuing alternative remedies such as appointing more impartial directors, offering to sell her shares or pursuing an unfair prejudice remedy. The court emphasised the nature of the family business as part of the family estate and the inappropriateness of the remedy sought in the circumstances.

The factor of polygamy is clearly an important element which has to be taken into account in any model of the Chinese family firm because it affects the dynamics of the relationships between mother and sons and groups of syblings. These are some of the factors which Wong has recently considered but without reference to polygamy.[147] Although this practice may be on the

---

142 P B Ebrey, "Family Instructions" in *The Chinese Adapting the Past, Building the Future*, eds R F Dernberger, K J DeWoskin et al, The University of Michigan Center for Chinese Studies (1986).
143 Cf *Re Estate of Kwan Kai Ming*, deceased, 30 December 1994, HK MD No 2996 of 1990, unreported; *Tsao Chin Lan v Tin Ka Kung* 20 December 1994, HK Action No A7605 of 1991, unreported.
144 These include *Re Taiwa Land Investment Co Ltd* [1981] HKLR 297; *Re Lai Kan Co Ltd* and *Re Safe Steel Furniture Factory Ltd* [1988] HKLR 257; *Re Bondwood Development* [1990] 1 HKLR 200; *Yuen San Fai v Yun Jip Auto Services Ltd* (1992) 1 HKC 234; *Lou Thiam Siong v Hwa Own Co (Hong Kong) Ltd* (1988) CWU No 170 of 1988; *Deacon Te Ken Chiu v Ronald Li Kai Chu* [1991] 1 HKLR; *Re Medavision Ltd* (1993) 2 HKC 629; *Prime Aim International Ltd v Cosmos Pavis International Ltd* (1994) 2 HKC 545.
145 Between 1980 and 1995 there were circa 270 petitions issued in the High Court on the basis of just and equitable winding up, the majority of which made alternative claims on the basis of unfairly prejudicial conduct.
146 HK 1988 No CWN 185, unreported.
147 S L Wong, "The Chinese Family Firm Revisited: Hidden Dimensions" presented at conference entitled *The Rise of Business Corporations in China from Ming to Present*, Centre of Asian Studies, The University of Hong Kong 12-13 July 1996.

decline in Hong Kong it is clearly alive and well elsewhere, such as Thailand.[148] But the effects of these relationship is felt today both in the success of "interrelated" networks of associated companies driven by a desire to maintain and increase their family wealth and the occasional disintegration of companies or their controlling constellations of shareholders when extended polygamous family relationships break down.

In the UK context Charkham emphasises the double ancestry of listed companies. One type the classic joint stock company had separation of ownership and control from its very inception. The other is the registered company which after *Salomon v Salomon & Co Ltd*[149] was often used as a family business vehicle with owner managers. According to Charkham:

> Such businesses often stayed private for a long while, and either died[150] or were absorbed. Of the successful a relative few were floated later; even so, they retained most of the characteristics of the family business with few if any outsiders on the board. Many of them, if truth be told, made the transition without changing habits, in the mistaken belief that it was they, the proprietors, who were conferring a favour on those who subscribe for some shares in their business, an error which occasionally persists.[151]

This double ancestry is reflected in the way people think about boards and the role of directors. A world of difference exists between a committee of owner managers in a private company (and by analogy a Chinese family dominated HKSE listed company) and a board of a great public company on which no one owns a significant shareholding. The question is whether it is appropriate to use the same legal and/or corporate governance regime for both.

Conclusion

In some ways the Chinese family corporation may be likened to a jungle in which firms live and die relatively rapidly or split into smaller organisms. "Plants die but the Jungle keeps going on". The underlying fundamental elements of its inner core are unstable at a larger scale and in the second or third generations. The holistic way in which the family estate is inextricably identified as the corporate business renders regulation and governance problematic, even more so as the legitimacy of the power structure breaks down over time, without modern management structures or personnel to bridge the gap.

Hwang has argued, in a view markedly different from that of Redding, that a fragmentation of family business is not the only future that can be imagined.

---

148 Suehiro, supra n 57.
149 [1947] AC 22.
150 Cf P Leach, The Family Business (1995) Director Publications, (Stoy Centre for Family Business), London, 1995. The Stoy figures show that while 75% of UK companies are family run, only 30% of UK family business make it to the second generation and just 14% to the third, P Beresford, "The Independent Ones" (1995) Director (November issue) 109-15 at 113. For problems of succession in UK family companies see J Oliver, "Who's Next?" (1996) *Management Today* July, 56-8.
151 Charkham, supra, n 4 at 260-1. For a study of this double ancestry in the Australian context, see P Redmond, *Companies and Securities Law: Commentary and Materials* (2nd ed, 1992), LBC, Sydney.

While Confucian family centred work values may guide small businesses, there are other long established systems of values upon which managers of expanding businesses may rely. Legalisation is identified as such a system which he defines in terms of the rights of the individual and equitable reward for individual effort. He concludes from his study of Taiwanese organisations that Chinese organisations become more effective only as they move away from structures reliant upon traditional Confucian values and toward structures based upon a more overt rationality.[152] There is also considerable evidence in the early development of the overseas Chinese Kongsi of an attempt to develop a kind of civil society with elected officials and other institutions when Chinese businessmen were without state and family.[153]

The HKSE and SFC will have to tread carefully, lest many more companies, tiring of what is often perceived as an increasingly alien and intrusive regulatory regime, opt for privatisation.[154] That is not to say that they should be less rigorous in enforcement but rather more subtle. Introducing the independent NED regime was an interesting development, particularly in the light of the sometimes easy going enforcement of the listing rules combined with the occasional cat and mouse game with those companies who are reluctant to comply. Herbet Hui's recent public statement that he was considering beefing up the guidelines on directors' resignation announcements to make the reasons for withdrawal from the boards of listed companies public was just one example of this.[155] But the whole scenario is indicative of the underlying problems outlined in this paper. Hong Kong has its corporate cowboys[156] and directors who attempt to pay themselves excessive remuneration[157] or bigger listed companies by selling assets to them at huge overvalues[158] as do other economies to a greater or lesser extent. Secrecy is endemic and the Securities (Disclosure of Interests) Ordinance 1988 has only chipped away at the surface since non director substantial shareholders do not

---

152 K K Hwang, "Modernisation of the Chinese Family Business" (1990) 25 *International Journal of Psychology* 593-618 discussed in Smith and Wang supra, n 101.
153 T P Wang, *The Origins of Chinese Kongsi*, Pelanduk Publications, Malaysia, 1994.
154 There were 16 privatisations of public companies in 1991-2; 24 in 1992-3 and almost 30 in 1993-4. As a result, the SFC has altered the share buyback code to protect the bargaining position of the minority.
155 A Ngai, "Open Door Looms for Boardroom Brawls", *Sunday Morning Post* 12 February 1995.
156 See eg, the recent adventures of Mr Arthur Lai in *Chingtung Futures Ltd v Arthur Lai*, [1994] 1 HKLR 95 and R Gluckman, "MKI How an Investor's Sweet Dream became a Nightmare", (1995) Vol 4 No 3 *Asia Inc* at 26.
157 See P Lawton, "Director's Remuneration, Benefits and Extractions, an Analysis of their Uses Abuses and Controls in the Corporate Governance Context of Hong Kong" (1995) 4 *AJCL* 430.
158 In the last two years there have been two spectacular instances of "corporate raiders" purchasing a sufficiently large shareholding in listed companies to gain de facto control without triggering a TOB. The raiders have then proceeded to milk the companies by transferring assets to them at high overvalues. The victims tended to be well established, cash rich and with an untypically wide spread of shareholdings for Hong Kong. Cf Reports by Inspectors of Investigations under s 143(1)(C) of the Companies Ordinance by Mr Nicholas Allen into the affairs of the Allied Group Ltd and by John Robert Lees into the affairs of Tomson Pacific Ltd and World Trade Centre Group Ltd. For an example in the context of a private company see *Mun Won Co Ltd and The Singapore-Johore Express (PTE) Ltd v Tay Vi Bing* (1989) HK No A2553, unreported.

have to make disclosure in respect of shares held under a discretionary trust which becomes a new instrument in maintaining family cohesion in the centralised and early segmented stages of a family firm's life.

Hong Kong does not have the luxury like the UK, of a real dual root to the origins of its listed companies, except for a few examples like Hong Kong Bank, the majority of its listed companies commenced life as private companies (discounting the recent listing of mainland enterprises). Not just private companies but Chinese family firms. As listed companies they are potentially unstable within a few years or generations of the founder's death. The problems of boards and governance are more acute. A legal and corporate governance regime needs to be explored which readily allows a synthesis of the strategic options available to such firms for longer term survival, namely, a series of strategic alliances with Japanese or Western companies with advanced technology and international brand names or alternatively the slow but sure rationalisation, professionalisation and bureaucratisation of control with the professional staff to make it work.

As Faure has recently put it:

> Established for the purpose of business, the enterprise can break away from family ownership and management, even though it does not always do so. Where it intersects with the financial market, however, the demands of the financial market tend to leave their marks on the business: the market demands accountability of the chief executive and some transparency in their managerial decisions. These demands do not mean that the chief executive cannot pass his position to his offspring, but it does mean that even if he does, his offspring no longer runs an enterprise that portrays itself as a family.[159]

But even if this is the case the factors outlined in this paper indicate that there are important differences in cultural outlook and expectations which affect the local response to the regulatory regime.

In the forthcoming review of Hong Kong's corporate law regime Ermano Pascutto proposes to draw upon a variety of corporate law models, mostly common law based, for the purpose of determining a Companies Ordinance for the 21st century. In his inception report Pascutto emphasises that the UK model of corporate law, often the inspiration for Hong Kong's regime, may not be the way of the future. He quotes Gower:[160]

> The major questions still unresolved, and likely to remain unresolved, can really be reduced to one: Has our system of Company Law (evolved in the 19th Century) adapted itself adequately to the needs of the 20th and the likely challenges of the 21st. To suggest that it has not, may seem churlish ... (O)ur system of Company Law was, until recently, the model widely followed in the Common Law countries. That leading role has now been taken over by the United States (influencing Canada, Australia and New Zealand) and we cannot hope to recover it.

Pascutto's inception report goes on to emphasise the influence of the United States and in recent times that of the Canadian system on recent reforms in New Zealand. Australian legislation is dismissed for its complexity and its failure to clearly distinguish between securities law matters and company law.

---

159 Faure supra n 26 at 26-7.
160 *Gower's Principles of Modern Company Law*, 5th ed (1992), at p 70.

It is regarded as "outdated and dense in form".[161] Australian corporate legislation is currently going through a process of simplification. In regard to the Asian context the inception report states:

> In conducting the review, reference should be had to the commercial and economic context in which the Companies Ordinance operates. Developments in companies legislation in other parts of Asia (where similar economic forces are at work) could be instructive. For example, Singapore and Malaysia currently have legislation in place modelled on the UK Companies Act 1948 and the Australian Uniform Companies Act 1961. Any plans for reform of these statutes would be of interest. Finally, any review of the Companies Ordinance must be done with an awareness of the recently enacted Company Law of the People's Republic of China.[162]

This, with respect, emphasises economic forces and fails to give due weight to, inter alia, the role of culture in the organisation, structure and management of Hong Kong companies. It is submitted that this is a serious oversight.

---

161 New Zealand Law Commission, *Company Law Reform and Restatement*, Report No 9, at p 11.
162 Ermano Pascutto, Hong Kong Companies Ordinance Inception Report: An Ordinance for the 21st Century at para 2.1.1.2.

[16]

Company Law and the Limits of the Rule of Law in China

*Professor Roman Tomasic**

Introduction[1]

The commencement of the new body of company law in China on 1 July 1994 represents a significant milestone in the development of commercial law in China. The enactment of this new legislation in December 1993 reflects a commitment on the part of the national government of China to a range of company law principles which would be familiar to many western lawyers. While it is tempting to dismiss this rather brief piece of legislation as being a somewhat simplistic attempt to introduce a modern company law regime into China, this new company law needs to be seen in context; it is the first body of such law to be enacted in China since the formation of the People's Republic of China in 1949.

The new Company Law should also be seen in the context of the degree of progress which has been achieved in China in developing a more sophisticated legal system which requires a body of judges and lawyers who have experience in the conduct of business relations and in the handling of business disputes and claims. Moreover, the fact that this legislation has been introduced into what has up until recently been a non-market based society further emphasises the significant nature of these changes. It would therefore be unrealistic to be too critical of this legislation as it is likely that over the next decade or so the Company Law will be further refined as the need to do so arises. This article will not seek to provide any detailed analysis of this new law, as such an analysis can be found elsewhere.[2] Instead, my focus will be upon the implicit assumption of the company law that the rule of law is to introduced in regard to business activity which is affected by the Company Law.

The rule of law is ultimately a polemical rather than a useful analytical term.[3] However, it is an ideal which is commonly applied by foreign business, the media and by some legal advisers when discussing the impact of the Chinese legal system upon business transactions. It is an idea commonly associated with the writings of the British lawyer and political activist A V Dicey. Put briefly, Dicey argued that the British constitution was characterised by the rule of law and that this referred to three different expressions of the one principle: first, Dicey referred to

---

* Professor of Law and Head, School of Law, University of Canberra.
1 This is a revised version of a paper delivered at the Asia Pacific Economic Law Forum held on 8, 9 December 1994 at the Queensland University of Technology, Brisbane.
2 See for example, G G Wang and R Tomasic, *China's Company Law: An Annotation*, Butterworths Asia, Singapore, 1994.
3 It may be more appropriate to seek to evaluate the performance of the Chinese legal system by reference to the degree to which it meets the Weberian ideal of a logically formal rational legal system. See further: M Weber, *Economy and Society*, Vol 2, (G Roth and C Wittich (eds)), University of California Press, Berkeley, 1978, pp 880-92.

the absolute supremacy or predominance of regular law in contrast to prerogative, discretionary or arbitrary powers; second, Dicey's conception of the rule of law referred to the existence of equality of all subjects before the ordinary law, without any exemption from a duty of obedience to the law being given to officials or others in positions of power; third, Dicey saw the Constitution of the state as itself being the product of the development of private law by the courts, so that the state and its officials would ultimately be subject to the ordinary law of the land.[4]

Of course, there is a large degree of polemic and over-generalisation in Dicey's conception, and it is interesting to note that as early as 1917 Harold Laski observed that the concept was already "so theoretical and so beset on all hands by exceptions as to be hardly applicable at all." Similarly, Ivor Jennings has noted that the rule of law was "rather an unruly horse" given the many exceptions to the rule.[5] However, the notion of the rule of law as a protection against arbitrariness upon the part of the state has continued to be a widely echoed aspiration in recent years, with some writers even suggesting that it has become a new natural law as a normative ideal which all legal systems should strive to achieve.[6]

It should be said that Dicey was wrong to argue that the exercise of discretionary powers by government would inevitably lead to a loss of individual freedom, for as Cosgrove has observed, "[d]iscretionary power, when restrained by law, need not be arbitrary."[7] However, the preservation of the rule of law is usually associated with the existence of a robust independent judiciary which can provide an independent judicial review of a disputed case.[8]

In relation to the introduction of principles of legality and the rule of law in China, these ideas have been frequently reaffirmed in China since the Cultural Revolution. However, as one observer has noted, although "the Constitution and the law proclaim the equality of all under the law, but in fact party and government cadres are more 'equal' than ordinary citizens."[9] Of course, similar statements have been made about the reality of legal rights in western legal systems.

---

4 For a discussion of Dicey's expression of the Rule of Law doctrine see further: R A Cosgrove, *The Rule of Law: Albert Venn Dicey, Victorian Jurist*, Macmillan, London, 1980, pp 78-87.
5 Quoted by Cosgrove, ibid at pp 82-3.
6 Per J K Garner, *Administrative Law*, p 17; quoted by Cosgrove, ibid at p 85. For a recent Australian discussion of the constitutional aspects of the rule of law see: G de Q Walker, *The Rule of Law: Foundation of Constitutional Democracy*, Melbourne University Press, Melbourne, 1988.
7 Ibid at p 85.
8 For a recent and lucid review of the Rule of Law doctrine see: G F Gaus, "Public Reason and the Rule of Law", in *The Rule of Law, Nomos XXXVI*, ed I Shapiro, New York University Press, New York, 1994, pp 328-35.
9 Albert Hung-yee Chen, *An Introduction to the Legal System of the People's Republic of China*, Butterworths Asia, Singapore, 1993, p 4.

Rule of Law Claims in the China Company Law

Many Articles in the new China Company Law make explicit reference to the rule of law. These references are of two broad types.[10] First, and most commonly, the Company Law uses what may be called the "political" or prescriptive notion of the rule of law, namely, the notion of the rule of law as a command of the state under which the company and its promoters, officers and shareholders must comply with various rules and procedures laid down in the Law and in related legislation.[11]

Second, and much less frequently, the Company Law uses what has been called a "material" or permissive notion of the rule of law. The latter notion of the rule of law focuses upon various rights which are immune to an overriding command by the state. Thus, the rule of law has these two basic elements, command and rights. Because the China Company Law sees incorporation as a privilege which has been given to those who have satisfied stringent requirements, rather than as a right which is widely available, it is not surprising to see that the prime emphasis in the Company Law is upon command or prescription, rather than upon rights or permissive action.

The commonest expression of the prescriptive approach to the rule of law which is found in the Company Law is the use of the phrase "in accordance with this Law" or the phrase "in accordance with the law". This phrase is used at least 70 times in less than 50 pages of printed legislation. Other phrases such as "stipulated by this Law" or "as required by the law" are also used throughout the legislation. For example, Art 11 provides that the scope of a company's business is to be defined in its articles of association and that this shall be registered in accordance with the law." Article 37 states that the shareholder's meeting of a limited company is to "exercise its powers in accordance with this Law." Article 24 provides that the valuation of land use rights which are relied upon as a source of capital for the company is to take place "in accordance with the law and administrative regulations." Article 102 provides that the shareholders' meeting of a Joint Stock Company is required to "exercise its function and powers in accordance with this Law."

The almost ritual incantation of these general prescriptions may perhaps be explained as merely a reflection of a style of legislative drafting which would be unfamiliar to those accustomed to reading legislation such as the Corporations Law in Australia. It could be argued that the meaning of relevant articles of the China Company Law would not be impaired by the total elimination of these prescriptive phrases.

---

10 Neumann has observed that the rule of law has a dual significance. See F L Neumann, *The Rule of Law: Political Theory and the Legal System in Modern Society*, Berg Publishers, Leamington Spa, 1986, pp 45-6.
11 This political conception of law can, for example, be illustrated in the writings of Hobbes and in early political doctrines such as that of the divine right of kings.

However, such an approach would probably be in conflict with the "concession" theory of the corporation upon which this body of law is almost entirely based.[12]

The impression which is given by the China Company Law is that the privileges of incorporation and limited liability will be jealously guarded by the state and that the state will closely monitor the actions of incorporated companies. Furthermore, it might be said that the balance of these so-called rule of law provisions in the Company Law is heavily weighed in favour of the state, rather than in favour of the company or its shareholders. This is in contrast to the generally non-interventionist philosophy which dominates the approach of the courts and of regulators in countries such as Australia. Under this non-interventionist (and often self regulatory) philosophy, the courts will be reluctant to intervene in the internal affairs of a company unless the company and its members are unable to resolve a problem or unless there has been a fraud of some kind. This approach has sometimes been identified with the so-called business judgment rule.[13]

These non-interventionist principles are widely shared by business in Australia[14], although it is probably the case that this would not be the case in China, given that country's recent historical experience of state owned enterprises.[15] In earlier times, as Gordon Redding has observed, while the "direct positive involvement by government in business was rare" in imperial China, the "Confucian disdain for the world of business" and the failure of Chinese governments to seek to protect business activity led business to adopt a defensive family-centred

---

12 The concession theory provides that the corporation is an artificial entity which has been created by the state and it exists as a privilege granted by the state: see further D Bonham and D Soberman, "The Nature of Corporate Personality", in *Studies in Canadian Company Law*, ed J S Ziegel, Butterworths, Toronto, 1967, p 5. The concession theory is to be distinguished with other theories of the corporation, most notably, the contract model which rests upon the notion of a corporation as a series of contracts between its members and between the members and the company: see further F H Easterbrook and D R Fischel, *The Economic Structure of Corporate Law*, Harvard University Press, Cambridge, 1991, pp 1-39. Also see generally: R Tomasic and S Bottomley, *Corporations Law in Australia*, Federation Press, Sydney, (forthcoming 1995), Ch 2.
13 In *Kinsella v Russell Kinsella Pty Ltd (in liq)* (1986) 4 ACLC 215 at 223 the NSW Court of Appeal noted that "[c]ourts have traditionally and properly been cautious indeed in entering boardrooms and pronouncing upon the commercial justification of particular executive decisions." See other statements to this effect in: *Australian Metropolitan Life Assurance Co Ltd v Ure* (1923) 33 CLR 199 at 221-2 (by Isaacs J in the High Court of Australia); *Howard Smith Ltd v Ampol Petroleum Ltd* [1974] AC 821 at 823 (in the Privy Council); Also see the American Law Institute's *Principles of Corporate Governance*, American Law Institute, St Paul, Minn, 1994, at s 4.01(c).
14 See further, R Tomasic and S Bottomley, *Directing the Top 500: Corporate Governance and Accountability in Australian Companies*, Allen & Unwin, Sydney, 1993, pp 79-84.
15 See for example Fairbank's discussion of government control of the ancient Chinese salt monopoly up until the end of the nineteenth century: J K Fairbank, *The Great Chinese Revolution 1800-1985*, Harper & Row, New York, 1987, p 53.

approach to business activity.[16] It will be interesting to see how this traditional approach to business will accord with the ethos of China's so-called market socialism.

The China Company Law also contains a number of provisions which take a more permissive approach to the rule of law. For example, Art 1 of the new Company Law proclaims that it has as one of its goals the protection of "the lawful rights and interests of the companies, shareholders and creditors" and Art 4 gives shareholders the "right" to participate in important decision-making processes of the company. The latter article gives companies "the entire property rights of a legal person over its capital" and adds that companies shall have rights and liabilities "in accordance with the law". Article 14 also provides that the "lawful rights and interests of a company shall be protected by the law and may not be infringed." Further, a company is required by Art 15 to protect the lawful rights and interests of its employees. In relation to Limited Companies, Art 27 provides that once a company has satisfied the conditions for registration which are stipulated by the Company Law, the company has a right to be issued with a business licence.

While these more permissive Articles are important, it should be emphasised that they are subject to overriding general provisions in the Company Law, such as those in Art 14 which states, inter alia, that: "[w]hen engaging in business activities, a company shall abide by the law and observe professional ethics, enhance the building of socialist spiritual civilization and accept supervision of the government and the general public."

It will be clear from these various provisions that China has certainly sought to introduce a form of the rule of law ideology into its system for the regulation of companies. Detailed administrative rules and regulations are intended to facilitate the implementation of this new Law. However, the rule of law as an idea cannot be understood in isolation and must be related to what sociologists of law have referred to as the law in action. The interpretation of the Company Law must therefore take place in the wider social and economic context of China and its implementation will be affected by the judicial, regulatory and legal professional cultures which provide a backdrop to these new rules. Added to this will be the fact that commercial laws such as these are often implemented upon the basis of personal relationships, rather than by strictly legal means. Thus, it is said that in China relationships of trust are all important in business transactions and in other dealings,[17] although it could well be said that this is also true in regard to business transactions in western countries.[18]

---

16 S G Reading, *The Spirit of Chinese Capitalism*, Walter de Gruyter, New York, 1993, pp 119-21. See also H H Gerth and C W Mills (eds), *From Max Weber: Essays in Sociology*, Routledge & Kegan Paul, 1977, pp 440-1.
17 C A G Jones, "Capitalism, Globalization and Rule of Law: An Alternative Trajectory of Legal Change in China" (1994) 3 *Social and Legal Studies* 195.
18 See for example, S Macaulay, "Non-contractual relations in business" (1963) 28 *American Sociological Review* 55.

Some Limits of the Rule of Law under Western Capitalism

A system of rational legal rules is often seen as an essential foundation upon which western market societies have been built. Furthermore, the rule of law is often touted as being a constitutive principle in western legal systems. As noted earlier, the rule of law and a rational legal system require the existence of a robustly independent judiciary. This aspect of the rule of law was, for example, powerfully expressed in the 1803 US Supreme Court opinion in *Marbury v Madison* where it was said that it is for the court to determine what the law is when issues of constitutional validity arise.[19] Having said this, it should be said that although the judiciary in western legal systems is generally autonomous, its members are nevertheless part of a broader social and political elite which administers the modern state, with shared values and similar social backgrounds to those in other arms of government.[20]

The existence of judicial review of the actions of state officials and agencies may be seen as another manifestation of this rule of law ideology. Consequently, the exercise of discretionary powers by executive agencies may be subject to scrutiny and control upon the basis of recognised legal principles. The fact that most discretionary decisions are never reviewed is largely irrelevant, as the mere possibility of such a review occurring satisfies the claims of the rule of law theory. However, this possibility of judicial review can sometimes be extremely remote when access to justice considerations, such as the cost of justice, are raised. A legal realist assessment of the rule of law in such contexts must lead to a conclusion that the mere theoretical possibility of its operation is a de facto denial of the rule.

Some might go further and suggest that even if it is possible to have a matter reviewed by the courts, the courts may be biased against, or unsympathetic towards, the particular claimant; as is often said by feminists and aboriginal activists in Australia.[21] Moreover, it can be shown that, given very high conviction rates, the function of trial courts is largely to convict[22]; and similarly, that the function of much lower court civil activity is to facilitate debt collection by creditors.[23] In the rare cases in which the right of appeal is taken, this serves largely to legitimise the

---

19 1 Cranch 137 (1803). It is interesting to note that *Marbury v Madison* has been described as the most significant lawsuit in American history: L Friedman, *Milestones*, West Publishing Co, St Paul, Minn, 1976, p 73.
20 See generally, A Patterson, *The Law Lords*, Macmillan, London, 1982; A Cox, *The Role of the Supreme Court in American Government*, Oxford University Press, London, 1978; F Rodell, *Nine Men: A Political History of the Supreme Court from 1790 to 1955*, Random House, New York, 1955.
21 See generally, R Graycar and J Morgan, *The Hidden Gender of Law*, Federation Press, Sydney. E Eggleston, *Fear, Favour or Affection: Aboriginals and the Criminal Law in Victoria, South Australia and Western Australia*, Australian National University Press, Canberra, 1976.
22 D McBarnet, D, *Conviction: Law, The State and the Construction of Justice*, MacMillan, London, 1981.
23 D Caplovitz, *Consumers in Trouble: A Study of Debtors in Default*, Free Press, New York, 1974.

original decision-making process.²⁴ Courts in western legal systems therefore play important parts in creating and articulating system maintaining ideologies in market societies, even if in reality the ideology is not matched by practice.²⁵

Despite criticisms which might be made of its implementation, it can nevertheless be argued that the rule of law in western societies is a powerful ideology which serves to unify a legal system in a state of on-going systemic disintegration and potential imbalance. The rule of law also serves to legitimise decision-making processes and as such serves as a symbolic reassurance of equality before the law.²⁶ This is similar to the role of the nation as the integrating principle in the modern state. As Franz Neumann has observed, the nation "is the unifying link between the individual and the state in the nineteenth and twentieth centuries. The modern state needs a legitimation."²⁷ The same can be said of the need of the legal system for a legitimation such as the rule of law ideology.

If we turn from constitutional principles, where the rule of law doctrine has been most fully developed, to the area of corporate law, the operation of this principle is somewhat more subtle, and sometimes seemingly non-existent due to the operation of considerable judicial restraint. The paradox of western systems of company law is that these laws have grown rapidly in size in recent decades, seeming to suggest that we are witnessing a veritable explosion of interest in the rule of law doctrine. While this may superficially be so, at least for those with a professional interest in corporate law, such as lawyers and judges, it is far from clear that business would see corporate law in similar terms.

Indeed, it can be said that corporate law is something which is by and large left to corporate advisers as most directors of companies would pay scant if any regard for the details of corporate law. Where corporate law is called upon, this is often for the purposes of legitimising the actions of management, as Mary Stokes has suggested.²⁸ Similar arguments have been put by other scholars such as the American legal historian Willard Hurst.²⁹ This conclusion is also supported by empirical findings from a

---

24 See generally: R Cotterrell, *The Sociology of Law: An Introduction*, 2nd ed, Butterworths, London, 1992, pp 238-9.
25 Ibid at pp 225-6. Also see: J Brigham, *The Cult of the Court*, Temple University Press, Philadelphia, 1989.
26 For a more detailed discussion of this point, see further: R Tomasic, "Ideology and Coherence in the Australian Legal Order", in *A Sociology of Australian Society: Introductory Readings*, 2nd ed, eds J M Najman and J S Western, Macmillan, Melbourne, 1993, pp 139-77.
27 F L Neumann, *The Rule of Law: Political Theory and the Legal System in Modern Society*, Berg Publishers, Leamington Spa, 1986, p 205.
28 M Stokes, "Company Law and Legal Theory", in *Legal Theory and Common Law*, ed W Twining, Basil Blackwell, Oxford, 1986, at pp 156, 160. Also see D Sugarman and G R Rubin, "Towards a New History of Law and Material Society in England 1750-1914", in *Law, Economy and Society, 1750-1914*, eds D Sugarman and G R Rubin, Professional Books, Abingdon, 1984, pp 12-13.
29 W Hurst, *Law and Social Order in the United States*, Cornell University Press, Ithaca, 1977, pp 243-4; and W Hurst, *Law and Markets in United States History*, University of Wisconsin Press, Madison, 1982, pp 48-9.

recent national survey of directors of top 500 Australian companies which found that most company directors had a minimal knowledge of basic corporate law rules and sometimes hold notions regarding their duties of directors which are at odds with the precise legal formulation of these matters.[30] Of far greater importance to corporate officers are such matters as corporate culture and peer group values.[31]

This attitude springs from the fact that, historically, commercial law has tended to emerge from the customs and values of merchants and businessmen, what used to be known as the lex mercatoria which came to be incorporated into common law principles, some of which have now been codified.[32] More recently, company law legislation has reflected a codification of common law principles, the formalisation of bureaucratic arrangements for entry into occupations in the area of corporate law (such as for the licensing of brokers, auditors, and liquidators) and the introduction of new structures such as those covered by the Australian Securities Commission Act. So much of the apparent legislative growth in recent years has been institutional and codificatory in nature and this legislation has not greatly departed from fundamental principles of company law.

As has been suggested in the above discussion, it can be argued that there is an important symbolic dimension in the rule of law ideology in western societies. This is not to suggest that there are not occasions when this ideology is actually true to its word, although it could be argued that this is so largely for legitimisation and system maintenance purposes. In relation to corporate law, the extent to which corporate regulatory agencies exercise their discretion to exempt corporations from having to comply with company law provisions may be seen as a means of softening the potential harshness upon business of strict compliance with technical legal provisions. In these circumstances, the company law breaches which tend to be excused in this way are often down-played as being merely "technical breaches."

For example, in Australia in the 1993-94 year, a total of 4050 standard applications were made for exemption of companies from a provision of the Corporations Law, for a modification of the law or the use of discretionary powers by the Australian Securities Commission. A further 610 such applications were made in relation to more minor matters. In relation to takeovers, a total of 138 applications were made (and 117

---

30 R Tomasic and S Bottomley, *Directing the Top 500: Corporate Governance and Accountability in Australian Companies*, Allen & Unwin, Sydney, 1993.

31 This is in conformity with American findings reported by writers such as C Stone, *Where the Law Ends: The Social Control of Corporate Behavior*, Harper & Row, New York, 1975; R Jackall, *Moral Mazes: The World of Corporate Managers*, Oxford University Press, New York, 1988. Also see generally in regard to the importance of peer group influences in regard to the securities industry: R Tomasic, *Casino Capitalism? Insider Trading in Australia*, Australian Institute of Criminology, Canberra, 1991.

32 See generally, N S B Gras, *Business and Capitalism: An Introduction to Business History*, FS Crofts & Co, New York, 1946, p 42. Also see generally, M Weber, *Economy and Society*, Vol 1, eds G Roth and C Wittich, University of California Press, Berkeley, 1978, pp 319-21.

478 (1995) 4 Australian Journal of Corporate Law

were granted) to modify the operation of the takeover provisions of the Corporations Law. A further 63 applications were made (and 59 were approved) to exempt compliance with these takeover provisions.[33] This again suggests that the rule of law in corporations law matters has a large symbolic dimension as compliance with the provisions of the law is formally avoided in the above ways. This cannot but serve to undermine the claims that the rule of law is characteristic of legal decision-making in relation to business in market-based societies. Such claims simply cannot be sustained upon the basis of the empirical evidence. The rule of law is far from being perceived as an inflexible requirement of western legal systems.

Challenges to the Rule of Law in China's Business Relations

As has been argued above, the ideology of the rule of law is a powerful ideology which is used to legitimise the legal and regulatory systems of market based societies, even though this ideology often fails to match commercial reality. However, where the rule of law ideology leads to less blatant exercises of power, this is clearly a consequence of the rule which should be welcomed.[34]

It is interesting to note that some of the greatest threats to the legitimacy of the new China Company Law are likely to come from the failure of the Chinese legal system to be able to adequately reproduce the rhetoric of the rule of law. I have already noted that the new Company Law makes a valiant attempt to pay homage to these values, albeit with a heavy emphasis upon the prescriptive and state oriented dimensions of this doctrine.

However, the China Company Law does not exist in isolation. It is obviously part of a wider legal and regulatory infrastructure which needs to convincingly articulate similar aspirations if it is to be seen to have a wider legitimacy.[35] The recent international press outcry concerning the resumption of property rights originally given to McDonald's to allow it to operate its largest world restaurant in Beijing, perhaps strikes at the rationality of Chinese legal arrangements.[36] Similarly, the legal action which has recently been commenced in the United States by Lehman Brothers against two of the largest Chinese government-owned companies for the alleged failure of these companies to pay debts

---

33 Australian Securities Commission, Annual Report, 1993/94, Canberra, AGPS, p 50.
34 See generally, E P Thompson, *Whigs and Hunters: The Origins of the Black Act*, Penguin Books, Harmondsworth, 1975, pp 258-69.
35 See generally, Albert Hung-yee Chen, *An Introduction to the Legal System of the People's Republic of China*, Butterworths Asia, Singapore, 1993.
36 T Plafker, "Is this the end of a beautiful friendship?", *Sunday Morning Post* (HK), 27 November 1994 at 6. Also see "Deal is just not words", editorial in *South China Morning Post*, 29 November 1994 at 26.

incurred by the companies through losses of about US$100m in foreign exchange and swap markets also raised questions about the commitment to rule of law ideals in China.[37]

The prevalence of fake bankruptcies among government-owned Chinese companies which have borrowed heavily from foreign sources also may be seen as challenging the credibility of the Chinese legal system when dealing with business matters.[38] The legal system has had difficulties in dealing with such problems as is evident from the fact that 31 foreign banks recently wrote to the Chinese Vice Premier Zhu Rongji seeking his assistance in collecting some US$600m which was owed by state enterprises.[39] This bankruptcy problem is probably the greatest threat to the integrity of Chinese government-owned enterprises, and this seems to be recognised by the China State Council, although its primary focus seems to have been upon the requirement that the enterprises make adequate provision for their employees.[40] It is clearly recognised in China that the proliferation of economic crime in China has the potential to undermine the legitimacy of the China Communist Party and some efforts are clearly being made to combat this corruption.[41] It may of course undermine the attempts to establish a rational legal order in which business can operate.

However, this article will not discuss any of these threats to the introduction of the rule of law in China. Instead, I want to look at just one recent case, that involving the Chinese-Australian businessman, James Peng Jiandong, or what will be referred to as the Peng case. Unlike McDonald's or Lehman Brothers, which are large enough to look after themselves, the Peng case is an illustration of the problems which smaller businessmen, especially those of Chinese ethnicity, may have in seeking to operate in the environment of China's market socialism.

The Australian Government has expressed great concerns about the handling of this case. For example, the Australian Minister for Trade, Senator Bob McMullan, has reportedly observed that the lack of confidence in the Chinese legal system which the Peng case has created, will be likely to discourage Australians from doing business in China.[42] After the enormous debt problems facing Chinese government-owned enterprises, the international impact of the Peng case probably represents one of the greatest threats to the acceptance of the

---

37 D Ibison, "Judgment day for Lehmans", *Sunday Morning Post* (HK), 27 November 1994 at 5. K Wong, "China loan row intensifies: Lehman threat to freeze assets", *Sunday Morning Post* (HK), 20 November 1994 at 1 (Money).
38 See further, R Tsang, "State-run companies fake bankruptcy to avoid debt", *South China Morning Post*, 14 November 1994 at 10 (Business Post).
39 "Review and Outlook" (Editorial), *The Wall Street Journal*, 18 November 1994.
40 "State Council tells bankrupt firms to pay up", *South China Morning Post*, 19 November 1994 at 4 (Business Post); also see D Kwan, "Bankruptcy warning", *South China Morning Post*, 19 November 1994 at 9.
41 "China outlines legal strategy to combat economic crime", *Sunday Morning Post* (HK), 27 November 1994.
42 "China risks investment: McMullan", *The Canberra Times*, 16 September 1994 at 3. Also see: L Evans, "Free businessman, China told", *The Canberra Times*, 11 September 1994 at 5.

proposition that the rule of law ideology has been introduced in China. Perhaps the Peng case should also be seen as an indicator of how the China Company Law will be applied.

The Peng case seems to be a litmus test of the problems being faced by the Chinese legal system in seeking to adjust to the norms of a market society.[43] The widespread international publicity which this case has received must be a cause of great concern to authorities in Beijing.[44] Of greatest concern is the fact that a commercial dispute between a foreign businessman and a state-owned enterprise all too readily can escalate into a criminal prosecution, especially if overseas Chinese are involved. As one journalist observed in the context of this case, "China seems to have a propensity to metamorphose any contractual or money dispute into an allegation of fraud or stealing state secrets, as a means to apply pressure on a foreign party."[45]

Another journalist recently observed in regard to the Peng case that it had "become a test case for the rule of law in China's international business dealings".[46] As some official corruption seems to be involved in this case, it is interesting to note the reported comments made by Liang Guoqing, Deputy Procurator-General and a leading figure in the fight against official corruption, who said recently that corruption had spread among officials at all levels and that "[t]hey use their power to blackmail, demand bribes, embezzle and pursue private interests."[47] Even Vice-Premier Zhu Rongji has acknowledged that the Peng case reflects badly upon the operation of the Chinese legal system.[48]

The facts of the Peng case are generally known, although it is useful to restate these here briefly for the purposes of readers who are unfamiliar

---

43 While the Peng case is not the only case of its kind, the publicity surrounding it and the intransigence of the Shenzhen authorities in pursuing this case is unusual. Other similar cases have involved American businessmen Dr Philip Cheung Hui-ho and Chong Kwee-sung.
44 For an Australian report, see M Harris, "Shanghaied: How China kidnapped an Australian citizen", *The Sydney Morning Herald*, 2 April 1994 at 14. Also see S Holberton, "Chinese dream sours for high-flying entrepreneur: The detention of 'Jimmy' Peng on suspicion of corruption has turned the spotlight on a secretive and primitive legal system", *The Financial Times*, 23/24 July 1994 at 3; "Judicial System Faces a test", (Editorial), *South China Morning Post*, 19 November 1994. "Review and Outlook", (Editorial), *Asian Wall Street Journal*, 1 September 1994; "Businessman is Charged in China", *Asian Wall Street Journal*, 5 August 1994; R MacPherson, "Chinese-Australian trapped aboard China's Midnight Express", Agence France-Presse, 22 June 1994.
45 Frankie Fook-Lun Leung, "Rule of Law: The Problem of Being Chinese", *Asian Wall Street Journal*, 2 June 1994 at 6. Leung suggests that this seems to be especially a problem for overseas Chinese businessmen who penetrate the Chinese economy at much lower levels than multinationals and as a result there is a suspicion among these businessmen that Chinese officials feel more at liberty to use high-handed legal methods with such persons.
46 S Long, "Boom town trial tests terms of doing business with China", *The Guardian*, 17 November 1994 at 17.
47 C Field, "Spirit of the Wild West lives on in the shimmering East", *The Times of London*, 23 August 1994.
48 G Crowthall, "Australian faces corruption trial", *South China Morning Post*, 14 June 1994 at 1.

with them.[49] Peng had been born in China (in Jieyang county in Guandong), and arrived in Australia in 1989, becoming an Australian citizen two years later. He then returned to Hong Kong to pursue various business interests in southern China. Peng had a private company in Hong Kong, Panco Industrial (Holdings) Ltd. Through this private company, Peng controlled more than a third of a joint venture garment company, Champaign Industrial Co, which had taken over a former state enterprise. Champaign became part of the first Sino-foreign joint venture to be listed on a Chinese stock exchange (on 26 February 1990) and was transformed from a loss-making state-owned enterprise into a successful manufacturing and property group.

In early 1992, a disagreement apparently arose between Peng and Shenzhen authorities and this led to an investigation of the company by the Bank of China which then seized Champaign's accounts and froze its bank accounts.[50] Various Shenzhen officials had also felt deceived by Peng. According to an August 1993 report by the committee which had been appointed to restructure Champaign, in July 1988 a state-owned company, Xinye, converted its ordinary shares in Champaign into preference shares so that it would become entitled to a dividend payment of 350,000 yuan. However, two months later, Peng revealed the company's real assets. This had the effect of increasing the company's net worth by 25.7m yuan and giving Panco a windfall gain of 24.6m yuan. Apparently in an effort to realise this windfall, in 1991 Peng sought to sell Panco, which then owned some 51% of Champaign, but this deal fell through, apparently because of moves by the Shenzhen government to stop the sale (to Lolliman) going through. Shortly thereafter, the

---

49 This account is drawn upon the following press reports: S Holberton, "Chinese dream sours for high-flying entrepreneur: The detention of 'Jimmy' Peng on suspicion of corruption has turned the spotlight on a secretive and primitive legal system", *The Financial Times*, 23/24 July 1994 at 3; C Field, "Spirit of the Wild West lives on in the shimmering East", *The Times of London*, 23 August 1994; M Harris, "Shanghaied: How China kidnapped an Australian citizen", *The Sydney Morning Herald*, 2 April 1994 at 14; D Kwan, "Peng denies charges amid tight security", *South China Morning Post*, 17 November 1994 at 1, 15; D Kwan, "Peng to go on trial for graft 'next week' ", *South China Morning Post*, 8 November 1994 at 9; Frankie Fook-Lun Leung, "Rule of Law: The Problem of Being Chinese", *Asian Wall Street Journal*, 2 June 1994 at 6; S Long, "Boom town trial tests terms of doing business with China", *The Guardian*, 17 November 1994 at 17; R MacPherson, "Chinese-Australian trapped aboard China's Midnight Express", Agence France-Presse, 22 June 1994; R Mathewson, " 'Cleared' Peng to face new charges", *South China Morning Post*, 6 November 1994 at 1, 7; R Mathewson, "Experts say Peng charges ominous", *South China Morning Post*, 6 November 1994 at 1, 7; R Mathewson, "Shenzhen launching new bid to try Peng", *South China Morning Post*, 30 October 1994 at 1, 2; R Mathewson, "Storm rising over jailing of businessman", *South China Morning Post*, 15 May 1994 at 4; Lina Shen-Peng, "The Perils of Doing Business in China", *Wall Street Journal*, 11 November 1994; Lina Shen-Peng, "Rule of Law Must Prevail in China", *Asian Wall Street Journal*, 9 November 1994 at 8; P Stein, "Unforeseen Risk", *Asian Wall Street Journal*, 23 May 1994 at 1; P Stein, "Foreign Businesspeople Find Dissidents Aren't Only Ones China Puts in Jail", *Wall Street Journal*, 25 May 1994 at 13; Wall Street Journal (Editorial), "Until Macau Comes Home", *Asian Wall Street Journal*, 1 September 1994 at 6.
50 It has been reported that Peng always refused to offer bribes to officials: *South China Morning Post*, 1 May 1994 at 6.

People's Bank of China sent inspectors into Champaign, it seized its account books and it also alleged that Panco was not the legal owner of shares in Champaign.[51] Loans which had been provided by Chinese banks were called in early, but Champaign was able to stay afloat.

On 7 July 1992 trading in Champaign shares on the Shenzhen stock exchange was suspended. In December, the Shenzhen Intermediate People's Court then ruled against Peng's company Panco. In March 1993 the Shenzhen Municipal People's Government issued orders to restructure Champaign. However, in May 1993, Peng won a ruling from the Guondong Higher People's Court in relation to this dispute with his Shenzhen joint venture partners, with the appeal court ruling that Panco's investment in Champaign was legal.

Despite this ruling by the appeal court, the Shenzhen authorities expropriated the shares in Champaign which were controlled by Peng. Assets of Champaign were seized and redistributed by Champaign without the approval of the joint venture company's majority shareholder. In September 1993 Champaign was restructured after a meeting of Champaign was held at which Panco and its majority shareholders were not represented. In the process, Panco lost its shares in the joint venture company without being given any compensation and despite a statement by the Hong Kong Supreme Court that the seizure of these shares was illegal. Panco's stake in Champaign had been valued at about HK$600m at that time.[52]

Peng was about to sue Shenzhen authorities for the return of the expropriated holdings in Champaign when he was imprisoned, with the assistance of Macau police. This detention seemed to be aimed at pre-empting further legal action by Peng against the Shenzhen government. It may be noted that by July 1992 Peng had resigned as chairman of both Champaign and Panco and had sold his controlling interest in Champaign.

On 13 October 1993, Peng was taken from his hotel room at Macau's Mandarin Oriental Hotel by two policemen and kept in custody overnight on suspicion of a visa problem. The next day Peng allegedly agreed to voluntarily return to China to assist in police inquiries. Peng was asked to sign a statement written in Portuguese, a language that was foreign to him, and he was then delivered by Portuguese authorities to police at the China border. Portuguese authorities insist that Peng's return to China was voluntary.[53] Peng was then held for 9 months without

---

51 S Holberton, "Chinese dream sours for high-flying entrepreneur: The detention of 'Jimmy' Peng on suspicion of corruption has turned the spotlight on a secretive and primitive legal system", *The Financial Times*, 23/24 July 1994 at 3.
52 It may be of interest to note that shares in Champaign had been classified as A shares, which can only be traded by Chinese nationals. However, the strict separation between A and B shares now seems to be breaking down in Shenzhen. Although China does not formally provide for dual citizenship, one lawyer has noted that informally it does tend to treat overseas Chinese as mainland Chinese citizens: Frankie Fook-Lun Leung, "Rule of Law: The Problem of Being Chinese", *Asian Wall Street Journal*, 2 June 1994 at 6.
53 The Australian Government has protested to the Macau authorities about these actions and these authorities have now insisted upon formal extradition procedures

access to his lawyers or his family. The protracted detention of Peng would usually be regarded as illegal, but for the existence of a procedure whereby detention for a period of longer than two months without charge can be approved by the National People's Congress Standing Committee. Such approval was apparently obtained in this case because of the alleged complexity of the Peng case. However, the existence of this NPC approval has never been substantiated.[54]

It is interesting to note that it was not until November 1994 that the Shenzhen authorities acknowledged that they had abducted Peng from Macau. However, they stated that this had been done because they believed that he was guilty. The second in command of the Shenzhen Procuratorate, Luo Jinquan, is reported to have said that "Peng had committed an offence so they [the procuratorate] decided he had to be captured."[55] It would be difficult to imagine the Australian Government taking a similar attitude to, for example, the Australian entrepreneur, Christopher Skase, who has been the subject of extremely protracted extradition proceedings in Spain. In the West, in the rare cases when forceful police abduction has occurred from another country, it has tended to be reserved for cases with very high political or moral significance.[56] It is very difficult to see how such illegal actions as occurred in abducting James Peng could be justified in a Western legal system let alone being allowed to sustain further legal proceedings against him.

The reported involvement in this case of Ding Peng, the niece of paramount leader Deng Xiaoping, seems to have made satisfactory resolution of the Peng case even more difficult.[57] Ms Deng was apparently originally hired by James Peng to seek to improve his communications with Shenzhen officialdom and she was paid HK$100,000 a month for her services. *The Financial Times* has noted that, subsequently, Ms Deng and an associate sought to transfer Panco's shareholding in Champaign, which was valued at HK$450m, to a mainland-owned Hong Kong company with which they were associated. Peng then sought to prevent this transfer by obtaining an injunction from

---

before persons are handed over to China: R Mathewson, "Legal Department in Macau learned of businessman's plight one month later", *South China Morning Post*, 17 July 1994 at 5.

54 D Kwan, "Probe on Peng has increased – official", *South China Morning Post*, 22 July 1994 at 1; *South China Morning Post*, 13 October 1994 at 9. Also, the failure of the Chinese authorities to inform Peng's family of his arrest until three days after it had occurred was also a violation of Art 43 of China's Criminal Procedure Law which requires that this notification must occur within 24 hours.
55 D Kwan, "Peng denies charges amid tight security", *South China Morning Post*, 17 November 1994 at 1.
56 One can think of few such cases, such as the Israeli abduction of a Nazi mass murderer or the American abduction of a major drug baron such as General Noriega.
57 N Cater, "Corruption case against Peng fails", *South China Morning Post*, 9 October 1994 at 7; S Holberton, "Chinese dream sours for high-flying entrepreneur: The detention of 'Jimmy' Peng on suspicion of corruption has turned the spotlight on a secretive and primitive legal system", *The Financial Times*, 23/24 July 1994 at 3; Lina Shen-Peng, "The Perils of Doing Business in China", *Wall Street Journal*, 11 November 1994.

the Hong Kong Supreme Court. Thereafter, Peng was apprehended in Macau after he lodged a suit before the Shenzhen Intermediate People's Court. However, the court refused to accept his application to commence legal proceedings against Ding Peng and her business partner Zheng Lielie. Ding Peng has reportedly hired a Sydney firm of solicitors to seek to obtain documents in Australia which belong to James Peng. Shenzhen prosecutors had apparently also travelled to Sydney in an effort to obtain more information about Peng.[58]

In August 1994, Peng was charged with embezzling US$1.4m from Champaign when he was its chairman. However these charges were thrown out by the Shenzhen courts upon the basis that there was not enough evidence. These funds had been invested by Peng in Australia upon behalf of Champaign. However, the prosecutor was given a further month in which to obtain further evidence. It now seems that the Shenzhen prosecutors have acknowledged that the sums invested by Peng in Australia were invested for company purposes in the name of Champaign. However, the new charges which have been laid on 14 October (but only reported in early November) seem to be a variation of earlier charges laid against Peng. Peng's lawyers have denied these charges and presented evidence to rebut them, including a statement from the international accounting firm Arthur Anderson which claims that not only had Peng not embezzled funds from Champaign, but that he was actually owed at least two million yuan by the company.[59]

It is interesting to note in passing that under the Chinese Criminal Procedure Laws it is an offence for "state personnel who take advantage of their office to engage in corruption involving articles of public property." This Law had been revised in recent years to provide that the phrase "state personnel" included managers and executives of joint venture companies in China. Peng was therefore subject to this provision if a case against him could be established. A conviction under this provision of the Criminal Procedure Law is subject to life imprisonment or to a death penalty. It should also be noted that there is no presumption of innocence under China's criminal law, so that, as one legal expert from the University of Hong Kong has said, "once charges have been laid by the procurate, which is an organ of the state, the unspoken assumption is that he is guilty."[60]

It is easy to see the misfortune of James Peng as the result of a groundless vendetta by various senior officials in China. This is clearly the view of many friends, lawyers and politicians who are fighting for his release.[61] It is also a view which has been suggested by editorial writers.[62] However, this case clearly has wider implications, in regard to the

---

58 R Mathewson, "Shenzhen launches new bid to try Peng", *South China Morning Post*, 30 October 1994 at 2.
59 D Kwan, "Peng denies charges amid tight security", *South China Morning Post*, 17 November 1994 at 1, 15.
60 R Mathewson, " 'Cleared' Peng to face new charges", *South China Morning Post*, 6 November 1994 at 7.
61 *South China Morning Post*, 9 October 1994 at 12.
62 "Judicial system faces a test", *South China Morning Post*, 19 November 1994.

implementation of the rule of law in the Chinese legal system. A correspondent for *The Financial Times* has quoted a Hong Kong lawyer who has said of this case that "[t]he Shenzhen authorities have shown a flagrant disregard for the rights of shareholders and creditors, which are basic rights enshrined in all company law."[63]

Furthermore, in an article by Dr Huang Chen-Ya, in the *South China Morning Post* appearing in August 1994, it was noted that it would be wrong for persons who were not ethnic Chinese to believe that they could avoid Peng's fate. Dr Huang persuasively argued that the failure of the central authorities in China to punish corrupt cadres in cases such as these is likely to provoke similar detention of non-Chinese businessmen in the event of a business dispute arising.[64] Others have made similar cautionary statements.[65] It is interesting to note that Mrs Shen-Peng, in her pleas to the Chinese authorities and in her articles in the international press, has laid emphasis upon achieving the ideal of the rule of law in China.[66] These sentiments were echoed by the *South China Morning Post* when it said of this case that:

> The rule of law has been severely tested by the manner in which the charges were brought and then altered to suit the whim of the Shenzhen authorities. The original case against Peng, which took 10 months to put together, was thrown out by the Intermediate People's Court in Shenzhen. The prosecutor was instructed to find more evidence. In any reliable system of justice, lack of evidence would lead to acquittal. But this court effectively gave the authorities leave to try a man twice for the same offence — contrary to what common law legal systems consider acceptable. Worse, when the prosecution came back, it did not bring more evidence, but claimed new alleged offences, as if recognising it did not have a case with the first charge ... [67]

The *South China Morning Post* was relatively kind in its criticisms, compared to those of the *Wall Street Journal* which has recently attacked the guanxi system (or the reliance upon high powered Chinese personal connections) as a basis for business in China, and it went on to attack what it described as "China's legal nonsystem" which was evident in cases such as this.[68] While this may be an overstatement it is a reflection of the depth of international concerns about this implications of this case. There is no doubt that the Peng case is a disaster for the international credibility of the Chinese legal system and its business regulatory apparatus. In view of the apparent (if limited) involvement of officials and persons of influence from Beijing, the case cannot be dismissed as a

---

63 S Holberton, "Chinese dream sours for high-flying entrepreneur: The detention of 'Jimmy' Peng on suspicion of corruption has turned the spotlight on a secretive and primitive legal system", *The Financial Times*, 23/24 July 1994 at 3.
64 *South China Morning Post*, 7 August 1994 at 17.
65 See comments by Mr John Kamm, a prominent American human rights lobbyist, reported by R Mathewson, "Storm rising over jailing of businessman", *South China Morning Post*, 15 May 1994 at 4. Kamm reportedly observed that Mr Peng's case "is a striking example of the law-unto-themselves attitude of the security forces."
66 Lina Shen-Peng, "The Perils of Doing Business in China", *Wall Street Journal*, 11 November 1994.
67 "Judicial system faces a test", *South China Morning Post*, 19 November 1994.
68 "China Business", (Editorial), *Wall Street Journal*, 18 November 1994.

mere local aberration. The Beijing authorities were clearly content to leave the matter in the hands of local authorities as is evident from the report that the Australian Foreign Minister, Gareth Evans, was told by China's Premier Li Peng and Foreign Minister Qian Qichen that the James Peng case was not an appropriate case for discussion with visiting government officials who were concerned with the treatment of their nationals.[69] It is clear that this case could not have come at a worse time for the new system of Company Law which has been introduced in China in 1994 as the legacy of the case, and of others like it[70], will be likely to undermine business confidence in the Chinese legal system for some time to come.

Conclusions

The maintenance of a legal system which can make credible claims to sustaining the rule of law is an important backdrop for market economies, even if most transactions between business persons and corporations rely more on trust and personal relationships than upon the application of legal principles. I have argued that the rule of law is an important ideology which the modern nation state seeks to sustain, even if from time to time rule of law claims sound somewhat hollow. Of course, the rule of law doctrine has developed in western countries over the last three hundred years or so. It would be surprising if it could be quickly implanted and widely accepted within a body politic such as China.

It is clear that significant efforts are being made to move in this direction in China, but challenges to the rule of law doctrine, such as the Peng case, may cause some damage to the acceptance of law reforms based upon this conception. However, unfortunate episodes such as the Peng case, may provoke sufficient loss of face upon the part of those whose task it is to fashion the ideologies of the state, and this includes the judiciary, that decisive action may be taken to deal with such embarrassing cases. It is important that the new China Company Law be given a chance to work as it is a fundamental vehicle for achieving a market economy.

The new law is such an important development in China's business law that it would be tragic if it was to be undermined by a widespread cynicism about the possibility of introducing a rational legal system which is concerned with advancing rule of law values. This is not to suggest that the rule of law is an unqualified good, for it is not, but, so long as its limitations are recognised, it can serve as an important bulwark against arbitrary power in the modern state. It is to be hoped that, given the symbolic significance which it has assumed, the Peng case may yet

---

69 G Crothall, "Li 'relaxed' over reforms in territory", *South China Morning Post*, 3 April 1994 at 6.
70 *The South China Morning Post*, "China's risky business", recently reported that of 16 Hong Kong people who are presently detained in China, some 15 were there on business, (November 1994).

provide an opportunity for a major judicial statement of the importance of the rule of law as an aspiration for China's changing legal system.

[17]

CREATIVE NORM DESTRUCTION: THE EVOLUTION OF NONLEGAL RULES IN JAPANESE CORPORATE GOVERNANCE

Curtis J. Milhaupt[†]

This Article analyzes the origins, persistence, and current evolution of a series of nonlegal rules (norms) that have played an important role in Japanese corporate governance. The central features of the governance environment examined here include: (1) the main bank system, in which banks voluntarily restructure loans to some distressed borrowers, (2) a social distaste for hostile takeovers, (3) implicit promises of employment stability, and (4) belief systems about the proper role and structure of the board of directors.

I show that, despite virtually ubiquitous claims to the contrary, these norms do not enjoy a long history of practice in Japan, but rather emerged only in the immediate postwar period. I hypothesize that they emerged for two reasons: First, they served as a low-cost substitute for a troubled formal institutional environment beset by the "transplant effect" that imperils legal reform in transition economies today. Second, they provided private benefits to the small number of interest groups that emerged intact from World War II. The flow of private benefits to norm adherents explains the persistence of the norms despite clear evidence of their inefficiency over the past decade.

I demonstrate that current models of norm reform, which emphasize the role of exogenous shocks, the workings of norm entrepreneurs, and increased information, explain why the norms of Japanese corporate governance are currently evolving.

Finally, extrapolating from Japan's experience, I suggest how norm analysis can contribute to the two most pressing questions in comparative corporate governance today: whether law matters to corporate governance and whether diverse systems of corporate governance are converging toward the Anglo-American model. As to both questions, closer attention to norms reveals shortcomings in the existing literature. Specifically, the empirical model underlying the "law matters" literature is shown to be inconsistent with historical experience and overly attentive to formal

---

[†] Fuyo Professor of Law and Director, Center for Japanese Legal Studies, Columbia Law School. This Article grew out of a series of interviews I held in Tokyo with approximately twenty-five government officials, lawyers, investment bankers, and corporate managers in June of 2000. Since several interviewees requested anonymity, I have cited to my interview transcripts without disclosing the identity of the interviewee. Interested (or skeptical) readers may review redacted transcripts upon request. I owe my interviewees a large debt of gratitude. Prior drafts were improved by comments from Robert Ellickson, Koichi Hamada, Michiyo Hamada, Hugh Patrick, Gary Saxonhouse, Mark West, my symposium commentator Reinier Kraakman, and symposium or workshop participants at Columbia University, University of Michigan, University of Pennsylvania, and Vanderbilt University Law Schools, and the American Law and Economics Association Annual Meeting. I also benefited from discussions with Melvin Eisenberg.

rules enforced by courts. Bold claims that we are witnessing rapid convergence toward a shareholder-centered ideology, which in turn will drive convergence of corporate law and practices, are only partially supported by the Japanese experience to date. Rather than the "end of history" for corporate law, we are witnessing an ongoing struggle to align the formal and informal components of the governance regimes of many transition economies, including Japan's.

INTRODUCTION

As this Symposium attests, the role of norms in the corporation has only recently attracted the attention of legal scholars.[1] This is curious, given the depth of analysis previously devoted to the role social norms play in governing collective behavior among cattle ranchers, diamond merchants, sumo wrestlers, and other exotica.[2] The importance, if not the novelty, of these well-studied groups pales in comparison to the corporation, arguably the most ingenious private organization ever devised.

Perhaps even more curiously, social norms have been virtually ignored in the comparative corporate governance debates of the past decade. The omission of norms from this body of literature is particularly stark. It is now widely recognized, for example, that legal protections for minority investors are a key variable in determining patterns of corporate ownership and finance around the world. Yet the literature to date (which ironically has been dominated by economists) displays a rather naïve fixation on *formal* legal protections and judicial enforcement to the exclusion of other alternatives. To take another example, analysis of complements and substitutes has been used powerfully to explain major phenomena in comparative corporate law, including the stickiness of institutional change and the unintended consequences of legal transplants. But this conceptual framework has not been brought to bear on the interaction between legal and nonlegal rules in the governance of firms. Perhaps most glaringly, for all the recent discussion of global convergence on a shareholder-centered model of corporate governance, there have been remarkably few careful examinations of the linkage between corporate norm shifts and

---

[1] Two noteworthy exceptions are Melvin A. Eisenberg, *Corporate Law and Social Norms*, 99 COLUM. L. REV. 1253 (1999), and Edward B. Rock, *Saints and Sinners: How Does Delaware Corporate Law Work?*, 44 UCLA L. REV. 1009 (1997).

[2] ROBERT C. ELLICKSON, ORDER WITHOUT LAW: HOW NEIGHBORS SETTLE DISPUTES (1991) (cattle ranchers); Lisa Bernstein, *Opting Out of the Legal System: Extralegal Contractual Relations in the Diamond Industry*, 21 J. LEGAL STUD. 115 (1992) (diamond merchants); Mark D. West, *Legal Rules and Social Norms in Japan's Secret World of Sumo*, 26 J. LEGAL STUD. 165 (1997) (sumo wrestlers).

changes in corporate law and practice.

As a modest step toward filling these gaps in the literature, in this Article I examine the creation, persistence, and evolution of a series of highly complementary, nonlegally enforceable practices that shaped postwar corporate governance for large Japanese firms. I examine four central features of the governance environment: (1) the "main bank" system and its role in corporate monitoring, (2) the absence of an external market for corporate control, (3) the structure and role of Japanese boards, and (4) the lifetime employment system. Examining these components of Japanese corporate governance is certainly not novel. Analyzing them as norms, however, yields some fresh insights into how nonlegal rules interacted with the legal system during the heyday of Japanese corporate governance, why the norm-based system persisted long after evidence of its inefficiency emerged, and how (or whether) Japan is currently adapting to a shareholder-centered ideology of corporate governance. Most interestingly, Japan's experience with corporate norms—which as we shall see is intimately related to its *three* experiences as a transition economy—sheds light on a current debate about the role of law in corporate governance. This debate is itself an outgrowth of the past decade of institutional disarray in many transition economies of Eastern Europe and Asia.

This Article has two principal aims: First, to contribute to the limited store of primary research on norms by analyzing their role in the governance of firms in the world's second largest economy. Primary research on norms of all types is in short supply, but research on the operation of norms among organizations is virtually nonexistent.[3] The second aim is to draw attention to the lack of norm analysis in comparative corporate governance scholarship. The Article does so by illustrating, based on the Japanese experience, how norm analysis contributes to the two most interesting questions in comparative corporate governance today: Do legal differences explain cross-country differences in corporate ownership and finance, and are corporate governance systems converging?

The Article is organized as follows: Part I describes four norms that are intimately connected to Japanese corporate governance practices in the postwar period. Part II demonstrates, despite numerous claims to the contrary, that each of these norms first emerged in the

---

[3] The sole exception may be an article prepared for this Symposium. Robert Cooter & Melvin A. Eisenberg, *Good Agent Character, Fairness, and Efficiency in Firms*, 149 U. PA. L. REV. 1717 (2001).

postwar period and represents a break with past practices. This insight provides important clues about the origins and durability of the norm-based system. I hypothesize that the new norms emerged as both low-cost substitutes for legal rules in the institutional turmoil of the immediate postwar period and as a fount of private benefits for the few organized groups left intact after the war and Allied occupation. Normative corporate governance, I argue, was a postwar Japanese invention understandable through the lenses of transaction cost economics and public choice theory. Part III explores the ongoing evolution of the postwar norms of Japanese corporate governance, reflecting shifts in the relative costs of using legal versus nonlegal rules, reconfigurations of the players in Japanese corporate governance, increased information, and the workings of norm reformers, including those within the government. Drawing on the creation and destruction of nonlegal rules in corporate Japan, Part IV highlights the contribution of norm analysis to the two key debates in comparative corporate law scholarship today.

Before proceeding, a definition and two caveats are in order. One of the principal problems with norm analysis is the lack of agreement on the definition of the term. In this Article, I have adopted Richard Posner's definition: a norm is "a rule that is not promulgated by an official source, such as a court or a legislature, nor enforced by the threat of legal sanctions, yet is regularly complied with."[4] This definition does not require that a rule be internalized as a preference[5] or that it be deeply rooted in the culture that complies with it. Unlike many other definitions in use, it does not place particular emphasis on social enforcement, thus highlighting the possibility that norms can be self-enforcing if compliance generates private benefits. The first caveat is that, for reasons made clear below, several of the rules I am about to discuss fall marginally outside that definition because they depend in some way on the government for promulgation or enforcement. I have included them because their informal character substantially outweighs the support they draw from the state and because the intermeshing of norms and state-generated rules is one of the key themes emerging from our inquiry. The second caveat is that these norms apply only to the governance of large, publicly held firms.

---

[4] Richard A. Posner, *Social Norms and the Law: An Economic Approach*, 87 AM. ECON. REV., PAPERS AND PROCS. OF THE HUNDRED AND NINTH ANN. MEETING OF THE AM. ECON. ASS'N, May 1997, at 365, 365.

[5] *Id.* at 365 n.1.

I. Four Nonlegal Rules of Japanese Corporate Governance

The stylized account of Japanese corporate governance for large firms contains several key features: the "main bank" system, in which banks are said to perform the key monitoring role over their client firms; the concomitant absence of an external market for corporate control; employee-dominated boards that focus on day-to-day management rather than monitoring; and the lifetime employment system, in which certain employees enjoy implicit promises of career-long job stability. This Part examines the normative features of these arrangements. My point here is not that law is irrelevant to Japanese corporate governance.[6] Rather, it is to highlight the distinction between institutions (endogenously generated, self-enforcing informal rules, including beliefs) and law,[7] and to show how important the former are to the Japanese firm.

A. Norms Governing the Main Bank System

Perhaps the principal distinguishing feature of Japanese corporate governance is the main bank system. The main bank, at least as it operated in its heyday, can be characterized as the largest single lender to a corporate client as well as one of its principal shareholders. As a central repository of information on the borrower, the main bank was well positioned to play a key role in monitoring the firm's management and rendering assistance in case of managerial crisis or financial failure.[8] This assistance could include loan forgiveness and guarantees of outstanding and new indebtedness.

The main bank is not a legal institution. Its function is not de-

---

[6] I have argued elsewhere that the formal legal structure in Japan supports corporate private ordering in crucial ways. Curtis J. Milhaupt, *A Relational Theory of Japanese Corporate Governance: Contract, Culture, and the Rule of Law*, 37 HARV. INT'L L.J. 3 (1996); *see also* J. MARK RAMSEYER & MINORU NAKAZATO, JAPANESE LAW: AN ECONOMIC APPROACH 2-3 (1999) (arguing that the Japanese legal system provides proper incentives for economic growth).

[7] I am following the lead of Stanford economist Masahiko Aoki in drawing this distinction. Aoki focuses exclusively on the main bank system. *See* Masahiko Aoki, A Note on the Role of Banking in Developing Economies in the Aftermath of the East Asian Crisis (1999) (unpublished manuscript, on file with author).

[8] I make no claims here about the quality or economic effects of main bank monitoring. Those questions are currently being reassessed in light of Japan's economic malaise. *See, e.g.*, Christopher W. Anderson & Terry Campbell II, Corporate Governance of Japanese Banks 30 (2000) (unpublished manuscript, on file with Social Science Research Network), *available at* http://papers.ssrn.com/sol3/papers.cfm?cfid=428604&cftoken=85393283&abstract_id=231950.

fined in any statute or regulation. Nor are any special obligations to borrowers specified contractually.[9] Rather, the main bank system rests on a social presumption. A "prominent part of the business ideology surrounding the main bank system"[10] is the expectation on the part of the bank, the borrower, and all relevant business and governmental actors that a main bank informally restructures a large failing company rather than foreclosing on its loans. In these informal workout scenarios, the main bank typically waives a portion of the debt in return for a restructuring plan by the borrower.[11] Although the main bank almost always has a first priority security interest in the collateral of the debtor, the bank, in effect, voluntarily subordinates its interest to that of the other lenders.

Why does the main bank undertake this role? This question is the subject of a vast literature that I will not summarize here. The key for present purposes is that, as Geoffrey Miller and I have argued elsewhere, the entire main bank system is supported by a cluster of norms that encourage banks to support weak firms (at least those for which a return to solvency and profitability are possible) in return for a non-legally enforceable promise by the government to prevent bank failure.[12] Indeed, until the early 1990s, there was not a single Japanese

---

[9] See Aoki, supra note 7; see also J. Mark Ramseyer, *Explicit Reasons for Implicit Contracts: The Legal Logic to the Japanese Main Bank System*, in THE JAPANESE MAIN BANK SYSTEM: ITS RELEVANCE FOR DEVELOPING AND TRANSFORMING ECONOMIES 231, 231 (Masahiko Aoki & Hugh Patrick eds., 1994) (describing the main bank system as a "nexus of implied contracts" or "promises . . . never made").

[10] Paul Sheard, *The Main Bank System and Corporate Monitoring and Control in Japan*, 11 J. ECON. BEHAV. & ORG. 399, 407 (1989).

[11] See Phred Dvorak, *Japan Readies New Remedy on Bank Debt*, WALL ST. J., Mar. 5, 2001, at A14 (reporting that 235 companies received informal debt waivers from 1985 to April 2000).

[12] Curtis J. Milhaupt & Geoffrey P. Miller, *Cooperation, Conflict, and Convergence in Japanese Finance: Evidence from the "Jusen" Problem*, 29 LAW & POL'Y INT'L BUS. 1, 19-20 (1997). Paraphrasing slightly, we described the norms in the following terms:

- *Survival of the Weakest*: Policies (rates) are set to permit the survival of the weakest member of the group. The weakest member of the group is often the one most likely to defect from the group's norms because the benefit this member obtains from abiding by those norms may be outweighed by the benefit it can obtain through defection. Because defection by one member can threaten the entire structure, the weakest member has a credible threat that places it in a strong bargaining position vis-à-vis its counterparts. In consequence, the substantive norms of the group are likely to protect the weakest member in order to insure this member's continuing loyalty to the group.

The norm of Survival of the Weakest benefits the stronger as well as the weaker members. In addition to enhancing the durability of the group as a whole, the Survival of the Weakest norm may support pricing arrangements that allow the weakest member to stay in business while allowing more efficient producers to

bank failure in the postwar period.

B. *The Norm Against Hostile Takeovers*

Closely linked to the main bank system is the second major distinguishing characteristic of Japanese corporate governance, the absence of a market for corporate control. Indeed, there have been virtually no contested bids among Japanese firms in the postwar period. Hostile takeovers have thus played no disciplining role over Japanese management. This function, to the extent it existed, was subsumed within the operation of the main bank system itself. Failing firms were often restructured under the guidance of the main bank, generally resulting in the replacement of existing management. Transfers of corporate assets are so heavily intermediated by banks that the tender offer process was used only three times from its inception in 1971 through 1990.[13]

---

earn supercompetitive profits.

- *No Exit (No Failure)*: Almost a corollary of the principle of Survival of the Weakest is that of No Exit: no group member is allowed to exit (fail). This enhances stability both by preventing failure by weaker members and by increasing public confidence in the management of the group.
- *Responsibility and Equitable Subordination*: When the danger of financial failure grows, the parent or principal source of funding for the failing entity is expected to take responsibility by extending financial assistance and by subordinating its claims to those of other creditors, even if not legally required to do so. This norm encourages monitoring by stronger group members by imposing both monetary and reputational costs on stronger players who allow smaller players under their jurisdiction to fall into difficulty.
- *Implicit Government Insurance*: The preceding norms lead naturally to a substantive norm of implicit insurance provided by the government. If strong members are expected to assist weaker members and if no member of the group is allowed to fail, some entity must backstop the strong members. Thus, an implicit grant of government insurance is inherent in the operation of the other norms. Put differently, the Responsibility and Equitable Subordination norm extends even to the government.

There are a few examples of bank defection from these norms in the 1970s and 1980s. However, the most prominent of these, involving the bankruptcy of Sanko Steamship Co. in 1985, actually underscores the existence of powerful nonlegal rules in the banking industry. Sanko was forced to file for protection from its creditors in 1985 when its three principal lenders refused to extend additional financing to the struggling firm. But prior to the banks' defection, both Sanko and the government defected as well: Sanko resisted the banks' attempts to play a larger role in its management, and the government refused to provide explicit guarantees to the banks. *See Japanese Shipping Firm Sinks*, CHICAGO SUN-TIMES, Aug. 14, 1985, *available at* 1985 WL 3576487; Masayoshi Kanabayashi, *Japan's Sanko Faces Pressure To Seek Relief*, WALL ST. J., Aug. 13, 1985, *available at* 1985 WL-WSJ 225942.

[13] Hideki Kanda, *Comparative Corporate Governance Country Report: Japan, in*

To be sure, there are legal and structural impediments to hostile takeovers in Japan. The most formidable is the practice of stable cross-shareholding among Japanese firms and banks, most prominently in the form of the *keiretsu* corporate groups. As Mark Ramseyer has noted, while these obstacles do not prevent hostile takeovers, they do make them more expensive relative to the alternatives.[14] There may also be a host of more subtle reasons for the lack of hostile takeover activity. For example, because a high percentage of directors of public firms are alumni cohorts of a small number of prestigious universities, the managers of the erstwhile bidder and target could well be classmates, particularly given the seniority-based promotion system of most large firms.[15]

Interesting for our purposes, however, is the fact that these impediments are shrouded in a firmly established social norm. The shared understanding that Japanese managers do not sell their companies, particularly to an uninvited bidder, is repeated like a mantra in virtually every domestic and foreign commentary on Japanese mergers and acquisitions ("M&A"). The following account of the norm by a foreign observer is representative:

> [T]he Japanese company is an extension of the concept of the family; the company cannot be separated from the people who comprise it. The sale of a Japanese business, therefore, is said to have the flavor of the sale of people. It is said to be immoral. Even the Japanese vocabulary used in acquisitions supports this view. The purchase of a company in Japan is called "*nottori*," which can be translated as "a hijacking."[16]

It is impossible to determine whether the structural impediments, the subtle factors, the norm, or some combination of the above is actually doing the work of dampening the market for corporate control in Japan. Nonetheless, the very existence of such a pervasive social

---

COMPARATIVE CORPORATE GOVERNANCE: THE STATE OF THE ART AND EMERGING RESEARCH 921, 934 (Klaus Hopt et al. eds., 1998).

[14] J. Mark Ramseyer, *Takeovers in Japan: Opportunism, Ideology, and Corporate Control*, 35 UCLA L. REV. 1, 38 (1987). For an excellent overview of obstacles to mergers and acquisitions ("M&A") in Japan, see Berkeley Scott, *M&A Japan: An Update from Morgan Stanley*, BUS. INSIGHT JAPAN, Nov. 1998, *at* http://bi-japan.com/1998/nov/bijapan-www/zashi/dm2.htm.

[15] This possibility emerged from a discussion with Robert Rasmussen. Indeed, just under fifty percent of the presidents of firms having capital of at least ¥100 billion in 1995 were graduates of the University of Tokyo. Setsuo Miyazawa & Hiroshi Otsuka, *Legal Education and the Reproduction of the Elite in Japan*, 1 ASIAN-PAC. L. & POL'Y J. 1, 20 & tbl.25 (2000), *available at* http://www.hawaii.edu/aplpj/1/02.html.

[16] Kelly Charles Crabb, *The Reality of Extralegal Barriers to Mergers and Acquisitions in Japan*, 21 INT'L LAW. 97, 116 (1987) (citations omitted).

understanding seems significant. Even if its effects are overwhelmed by more prosaic disincentives to hostile bids, the emergence and persistence of a "trivial" social norm remains to be explained.

C. *Beliefs About Board Structure and Role*

There is a sizeable gap between Japanese corporate law and practice on the composition and role of the board of directors. In contrast to the German system of codetermination, Japanese law does not require employee participation at the board level. Yet Japanese boards are comprised almost exclusively of managers who have served the corporation throughout their career and are viewed as employee representatives.[17] Legally, the Japanese board is charged with monitoring corporate activity and vested with the authority to make important managerial decisions.[18] In fact, boards have not traditionally emphasized their monitoring role. Moreover, it is commonly understood that a few senior directors (acting as an informal management committee) or a representative director (who is virtually always the president) have the ultimate decisionmaking authority in the corporation, rather than the board as a whole. These discrepancies between law and practice recently led a blue ribbon corporate governance panel to conclude that "[i]t is questionable whether the Japanese board of directors actually complies with the Commercial Code's stipulation that it function[] as the body which decides on corporate will and exercises corporate oversight."[19]

The gaps between law and practice can be traced to beliefs about the board's proper function in the Japanese system. Election to the board has traditionally been viewed almost exclusively as the crowning achievement in a long career with the firm that begins upon graduation from college. As noted above, virtually all members of the board have traditionally been members of senior management (typically one from each of the company's major divisions).[20] Indeed, the Commercial Code does not even recognize officers as a distinct corporate organ, suggesting that the concepts are indistinct. The fact that senior managers are almost never hired away from competitors or firms in

---

[17] CORPORATE GOVERNANCE COMM., CORPORATE GOVERNANCE FORUM OF JAPAN, CORPORATE GOVERNANCE PRINCIPLES—A JAPANESE VIEW 41-42 (1998).
[18] SHŌHŌ [Commercial code], Law No. 48 of 1899, art. 260.
[19] CORPORATE GOVERNANCE COMM., *supra* note 17, at 49.
[20] *Id.*; *see also* WILLIAM M. MERCER COMPANIES LLC, TORISHIMARIYAKU INOBEISHON [DIRECTOR INNOVATION] 49 (1999) [hereinafter DIRECTOR INNOVATION].

other industries reinforces the perception that directors represent employees or, at most, divisions of the firm.

This belief system shaped the two defining characteristics of the traditional Japanese board, its large size and lack of independent directors.[21] A survey of all listed companies in Japan found that the boards of firms with more than 1000 employees had an average of 17.7 directors. Among the same firms, 22% had 20 to 24 directors and 10% had 25 or more directors.[22] The friendly merger of two large Japanese banks once created a board of 67.[23]

The common practice of having a very large board composed almost exclusively of senior managers is consistent with the view of board seats as incentive devices for loyal employees. The practice, however, is harder to square with the legal conception of the board as the locus of corporate monitoring and strategic decisionmaking.[24]

D. *Lifetime Employment*

Another principal feature of Japanese corporate structure is the "lifetime" employment system, which covers white-collar and most blue-collar workers in large firms. In this system, the mutual expectation of employer and employee is that the employee will enjoy continuous employment until the mandatory retirement age. Wages that undercompensate for productivity at the outset of the employment relationship are eventually offset by wages that overcompensate for productivity in the latter stages of the employee's career. Semi-annual bonuses, an integral part of the salary structure, are loosely tied to firm performance and pensions are generally not portable. Because labor mobility is limited and the employee has in effect posted a bond at the outset of the employment relationship that will only be fully recouped upon retirement, employees have a significant vested interest

---

[21] *See* CORPORATE GOVERNANCE COMM., *supra* note 17, at 41-42 (noting the difficulties of achieving board independence).

[22] DIRECTOR INNOVATION, *supra* note 20, at 20-21. A study by Steven Kaplan found that Japanese firms had a median of 21 directors, while U.S. firms had a median of 15. Steven N. Kaplan & J. Mark Ramseyer, *Those Japanese Firms with Their Disdain for Shareholders: Another Fable for the Academy*, 74 WASH. U. L.Q. 403, 410 (1996).

[23] *The Skies Are Darkening over Japan's Big Bank Mergers*, ECONOMIST, May 27, 2000, at 75.

[24] CORPORATE GOVERNANCE COMM., *supra* note 17, at 49. CalPERS believes the Japanese view of the board as a status position bestowed upon long-term employees as a reward for loyal service is in direct conflict with the monitoring and decisionmaking role of the board. CalPERS, *Japan Market Principles*, http://www.calpers-governance.org/principles/international/japan/page04.asp (1999).

in the continued viability and success of their firms.

Lifetime employment is not legally mandated. Nonetheless, treating lifetime employment as a norm requires qualification, because law has played an important role in shaping this institution. Japanese courts have supported the lifetime employment system by supplying bargaining endowments to both employers and employees, resulting in malleable, long-term employment patterns.[25] For employees, judicial precedent places substantial constraints on an employer's ability to dismiss workers even where layoffs are motivated by economic necessity. For employers, doctrine supports adjustment of work rules and ambiguous demarcation of job requirements, providing flexibility in worker assignments and transfers. Thus, important aspects of lifetime employment *are* legally enforceable.

At the same time, however, it is unlikely that the threat of legal sanction was the primary motivation of Japanese firms in entering into long-term, open-ended employment relationships with key workers. While some cases on abusive dismissal predate the emergence of lifetime employment practices, the Supreme Court did not affirm the standards developed in the lower courts until 1975. Furthermore, many of the important cases restricting layoffs arose out of the oil crisis of the 1970s and the yen crisis of the 1980s, long after lifetime employment practices were firmly entrenched. More importantly, the judicial standards for dismissal apply to a much larger universe of employees than those covered by lifetime employment,[26] indicating that implicit promises of career-long employment security are not the only available response to the legal requirements.

Professors Ronald Gilson and Mark Roe hypothesize that lifetime employment grew out of a political deal in which favored workers were granted employment security in return for labor peace and cooperation.[27] They characterize lifetime employment as "political" to emphasize the noneconomic rationale driving the formation of the institution. But their account is consistent with the view that lifetime employment arose out of a larger social pact to bring stability to post-

---

[25] For further analysis of the importance of judge-made law in the development of Japanese employment practices, see Takashi Araki, *Flexibility in Japanese Employment Relations and the Role of the Judiciary*, in JAPANESE COMMERCIAL LAW IN AN ERA OF INTERNATIONALIZATION 249 (Hiroshi Oda ed., 1994).

[26] *Id.* at 253-54.

[27] Ronald J. Gilson & Mark J. Roe, *Lifetime Employment: Labor Peace and the Evolution of Japanese Corporate Governance*, 99 COLUM. L. REV. 508, 522-23 (1999).

war Japan.[28] Indeed, the origins of lifetime employment are echoed in the judicial standards on abusive dismissal, under which layoffs must be "objectively reasonable and socially appropriate."[29] Viewed in this light, lifetime employment is a social norm that has been sanctioned and diffused by the state.[30]

* *

It is now common to analyze corporate governance institutions in a given country as a system of complementary components, meaning that the system as a whole is greater than the sum of the individual parts.[31] The nonlegal rules of Japanese corporate governance, particularly in conjunction with cross-shareholding practices, clearly constitute a complementary system. Bank monitoring, for example, has greater impact where share ownership is concentrated and lifetime employment is the norm; it would have less effect where ownership is dispersed, the market for corporate control is active, or senior managers are recruited from outside the firm.[32] A tradition of nonlegal governance may itself be complementary to bank monitoring. It has been argued that bank monitoring is actually enhanced by a low level of legal enforcement, since it reduces liability disincentives to active participation in the oversight of client firms.[33] The absence of a hostile takeover market in a system of bank monitoring, in turn, makes credible the implicit promise of lifetime employment, which reinforces beliefs about the proper role of management and the structure of the board.

Less well understood, however, is a question the seminal literature explicitly sidesteps: how are diverse actors led to pursue coherent policies and practices that result in complementary systems?[34] We

---

[28] In fact, Gilson and Roe expressly leave room for this interpretation. *Id.* at 523 (hypothesizing that the deal was "cemented by an emergent norm or 'macro' political understanding").

[29] Ichikawa v. Nihon Shokuen Seizō Co., 29 MINSHŪ 456, 458 (Sup. Ct., Apr. 25, 1975).

[30] For a similar conclusion, see Daniel H. Foote, *Judicial Creation of Norms in Japanese Labor Law: Activism in the Service of—Stability?*, 43 UCLA L. REV. 635, 651 (1996).

[31] The seminal article is Paul Milgrom & John Roberts, *Complementarities and Systems: Understanding Japanese Economic Organization*, 9 ESTUDIOS ECONOMICOS 3 (1994).

[32] These examples come from Hideki Kanda, *Japan's Financial Big Bang: Its Impact on the Legal System and Corporate Governance*, in CRISIS AND CHANGE IN THE JAPANESE FINANCIAL SYSTEM 277, 281-82 (Takeo Hoshi & Hugh Patrick eds., 2000).

[33] *Id.* at 284.

[34] Milgrom & Roberts, *supra* note 31, at 19.

turn now to this question. As we will see, in Japan individual governance components were bonded into a complementary whole by normative glue emerging out of the distinctive environment surrounding World War II.

II. NORM CREATION AND THE DEMAND FOR CORPORATE LAW

Why did these corporate governance norms emerge and how did they interact with the corporate law? Fortunately, it is possible to identify the historical period in which all of the corporate norms just discussed emerged. Knowing the historical context makes it possible to develop a hypothesis about how the norms emerged and why they persisted.

A. *Origins and Persistence of Normative Corporate Governance*

Tracing the origins of social norms is no small task, and I do not claim to have definitive historical evidence linking the emergence of normative corporate governance in Japan to the actions of individual actors. Yet one thing is clear: although claims to the contrary are virtually ubiquitous, none of the norms just described is deeply rooted in Japanese culture or reflects longstanding business customs.

On the contrary, the corporate governance norms surveyed above are a postwar Japanese invention.[35] Indeed, evidence of common prewar practices contrary to each of the four norms is not hard to find. For example, the main bank system did not exist in the first major phase of modern Japanese economic growth, the Meiji and Taisho periods (1868-1925), nor did any system of bank-oriented corporate governance.[36] Crucially, the government's implicit insurance against bank failure, which animates the main bank norms, was not in place

---

[35] Strictly speaking, the institution that would become the postwar main bank system had its origins in wartime loan syndicates guided by the government. Juro Teranishi, *Loan Syndication in War-Time Japan and the Origins of the Main Bank System, in* THE JAPANESE MAIN BANK SYSTEM, *supra* note 9, at 51.

The governance of firms is not the only place where a bit of digging reveals the shallowness of Japanese claims to deep historical roots. *See* MIRROR OF MODERNITY: INVENTED TRADITIONS OF MODERN JAPAN (Stephen Vlastos ed., 1998) (finding recent origins of many "age old" Japanese practices and cultural icons, including the rituals of sumo wrestling, aversion to litigation, and domesticity ideals).

[36] Yoshiro Miwa & J. Mark Ramseyer, Banks and Economic Growth: Implications from Japanese History 33-35 (Aug. 2000) (unpublished manuscript, on file with Social Science Research Network), *available at* http://papers.ssrn.com/sol3/papers.cfm?cfid=428604&cftoken=85393283&abstractid=239957.

before World War II. At least in the 1920s and 1930s, the Japanese government did not interfere with market discipline on banks, and bank failures were numerous.[37]

Mergers and acquisitions were also common in the Meiji Period. The family-controlled conglomerates known as *zaibatsu* frequently used acquisitions, including hostile takeover bids, as a strategic means of entering and developing industries.[38] Moreover, in the 1950s, several former *zaibatsu* firms were threatened by hostile bids. Managerial fear of hostile bids may have been an impetus for the practice of cross-shareholding, which emerged about this time.[39]

Finally, prewar practices at the board and employee levels also differed from the patterns previously discussed in this Article. For example, there is evidence that during the turn of the last century outside directors served on many boards and played an important role in monitoring firms.[40] Perhaps most surprisingly, employment relations through World War II are best described as *in*secure, as high rates of turnover and a mutual lack of long-term commitment on the part of employers and employees predominated.[41] In short, prewar Japanese corporate governance shared more traits with the present Anglo-American system than with its postwar reincarnation.

Why did norms at odds with past practices emerge to create the defining characteristics of postwar Japanese corporate governance?

---

[37] NIHON GINKŌ [BANK OF JAPAN], SENZENKI NI OKERU HATAN GINKŌ SEIRI NO JIREI [EXAMPLES OF FAILED BANK RESOLUTIONS IN THE PREWAR PERIOD] (1998) (showing major capital and deposit write-offs for failed banks during a financial crisis in the 1920s).

[38] *See* TOMATSU & CO., YOKU WAKARU M&A [UNDERSTANDING M&A] 28 (2000); Zenichi Shishido, Reform in Japanese Corporate Law and Corporate Governance: Current Changes in Historical Perspective 2 (Nov. 4-5, 1999) (unpublished manuscript, on file with author).

[39] *See* Randall Morck & Masao Nakamura, Japanese Corporate Governance and Macroeconomic Problems 8-9 (Apr. 2000) (unpublished manuscript, on file with Social Science Research Network), *available at* http://papers.ssrn.com/sol3/papers.taf?cfid=428604&cftoken=85393283&abstract_id=235758.

[40] Yoshiro Miwa & J. Mark Ramseyer, The Value of Prominent Directors: Lessons in Corporate Governance from Transitional Japan 6-7 (Nov. 2000) (unpublished manuscript, on file with Social Science Research Network), *available at* http://papers.ssrn.com/sol3/papers.cfm?cfid=428604&cftoken=85393283&abstract_id=192388.

[41] *See, e.g.*, ANDREW GORDON, THE EVOLUTION OF LABOR RELATIONS IN JAPAN: HEAVY INDUSTRY 1853-1955, at 132-61 (1985) (discussing pre-World War II trends in employment relations and variations in commitment level); Gilson & Roe, *supra* note 27, at 518-20 ("Stable employment is *not* a continuous Japanese cultural tradition.... Yearly turnover rates of around seventy-five percent were the norm in most industries during World War I."); Shishido, *supra* note 38, at 3.

Part of the answer, as other scholars have recognized, is that World War II created new patterns of interaction between government and industry that left an indelible mark on Japan's economic structures.[42] The National General Mobilization Law, enacted in 1938, provides insight into how the exigencies of wartime production could have reoriented thinking about the organization of firms.[43] The purpose of the law, which vested the government with vast power over all facets of labor, capital, contracting, and the operation of commercial enterprises, was "the control and operation of human and material resources in order that the nation may be enabled to display its total power most effectively for the realization of national defense purposes in time of war."[44] Main bank practices, for example, have been traced to wartime financing directives issued by the Ministry of Finance to the banking industry. And the impact of this regime appears to have been even more pervasive than the banking and finance scholars have indicated. A recent Japanese newspaper editorial suggests that the law "cast a spell" over Japan, serving as both catalyst for the economic dynamism of the 1980s and albatross in the long recession of the 1990s.[45]

Important as these influences no doubt were, it is difficult to credit wartime production alone with shaping the corporate governance norms of the next half century. After all, the National General Mobilization Law was repealed fifty-five years ago. The Japan of the 1970s to 1990s bears little economic, political, or social resemblance to the Japan of the 1930s and 1940s. Two central insights from standard norm scholarship help enrich the scanty existing account of the emergence and persistence of Japanese corporate norms. First, norms can sometimes supply a governance framework at lower cost than formal rules. Second, norms are subject to strategic manipulation, including manipulation by the state. In the remainder of this Part, I draw on these insights to explain the rise and persistence of normative corporate governance in postwar Japan.

One of norm scholarship's principal contributions to date lies in showing that over a wide range of human activity, informal norms provide more efficient mechanisms to govern conduct than legal

---

[42] *See, e.g.*, Teranishi, *supra* note 35, at 65-66, 75-80 (discussing the Japanese government's intervention into business during World War II and its effects on the postwar period).

[43] Kokka sōdōinhō, Law No. 19 of 1938.

[44] *Id.* art. 1.

[45] Mitsuo Miura, *Economic Forum: Breaking Free from Stranglehold of Wartime Regime*, YOMIURI SHIMBUN, May 3, 2000.

rules.[46] Applying this insight to Japan, it is highly plausible that in the immediate postwar environment, nonlegal rules supplied a corporate governance framework at lower cost than the legal system. To understand why, consider the extant legal system as it impacted corporate conduct. Japan's Commercial Code, a late-nineteenth-century German transplant, was extensively amended in 1950 under the influence of the occupation reformers to imbue the law with American notions of shareholders' rights. Among other changes, the amended Code enabled shareholders to access corporate records, bring derivative suits, vote cumulatively, and receive share appraisals in mergers. In short, minority investor legal protections were enhanced in precisely the ways that modern reformers suggest is crucial for good corporate governance in transition economies.[47] While the amendments eventually received support from the business community, academic and practitioner commentary was initially highly critical of the drastic increases in shareholder rights,[48] which co-existed awkwardly with the Code's emphasis on creditor protections. A board of directors and concepts of director accountability were also introduced into the Code at this time.[49] Yet the new board of directors overlapped with the Code's preexisting, German-style statutory auditor system, which was also designed to monitor corporate compliance. Thus, from its inception, the board was functionally orphaned by the statutory scheme.

Japanese securities laws also had been recently transplanted from abroad. The occupation reformers refused to reopen Japanese securities exchanges after the war until a statute resembling the U.S. securities laws was enacted. This was accomplished with the Securities Exchange Act of 1948, which is based heavily on the U.S. Securities Act of 1933 and Securities Exchange Act of 1934. The statute emphasizes investor protection and features a broad antifraud rule based directly

---

[46] The comparative advantages of private versus public ordering are a mainstay of the norm literature. *See, e.g.*, ELLICKSON, *supra* note 2 (concluding that value-maximizing norms, not law, are central to social order); Bernstein, *supra* note 2, at 157 (arguing that private dispute resolution in the diamond industry is superior to recourse to the legal system); Janet T. Landa, *Personal Versus Impersonal Trade: The Size of Trading Groups and Contract Law*, 4 INT'L. REV. L. & ECON. 15 (1984) (arguing that trade groups are a response to inefficient legal structures).

[47] *See infra* Part IV.A.

[48] Mark D. West, *The Puzzling Divergence of Corporate Law: Evidence and Explanations from Japan and the United States*, 150 U. PA. L. REV. (forthcoming 2001), *available at* http://papers.ssrn.com/sol3/papers.cfm?cfid=428604&cftoken=85393283&abstract_id =251028.

[49] *Id.*

on section 10 of the 1934 Act.[50] An independent SEC-style agency was established to enforce the securities laws.[51] As with the corporate law, however, the new securities laws rested uneasily with national sentiment and the creditor orientation of the corporate law. Important features of the new securities law regime, including the SEC-style agency, were either repealed as soon as the occupation ended or atrophied in the ensuing decades.

The bankruptcy regime—"a dislocated set of procedures that has developed haphazardly according to historical circumstance"[52]—was similarly not conducive to efficient utilization. Some parts of the corporate reorganization regime are influenced by German law and date to the 1920s; other parts were added in the wake of the occupation and are modeled on U.S. law. In general terms, the problem is that some reorganization options differ little from a private workout (providing scant incentive to use the state's ground rules), while other options are so procedurally rigid as to be highly unattractive.

In view of the more recent transition economy experience, it is not surprising that this legal regime was overridden by private ordering and thus had little impact on corporate practices. Indeed, it would have been more surprising if Japan had somehow escaped the "transplant effect"—the inability of countries to assimilate foreign laws rapidly, particularly in the absence of smoothing agents such as a legal profession familiar with the new statutes.[53] The transplant effect was all the more likely to occur in transitional Japan since enforcement of the rights and protections contemplated by the new statutes depended upon a small, newly independent judiciary with limited enforcement powers and a procedural landscape devoid of enforcement incentives for legal professionals.

In some areas, norms likely prevailed because state-set ground rules for economic activity were inadequately specified—a situation that persisted until very recently. The No Hostile Takeover norm pro-

---

[50] On the origins of Japanese securities law, see Curtis J. Milhaupt, *Managing the Market: The Ministry of Finance and Securities Regulation in Japan*, 30 STAN. J. INT'L L. 423 (1994).

[51] *Id.* at 432-33.

[52] Stacey Steele, *Evaluating the New Japanese Civil Rehabilitation Law*, 2 AUSTRALIAN J. ASIAN L. 53, 56 (2000).

[53] The transplant effect has most recently afflicted the transition economies of Eastern Europe. *See* Daniel Berkowitz et al., Economic Development, Legality, and the Transplant Effect 4 (Nov. 1999) (unpublished manuscript, on file with Social Science Research Network), *available at* http://papers.ssrn.com/sol3/papers.taf?cfid=428604&cftoken=85393283&abstract_id=183269.

vides an informative example. Until 1990, there were no share ownership disclosure requirements under the securities laws. Thus, it was possible for a raider or greenmailer to secretly amass shares of a public company and spring itself upon an unsuspecting management. Procedural safeguards in tender offers as well as securities antifraud rules remained underdeveloped through the 1980s. To this day, the Commercial Code provides managers with little flexibility to craft defensive measures to fend off unsolicited bids. In such an environment, a social norm denigrating hostile takeovers as unethical could operate as a low-cost substitute for an extensive system of formal ground rules for M&A activity and as a complement to the structural obstacle posed by cross-shareholding practices. Even if the norm is superfluous in those roles, it may have emerged as a convenient and self-serving shorthand for a complex institutional reality. Alternatively, it may persist largely as a historical vestige of an era (particularly before the rise of cross-shareholding) when it did play a role in dampening takeover activity.

Standing alone, however, the explanation from transaction cost economizing confronts both empirical and theoretical problems. While the Japanese legal and economic environments have evolved significantly since the occupation, the nonlegal rules emerging in the immediate postwar period continued to pervade the corporate governance regime. Most acutely, explanations from efficiency alone fail to account for the past decade, in which Japanese firms and banks adhering to the norms have lost international competitiveness (see Table 1). Theoretically problematic is the assumption that dispersed actors sustained, for many decades, a high degree of coordination in the face of a collective action problem. While it is collectively rational for each of the players of Japanese corporate governance to continue adhering to the norms if the per-firm benefit to the economy of private ordering exceeds the per-firm cost, it is individually rational for each firm to defect from those norms where the gains from launching a hostile takeover or failing to rescue a troubled borrower, for example, exceed the firm-specific benefits of norm compliance. This analysis suggests that normative corporate governance would not be a stable equilibrium unless (1) the postwar norms were immediately and universally internalized, (2) a coordination mechanism exists, or (3) there are substantial private benefits to norm compliance.

Table 1: Japan's World Competitiveness Ranking 1986-2000[54]

1986-1993	1
1994	3
1995	4
1996	4
1997	9
1998	18
1999	16
2000	17

Thus, in order for our explanation to be complete, we need an account not only of the creation of the norms, but also of their persistence despite changes in the transaction cost environment and evidence of their eventual inefficiency. I discount the rapid internalization of the new norms as an explanation because no convincing theory exists to explain such a phenomenon. Rather, two causes of inefficient norm persistence seem particularly relevant to our account.[55] First, information lags bedevil the efforts of any group to maintain efficient norms in the face of changing environments and technologies. Even if old norms are gradually replaced, the inefficient norm governs during the transition period. As Table 1 suggests, the deterioration in Japanese productivity was precipitous. Perhaps not surprisingly, early signs of inefficiencies in normative corporate governance were dismissed as aberrational and the system veered perilously close to collapse before norm reform began in earnest.

Second and perhaps more importantly, norms may be created and maintained for the private benefits they provide to favored groups. The circumstantial evidence of norm capture in Japan is compelling. World War II and its aftermath destroyed many organized interest groups in Japan.[56] Several groups, however, including the bureaucracy

---

[54] INT'L INST. FOR MGMT. DEV., WORLD COMPETITIVENESS REPORT (various years); INT'L INST. FOR MGMT. DEV., WORLD COMPETITIVENESS YEARBOOK (various years). In citing these rankings, I am conscious of the criticism directed at the notion of "world" or "international competitiveness." *See, e.g.,* PAUL KRUGMAN, POP INTERNATIONALISM 10 (1996) (suggesting that the term is misleading and simply another way of saying "productivity"). Even if the term is open to criticism, the rankings are illustrative of the deterioration in Japan's productivity vis-à-vis that of other countries.

[55] *See, e.g.,* Eric A. Posner, *Law, Economics, and Inefficient Norms,* 144 U. PA. L. REV. 1697, 1711-19 (1996) (discussing information lags and strategic behavior as causes of inefficient norms).

[56] MANCUR OLSON, THE RISE AND DECLINE OF NATIONS 75-76 (1982).

(particularly the Ministry of Finance), leaders of major commercial banks, and corporate managers of the former *zaibatsu*, not only survived the occupation intact, but by design or serendipity actually enjoyed enhanced power as a result of the political and economic purges.[57] Whatever initial comparative advantage norms may have enjoyed over legal rules in postwar Japan, the norms of Japanese corporate governance also clearly benefited the interest groups left standing after the occupation. As Mark Ramseyer has argued, a no-takeover ideology benefits managers of large corporations both by insuring them against economic losses in a takeover and by justifying managerial power.[58] The norm on board role and structure, with its self-serving emphasis on employee loyalty and the exclusion of outsiders, performs a similar role. The main bank system allowed large banks to extract rents from their borrowers.[59] Financial regulators, in turn, benefited from enhanced discretion and public prestige accruing to the managers of a highly informal financial system that avoided bank failure. More tangibly, they also derived rents from banks in the form of a highly institutionalized system of lucrative post-retirement employment opportunities with regulated firms.

Normative corporate governance can thus be viewed as a largely self-enforcing, informal response to the postwar legal environment. Crucially, because powerful governmental actors also derived private benefits from norm compliance, there was a built-in coordination mechanism to overcome the collective action problem. The norms were relatively impervious to change, despite their eventual inefficiency for society as a whole, because they continued to generate significant private benefits to powerful groups.

---

[57] The occupation authorities chose to rule *through* the bureaucracy, in particular the Ministry of Finance, insulating it from major reform. The economic purge of wartime executives and breakup of powerful "city" banks closely allied with *zaibatsu* were either abandoned or diluted as reverse-course policies gained ascendance in the years following Japan's surrender. JOHN W. DOWER, EMBRACING DEFEAT: JAPAN IN THE WAKE OF WORLD WAR II 532-33, 544-45 (1999). Ironically, the dissolution of the *zaibatsu* actually reinforced the rights of corporate insiders by creating the ideal conditions for a pure internal promotion system insulated from both family succession problems and outside directors. Fabrizio Barca et al., Post-War Institutions: The Divergence of Italian and Japanese Corporate Governance Models 23-24 (1998) (unpublished manuscript, on file with author).

[58] Ramseyer, *supra* note 14, at 12-13.

[59] David E. Weinstein & Yishay Yafeh, *On the Costs of a Bank-Centered Financial System: Evidence from the Changing Main Bank Relations in Japan*, 53 J. FIN. 635, 639 (1998).

B. *The Interaction of Corporate Norms and Law*

Not suprisingly, heavy reliance on nonlegal rules reduced demand for corporate law and legal professionals in postwar Japan. The main bank system redirected some of the most complex corporate reorganizations away from the legal system, replacing the judge and court-appointed receiver in a formal bankruptcy proceeding.[60] The main bank system also provided a substitute for the accountants and credit rating agencies who specialize in corporate monitoring and disclosure for the benefit of corporate claimants in more capital-market-driven financial systems.

Similarly, private ordering provided substitutes for legal procedures designed to protect shareholder rights. The concentration of large blocks of stock in the hands of banks and other institutional investors and the organization of many firms into *keiretsu* corporate groups with a main bank at the center provided mechanisms of voice and access to information for many Japanese institutional shareholders that were less costly and more effective than Commercial Code mechanisms. This was particularly true because, until recently, procedural requirements made shareholder derivative litigation very costly.[61]

Norms were also used to bypass roadblocks in the legal system for investor protection. As noted above, Japanese securities law contains a broad antifraud provision facially similar to Rule 10b-5.[62] Yet, in contrast to the situation in the United States, the Japanese provision is the basis of *no* private securities fraud litigation (and virtually no public enforcement either, at least until very recently). The ostensible legal reason is prosaic: the antifraud provision does not expressly contemplate suits by private claimants, and Japanese courts do not recognize implied private rights of action. The normative response was creative: instead of suing, aggrieved investors relied on an informal norm in

---

[60] To be sure, rapid economic growth in the 1970s and 1980s kept the number of corporate reorganizations low in any event.

[61] Japanese law contains a shareholder derivative suit mechanism, which was adopted in 1950 and is similar to that found in U.S. state corporate codes. Shareholders who satisfy minimal standing requirements can bring suit against directors for breach of duty. Yet until recently, this mechanism was virtually moribund in Japan. Derivative suits were rare because enforcement problems raised the cost of the procedure relative to private alternatives. Until a statutory amendment in 1993, most Japanese courts held that the amount of the filing fee required to initiate such a suit should be tied to the amount in controversy. This posed a formidable barrier to litigation, since the damages sought in derivative suits are often substantial.

[62] *Supra* text accompanying notes 50-51.

the securities industry under which large brokers implicitly indemnified important customers for investment losses.[63] In order to seek redress for losses in securities transactions, investors began turning to the courts in large numbers (claiming breach of contract or tortious injury) only after this practice was prohibited in the early 1990s.

Table 2 provides data on the demand for law in the governance of Japanese firms. While the measurement is imperfect, Table 2 highlights the traditional infrequency of direct resort to the standard legal mechanisms for resolving disputes and organizing relations among shareholders, managers, and creditors. It is of course both possible and likely that the legal regime nonetheless affected private ordering. It also bears noting that resort to these mechanisms is becoming more routine, a development that is explored in the next part of the Article.

Table 2: Demand for Corporate Law[64]

Number of Tender Offers for Public Companies 1971-1999	51
Number of Shareholder Derivative Suits Filed 1950-1990	23
Number of Private Securities Fraud Cases Brought Under the Securities Exchange Law 1950-2000	0
Average Annual Number of Criminal Cases Brought Under the Securities Exchange Law 1989-1998	3
Percentage of Corporate Insolvencies Resolved Through the Legal System 1980-1990	10

The process of Commercial Code reform in Japan also indicates an historically sluggish demand for corporate law. Traditionally, most corporate law reforms were not the result of competitive or even interest group pressures, as private actors sought a more efficient or privately beneficial formal governance framework. Rather, changes were prompted by one of two impulses. Some were theoretically appealing

---

[63] Milhaupt, *supra* note 50, at 460.

[64] Data on tender offers are from Keisho Komoto, *The Present Status of Takeover Bids (TOB) and Their Effect on Stock Prices*, 147 NLI RESEARCH 8 (2000), and Kanda, *supra* note 13, at 934; data on shareholder derivative suits are from 196 BESSATSU SHŌJI HŌMU 475-82 (1997); data on securities fraud cases by regulators are calculated from SHIHŌ TOKEI NEMPŌ [ANNUAL OF JUDICIAL STATISTICS] (various years); data on insolvencies are calculated from Frank Packer & Marc Ryser, The Governance of Failure: An Anatomy of Corporate Bankruptcy in Japan 57 tbl.1 (1992) (unpublished manuscript, on file with the Columbia University School of Business, Center on Japanese Economics and Business).

revisions made by the scholars and Justice Ministry officials in charge of Commercial Code reform ("theory pushed" rather than "demand pulled" reforms in the words of one scholar[65]); others were responses to exogenous shocks such as political scandals.[66] For this reason, throughout postwar Commercial Code history, many legal reforms have had little or no effect on Japanese corporate practices.[67] Only the small number of recent demand-pulled reforms discussed in Part III of this Article have led to significant changes in practice.

At least partly as a result of the substitution effect between private and public ordering, as Table 3 indicates, Japan has the smallest formal legal system of any major industrialized country. Table 3 must be interpreted with considerable care, because it understates the size of the Japanese lawyer population in failing to include significant numbers of quasi-legal professionals and an even larger number of law-trained public and private sector employees who perform lawyer-like tasks. Notwithstanding this caveat, however, Japan has only about 1000 corporate and securities lawyers as those terms would be understood in the United States. The Japanese legal system is small even in comparison to the German and French legal systems, which served as models for Japan during its first modern phase of legal transplanting. Particularly noteworthy is the small number of judges in Japan.

---

[65] Shishido, *supra* note 38, at 9.
[66] West, *supra* note 48.
[67] Shishido, *supra* note 38.

Table 3: International Comparison of Judicial Systems (1997)[68]

	U.S.	England	Germany	France	Japan
Legal Profession	940,508	82,653	111,315	35,695	19,733
Per 100,000 Population	352.5	158.3	135.7	61.3	15.7
Lawyers	906,611	80,868	85,105	29,395	16,368
Per 100,000 Population	339.87	154.89	103.77	50.15	13.0
Judges	30,888	3170	20,999	4900	2093
Per 100,000 Population	11.6	6.07	25.6	8.4	1.7

C. Evaluation

The process I have described is a mutually reinforcing cycle. The formal institutional environment is problematic, leading those with the most at stake to generate alternative practices. Powerful interest groups (including some state actors) select norms consistent with their own self-interest. A process of what might be called "social codification" occurs as the favored groups become contented with the informal institutions and memories of inconsistent practices fade. Pervasive resort to norms reduces demand for law and legal reform. Lack of competition from the legal system, in turn, contributes to the durability of the norms.

While the norm literature recognizes complementarities between public and private ordering, scholars have focused attention almost exclusively on the "expressive function" of law. Similarly, it is now well understood that the state can draw in more private enforcement of a norm by enacting it into law.[69] Indeed, we saw an example of this in lifetime employment, where the courts confirmed and diffused a social norm in favor of employment security.[70] But Japan's experience demonstrates that the state also reinforces norms by simply failing to

---

[68] Saikō Saibansho [Supreme Court of Japan], *21-Seiki no shihō seido wo kangaeru* [*On the Legal System of the 21st Century*] tbl.16 (2000), http://www.courts.go.jp/pre21/16.gif.

[69] *See* Robert D. Cooter, *Law from Order: Economic Development and the Jurisprudence of Social Norms*, in A NOT-SO-DISMAL SCIENCE 242 (Mancur Olson & Satu Kähkönen eds., 2000) (stating that the backing of state officials increases the effectiveness of private enforcement and lowers its costs).

[70] *See supra* Part I.D.

mobilize its lawmaking power against them. To be sure, the state actively promoted normative governance by directly supporting the payoffs from norm compliance and by occasionally serving as enforcer of ostensibly private commitments. The operation of the main bank system is perhaps the best example of the government's overt role in norm enforcement.

More subtly, however, the state exercised its monopoly power over the legal system to raise the cost of norm deviation.[71] For example, the Lifetime Employment norm may have been less stable if the government had not strictly regulated headhunting.[72] The No Hostile Takeover norm and belief system about corporate boards were buttressed by low-quality corporate and financial disclosure.[73] More firms may have used the tender offer process for both friendly and hostile deals in a more robust environment for financial disclosure, since lack of information is a serious obstacle to corporate acquisitions. Similarly, boards of directors may have become more attuned to monitoring and shareholder accountability under a more stringent disclosure regime, particularly if costly procedural barriers to derivative litigation had been removed more promptly. As the next section of the Article shows, these norms began breaking down rapidly once their inefficiency was publicly revealed.

The Japanese experience also casts light on a mainstay of the norms literature: the debate over the comparative advantages of public versus private ordering. The question is whether norms or law should be preferred as a tool of social governance. Jonathan Macey, for example, has asserted a categorical public-choice-based preference for private ordering, on the ground that legal rules exist where norms

---

[71] This inertial approach to norm reinforcement is particularly effective in systems like Japan's that adhere to a norm of regulatory prohibition. This is a shared social understanding among regulated groups that conduct not explicitly approved by law is prohibited. Hideki Kanda, *Politics, Formalism, and the Elusive Goal of Investor Protection: Regulation of Structured Investment Funds in Japan*, 12 U. PA. J. INT'L BUS. L. 569, 582 (1991). While adherence to the norm lowers the cost of lawmaking, it also greatly reduces private innovation around inefficient rules—and inefficient norms to the extent they would otherwise be eroded by new law—or channels that innovation into corruption or organized criminal activity. *See* Curtis J. Milhaupt & Mark D. West, *The Dark Side of Private Ordering: An Institutional and Empirical Analysis of Organized Crime*, 67 U. CHI. L. REV. 41, 43 (2000) (arguing that organized crime is "the dark side of private ordering—an entrepreneurial response to inefficiencies in the property rights and enforcement framework supplied by the state").

[72] Gilson & Roe, *supra* note 27, at 527-28.

[73] *See* Richard H. McAdams, *The Origin, Development, and Regulation of Norms*, 96 MICH. L. REV. 338, 392 (1997) (noting that "law can manipulate norms by manipulating information").

alone would be suitable because organized groups demand laws from politicians.[74] Other scholars have voiced suspicion that norms will usually not be fully efficient, because they arise in situations that depart from the classic model of perfect competition.[75] In the Japanese case, norms did provide a comparatively efficient governance structure when the legal framework for corporate conduct was unfamiliar, incomplete, and weakly supported with enforcement incentives. But Japan's experience suggests that the converse of Macey's claim can also be true: norms may persist where legal rules would be more efficient due to the same capture phenomenon that is well understood in the regulatory context.

One of the reasons Japan's ongoing recession has been so prolonged and severe is that norms had to be undermined before elements of the legal framework critical to recovery could be erected. This was most apparent in banking, where a legal structure for handling bank failures had to be built virtually from scratch before any progress could be made toward resolving the nonperforming loan problem. Before the political process could be engaged to create such a structure, however, the underlying social norms that aggrandized the No Failure principle for banks (and thus precluded the operation of market forces in the banking industry) had to be undermined.[76]

III. CREATIVE NORM DESTRUCTION

Despite their tenacity, the postwar norms of Japanese corporate governance are being destroyed by a confluence of forces. Norm reform is taking place for the reasons predicted in the models developed by norm scholars:[77] exogenous shocks are altering cost-benefit conditions and group membership, increased information is giving

---

[74] Jonathan R. Macey, *Public and Private Ordering and the Production of Legitimate and Illegitimate Legal Rules*, 82 CORNELL L. REV. 1123, 1124 (1997).

[75] Avery Katz, *Taking Private Ordering Seriously*, 144 U. PA. L. REV. 1745, 1749 (1996). Katz is careful to add, however, that because state-set norms may suffer from the same limitations, a priori there is no basis for preferring public or private lawmaking.

[76] *See* Curtis J. Milhaupt, *Japan's Experience with Deposit Insurance and Failing Banks: Implications for Financial Regulatory Design?*, 17 MONETARY & ECON. STUD. 21, 23 (1999) [hereinafter Milhaupt, *Deposit Insurance*].

[77] *See* Robert C. Ellickson, The Evolution of Social Norms: A Perspective from the Legal Academy 7 (July 1999) (unpublished manuscript, on file with Social Science Research Network), *available at* http://papers.ssrn.com/sol3/papers.cfm?cfid=428604&cftoken=85393283&abstractid=191392.

rise to norm shopping, agents specially suited to lead the process of norm change are emerging, and state actors are engaging in norm manipulation. I take up the process of norm reform for each of the nonlegal rules examined above.

A. Main Bank Norms

The norms supporting the operation of the main bank system have been under stress for most of the past decade. A complete appreciation of their gradual demise would require recounting the bubble economy, the ensuing banking crisis, and the tortured efforts to build a viable financial regulatory structure in Japan, a task that I will not undertake here.[78] Instead, I wish to highlight three developments that are destroying the main bank norms as traditionally understood: (1) a change in the economics of the operation of these norms, (2) a shift in belief systems about bank governance and corporate governance, and (3) a quirky exogenous shock that delivered a blow to the norms at the heart of the main bank system.

The first step in the destruction process is a dramatic change in the payoff structure to banks that abide by the main bank norms. For most of the postwar period, there was a compelling economic logic to the main bank system. Banks delegated monitoring and restructuring responsibilities for a given firm to its main bank, which possessed superior information about the firm's operations and prospects. As noted above, main banks were willing to perform this role at least in part because they extracted rents from their borrowers.[79] In turn, the importance of the main bank institution to the economy insulated banks from failure and ensured a steady stream of regulatory rents, which provided incentive to continue behaving as a "good" main bank.[80]

This logic began to unravel, however, when the moral hazard implicit in the main bank norms peaked in the bubble period of the 1980s, resulting in a massive nonperforming loan problem. By the mid-1990s, the international financial community began to perceive an unusual form of systemic risk arising from the norm-supplied safety net. While not expressed precisely in these terms, the market worried

---

[78] For analysis, see Milhaupt, *Deposit Insurance*, supra note 76; Milhaupt & Miller, supra note 12.

[79] Weinstein & Yafeh, supra note 59, at 639.

[80] Takeo Hoshi & Hugh Patrick, *The Japanese Financial System: An Introductory Overview*, in CRISIS AND CHANGE IN THE JAPANESE FINANCIAL SYSTEM, supra note 32, at 1, 7.

that regulators would undermine the strength of major Japanese banks by enforcing the Equitable Subordination norm—that is, pressuring the banks to bear more than their pro rata share of losses in connection with the collapse of weak institutions to which they had lent heavily—and by enforcing the No Failure norm by orchestrating acquisitions of institutions that should have been allowed to fail. The price exacted for these concerns was labeled the "Japan Premium," an additional risk premium charged by non-Japanese banks on loans to Japanese banks in international money markets. At one time the Japan Premium exceeded 100 basis points (one percent), a large premium given the razor thin margins in this area of finance. Crucially, until a major Japanese bank was allowed to fail in late 1997, the same premium was charged to *all* Japanese banks regardless of individual financial strength, a clear indication that the premium reflected systemic risk arising from the implicit regulatory scheme.[81]

The second step in the destruction of the main bank norms is a significant shift in beliefs about the benefits of bank-oriented corporate finance and governance. Not long ago, Japan was a model for developing economies in Asia and Eastern Europe. In contrast to the United States, Japan had not politically hamstrung large financial intermediaries from playing a role in corporate governance. Banks solved agency and information problems inherent in stock market driven systems, led to far-sighted alliances between capital and production, and served as pliant partners of government in carrying out industrial policy (or so the argument went). But in the wake of the Asian financial crisis and Japan's long recession, "relationship financing" became "crony capitalism." Easy credit policies inherent in bank-oriented systems are now linked with monitoring lapses and poor corporate performance.[82]

The third and perhaps most interesting step in the destruction of main bank norms is the nationalization and reprivatization of the Long-Term Credit Bank ("LTCB"), one of postwar Japan's largest and most politically connected banks. LTCB, which served as the main bank for many important firms, became insolvent and was temporarily nationalized in 1998. It was later sold to Ripplewood, a group of foreign investors including Citigroup and GE Capital, when no Japanese

---

[81] Milhaupt, *Deposit Insurance, supra* note 76; Milhaupt & Miller, *supra* note 12.

[82] *See, e.g.*, Anderson & Campbell, *supra* note 8, at 1 (finding that ineffective governance exacerbated the Japanese banking crisis and delayed restructuring); Randall Morck & Masao Nakamura, *Banks and Corporate Control in Japan*, 54 J. FIN. 319, 319-20 (1999) (reassessing the efficacy of Japanese bank governance of firms).

buyer for the bank could be found. The acquisition agreement gave Ripplewood the option to return to the government any assets (loans) that decline from March 1, 2000 book value by twenty percent or more within three years. The put option is lost, however, if the bank (renamed Shinsei Bank) accepts a borrower's request for loan forgiveness.

Whether intended by the government or not, by altering the bank's incentive structure in this way, the Shinsei deal threatens the bank's nonlegal commitment to failing borrowers. Since loan forgiveness is a central feature of the main bank system as traditionally understood, the agreement undermines a crucial informal rule in Japanese finance. Indeed, in several recent cases, including the high profile bankruptcy of Sogo Department Store, Shinsei refused requests to write off loans to failing borrowers, leaving the firms no choice but to resort to legal protection under the bankruptcy regime.[83] This prompted a Japanese newspaper to grouse that the bank had "ignored traditional Japanese thinking by rejecting a plan to forgive Sogo's debts."[84] As a result, Shinsei's status as a main bank, and the continued viability of the norm-based main bank institution itself, are in question.[85] Standard & Poor's, for example, recently noted "increasing uncertainties over the system of credit support for major Japanese companies, which many Japanese borrowers and lenders had taken for granted."[86] The report concludes that "[t]he long-held perception . . . that major Japanese companies are too big to fail is no longer valid."[87]

---

[83] *Reborn LTCB Has a Western Look*, NIKKEI WKLY., June 12, 2000, *available at* http://ptg.djnr.com/ccroot/asp/publib/story.asp.

[84] *Analysis: Sogo's Collapse May Bring About New Financial Order*, YOMIURI SHIMBUN, July 19, 2000.

[85] *Analysis: Shinsei Bank Carries a Heavy Burden of LTCB Legacy*, YOMIURI SHIMBUN, June 7, 2000 (quoting one bank executive as stating, "[i]t has become difficult to see Shinsei Bank playing the role of a main bank"). Some in the industry suggest that if Shinsei is unwilling to forgive debts, it will be excluded from the Japanese banking community and will need to rely on foreign capital. *Id.* This refers to the fact that LTCB did not rely on deposits for capital, but instead raised funds by issuing debentures to Japanese institutional investors.

[86] Jitendra Joshi, *Dangers Grow for Japan Inc.'s Credit Quality: Standard and Poor's*, AGENCE FRANCE-PRESSE, July 18, 2000.

[87] Gillian Tett, *Japanese Haunted by Turmoil of '98*, FIN. TIMES, July 20, 2000, at 25, *available at* http://globalarchive.ft.com/globalarchive/articles.html?id=000720000260&query=gillian+tett. Shinsei is not the only bank playing by new rules. Other major Japanese banks refused to extend debt forgiveness programs to a real estate group, which was forced to file for liquidation.

B. *The No Hostile Takeover Norm*

Looking back, scholars may date the beginning of the end of the No Hostile Takeover norm to January 24, 2000. On that date, a Japanese firm called M&A Consulting, Inc. ("MAC") launched a hostile tender offer for Shoei Corporation, a member of the Fuyo *keiretsu*. This was one of the first postwar hostile takeover bids for a Japanese corporation *by* a Japanese corporation.

The bid was motivated by a desire to destroy the No Hostile Takeover norm.[88] This is evident from the nature of the offer itself and from MAC's own public pronouncements. For example, although the market price of Shoei shares quickly reached and then surpassed the offering price of ¥1000 per share (a fourteen percent premium over Shoei's closing price on the day prior to the offer), MAC steadfastly refused to raise its bid. Even in the midst of the offering period, the bidder's CEO publicly admitted that he never expected to win a controlling stake in Shoei because Fuyo group companies owned approximately sixty percent of its shares and were unlikely to tender them in the bid.[89]

MAC's own publicity materials emphasize its norm reform mission. The materials stress that the firm is "[n]ot bound by conventional ideas and practices."[90] They describe MAC as "an active market player that is making its mark on corporate Japan."[91] The company professes a "Firm Belief in the Market Economy" and views "M&A as one of the powerful tools for dynamic restructuring."[92]

What makes the bid even more interesting is the man behind it. The CEO of MAC is Yoshiaki Murakami, formerly a senior official at the Ministry of International Trade and Industry ("MITI"), traditionally one of the most elite positions in Japanese society. Murakami is a textbook example of what Robert Ellickson calls a change agent. Change agents are low-cost suppliers of new norms because they pos-

---

[88] At least this was the primary purpose of the bid as represented to me by one of the principals. Interview transcript I (Tokyo, June 27, 2000). This is not to say that the motives of the bidder were purely altruistic. Indeed, as explained below, the bidder had reason to expect both tangible and intangible benefits from a breakdown in the norm. *See infra* text accompanying notes 94-98.

[89] Peter Landers, *First Japanese To Seek Hostile Takeover Expects To Fall Short, Seek Board Seat*, WALL ST. J., Feb. 11, 2000, at A12.

[90] Introduction to M&A Consulting (June 2000) (unpublished materials, on file with author).

[91] *Id.*

[92] *Id.*

sess attributes such as technical knowledge and leadership skills that reduce the opportunity costs of norm reform. Moreover, change agents can anticipate both tangible and intangible benefits from the acceptance of the new norm. More specifically, Murakami displays both of the traits Ellickson identifies with the "norm entrepreneur," a subspecies of change agent. First, Murakami "possess[es] a relatively high level of technical knowledge relevant to the norms within his specialty."[93] At MITI, Murakami spent much of his career on industrial policy, corporate governance, and M&A issues. He was thus intimately familiar with the legal and social institutions surrounding Japanese M&A. Second, he "is likely to be cognizant that there are appreciative experts (often, close associates in a social subgroup) who are likely immediately to esteem the norm entrepreneur for trying to change the social practice at issue."[94] Murakami's efforts were generally applauded in the Japanese and foreign financial press,[95] the legal and investment banking communities,[96] and by his former colleagues at MITI, where corporate governance reform is now a major preoccupation.[97] Whether Murakami anticipated such widespread applause is unknowable. Yet Murakami has long-standing political ambitions,[98] and at the very least he may have anticipated a major boost in name recognition as a result of his norm reform effort. More tangibly, he saw a business opportunity as a consultant in a robust market for corporate control.

The bid was financed by Orix Corporation, a leasing and financial services company that is viewed in Japan as a corporate nonconformist.[99] The CEO of Orix, Yoshihiko Miyauchi, played a supporting role

---

[93] Ellickson, *supra* note 77, at 19.
[94] *Id.*
[95] *See, e.g.*, *Nihon sho "Tettaiteki baishū"*, [*The Meaning of Japan's First "Hostile Acquisition"*], NIHON KEIZAI SHIMBUN, Jan. 27, 2000, at 3 ("Although it is a mini-deal by world standards, [MAC's bid for Shoei] is a fitting way to begin the year 2000 for Japan, a runner that is being lapped in the race among capitalist countries."); Peter Landers, *A Hostile Takeover Bid Elbows Its Way into Usually Polite Japan*, WALL ST. J., Jan. 25, 2000, at A13 ("[T]he struggle for Shoei could become a milestone in Japanese corporate history.").
[96] Interview Transcript B (Tokyo, June 20, 2000); Interview Transcript H (Tokyo, June 27, 2000); Interview Transcript K (Tokyo, June 27, 2000). Most lawyers and investment bankers did see shortcomings in the Shoei bid as a precedent, however, given its small size and failure to attract *keiretsu* shareholders.
[97] Interview Transcript M (Tokyo, June 28, 2000).
[98] Interview Transcript I, *supra* note 88.
[99] Phred Dvorak, *Japan's Orix Burnishes Its Reputation as Maverick by Bankrolling Hostile Bid*, WALL ST. J., Jan. 27, 2000, at A16 ("Orix group . . . is known for playing outside the rules that traditionally governed corporations.").

in the cast of norm entrepreneurs. He is described by the *Wall Street Journal* as "a well-known advocate of shareholder rights and deregulation."[100] One Japanese banker, reflecting on Orix's support for Japan's most highly publicized hostile bid, commented, "That's the type of thing Orix would do. Big Japanese banks wouldn't dare—they worry too much about what others would think." [101]

As expected, the bid failed when the Fuyo group companies refused to tender their shares. Ultimately, MAC increased its stake in Shoei by just a few percent. But this did not stop Murakami from claiming victory. On this point, he may have been correct. By many accounts, this small, quixotic, and unsuccessful bid helped tenderize the market for corporate control in Japan.[102]

C. *Board Role and Structure*

Professor Melvin Eisenberg has written perceptively about the normative underpinnings of the increased level of directorial care in the United States over the past decade. Eisenberg argues that because neither an increase in the threat of liability nor the prospect of gain can account for this change, the increased level of care must be due to a shift in social norms about the board's obligations.[103] Ultimately, he traces this norm shift to a change in the belief system of the business community about the board's duty of care, functions, and structure. Corporate governance has changed over the past twenty years as the dominant conception of the board moved from a managerial model to a monitoring model.[104] In Eisenberg's view, this change in belief system was due to new information about managerial efficiency that was transmitted by takeover premiums. The legal system reinforced the shift, as a series of Delaware cases created a new image of the board's proper role in corporate governance.[105]

The process that Professor Eisenberg describes for American boards has parallels in many recent developments in Japan. A significant shift in mindset—or at least rhetoric—among boards of major Japanese corporations is apparent, with the managerial model being

---

[100] Landers, *supra* note 95.
[101] Phred Dvorak, *Orix Takes a Maverick Stance in Japan*, ASIAN WALL ST. J., Jan. 27, 2000, at 1 (internal quotation omitted).
[102] *See* Interview Transcript K, *supra* note 96; Interview Transcript M, *supra* note 97.
[103] Eisenberg, *supra* note 1, at 1266-71.
[104] *Id.* at 1278-82.
[105] *Id.* at 1269-71, 1278-82.

replaced by the monitoring model. Consistent with Eisenberg's analysis of the U.S. situation, the threat of liability or prospect of gain is not sufficient to account for the heightened concern for corporate performance among Japanese managers. Until a major decision involving the directors of Daiwa Bank was rendered in the fall of 2000, the only cases in which directors of public companies had ever been found liable to their shareholders for breach of the duty of care involved unambiguous violations of domestic law, such as violations of the Commercial Code.[106] The *Daiwa Bank* case itself, which involves a *Caremark*-like failure-to-monitor claim, represents egregious directorial nonfeasance regarding violations of foreign (U.S.) law.[107] Thus, for all but a tiny fraction of Japanese directors, the threat of personal liability is small. Nor is increased income from enhanced performance likely to be the principal motivation for the change in mindset. Stock price, while a factor in executive compensation in Japan, does not have the high-powered incentive effects on management that it does in the United States because stock options are a very recent and limited component of executive compensation. Rather, Japan's waning international competitiveness and the stream of negative publicity surrounding managerial performance in the bubble period appear to have motivated the shift in beliefs about the directors' role.

While the threat of liability alone may not have been a rational reason to reshape the board's structure and function, the Japanese courts are helping to catalyze the change in directorial mindset. In the process of deciding a rash of shareholder derivative litigation that broke out when procedural barriers were removed in 1993, the courts are educating directors about the scope and content of their obligations. These cases have focused a spotlight on board conduct and, for the first time, put some interpretive flesh on the Commercial Code's skeletal description of directorial duties to the corporation.

The *Daiwa Bank* case is perhaps the best example of this process. Shareholders of Daiwa Bank derivatively sued eleven current and former directors for failing to uncover and report to U.S. authorities massive unauthorized trading in the New York branch that resulted in almost $1.5 billion in losses and fines. When eleven years of unauthorized trades were finally revealed by the rogue trader's confession,

---

[106] HIDEAKI KUBORI ET AL., TORISHIMARIYAKU NO SEKININ: DAIHYŌ SOSHŌ JIDAI NO RISUKU KANRI [THE LIABILITIES OF DIRECTORS: RISK MANAGEMENT IN THE AGE OF SHAREHOLDER DERIVATIVE LITIGATION] 102 (1999).

[107] Nishimura v. Abekawa (The Daiwa Bank Case), 199 SHIRYŌBAN SHŌJI HŌMU 248 (D. Ct., Sept. 20, 2000).

senior bank management reported the problem to Japan's Ministry of Finance. The Ministry suggested that disclosure to the Federal Reserve, which had jurisdiction over the branch, be delayed to avoid instability in the Japanese financial system. Acting at the Ministry's suggestion, Daiwa filed a misleading Call Report with the U.S. banking regulators. When the Federal Reserve eventually discovered the problem, it fined the bank $340 million and revoked the bank's license to operate in the United States. The Osaka District Court found the directors liable for breach of duty, and ordered them to pay about $775 million in damages. In a passage that nicely illustrates the tension between old and new rules governing Japanese managers, the court found that "the defendant [directors] had persisted in following informal local rules that only apply in Japan, despite the fact that [the firm's operations] had expanded on a global scale."[108]

As educators of management, the Japanese courts are performing a modest version of the role Professor Edward Rock described for the Delaware courts.[109] While the Japanese case law does not explicitly reference Delaware jurisprudence, it is hard to imagine that the courts (and by extension boards of directors) are not influenced by it. Virtually every scholarly analysis of the Japanese board's role in corporate governance now refers to landmark Delaware cases such as *Van Gorkom*,[110] *Unocal*,[111] and *Caremark*.[112]

Again, as in the United States, the takeover market (albeit a diluted version thereof) played a role in delivering the bad news about managerial inefficiency to Japanese boards. Leading business journals and even a research committee working under the auspices of MITI have recently published lists of companies that, by various measures, are attractive acquisition targets.[113] As the MITI research committee's

---

[108] *Id.* at 255.

[109] *See* Rock, *supra* note 1, at 1016 ("[T]he Delaware courts generate in the first instance the legal standards of conduct . . . largely through what can best be thought of as 'corporate law sermons.' . . . Taken as a whole, the Delaware opinions can be understood as providing a set of parables . . . .").

[110] Smith v. Van Gorkom, 488 A.2d 858 (Del. 1985).

[111] Unocal Corp. v. Mesa Petroleum Co., 493 A.2d 946 (Del. 1985).

[112] *In re* Caremark Int'l Inc. Derivative Litig., 698 A.2d 959 (Del. Ch. 1996); *see, e.g.*, Seiichi Okazaki, *M&A no koshō to torishimariyaku no keiei handan* [*M&A Negotiations and Directors' Business Judgment*], 1562 SHŌJI HŌMU 18 (2000) (Part I), 1563 SHŌJI HŌMU 27 (Part II), and 1566 SHŌJI HŌMU 22 (Part III).

[113] *See, e.g.*, MBO KENKYŪ KAI [MBO RESEARCH GROUP], WAGA KUNI NI OKERU MBO DONYŪ NO IGI TO SONO FUKYŪ NI MUKETE NO KADAI [THE SIGNIFICANCE OF THE INTRODUCTION OF MBOS INTO OUR COUNTRY AND ISSUES RELATED TO THEIR DIFFUSION] 3, 4 (1999) [hereinafter MBO RESEARCH GROUP] (listing attractive targets

report notes:

> Among Japanese firms, many have balance sheets loaded with non-performing assets.... There are 33 publicly traded firms [identified by name in the report] in which net cash balances exceed market capitalization. In an age in which efficiency is given higher priority than expansion, managers must bear fundamental responsibility for such inefficient utilization of assets.[114]

This report represents perhaps the most blatant of several recent attempts at norm manipulation by state actors.

Unlike the situation in the United States, however, the evolution of Japanese norms on board role and structure can also be traced to the work of an identifiable norm entrepreneur. In 1997, Sony undertook significant board reform, shrinking the size of its board from thirty-eight to ten (seven executive and three outside directors) and introducing the executive officer [*shikkō yakuin*] structure, which has no legal foundation under the Japanese Commercial Code. The seven executive directors and twenty-seven presidents of the various Sony companies comprise the executive officers.[115] Sony's reform, which was widely reported in the business and legal press, appears to have been a tipping point in board belief systems. Orix and other major firms quickly followed Sony's extra-legal innovation. Within one year of Sony's move, over 100 firms had adopted similar reforms.[116] Within two years, the number of adopting firms approached 200.[117]

This extralegal arrangement does have a significant legal advantage for the firms adopting it. Because the Japanese Commercial Code does not recognize officers as a corporate organ, only directors (and statutory auditors) are liable to the corporation for breaches of duty. Thus, Sony-style board reform not only facilitates board monitoring and strategic decision making, it also reduces the available tar-

---

based on Net Cash to Market Capitalization Ratio and Takeover Recovery Cost Ratio); Masatoshi Kikuchi, *TOB sareyasui kigyō 25 sha* [*25 Firms for Which a Tender Offer Could Easily Be Made*], EKONOMISUTO, Mar. 14, 2000, at 60, 61 (listing attractive targets based on asset values and other factors).

[114] MBO RESEARCH GROUP, *supra* note 113, at 3.

[115] TETSUO NIWA, SHIKKŌ YAKUIN SEI [THE EXECUTIVE OFFICER SYSTEM] 18 (2000).

[116] DIRECTOR INNOVATION, *supra* note 20, at 20-21. This marked Sony's second pioneering departure from the regulatory prohibition norm. In 1995, it bypassed legal obstacles to the issuance of stock options through creative use of bonds with detachable warrants.

[117] *Shikkō yakuin donyū kasoku* [*Acceleration of Adoption of Executive Officer System*], NIHON KEIZAI SHIMBUN, June 25, 1999, at 3 (indicating that 179 companies adopted the system).

gets of shareholder derivative litigation.[118]

D. *Lifetime Employment*

Lifetime employment remains the stickiest of all the corporate governance norms. On one hand are data portending an eventual decline in this institution. A Labor Ministry survey indicates that many major firms plan to eliminate jobs, and the rate of soon-to-be college graduates who have yet to find employment is at a record high, indicating that firms have cut intake into the lifetime employment system.[119] Moreover, the market appears to be rewarding firms that depart from the norm, and punishing those that continue to abide by it.[120] There have been several large layoffs recently, including 20,000 at NTT, 21,000 at Nissan, and 17,000 at Sony. Anecdotal evidence also suggests that younger workers place higher value on merit-based pay and promotions over long-term job security.

Yet adherence to the job security norm is dying hard, despite widespread acknowledgment of serious over-employment in the ranks of middle management. As one Japanese newspaper recently put it (complete with misrepresentation of history), "Most Japanese companies intend to maintain the lifetime employment system, despite growing criticism that the centuries-old practice is destroying the economy."[121] The large layoffs to date have mostly involved firms already at the fringes of Japanese corporate norm compliance, such as Sony and Nissan, which is now controlled by Renault. A recent survey indicates

---

[118] Indeed, popular "how to" books on the officer system aimed at white-collar workers tout this legal advantage. *See* MANABU HAYASHIDA & MAMORU NANAMURA, JINZAI KATSUYŌ BIGU BAN [THE BIG BANG IN UTILIZING HUMAN RESOURCES] 138 (2000). If these board reforms were motivated solely by the fear of liability, *see* Mark D. West, Why Shareholders Sue: The Evidence from Japan 11 (Nov. 2000) (unpublished manuscript, on file with Social Science Research Network), *available at* http://papers.ssrn.com/sol3/papers.cfm?cfid=428604&cftoken=85393283&abstract_id =251012, they would appear to be an overreaction to the legal environment. It is also possible that the executive officer system merely ratifies existing practice, in which actual decisionmaking authority is vested not in the whole board, but in a small subset of the most senior board members.

[119] Shuichi Ito, *The Changing Corporate Climate in Japan*, J. JAPANESE TRADE & INDUSTRY, Mar. 1, 2000, *available at* 2000 WL 19832771.

[120] There are several reports of abnormal returns on the stock of firms that announce layoffs. *See* Kishiko Hisada et al., *Japan Sticks to Lifetime Job System*, ASAHI SHIMBUN, Dec. 2, 1999, at 4, *available at* 1999 WL 17701748 (reporting that one corporation's stock price more than doubled after it announced layoff plans); Shishido, *supra* note 38, at 7. Moody's Investor Service lowered the ratings of companies that intend to maintain lifetime employment. Hisada et al., *supra*, at 4.

[121] Hisada et al., *supra* note 120, at 1.

that a majority of companies plan to maintain the lifetime employment system; most are seeking to reduce employment through natural or incentivized attrition.[122] Finally, a comprehensive study of survey results and qualitative data has found little support for the rhetorical claim that lifetime employment practices are coming to an end.[123]

IV. NORMS IN COMPARATIVE CORPORATE LAW SCHOLARSHIP

As noted in the Introduction, norms have been largely ignored in the comparative corporate governance debates of the past decade. Perhaps this was understandable in the first phase of such scholarship, which was preoccupied with exposing the political leitmotif of a given country's financial laws and resulting corporate structures. Grappling with norms seems inevitable, however, now that scholarly attention has turned toward two interrelated questions: whether law matters to corporate ownership and finance around the world and whether corporate governance systems are converging, particularly toward an Anglo-American, shareholder-centered model. In this Part, I draw on Japan's experience with norms and corporate governance to inform analysis of these questions.

A. *(Non)Law Matters*

Comparative corporate law scholarship appears to have entered a new era. Politics is out; law is in. For a decade, the literature was dominated by a search for the effects of politics on corporate governance structures. Large financial intermediaries and concentrated shareholdings were viewed as attractive (or at least equally compelling) alternatives to stock markets and dispersed ownership, since political contingencies, not economic rationale, were deemed to be determinative of corporate finance, structure, and monitoring. Now a provocative new line of empirical scholarship has emerged to challenge this view. This literature, which is dominated by economists, holds that variations in law and its enforcement are key to understanding why corporate ownership and finance differ across countries.[124] A

---

[122] *Id.* at 3.

[123] *See* Takao Kato, The End of "Lifetime Employment" in Japan?: Evidence from National Surveys and Field Research (Jan. 31, 2001) (unpublished manuscript, on file with author).

[124] For a review of this literature by its principal proponents, see Rafael La Porta et al., Investor Protection and Corporate Governance (2000) (unpublished manuscript, on file with Social Science Research Network), *available at* http://papers.ssrn.com/

series of studies shows that the origin of a given country's legal system and the quality of its law enforcement are statistically correlated with patterns of share ownership, the cost of capital, and other corporate governance variables. In contrast to the political approach, this scholarship suggests that dispersed ownership is a sign of good legal protection of minority investors. Because common law systems apparently outperform civil law regimes on investor protection, more robust capital markets and more dispersed ownership exist in countries adhering to the common law tradition.[125]

Few legal academics would dispute the assertion that corporate, securities, and bankruptcy law matter to corporate governance, and the statistical significance of the results in these studies must be taken seriously. Yet the empirical results are more puzzling than the authors of these studies admit and the implications for reform more attenuated than a naïve reading of the literature would suggest. Here I wish to highlight several problems and limitations inherent in the new "law matters" literature by bringing norms, particularly Japan's experience with norms and corporate governance, into focus.

First, the statistical correlation between formal legal protections and corporate governance patterns revealed by these studies is in tension with the results of important natural experiments in transition economies, including Japan's. In a recent paper, the authors of the seminal "law matters" literature imply that the occupation legal reforms had a significant impact on Japanese corporate governance.[126] As we have seen, however, enhanced investor protections in the corporate and securities laws of precisely the type recommended in the new literature had virtually no impact on Japanese corporate practices or shareholding patterns for several decades. Share ownership was widely dispersed in the immediate postwar period, but this was the direct result of the forced dissolution of the *zaibatsu*, a key occupation policy. In fact, as Table 4 shows, the decades following the occupation-imposed improvements in formal legal protection of minority investors in Japan are characterized by a steady *concentration* of share ownership in the hands of large financial and corporate investors. This is not surprising, given the complementarities between concentrated share ownership, particularly by financial institutions, and the

---

sol3/papers.cfm?cfid=408152&cftoken=41757136&abstract_id=183908.
[125] *See id.* at 29 ("[S]trong investor protection is associated with effective corporate governance, as reflected in valuable and broad financial markets, dispersed ownership of shares, and efficient allocation of capital across firms.").
[126] *Id.* at 25.

operation of nonlegal rules on takeovers, main bank operations, board structure, and employment. Unsurprising, perhaps, but in direct tension with the thrust of the "law matters" literature. Significant changes in share ownership patterns became evident only recently, coinciding with the breakdown of normative corporate governance and the formation of coalitions to lobby for reform of corporate law.[127]

Table 4: Share Ownership of Japanese Public Companies (Selected Shareholders)[128]

Year	Financial Institutions	Corporations	Individuals	Foreigners (Corp. & Indiv.)
1949	9.9%	5.6%	69.1%	-
1950	12.6%	11.0%	61.3%	-
1955	23.6%	13.2%	53.2%	1.7%
1960	30.6%	17.8%	46.3%	1.3%
1965	29.0%	18.4%	44.8%	1.8%
1970	32.3%	23.1%	39.9%	3.2%
1975	36.0%	26.3%	33.5%	2.6%
1980	38.8%	26.0%	29.2%	4.0%
1985	42.2%	24.1%	25.5%	5.7%
1990	45.2%	25.2%	23.1%	4.2%
1995	41.4%	23.6%	23.6%	9.4%
1996	41.3%	23.8%	23.6%	9.8%
1997	40.2%	24.1%	24.6%	9.8%
1998	39.3%	24.1%	25.4%	10.0%
1999	36.1%	23.7%	26.4%	12.4%

Second, norm analysis exposes theoretical weaknesses in the speci-

---

[127] On the relationship between coalitions and corporate law reform, see John C. Coffee, Jr., Convergence and Its Critics: What are the Preconditions to the Separation of Ownership and Control? (Sept. 12, 2000) (unpublished manuscript, on file with Social Science Research Network), available at http://papers.ssrn.com/sol3/papers.cfm?cfid=428604&cftoken=85393283&abstract_id=241782. One good example is the re-establishment of an independent securities regulator in Japan. As noted above, the occupation reformers created an SEC-style agency, but it was viewed as irrelevant and disbanded as soon as they left. It took forty years for it to be reestablished, after a series of scandals in the 1980s and 1990s created widespread dissatisfaction with the largely informal and nontransparent regulation of the Ministry of Finance.

[128] Zenkoku shōken torihiki kyōgikai [Securities Exchange Council of Japan], *Heisei 11 nendo kabushiki bunpu jōkyō chōsa kekka ni tsuite* [*On the Results of the 1999 Survey of Share Distribution*], at 10, Graph I-3, June 26, 2000.

fication of the model underlying the "law matters" literature. In the model, ownership concentration, external finance, or some other corporate governance variable is regressed on a set of variables designed to control for the quality of legal protection afforded investors, including both shareholders and creditors. Some variables measure substantive shareholder protections, with a focus on voting rights in the election of directors and other important corporate matters. Others quantify substantive creditor rights in liquidation and reorganization procedures when borrowers default. The model also includes summary variables such as survey-based estimates of the "rule of law" and the "efficiency of the judicial system," which are designed to control for the quality of law enforcement. While the model has produced statistically significant correlations between the legal variables and the corporate governance variables, it is not clear what is being measured. The extent to which legal rules are enforced is not necessarily a function of the "quality" of a legal system or the "efficiency" of the judiciary, even assuming those attributes can be quantified. We have seen that on the level of positive law, several areas of Japanese corporate and securities regulation are virtually identical to the American provisions on which they were based, yet levels of enforcement of these provisions differ dramatically between the two countries for reasons that are unlikely to be captured in the standard indices. Moreover, while it is firmly established that social norms can substitute for law on the level of substance, remedies, and enforcement, the model does not—and probably cannot—control for these substitution effects. In short, the "law matters" model is operationalized in a manner that is inconsistent with legal theory and historical experience.

So then, what to make of the results? Perhaps, as the authors themselves suggest, the legal variables are simply a proxy for climates that are hostile or friendly toward institutional development.[129] Indeed, it would be interesting to investigate further the correlation between legal regimes and normative environments. Some preliminary work along these lines has been done,[130] but the field is wide open for inquiry.

Third, the empiricists may have reversed the actual chain of causa-

---

[129] Rafael La Porta et al., *Legal Determinants of External Finance*, 52 J. FIN. 1131, 1149 (1997).

[130] *See, e.g.*, Rafael La Porta et al., *Trust in Large Organizations*, 87 AM. ECON. REV., PAPERS AND PROCS. OF THE HUNDRED AND NINTH ANN. MEETING OF THE AM. ECON. ASS'N, May 1997, at 333 (finding that countries with more dominant hierarchical religions have, among other things, less efficient judiciaries and more corruption).

tion between law and corporate governance. Law and its enforcement may not determine the structure of corporate groups; rather, important corporate and financial groups in a given society may drive the development of legal institutions and enforcement practices by affecting the demand for law, at least in part through norm creation and destruction.[131] This, at least, is what I have argued above with respect to Japan. Another salient example of this phenomenon is the prevalence of concentrated share ownership throughout East Asia. In many of these countries, family control and succession is a socially valued practice that has persisted through innumerable changes in legal regime. It takes a legal centrist in the extreme to believe that the South Korean *chaebol*, for example, could be disbanded (or never would have emerged) if the corporate code simply contained provisions on cumulative voting, preemptive rights, and the other minority protections emphasized in the empirical literature. Where powerful enterprise groups already exist, they constitute major antagonists against the adoption and enforcement of laws that alter the balance of power between controlling and minority shareholders. At the very least, the Japanese example indicates that significant time lags—half a century in Japan's case—may be present between legal reforms and corporate governance effects.

This causation analysis provides broader perspective on Professor John Coffee's argument that legal developments tend to lag behind economic change.[132] Sometimes, as Coffee argues, legal developments must await the formation of motivated coalitions to lobby for new protections. Probably more often, however, motivated coalitions block or dilute legal developments adverse to their narrow interests. At other times, particularly when law is shaped by foreign advisors or occupying

---

[131] The authors of the empirical studies seek to rebut this criticism by claiming that legal origin is exogenous and pointing out that the legal origin variable remains significant even when holding other variables constant. It is unlikely that a legal system is completely exogenous, however, even where a colonizing or occupying force has imposed it. More importantly, the validity of the classification scheme used to create the legal origin variable is highly suspect. For example, these studies list Japan as belonging to the German civil law family. This is partially, but only partially, true of Japan's five major codes, which were adopted around the turn of the last century. But many subsequent Commercial Code revisions and important economic regulatory statutes are of U.S. origin. German law has had only a minor influence on postwar Japanese legal developments. Thus, the classification for Japan is only partially accurate and no theory is offered to explain why legal origin, as opposed to subsequent legal developments, would be determinative of corporate governance patterns. It would not be surprising if the classifications of legal origin for other countries in the study were subject to similar defects.

[132] Coffee, *supra* note 127, at 9.

forces, legal developments outpace the absorptive capacities of society.

Fourth, the policy implications of these studies are open to multiple interpretations. As other commentators have pointed out, it may be overly optimistic to interpret these studies as suggesting that countries simply need to improve their corporate law (that is, to enact the list of investor protections that correlate empirically with desirable results) in order to improve corporate governance. A less sanguine view is that legal rules are highly complementary within a given legal system, so that legal improvements require reforms of entire legal systems.[133] Norm analysis, and the Japanese experience with norms in particular, suggests an even more pessimistic interpretation: the complementarities at work in corporate structure and finance go well beyond the components of the formal legal system, encompassing social norms and their enforcement. The good news here is that norms are subject to change; the bad news is that the process may be even more difficult and unpredictable than reforming entire legal systems. In the Japanese case, we have seen that corporate norms may be the product of interest group dynamics and that their informal character can subject the process of reform to the happenstance of exogenous shocks and the appearance of norm reformers. If, as seems most plausible, differences in corporate finance and governance are due to institutional (and not exclusively legal) differences, including the constraints people carry in their own heads, a vast amount of social engineering remains even after legislators and courts begin to function. Japan's ongoing struggle to reform its corporate governance and financial system indicates the importance and difficulty of changing mindsets, not just legal rules.

Although nothing in the postwar Japanese experience refutes the empirical finding that law matters to corporate governance and finance, the Japanese case seriously challenges researchers and policymakers to refine their understanding of this relationship. For example, Japan shows that substitutes to legal institutions can operate effectively and at low cost, at least in certain environments. Thus, questions such as how nonlegally enforceable constraints emerge and persist, whether they are efficient in comparison to available alternatives, and the policy implications of norm-based governance deserve

---

[133] Erik Berglöf & Ernst-Ludwig von Thadden, The Changing Corporate Governance Paradigm: Implications for Transition and Developing Countries 5 (June 1999) (unpublished manuscript, on file with Social Science Research Network), *available at* http://papers.ssrn.com/sol3/papers.cfm?cfid=428604&cftoken=85393283 &abstract_id=183708.

increased scholarly attention. Norm analysis suggests the need to reconceptualize the linkage between the "rule of law" and economic structures to accommodate more than the simple focus on formal rules enforced by courts that dominates the early phases of the new comparative corporate governance literature.

B. *Normative Convergence*

One of the few exceptions to the absence of norms from the comparative corporate governance literature is a recent article by Professors Henry Hansmann and Reinier Kraakman entitled *The End of History for Corporate Law*.[134] Despite the title, Hansmann and Kraakman seem principally concerned not with law, but with ideology. Indeed, they assert that corporate *law* had largely converged worldwide by the end of the nineteenth century.[135] Yet basic legal convergence clearly did not dictate twentieth-century global consensus on the appropriate structure, financing, or conduct of corporate affairs. Thus, the central claims of the paper relate to corporate norms—which for Hansmann and Kraakman means ideologies about how firms ought to be run— and their impact on corporate practices. They argue:

> [A]t the beginning of the twenty-first century we are witnessing rapid convergence on the standard shareholder-oriented model as a normative view of corporate structure and governance. We should also expect this normative convergence to produce substantial convergence in the practices of corporate governance and in corporate law.[136]

These are bold claims, the accuracy of which has crucial implications for corporate actors and scholars everywhere. It is fair to ask whether the two claims in this passage accurately describe developments in Japan, the world's second largest economy and longstanding model of bank-centered corporate governance. Is Japan rapidly embracing a shareholder-centered ideology? Part III of this Article suggests that the answer is both yes and no. Certainly there are signs of important norm shifts under way in Japanese business and government: increased acceptance of the takeover as a legitimate tool of corporate strategy and monitoring (and a concomitant reduction of legal and structural impediments to M&A), a heightened awareness of shareholders' economic expectations, a change in managerial mindset

---

[134] Henry Hansmann & Reinier Kraakman, *The End of History for Corporate Law*, 89 GEO. L.J. 439 (2001).

[135] *Id.* at 439.

[136] *Id.* at 443.

about its proper role in running the firm, diminished social expectations of forbearance on the part of banks and their regulators, and rising ambivalence about the benefits of seniority-based employment practices. These shifts are palpable and important. Taken together with the emerging evidence of parallel norm shifts under way in Europe, they portend a much narrower ideological spectrum on how and for whose benefit firms should be managed.

At the same time, the rapidity and extent of Japanese normative convergence toward the Anglo-American model should not be overstated. While signs of norm shifts are very recent, evidence of the inefficiency of the old norm structure surfaced nearly a decade ago. And signs of norm stickiness are abundant. To take just one example, the U.K. telecommunications firm Cable & Wireless, which recently made a contested bid for a Japanese firm, interviewed seventeen Japanese law firms, including several with which it had ongoing professional relationships, before it found a single one willing to represent it in connection with its bid.[137] Similar reputational concerns serve as a continuing constraint on domestic financing for hostile bidders.[138]

Complete analysis of Hansmann and Kraakman's first claim would require a deeper inquiry into the process of norm change than is possible here. But three cautionary notes suggest that it may be premature to consign alternate corporate governance models (all of which, ultimately, rest on a thick bed of nonlegal practices and customs) to the dustbin of history. First, the informality of norms can frustrate their reform because there is no established procedure for norm amendment.[139] Whether existing norms in a given system are malleable or rigid turns on the magnitude of private benefits they generate and the willingness of state actors to participate in the norm manipulation process. Second, like law, norms are deeply intertwined with special interests. A priori, there is no basis for concluding that norm reform is more impervious to the effects of capture than its legal counterpart. Thus, there is no reason to believe that corporate governance norms around the world are poised to yield uniformly to a more efficient set of norms. Third, it seems unlikely that countries can embrace the shareholder supremacy norm for corporate activity

---

[137] Interview Transcript N (Tokyo, June 29, 2000).

[138] Interview Transcript A (Tokyo, June 19, 2000); Interview Transcript J (Tokyo, June 27, 2000).

[139] Robert D. Cooter, *Decentralized Law for a Complex Economy: The Structural Approach to Adjudicating the New Law Merchant*, 144 U. PA. L. REV. 1643, 1655 (1996) (discussing H.L.A. HART, THE CONCEPT OF LAW (1961)).

without wholesale revision of deeply entrenched views and practices in other areas of society.

Turn now to the linkage between normative convergence and convergence of corporate law and practices. Japan provides modest support for the claim that normative convergence is leading to changes in corporate governance practices. At the margins, for example, norm shifts are influencing the selection of governance technologies. One example is increased interest in the management buyout as an acquisition technique. Perceived consistency between the MBO and past Japanese business practices is often stressed, even by the government, as a reason why this technique may be appropriate for Japan.[140] The MBO is attractive because it has the potential to meld two conflicting Japanese norms: the emergent concept of shareholder primacy and the more longstanding focus on employee welfare. To date, however, while MBO funding is available, few deals have emerged because the technique has not caught on with Japanese managers.[141]

Yet normative convergence does not necessarily imply that formal convergence will follow inexorably. Sometimes normative convergence outpaces legal reform and must coexist at least temporarily with conflicting institutions. Japanese board reform is a good example of this phenomenon. While Sony-style board reform was driven in part by normative convergence, it has not yet led to changes in corporate law. There is no legal recognition of executive officers as a corporate organ, and thus executive officers are not legally accountable to shareholders.[142] Nor for that matter has normative convergence in this area led to complete functional convergence. Japanese directors and officers still play different roles than their U.S. counterparts.

What seems more probable than a tight correlation between normative and formal convergence is a regime of *constrained pluralism* among national corporate governance practices. That is, for all but the most international of firms, practices will continue to diverge, based as they are on a welter of different informal understandings and

---

[140] MBO RESEARCH GROUP, *supra* note 113, at 7 (1999) (emphasizing that the MBO may be comparatively easy to introduce into Japan because, in contrast to other forms of M&A, (1) it is similar to an existing Japanese business practice known as *norenwake* and (2) it generally does not entail mass layoffs).

[141] Interview Transcript K, *supra* note 96.

[142] Proposals to amend the Commercial Code to legally recognize executive officers and subject them to derivative suits are pending, however. *Shikkō yakuin ni mo hōteki sekinin* [*Legal Liability for Executive Officers Too*], NIHON KEIZAI SHIMBUN, Dec. 5, 2000, at 1.

exogenous stimuli. But those practices will operate within a spectrum of acceptable corporate governance goals and beneficiaries made narrower by general consensus on major issues such as the need to prevent expropriation of minority investments and the responsibility of management to explain its decisions to shareholders.

At a fairly high level of generality, then, Professors Hansmann and Kraakman have provided a provocative account of one of the principal mechanisms driving corporate convergence: the ascendance of the shareholder primacy norm. In so doing, they have highlighted an understudied aspect of comparative corporate governance. Ultimately, however, their claims may be overstated, deflecting attention from what promises to be the key challenge for many transition countries, including Japan, in the decade ahead—the struggle to realign the formal and informal components of their corporate governance institutions into a complementary whole. As the experience of Japan and other transition economies over the past decade suggests, this process will be complicated by the extraordinarily unpredictable process of changing institutions by changing the way people think. For the economic and political actors in these countries, it is not the end of history, but the beginning of time.

Conclusion

Nonlegal rules and their relationship to formal institutions are important to our understanding of Japanese corporate governance. Inquiry into the origins of prevailing corporate norms reveals that, contrary to common assertions, none enjoy a long history of practice in Japan. Rather, these norms appear to have emerged in response to the peculiarities of the formal postwar institutional environment. Norms provided a low-cost substitute for legal governance mechanisms in the institutional turmoil of the immediate postwar period, when Japan was beset by the transplant effect that so commonly disrupts legal reform in transitional societies. The norms arising at that time had particular resiliency because they supplied private benefits to interest groups left intact after the war, including key governmental actors.

Today, the norms of postwar Japanese corporate governance are being destroyed—some dramatically, others more gradually—by a confluence of forces captured in the academic models of norm reform: increased information, exogenous shocks, the workings of norm entrepreneurs, and state-led norm manipulation.

Examination of the postwar Japanese experience with norms and corporate law highlights the absence of norm analysis in comparative corporate law scholarship. Bringing norms into focus contributes to the debates on convergence and corporate law enforcement that dominate the literature today and highlights several weaknesses in existing analyses of these issues.

[18]

Delusions of Hostility:
The Marginal Role of Hostile Takeovers in Japanese Corporate Governance Remains Unchanged

Dan W. Puchniak *

I. Introduction
II. The Impact of *Failed* Hostile Takeovers is Limited to Increasing Ex Ante Threat
III. Failed Hostile Takeovers Did Not Increase Ex Ante Threat Because They Were Not a Novel Feature of the Lost Decade Recovery
IV. The Continued History of Failed Hostile Takeovers During the Lost Decade Recovery Reconfirmed Their Marginal Role in Japanese Corporate Governance
V. The Increase in Japanese Takeover *Bids* is Not Evidence of an Increase in the *Ex Ante* Threat of Hostile Takeovers
VI. Japanese Managers Did Not React Swiftly to the Purported Threat of Failed Hostile Takeovers
VII. Japan's "Barriers" to Hostile Takeovers Began to Rebuild During the Lost Decade Recovery
VIII. Conclusion

I. Introduction

Two decades ago, a love for hostile takeovers was largely limited to some American academics and highflying investment bankers on Wall Street who lived by the mantra "greed is good." Today, hostile takeovers are widely embraced by mainstream governments, academics, and corporate governance pundits around the world who assume that hostile takeovers are a prerequisite for an efficient system of corporate governance. This is a dubious assumption. [1]

---

* This is an updated and condensed version of an article that was first published in the Berkeley Business Law Journal. I would like to thank the Berkeley Business Law Journal for their permission to reprint the article and excellent work editing the original published version. See, D.W. Puchniak, The Efficiency of Friendliness: Japanese Corporate Governance Succeeds Again without Hostile Takeovers, in: Berkeley Business Law Journal 5 (2008) 195. I would like to thank Kyushu University and the Japanese Government for supporting the research for this article. Thanks also to John O. Haley, Kent Anderson, Leon Wolff, Luke Nottage, Tom Ginsburg, Kenichi Osugi, Mitsuhiro Kamiya, Michiaki Abe, Caslav Pejovic, Mark Fenwick and Hyeok Joon Rho for providing comments on earlier drafts. Special thanks to Harald Baum for excellent comments and editing. To my wife and best friend, Norah, thank you for being you.

Recent economic history suggests that hostile takeovers are anything but a prerequisite for an efficient system of corporate governance. Japan's miraculous rise from its postwar ruins to the world's second-largest economy was built on a system of corporate governance that thrived because of—not despite—the *absence* of hostile takeovers. This historical fact is well-known and widely accepted. Based on this alone, the assumption that hostile takeovers are a prerequisite for efficient corporate governance appears ahistorical and misguided.

However, with the burst of the bubble in the early 1990s and the "lost decade" of economic ruin that followed, the Japanese corporate governance model was widely viewed as a failed economic experiment. Its success without hostile takeovers was deemed irrelevant. Concurrently, in the 1990s, America's unprecedented accumulation of wealth propelled it to the position of the world's sole economic superpower. America's success was largely attributed to its unique market-based corporate governance model, which was purportedly driven by hostile takeovers. Global competition led governments around the world to "play catch-up" by developing their own hostile takeover regimes. The increasing prevalence of hostile takeovers throughout the developed world, especially in continental Europe, became "evidence" of their efficiency and necessity. The received wisdom became that countries either embrace a hostile takeovers regime (in some form) or accept suboptimal economic performance.

It is in this context that Japan's recent economic recovery from its now infamous "lost decade" provides a poignant counterexample. From 1997 to 2007, Japan transformed itself from being on the brink of one of the largest economic meltdowns in modern economic history to experiencing (from 2002 to 2007) its longest period of postwar economic expansion. This astounding recovery (hereinafter "the lost decade recovery") was defined by massive reallocations of capital from inefficient firms and industries to more efficient ones. If one accepts that hostile takeovers are an essential mechanism for an efficient system of corporate governance—particularly in periods of restructuring—then one would expect that hostile takeovers played a major role in Japan's remarkable lost decade recovery.

This was not the case. In fact, the role of hostile takeovers was minimal. There was not a *single* successful hostile takeover of a major Japanese company during the lost decade recovery. Instead, true to its postwar tradition, corporate Japan successfully restructured through government intervention, bank-driven reallocation of capital, and orchestrated, friendly mergers—the antitheses of the American corporate governance model premised on hostile takeovers.

The conspicuous absence of hostile takeovers in Japan's lost decade recovery is even more remarkable considering that, in the opinion of most experts, market conditions for

---

1 For more detailed footnotes supporting statements made in the introduction, see D.W. PUCHNIAK, The Efficiency of Friendliness: Japanese Corporate Governance Succeeds Again without Hostile Takeovers, in: Berkeley Business Law Journal 5 (2008) 195, 197-204.

hostile takeovers during the lost decade recovery were close to optimal. Prior to and during the recovery, the bust-up values of a substantial percentage of Japan's listed companies were considerably more than their cumulative stock price. Stable shareholdings between firms, which were widely viewed as the most significant barrier to hostile takeovers in Japan, had substantially declined to levels that many claimed made them increasingly irrelevant. Shareholder activism, spurred on by charismatic cultural icons and buttressed by a substantial increase in foreign shareholders, led many to suggest that Japan's purported cultural aversion to hostile takeovers was no longer a major hindrance. Reforms to Japan's corporate law regime essentially made Delaware takeover jurisprudence part of Japan's legal framework. Indeed, many corporate governance experts considered Japan to be a utopia for hostile takeovers. Yet despite the pro-hostile takeover environment that emerged, there was not a single successful hostile takeover bid either prior to or during Japan's lost decade recovery.

Ironically, not only were successful hostile takeovers absent during the lost decade recovery, but the recovery appears to have reinforced the traditional Japanese corporate governance model (in which hostile takeovers play absolutely no role). Despite the poison pill being made legally available, banks and companies opted to substantially rebuild their cross-shareholdings. Shareholder activism was quelled by the prosecution and demise of Horie and Murakami—the two *de facto* leaders of the shareholder activism movement. The ostensibly "more efficient" US-style board structure, with its mandatory "independent" directors, was adopted by less than three percent of Japan's listed companies. These facts clearly demonstrate that the lost decade recovery inspired a movement *away* from, not towards, the American governance model based on hostile takeovers.

The conclusion that hostile takeovers played a minimal role in Japan's lost decade recovery will likely surprise both casual observers and Japan experts. This is because for two decades, a hopeful cadre of journalists, academics, lawyers, and M&A consultants has produced a veritable library of literature explaining why Japan has been on the brink of a vigorous hostile takeovers market similar to that in the United States. Recently, a number of luminaries in the field have even drawn strained comparisons between the *de minimis* effect that repeated *failed* attempted hostile takeovers had during Japan's lost decade recovery with the dramatic effect that the vigorous hostile takeovers market had on restructuring corporate America in the late 1980s. The myopic focus on predicting the arrival of hostile takeovers in Japan and straining to find comparisons with the evolution of American corporate governance has distorted the literature by creating the false impression that hostile takeovers have become an important mechanism in Japanese corporate governance. They have not.

This article aims to correct this distortion. It exposes, with the aid of case studies and empirical evidence, the fundamental flaws in claims by numerous Japan experts that hostile takeovers played a significant role in the lost decade recovery. The conclusion reached is that there is no credible evidence that hostile takeovers played anything more than a *de minimis* role in the recovery. This should not surprise. Hostile takeovers have consistently played only a marginal role in postwar Japanese corporate governance.

Admittedly, the goal of this article is humble. It is limited to disproving the evidence that hostile takeovers were a significant force in the lost decade recovery. This article does not attempt to provide a positive explanation for how Japanese corporate governance—in the absence of hostile takeovers—engineered the recovery (in another recently published article, I make this more ambitious positive argument).

Despite this article's humble goal, I believe it has substantial merit. Japan's economic prowess makes it one of a select group of countries that is viewed by comparative corporate law and governance scholars as a potential model for improving corporate governance around the world. Particularly since the emergence of the current global financial crisis, Japan's lost decade and recovery have taken on a heightened importance as prominent policymakers have dissected this period in Japan's economic history for clues of how to deal with the financial crisis. Thus, a fundamental misunderstanding of the role that hostile takeovers played in the lost decade recovery may negatively impact on critically important corporate governance reforms that are now being undertaken around the world to remedy the defects that may have instigated the financial crisis.

The balance of this article will proceed as follows. Section two explains why the absence of *successful* hostile takeovers in Japan logically undermines any claim that hostile takeovers had an *ex post* effect on corporate governance during the lost decade recovery. Section three outlines Japan's long history of *failed* hostile takeovers to debunk the argument that the "novelty" of hostile takeover *attempts* during the lost decade increased their *ex ante* threat. Section four demonstrates that the marginal nature of hostile takeovers remained unchanged during the lost decade recovery. Section five explains the fundamental flaw in attempts to equate the substantial increase in takeover *bids* during the lost decade with an increase in the *ex ante* threat of hostile takeovers. Section six empirically demonstrates that during the recent recovery Japanese managers failed to embrace new legally available defensive measures to protect themselves from the purported threat of hostile takeovers—buttressing the conclusion that there was no significant threat at all. Lastly, section seven explains how Japan's "barriers" to hostile takeovers began to rebuild during the lost decade recovery—suggesting that hostile takeovers will remain a marginal force in Japanese corporate governance in the foreseeable future.

II. The Impact of *Failed* Hostile Takeovers is Limited to Increasing *Ex Ante* Threat

The absence of successful hostile takeovers during the lost decade recovery is a historical fact.[2] This fact presents a problem for the cadre of corporate governance experts who are intent on drawing strained comparisons between Japan's non-existent hostile takeovers market during the lost decade recovery and the vigorous hostile takeovers market that drove restructuring in the United States during the 1980s.[3] As a result, some experts have tried to rely on failed hostile takeover attempts as evidence that hostile takeovers played a significant role in Japan's lost decade recovery.[4] This argument is seriously flawed.

From a corporate governance perspective, hostile takeovers are important because, given that share price reflects expected company performance, outsiders who believe that they can improve a company's performance have an incentive to acquire its shares. In theory, competition among outsiders ensures that the company's resources will be acquired by the outsider who can run the company most efficiently. Efficiency is increased *ex post* as the acquirer replaces management who is either less competent or not acting in the best interest of shareholders. In this way, hostile takeovers ensure that managers and companies that do not maximize shareholder value do not survive. In addition, hostile takeovers raise efficiency *ex ante* because the threat of hostile takeovers forces incumbent management to maximize shareholder value and reduce agency costs.[5]

---

2   *Ibid.* 200.
3   C.J. MILHAUPT, In the Shadow of Delaware? The Rise of Hostile Takeovers in Japan, in: Columbia Law Review 105 (2005) 2171, 2176, 2189. For a synopsis of Milhaupt's article see, C.J. MILHAUPT, In the Shadow of Delaware? The Rise of Hostile Takeovers in Japan (synopsis), in: Journal of Japanese Law 21 (2006) 199. See also, C.T. HINES ET AL., Doing Deals In Japan: An Analysis of Recent Trends and Developments For The U.S. Practitioner, in: 2006 Columbia Business Law Review (2006), 355, 360; J.B. JACOBS, Implementing Japan's New Anti-Takeover Defense Guidelines: Part I: Some Lessons from Delaware's Experience in Crafting "Fair" Takeover Rules, in: 2 New York University Journal of Law & Business 2 (2006) 323, 327.
4   According to Schaede, "whether or not a hostile bid is launched or eventually successful is not as relevant as the potential threat of a hostile takeover introducing managerial discipline." U. SCHAEDE, Competition for Corporate Control: Institutional Investors, Investment Funds, and Hostile Takeover in Japan, in: Center on Japanese Economy and Business, Working Paper Series 4 (Columbia University 2006) 25-26,
    http://app.cul.columbia.edu:8080/ac/bitstream/10022/AC:P:258/1/fulltext.pdf;
    MILHAUPT, *supra* note 3, 2183; see also R.J. GILSON, The Missing Infrastructure, in: 2004 Columbia Business Law Review (2004), 29; D.G. GRUENER, Note, Chilled To The Pill: The Japanese Judiciary's Cool Reception Of The Poison Pill And Potential Repercussions, in: University of Pittsburgh Law Review 67 (2006) 871, 895; C. CARYL, End of a Rebel Culture? in: Newsweek International, 30 January, 2006; M. NAKAMOTO, A Takeover Battle Launched by the Upstart Livedoor is a Test of How Much Big Corporate Groups Can Protect Themselves Against Unwanted Attention, in: Financial Times, 22 March, 2005.
5   M. BURKART / F. PANUNZI, Takeover, in: European Corporate Governance Institute, Finance Working Paper No. 118 (2006) 3, *http://ssrn.com/abstract_id=884080.*

The *ex post* efficiency gains achieved by replacing underperforming management obviously do not arise in the case of failed hostile takeovers because incumbent management maintains their position *ex post*. In turn, the claim that failed hostile takeovers impact corporate governance is largely based on the assumption that they raise efficiency *ex ante* by increasing the perceived threat of successful hostile takeovers. Therefore, those who claim that failed hostile takeovers in Japan have significantly affected corporate governance are more accurately claiming that failed hostile takeovers have significantly increased the *ex ante threat* of successful hostile takeovers. As explained below, case study and empirical evidence do not support this conclusion.

III. Failed Hostile Takeovers Did Not Increase Ex Ante Threat Because They Were Not a Novel Feature of the Lost Decade Recovery

In order to argue that failed hostile takeovers increased efficiency *ex ante* during the lost decade recovery, hopeful M&A pundits have erroneously claimed that hostile takeover attempts were a novel feature of the recovery. Labeling hostile takeover attempts as novel allowed experts to suggest that, even though all of the takeover attempts during the lost decade recovery failed, the novelty of the attempts increased the perceived threat of hostile takeovers and thus increased the *ex ante* efficiency of hostile takeovers in Japan.

A leading article by Milhaupt, which is based on a number of failed (but no successful) hostile takeover attempts between 2000 and 2005, illustrates how experts have exaggerated the novelty and significance of failed hostile takeovers during the lost decade recovery.[6] Milhaupt admits that there were not any successful hostile takeovers during the recovery.[7] However, he then erroneously declares that, "the unthinkable has happened", "hostile takeovers have arrived in Japan".[8] Such a claim suggests that the mere presence of hostile takeover attempts during the lost decade recovery represented a dramatic shift in Japanese corporate governance. This is an error.

That hostile takeovers were attempted during the lost decade recovery is far from "unthinkable". To the contrary, for decades the control rights of asset-rich Japanese companies with languishing stock prices have been sporadically targeted by maverick Japanese and foreign investors.[9] Target companies in Japan have consistently used defensive measures, which have normally involved relying on assistance from friendly

---

6　See MILHAUPT, *supra* note 3, 2177-2181.
7　See *ibid.* 2181, 2184.
8　*Ibid.* 2171-2172.
9　M. TOKUMOTO, The Role of the Japanese Courts in Hostile Takeovers, in: Law in Japan 27 (2001) 1, 3-5.

stable shareholders, to prevent acquirers from successfully gaining control.[10] On numerous occasions over the past several decades, acquirers have responded to these defensive measures by commencing legal proceedings in which they attempted to have the court set aside defensive measures on the basis that their "primary purpose" was to entrench target management and not to increase shareholder value.[11] In some instances, acquirers have succeeded in having Japanese courts strike down defensive measures.[12] In other instances (more often in the 1980s than during the lost decade recovery), aggressive shareholders have pressured target management to repurchase shares at a significant premium to avoid being acquired and to maintain their ultimate control.[13] These facts about Japan's hostile takeover environment over the last several decades are unremarkable when compared to the United States and to many other developed countries.

However, what distinguishes Japan from the United States, and most other developed countries, is that attempted hostile takeovers have been almost universally unsuccessful in removing control from target management.[14] This did not change during the lost decade recovery. In addition, the trend that hostile takeovers have been attempted mainly by those outside of Japan's established business community remained largely intact. Both the consistent failure of hostile takeovers to remove *de facto* control rights from Japanese management and their status as being driven mainly by marginal players in the business community have relegated hostile takeovers to a footnote in postwar Japanese corporate governance—even during the lost decade recovery.

An examination of the failed hostile takeover attempts in Japan prior to the burst of the bubble (which occurred in 1989–1990) demonstrates that failed hostile takeovers existed long before the lost decade recovery. Two of the most notorious large-scale hostile takeover attempts in the 1980s were Video Seller's attempt to take over Fujiya and Trafalgar-Glen's attempt to take over Minebea Company.[15] While the Video Seller's takeover attempt was driven by aggressive Japanese private investors and Trafalgar-Glen's attempt by aggressive foreign investors, they shared a number of characteristics that are typical of failed hostile takeovers in Japan: (1) the hostile takeover targets were both large, well-established Japanese companies listed on the Tokyo Stock Exchange (TSE) (2) both targets had high asset values and languishing stock prices; (3) the

---

10 W.C. KESTER, Japanese Takeovers: The Global Contest for Corporate Control (Harvard Business School Press, 1990) 256; TOKUMOTO, *supra* note 9, 5-11; M. KAMIYA, The Possible Implications of Japanese Court Decisions on Defensive Measures for Japanese Corporate Governance, presented at Kyushu University's Corporate Governance in East Asia Conference, 10 February, 2007 (unpublished paper, on file with author), 5.
11 S. MARTIN, The Ultimate Barrier Revisited: Mergers and Acquisitions in Japan, in: Oda (ed.), Japanese Commercial Law. In an Era of Internationalization (London, Kluwer Academic, 1994) 55; TOKUMOTO, *supra* note 9, 5-11.
12 See, *e.g.*, *Shuwa v. Inageya*, Tokyo District Court, 2 July 1989, Hanrei Jihô 1317, 28.
13 KESTER, *supra* note 10, 237-262.
14 PUCHNIAK, *supra* note 1, 232.
15 KESTER, *supra* note 10, 239-244, 254-58.

acquirers were not part of Japan's business establishment; (4) the management of the target companies relied on friendly stable shareholders and other defensive tactics to dilute the acquirer's stake; and (5) management was ultimately successful in maintaining control.[16]

The Video Seller and Trafalgar-Glen cases reflect a wider trend of pre-bubble hostile share acquisitions in which management was able to maintain a firm grip on ultimate control. Every year from the late 1970s until the burst of the bubble in the late 1980s, there were several major share acquisitions of large listed Japanese companies by maverick Japanese investors with hostile intents.[17] Although virtually every hostile share acquisition failed to remove control from management, many ended "successfully" for the acquirers as they "greenmailed" management of the target companies into repurchasing the shares they acquired at a premium in order to maintain their control.[18] This trend was particularly pervasive from 1984 to 1988, during which Japan witnessed a rash of 23 successful greenmail transactions.[19] None of these transactions removed ultimate control from entrenched managers, indicating that although these greenmail attempts "succeeded," the threat they ultimately posed to the control rights of Japanese management was marginal.

Koshin's acquisition of Kokusai Kogyo in December 1988 is the only case during the entire pre-bubble era in which a hostile acquirer successfully (albeit temporarily) removed ultimate control from incumbent management.[20] However, upon closer examination, even this supposed hostile takeover is evidence of the inability of hostile acquirers to remove successfully ultimate control from incumbent Japanese management.[21]

Early in 1989, immediately following Koshin's supposedly "successful" hostile takeover, the transaction was mired in criminal allegations related to Koshin's on-market acquisition of the target's shares. The allegations led Japanese regulators to indict numerous parties involved in the takeover on charges of insider trading, stock price manipulation, violations of banking regulations, and tax fraud.[22] Under the pressure of

---

16 *Ibid.*
17 *Ibid.* 247-248.
18 *Ibid.* 237-262.
19 *Ibid.* 247-248.
20 In December 1988, Koshin exercised its rights as a holder of over three percent of Kokusai Kogyo's shares and requisitioned an extraordinary general meeting. In the meeting, Koshin used its majority stake to elect 15 new outside directors. This gave Koshin a majority of the directors on the board and ultimate control of Kokusai Kogyo. JOE J. LUFKIN, Flash in the Pan, in: IR Magazine 2000,
    http://www.thecrossbordergroup.com/ir_archive/pages/798/June+2000.stm?article_id=9435;
    J. STERNGOLD, Light Penalty for Speculator in Japan Stock Manipulation, in: New York Times, 20 May, 1993.
21 Arguably, this makes Koshin's acquisition of Kokusai Kogyo the only successful hostile takeover of a major corporation in postwar Japan.
22 Perhaps, the most disturbing allegation was that four of Kokusai Kogyo's senior executives had inside information about Koshin's plan to attempt a hostile takeover and then purchased

this enormous scandal, within a few months of this "successful" hostile takeover, Koshin lost control of Kokusai Kogyo's board.[23] A little over a year later, Mitsuhiro Kotani, the infamous greenmailer who led Koshin's hostile takeover, was pressured to resign as Chairman of Kokusai's board and was later convicted of tax evasion charges in a related transaction.[24]

Rather than serve as a threatening precedent to Japan's entrenched incumbent management, Koshin's disastrous and temporary takeover of Kokusai Kogyo did the opposite. It reinforced the image of hostile takeovers in the pre-bubble era as marginal players in corporate governance that were doomed to ultimate failure. During the lost decade recovery, this historical trend of failed hostile takeovers—which presented a marginal threat to the control of entrenched corporate management—continued.

In addition, as was the case during the lost decade recovery, prior to the burst of the bubble, Japanese courts played a significant role in regulating hostile takeover attempts.[25] In the late 1980s, it was common for companies to issue shares to friendly shareholders as a defensive measure to dilute the hostile acquirer's stake.[26] In several of these cases, hostile acquirers responded to these defensive measures by commencing injunctive proceedings, under Article 280-10 of the *Commercial Code*, to suspend the issuance of shares by the target company.[27]

---

shares based on that information, which they later sold at a profit when Koshin began secretly acquiring shares on the open market. J. STERNGOLD, Four Arrested in Japan in Stock-Trade Scandal, in: New York Times, 20 May, 1993; S. WAGSTYL, Insider Trading Suspected in Japan's Latest Share Scandal, in: Financial Times, 15 June, 1990; see generally "Fugitive Businessman Arrested in Sydney", Daily Yomiuri, 17 October, 1990; "Kotani Associate Hid 1 Billion Yen", Daily Yomiuri, 12 April, 1991; "Stock Speculator Gets Prison Sentence for Tax Evasion", Japan Economic Newswire, 27 April, 1992; "Sumitomo Executives Resign Amid Loan Scandal", United Press International, 16 October, 1990; "10-YR Imprisonment Demanded for Janome Extorter", Jiji Press Ticker, 20 December, 1999.

23 On February 23, 1989, ten members resigned from Kokusai Kogyo's board. Seven of the directors that resigned had been placed on the board by Koshin in the December 1988 extraordinary shareholders' meeting in which Koshin removed ultimate control from incumbent management by electing a majority of directors to the board. Following the resignation of Koshin's seven directors, Kokusai Kogyo's board was composed of 11 original members (i.e., those on the board prior to the takeover) and eight members placed on the board by Koshin. Thus, incumbent management had regained substantial control of Kokusai Kogyo. "10 Resign From Kokusai Kogyo Board", Jiji Press Ticker, 23 February, 1989.

24 KESTER, *supra* note 10, 17; "Corporate Raider Given Suspended Sentence", Asahi News Server, 19 May, 1993.

25 In his article in 2000, Minoru Tokumoto, discusses four cases in the late 1980s in which the court issued judgments in response to proceedings commenced in reaction to defensive measures implemented by a target company in the context of a hostile takeover attempt. TOKUMOTO, *supra* note 9.

26 See *e.g.*, KESTER, *supra* note 10, 256; KAMIYA, *supra* note 10, 5; TOKUMOTO, *supra* note 9, 5-11.

27 See TOKUMOTO, *supra* note 9, 5-11; see also MARTIN, *supra* note 11, 55.

In the late 1980s, as a result of a number of cases being brought before the court, a judicial test was developed for determining the circumstances under which target management could issue shares to friendly shareholders. According to this test, if the primary purpose of the issuance were to raise capital for the target company then the court would not suspend the issuance.[28] The jurisprudence surrounding this test, which came to be known as the "primary purpose test", illustrates that the involvement of Japanese courts in hostile takeover battles was also not a novel feature of the recent recovery.[29]

Failed hostile takeover attempts, and the court's role in policing them, did not end with the burst of the bubble. In November 1989, just as the bubble was about to burst, T. Boone Pickens, a Texas billionaire and infamous American corporate raider, commenced a high profile hostile takeover attempt against Koito Manufacturing, a parts supplier and member of the Toyota *keiretsu*.[30] The Pickens-Koito takeover battle began when Pickens, who was widely criticized by the Japanese business establishment, secretly acquired a twenty percent stake in Koito from a well-known Japanese greenmailer.[31]

This sparked a two-year takeover battle that included an unsuccessful court action by Pickens to use his shareholdings to gain information about Koito's finances, complaints by Pickens to the United States Congress that Koito's stable shareholding relationships amounted to unfair trade practices and the refusal by Koito to allow Pickens any representation on the board.[32] In 1991, Pickens finally admitted that he could not defeat Koito with its stable Toyota *keiretsu* shareholders and sold the shares he had acquired without a profit. [33] As expected, Koito's management remained firmly entrenched.

In 1996, Japan experienced another high profile hostile takeover attempt when Masayoshi Son, of Softbank and Yahoo! fame, joined forces with Rupert Murdoch, the Australian media baron and takeover mogul, to acquire TV Asahi, one of Japan's five main private broadcasters.[34] Similar to T. Boone Pickens' attempt, the hostile takeover attempt by Son and Murdoch was "widely abhorred by the [Japanese business] estab-

---

28 TOKUMOTO, *supra* note 9, 4.
29 See Corporate Value Study Group, METI-Sponsored Corporate Value Report 2005, 13: available at *http://www.meti.go.jp/policy/economic_oganiza-tion/pdf/houkokusyo_hontai_eng. pdf*. For a summary of the Corporate Value Report 2005, see Corporate Study Group, Corporate Value Report 2005 (Abstract), in: Journal of Japanese Law 21 (2006) 137. For a concise explanation of how the corporate value report relates to Japan's new regime for regulating hostile takeovers see, H. BAUM, Takeover Defenses in Japan: Corporate Value Reports and Guidelines, in: Journal of Japanese Law 21 (2006) 131.
30 P.C. REICH, T. Boone Pickens and Corporate Governance in Japan: A Retrospective View of Three Sides of the Story and Recent Developments, in: Law in Japan 27 (2001) 27.
31 *Ibid.* 29.
32 See *ibid.* 29-36.
33 See D. IBISON, Prospect of Takeovers Becomes Hot Topic, in: Financial Times, 30 March, 2005; REICH, *supra* note 30, 31-33.
34 "Media Mould-Breakers", Campaign, 24 March, 2006.

lishment".[35] After Son and Murdoch managed to acquire a twenty-one percent stake in TV Asahi, the entire Asahi media group rallied around TV Asahi.[36] Three months later, Son and Murdoch "cried uncle," selling their TV Asahi shares to Asahi Daily Shimbun (the group's daily newspaper) at no profit.[37] The control of TV Asahi's management was never seriously threatened by the failed hostile takeover attempt.

The pervasiveness of failed hostile takeover attempts prior to the burst of the bubble and during the lost decade demonstrates that they were not a novel feature of the lost decade recovery. The court's involvement in regulating Japan's lackluster hostile takeover regime is also not new to the recovery. Indeed, even claims by experts that failed hostile takeover attempts represent a revolution in Japanese corporate governance are not novel.

In 1991, Carl Kester, in his leading book on Japanese takeovers, claimed that failed hostile takeovers suggested a dramatic shift in Japanese corporate governance towards the American hostile takeovers-based model.[38] Kester also predicted, based on the failed hostile takeover attempts of the 1970s and 1980s (particularly, Video Seller and Trafalgar-Glen), that Japan would develop "a newly active market for corporate control" that would "no doubt" feature a "few surprising and notable successful hostile takeovers".[39] As two decades have passed since Kester published his book and there have been no "surprising [or] notable successful hostile takeovers", his predictions are obviously incorrect. The inaccuracy of Kester's predictions further casts doubt on similar, more recent, predictions by experts that "novel" hostile takeover attempts during the lost decade recovery represent a dramatic shift towards the American governance model.

In sum, the history of failed hostile takeovers by maverick investors prior to the lost decade recovery is important because it illustrates that the hostile takeover attempts that occurred during the lost decade recovery were not novel. Aggressive investors attempting to exploit asset rich companies with floundering stock prices have long been a part of Japanese corporate governance. The use of defensive measures and court actions in the context of these hostile takeover battles is also nothing new. Even claims by experts that rely on failed hostile takeover attempts as evidence of the arrival of an American-style market for corporate control have a long history. Far from being "unthinkable," the failed hostile takeover attempts during the lost decade recovery and the familiar predicttions by experts that these mere attempts suggest a dramatic shift in Japanese corporate governance were completely predictable.

---

35 *Ibid.*
36 *Ibid.*
37 NAKAMOTO, *supra* note 4.
38 KESTER, *supra* note 10, 239.
39 *Ibid.* 18 and 239.

IV. The Continued History of Failed Hostile Takeovers During the Lost Decade Recovery Reconfirmed Their Marginal Role in Japanese Corporate Governance

The continued history of failed hostile takeovers during the lost decade recovery created a serious problem for experts who were intent on demonstrating that Japan developed a hostile takeovers market reminiscent of the United States in the 1980s.[40] This led many experts to exaggerate the significance and pervasiveness of hostile takeovers during the lost decade recovery. In some cases, experts reported hostile takeovers when none existed.[41] In other cases, overly exuberant pundits prematurely claimed that "Japan's first successful hostile takeover was nearing completion," only to see the hostile bid soundly defeated in traditional fashion.[42] In yet other cases, a number of experts accurately acknowledged the persistent failure of hostile takeovers during the lost decade recovery, but then erroneously claimed that these failures were of "epoch-making significance";[43] the "nail in the coffin for ….. old Japan Inc.";[44] and marked "the advent of an era of hostile takeovers [in Japan]."[45] As in the past, failed hostile takeovers merely reconfirmed that Japanese management, not shareholders, maintained a firm grip on corporate control—precisely the opposite of the dramatic shift in Japanese corporate governance that many experts claimed these failed hostile takeovers to represent.[46]

Before examining the details of the most prominent failed hostile takeovers during the lost decade recovery, it is necessary to re-examine transactions that have been held out to be hostile takeovers, which upon closer inspection, were not. A number of experts who credit hostile takeovers with transforming Japanese corporate governance during the lost decade recovery cite the 1999 acquisition by Cable & Wireless ("C&W") of International Digital Communications ("IDC") and the 2000 acquisition by Boehringer

---

40 See *supra* note 2.
41 See U. SCHAEDE, The Strategic Logic of Japanese Keiretsu, Main Banks and Cross-Shareholdings, Revisited; Center on Japanese Economy and Business, Working Paper No. 247, 2006, 32, *http://app.cul.columbia.edu:8080/ac/bitstream/10022/AC:P:259/1/fulltext.pdf;* "A&O Must Make the Most of Its Long-Awaited Japanese Entry", Lawyer, 19 March, 2007; N. MATSUKO, 'Market for Corporate Control' for Better Governance in Japan, in: Economic Conference and Symposium, Corporate Governance in the New Japan, 3 November, 2003, 4 (unpublished PowerPoint presentation, on file with author); HINES ET AL., *supra* note 3, 225; R. NEFF, Japan: Land of the Hostile Takeover?, in: Business Week, 13 March, 2000; H. MIYAJIMA / F. KUROKI, The Unwinding of Cross-Shareholding in Japan, in: Aoki et al. (ed.), Corporate Governance in Japan (Oxford University Press, 2007) 79, 119.
42 C. SMITH, Will Livedoor Open the Door?, in: Deal, 8 July, 2005.
43 "M&As shake Japan's corporate mindset, give hope for future", Nikkei Weekly, 11 December, 2006; see also, MILHAUPT, *supra* note 3, 2173-2174, 2216.
44 M. FACKLER, Mergers and Acquisitions No Longer Shock Japanese, in: New York Times, 29 March, 2007.
45 "Reality check for new-media mirage", Weekend Australian, 21 January, 2006.
46 G. JACKSON / H. MIYAJIM, Introduction, in: Aoki et al. (eds.), Corporate Governance in Japan (Oxford University Press, 2007) 9.

Ingelheim ("B&I") of SSP as the beginning of Japan's "new era of hostile takeovers."[47] Despite such claims, both of these transactions were friendly acquisitions that bared no resemblance to a hostile takeover.

One such example was C&W's acquisition of IDC. Although dubbed as one of Japan's first "successful hostile takeovers," it was nothing of the sort.[48] In 1998, the early stages of the IDC transaction occurred when IDC, a Japanese international telecom company, tendered for advice on its upcoming sale.[49] Almost everyone in the market saw the tender as a mere formality because it was widely assumed that IDC was destined to be bought by NTT, Japan's former state telephone monopoly.[50] However, in March 1999, C&W, a British international telecom company, which was already a large stable shareholder of IDC, made a surprising offer to purchase it.[51] NTT quickly countered with an offer of its own.[52]

IDC's board held an extraordinary meeting to consider the two competing offers and expressed its general preference for the specific terms of the NTT offer.[53] Following IDC's board meeting, C&W revised the terms of its offer and significantly increased the premium of its bid on two occasions in response to counter offers made by NTT.[54] IDC's board remained neutral throughout the balance of the transaction and offered no further recommendations.[55] At no time did IDC's management-controlled board attempt to use any takeover defenses or suggest which bid its shareholders should support based on C&W's revised offers.[56] In fact, the only recommendations following C&W's revised offers were from Toyota and Itochu, two of IDC's major stable friendly shareholders, who publicly announced their decision to sell their 17.7 percent stake in IDC to C&W.[57] In the end, a resounding 134 of IDC's 141 major stable shareholders chose to tender their shares to C&W.[58] C&W ultimately acquired control of IDC because its

---

47 See, *e.g.*, GILSON, *supra* note 4, 23; HINES ET AL., *supra* note 3, footnote 225; MATSUKO, *supra* note 41; "Weapons Needed to Fight Takeovers", Nikkei Weekly, 27 September, 2004.
48 HINES ET AL., *supra* note 3, footnote 225; JACKSON / MIYAJIMA, *supra* note 46, 15; MATSUKO, *supra* note 41; See, D.H. WHITTAKER / M. HAYAKAWA, Contesting "Corporate Value "Through Takeover Bids in Japan, in: Journal of Japanese Law 23 (2007) 5, footnote 2. See also E. COLCERA, The Market for Corporate Control in Japan (Springer, New York, 2007), 60-62 and 109.
49 COLCERA, *supra* note 48; "Shareholder Power", Economist, 27 November, 1999.
50 Economist, 27 November, 1999, *supra* note 49.
51 See *ibid;* "IDC's Board Votes in Favor of NTT's Takeover Offer", Japan Times, 15 April, 1999.
52 Economist, November 27 1999, *supra* note 49.
53 COLCERA, *supra* note 48, 110.
54 "C&W Makes New Takeover Bid for IDC", Japan Times, 6 May, 1999; "C&W Secures 97.69% Stake in IDC", Japan Times, 16 June, 1999.
55 COLCERA, *supra* note 48, 109.
56 *Ibid.*
57 "C&W Wins IDC Stakes", Japan Times, 9 June 1999.
58 Japan Times, 16 June, 1999, *supra* note 54.

revised offers were unopposed by IDC's management and supported by IDC's stable friendly shareholders—precisely the opposite of a hostile takeover.

Like the IDC transaction, the acquisition in 2000 of SSP, Japan's fourth-largest supplier of over-the-counter drugs, by B&I, a large German drug company, is also erroneously described as one of Japan's "first successful hostile takeovers."[59] Despite these claims, from the outset, B&I's acquisition lacked the hallmarks of a hostile takeover. B&I and SSP were long-time business partners, with SSP acting as the distributor for B&I's products in Japan.[60] B&I also had a seat on SSP's board and was a significant stable shareholder of SSP, with a 19.6 percent stake—hardly the profile of a corporate raider.[61]

In 2000, B&I made a successful unsolicited bid for a controlling stake in SSP, offering a forty-two percent premium to SSP's shareholders.[62] There is no evidence that the bid was hostile in nature. To the contrary, B&I actively assured investors that the bid was not hostile and SSP's management remained neutral throughout the entire bid.[63] B&I's friendly relationship with SSP's incumbent management is evident from the fact that B&I chose to leave all of SSP's management in place after its acquisition was complete—something that does not always occur even in friendly takeovers.[64]

Experts also refer to the 2004 Sumitomo Trust-UFJ dispute as evidence that Japan developed a hostile takeovers regime during the recent recovery.[65] Again, this claim is confused. The Sumitomo Trust-UFJ dispute did not even involve a hostile takeover *bid*, let alone a successful hostile takeover. The dispute, however, did involve an interesting contractual issue and competing merger bids between Japan's largest banks, but that misses the point. It is simply misleading to portray the Sumitomo Trust-UFJ dispute as an "epoch changing" transaction that marked a new era of hostile takeovers in Japan.[66]

The facts in the Sumitomo Trust-UFJ case are straightforward. In May 2004, UFJ Holdings entered into a memorandum of agreement to sell its most profitable entity, UFJ Trust Bank, to Sumitomo Trust.[67] A term of the agreement was that Sumitomo Trust had the exclusive right to acquire UFJ Trust Bank during a two-year period and that neither party could engage in discussions with third parties that could have interfered

---

59 See MATSUKO, *supra* note 41; NEFF, *supra* note 41; see also " Ever So Polite", Economist, 17 February, 2001; CORPORATE VALUE REPORT 2005, *supra* note 29, 14. See also generally, WHITTAKER / HAYAKAWA, *supra* note 48, footnote 2.
60 COLCERA, *supra* note 48, 59.
61 J. CHOY, Win or Lose, More Players Join Japan's Mergers and Acquisitions Game, in: Japan Economic Institute (JEI Report No. 9 Mar. 3, 2000).
62 *Ibid;* SMITH, *supra* note 42.
63 SMITH, *supra* note 42.
64 *Ibid.*
65 MILHAUPT, *supra* note 3, 2177-2178.
66 See *ibid.* 2173-2174, 2177-2184.
67 See *ibid.* 2177-2178.

with the potential acquisition ("the no shop clause").[68] In July 2004, UFJ appeared to violate this "no shop clause" by having discussions with Mitsubishi Tokyo Financial Group (MTFG) about a transaction in which MTFG would acquire all of UFJ's business operations, including UFJ Trust Bank.[69]

In response to the MTFG-UFJ discussions, Sumitomo Trust commenced legal proceedings to stop the MTFG-UFJ transaction on the basis that it breached the "no shop clause."[70] After Sumitomo Trust's legal action failed, it publicly threatened to launch a hostile bid for UFJ. However, in the end, Sumitomo's threat of launching a hostile takeover bid was just a threat. In the fall of 2005, the MTFG-UFJ merger closed and Sumitomo Trust did not launch a hostile takeover bid.[71] Characterizing the MTFG-UFJ transaction as evidence of Japan developing a U.S.-style hostile takeovers market is simply inaccurate.[72]

If mis-describing friendly transactions or contractual disputes as hostile takeovers is confusing, then mistaking takeover *bids* with actual hostile takeovers compounds the problem. In a recent article, Ulrike Schaede, an Associate Professor of Japanese Business at the University of California, claims that "in 2005 a total of 53 successful hostile takeovers were recorded [in Japan]".[73] In reality, there was not a single successful hostile takeover in Japan in 2005. It is likely, therefore, that Schaede has confused takeover *bids* (many of which were not hostile) with successful hostile takeovers.[74] As takeover bids in Japan do not even serve as a valid proxy for the *threat* of hostile takeovers (see next subsection below), these 53 cases do not lend support to her conclusion that hostile takeovers became a significant feature of Japanese corporate governance during the recent recovery.[75] In another article, *The Lawyer Magazine* reports that, in August 2006, Japan experienced its "first-ever hostile takeover" when Oji Paper acquired Hokuetsu Paper Mills.[76] As described in more detail below, Oji's bid for Hokuetsu was defeated. The claim by *The Lawyer Magazine* is simply wrong.

Despite the exaggerations, mis-descriptions and false claims by experts, there were several failed hostile takeover attempts that actually did occur prior to and during the lost decade recovery. These failed hostile takeovers are noteworthy because they illustrate the ability of entrenched Japanese management to defeat consistently hostile take-

---

68 See *ibid.*
69 *Ibid.*
70 *Ibid.*
71 *Ibid.*
72 *Ibid.* 2182-2183.
73 SCHAEDE, *supra* note 41, 32.
74 The total number of takeover bids in Japan in 2005 was 53—which is the same as the purported number of "successful hostile takeovers" reported by Schaede. See RECOF's webpage for a chart displaying the number of takeover bids in Japan from 1972 until present: *http://www.recof.co.jp.*
75 SCHAEDE, *supra* note 41, 32.
76 LAWYER, 19 March, 2007, supra note 41.

overs. In addition, they demonstrate that hostile takeovers are still largely launched by those outside of Japan's established business community and that relying on friendly stable shareholders is still a primary mechanism for incumbent management to defeat hostile attempts. In this sense, the failed hostile takeovers of the lost decade recovery are a continuation of the history of failed hostile takeovers in Japan over the past several decades.

In January 2000, Yoshiaki Murakami, a man described at the time as "a corporate raider" who preached "a very American sounding gospel of shareholders' rights and free markets," launched what many claim was Japan's first domestic hostile takeover bid.[77] Through his takeover boutique, M&A Consulting ("MAC"), Murakami targeted Shoei Corporation, a little-known electronics and real estate company that was part of the Fuyo (Fuji Bank) *keiretsu*. Shoei's cumulative stock price of $66 million and $570 million in liquid assets made it characteristic of a significant percentage of companies on the TSE that made Western pundits repeatedly predict that a wave of hostile takeovers in Japan was inevitable.[78]

On January 24, 2000, MAC made a tender offer for all of Shoei's outstanding shares, with a forty percent premium over the 1999 market price.[79] Murakami's move made media headlines, but as an unwelcome outsider, he garnered little respect from Shoei's president, who refused to speak with him.[80] Despite the substantial premium offered, MAC's bid failed miserably, accumulating only 6.5 percent of Shoei's shares.[81] The reason for the failure was predictable. In traditional fashion and unlike the American takeover market, stable and friendly shareholders gave unconditional support to existing management and refused to tender their shares to the "unwelcome bidder" regardless of the premium.[82]

In December 2003, the next widely publicized hostile takeover attempt took place when Steel Partners, an aggressive American buyout fund, attempted to takeover Sotoh, a wool fabric company, and Yushiro Chemical Industry.[83] Both companies were extremely attractive takeover targets since their cumulative stock prices were lower than their liquidated asset values and they had significant cash holdings.[84] Steel Partners, which already had a ten percent stake in each of the companies, made takeover bids for each company with a thirty percent premium over their previous closing prices.[85]

---

77 "Challenging Japan's Cozy Corporate Culture", Time Asia, 7 February, 2000.
78 Ibid.
79 COLCERA, *supra* note 48, 110.
80 TIME ASIA, 7 February, 2000.
81 COLCERA, *supra* note 48, 110.
82 P. LEE, A New Generation Embraces M&A, in: Euromoney, February 2006.
83 See MILHAUPT, *supra* note 3, 2180-2181.
84 See *Ibid.* 2180.
85 *Ibid.* 2180-2181.

In both cases, incumbent management "immediately announced their opposition to the unsolicited bids and, as a defensive measure," substantially increased their dividends.[86] The substantial increase in dividends caused the share price of both companies to increase dramatically. As a result, Steel Partners' hostile bids failed miserably because they no longer offered a substantial premium to shareholders.[87] In 2005, after Sotoh's management decided that the threat of a hostile takeover was no longer imminent they decreased dividends to pre-bid levels.[88] The tactic used by Sotoh's management to "pay off" its shareholders with a short-term dividend increase, to maintain their power, is reminiscent of Japanese managers using corporate funds to 'pay off' greenmailers in the 1980s.

In 2005, Livedoor's failed hostile takeover of Nippon Broadcasting System ("NBS") caused a media circus that rivaled any business story in recent memory.[89] Public interest in the attempted hostile takeover was fueled by Livedoor's flamboyant 32-year-old president and university dropout, Takafumi Horie, who became a billionaire and cultural icon through a dotcom company he started named Livin' on the Edge (later renamed Livedoor).[90] Horie's spiky-hair, "Cheshire cat" grin, silver-blue Ferrari, bikini-clad girlfriend and t-shirt and jeans business attire mesmerized the Japanese public.[91] It seemed that Japanese people, especially the younger generation, could not get enough of this brash young entrepreneur taking on Japan's corporate old guard who had fallen out of favor during the lost decade.[92]

Experts and academics fell into the "Horie-hype" and pointed to Horie as evidence of a dramatic shift in Japanese corporate governance.[93] Some experts posited that the day Horie launched Livedoor's bid for NBS marked the "advent of an era of hostile takeovers" in Japan.[94] Other experts claimed that Livedoor's takeover attempt sparked "a revolution in [Japan's market for] corporate control."[95] Some other experts even erroneously credited Horie with pulling off Japan's first-ever successful hostile takeover

---

86 See *Ibid.* 2181; "Hostile Bids are Back Again: Who Should Rejoice?", Economist, 21 February, 2004.
87 See MILHAUPT, *supra* note 3, 2181.
88 COLCERA, *supra* note 48, 113-114
89 See C. ALGER, The Livedoor Looking Glass: Examining The Limits Of Hostile Takeover Bids In Japan, in: New York University Journal of Law and Business 3 (2006) 309, 319; GRUENER, *supra* note 4, 878; J. KINGSTON, The Beginning of the End for Japan Inc., in: International Herald Tribune, 1 April, 2005.
90 MILHAUPT, *supra* note 3, 2181.
91 "Stirred by Flashy Entrepreneur", New York Times, 19 January, 2006.
92 See KINGSTON, *supra* note 89; "The Battle for Corporate Control: The Outlook for M&A in Japan", Economist Intelligence Unit (2005) 11-13.
93 ECONOMIST INTELLIGENCE UNIT 2005, *supra* note 92, 11-13.
94 "Reality check for new-media mirage", Weekend Australian, 21 January, 2006; "Livedoor May Have Opened Door to Era of Hostile Takeovers", Japan Economic Newswire, 23 February, 2005.
95 ECONOMIST INTELLIGENCE UNIT, *supra* 92, 7.

before the Livedoor bid was even complete.[96] In the end, similar to most other trends in Japan, the "Horie-hype" faded quickly.[97] Livedoor's hostile bid failed in traditional fashion with stable friendly shareholders coming to NBS' rescue and Horie being disgraced by an accounting fraud and stock market manipulation conviction that sent him from his Roppongi Hills penthouse to the "Japanese big house."[98]

All 'Horie-hype' aside, the Livedoor case was simply another example of a maverick Japanese investor being defeated by incumbent Japanese management with help from friendly stable shareholders. The Livedoor case arose out of an unusual cross-shareholding relationship that existed between NBS and Fuji TV, which were both part of the same media conglomerate (the Fujisankei Communications Group).[99] Fuji TV, Japan's largest private television company, was technically controlled by NBS, a much smaller radio station, by virtue of the fact that NBS owned 22.5 percent of Fuji TV's shares, while Fuji TV owned only 12.4 percent of NBS' shares.[100] This created the perverse incentive for corporate raiders to target the much less valuable NBS to gain *de facto* control of Fuji TV.

To rectify this situation, on January 17, 2005, Fuji TV announced an all-cash offer for all of the outstanding shares of NBS. Fuji TV's bid was below the market price for NBS shares, which (as explained below) was characteristic of takeover bids in Japan prior to and during the lost decade recovery.[101] Despite the below market offer, the takeover bid was immediately approved by Fuji TV's management, which was also predictable during Japan's lost decade recovery.[102]

However, unbeknownst to NBS and Fuji TV, during the tender offer period, Livedoor was secretly acquiring NBS shares in after-hours trading.[103] On February 8, 2005, before Fuji TV's tender offer period had expired, Livedoor made the shocking announcement that it had acquired 29.6 percent of NBS' shares (bringing its stake up to thirty-eight percent) and intended to acquire the remainder.[104] NBS responded quickly with defensive measures by announcing that it would issue warrants to Fuji TV, which if exercised, would dramatically increase NBS' share capital by 140 percent and dilute Livedoor's stake in NBS to less than twenty percent.[105]

---

96 SMITH, *supra* note 42; see CORPORATE VALUE REPORT 2005, *supra* note 29, 14.
97 NIKKEI, *supra* note 43.
98 See ALGER, *supra* note 89, 321; ECONOMIST INTELLIGENCE UNIT, *supra* note 92; "Livedoor Founder Horie Given 2 1/2-Year Prison Term", Japan Economic Newswire, 16 March, 2007.
99 ALGER, *supra* note 89, 319.
100 *Ibid.*
101 *Ibid.*; ECONOMIST INTELLIGENCE UNIT, *supra* note 92.
102 ECONOMIST INTELLIGENCE UNIT, *supra* note 92.
103 ALGER, *supra* note 89, 319; HINES ET AL., *supra* note 3, 375-376.
104 ALGER, *supra* note 89, 319; MILHAUPT, *supra* note 3, 2179.
105 ALGER, *supra* note 89, 319; GRUENER, *supra* note 4, 879; NAKAMOTO, *supra* note 4.

In response to NBS' defensive actions, Livedoor sought an injunction from the court to stop the issuance of the NBS warrants. The fact that the warrants, if exercised, would have more than doubled NBS' capital made it virtually impossible for NBS to argue convincingly that the "primary purpose" of the issuance was to raise capital and not to entrench management.[106] Therefore, unsurprisingly, in light of the well-established "primary purpose test," the Tokyo District Court granted NBS' injunction, which was affirmed on appeal by the Tokyo High Court.[107]

Livedoor's court victory prompted Fuji TV's management to fight back using traditional defensive tactics. Fuji TV called on its friendly stable shareholders to increase their NBS holdings and convinced Softbank Investment to borrow fifteen percent of Fuji TV's shares from NBS—making Softbank Investment Fuji TV's largest shareholder.[108] As a result, Livedoor could no longer gain *de facto* control over the extremely valuable Fuji TV by controlling NBS. In addition, NBS' management received crucial support from its lifetime employees, as ninety percent of them signed a public statement supporting NBS' incumbent management over Horie and Livedoor.[109]

In April 2005, in an act that was tantamount to admitting defeat, Livedoor sold its NBS shares to Fuji TV at a marginal profit, which was just enough to allow Horie to "save face."[110] In the end, Livedoor was defeated because, in traditional fashion, stable and friendly shareholders rallied around incumbent management, "demonstrating that the era of a truly free stock market [was] still a long way off" in Japan.[111] In addition, the defeat emphasized that Japan's unique corporate governance, embodied here by lifetime employees, renders dubious any predictions of hostile takeovers that find support from American precedent.

In the year following Livedoor's failed hostile takeover, there were a number of other hostile takeover attempts. These attempts received far less coverage and were universally unsuccessful.[112] However, in the summer of 2006, hopeful hostile takeover pundits emerged again when Oji Paper launched its hostile takeover bid for Hokuetsu Paper Mills. Oji's bid reignited familiar claims of an "epoch-making" event that was sure to spark a "wave" of successful hostile takeovers in Japan.[113] Predictably, yet again, Oji's bid failed in traditional fashion with friendly stable shareholders rescuing Hokuetsu's management at the expense of individual minority shareholders.[114]

---

106 GRUENER, *supra* note 4, 879.
107 *Ibid.* 878-879; ALGER, *supra* note 89, 320.
108 ECONOMIST INTELLIGENCE UNIT, *supra* note 92, 11-13.
109 *Ibid.*
110 *Ibid.*
111 *Ibid;* see ALGER, *supra* note 89, 319-321.
112 PUCHNIAK, *supra* note 1, 246.
113 P. ALFORD, Japanese Paper Giants Practise Origami on Corporate Rule Book, in: Australian, 9 August, 2006; NIKKEI, *supra* note 43; "Oji's TOB First by Smokestack Firm, Heralds New M&A Era", Nikkei Weekly, 31 July, 2006.
114 See ALFORD, *supra* note 113; W. PESEK Jr., Japan's Barbarians Within, in: International

The particular facts in the Oji case are worth examining because they illustrate that, even as the lost decade recovery was coming to an end, incumbent Japanese management still maintained an iron grip on their *de facto* corporate control. In May 2006, the event that triggered Oji's unsolicited takeover bid occurred when Hokuetsu decided to expand the production capacity in its Niigata plant, posing a serious threat to profits in Japan's already saturated paper industry.[115] On July 3, 2006, in response to this threat, Oji's management informed Hokuetsu that it intended to acquire Hokuetsu and provided its plan for a post-merger integration.[116] As expected, Hokuetsu's management quickly began working behind the scenes to rally its friendly and stable shareholders to ward off Oji's unwelcome takeover attempt.[117]

On July 21, 2006, Hokuetsu's board put its defensive measures into action. The board decided that it would issue Mitsubishi, a friendly stable shareholder, 50 million shares at the discount price of 607 yen—which was approximately five percent below the previous closing price and ten percent below the high earlier in the year.[118] The share issuance would provide Mitsubishi with a twenty-four percent stake in Hokuetsu's expanded capital and ensure that Hokuetsu's management had a large block of stable friendly shares to protect them against Oji's attempted hostile takeover.[119] At the same meeting, the board voted itself a poison pill in the form of equity warrants issued to friendly stable shareholders, including Mitsubishi, which were exercisable in the event that Oji (or any other unwelcome acquirer) made an unsolicited tender offer.[120]

As to be predicted, Hokuetsu's defensive measures ensured the entrenchment of Hokuetsu's incumbent management, but blatantly disregarded minority shareholders. Without a seat on Hokuetsu's board, the average shareholder would have had no way of knowing that twenty-four percent of their company had been offered to Mitsubishi at a significant discount, that they were to be diluted by sixteen percent, and that a new poison pill protected management.[121] Minority shareholders also received scant protecttion from the so-called "independent committee"[122] that approved the poison pill, as it was made up of two retired auditors who had previously worked for Hokuetsu and a

---

Herald Tribune, 6 August, 2006.
115 ALFORD, *supra* note 113.
116 See K. OSUGI, What is Converging? Rules on Hostile Takeovers in Japan and the Convergence Debate, in: Asian-Pacific Law & Policy Journal 9 (2007) 143; "TOB 'Hostility' Limited by Tradition", Nikkei Weekly, 4 September, 2006; C. WRIGHT, Hostile Bid Subverts Japanese Politeness, in: Euromoney, September 2006.
117 ALFORD, *supra* note 113.
118 ALFORD, *supra* note 113; M. SANCHANTA, Oji Paper Gives Up on Hokuetsu Takeover, in: Financial Times, 6 September, 2006.
119 ALFORD, *supra* note 113.
120 *Ibid.*
121 *Ibid.*
122 HINES ET AL., *supra* note 3, 412-413.

Shinto priest—hardly a model for minority shareholder protection.[123] The TSE was similarly left in the dark by Hokuetsu's management-dominated board, which conveniently failed to mention Oji's takeover offer when it gave notice to the TSE (as required by the New TSE Listing Rules) about the board's plan to institute the poison pill.[124]

Finally, on July 23, 2006, after spending more than two weeks surreptitiously building an impenetrable barrier of takeover defenses, Hokuetsu's management formally rejected Oji's takeover offer.[125] Oji's president responded by publicly announcing that if Hokuetsu cancelled its planned placement of shares with Mitsubishi, Oji would make an on-market offer for 50.1 percent of Hokuetsu's shares at the premium price of 860 yen—thirty-five percent above the previous closing price.[126] The stock market quickly responded to Oji's potential offer by driving up Hokuetsu's shares to 825 yen.[127]

At this point, from an American shareholders' rights perspective, the planned placement by Hokuetsu's board of a quarter of the company with Mitsubishi for 607 yen per share, which now stood at a whopping twenty-six percent discount to the current market price, appeared unthinkable.[128] However, Hokuetsu's board would make its decision in Tokyo, not Delaware. So predictably, the placement of Hokuetsu's shares in Mitsubishi went through as planned.

Then, when it seemed that the shenanigans of Japanese management could not get any worse, Oji was blindsided again when Nippon Paper Group announced that it had acquired an 8.5 percent stake in Hokuetsu to help block the Oji bid.[129] Even more shocking, Nippon Paper's management-dominated board paid approximately 800 yen for the same shares that Mitsubishi was being handed for 607 yen—knowing full well that when Hokuetsu placed its shares with Mitsubishi it would significantly dilute Nippon Paper's stake.[130] For good measure, Nippon Paper's board also conveniently forgot to comply with the five percent reporting rule when it acquired its 8.5 percent blocking stake in Hokuetsu.[131]

This is where claims that Japan's hostile takeovers market dramatically changed during the lost decade recovery begin to unravel.[132] According to such claims, in the dramatically changed environment of the lost decade recovery, Japanese shareholders

---

123 ALFORD, *supra* note 113; "Barbarians Within the Gate", Economist, 12 August, 2006.
124 ALFORD, *supra* note 113.
125 NIKKEI WEEKLY, 2006, *supra* note 116.
126 ALFORD, *supra* note 113; WRIGHT, *supra* note 116.
127 ALFORD, *supra* note 113.
128 *Ibid;* ECONOMIST, *supra* note 123.
129 ECONOMIST, *supra* note 123.
130 ALFORD, *supra* note 113.
131 *Ibid.*
132 There have been a myriad of claims from experts that Japan developed a vigorous, American-style, hostile takeovers market during the recent recovery. See, PUCHNIAK, *supra* note 1, footnote 343.

should have challenged Hokuetsu's unreasonable defensive measures in court.[133] Conversely, Hokuetsu's friendly shareholders should not have sacrificed shareholder value in their own companies merely to save Hokuetsu's incumbent management. In Milhaupt's words, during the lost decade recovery it was "no longer considered acceptable [for Japanese boards]…..to support incumbent management…..regardless of the financial consequences to their own shareholders".[134] Based on such claims, there should have been a tirade of litigation challenging the "Shinto priest approved" poison pill; the sale of a quarter of Hokuetsu to Mitsubishi at an unreasonable discount; and the purchase of soon-to-be-diluted shares at an unjustifiable premium by Nippon Paper's management-dominated board.[135]

However, what "should have" happened, based on the predictions of hopeful hostile takeover pundits, did not. There was not a single legal proceeding commenced in the Oji-Hokuetsu case.[136] The brazen defensive measures by Hokuetsu's management and its friendly stable shareholders produced not a peep from nascent shareholders. Even Hokuetsu's foreign shareholders, who held twenty-five percent of the company, would not take the risk of challenging the defensive measures of Hokuetsu's corporate old guard.[137]

Finally, on August 30, 2006, without a legal action in sight, over thirty percent of Hokuetsu in the hands of two companies that were not on the share register a month before, and with a "Shinto priest approved" poison pill in place, Oji conceded defeat.[138] Oji's "epoch-making" bid for 50.1 percent of Hokuetsu, which received rave reviews from the international business community for making impeccable business sense, managed to net Oji a paltry 5.25 percent of Hokuetsu's shares—not exactly a menacing threat to Hokuetsu's entrenched management.[139] However, Oji's hostile attempt did achieve one thing. It made Oji a pariah in Japan's "old school" paper industry and left the Japanese bank that supported Oji's bid wondering why it ever went out on a limb to do so.[140]

The Oji case occurred as Japan's remarkable 5-year lost decade recovery was ending and its economy was transitioning into what appeared to be an era of sustained growth— before it was derailed by the global financial crisis. This example clearly illustrates that not much changed during the lost decade recovery as hostile takeovers continued to play a marginal role in corporate restructuring.[141] This is confirmed by a survey of Japanese

---

133 See MILHAUPT, *supra* note 3, 2202.
134 *Ibid.* 2186.
135 ALFORD, *supra* note 113.
136 See *Ibid.*
137 See WRIGHT, *supra* note 116.
138 See "Oji / Hokuetsu", Financial Times, 30 August, 2006.
139 SANCHANTA, *supra* note 118; see also "Under Pressure", Economist, 9 September, 2006.
140 See WRIGHT, *supra* note 116; NIKKEI, *supra* note 43.
141 See WRIGHT, *supra* note 116.

management shortly after the Oji bid, which reported that seventy-seven percent of Japanese executives said that they would not consider attempting a hostile takeover.[142] However, in the same survey, ninety-three percent expected friendly corporate acquisitions to continue to increase in Japan.[143] This suggests that the "efficiency of friendliness," which drove the lost decade recovery, will likely continue to be the *modus operandi* in Japanese corporate governance for the foreseeable future. Indeed, since Oji's bid failed, friendly takeovers have persisted and Japan remains the only developed country in which there has yet to be a successful hostile takeover bid.[144]

V. The Increase in Japanese Takeover *Bids* is Not Evidence of an Increase in the *Ex Ante* Threat of Hostile Takeovers

A technical point that must be addressed before moving on is the claim by some experts that an increase in the number of takeover bids in Japan during the lost decade and lost decade recovery demonstrates that Japan developed, or was developing, an American-style hostile takeovers regime.[145] This claim would be accurate if takeover bids in Japan were tantamount to takeover bids in the United States. However, they are not. The significant discrepancy between what is considered a takeover bid in Japan and the United States makes conclusions based on comparisons between them erroneous.

In the United States, the number of takeover bids has come to be viewed as a proxy for the threat level of hostile takeovers.[146] This is because, contrary to mergers, takeover bids allow bidders to bypass management by making an offer directly to target shareholders.[147] This allows takeover bidders to assume control of target companies without management's approval (i.e., via a hostile takeover) and then to replace unskilled or underperforming management to improve company performance.[148]

---

142 "Top Execs Split on Approval for Oji's Run at Hokuetsu", Nikkei Weekly, 11 September, 2006.
143 *Ibid.*
144 In fact, the most recent significant failed attempted hostile takeover involved the high profile failure of Steel Partners to take over Bulldog Sauce. OSUGI, *supra* note 116, 158-159; NELS HANSEN, Japan's First Poison Pill Case, Bulldog Sauce vs. Steel Partners: A Comparative and Institutional Analysis, in: Journal of Japanese Law 26 (2008)139. In addition, at the end of 2007, there were renewed claims that Japan had just experienced its "first hostile takeover." Again, these claims were overly exaggerated and ultimately false. See "Hostility, of Sorts", Economist, 22 December, 2007.
145 COLCERA, *supra* note 48, 48-52; SCHAEDE, *supra* note 4, 22; SCHAEDE, *supra* note 41, 32.
146 See D.G. BAIRD / R.K. RASMUSSEN, Private Debt and the Missing Lever of Corporate Governance, in: University of Pennsylvania Law Review 154 (2006) 1243; B. HOLMSTROM/ S.N. KAPLAN, Corporate Governance and Merger Activity in the United States: Making Sense of the 1980s and 1990s, in: The Journal of Economic Perspectives, 15 (2001) 125.
147 BURKART / PANUNZI, *supra* note 4, 2.
148 *Ibid.* 3.

During the vigorous hostile takeovers market in 1980s America, takeover bids were the primary means for initiating and executing hostile takeovers.[149] In the 1980s, the United States was an epicenter for hostile takeovers, as over half of all major American companies received hostile takeover bids.[150] In 1988 alone, there were over 200 hostile takeover bids and 85 successful hostile takeovers.[151] As such, during the 1980s, the threat of a hostile takeover bid and a subsequent overhaul of management was a real prospect for every CEO of a listed American company. Many experts claim that, in the late 1980s, this *ex ante* threat of being subject to a hostile bid, with the real prospect of being taken over, forced American executives to focus on maximizing shareholder value and reducing agency costs, which successfully drove the restructuring of corporate America.[152]

In Japan, prior to 1990, there were virtually no takeover bids.[153] From 1990 until 1997, takeover bids increased modestly to less than 10 bids per year. However, since 1997, there has been a substantial increase in the number of takeover bids from about 20 in 1999, 30 in 2001, 40 in 2004, and 50 in 2005.[154] According to American precedent, this increase in takeover bids should have significantly increased the threat of hostile takeovers in Japan. Indeed, several experts have pointed to the increase in the number of takeover bids as evidence that the threat of hostile takeovers significantly increased in Japan during the lost decade and lost decade recovery.[155]

However, comparing Japanese and American takeover bids is like comparing "apples and oranges." Compared to their American counterparts, Japanese takeover bid rules are extremely broad.[156] In Japan, with only a few limited exceptions, a proposed purchase of shares will be considered a takeover bid whenever shares are acquired outside of the securities market.[157] In the United States, for a proposed purchase of shares to be considered a takeover bid it generally must meet eight criteria including that the offer price is higher than the market price (i.e., the offer includes a 'premium').[158]

---

149 *Ibid.* 1.
150 HOLMSTROM / KAPLAN, *supra* note 146, 125.
151 M. MARTYNOVA / L. RENNEBOOG, Takeover Waves: Triggers, Performance and Motives, in: ECGI Finance Working Paper No. 97 (2005) 8, *http://ssrn.com/abstract=880379*.
152 M.J. ROE, Political Preconditions to Separating Ownership from Corporate Control, in: Stanford Law Review 53 (2000) 539, 558; see also BURKAT / PANUNZI, *supra* note 4, 9, 24; HOLMSTROM / KAPLAN, *supra* note 146, 125.
153 KESTER, *supra* note 10, 99; C.J. MILHAUPT / M.D. WEST, Institutional Change and M&A in Japan: Diversity Through Deals, 2001, 36 (forthcoming in C.J. MILHAUPT, Global Markets, in: Domestic Institutions), *http://papers.ssrn.com/abstract=290744*.
154 COLCERA, *supra* note 48, 49.
155 SCHAEDE, *supra* note 4, 22-26.
156 K. KOMOTO, The Present Status of Takeover Bids (TOB) and Their Effect on Stock Prices, in: NLI Research No.147 (2000) 8-9,
http://www.nli-research.co.jp/english/economics/2000/eco0012a.pdf.
157 *Ibid.*
158 D.A. OESTERKE, The Rise and Fall of Street Sweep Takeovers, in: Duke Law Journal 1989,

According to two studies conducted on takeover bids in Japan in the post-bubble era, almost half of the takeover bids had an offer price below the market price (i.e., a "negative premium").[159] Therefore, on this basis alone, half of the post-bubble takeover bids would not be considered takeover bids under United States law. More importantly, these negative premium bids present absolutely no *ex ante* threat to management to maximize shareholder value or control agency costs. To the contrary, management may feel they can allow the company's share price to decline if there are negative premium bids in the market.

A related peculiarity in Japanese takeover bids is that the average premium offered to shareholders was (and is) extremely low compared to the premium offered to shareholders in American takeover bids (and in bids in all other countries). In the United States, the average premium offered to shareholders in takeover bids is about forty-five percent above the market price.[160] In Japan, during the lost decade, the average premium offered to shareholders in takeover bids was *minus* 4.72 percent.[161] According to one study that examined takeover bids from 1990 to 2002, Japan held the unique distinction of being the *only* country in the world that had an average *negative* bid premium.[162] Even during the lost decade recovery, when premiums were said to have increased, the average premium offered was a modest ten percent, which is well below the forty-five percent offered in the United States.[163]

Takeover bid premiums in Japan were considerably lower than in the United States (and all other developed countries) because a significant portion of Japanese takeover bids involved friendly pre-negotiated deals between bidders and target companies.[164] In these so-called "takeover bids," the offer price is arranged between the acquirer and main shareholders (with approval from 'target' management) prior to the offer being made and there is no competition between potential acquirers. This is in sharp contrast to American takeover bids where prearranged friendly offers to a single bidder, which normally have a small or negative premium, are not considered takeover bids.[165] These low premium prearranged takeovers, which predominated in Japan during the lost decade and lost decade recovery, do nothing to increase the threat of hostile takeovers. In fact, they are welcomed by incumbent management as they may present an oppor-

---

202, footnote 92.
159 KOMOTO, *supra* note 156, 10; MILHAUPT / WEST, *supra* note 153, 17.
160 S. ROSSI / P.F. VOLPIN, Cross-Country Determinants of Mergers and Acquisitions, in: Journal of Financial Economics 74 (2004) 282.
161 MILHAUPT / WEST, *supra* note 153, 17.
162 ROSSI / VOLPIN, *supra* note 160, 282.
163 See H. MIYAJIMA, Analyzing the Role of M&As for Japanese Companies, in: RIETI Report No. 076 (2006), http://www.rieti.go.jp/en/rieti_report/076.html; ROSSI / VOLPIN, *supra* note 160, 282.
164 KOMOTO, *supra* note 156, 11.
165 *Ibid.* 10.

tunity to be rescued from hidden liabilities (which may be the reason for the negative premium bids) that have not been disclosed to the market.[166]

Even the rare Japanese takeover bids that included premiums similar to typical American takeover bids have failed.[167] Again, this is in contrast to the United States, where about thirty-five percent of hostile bids succeed, and the European Union, where fifty percent of hostile bids are successful.[168] Obviously, with a zero percent success rate, even takeover bids that do offer a substantial premium, will not pose the same level of threat as takeover bids in the United States or European Union, where there is a significant chance that a takeover bid will result in a successful hostile takeover.

Finally, even if all of the significant differences between Japanese and American takeover bids are ignored, the total number of takeover bids in the United States during the late 1980s still dwarfs the number in Japan during the lost decade and lost decade recovery. In the United States, during the last five years of the 1980s, there was approximately three times the number of takeover bids as in Japan during the lost decade and lost decade recovery—which lasted over 15 years.[169] Of course, this overlooks a significant percentage of so-called Japanese "takeover bids" which were not a proxy for hostility in the market.

In sum, it is undeniable that there was an increase in takeover bids in Japan during the lost decade and lost decade recovery. However, this increase is not comparable to that of the United States in the 1980s—in either the nature or frequency of the bids. This is because a significant percentage of Japanese "takeover bids" were friendly, negotiated deals with low or negative premiums. In addition, all of the bids offering premiums equivalent to those in the United States failed. As such, the raw number of so-called "takeover bids" in Japan during the lost decade and lost decade recovery is not a reliable proxy for the threat of hostile takeovers. If anything, especially during the lost decade, it is more likely that Japanese takeover bids acted as a proxy for perversity in the market (i.e., stronger companies rescuing weaker ones with undisclosed liabilities, which may explain negative premium bids) than as threats of hostile takeovers.[170]

---

166 *Ibid.* 12-13.
167 *Ibid.* 12.
168 CORPORATE VALUE REPORT 2005, *supra* note 29, 12.
169 PUCHNIAK, *supra* note 1, footnote 381.
170 See D.W. PUCHNIAK, Perverse Main Bank Rescue in the Lost Decade: Proof that Unique Institutional Incentives Drive Japanese Corporate Governance, in: Pacific Rim Law & Policy Journal 16 (2007) 13, 20-24.

VI. JAPANESE MANAGERS DID NOT REACT SWIFTLY TO THE PURPORTED THREAT OF FAILED HOSTILE TAKEOVERS

Another way to gauge the effect of failed hostile takeovers on corporate governance during the lost decade recovery is to attempt to measure the subjective threat felt by Japanese managers as a result of failed hostile takeovers. From a corporate governance perspective, the threat of hostile takeovers only becomes significant if it is serious enough to influence managerial behavior.[171] A clear indication that management perceives the threat of hostile takeovers as serious is when management takes steps to protect itself against hostile takeovers. During the 1980s, the serious threat of hostile takeovers in the United States drove managers to take a number of defensive actions. Two of the most significant actions were adopting poison pills and increasing the prominence of independent directors on American boards—both of which were effective in guarding against hostile takeovers.[172]

In November 1985, the Delaware Supreme Court upheld a company's right to adopt the poison pill as a takeover defense.[173] Shortly after the court's "authorization of the pill," over 1000 American companies adopted this defensive technique. Furthermore, by the mid-1990s, over sixty percent of all listed American companies had adopted the pill.[174] This is definitive evidence that, in the late 1980s, the threat of hostile takeovers was serious enough to drive managerial action in the majority of American companies.

Prior to 2001, the poison pill was not available under Japanese law. In 2001, a *Commercial Code* amendment made a version of the poison pill technically available in Japan.[175] However, despite efforts by large law firms to market the pill and predictions by experts that the pill may be widely adopted, no Japanese companies adopted it.[176]

---

171 MIYAJIMA / KUROKI, *supra* note 41, 79 and 85.
172 R. MONKS / N. MINOW, Corporate Governance, (3d ed., 2004) 227, 248; see also BAIRD / RASMUSSEN, *supra* note 146, 1244; L.A. BEBCHUK / A. COHEN, The Costs of Entrenched Boards, in: Journal of Financial Economics 78 (2005) 409, 410; L.A. BEBCHUK ET AL., The Powerful Anti-takeover Force of Staggered Boards: Theory Evidence and Policy, in: Stanford Law Review 54 (2002) 887, 895; GILSON, *supra* note 4, 33-34; GRUENER, *supra* note 4, 873.
173 *Moran v. Household Int'l. Inc.*, 500 Atlantic Reporter 1346 (Delaware Supreme Court 1985); see generally GILSON, *supra* note 4, 33-34.
174 BEBCHUK / COHEN, *supra* note 172, 413; MONKS / MINOW, *supra* note 172, 237.
175 C.J. MILHAUPT, A Lost Decade for Japanese Corporate Governance Reform?, in: The Center for Law and Economic Studies, Working Paper Series No. 234 (Columbia Law School, 2003), footnote 24 , *http://ssrn.com/abstract=442960*. See also, S. KOZUKA, The Use of Stock Options as Defensive Measures: The Impact of the 2001 Amendments to the Corporate Law on Corporate Controls in Japan, in: Journal of Japanese Law 15 (2003) 135.
176 See GILSON, *supra* note 4, 23-24; C.J. MILHAUPT, Foreword To The Hostile M&A Conference Issue, in: Columbia Business Law Review 2004, 1, 5-7; H. KANDA, Does Corporate Law Really Matter In Hostile Takeovers?: Commenting on Professor Gilson and Chancellor Chandler, in: Columbia Business Law Review 2004, 75; Z. SHISHIDO, Changes in Japanese Corporate Law and Governance: Revisiting the Convergence Debate, in: Law and Econo-

This failure to adopt the pill may have been because, although it was technically available, its legal status was still uncertain.[177]

Then, in 2005, the government responded to the uncertainty of the legality of the poison pill by releasing the Takeover Guidelines which "officially sanctioned" the poison pill and imported Delaware takeover jurisprudence into Japan.[178] Both the government and large law firms actively encouraged listed companies to adopt the "officially sanctioned" poison pill.[179] Based on American experience in the 1980s, it was assumed that "officially sanctioning" the pill would cause a wave of companies to adopt it.[180] Central to this assumption was the erroneous belief that Japanese managers were seriously threatened by hostile takeovers during the lost decade recovery—regardless of the fact that all hostile takeover bids had failed.

However, despite the 2001 *Commercial Code* amendment, the "official sanctioning" of the pill, and the government and law firms' attempts to market the pill, the adoption of the pill during the lost decade recovery was, at best, "limited and gradual".[181] In 2005, only eight out of Japan's 4,000 listed companies adopted the poison pill at their annual general shareholders' meeting.[182] Even by 2006, as the lost decade recovery ended and what was to be Japan's period of sustained growth commenced, still less than two percent of Japan's listed companies had adopted the pill.[183] In sum, during the lost decade recovery, very few Japanese managers feared hostile takeovers enough to implement the poison pill. This empirical evidence also calls into question predictions by experts who expected Japan to rush to adopt the pill based on the past experience in American corporate governance during the 1980s.[184]

---

mics Workshop, Paper 1 (University of California Berkeley 2004) 11-12, *http://repositories.cdlib.org/berkeley_law_econ/ Fall2004/1/*.

177 KANDA, *supra* note 176, 70-71; MILHAUPT, *supra* note 176, 5.
178 See MILHAUPT, *supra* note 3, 2173-2174 and 2200.
179 See *ibid.* 2206-2208; see also ECONOMIST, *supra* note 139.
180 See HINES ET AL., *supra* note 3, 374-375; MILHAUPT, *supra* note 3, 2200-2201; SCHAEDE, *supra* note 4, 24-25.
181 GRUENER, *supra* note 4, 873-874; HINES ET AL., *supra* note 3, 408.
182 GRUENER, *supra* note 4, 873; OSUGI, *supra* note 116.
183 According to the Ministry of Economy, Trade and Industry, by March 2006, 48 companies had introduced the poison pill out of Japan's approximately 4000 listed companies. Corporate Value Study Group, Corporate Value Report 2006, 7, footnote 7, *http://www.meti.go.jp/policy/economic_oganization/pdf/houkoku06*. For a summary of the Corporate Value Report 2006, see Corporate Study Group, Corporate Value Report 2006 (Abstract), in: Journal of Japanese Law 21 (2006) 140. There are reports that, by the end of 2007, slightly less than ten percent of listed companies had adopted the poison pill. OSUGI, *supra* note 116, 158. However, in the context of this paper, adoption of the pill after the end of the lost decade recovery (i.e., mid-2006) is irrelevant because it tells us nothing about the *ex ante* threat of hostile takeovers *during* or *preceding* the recent recovery—which is what this paper focuses on.
184 See MILHAUPT, *supra* note 3, 2200; CANADIAN INVESTOR RELATIONS INSTITUTE, The Year of the Poison Pill (August 2005), *http://www.ciri.org/resources/reading_room/articles/shareholder/?article_id=953*.

Also in the 1980s, the rise of the poison pill in the United States was accompanied by an increase in the prominence of independent directors on American boards.[185] Delaware jurisprudence made the independence of boards a central criterion for justifying the appropriateness of defensive actions taken in response to hostile takeover bids.[186] This resulted in a significant increase in the number and quality of independent directors on American boards as management attempted to insulate themselves from the serious threat of hostile takeovers.[187]

In 2002, the *Commercial Code* was amended to allow Japanese companies to opt out of the traditional Japanese-style board featuring the statutory auditor and to adopt instead an American-style board with an "independent committee system."[188] Firms that opted for the American-style board were required to establish "independent" board committees for the audit, nomination, and compensation functions, which take the place of the statutory auditor.[189] A key element of the American-style board is that it legally mandates a separation between directors and executive officers, which is synonymous in the traditional Japanese-style statutory auditor system.[190]

The combination of the separation between directors and executive officers and the increased independence of the committee system should have made American-style boards an attractive option for companies that felt threatened by hostile takeovers because it increased their ability to justify the adoption of takeover defenses. This was especially true after the release of the 2005 Takeover Guidelines, which transplanted Delaware takeover jurisprudence into Japan. Indeed, after the Takeover Guidelines were released, Milhaupt predicted "there could be a spike in adoptions of the U.S.-style board committee system" because the independent committees played a large role in Delaware takeover jurisprudence.[191]

Milhaupt's prediction proved to be incorrect. In fact, the opposite has happened. Since 2002, less than three percent of Japan's listed companies have chosen to adopt an American-style board.[192] In addition, over three-quarters of the companies that have adopted an American-style board did so in 2003 (the year following the amendment).[193] Thus, the number of companies that decided to adopt the American-style board was considerably lower after the Takeover Guidelines were implemented in 2005 than in 2002,

---

185 GILSON, *supra* note 4, 33-34; MONKS / MINOW, *supra* note 172, 227, 248.
186 GILSON, *supra* note 4, 34.
187 MONKS / MINOW, *supra* note 172, 227, 248; see also GILSON, *supra* note 4, 33-34.
188 See D.W. PUCHNIAK, The 2002 Reform of the Management of Large Corporations in Japan, in: Australian Journal of Asian Law 5 (2003) 42, 46.
189 See *ibid.* 49-56; MILHAUPT, *supra* note 3, 2187.
190 See MILHAUPT, *supra* note 3, 2187; PUCHNIAK, *supra* note 188, 50, 55-56.
191 MILHAUPT, *supra* note 3, 2202.
192 P. LAWLEY, Panacea or Placebo? An Empirical Analysis of the Effect of the Japanese Committee System Corporate Governance Law Reform, in: Asian-Pacific Law & Policy Journal 9 (2007) 106; OSUGI, *supra* note 116, 158.
193 LAWLEY, *supra* note 192.

after the amendment was first introduced.[194] The fact that so few listed companies have chosen to adopt this change, especially after the Takeover Guidelines imported Delaware takeover jurisprudence, illustrates that the threat of hostile takeovers during the lost decade recovery was not serious enough to influence the actions of the vast majority of Japanese managers.

The failure of Japanese companies to adopt quickly the poison pill and the American-style board is even more of a surprise, considering that 2003 witnessed a postwar low in cross-shareholding and a postwar high of foreign shareholding and shareholder activism. The most logical explanation for the failure of Japanese companies to implement quickly these defensive tactics is that managers did not perceive the threat of hostile takeovers as serious enough to take action. The flawed predictions of a rush to the poison pill and American-style boards should serve as yet another reminder that Japanese corporate governance cannot be understood based on United States' precedent—especially the American hostile takeovers environment of the 1980s.

VII. Japan's "Barriers" to Hostile Takeovers Began to Rebuild During the Lost Decade Recovery

Interestingly, in spite of the litany of predictions that the lost decade recovery would produce a US-style market for corporate control, it in fact produced the opposite—a rebuilding of Japan's traditional barriers to hostile takeovers. The lost decade recovery saw a dramatic return to cross-shareholding.[195] Since 2004, shares held by non-financial companies, which are commonly seen as cross-shareholdings, have rapidly expanded by over thirty percent and the three mega-banks have increased their cross-shareholdings.[196] The return to cross-shareholding, which occurred at the same time the Japanese economy was returning to economic normalcy (prior to the global financial crisis), suggests that Japanese companies sold their cross-shareholdings during the lost decade out of a necessity to raise capital—not because they thought the main bank system or cross-shareholding was fundamentally flawed.[197] It is also worth noting that the recent growth in cross-shareholding occurred despite the fact that the poison pill was "officially sanctioned" by the Japanese government. This calls into question the claim by Milhaupt

---

194 *Ibid.*
195 See Y. TAKI ET AL., Options Available for Japanese Companies in a Globalized Market Environment, in: NRI Papers No. 111 (2006) 5,
  http://www.nri.co.jp/english/opinion/papers/2006/pdf/np2006111.pdf;
  W. PESEK, Welcome Back, Japan Inc., in: New York Sun, 19 September, 2006; "Cross-holding Revives as Takeover Shield", Nikkei Weekly, 29 January, 2007.
196 NIKKEI, *supra* note 195.
197 KANDA, *supra* note 176, 70.

and West that cross-shareholding existed in Japan because Japan's corporate law did not allow for American-style defenses—particularly the poison pill.[198]

As the lost decade recovery ended, reports of enthusiasm for hostile takeovers in corporate Japan also waned and even reversed course.[199] In 2005, during Livedoor's hostile takeover attempt, Horie, the founder and CEO of Livedoor, was perceived by a large portion of the Japanese public as the face of Japan's rapidly evolving business culture.[200] His hostile attempt to take over Fuji TV was viewed as evidence that American-style hostile takeovers had finally arrived in Japan.[201] As explained above, even in the wake of Livedoor's failure, many pundits erroneously viewed Horie's mere attempt to challenge the Japanese old guard as a watershed moment marking the beginning of an era of hostile takeovers in Japan.[202]

However, in 2006, all of this quickly changed when Horie was arrested and indicted on allegations of accounting fraud and stock market manipulation.[203] The scandal spurred a massive two-day sell-off on the TSE. The volume of selling was so great that the TSE was forced to close early, a move that was seen as a "blow to the nation's pride."[204] This caused markets around the world to fall and was dubbed by the news media as the "Livedoor shock."[205] Horie was disgraced, as Livedoor's share price plummeted in a month from 696 yen to 61 yen and in April, the stock was delisted from the TSE.[206]

The picture of Horie solemnly bowing before a trial judge in Tokyo, with his trademark spiky-hair fully cropped and wearing a conservative "salary man" black suit, was a stark contrast to the once renegade shareholder activist who was famous for flamboyantly challenging Japan's conservative business culture.[207] In March 2007, Horie was sentenced to two and a half years in prison. Given that Japanese courts rarely impose jail terms for securities violations, many viewed this sentence as extremely harsh.[208]

---

198 See HINES ET AL., *supra* note 3, 374-375; MILHAUPT, *supra* note 3, 2173-2174; MILHAUPT / WEST, *supra* note 153, 22, 47.
199 See OSUGI, *supra* note 116, 156-157; see also ALFORD, *supra* note 113; D. IBISON, Koizumi Drops FDI Pledge on M&A Fears, in: Financial Times, 2 February, 2006; ECONOMIST, *supra* note 139.
200 HINES ET AL., *supra* note 3, footnote 227.
201 *Ibid.* 376-77; GRUENER, *supra* note 4, 873 and 895; ECONOMIST INTELLIGENCE UNIT, *supra* note 92, 7.
202 See CARYL, *supra* note 4; KINGSTON, *supra* note 89; NAKAMOTO, *supra* note 4. See more generally, WHITTAKER / HAYAKAWA, *supra* note 48, 5.
203 OSUGI, *supra* note 116.
204 "Stirred by Flashy Entrepreneur", New York Times, 19 January, 2006.
205 ALGER, *supra* note 89, 323.
206 HINES ET AL., *supra* note 3, footnote 227.
207 M. NAKAMOTO, Ex-Livedoor Chief Horie Pleads Not Guilty, in: Financial Times, 5 September, 2006.
208 JAPAN ECONOMIC NEWSWIRE, *supra* note 98; "Livedoor Internet Guru Jailed for Faking Profits", Evening Standard, 16 March, 2007.

Murakami, the CEO of MAC, who was the other *de facto* leader of shareholder activism in Japan during the recent recovery, was also disgraced by criminal charges. In June 2006, Murakami was arrested on allegations of insider trading that took place during the infamous Livedoor hostile takeover attempt.[209] As Murakami awaited trial, most commentators saw the case against him as weak but nevertheless expected that he may receive a harsh sentence to send a message to "all those wannabe [corporate raiders] to reassess their approach to the market." [210] As suspected, on July 19, 2007, Murakami received the harshest sentence for insider trading ever issued by a Japanese court.[211] During the sentencing, the judge called Murakami's "profit first attitude .... horrifying."[212]

The imprisonment and disgrace of Japan's two most prominent shareholder activists, who were widely viewed as the face of hostile takeovers in Japan, has caused a "chilling effect" in Japan's takeover market.[213] Combined with the rise in cross-shareholding, these sentences serve as yet another caution for those who, for the last two decades, have been perpetually predicting the arrival of American-style hostile takeovers in Japan.[214] They further illustrate how Japan's unique form of corporate governance continues to persist and dominate.

VIII. CONCLUSION

The lesson from Japan's lost decade recovery is simple. Hostile takeovers play a marginal role in Japanese corporate governance. This has been the case throughout the postwar period. The lost decade recovery was no exception.

The magnitude of the distorted literature which creates the false impression that hostile takeovers have come to play an important role in Japanese corporate governance is somewhat curious. It is surprising to see one capable scholar after another, over a period of decades, repeat the same mistake by erroneously predicting the arrival of American-style hostile takeovers in Japan. The mantra that global corporate governance will inevitably evolve towards the "optimally efficient" American model appears to have made otherwise bright and careful scholars have "delusions of hostility".

Hopefully, this article will cure such delusions. After all, correctly understanding the reality of Japan's unique system of corporate governance is far more enriching than toiling to reconstruct the Japanese facts to fit a preconceived notion of what good corporate governance ought to be.

---

209 A. FUKUDA, Japanese Investors Face Stricter Disclosure Rules, in: International Herald Tribune, 28 December, 2006.
210 S. HERMAN, Latest Shot Fired In Battle Between Japan Inc., in: United States Federal News, 13 June, 2006.
211 See "Murakami Gets 2-yr Term", Daily Yomiuri, 20 July, 2007.
212 See *ibid.*
213 HERMAN, *supra* note 210.
214 ECONOMIST INTELLIGENCE UNIT, *supra* note 92, 27.

Name Index

Abbott, Kenneth W. xiii, 332
Acuff, Frank L. 231
Ahn, Dukgeun 332, 342
Akinbami, xvii
Alvarez, J.E. xv
Armen 269–72, 274, 275
Anderson, K. xxix
Anh, Phi 251
Annan, K.A. xiii
Antons, C. xii, xix, xxv
Aoki, Masahiko 274–5
Appelbaum, Richard P. xiv, 3–24
Aquinas, Thomas 28
Araki, Ichiro 332, 335, 341, 351
Arner, Douglas W. xv, 25–69
Arora, T. xi
Arrighi, Giovanni 11, 12, 13–14
Asanuma, Banri 274
Augustine, St 240, 241
Axelrod, Robert 257, 262
Axtell, Roger E. 231

Babbie, Earl 246, 248
Barton, Clifton 247
Baruma, I. Xiv
Bayoumi, T. xx
Becker, Gary Stanley 5
Beresford, Melanie 98
Berle, Adolf 129, 131, 136
Bernstein, Lisa 259
Biddulph, S. xxiii
Birch, D. xii
Birnbaum, David G. 17, 18
Björkman, Ingmar 406
Black, Julia 97
Black III, W.L.R. xiii
Boettcher, J.G. xxvii
Bonacich, Edna 17
Booth, Charles D. xv, 25–69
Borden, George A. 231
Bowman, G.W. xiii
Brandt, Loren xxiii, 85
Brett, Jeanne M. 232, 233

Buckley, S. xxvi
Byamugisha, Frank 40

Canaan, Edwin 36
Carlier, Amanda 97
Carlton, Dennis 269
Carruthers, B.G. xxii
Casadesus-Masanell, Ramon 297
Chan, Charlie 232, 236, 241
Chan, Joseph 17, 18
Chang, Chun 88
Charkham, Jonathan 407–8, 410, 419
Chase-Dunn, Christopher 12
Che, Jiahua 88
Cheah, Eric 149
Chen, J. xvi, xxi, xxii, xxiii
Chen, Shi-Zeng 3
Chen, Su 363–90
Chen, Zhu 232, 236
Cheng, Francis Man-Piu 17, 18, 19
Cheng, Yik Hung 19
Chesterman, S. xiii, xiv
Chiappori, Pierre-Andre 297
Chiba, Masaji 128–9
Child, John 398, 407, 411, 412, 413
Chung, Johnny Chien Chuen 3
Clague, Douglas 402
Clarke, Donald C. xvi, xxi, xxiii, 71–93, 102
Clinton, Bill 3, 4, 314, 315
Coase, Ronald 274
Coffee, John 481
Cohen, Louis 246
Cohen, S.J. xxviii
Colatrella, M.T. xxvii, xxviii
Collyns, C. xx
Conaway, Wayne A. 231
Confucius 28, 397
Conley, J.M. xxv
Cooney, S. xxiii
Corn, Ian 237
Cosgrove, R.A. 424
Cossman, B. xi
Cotterrell, Roger 246

Crawford, Robert 269–72, 274, 275
Crocker, Keith 272
Crouch, Harold 145
Cunningham, Jim 17
Cuong, Phung Quang 115

Dalton, Russell J. 99
Dang, Hung Vo 103
Dau, Anh Tuan 110
Deakin, S. xv–xvi
de Soto, Hernando 34–5, 39, 45, 103, 262
de Sousa Santos, Boaventura xii, xxiv, 6
de Vydler, Stefan 98
Deng, Xiao Ping xxi 436
Dezalay, Yves xiv, 6–9, 12
Dicey, A.V. 423–4
Ding, Peng 436, 437
Do, Anh Tuan 97, 110
Doanh, Kinh 251
Draper, P. xx
Durkheim, Emile 5
Dyer, Jeffrey H. 275

Edwards, Jeremy 393
Eisenberg, Melvin 472–3
Elegant, Robert S. 11
Ellickson, Robert 470–71
Ellis, P. xxvi
Evans, Gareth 439
Evans-Pritchard, A. xxi

Faure, David 415, 421
Fauvarque-Cosson, B. xi
Fei, Xiaotong 397, 398
Fforde, Adam 98, 99
Fidler, D.P. xiii, xiv
Fischer, Klaus 393
Freidman, L.M. xiv
Friedman, Milton 28
Fu, H. xxviii
Fung, J.K.W. xx

Gainsborough, Martin 98, 247
Gao, Henry 344
Garnaut, R. xvi
Garth, Bryant 6–9, 12
Gates, Bill 232, 236
Gaubatz, K.T. xi
Geertz, Clifford xviii, 129
Gereffi, Gary 14–15

Gerlach, Michael L. 16
Gessner, V. xvii
Gilbert, Daniel T. 238
Gillard, Julia xiii
Gillespie, John xvi, xx, xxiv, 95–122
Gilmore, Grant 245
Gilson, Ronald 275, 392, 451
Ginsburg, T. xv, xvi, xvii, xix, xx, xxvii
Glenn, H.P. xii
Gold, Thomas 99
Goldsmith, Raymond 32, 33
Gower, L.C.B. 421
Granovetter, Mark 11, 16
Green, S.K. xxiii
Guthrie, Doug xxvi, 99

Hakansson, Håkan 16
Haley, John O. xxviii, 101
Hall, Edward T. 231
Hall, P.A. xxi
Halliday, T.D. xxii
Hamashita, Takeshi 12
Hamilton, Gary G. 11, 14, 15, 16, 397, 398
Hampden-Turner, Charles 231
Hansmann, Henry xiv, xxviii, 483, 484, 486
Hart, H.L.A. 252
Harvey, David 6
Haselmann, Rainer 68
Hattori, Tamio 416
Hayek, Friedrich 28, 97
Heller, T.C. xviii
Henderson, D.F. xviii
Herron, D. xxvii
Hill, Stephen 406, 407
Hilmer, Frederick C. 410
Hira, Anil 110
Hirst, Paul Q. 6
Ho Zhu 229
Hoang, Quoc Viet 105
Hobbes, Thomas 252
Hoetker, G. xxvii
Hofstede, Geert 231, 234, 413–14
Hong, Zhaohui 88
Hooker, Barry 143
Hopkins, Terrance 14
Horie, Takafumi 491, 505–6, 507, 519
Hosokawa, Morihiro 314
Hsu, Berry F.C. xv, 25–69
Huang, Chen-Ya 438
Huang, Johnny 4

Hui, Herbert 420
Hui, Po-keung 13
Hu Jinato, President xxi
Hutchings, K. xxv, xxvi
Hurst, Willard 429
Hutson, C.R. 16
Hwang, Kwang-Kuo 419–20

Ibrahim, Anwar 144, 149
Iida, Keisuke 332, 335

Jaffee, Dwight M. 41
Janisik, R.J. xxvi
Jayasuriya, K. xii, xxv
Jennings, Ivor 424
Johnson, S. xx
Jolowicz, Anthony 146
Jordan, Michael 232, 236

Kanda, H. xix
Kanter, Rosabeth Moss 237
Kao, Cheng-shu 11, 16
Kawakatsu, Heita 12
Kawashima, Fujio 332, 335
Kawashima, T. xxvi–xxvii
Keefer, Philip 80–81, 82, 89
Keleman, R.D. xiv, xxviii
Kennedy, D. xii
Kerkvliet, Benedict 103
Kester, Carl 499
Keynes, John Maynard 28, 36
Kim, Annette M. 104
Kim, Hwa-Jin xvii, xxiv, 153–86
King, Robert G. 33
Kingman, Matt 19
Kirby, William C. 395
Klein, Benjamin 269–72, 274, 275
Knack, Stephen 80–81, 82, 89
Kobayashi, I. xxvii
Kochhar, K. xx
Korobkin, Russell B. 250
Kotani, Mitsuhiro 497
Kotz, H. xviii–xix
Kraakman, Reinier xiv, xxviii, 483, 484, 486
Kuroda, K. xxv
Kuzuhara, K. xxvii

La Porta, Rafael xv, 32
Langer, Ellen 236
Laski, Harold 424

Lawan, Thanadsillapakul 354
Lawton, Philip xxix, 391–422
Leaptrott, Nan 231
Lee Kuan Yew 9
Lee Qiang 227
Lejot, Paul xv, 25–69
Levine, Ross 33
Levy, Marion J. 5
Li Ka Shing 228, 403
Li Qiang 229
Li Zhang 226
Li, David 87–8
Li, Guo 85
Li, Peng 439
Liang, Guoqing 433
Lin, Li-Wen xviii, xxiv, 187–220
Lingle, C. xiii
Liu, L.S. xxiv
Llewellyn, Karl 245, 263
Lo, V.I. xxviii
Locke, John 28
López-de-Silanes, Florencio xv, 32
Luat, Phap 251
Luo, Jinquan 436

MacArthur, M.C. xi
Macauley, Stewart 246, 262
Macey, Jonathan R. 177, 465, 466
Macintyre, A. xi
Macneil, Ian R. 99, 249, 263
Mahbubani, K. xi, xiii
Malone, Patrick S. 238
Manion, Lawrence 246
Mao Tse-Tung (Zedong) xxi, 232, 236
Markovits, Inga 190
Marx, Karl 5, 28, 34
Masten, Scott 269, 272
McMillan, John 74, 99, 245, 246, 253, 254, 257, 258, 259, 260–62, 263
McMullan, Bob 432
Means, Gardiner 129–30, 131, 136
Meehan, James Jr 269
Menski, W. xviii, xxi
Meyer, John W. 6
Milgrom, Paul 269
Milhaupt, Curtis J. xv, xxix, 105, 150, 441–87, 494, 510, 517, 518
Miller, Geoffrey 177, 446
Miller, Jonathan 205, 207, 208
Ming Xu 226

Mitton, T. xx
Miwa, Yoshiro xxvii, 267–98
Miyauchi, Yoshihiko 471
Murray, G. xxv, xxvi
Morrison, Keith 246
Murrell P. xxiii
Morrison, Terry 231
Murakami, Yoshiaki 470–71, 472, 491, 504, 520
Murdoch, Rupert 498–9

Nakagawa, Junji xxviii, 331–61
Naughton, B. xi, xvi
Neumann, Franz xi, 429
Ng, Ringo 17, 18
Nguyen, Nien 105
Nguyen, Phuong Quynh Trang 110
Nguyen, Quan H. xxvi, 245–66
Nguyen, Sa 106
Nguyen, Thi Thom 104
Noda, Y. xv
Nonini, Donald M. 11, 15
Norlund, Irene 99
North, Douglass C. xviii, 29, 30, 32, 34, 72, 77, 79–80, 81, 82, 91, 101, 250, 263
Nottage, L. xxix

Obama, Barak xiii
Obiora, L. xii
Olson, Mancur 29–30
Ong, Aihwa 6, 11, 15
Orrú, Marco 11

Page, J. xv
Palmkvist, Gösta 103
Pao, Y.K. 403
Parker, Christine 96, 97
Parkin, J. xxvi
Parsons, Talcott 5
Pascutto, Ermano 421
Pattison, P. xxvii
Pearce II, John A. xxv, 223–30
Peerenboom, R. xix, xx, xxiv
Pekkanen, Saadia M. xxviii, 299–329, 332, 334, 335
Peng Jiandong, James 432–9
Perloff, Jeffrey 269
Pham, Chi Lan 110
Pham, Duy Nghia 107
Pickens, T. Boone 498
Pistor, Katharina xv–xvi, xxiii, 68, 105, 128, 189

Plato 28
Port, K.L. xxviii
Posner, Richard 444
Potter, P.B. xxi
Puchniak, Dan W. xxix, 489–520

Qian, Qichen 439
Qian, Yingyi 88
Quinn, Brian 100

Ramli, Tajuddin 149
Ramseyer, J. Mark xxvii, 267–98
Ramseyer, Mark 448, 460
Rawski, T.G. xxiii
Redding, S. Gordon 247, 394, 401, 402, 409, 416, 417, 419, 426
Reid, Anthony 247
Renaud, Bertrand 41
Reynolds, Kenneth 272
Roberts, John 269
Robertson, Roland 6
Robinson, Joan 36
Robinson, Richard B. Jr xxv, 223–30
Robinson, Robert J. 239
Rock, Edward 474
Rodriguez-Garavito, C.A. xii
Rodrik, Dani 82
Roe, Mark 131, 275, 391–2, 451
Romano, Roberta 393
Rousseau, Peter L. 32
Rozelle, Scott 85
Rubin, Jeff 232, 240
Ruskola, T. xii

Sahlins, Marshall D. 5
Sakamoto, Yoshihiro 320, 321
Salacuse, Jeswald W. 232, 233, 236, 237
Salanie, Bernard 297
Salim, Mohammad Rizal xvii, xxiv, 123–51
Sander, Frank 232, 240
Sanders, S. xiii
Schaan, J.L. 412
Schaede, Ulrike 101, 503
Schirato, T. xii
Schumpeter, Joseph 36
Scott, John P. 400, 408
Scott, Robert E. 245
Sebenius, James K. xxv, 231–43
Service, Elman R. 5
Shen-Peng, Lina 438

Shleifer, Andrei xv, 29, 32
Sibbitt, E.C. xiv, xxviii
Skase, Christopher 436
Sloane, Patricia 142
Smart, Alan 16
Smart, Josephine 16
Smith, A.O. 273–4
Smith, Adam 28, 34
Snyder, Edward 269
Solomon, Gerald 3
Son, Masayoshi 498–9
Son, Thanh 97
Song, L. xvi
Soskice, D. xxi
Spulber, Daniel F. 297
Stewart, Rosemary 406–7
Stiglitz, Joseph E. xv, 261
Stokes, Mary 429
Stout, L. xvii
Stromseth, Jonathan R. 110
Suehiro, Akira 416
Sung, Yun-wing 18
Sunny Zhou 224, 225, 230
Sylla, Richard 32

Tamirisa, N. xx
Tanase, T. xxvii
Taylor, V. xii, xxv, xxvii
Tenev, Stoyen 103
Teubner, G. xvii
Thomas, George M. 6
Thompson, Grahame 6, 11
Tomasic, Roman xvii, xxii, xxix, 423–40
Tönnies, Ferdinand 5
Tran, Huu Huynh 110
Treitel, G.H. 252
Tricker, Robert I. 399
Trocki, Carl A. 12–13
Trompenaars, Fons 231, 413–14
Trubek, David xiii, 74
Truong, Thai Vinh 251
Truong, Thanh Duc 106
Tsang, Paul C.M. 17

Upham, F. xi

Valcke, C. xii
Vandenbergh, Michael 198
Vig, Vikrant 68
Vishny, Robert W. xv, 32

Wallerstein, Immanuel 11, 14
Walters, R.J. xxv
Walton, Steven R. 17, 18
Wang Li 224, 225
Wang, Yijiang 88
Wank, David 99
Watson, Alan 127, 192
Wayne, John 232, 236, 241
Weber, Max 5, 34, 71, 74, 75, 78, 91
Weiss, J. xiii
Weiss, Stephen E. 232, 240
Weitzman, Martin L. 86–7
Wellons, P.A. xxiii
Whitely, Richard 15–16
Whiting, S. xxiii
Whitman, J.Q. xii
Williams, C.A. xxv
Williamson, Oliver 252, 269, 271, 274, 275
Willis, T.H. 16
Winn, Jane K. 99
Wolff, L. xi, xxix
Wong, B.K.Y. xxvii, xxviii
Wong, Gilbert 408–9
Wong, Keniel 408
Wong, Siu-lun 11, 401, 403, 413, 415, 417, 418
Wong, Victor Witt H. 17
Woodiwiss, A. xx
Woodruff, Christopher M. 74, 99, 245, 246, 253, 254, 257, 258, 259, 260–62
Wu Bing 229
WuDunn, Sheryl 6

Xie, Zengyi 363–90
Xu, Chenggang 86–7

Yamanouchi, N. xxviii
Yamashita, Kazuhito 352
Yang, Mayfair Mei-hui 10–11
Yatim, Rais 145
Yell, S. xii
Yi, L.M. xxvi

Zeitlin, Maurice 131
Zhang, D. xxv
Zhang, Z. xxii
Zheng, Lielie 437
Zhu, Rongji 432, 433
Zhu, Y. xxiii
Zuckerman, Adrian 146
Zweigert, K. xviii–xix